The Great Painters of the Italian
RENAISSANCE

Volume II
The Triumph of Color

EBERHARD KÖNIG (Editor)

The Great Painters of the Italian
RENAISSANCE

Volume II
The Triumph of Color

h.f.ullmann

Contents

Frontispiece:
Leonardo da Vinci
The Annunciation, ca 1470–1473
Oil and tempera on wood, 98 x 217 cm
Galleria degli Uffizi, Florence

The Victory of *Colore* over *Disegno*

NETHERLANDISH PAINTING AND ITALIAN ART

During the years after 1300, Giotto, moving from Padua to Florence, and the Lorenzetti brothers in Siena, had set artistic standards for the whole of Latin Europe. Their grasp of reality was convincing, but at the same time they, and to an even greater extent Simone Martini, sanctioned the confrontation of a late courtly dream with the adversity of the times. Many Northerners who were not painters had encountered such art on their travels, while individual painters, like most princely patrons, had in contrast seen at home only more transportable works of art, small-format paintings.

Throughout the 14th century, Northern Europe, with its delicate art, had had but little to offer Italian artists. This changed around 1400. The accomplished rendering of nature, mastered by the French book illustrators of the time of the Duc de Berry (1340–1416), became as much of a challenge for painters such as Gentile da Fabriano (Volume I, pages 201–203) as the first innovations in coloring and the virtuoso use of gold leaf. Pictorial culture on both sides of the Alps, however, was moving away from the preciousness of the materials to the skill of the artist. Increasingly it came to be expected that the sheen of precious metals should be conveyed by the artist's skill in optical illusion and not by their actual presence.

It is particularly in the handling of light that the eras diverge. There was an appreciable decrease in the application of metal foil, which reflected light, and artists endeavored instead to capture light in the uniform medium of paint. This change from objective presence to artistic representation encouraged the development, even the invention, of new techniques. From their beginnings in Paris around 1400, these new approaches made a breakthrough in the 1420s, precisely when Brunelleschi, Donatello, and Masaccio were giving a new direction to the outlook of sculptors and paintings in Florence with geometrically constructed perspective. In the Netherlands, a new technique had come to maturity that employed oil as the main binder: Jan van Eyck (ca. 1386–1441) had, as Vasari assures us, invented oil painting.

An objection to this dogmatic statement could be that old binders such as egg whites and yolks, used with tempers, by no means disappeared from one day to the next, since with every new pigment (that is, powdered colorant) a new decision had to be made as to whether oil was at all suitable for the purpose, or whether it would not be better in some cases to retain the old media. In addition, painters such as Ghirlandaio sometimes imitated the effects of early Netherlandish painting so deceptively with the use of older materials that one could believe one was standing in front of an oil painting (Volume 1, page 27). But art historians have been content with this simplification, because a preserved painting does not incorporate complex developments but only the resulting image.

An example is to be found at the beginning of this volume. Around 1435 Jan van Eyck succeeded in his so-called *Rolin Madonna* (page 7), on an almost square area (66 x 62 cm), to direct the gaze from a convincingly captured inner space, as it were, toward the whole world. Without mathematically correct perspective, the gaze is directed alternately by geometric means and accessible routes: from floor tiles aligned in perspective, a flight of four strongly abbreviated steps lead into a garden, and after passing flower borders one reaches a further flight of steps leading to a battlemented parapet. Two men in the center of the image indulge the urge to gaze: one looks down between the battlements, while the other presses close to him in the attempt to enjoy the same breathtaking vista. A river separates two cities linked by a bridge; a fortified island occupies the point at which the straight course of the river changes to gentle curves. Snow-covered mountains on the horizon make it clear that this wide stream is flowing down toward the observer, as it were, from the Alps.

It is difficult to comprehend here what was so excitingly modern in this image at the time of its creation. The sensation is by no means restricted to the density of paint, the materiality, and the light-flooded landscape with its inexhaustible feast for the eyes. Gothic forms have given way to round arches which originate in the Romanesque period, but lead to the Renaissance.

Jan van Eyck
The Madonna and Child with Chancellor Rolin (Rolin Madonna), ca. 1435
Oil on oak, 66 x 62 cm
Musée du Louvre, Paris

This painting comes from Autun; up to the French Revolution it was kept in the private chapel of the Burgundian chancellor Nicolas Rolin (1376–1462), who was painted by Rogier van der Weyden in a highly similar style in a large altarpiece in Beaune. Nevertheless, it is doubtful whether the supplicant in the so-called *Rolin Madonna* is really intended to be Rolin, for he wears brocade and a short robe, which would not have been appropriate for the chancellor, who was not raised to the nobility until 1424.

It could, however, be a commemorative portrait of John the Fearless, Duke of Burgundy, who was murdered on a bridge in 1419, and on whose appearance Rolin had modeled his own. Whoever the supplicant may be, he is praying to the Christ Child to be allowed to cross the bridge shown in the center to the city of churches; at the same time, the peacocks and magpies and the capital relief above his head depicting the Fall of Man proclaim him a sinner, who is presumably seen reading the penitential psalms.

The painter has refrained from the idealization of his earthbound figures, as though he consciously wanted to capture them in their accidental appearance.

The most interesting aspect is the eye level of the two large figures. Following a courtly convention, Jan van Eyck differentiates with care: the praying figure's gaze is directed just below the line of the horizon, while the Virgin Mary's humbly downcast eyes are slightly above the level of his, so that the painter does not permit the supplicant to gaze openly into the face of the Mother of God. Around 1435, of all times, the architect and theorist Leon Battista Alberti (1404–1472) demanded in Florence that the eye level of main figures should reach the horizon, to make it possible for both painter and observer to gauge the dimensions of the persons portrayed. In Tuscany, Alberti's rule was only rarely observed; but clearly Jan van Eyck stumbled on the same equation of figure and landscape of his own accord, without the influence of any theory.

Not the *Rolin Madonna* itself, but similar paintings reached Italy at an early stage. Their truth to life and spatial effect was impressive. Certainly it was understood how close these paintings, however diverse, came to their own concept of art.

Nevertheless it was possible to keep one's distance from Flemish painting, with its luxuriant use of color, and its tendency, above all to the severe theorists of later centuries, to surrender so lightly to the incidental. The intention and ability of early Netherlandish masters not to reconstruct nature, but to comprehend the nature of things from the surface down, as it were, were seen equally as a merit and a fault. Instead of starting from the concept of *disegno* to create the world anew in his own head as an *invenzione*, a painter such as Jan van Eyck saw his task as the comprehension of God's creation in its inexhaustible multiplicity.

The most convincing advantages of the new techniques were seen in the portrait, aided by the circumstance that, as a result of the close trade relations with the Flemish cities, members of Italian families who had traveled in the Netherlands had had their portraits painted there. The rejection of idealization was in harmony with the humanist notion that it was better to be good than to appear to be good; thus even a proud Italian endured the merciless gaze of a Jan van Eyck.

In his *Portrait of a Man Wearing a Turban* of 1433 (above), in which one is tempted to recognize a self-portrait, Jan van Eyck succeeds in capturing with cold reason the sharp eyes, narrow mouth, and aging skin of his subject. He shows the head with the face turned to the left and the eyes gazing steadfastly at the observer. The sumptuous turban creates a stunning effect; it is in the Burgundian fashion of the 1430s, which was to reach the Florence of the Medici from the ducal court in Burgundy. Before Florentines were confronted with the portrait art of Van Eyck, they were used to seeing portraits in profile (Volume 1, page 450); the three-quarter turn demanded greater skill on the part of the painter and clearly was also another sensation coming from the North.

Above left:
Jan van Eyck
Portrait of a Man Wearing a Turban, 1433
Oil on oak, 26 x 19 cm
National Gallery, London

Early Netherlandish painters liked to portray married couples in pairs of pictures, with the man on the right, that is, the left as seen by the observer. The fact that the subject here faces in the opposite direction makes it clear that this is a single work. Nevertheless, and although the painting does not correspond in terms of either format or date with the explicitly titled portrait of Jan's wife (Groeninge Museum, Bruges), arguments are being mustered to declare it a self-portrait. This portrait fascinates with the alertness of the subject's penetrating gaze, but this is not the only face depicted by Jan van Eyck to gaze so resolutely at the observer. The turban suggests for the first time in art history that the painter was aware of the triumphal effect of red.

Above right:
Antonello da Messina
Portrait of a Man (Il Condottiere), 1475
Oil on wood, 35 x 28 cm
Musée du Louvre, Paris

The extent to which a good portrait that has been preserved without a name can stimulate the imagination is shown by the epithet that has traditionally been bestowed on this energetic-looking man: Il Condottiere, the hired soldier. With portraits such as these, both painters and clients were clearly concerned to conceal social status. This is related to the basic conviction of learned humanists that it is the person who matters, and not his rank.

The first Italian painter to follow Jan van Eyck's approach was Antonello da Messina, who has already been discussed at the beginning of Volume I (pages 25, 28); this Sicilian artist adopted both the technique and the portrait type used by his Flemish colleague. He even schematically took over Van Eyck's characteristic complex treatment of light (page 9). One might have expected that subtle painting of light would open up the relief of a face from the side turned toward the observer. The contour of the nose, above all, could be expressively conveyed. However, the famous Flemish painter clearly wanted the nose, as it were, to cast its shadow on the face; this increases the sculptural effect in his work, and even more decisively in the work of Antonello.

Not all early Netherlandish painters observed these maxims; the difference is seen in the more gently lit male portrait in the Uffizi by Hans Memling (below, left), perhaps painted in the same year, 1478, in which Antonello created his famous *Portrait of a Young Man* (below, right). Traditionally, very dark backgrounds had been preferred in portrait painting, as with the *Portrait of a Man with Turban* (page 8). Both these paintings break with this tradition. They place the subject in a landscape, and at the same time their painters free themselves in their different ways from Alberti's instructions as to eye level and horizon. Antonello builds up the figure above a small parapet,

creating the impression that one is looking down from a great height at its upper edge. The silhouette of the landscape however is below the man's shoulder, so that the head is outlined against the threateningly gloomy sky. This allows the landscape to be equated with the shoulder and the sky with the head. Memling, however, composes the background like a shining collar around the neck.

Which of the two artists was the innovator here is not easy to say. Netherlandish portraits with landscapes hardly existed before Memling; in Antonello's work, on the other had, the Berlin painting from the year before his death was a late exception. It may be that the Sicilian, who visited many princely courts, found his stimulus in Urbino, rather than transmitted by a Flemish portrait. It was in Urbino that the two panels were preserved on which Piero della Francesca had portrayed the married couple Battista Sforza and Federico da Montefeltro, around 1465 to after 1472, but certainly before 1476 (Volume I, pages 360, 361); they may derive from Domenico Veneziano's *Profile Portrait of a Young Woman* in the Berlin Gemäldegalerie (Volume I, page 450) and for the first time define landscape as shoulder and sky as head, additionally varying the lines of collar and neck-chain in the landscape. We may attribute the invention of such portraits to the great master of *disegno*, whose style also influenced the young Raphael from Urbino (pages 218, 219).

Below left:
Hans Memling
Portrait of a Man, ca. 1478–1480
Oil on oak, 28 x 27 cm
Galleria degli Uffizi, Florence

Unfortunately, the date of the arrival in Italy of this painting is totally obscure. It was bought for the Uffizi in 1836 as a work by Antonello; today there is no doubt that this is a particularly typical and outstanding work by Hans Memling, who reached Bruges from Seligenstadt near Aschaffenburg by way of Cologne and Brussels, and worked there for clients from all parts of Europe. The little wooden parapet and the letter in the man's hand seem to be owed to Italian influence.

Below right:
Antonello da Messina
Portrait of a Young Man, 1478
Wood, 20.4 x 14.5 cm
Gemäldegalerie, Staatliche Museen, Berlin

The sky with the view of the landscape was so disconcerting in the past that it was sometimes thought it had been painted retrospectively to cover a monochrome dark background, under the influence of Memling's portraits in front of a landscape. However, this viewpoint has since been refuted, so that the painting in its entirety is now considered the most important legacy of the Sicilian master to Venetian painting. The inscription below advises modesty in prosperity and wisdom in times of need: *prosperans modestvs esto infortvnavs vero prvdens.*

We do not know whether we have Italy or the North to thank for the concept of the portrait with landscape; there were examples in Florence as early as the time of the severe profile in tempera (Volume I, page 450). Even Memling may have known of works such as Piero della Francesca's portraits; personal contact between the artists come into play here. In Italy, however, there were not only paintings imported from the North that attracted attention, but also masters who came from the North. That Jean Fouquet had traveled to Rome from Tours before 1447 was known to Vasari a hundred years later, because he admired that papal portrait by the French artist in Rome, which was later to inspire Raphael (Volume I, page 15).

Pilgrimages in the Holy Years of 1450 and 1500 brought artists to the Eternal City. But the most powerful effect was exercised by the court in Urbino, where Federico da Montefeltro (in power 1444–1482)

set up a Court of the Muses in the spectacular new Ducal Palace. The Duke, whom Piero della Francesca portrayed several times (Volume I, pages 361, 366), also had himself painted reading a folio (Volume I, page 367). This harmonious painting manifests a curious disparity, depicting Federico, a war veteran, both as *gonfaloniere*, that is, army commander, of the Pope, and also as a scholar with a passion for reading. It is thus no contradiction when Federico, as in Piero's *Montefeltro Altarpiece* (Volume I, page 366), wears his armor as he sits in the study with the little heir to his dukedom. The portrait was painted in Urbino by a workshop that included not only Italians, but also painters from all over Europe; it is attributed to the Spaniard Pedro Berruguete (ca. 1450–1504).

Among these painters, whom Federico brought to Urbino in the 1470s, Joos van Wassenhove took up a leading position from 1471. Today he is commonly

Above left:
Justus van Ghent
Dante, 1472–1474
From the *Studiolo* in Urbino
Oil on wood, 111 x 64 cm
Musée du Louvre, Paris

In the 14th and 15th centuries there was a certain degree of awareness of Dante's facial appearance, at least to the extent that the poet, with his gaunt features and in unpretentious dress, was shown by preference in strict profile, even at times when the three-quarter profile had become established (as later with Raphael; see page 235). As poet laureate, he wears a laurel crown; he holds his book closed, in order to hold forth with a restrained gesture.

known as Justus van Ghent: around 1460 he turns up in Ghent; he died around 1480, probably in Urbino. Together with Melozzo da Forlì, who came from the Romagna and in 1475 captured the founding of the Vatican Library in a mural in Rome (Volume I, page 561), and Pedro Berruguete, who later returned to his home in Spain, the master from Ghent created painted panels which were inserted in the wooden paneling of the *studiolo*.

The most comprehensive series is composed of paintings that are designed in a lifelike manner as portraits, but show almost exclusively the great authors of the past, to whom a library owes its treasures (page 10). The paintings, which culminate in a brilliant portrait of the reigning pope, Sixtus IV (page 11), demonstrate the complete adoption of the techniques from the North by painters of the South, although researchers, as usual, are not agreed about the relative contributions of the masters.

Opposite page, right:
Justus van Ghent and Pedro Berruguete
Plato, 1472–1474
From the *Studiolo* in Urbino
Oil on wood, 111 x 64 cm
Musée du Louvre, Paris

In the days of Federico da Montefeltro, there was not yet such a strong distinction between biblical and classical antiquity for Greek philosophers to be differentiated in appearance from Old Testament characters or the Apostles. Thus Plato looks like a prophet and wears the costly clothing imagined by these two painters, influenced by Burgundian fashion. A richer layer of painting covers the original image; today it is attributed to Pedro Berruguete, who had come to Urbino from Spain.

Pedro Berruguete
Pope Sixtus IV, 1474–1476
From the *Studiolo* in Urbino
Oil on wood, 116 x 56 cm
Musée du Louvre, Paris

The most lifelike image among the half-figures in Federico da Montefeltro's *studiolo* in the Ducal Palace at Urbino shows the only contemporary of the clients and painters: Pope Sixtus IV (pope 1471–1484). Melozzo da Forlì immortalized him most impressively in the fresco of the founding of the Vatican Library (Volume I, page 561). In Urbino, however, the layer of painting with the portrait of the Duke (Volume I, page 367) replaces a quite different depiction. This presumably goes back to the Pope's appointment of the Duke as his army commander, or *gonfaloniere*, in 1474. Since his insignia are to be found only in more recent layers of painting, these have been separated according to contribution, and are today ascribed, together with the portrait of the Pope, to Pedro Berruguete.

XYSTO IIII PONT MAX

Changing Times in Florence

While Joos van Wassenhove was a leading member of a princely workshop in Italy (pages 10, 11), it was his brother-in-law, a master in Ghent, who painted the picture that had the most decisive influence on Italian art history (page 12): Hugo van der Goes (ca. 1440–1482) created a triptych for the Florentine Portinari family that reached Florence in 1480, and found its place in Santa Maria Nuova until 1919 with those monks who ran an influential studio around 1400 with Don Lorenzo Monaco (Volume I, page 200). While, as late as the 1420s, indigenous painters destroyed the workshop of the outsider Gentile da Fabriano (Volume I, page 201), the generation of painters active around 1480 concerned themselves creatively with Hugo's work.

The *Portinari Altarpiece* with its overpowering use of color surpassed the portraits and the small, more easily transportable works known in Italy up to that point. At the same time, its choice of themes brought in a new element: in Florence the *Adoration of the Magi* had been painted more often than anywhere else, for example as the theme of Gozzoli's frescoes in the Medici Palace (Volume I, pages 376–389).

Hugo van der Goes: *Adoration of the Shepherds,* ca. 1475
Central panel of the *Portinari Altarpiece*
Oil on oak, 249 x 200 cm
Galleria degli Uffizi, Florence

Behind one of those traditionally famous flower still-lifes lies the naked Christ Child. Angels have hastened to the scene from all sides; some are still floating in the air. The first three shepherds are just arriving, touching in their awkward coarseness, which is all at once transformed into a deep human comprehension by the realization that they are worshipping their Savior—a wonderful tribute to humanist thought, which is concerned with the core of the individual and not the mere appearance.

The change from the fantastic to the simplicity of genre painting fascinated both clients and painters, since in an unexpected way it also incorporated the humanist ideal, which elevates plain and simple truth above colorful pomp. Hugo's panel inspired Domenico Ghirlandaio to create his most beautiful painting in 1485 (above).

Domenico Ghirlandaio
Adoration of the Shepherds, 1485
Mixed media with oil on wood, 167 x 167 cm
Cappella Sassetti, Santa Trinità, Florence

As the main event of this altar painting, venerated by the founding couple in the fresco, Ghirlandaio shows, in a city that had adopted the Three Magi as patrons, the *Adoration of the Shepherds*, though with the triumphal procession of the Magi in the background. Joseph turns toward this, or toward the star, while Mary, in a pictorial formula known from other Flemish paintings, worships the Child, and three shepherds, as in Hugo's work, move toward him.

Alessio Baldovinetti
The Annunciation, 1457
Tempera on wood, 167 x 137 cm
Galleria degli Uffizi, Florence

After the death of Fra Angelico, Baldovinetti
again adopted the pictorial convention, not favored
by the latter, in which Mary is seen standing. The
architectural depiction owes a great deal to the
Dominican monk; but the coloring of the arches and
the alternation of light and dark with the golden capitals,
as well as the colorfulness of the garments, show that a
new splendor was entering Florence. However, it is
technique rather than the painter's aesthetic orientation
that produces the austere, dry effect of the painting.

In the Netherlands, fine painting was preserved in
minute detail, which also caused it to be disparaged by
severe art critics. For this reason it was only rarely that
painters welcomed such foreign themes as the shepherds
of the *Portinari Altarpiece* (page 12). The continuity of
an indigenous formula beyond technical change is shown
by two paintings of the Annunciation, a generation apart,
which nevertheless with surprising faithfulness follow a
pictorial pattern whose basic features had been known in
Florence since about 1350, and which we have already
met in Donatello's *Cavalcanti Tabernacle* (Volume I, page
223). Around 1457, Alessio Baldovinetti (1425–1499)

repeated the arrangement: Gabriel approaches from the
left and falls to his knees, while Mary, standing, turns
toward him from her prayer book (above). In this
version, which was taken up in book illustrations and
prints, for example by Francesco Rosselli (ca.
1445–before 1513), the angel wears a kind of peplum,
that is, a finely pleated, double-belted garment, here
painted in red, over a light blue tunic. Gabriel folds his
arms, while Mary allows her cloak to drop to show the
robe and girdle that cover her conceiving womb.

In the early 1480s, which were defined by the exciting
encounter with the *Portinari Altarpiece,* the Virgin Mary

remained almost unaltered by Lorenzo di Credi (1459–1537); the angel, however, was given a cloak of costly crimson and luscious green, which contrasts with the delicate white undergarment (above). Although all the other fabrics are paler in color, this later painting has much stronger color contrasts.

The flat relief of Baldovinetti is here broken up. As though Lorenzo di Credi wished consciously to place himself in the tradition of the *Rolin Madonna* (page 7), he opens up the Virgin's princely chamber with three arches. Jan van Eyck's idea was not known to him from the example in Autun, which, however, had admittedly found widespread imitation. Rogier van der Weyden (ca. 1399–1464) and other artists had already curbed their curiosity and eliminated the infinity of details. Lorenzo di Credi, however, not only keeps his distance from the older painting in Florence, but also from the early Netherlandish models: by making the garden limitless, clearing the path, and simplifying the plants, he proves how little the Florentine *disegno* had in common with the colorful sensations of Flanders. But what the painter was particularly able to gain from the use of oil was the atmospheric total effect of the painting.

Lorenzo di Credi
The Annunciation, ca. 1480–1485
Oil on wood, 88 x 71 cm, Galleria degli Uffizi, Florence

Above a strip painted in golden-brown camaïeu, which shows the scenes from Genesis of the Creation of Eve, the Fall, and the Expulsion from Paradise (still a little in the style of Masaccio: Volume I, page 233), this artist, who studied under Verrocchio and learned the art of painting side by side with Leonardo, supplies an adjusted version of the spatial arrangement of the *Rolin Madonna* (page 7), with a floor meticulously freed from all unevenness and a nature robbed of all accidental elements. Nevertheless, Lorenzo di Credi succeeds in creating a strongly atmospheric effect with the new colors.

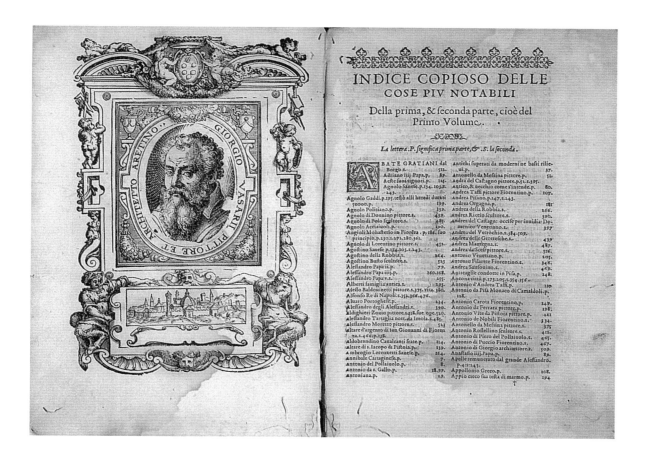

DISEGNO AND *COLORE*:
LINGUISTIC USAGE AND ART THEORY

In planning a history of Italian painting in two separate volumes, first pursuing the triumph of drawing (*disegno*) up to Michelangelo Buonarroti, and then confronting it with the triumph of color (*colore*) almost a century later, we are making a traditional distinction from the beginnings of modern art historiography into a guiding principle. It is associated with Giorgio Vasari, who was born in Arezzo in 1511, lived in Florence from 1524, came to Rome for the first time in 1531, encountered Michelangelo there and came to admire him above all else. In the contemporary discussions of his time, Vasari always took Michelangelo's side and energetically stressed the contrast between him and the Venetian Titian; the discrepancy between the two masters is summed up in the values of *disegno* and *colore*.

None of Vasari's paintings has really entered the consciousness of posterity. His most important work was an office building with a princely top floor, which is famous today, but not because it is, in its own way, brilliant architecture: it is the Uffizi in Florence. It was in the service of Cosimo de' Medici, who became

Grand Duke in 1555, thus completing the rise of his family from bankers to members of the grand aristocracy of Europe, that Vasari found his decisive role. In Florence and in the Tuscan possessions of the Medici, he was as competent to deal with his master's new artistic projects as with the heritage of earlier generations. Like a modern conservator, he had, for example, to find places for works whose location was disputed. At times he had to make difficult decisions. That Masaccio's *Trinity* fresco in Santa Maria Novella (Volume I, page 17), for instance, is very well preserved, is due to the fact that the wall in question was covered by an altarpiece of Vasari's, after he himself had honored the merits of that revolutionary fresco of the 1420s.

Vasari also contributed decisively to the ennoblement of the status of the artist. His positively princely self-portrait (page 17) from the period of his greatest recognition insistently draws attention to the gold chain with a medal of Pope Pius V (in office 1566–1572). Titian, for example, immortalized himself in similar fashion (Volume I, page 9), but without betraying the

Portrait of Giorgio Vasari, presumably from a self-portrait
Woodcut
From Giorgio Vasari: *Le Vite de' più eccellenti pittori, scultori e architettori*, 2nd edition, 1568

Vasari's multi-volume publication of the lives of famous painters, beginning with Cimabue and culminating in Michelangelo (clearly also encompassing further figures of his own time), is illustrated throughout with portraits of the masters discussed, most of them with clearly very reliable features. Vasari himself appears in a full-page reproduction of his great self-portrait, which today belongs to the unique collection of self-portraits in the Uffizi (page 17).

origin of his gold chain, actually a double one in his case. This princely distinction was to become a commonplace for artistic success throughout Europe.

Vasari's efforts to give the artist a new social status began with his own education. He had learned the craft of the painter in Arezzo, and by 1527 had attained the status of a learned scholar at the court of the Medici in Florence, and could thus see himself as a *pictor doctus*. His talent as a writer was to put all the other abilities of this gifted man in the shade. The *Vite de' piú eccellenti architetti, pittori, et scultori italiani* (*Lives of the Most Excellent Architects, Painters and Sculptors*, widely known simply as the *Lives of the Artists* or just the *Lives*), was revised during the years from which the portrait dates, and substantially altered, expanded, and republished in 1568 (with the title changing slightly as well).

Though concepts are codified by books, in general they do not come into being with the book. Vasari's style was developed from the linguistic usage of his day. The contrast of *disegno* and *colore* was his own intellectual construct, but the concept, which had taken shape in the studio, had encompassed other areas of life before the first publication of Vasari's *Lives*. Words that on the one hand designated stages of the creation of paintings, but on the other hand also embraced perceptible phenomena of aesthetic effect, had become general characteristics of art.

Here a brief glance back at the 1420s is informative. In Florence, the revolutionizing of what could be meant by an image had been by no means merely a mechanistic or mathematical change, but an attack on the core of art. From then on, the relationship of painter and observer with figure and space was defined with judicious understanding. Rational measurements were used for guidance; the painter who wanted to show foreshortened space would start from the right-hand corner, and he relied on the fact that the observer would perceive the system of lines in the image in the same orthogonal manner. Light served as clarification of the arrangement of the space, not as an atmospheric bonus. Since this development coincided with a return to classical antiquity, which incidentally had no concept of perspective, many a decisive criterion was immediately added. The preserved remains of classical sculpture were looked on with new eyes; the meaning of the classical contrapposto was recognized, and the human figure was understood as a mass in light and as a body with gravity, so that, all at once, Masaccio's figures cast shadows.

All this was most easily grasped in the traditional technique of the fresco. This required advance planning merely from the point of view of distribution of labor, for only a painter who had intelligently organized his day's labors could convincingly conclude his work. In the separate steps of his work, he had first to develop a concept of the whole; if he wished to make fundamental changes to his image, he had to dismantle the plaster, in other words actually destroy his painting. The paint had rights only in so far as it gave more lifelike shape to what was already unalterably created in its core. The ultimately valid layer of the image, in addition, came into being

under pressure of time; when the planned "day's work" (*giornata*) was in place, the painter could not delay, because dry plaster would no longer accept the paint as efficiently.

Ornamentation and everything else unrelated to the artist's understanding only delayed the work. This was not true to the same extent of panel paintings, but even the tempera technique that was usual for these was resistant to excessively intense reworking. Adding layers to each other was not recommended, even when this allowed greater leisure in working. The Florentines were more willing than others to bow to these requirements. In Florence the fresco paradigmatically typified the aesthetic; it had found a new significance with the development of perspective.

Giorgio Vasari
Self-Portrait, 1566–1568
Oil on wood, 100.5 x 80 cm
Galleria degli Uffizi, Florence

Of princely form, this work is larger than Titian's contemporary *Self-Portrait* (Volume I, page 9) and has almost the same dimensions as the latter's portrait of Pietro Aretino (page 18). It shows the artist as a draftsman, far from any danger of spattering himself with paint. Dignified in his black garments, he is distinguished as a nobleman by a chain with the arms of Pope Pius V, elected in 1566. Despite all the verbally invoked contrasts with the Venetian portraits of the time, Titian's manner of capturing a figure seems to have been adopted by, of all people, Vasari, who in general was only too eager to distance himself from the Venetian master.

Titian
Portrait of Pietro Aretino, ca. 1545
Oil on canvas, 96.7 x 77.6 cm
Galleria Palatina, Palazzo Pitti, Florence

It is tempting to date this splendid painting precisely to the year in which the writer Pietro from Arezzo, who after long service to the Medici had found refuge in Venice, mounted a violent attack on Michelangelo's *Last Judgment* (Volume I, page 639). This dating makes the portrait a token of the friendship of the leading master of *colore*, who here celebrates the opponent of the most important champion of *disegno*. But such relationships are fragile: Aretino was so imbued with the Tuscan aesthetic that he was repelled by the sketchiness of the painting, which was perhaps not even finished. Nevertheless, Titian's portrayal is an impressive testimony to the consciousness of the times. Who else would create such a majestic image of a salacious author who was constantly coming into conflict with popes and princes.

There is also a parallel with rhetoric that should not be overlooked. With the fresco as the central concern of painting, artistic ambition in Florence was directed at the grand form and at the same time the succinct, which tolerated nothing but the decisive statement. With his *Last Judgment* in the Sistine Chapel (Volume I, page 639) Michelangelo had given an unprecedented finale to this development. Not all who had received their cultural education in Tuscany cared to follow the Titan in his final radical stage; and it may even have provided a stimulus for mockery. Pietro Aretino (1492–1556), a shrewd literary figure whose surname indicates that, like Vasari, he came from Arezzo, and who died in Venice, attempted in a celebrated letter of 1545 to ridicule Michelangelo's work in the coarsest possible way (without, incidentally, ever having seen it!).

In doing so, from his Venetian residence he in fact took up a position against everything that was sacred to Vasari, at the same time placing himself on the side of Michelangelo's greatest rival, Titian, who around the same time created an enchanting portrait of Aretino (page 18). But such partisanship in favor of one of the two greatest painters of his time did not mean much to a cynic like Aretino. He would not accept Titian's portrait of himself, because it was painted in swift strokes and remained partly incomplete. He was not satisfied with "dashed-off work" precisely because from his childhood he had been used to Florentine paintings, had served the Medici family (Pope Clement VII and Giovanni delle Bande Nere), and had never quite become a Venetian. This fits with Aretino's later relationship with Michelangelo: despite his sharp words of 1545, Aretino in his own later years even praised the master and boasted of his acquaintance, even friendship, with him.

Moreover, the writer Aretino cultivated in his own linguistic usage the terms *disegno* and *colore*, just as did Vasari, who for his part considered himself, in this specific aspect, the disciple of Michelangelo. Aretino, of all people, even included these paired concepts in several written statements on his own art: in 1538 he wrote with false modesty to Pietro Bembo that his literary work was suffering from weakness of *disegno* and taking refuge in the triviality of coloring; here he actually uses the words *debolezza del disegno* and *trivialità del colorito*. Two years earlier, in his *Ragionamenti*, Aretino had already compared his own way of drawing portraits in words with Titian's hasty application of paint, but had attributed true effort, in literature too, to *disegno*; according to him, color creates only a beautiful appearance, which cannot deceive us with regard to the true character of the work.

Now Pietro Aretino was much too vain, too vacillating and malicious to be regarded as a real authority. His maneuvering between Titian's Venice and the Tuscan tradition as manifested in Michelangelo is therefore less important than his language, which transfers the contrast drawn from painting to artistic creativity in general, interpreting *disegno* as the basic structural idea, and *colore* as the pleasing outward appearance. Aretino's words show that Vasari's codification is oddly out of date, and this is confirmed by another circumstance: the literary man clearly has no problems with the painter's claim to be no longer regarded as a craftsman, but to be part of nobler society as a *pictor doctus*, for he basks in the favor of Titian and also makes claim to the affection of Michelangelo.

We will seek in vain in the Renaissance for a theoretical position that sees the work of the painter exclusively in terms of color. But there are interesting positions between the two extremes, even though, time and again, rational control (that is, the intellectual core of *disegno*) is valued more highly than any color; they can hardly dispense with a reference to Michelangelo, but also include Leonardo, whose extremely subtle theory of art was only fragmentarily accessible to the public.

In this context, we should think of the Milanese painter Giovanni Paolo Lomazzo (1538–1600), who went blind at an early age, and who mediates between the intellectual origin of the artistic themes and work of the painter in a different way from the older artist Vasari. For Lomazzo, the social status of the artist is hardly a problem any more; he takes the role of the *pictor doctus* for granted, and does not in any case concern himself with lesser spirits. In his wide-ranging *Trattato dell'arte della pittura* of 1584 he even demands an enormous degree of culture of the painter, quite in line with the demands that Leonardo made of his art; and here the possibilities arise of formulating what is to be depicted from painting itself, and not from the height of the culture that has been attained. At the same time, the age of the academies and of the codification of art has begun; Lomazzo's *Self-Portrait* (below), perhaps dating from the same year, 1568, in which Vasari's *Lives* appeared in their definitive form, bears witness to this.

Giovanni Paolo Lomazzo
Self-Portrait, ca. 1568
Oil on canvas, 56 x 44 cm
Pinacoteca di Brera, Milan

The young painter has depicted himself as a *nabàd*, in Italian *abate*, that is, abbot of the Accademia dei Facchini di Val di Blenio, which he ran for a number of years. This peculiar association of artists of the most varied kinds, who conversed with each other in a Ticino dialect difficult for others to understand, was under the patronage of Bacchus; this is why the painter is crowned with vine leaves. In an inscription, he identifies himself with the name by which he was known in this community, where occult interests were pursued. At that time, this was by no means in conflict with acute intellectuality, but the Dionysian aspect introduces another element that, unlike *disegno* and *colore*, no longer belongs to the concept of the artist's intellectual control.

FLORENCE AND VENICE

The categories *disegno* and *colore* were in use long before the publication of Vasari's *Lives*, for this way of thinking had already made its way from the realm of painting into other arts. Vasari polemically attempted to characterize the contrast by assigning two centers: Florence and Venice. With all its pleasure in new color effects from the North, Florence stayed true to *disegno*. In Venice, the Sicilian Antonello da Messina was triumphant. Many a painter altered his way of working in Venice, while in Florence a man such as Lorenzo di Credi stayed true to the old principles, even though clothed in new garments.

This view of history is a simplistic one, and takes no account of contrasting elements such as climatic influences. A resident of the lagoon by no means sees the world differently from a Tuscan. But in the damp air of Venice the fresco technique soon deteriorates; for this

reason, painters there made more energetic efforts to develop the image released from the wall. Even monumental formats of dimensions which actually only fitted in the spaces for which they were intended were if possible not created directly on the wall, in which salt water tended to stagnate.

The most important support medium until about 1500, even in Venice, remained panels of poplar; but then, and in fact even earlier than anywhere else, the painting on canvas was to assert itself in Venice. Oil was most suitable as a binder. In Flanders, however, oil painting was not at first used for canvas, but for oak panels. With the use of new media the work process also changed, for the cloth had to be prepared differently; soon the idea took hold of replacing the *gesso* (plaster) surfaces of panel painting, whose hard brilliance was reminiscent of the white plaster of fresco painting, with

Giorgio Vasari
View of the Uffizi, façade facing the Arno, 1560–1574
Florence

Most old cities, in one way or another, lie by water; but cities that are traversed by rivers such as the Arno are hardly ever seen from the water. Not even bridges such as the Ponte Vecchio, on which Vasari built a gallery, offered a view of the buildings by the river. Even today, this is expressed by the popular views of the Uffizi. The façades, leading like a cul-de-sac to the river, of the deliberately similar entrances to the offices (uffizi) of the Medici administration, are often portrayed, but not the view of the building reflected in the river. With its clear contours and the exceptionally rational arrangement of the whole, Vasari's most important structure takes its place in an architectural tradition to which everything "painterly" is foreign.

Antonio Canale, called Canaletto
Campo San Rocco, post-1730
Oil on canvas, 47 x 80 cm
Woburn Abbey Art Gallery, Woburn

The façade of the Scuola di San Rocco in Venice, completed by Bartolomeo Bon in 1549, predates Vasari's Uffizi by two decades. As in Florence, there were guidelines of practical utility to be followed, and thus a series of architectural elements had to be relied upon. However, this astounding architect works with a very much more sculptural pattern, which, particularly in the version of the painting created almost 200 years later, seems attuned to the atmosphere of its city in a very different way from Vasari's Uffizi.

tinted ground coats. Antonello still built up his colors on white, while Titian often worked on brown surfaces. This had significant consequences for drawing; for while contours stand out against a smooth white surface, in later Venetian painting on canvas they lose their powerful dimension.

Like the discovery of perspective in Florence, oil painting is among the innovations that characterize the beginning of the new era in Europe. Its further development in Venice, but equally in Leonardo's Milan, belonged to the future. It established itself not only as a painting technique, but also as a way of capturing the world in the image. Just as the development in Florence was not restricted to geometry, the benefit of oil painting was not exhausted by the chemistry of pigment and binder. Rather, it offered solutions for intellectual and aesthetic problems, which had already been posed in art. The new calculation of space and surface in Florence and the new binders that were now being used in Venice for painting in oil on canvas were of less influence on practical work than on the basic concept of painting.

If drawing and color had been only basic categories of painting, they would in principle always have had equal and related rights throughout history. But this was not the case. In fact their development took its course analogously to the role of *disegno,* whether as a mental concept or as a sketch on a light-colored ground, to *colore,* the valid color version, or the optical reproduction of what appeared to the eyes. Just as almost every painter first draws and then applies paint, the triumph of drawing too preceded the triumph of color in the great historical context.

As a result, the contours of the history of Italian Renaissance painting become smooth, and the contrast is no longer one of *disegno* and *colore,* but of the move from drawing to painting, up to the arrival of the Baroque. The conclusion is formed by a second Michelangelo—Caravaggio, who was born Michelangelo Merisi. Traditional art history unhesitatingly categorizes him in that era which followed the Renaissance and Mannerism. But anyone who, passing through museums such as the Berlin Gemäldegalerie, is constantly obliged to observe Caravaggio and Rubens side by side, can hardly avoid drawing a sharp line between them. In a clearly paradoxical situation the Italian painter, although he was positively proud of never having made a drawing, can still be classified in the tradition of draftsmanship, while the divinely gifted draftsman Rubens could only design in terms of painting, even when working on paper. This was something the Flemish artist learned in Venice, even though he spent much more time in Rome.

Sandro Botticelli
The Madonna and Child Between John the Baptist and John the Evangelist (Bardi Altarpiece), 1484
Tempera on wood, 185 x 180
Gemäldegalerie, Staatliche Museen, Berlin

This excellently documented painting for the Bardi family comes from Santo Spirito in Florence and places the two Johns on either side of the throne: the Baptist, seen as the one crying in the wilderness, on the right, and the Evangelist, shown as an aged man, on the left. In their postures the two saints create a sort of understanding between the observer and the throne of Mary. The Virgin, with a modest indication of her gift of milk, shows that she is a True Mother. To be understood as a trompe l'œil, the little panel with an image of the Crucifixion on a gold ground, below center, is intended as a reminder at Mass of the sacrifice of the Savior, and leans against a sort of metal container such as might be used to store the Blessed Sacrament. The inset image with architectural motifs places the observer in a garden, though the plants are tied in such a way that they form niches for the figures.

THE *SACRA CONVERSAZIONE* IN FLORENCE AND VENICE

Italian retables of the 14th century are ordered around a divine apparition—usually an image of the enthroned Madonna—with innumerable variations of standing saints. For these, individual panels were added, which were separated by decorative architecture. As long as this was the case, the question of the point in time of what was depicted did not arise at all, because there was no unity in the image. In fact, it is a peculiar ensemble that is formed when, for example (above), the Christ Child, according to the Gospels of the same age as the two Johns, is shown with the Baptist as a mature adult and the Evangelist as an old man. This becomes noticeable only when Botticelli presents the three contemporaries at the same time at three different ages.

Masaccio's Pisa altarpiece (Volume I, 240–243) was still divided into separate panels. Each image was autonomous; but from the time that painters such as Fra Angelico (Volume I, pages 268, 271, 273) and Domenico Veneziano (Volume I, page 311) removed the borders between the throne and the subsidiary figures, such retables give the impression of an audience at court with figures actually present, as advisers or petitioners, sometimes both at the same time. With perspective, which helped the creation of convincing spaces, the rewarding idea was formed that it was not only a continuing space that was shown in the image area, but also a single moment. But there cannot be a unity of place and time in such images.

With regard to the arrangement of the saints, the clients were by no means as free and easy as one likes to think. The ensembles as a rule resulted from the liturgical needs of the individual chapels. Altarpieces were dedicated to a specific saint before being provided with a retable; the sponsors of the altarpiece of course had to be included in the picture. If one checks a specific case, one will most often find a meaningful arrangement for each endowment of an altarpiece. Rarely or never do the names of the clients play a part; not only are they missing when, as in Piero della Francesca's monumental panel, the client was Federico da Montefeltro, whose name is not linked to that of any notable saint (Volume I, page 366), but because the client's influence simply would not have justified this. In praying, as with the situation at court, it was the practice to address oneself first to the subsidiary figures and implore their intercession with Mary and the Christ Child.

Such images are known as a *sacra conversazione*, "holy conversation," but the saints usually stand directly side by side, and hardly communicate with looks, almost never by conversation. Supplicants are rarely included; the saints hardly concern themselves with them; even in Piero's painting, the Duke of Urbino kneels in isolation in front of the dense throng of angels and saints. At times, the minor figures point toward the center, but usually only as if in a centrally composed ballet.

Both Florence and Venice knew the pictorial type of the *sacra conversazione*; in both cities in the 1440s the picture surface and space were standardized (Volume I, pages 268, 311; Volume II, pages 56–57). Jan van Eyck may again have been the precursor with an admittedly very small painting, the *Madonna of Canon van der Paele* of 1436 (Groeninge Museum, Bruges). The differences between the two Italian cities are all the more astonishing; this, in spite of the almost simultaneous first appearance, is due to a time shift in the further course of events. In Florence, the theme was already flourishing in the lifetime of Fra Angelico, around 1450, while it was not until a generation later, starting from the years when Antonello da Messina lived in their city, that Venetians really became attached to the theme.

A much disputed question is: who actually established the characteristic type for Venice, the Sicilian Antonello or perhaps Giovanni Bellini? Only a few splendid examples of Bellini's are preserved (right); but the earliest was created by Zoppo in 1471 (page 125).

While in Florence, and precisely in Brunelleschi's newly built Renaissance churches, landscape formats were customary, and therefore the altarpiece, with a few exceptions, hardly rose above the height of a square (page 22), painters in Venice, particularly Bellini, with his fine altarpiece in San Zaccaria (right), created the illusion of standing in front of a stately chapel, which opens behind the altar into the open air. The coloration additionally helps the recognition of mostly noble reliefs, while the Venetians tried to deceive the eye with their use of light in painting.

Giovanni Bellini
The Madonna and Child Enthroned with Saints (Madonna of San Zaccaria), 1505
Oil on wood, transferred to canvas, 500 x 235 cm
San Zaccaria, Venice

Peter with his keys and the Church Father Jerome in the robes of a cardinal flank the throne; they represent the Church and the correct understanding of the Scriptures, while the two female saints quietly turn toward the Mother and Child. There is no speech or "conversation" here. When the French armies under Napoleon removed works of art from Venice, some formats—in this case the enormous size—proved to be unsuitable; they then simply cut a piece off. In this case, the top of the upper arch is missing. The painting has long been returned to its old frame above a side altar; only the illusion has been disturbed. By agreement with the craftsmen who created the frame, the painter had actually wanted to encourage the idea that an arch had been opened up in the church wall, allowing a view of a space opening in one of the sides, enclosed by a sort of apse niche.

CHANGES IN NORTHERN ITALY

Technical solutions presuppose a need for them; they respond to problems posed in the course of cultural development. Gutenberg's introduction of printing could only become established because around the middle of the 15th century the time had come for a new way of making books accessible. That something unknown until that time in art history should prove its worth demands an analogous inclination toward the new. That the profusion of color and creative possibilities such as those conveyed by means of oil painting by Antonello da Messina could establish themselves in Venice with so much more vitality must have something to do with a specifically local predisposition.

This should not be understood as a statement that "the Venetian" had always seen the world differently from "the Florentine." But in fact, Northern Italian painting in the late 14th century already shows tendencies otherwise found only in Naples, or in the case of masters such as Gentile da Fabriano (Volume I, pages 201–203). The first chapter of this volume will deal with trends of this kind. Even more decisive were the first signs in the early work of Giovanni Bellini (ca. 1430–1516).

Bellini had grown up in a family of painters; his father Jacopo (ca. 1400–1470/71) had also transmitted to his sons some of the influence of Gentile da Fabriano's painting. But while the eldest son, Gentile

Andrea Mantegna
Christ on the Mount of Olives, ca. 1455
Tempera on wood, 63 x 80 cm
National Gallery, London

Here Mantegna seems to have been concerned with completeness. On the opposite side of the Brook Kidron in the right foreground, we see the hill in front of which the three favorite disciples are sleeping. In the background, Judas is approaching as leader of the officials who are to take Jesus prisoner and bring him to Jerusalem, whose proud walls rise at the back. Not the Chalice of Sorrow mentioned in the gospels, but the signs of his Passion, the *arma Christi,* are shown to the praying Christ by angels. The world is stony, as though the painting were a powerfully colored stone relief. So that the enemies of the Lord can be seen, the painter has felled some of the trees by the brook, of which only stumps remain.

(1429–1507), was to paint in rather dry and two-dimensional style throughout his life, Giovanni at an early stage developed an interest in light, color, and space. He soon emancipated himself from the art of his father, probably also learning from his brother-in-law Mantegna (1429/30–1506), who had grown up in Padua; but the decisive contribution that he was to make to the history of European painting cannot be understood on the basis of a network of family relationships alone.

To illustrate this, let us here repeat one of the most revealing comparisons in art history. Mantegna and Giovanni Bellini, almost at the same time, painted the scene of daybreak on Good Friday on quite small panels (pages 24, 25). They perceive the story in similar ways, since they are both concerned with showing the end of the night on the Mount of Olives. While the favorite disciples are fast asleep, Judas is already bringing Christ's pursuers to the scene. They still have to cross the Brook Kidron. Meanwhile Jesus is unaware of all this, for he is caught up in mortal fear and has turned toward the heavens to pray. Here Mantegna shows him with all the instruments of torture of the Passion, but Bellini shows only the

chalice. This difference in motif already tells us something about the contrast between the two brothers-in-law of the same age: Mantegna is interested in Jerusalem, Bellini in the garden of Gethsemane. With Mantegna, the Mount of Olives is built up in convex fashion, from slabs of stone layered diagonally, a hard surface for the suffering Christ to kneel upon, while Bellini provides a sandy hollow for him, leading to a rock whose structures are folded vertically. In Mantegna's image the landscape intrudes on the view, in Bellini's it opens up; one painting is dominated by nocturnal darkness, while in the other the early morning light breaks through much more energetically, already allowing the walls of the mountain on the left to glow brightly.

Mantegna's sky seems to be closed in by its colors, while Bellini seems to have captured its airy quality. Instead of forming relief-like bands of firm consistency, his clouds gather into a painterly form that dissolves toward their edges. Mantegna was later to make his already lively coloring even stronger with the use of oils, but for the Venetian Bellini, these would open up possibilities of which he was already dreaming in this image of 1459.

Giovanni Bellini
Christ on the Mount of Olives, 1459
Tempera on wood, 81 x 127 cm
National Gallery, London

In this version of the scene, Christ learns of his Passion by means of the airy, light-filled figure of a putto, who shows him the chalice, painted in an equally non-material style. As though in a hollow, the three favorite disciples are resting, dispersed across the terrain. That the figures have come here from the garden of Gethsemane is shown by the fence with the open garden gate on the right. In the central area, and in fact in the center of the image, Judas and his companions appear; they must cross the bridge and the steps on the left in order to capture Jesus. A strangely barren landscape opens up vividly in the distance; nothing here suggests Jerusalem and the Crucifixion.

Leonardo's Workshop
The Madonna with the Spindle, post-1510
Oil on wood, transferred to canvas, 50.2 x 36.4 cm
Private collection, New York

As though from the depths of an alpine landscape, such as has been immortalized by the *Mona Lisa* (page 201), the Virgin Mary turns in an astonishing twist to the right, where the Christ Child is gazing with great attention at a small cross that has been given to him as though it were a toy. Here we must be aware of the devotion to the Cross, persisting from the Middle Ages into modern times, in which the wood to which Christ was nailed is revered as bringing salvation. Presumably for reasons of conservation, this classic oil painting on a wooden panel was transferred to canvas.

On the brink of the 16th century, the influences of the Netherlands and the clearly far-reaching encounter with Antonello da Messina had long been assimilated in Venice. At this time a remarkable role is played by Leonardo, whose stay in the city remains enigmatic today. As a Florentine, he was among those artists who had had to come to terms with the shock of the *Portinari Altarpiece* (page 12). To a greater extent than any other artist, he concerned himself with the new possibilities. Clearly he wanted to free his art from the aesthetic of the fresco; for that reason he unfortunately executed his *Last Supper* in Milan (pages 190–191) using an unsuitable technique.

A defining factor for Leonardo himself and for his posthumous fame was the circumstance that because of his engagement with the interminably slow method of working in oil, important pictures such as his *Adoration of the Magi* (page 172) remained incomplete. Many images that show features of his art are still disputed today, for, at least in Milan, the master surrounded himself with young people whom he taught to paint, and who apparently also worked for him. One of his

Titian
Mary Magdalene, 1565
Oil on canvas, 118 x 97 cm
Hermitage, St. Petersburg

Images of penitence, for which Mary Magdalene, according to legend, retired to Sainte-Baume in Provence, demanded a figure in a landscape, and could have a strongly erotic aspect or, as here, a psychological effect, in which the landscape shares. The general development toward the picturesque, we should not forget, includes the enlargement of the canvases. This painting comes from Titian's posthumous estate, and was sold in 1581 by Titian's son Pomponio, with the entire stock, to Cristoforo Barbarigo, and came into the possession of the Tsar of Russia in 1850 as part of the collection of an important Venetian family.

compositions, at least, is most likely the source of a type of the Madonna in front of a wild landscape (page 26), which is prefigured in some studies and of which several examples survive. None of these are indisputably by his own hand alone; but they betray a great deal of what Leonardo was able to draw from the new possibilities of painting, even in terms of content.

Painting could now link figure and landscape together in such a way that inner drama was already built into the depth of the image. Against a sublime alpine landscape, mother and child turn aside to meditate on the cross, which, however small, is capable as a divine sign of putting the whole world under its spell. But in his painting, which is also not very large, the painter was able to capture *this* world as well.

This was the starting point for Giorgione and his pupils. Above all, the saints in a landscape of the long-lived Titian probe the extent to which painting, ever more freely executed, can link the depths of the soul with the expressive values of the landscape. Here the step from Venetian *colore* to the picturesqueness of the Baroque has almost been completed.

COLOR IN THE FRESCO: RAPHAEL

When writing art history it is necessary to start with theories. But these should never be absolute, for the artist has yet to be found who followed theories logically all his life—even his own. Individual attempts at stylization of this kind are known above all in the last two centuries; their representatives, such as Johannes Itten at the Bauhaus, however, have either remained shadowy, or are notable precisely for striking contradictions between theory and practice. In historical reality, theory even serves rather to explain and justify creative work retrospectively. One need only think of Picasso and Braque, whose Cubist paintings were interpreted by Daniel Kahnweiler in such a way as to suggest the two painters had first discovered intellectually what they sought experimentally in the course of painting.

Greatness in art, however, includes in particular the ability to cross borderlines. Color did have its advocates, but theorists could not imagine working exclusively on the basis of color, if only because such a process was contrary to the actual manner of working. This had to be built up as *disegno* as an intellectual concept and in most cases as a drawing.

Drawing as a principle was emphasized in the work of masters such as Botticelli, even in the application of color. This tendency, which stresses contour even in color effect, leads to a tremendous triumph on the part of *disegno* as concept and drawing as a system of lines in Michelangelo's frescoes and the few panels executed by him. Other artists of genius, however, abandon sharpness of line as soon as they glance at their objects, and then in drawing. In Leonardo's drawings there is an atmospheric note when the objects are, as it were, dissected in a timeless and placeless way; for the master opens up what he sees by means of subtly modified light. The longer and more abundantly he then draws, the more strongly painterly features appear on the paper (page 198).

This volume begins with Leonardo's Archangel Gabriel (page 2); he has been taken from precisely that Florentine *Annunciation* whose Mary creates such a strangely cold and draftsmanlike effect that some would prefer to attribute her to a follower of Domenico Ghirlandaio (pages 162–163). This part of the painting has its place because the executed painting with its subtle values almost allows the lines to be forgotten in the soft light and *sfumato*. The Florentine Leonardo, who had been trained under Verrocchio in a tradition building logically on drawing and precise conceptuality, realized that the line, such as a painter needs to keep in mind and in his hand, does not exist at all in nature.

If we speak of the triumph of color in this volume, this also refers to a decisive change in Leonardo's work.

From his observation of nature, he disputes the true existence of the most important method of ordering of the visual artist, the line in drawing. Drawing, the central practice in the designing process, becomes an aid to the endlessly long process of painting, and disappears into color.

The fresco technique, with its insistently rapid completion, could not be appropriate to such a painter: the technical failure of the *Last Supper* (pages 190–191) was the result. But other artists have made surprisingly successful efforts to free themselves from the line in fresco. While Michelangelo in the Sistine Chapel always makes use of the contour as a powerful aid to seeing, Raphael succeeds in his more near-sightedly arranged frescoes in the rooms of the Vatican in developing a manner of painting in whose completion color alone still dominates. With astonishing virtuosity, Raphael also masters everything that was actually much more strikingly to be grasped in oil painting. He uses the representation of light as convincing materiality (page 245); he even succeeds, almost 200 years after Taddeo Gaddi's experiments with a night image (Volume I, page 117), in capturing the release of St. Peter from prison in a nocturnal mood that was barely imaginable until then (page 247).

Generally, however, as in the *School of Athens* (pages 29, 232) Raphael retains the brightness otherwise typical of fresco painting. According to the principles of a perspective converging at a vanishing point, he constructs the architecture in masterly fashion; and in doing so he unconsciously places himself in the succession of those Florentines, Masaccio and Donatello, who developed the new concepts of Italian painting in the 1420s. But in coloring in his paintings, he frees himself from the primacy of the line; volumes developed from color determine the total effect. Light and shade—even though, for example, the blue of Plato's cloak has almost entirely deteriorated—give the coloration a splendor that allows us to forget Raphael's beginnings as much as that art of *disegno*, anxiously concerned with the right concept and with sharply outlined drawing, from which he emerged.

In placing Aristotle and Plato in the center of the philosophers, Raphael thematizes the fundamental opposition which is also the concern of *colore* and *disegno*: the Aristotelian view validates the world perceived by the senses, while Plato's world of ideas is, as it were, *disegno* in the intellect. Here Aristotle is given the position of greater prestige, on the right; even if his facial features are reminiscent of Leonardo's self-portraits (see page 207), this perhaps also indicates that in our division between images and theories we are on the right path.

Raphael
The School of Athens, 1509
(detail page 232)
Stanza della Segnatura, Vatican, Rome

Plato and Aristotle are placed centrally in Raphael's depiction of an imaginary meeting of the philosophers and scholars of classical antiquity. The fact that this is not a historical moment links an image such as this with the altarpieces featuring a *sacra conversazione*. Here the two most important authors among the ancient philosophers are honored at the same time; this may also remind us that according to Renaissance thought the idea that a great individual was godlike (*divino*) was quite common. Their appearance in front of a bright blue sky at the same time gives both figures a particular strength of color, which is not lessened even by the fact that Plato's blue has clearly suffered severely.

Mannerism and Color

While Michelangelo spreads bright colors like sails between his confident contours, Leonardo was searching, even in his drawings, ever more intensively for the subtle gradations which develop in enormous variety in monochrome. From this point, of course, colorfulness becomes foreign to his images (page 172), particularly since in his painting he develops the tendency to keep

the color in check by means of distinctive shadows. In this way he opened up the path to chiaroscuro in painting, which was further energetically pursued by Giorgione, Titian, and other Venetians, until Caravaggio completed this tendency.

But the world around wanted to revel in color. Parmigianino (1503–1540) had come to Central Italy from Northern Italian Parma. An acute draftsman in his basic attitude, who entrusts the line with astonishing effects, he yet works out a treatment of light with fabulous color effects, which, however, allows the bright colors to emerge from areas of shadow, as with Leonardo's *sfumato* (page 30). Admittedly, Parmigianino replaces the canon of splendid primary colors with broken tones: his red looks like neither vermilion nor carmine, at most sometimes like crimson, and his blue is mixed with far too much white for the ultramarine still to glow deeply from it.

Veronese (1528–1588) is quite happy to do without chiaroscuro. The larger his paintings are, the more brilliant is their total coloration. He retained all his life a feeling for the radiant appearance of a single color. It may be more than a coincidence that he clothes his self-portrait in a green of unexampled luminosity and rich gradations. Incidentally, "Veronese green" is not in the same category as "Titian red." No pigment is actually named after Titian himself, but the term refers equally to a shade and to that paradoxical color effect that takes place with many paintings of the master's, when the observer is challenged to pursue the few clear indications of color that verge on the crimson further into the chiaroscuro. Veronese green on the other hand is a green earth, which is linked to the painter Paolo Caliari, known as Veronese, only in so far as both have become trade marks of Verona. However, the painter may, in the spirit of Mannerism, have alluded to this in the choice of his garment (page 31).

In his self-portrait, the painter presents himself in profile, a particularly difficult view for this task. His own face can only be seen in part, by means of optical diversions with several mirrors. But since Leonardo produced such self-portraits at least as drawings, and Titian as actual paintings (Volume I, page 9), with this development the young artist consciously places himself in their tradition.

Parmigianino
The Madonna with the Long Neck, ca. 1534
Oil on wood, 219 x 113 cm
Galleria degli Uffizi, Florence

This representation of the Mother of God is laden with heavy iconographic meaning by the sleep of the Christ Child, who already indicates his death on the Cross, the noticeably emphasized breast, in which the true motherhood of the Virgin is displayed, and the man in the background, who is certainly to be understood as a prophet with a prophecy of Christ's act of salvation. Important set-pieces, which were to return with much greater force in Baroque painting, are already incorporated in this painting: most noticeably, the triumphal curtain and the mighty column. From the start, the strange proportions were found disturbing; the painting soon acquired its nickname, under which it became world-famous. It inspires not so much devotion as aesthetic astonishment; this may be the reason that the picture was soon moved from the altar for which it was intended, to hang in the gallery.

Opposite page:
Veronese
The Feast in the House of Levi, 1573
(detail page 484–485)
Gallerie dell'Academia, Venice

It was precisely in this work, which precipitated the artist into the worst situation of his life, that Veronese created his finest self-portrait (left). Like a master of ceremonies, he stands in front of the monumental architecture, inviting guests and giving instructions to the servants, a prince and impresario at the same time, in his splendid gradations of green striking those jubilant notes that, apart from chiaroscuro, were so characteristic of painting in Venice.

Chiaroscuro Painting as a Sister Art of Music

One could actually describe the history of Italian painting, from the Florentine *disegno* to the Venetian *colore* that inspired the Baroque, as a path that by no means ends in the triumph of color, for painting noticeably moves away from bright coloration in clear light toward chiaroscuro, where a strong light is cast only on certain parts of the image. The change from wood to canvas, which was accompanied by color changes to the ground of the painting, drove out the radiant white of smoothly polished plaster in favor of brown on a linen base. The darker ground hinders the process of preliminary drawing on the surface of the image, and chiaroscuro also swallows up outlines. This leads away from drawing, but hardly benefits the coloration. Bright color is replaced by an overall tone tending toward brown, a single color that the observer has to perceive from the few areas illuminated by full light. However, swallowed outline does not constitute the triumph of color!

Now the change from *disegno* to *colore* also stimulated a move from intellectual approaches to art in favor of effects that do not appeal to the understanding. When Pietro Aretino transfers the pair of concepts from the visual arts to literature, he means that in literary writing *colore* serves toward deception, because it covers up the weaknesses of *disegno*, that is, the intellectual structure. That the other arts were similarly guided by reason is beyond debate. Music in particular, at least in its noble manifestations, had been considered since the days of classical antiquity as a sister of mathematics and geometry. But beyond all theory, it had the attraction that it addressed areas outside those of the intellect. Now a silent image is contrasted with music; but it was precisely this circumstance that stimulated artists.

In life itself, many painters tried their hand as musicians; Leonardo, in the letter of application that he wrote to the Sforzas in Milan, boasted of his many abilities; his talent at playing the lute was of greater value to him than all his skills in the visual arts. To vie with music as an art of harmony and melody by means of a silent painting was thus a challenge that went along with the triumphal progress of color in painting.

A canvas in the Palazzo Pitti was ascribed to Giorgione before the work was restored and recognized as that of the young Titian (below). Three men of rank, not traveling musicians, have come together for this so-called concert; the center position is taken up by a young man at a keyboard instrument, who turns in a

Titian
The Concert, ca. 1510
Oil on canvas, 86.5 x 123.5 cm
Galleria Palatina, Palazzo Pitti, Florence

The side figures, above all, have suffered a great deal with regard to their state of preservation, while the brilliantly depicted keyboard player in the center testifies to Titian's masterly touch. The scene is set in an elevated milieu, but the relationships between the individuals leave room for doubt, for example, as to whether music is here regarded as part of a concept of education, with the older man, a priest, as it were playing the part of teacher of two people of different temperaments. It is hardly a question of a concert, since the young man with the sumptuous headdress is not singing, and the priest is not holding the lute as though ready to play it. The main theme of the painting is clearly the way in which music unites the individuals represented.

Caravaggio
The Concert, ca. 1595
Oil on canvas, 92 x 118.5 cm
The Metropolitan Museum of Art, New York

This painting is confusing because it shows the young people not in the open air, as would be appropriate for a mythological scene, but in an interior space, which is most likely a studio, such as the artist was clearly able to set up thanks to Roman patrons such as Cardinal del Monte.

Caravaggio presents the youths, one of whom, on the right at the back, could even be a self-portrait, in the style of a still-life; the wings on the shoulders of the figure on the left at the back prevent the work from being understood simply as a kind of genre painting from the artist's immediate circle.

wonderful gesture toward a priest, who has brought his lute along, but is not playing it.

The persons are shown life-size, as half-length figures against a dark background. The chiaroscuro that was to conquer the world of painting from Venice already reigns. The lack of a specific theme—the three men are nameless, at least today, and were probably never intended to be identified—introduces another aspect that leads us away from the concept of the strictly fixed approach to painting in the *disegno*. The meaning of a picture such as this belongs to the realm of the arts and not of reason.

From here it is a short step to the young Caravaggio's *Concert*, painted three generations later (above). The Lombard painter in Rome also shows half-length figures making music, and in marked chiaroscuro. But these are not characters who appear at a domestic concert in their everyday clothes, as in Titian's painting. These are youths who bear no signs of their social

status. If they come from the immediate circle of the painter, they have divested themselves of their usual clothing, either for him or for the kind of music they are playing, in order to wrap themselves in cloths. The observer is taken to another world: that this is the world of Arcadian classical antiquity is confirmed by two gods who make their contribution here: Bacchus and Cupid.

If the painter had intended to show a performance in his own time, one of the youths would have stuck false wings to his shoulders in order to play Cupid. Nevertheless one cannot quite suppress the impression that Caravaggio is describing a classicistic fancy-dress show, performed by youths from his circle. But it is precisely in the rejection of the highly regarded motif of the mythological subject that this sort of genre painting burst through the self-imposed boundaries of a culture that placed a high value on intellect. In a metaphorical sense, color is triumphant in an art whose theorists wished it to be as dominant as possible.

VENICE, BOLOGNA, AND ROME

Titian
The Madonna with the Hare, ca. 1530
Oil on canvas, 74 x 84 cm
Musée du Louvre, Paris

A kind of poetically charged pastoral art had developed in
Venetian painting, and this influenced all Northern Italy.
Caravaggio developed his *Flight into Egypt* (page 35)
from pictures like this one, which depicts the Holy
Family as full-size figures in an oblong format in which
they would be unable to stand upright.

THE REST DURING THE FLIGHT INTO EGYPT: A PASTORAL, OR CARAVAGGIO'S FIRST GREAT WORK?

The writing of history is a catalogue of contradictions:
the more blatantly worlds collide, the livelier the debate
becomes. Ever since Walther Friedlaender's groundbreaking *Caravaggio Studies* of 1955, scholars have been
striving to reconcile the artist's sometimes violent and
often irreverent behavior with the sublimity of his
religious works. Accordingly, anyone who opens books
about Caravaggio may sometimes hardly believe what

meanings are read into the pictures. Jutta Held, writing
in 1996, is implacably opposed to the artist, and takes
the view that Caravaggio's pictures are significant only as
ammunition in the battle of the Counter Reformation
against the legitimization of the Old Church. A slightly
more enthusiastic account comes from Maurizio
Calvesi, who focuses solely on Christ.

The published conference papers of a colloquium in
Rome, held in 1996, show what blunders interpretation can make. Even the secular pictures of
Caravaggio's early years in Rome are given a mystical
interpretation, as if not only vases of flowers but also

madrigals about love were really only the Song of Solomon. Similarly, the goldfinch in the cage in the New York version of the *Lute Player* (page 521) becomes Christ in prison.

Even Michael Ondaatje, who calls a character in his novel *The English Patient* (1993) Caravaggio, knows that the Borghese *David* (page 491) is a double self-portrait. In this picture some contemporary art historians claim to detect nothing less than a central idea for the conversion of St. Augustine. Thinkers and theologians of Caravaggio's day, such as the Oratorian Cardinal, Baronio, are said to have inspired the artist.

Only the long-established—and still unexplained—dislike of intellectuals for Jesuits prevents somebody from seeing St. Ignatius of Loyola's *Exercises* as the source of the directness of Caravaggio's approach to work.

Whatever form an interpretation geared to the picture as well as to religious tradition might take, we shall explore an example from Caravaggio's years in Rome. His *Rest During the Flight into Egypt* (pages 36–37) depicts an episode in the childhood of Christ that does not feature in the Bible. The music helps us to understand the painting better. As an expert will

Tintoretto
The Flight into Egypt, between 1582 and 1587
Oil on canvas, 422 x 580 cm
Scuola Grande di Arciconfraternita di San Rocco,
Venice

In painting the *Rest During the Flight into Egypt* (pages 36–37), Caravaggio seems to have, as it were, subdued the dramatic impact of Tintoretto's version of that subject. The Venetian artist depicts the donkey emerging from the depths of the scene. The travel bundle lies in the center of the picture, near the spot where they are resting by the water, and Joseph is hesitantly fingering the halter.

Caravaggio
The Rest During the Flight into Egypt, ca. 1595
Oil on canvas, 135.5 x 166.5 cm
Galleria Doria Pamphilj, Rome

The composition fans out from an exquisite angel who is
playing music and who has his back to the viewer. He divides
the picture centrally with the outline of his right side and his
left wing, which projects vertically towards the viewer in the
foreground picture area. Nothing grows on the stony ground
to the left. Joseph, now an old man, sits there beside a still-life
consisting of a traveling bottle, basket, and a bundle. He is
wearing clothes of earth color and is holding a book of music,
from which the angel is playing a violin solo, whilst the
donkey's large eye peeps out from under the brown foliage.

realize, the music here is a motet from the *Marian Vespers*. These turn the painting into a Vesper Picture, in which Caravaggio evokes the hours the Virgin Mary spends with her child, the pastoral character of the angelic music, and the nearness of sleep and death.

Within the development of Caravaggio as a young man, the *Rest During the Flight into Egypt* in the Galleria Doria Pamphilj, Rome, occupies a key position. This subject, which is practically unknown in Italy, demands a landscape setting. In it, the artist gives the figures a slightly less than life-size quality, but makes them as impressively present as he does in his genre-pictures with half-length figures. A strong geometrical composition divides the oblong space into the barren half occupied by Joseph. Almost incidentally, behind the angel's wings, mother and child appear.

Both the pastoral character of the scenery and the angelic music have led some scholars to read the solo score, from which the angel is playing the violin, as a kind of lullaby. Or, to be more specific: whilst old age in the left-hand half of the picture is contrasted with youth as the quintessence of eternal life on the right, the eye is drawn from the stony earth on the left across the world to paradisical perspectives of eternity. At the same time, there are also allusions to the flowers and fruit in the Song of Solomon. The oratory of the still very young community of lay priests that Filippo Neri had founded was still searching for the spirit which would give music a totally new value within religious life.

That said, the intimate relationship between the angel and the old man holding the score leads our thoughts in quite different directions. In this figure Caravaggio's nude painting reaches its supreme expression in a most gentle and beautiful way. That said, he also has his impudent side. A piece of white drapery, fluttering magnificently around his naked body, conceals the intimate parts of his body from the viewer. If we turn the boy around, however, and imagine what the old man will be looking at, it will be clear how close this angelic figure in a Christian painting is to the Berlin Cupid (page 522).

The Rest During the Flight into Egypt is a northern subject. In Italy, landscape took second place to an image of the Madonna, to which Joseph and the donkey were generally loosely connected at some distance. In Venice, whose painting inspired Caravaggio time and again, there is no major example of this subject, though there probably are a few striking forerunners, by Titian, the *Madonna with the Hare*, for example, in the Louvre, Paris (page 34).

To me, however, what seems more important is the artist's harsh confrontation with Tintoretto's famous painting in the lower room of the Scuola di San Rocco in Venice, from about 1582 to 1587 (page 35). In a critical appropriation of this precursor of his own picture, whose Mannerist inadequacies needed clarification, Caravaggio equated the departure with the rest during the flight. He distinguished the landscape according to the adult figures, with the angel as a hinge between the two. However, in setting out some violin music for this angel to play—and for experts to decipher—Caravaggio was offering a key to the painting's meaning. As in his versions of the *Lute Player*, Caravaggio painted such a meticulous and know-ledgeable copy of a music book printed in Rome about 1520 and containing a motet of the time, that, although we can see only the initial Q, we can identify a passage from the Song of Solomon as the text appropriate to the music. As set to music by the Netherlands composer Noël Bauldewijn, it runs: *Quam pulchra es et quam decora carissima in deliciis. Statura tua assimilata est palmae et uba tua botris* ("How beautiful, how lovely you are, my beloved, you creature of bliss! As you stand there, you are like the palm tree and your breasts are like grapes"). This quotation from the Bible forms part of the *Vespers of the Virgin Mary*. It recurs in famous pieces of music, for example by Monteverdi.

The key word, vesper suggests the office of the Virgin Mary, a form of prayer that played a major role in the day of a pious Christian, especially in the late Middle Ages and the early modern period. Although the pressure of Protestant ridicule had helped to effect the Council of Trent's decision to rethink the whole notion of horary prayer for the laity, the term vesper has survived in the language of German Protestants up to the present day. Though the same word in German has degenerated into another word for supper, the word vespers refers to the hour of sunset, the end of the day's labors before nightfall. At such a time pious people were expected to meditate upon the Flight into Egypt as well as the Deposition of the Dead Christ. In the German tradition Vesperbild (vesper pictures), the forerunners of the *Pietà*, depict Our Lady of Sorrows with the dead Christ on her lap.

Caravaggio now merges together both strands of older traditions into a uniquely well thought through concept. He takes the old relationship of the Flight into Egypt to vespers so literally that, instead of depicting the fleeing Holy Family, usual in Italy, he chooses to show them resting, as befits the hour of sunset.

In his painting, the child is replete and the mother tired. With his acute appreciation of the everyday, Caravaggio makes the music a lullaby. However, at the same time as he clarifies the liturgical context, he also shows the Virgin Mary experiencing her first suffering during the flight into Egypt: a prelude to the tears she will shed beneath the Cross.

Ever since the time of classical art, sleep and death have been intimately linked. The everyday subject of a mother and child asleep becomes an indication of things to come, a symbol of death. This transforms the pastoral painting in the Galleria Doria Pamphilj into one of the most beautiful examples of how an artist of genius can make a profound and serious statement through an apparently charming genre-picture.

The text of the music from the Song of Songs (7: 6–7) is as follows: "How fair and how pleasant art thou, O love, for delights! This thy stature is like to a palm tree, and thy breasts to clusters of grapes." Like the secular madrigals of the *Lute Player*, it describes the beauty of a woman, on this occasion the bride, as recounted by the Song of Solomon in the Old Testament.

If it were only a matter of "How fair and how pleasant art thou," the angel's music would also evoke the beauty of art. Caravaggio's own contribution to the subject is the naked boy, around whose pure body he drapes an indescribably beautiful piece of white fabric. Accompanied by his violin—in other words in an art form, music, which is unattainable for the artist—this boy presents a song in praise of beauty. Though directed towards the Virgin Mary, the astonished exclamation "How fair and how pleasant art thou" might equally be applied to him.

Caravaggio's angel (page 36–37) is like a female figure in paintings by Annibale Carracci (1560–1609). In his painting, *Hercules at the Crossroads* (page 39), this great competitor depicted vice (of all things) in a very similar way. Yet it is not entirely clear how the two pictures relate as regards the time of their composition, for Carracci completed this painting about 1595, roughly the same time as Caravaggio was painting his *Rest During the Flight into Egypt*.

The angel has come from the world of nude painting, which issues, in turn, from the study of the body and confirms the artist's skill. This art is extended by the still-life of the musical instrument, and the basket and bottle. The character study of the man's face beside the ass's is also evidence of a form of animal painting that Caravaggio, as a city-dweller, only rarely attempted. The Virgin Mary and Child may have developed in the same way as the *Penitent Mary Magdalene* (page 504). The same young woman seems to have posed for this picture, too, with an infant who is so freshly observed that we suspect he too was painted direct from a model.

The synthetic nature of the landscape, with its stony area on the left and, on the right, what would now be called a moist biotope, suggests that the picture has been painted from memory rather than from nature. Just a short while after this picture, Caravaggio was to use the concept of *imitatio* direct from a posed model as the basis for something akin to a new theoretical method of narrative art: or, to put it another way, of historical painting.

Eberhard König

Annibale Carracci
Hercules at the Crossroads, ca. 1595
Oil on canvas, 167 x 237 cm
Museo Nazionale di Capodimonte, Naples

Carracci may have seen the lascivious potential in Caravaggio's exquisite figure (pages 36–37), seen from the back, turned the youth into a woman, and so defamed Caravaggio's art by casting her in the role of vice. Or perhaps the younger artist from Lombardy criticized the great painter from Bologna, then felt inspired by the woman figure, with her strong Mannerist overtones, to ask the boy who had modeled the angel for him to pose in a similar way. In that case, Caravaggio's sense of artistic beauty, whose epitome is the youthful nude, would have triumphed over Carracci's moral definition of vice.

In Search of Color:
From Giusto de' Menabuoi to Jacopo Bellini

PAINTING OF THE LATE 14TH CENTURY IN PADUA

One of the most important places today for becoming acquainted with Florentine art of the highest rank is the university city of Padua, on the mainland not far from Venice, and not appropriated by the Republic of Venice until the 15th century. It was in Padua that Giotto left his undisputed masterpiece (Volume I, pages 64–87); Donatello worked in the city (Volume I, pages 224–225); and if Vasari had known that the painter Giusto de' Menabuoi, who died around 1390 in Padua, was born around 1330 in Florence, he would have given the master a place in the consciousness of art history, instead of almost forgetting his work and dealing with him in his life, of all people, of the Venetian Vittore Carpaccio. Since Vasari had nothing to report about him, Giusto de' Menabuoi today is still among those artists whose name is hardly spoken by anyone. Even his greatest work goes almost unregarded in such an extended medieval city as Padua, particularly since the Cathedral, whose baptistery he decorated, has the least pulling power among the great monuments of the city.

There may, however, be another reason why this painter was largely forgotten: Giusto's painting does not fit easily into the familiar traditions, indeed it breaks out of the usual schemes. It does not look Florentine, indeed it is precisely in Padua that it distinguishes itself vitally from the clarity of Giotto. At best, this master can be linked with an only slightly older painter, Giovanni da Milano (active 1346–1369); but this at the same time takes all the talk of the difference between Northern Italy and Tuscany to the point of absurdity, for it is precisely that Lombard, who was born in Caversaccio near Como and died in Rome, but created his greatest work for the Florentine Franciscans of Santa Croce (Volume I, pages 120–121), who is closest to Giusto de' Menabuoi from Florence, though the latter was active only in Northern Italy throughout the whole of his known creative

career. Like Giovanni da Milano, in his painting Giusto, who worked first in Milan and from 1370 in Padua, went in search of new fire for color; this makes his frescoes, with their dark coloration, sometimes look as strange as though they came from the 19th century and not the Trecento.

In the Baptistery in Padua, in glowing colors and with a tremendous power, to be attributed to the smooth transition between radiant light-filled areas and deep darkness, the painter fashioned earthbound, bullheaded figures, gazing with large eyes. With skill and accuracy he portrays the most varied scenes in the densely ranked series from Genesis; at the same time, when dealing with background, he is by no means satisfied with unpretentious schemes for landscape and space.

Giusto is at his most disturbing in his painting of the dome (page 41). From the height of the Baptistery, Christ looks down in the form of a manifestation known from the Eastern Church as the Pantocrator, or ruler of the world, and likewise seen as a mosaic in the Florentine Baptistery. The dark complexion of the Savior may recall Byzantium and its influence on nearby Venice, but his features betray all of Giusto's singularity, as though he had intended to form such heads from the vital power of his imagination, regardless of all tradition. Even more strongly, the Virgin Mary appearing in ethereal pale blue demonstrates the master's special position: clearly he is concerned with surprising color effects, which at times acquire almost psychedelic qualities.

Throughout these frescoes one gains the impression that this eccentric from Florence pursued a vision of painting in Padua for which the media of the day did not suffice. The radiant brightness of mural painting elsewhere held no value for Giusto. He seeks effects to give power to the color. In this endeavor he develops a sort of chiaroscuro, long before art history was ready to use the term. It ensures that the outlines naturally laid

Giusto de' Menabuoi
The Manifestation of God, and the Virgin Mary Surrounded by Saints, post-1370
Dome fresco
Baptistery, Padua

The architecturally modest Baptistery next to the Cathedral in Padua owes its unprecedentedly splendid decoration—with a cycle of stories from Genesis, culminating in the image of All Saints in the dome and a kind of Pantocrator—to its function as the site of the tomb of Francesco I da Carrara, the ruler of the city, and his wife, Fina Buzzacarina. The images over a wide area correspond to one of the richest pictorial Bibles of the time around 1400, the Rovigo Bible, which is today divided between the British Library in London and the Rovigo city library.

out by the master at the start are repeatedly swallowed. The depiction thus loses in conceptuality but gains in atmosphere; and thus it moves in a direction to which other painters aspired more convincingly, and mostly without knowledge of the strange artist in Padua.

A more sober and satisfying effect, in comparison, is produced by the frescoes left behind in Padua by Altichiero (ca. 1330–ca. 1390) and Avanzo (who either died in 1376 or was still active in the early 15th century). Not much more is known about these two than about Giusto, particularly in view of the uncertainty of distinguishing the contributions of two artists who are sometimes named together.

Altichiero da Zevio came from the small town near Verona where some of his works are also preserved, Jacopo Avanzo on the other hand from Bologna. They worked together on a fresco cycle completed in 1379 in the great chapel of St. James of the Franciscan church, which was built in honor of St. Anthony of Padua and is still, under the name of the Santo, the destination of many pilgrims. These frescoes were not well known to

later art literature, so that at the beginning of modern art historiography they have met with as little interest as the works of Giusto de' Menabuoi.

At the most recent restoration it is believed that in a fresco found in the Chapel of St. James in the Santo, one of the two distinguishable hands abruptly broke off work and left it for the other master to complete. Since this cut-off point in the painting is datable by evidence of payments in May 1376, new weight can be given to a report from Bologna that a Jacopo Avanzi died shortly before that date.

Art historians cannot be very happy with this conclusion, for the painting of a spacious chapel next to the Santo in the years that followed had once been taken as a starting point for all attempts to distinguish the hands. Both the surname Avanzo and the Christian name Jacopo may have occurred a second time, for all earlier attempts to pin down Avanzo's work had tended to associate him with work of the early 15th century. This would fit with the opinions of other researchers who claimed to have found his signature in the

Altichiero da Zevio
The Adoration of the Magi, 1378(?)
Fresco
Oratorio di San Giorgio, Padua

Ingeniously, the *Nativity* and the *Adoration of the Magi* are placed side by side above the entrance door to the chapel; the painter shows the stable and the city of Bethlehem from two slightly different points of view. In the picturesque entourage, Altichiero's clarity is slightly intermingled with the painterly interest of the later stage of his style (page 45).

Opposite page: Altichiero da Zevio
The Crucifixion, 1378(?)
Fresco
Oratorio di San Giorgio, Padua

Like the works in the Santo itself, this commission came from the Lupi family; Raimondino Lupi, Marquess of Soranzo, had had the present-day Oratorio di San Giorgio built in front of the basilica as a funerary chapel. The entire altar wall is taken up by a monumental version of the highly populated Crucifixion scene, with many minor figures on horses. Painters north of the Alps took such paintings as a model for many variants.

stylistically more strongly developed frescoes of the Oratorio di San Giorgio (page 45).

The character of the painter who died in 1376 and has therefore recently been identified as Jacopo Avanzo is not easily grasped; his individuality is submerged in the general style of the Altichiero workshop. This is not the case with the hand given the same name in the Oratorio di San Giorgio. Altichiero clearly follows the example of Giotto, but is distinguished from the latter's clarity and draftsmanlike definition by his darker modeling. In the figure relief (pages 42, 44) he likes to place light-colored figures in the front row and to extend the dimension of depth with the darker garments of those standing further back. This tendency is stronger in a few frescoes such as the *Burial of St. Lucy* (page 45). Here the dark coloration is more intensely used, while the forms are softer and, in the aesthetic sense, placed in more painterly fashion.

If it is Avanzo we have before us in such wall paintings, then his style was very decidedly advanced in comparison with the old Veronese master Altichiero. Here color triumphs with the most subtle nuances and rich tones, above all in the cases of brown and crimson.

Blue, on the other hand, is largely eliminated from the colors of the clothing. If it is substantiated that the historical Jacopo Avanzo died as early as 1376, there is no question of attributing such painting to him, because it already noticeably strives after effects that were to flourish only in later painting.

A glance at the architecture underlines the difference: Altichiero loves a complex arrangement of figures within arches (page 44); this once again decisively links his painting with Giovanni da Milano (Volume I, page 109). He uses the alternation of stones popular in Northern Italy to decorative effect in the arches, and creates structures reminiscent of a stage wall in the ancient theater, known as *scenae frons*. In front of this, the action takes place with fine divisions between the individual figures, which are never agglomerated into amorphous groups. However, this constitutes the modernity of some frescoes in the Oratorio di San Giorgio; it is already proclaimed in the upper register of the entrance wall in the *Adoration of the Magi* (page 42), but then abruptly determines scenes in the lower register such as the *Burial of St. Lucy* (page 45).

Altichiero da Zevio
St. George Baptizes King Sevius of Cyrene, 1378 (?)
Fresco
Oratorio di San Giorgio, Padua

A whole wall is devoted to the St. George cycle. This gives the painter, as later with Carpaccio in San Giorgio degli Schiavoni (page 148), the opportunity to portray unusual scenes: after his victory over the dragon, about to be accomplished by the saint in Pisanello's fresco (page 50), Cyrene is converted with its royal family and the king has himself baptized by George.

Opposite page: Younger colleague of Altichiero da Zevio (Jacopo Avanzo?)
The Burial of St. Lucy, 1378(?)
Fresco
Oratorio di San Giorgio, Padua

The burial of important saints was part of the cult of relics. The responsibility for this fresco, with its unusually differentiated color values, was clearly a younger painter, who must either remain nameless or be identified by the name of Jacopo Avanzo. In that case he cannot be identical with the Bolognese of the same name who died as early as 1376, for in its materiality and subtlety this wall painting is already on the threshold of the 15th century.

Gardens of Paradise on both Sides of the Alps

Northern Italy was to be reached only with difficulty by crossing the Alps, but was involved, at least during the period around 1400, in more intensive exchanges with the North than the rest of Italy. The strongest mutual influences were between book illustrators, but the panel makers also shared common interests. While art in Florence, as Don Lorenzo Monaco's paintings show (Volume I, page 200), still stood by the strict ideals of the Trecento, in the succession to Giotto and Taddeo Gaddi, in Verona and then also in Venice there was an increasing feeling for detail, which was able to enliven a depiction. In the minor details, nature took up more and more space; it was the flowers and trees, the fine fabrics and precious accessories that became increasingly popular with both artists and clients.

Certainly the anonymous *Garden of Paradise* from Frankfurt (below) of 1410/20 did not reach Italy from the Upper Rhine valley; but it represents an art which, itself stimulated by Sienese 14th-century painting, went in search of nature and, predominantly in small formats,

had a retroactive effect in the South. In the present context, a change in the attitude to color is decisive here: even before oil was used experimentally as a binder, artists strained to make their coloration more lively and brilliant. Value was placed on the effect of the presence of the pigment on the surface, and this was what was fascinating in these pictures throughout Europe.

The Garden of Paradise, with its precious objects from nature, with its blossoms and little birds, incorporates this art in the most vivid fashion. It stands in total contrast to the period of its creation, which was marked in ecclesiastical terms by the Great Schism and unsuccessful councils, while politically it brought only unrest: a failed crusade against the threatened invasion by Sultan Bayazit's armies in the Danube area, wars between Christian rulers in many places, regicide in England, deposition of the German King Wenceslas, and finally the Hussite wars. In addition to the great upheavals in Europe, there were incessant guerrilla wars between the individual Italian states.

Upper Rhine Master
The Garden of Paradise, ca. 1410/20
Wood, 26.1 x 33.3 cm
Städel Museum, Frankfurt am Main

A white wall shields the Garden of Paradise, with its precious flowers and trees, from the rest of the world, which thus does not even need to be shown. The dark blue of the background reminds us of the sky, but does not give any illusion of the vault of the heavens. Only a corner of the garden is show, where a little stream springs, the Christ Child plays with saints while Mary is absorbed in reading, and angels and saints ponder on evil, which lies on the grass in the form of a dead monster.

Stefano da Zevio
The Garden of Paradise, ca. 1400
Tempera on wood
Museo di Castelvecchio, Verona

In antiquity, and later in poetry, a stream represents a place of delight, the *locus amoenus*. In this Madonna image it has become a delicate object of the goldsmith's art, much too small for the figures; but such painting cannot be judged by proportions. The flowery meadow is like a carpet spread out, spanning almost the whole area of the image, which is bounded by a finely chased gold ground.

There was a longing for "the pleasant place," the *locus amoenus*, a garden screened off from the world, where a little stream flows, time stands still, and evil is shut out. Certainly the artistic means employed by Stefano da Zevio are not quite the same as in the North (above). But the painters of the Soft Style are related in spirit; and they not only allow a new splendor of color, but are oriented toward nature in a way previously unknown, opening it up not from the point of view of light and space like the Florentine painters, but of picturesque detail. Here we find the most important of the multiple meanings of the word "painterly": joyous detail from nature is studied with new attention; it demands rich colors, and the painters who dedicated themselves to flowers and fine fabrics were already developing a new sense of materiality in their Gardens of Paradise, which, however, aesthetically belongs to the characteristics of the painterly, even if by 1400 it was hardly ready to renounce the strict outlines and the primacy of drawing.

PISANELLO AND JACOPO BELLINI

We are led out of the delightful world of the Garden of Paradise by a painter whose monumental works have nearly all been destroyed or could be uncovered only in shadowy form in the Ducal Palace in Mantua. His family came from Pisa, and thus from Tuscany, but his mother lived in Northern Italy, in Verona. His name appears for the first time in 1395 in the will, made in Pisa, of his father Puccio di Giovanni di Cerreto; later he was active in many places and on behalf of several high-ranking nobles. He was Antonio Pisanello (before 1395–1455).

The basis of his creative work was the careful recording of natural phenomena. He executed enchanting studies of animals and birds, which he then inserted into his few surviving paintings, in order to give greater credibility to the events they depicted.

As early as the 12th and 13th centuries, individual animals had been carefully recorded in pattern books, in convincing attitudes. Horses and dogs, but also eagles and falcons, had long been part of the tried and tested repertoire of painters and sculptors. A heightened sense of materiality developed in the case of fur and cloth; it was encouraged by a fashion in clothing that understood how to weave into precious fabrics everything needed by the nobility and the bourgeois who aimed at princely splendor for their self-portrayal.

The art of hunting here played a special role: it actually requires sporting skill, so should be aimed at practical needs. But this is contrasted with the luxury of a society that seeks to impress by means of fabrics and hats, bridles, saddles, and caparisons. This tendency is taken *ad absurdum* in a delightful drawing from the circle of Pisanello (above): a youth appears as a falconer with his hunting dogs, but instead of a horse he rides a mule, almost gets his feet tangled up in the gaily fluttering, scallop-edged trappings of his saddle, and in addition wears a hat which looks like a monstrous continuation of the hair of his head.

His short fur-trimmed cloak marks him as one of those who followed the Burgundian fashion for the *gens de robe courte*, the high-ranking nobility who wore short robes. While the costly embroidery of his cloak suggest the identification of the subject as a prince of the house of Este, its shrill exaggeration may rather encourage us to recognize a character typifying the maxim "pride comes before a fall."

An artist may be led by positively scientific interest when he records views of a horse from both front and back, and with the discipline of perspective chooses the two points of view exactly opposite to each other (above, left). As far as one can see, however, the structure

Above left: Pisanello
Two Views of a Horse, ca. 1438/39
Pen and ink drawing with brown ink and gray and brown wash, heightened with white, on paper, 19.9 x 16.5 cm
Département des Arts Graphiques, Musée du Louvre, Paris

An acute sense of the direction of the artist's gaze and of the systematic reproduction of the visible ensures that a horse is carefully recorded from two exactly opposite directions. In paintings, such studies then turn up as subtle contrasts (as with Domenico Veneziano, Volume I, page 247). Pisanello would have been able to observe the ornamentation of the horse in 1438/39 at the Council of Ferrara and Florence in the entourage of the Byzantine emperor John VIII Palaeologus; Pisanello commemorated that ruler in a medal.

Above right: Pisanello (or a follower)
Gentleman of the House of Este Hunting, 1430 or 1450
Pen drawing, modeled in brown, with gold highlights, on beige-toned paper, 22.5 x 17.5 cm
Institut Néerlandais, Paris

The pack of hunting dogs is portrayed with unerring accuracy, followed by a beardless, clearly very young gentleman. He seems a caricature of his caste, for he rides a mule rather than a horse and wears a hat that is bound to fall off as soon as the animal increases its speed. An old inscription claims that this sheet is by Cosimo Tura (page 124); today the drawing is believed to be a work by Pisanello or a follower.

Jacopo Bellini
The Nativity, 1440s
Pen drawing, brown wash, on parchment,
ca. 29 x 42.5 cm
fol. 33 of the volume of drawings
Département des Arts Graphiques, Musée du Louvre,
Paris

In the folio volume of sketches that Jacopo Bellini
bequeathed to his son Gentile, and which are today
in the Louvre in Paris, most of the drawings are in
upright format. As though he had intended to prepare
a predella in the customary landscape format, for the
Nativity he used a horizontal rectangle. With the
restricted number of figures in this scene, a gap is created
that is filled in almost an abstract way by the perspective
structure of the enormous stable. On this evidence,
Jacopo, who was in Florence in his early years, could
have become a fine master of *disegno*.

Pisanello
Two Men in Each of Two Studies
Pen and brown ink, traces of metal pen,
on parchment, 15.8 x 26.6 cm
Département des Arts Graphiques, Musée du Louvre,
Paris

Two men, differentiated by their hairstyles, sit on the
ground, trying to break up large sticks. This sensational
nude study, with its cheeky glance at the genitals, next
found only in Caravaggio, was first linked with
Pollaiuolo; but the drawing is so "painterly" that it is
rather the early Pisanello who comes to mind, since he
repeatedly studied the same object from different
directions.

of space never really interested Pisanello. Jacopo Bellini
from Venice (1396–1470?), only a few years his junior,
however, was quite obsessed by perspective calculations.
Both painters in their ways learned from Gentile da
Fabriano, who was a generation older than they and
astounded his contemporaries throughout Italy with his
new fascination with fabrics and details drawn of nature
(Volume I, page 200–203). Jacopo was in Florence with
him and there evidently discovered a taste for geometry.
He depicted the events in Bethlehem in two large
drawings. Certainly they do not portray the same stable,
but the alternating point of view is linked with similar
procedures of Pisanello's. This is not quite without
precedent in Northern Italy, for Giotto and, three
generations later, Altichiero (page 42) worked with
viewpoints that deal differently with the same space or
objects.

A man such as Pisanello fits wonderfully into a late
courtly culture which discovers its own likeness, likes it
to be commemorated in the classical tradition in a
medal, and also values hunting and the arts of war as
evidence of a noble life. The favorite saints are George
and Eustace. The former freed a kingdom and a king's
daughter by killing a dragon (page 50), while the other,
while out hunting, saw a vision of the crucified Christ

in the antlers of a stag (page 51). As examples of society, however, they served not only the feudal aristocracy scattered over the land, but also the distinguished people of the city, as is shown by Pisanello's fresco in Verona.

The society that could afford paintings clothed itself in the most costly fabrics, which linked the family coat of arms with personal mottos; it therefore also had a more acute sense of the painter's skill when he was able to reproduce such fabrics convincingly in paint. People recognized the unfamiliar, the eccentric, dealt with animals from distant lands, and were pleased when the painter showed greyhounds hunting a hare (page 51) or observed a guenon monkey at play in his drawings. But the shimmering creatures from their own forests, such as the kingfisher or the hoopoe, as well as the peacock, considered a rarity, but also quite commonplace creatures

such as roosters and hens, have become lasting treasures through the draftsman's hand.

At the same time, art, as it became ever more accurate, also became appropriate for reporting on its own time: Pisanello observed with great attention the entourage of the Byzantine emperor who had come to Italy in 1438–1439 for a council. The encounter with the Greeks, who brought a hint of the Orient with them, may have strengthened an important tendency in the creative work of Pisanello and his contemporaries. People were interested in ancient texts, and had access to archeologically interesting material throughout Italy; but since at the same time they knew that everything Greek was tirelessly praised in classical Roman literature, they were fascinated by the Greeks who actually turned up in their own time. The appearance of the Greek emperor and his court, however, stood in remarkable

Pisanello
St. George and the Princess, 1436–1438
Fresco, 223 cm in height
Sant'Anastasia, Verona

Of the wall painting above the entrance arch of the Cappella Pellegrini, the interior of which was also once painted by Pisanello, the right half has remained very comprehensible; it was removed and can therefore now be viewed at close quarters. Vasari particularly admired this work. Not shown here is the dragon, which appears on the left-hand side of the arch with a throng of evil wormlike creatures. The youthful knight-saint in his over-ornate armor is about to mount his charger in order to ride into the combat that was to make him famous.

Pisanello
The Vision of St. Eustace, 1436/1438(?)
Tempera on wood, 54.8 x 65.5 cm
National Gallery, London

Because of its thematic agreement with a lost fresco of
St. Eustace in the same Cappella Pellegrini above which
St. George appeared (page 50), this panel is attributed
to the same period, and it is believed that because of
its significantly better state of preservation it is possible
to have a better idea of the appearance of the lost
monumental painting. The way in which the horse
comes to a halt in front of the stag is impressive, because
the animal manifests its surprise more intensely than
its distinguished rider. The saint's turban may look
sumptuous, but is by no means as absurd as that of the
equestrian hunter (page 48, right).

contrast to what they had in front of their eyes in the
form of marble, coins, and medals from classical
antiquity. The Oriental splendor of the Byzantines, later
even the magnificence of the Turks, thus drove out the
evidence of silent monuments. When Pisanello depicts
something from antiquity or from the legends of the
saints, his experience of the Orient blots out everything
that was known of the Romans in Italy. At the same
time, he is able to differentiate when he shows
St. George in an oriental setting but makes St. Eustace a
nobleman of his own time.

The master seems never to have taken the difference
between wall and panel painting very seriously; this had
an unfortunate result for the condition of his few
preserved monumental paintings, for the costly materials

that he used in the *fresco secco* technique (painting on dry
plaster) were not durable. A panel such as that of
St. Eustace in London (below) will demonstrate the
coloration in which the highly densely structured fresco
from the story of St. George in Verona was created.

The sense of color asserts itself above all when new
significance is found in the minor details. While in the
depictions of the Garden of Paradise the feeling for the
pigment is sharpened, landscapes demand that the
painter capture the phenomena becoming indistinct
in the distance by means of the use of light and shade,
while blossoms portrayed in the foreground, in
particular when they stand out from dark bushes,
demand a confrontation between local color and
chiaroscuro.

Jacopo Bellini
The Madonna and Child with a Member of the Este family,
ca. 1440
Mixed media on wood, 60 x 40 cm
Musée du Louvre, Paris

Among the most unusual Virgin and Child images from the Middle Ages to the Renaissance is this panel, which shows a member of the Este family in prayer before the Christ Child, who is standing on Mary's lap. This picture places the heads of mother and child in front of a blue sky above a curving landscape backdrop. Mary is kneeling on her left leg and has bent her right leg in order to support the Child. The foreshortening seems too bold, and it is clear that the basic idea for the composition actually comes from the tradition of half-length depictions.

Two enchanting examples of landscape and flowers from the years up to 1440 are by Jacopo Bellini (1396?-1470?) and Pisanello. The gold ground customary for Madonnas until well into the 15th century was abandoned by the founder of the Bellini family of painters (left). His blue sky, arranged in horizontal stripes that lightens toward the horizon, is reminiscent of paintings such as the portrait of a woman in Berlin, which has for some time been attributed to Pollaiuolo, but still seems to me to be a major work by Domenico Veneziano (Volume I, page 450). In contrast to the painting of the master who came from Venice to Florence, under a similar sky Jacopo Bellini spreads out an atmospheric landscape, whose fine chiaroscuro may today still be influenced, at least in part, by its state of preservation.

A conflict arises for Jacopo Bellini from the need to show lights in the distance; these he does not develop from the color of the sky, preferring to use gold, which lies gleaming over the mountain tops. Gentile da Fabriano had already done the same in his panels for the *Strozzi Altarpiece* in Florence (Volume I, page 200–203), and it is noticeable how marked the influence of the older painter was on Jacopo Bellini, who had allowed himself to be thrashed on behalf of his master in a nocturnal attack on Florentine painters in the early 1420s.

Gentile da Fabriano also influenced Pisanello, with whom he may possibly even have worked in the Doge's Palace in Venice. Both are virtuosos in depicting opulent blossoms flashing up out of the dark. In the two portraits securely attributed to him, Pisanello places the figures in front of bushes enlivened with blossom. In the portrait of a woman, he does this with particular subtlety, allowing the sky to shine through behind the plants (page 53). The contours of the young woman, determined by courtly fashion, with her headdress, are echoed, as it were, in the background by the contrast between leaves and the blue of the sky, and suddenly one notices that the figure stands totally without a horizon in front of the translucent vault of heaven. This again links it with the Berlin portrait of a woman, which moves the subject to an astonishing height.

The link between the painters constitutes the basic difference between the Venetian in Florence and the Pisan in Northern Italy: austere strength, which tends to be associated with the bourgeois city on the Arno (although its aristocratic stratum, to which the young woman in Berlin certainly belongs, liked to put on princely airs), is replaced in Pisanello by a magic which partly arises from bizarre, fashionable elegance, but basically stems from the floral decoration borrowed from nature. The cold coloration corresponds to one extreme, while on the other hand the search for warm color tones which, for all the precision of its rendering, plays with emergence into the light and disappearance into the shadows, characterizes both Jacopo Bellini's Madonna and Pisanello's portraits of members of the Este family in Ferrara.

Pisanello
Portrait of Lucia or Ginevra d'Este, 1437 (?)
Mixed media on poplar, 42 x 39.6 cm
Musée du Louvre, Paris

Pisanello tackled the tasks of the portrait above all in
his medals; he adopted the view in strict profile, long
customary for that medium, for his two preserved portrait
panels: this lady of the house of Este in half-length view,
and the bust of Leonello d'Este, who came
to power in 1441 (Accademia Carrara, Bergamo).
Recently it has been suggested that one of the twin
sisters born in 1419, Ginevra d'Este (d. 1440) or Lucia,
is the subject of this image. Heraldic evidence speaks
in favor of Lucia, who married Carlo Gonzaga in 1437
and died the same year.

A First Upheaval in Venice: Antonio Vivarini and Giovanni d'Alemagna

Andrea del Castagno
God the Father, 1442
Fresco
Cappella di San Tarasio, San Zaccaria, Venice

Into the narrow fields of the Gothic choir vault, Andrea del Castagno, who had fled from Florence to Venice, fitted individual figures: God the Father and saints. They appear to be floating in front of the blue of the heavens; but it turns out that the earthbound painters who had at last discovered the force of gravity were still hardly suited to capture accurately the airy creatures with which the Christian power of imagination peoples the heavens. One gains the impression that Castagno's shadowy figures are in danger of suddenly tumbling down from their heights.

Vasari's distinction between the principles of *disegno* and *colore* must be seen in the context of the rivalry between Michelangelo and Titian in the mid-16th century. He follows their contrasting aesthetic far back into the past and reads it as a conflict between Florence and Rome on one side and the whole of Northern Italy on the other. This takes place with all the contradictions that arise from the facts that Giotto triumphed in Padua, the Pisan Pisanello impressed the world when working from Verona, and Domenico Veneziano in Florence is classed among the founders of that form of painting that pleased Vasari so much for its conceptual nature. With all the contradictions, which he builds up rather as a criterion of classification than as historical reality, the founder of art history never betrays his eminently lively artistic judgment in deference to local and regional patriotism.

In one respect Vasari is right: the new could not take root as quickly in Venice as elsewhere. I have spoken now and again of contradictions. Now it is time to move into that space where one can understand even Venetian reserve in the face of the new art from the south. It is the Cappella di San Tarasio, the original choir of the church of the Benedictine nuns, San Zaccaria, in Venice, exceptionally highly regarded in urban hierarchy. The main building, not completed until the 15th century, is dedicated to the prophet Zechariah, a choice of a figure from the Old Testament as patron saint that already formed one of the distinctive features of Venice. The church today still houses Bellini's magnificent late work, the *Madonna of San Zaccaria* (page 23), which can be regarded as the final point of the changes effected in the course of the 1440s.

In the chapel, four major works are crowded together, created within a short time of each other, and all following a similar concept. On each of three altars, rising to an impressive height of up to six meters (20 feet) with their gilded pinnacles, stands a narrow main panel, surrounded by many further painted panels and even sculptures; the two side altars, dedicated respectively to the Resurrection of Christ and to St. Sabina, were consecrated at the same time, in October 1443, as foundations by two nuns. In 1444, there followed the high altar, which in similar fashion places several saints around the Madonna and was paid for by the prioress (page 55).

These altars are part of an old tradition that apparently survived similarly north and south of the Alps. They demonstrate not so much the personal interests or indeed the names of their founders, but the quite substantial salutary power, for detailed inscriptions report what relics can be venerated here: in one sarcophagus, Pancratius lies together with Nereus and Achilles; in another St. Sabina; while the high altar alone contains parts of the bones of the saintly popes Stephen and Leo, of Gregory of Nazianzus, and of Theodore and Thomas. The chapel also housed, among other items, one of the Holy Innocents of Bethlehem.

This wealth of relics was demonstrated by magnificently colorful images on shining gold grounds facing the church interior, while the back of the high altar is painted in grisaille, that is, in monochrome. As if in a cabinet of relics, the saints were shown overlapping in several registers, each one in his or her own right. The painters responsible were Giovanni d'Alemagna and Antonio Vivarini, the one demonstrably in Murano from 1441 to 1450, the other born around 1418/20 and dying between 1476 and 1484. They were masters of subtle color effects, quite in the tradition of that charming art of the Soft Style which Gentile da Fabriano had brought to splendid flowering (Volume I, page 200–203) and which intensively characterized those painters born shortly before 1400, such as Pisanello and Jacopo Bellini.

Giovanni d'Alemagna and Antonio Vivarini, however, had to come to terms more intensively than the older artists with the new Florentine painting. The positively shocking effect of this strange art can be nowhere observed as vividly as in San Tarasio. Here Andrea del Castagno from Florence with his wild figures painted a similar series of saints around an apparition of God in the vault (page 54), uncompromising and without a trace of the tenderness that had wafted from the Garden of Paradise even to the altars of San Tarasio. The most astonishing thing about it is the date: the Florentine dated his daring images in August 1442. The altars were certainly in progress then, but they were not set up until two years later; an effect was to emanate from that strange art that did not fail to leave its traces on Giovanni d'Alemagna and Antonio Vivarini.

Antonio Vivarini and Giovanni d'Alemagna
Altarpiece with the Virgin Mary and Saints, 1444
Tempera on wood and inset wood carving,
600 x 320 cm
Cappella di San Tarasio, San Zaccaria, Venice

Among the three great altars set up in this chapel in
the early 1440s, the high altar is liturgically given the
highest status; but since it was clearly assembled from
heterogeneous parts, it is seldom reproduced in
illustrations. The main area is dominated by the Virgin
and Child. She was painted as early as 1385 by Stefano
da Sant'Agnese, and is flanked by standing saints, each of
which occupies a field framed by an arch. The two panels
on the right, like the predella, date from 1385; the date
of 1444 refers to the total arrangement, including the
back as well as the two saints on the left. The exuberant
carving, whose fleshy foliage is sumptuously gilded, above
all creates a magnificent effect. In abrupt contrast to the
wealth of color at the front, the back is worked in
grisaille; it groups a further number of saints around the
Man of Sorrows. Here the uniform style of Antonio
Vivarini and Giovanni d'Alemagna reigns. Only
individual panels at the front by these two painters, who
worked together in a workshop in Murano, are signed.
An inscription that gives information about the whole
altar is preserved only in very fragmentary form; its value
lies in the fact that it also names a woodcarver, Ludovico
da Forlì, which means that Giovanni d'Alemagna cannot,
as is sometimes suggested, have been the builder of the
altarpiece.

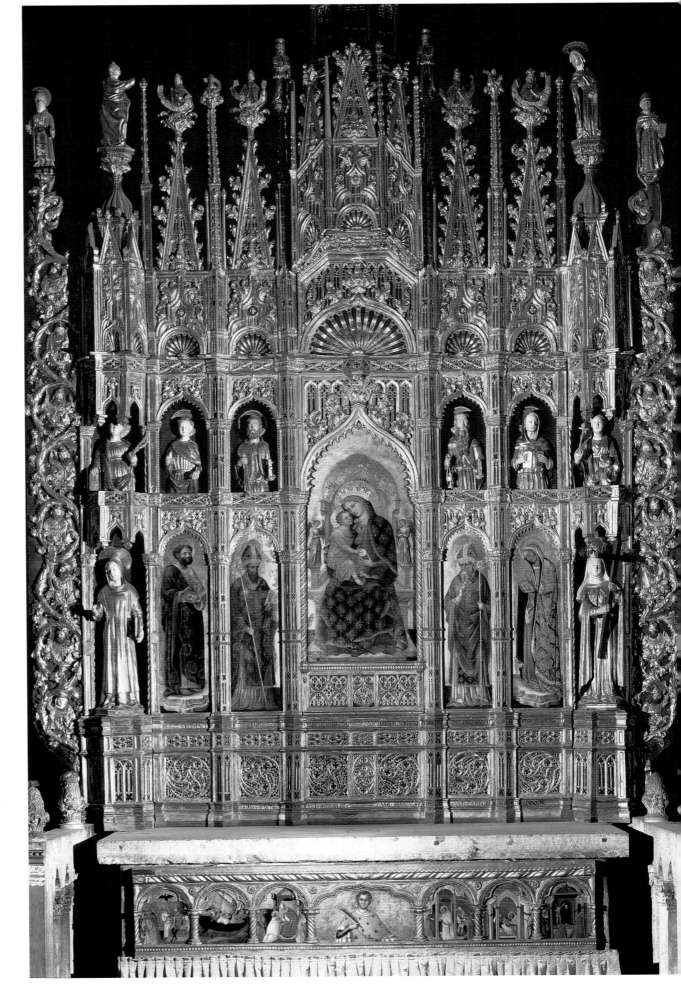

Antonio Vivarini and Giovanni d'Alemagna
Altarpiece of the Church Fathers, 1446
Egg tempera and oil on canvas, 344 x 203 cm
(central panel), 344 x 137 cm (side panels)
Gallerie dell'Accademia, Venice

The Church Fathers venerated here are Pope Gregory the Great; the translator of the Bible St. Jerome, shown here as a cardinal; and two bishops: Ambrose of Milan, who represents Christian hymnography, and Augustine of Hippo, who with his book *De Civitate Dei* (*The City of God*) had provided the most important political theology of the Middle Ages. In a space of the choir they surround the throne, also flanked by angels, of the Mother of God, on whose lap stands the naked Christ Child. The inscription for this altar image reads: *M.4.46 JOHANES ALAMANUS / ANTONIUS. DA. MURIANO* ("1446: Giovanni d'Alemagna, Antonio da Murano"). Antonio was to go down in history as founder of the Vivarini family of painters. The altarpiece is from the Sala dell'Albergo in the Scuola di Santa Maria della Carità; like Titian's *Presentation of the Virgin at the Temple* (pages 326–327), it remained in the old house that today contains the great art gallery of Venice, being moved to a different wall only in the 19th century when a staircase was built in.

Under the symbol of *caritas*, the Greek cross enclosed in two circles, and in front of a choir stall that bears this title for the Scuola, the four figures are assembled and provided with unusual attributes: Jerome, in whose name the Hieronymites cared for the Scuola, holds a model of the building and, of all his books, not the best known, but the text *On the Contempt of the World* (*De contemptu mundi*) with a detailed and easily legible quotation. Pope Gregory shows himself to be inspired by the dove of the Holy Spirit. Ambrose, with his threefold scourge, alludes to the episode of his forbidding the entrance of Emperor Theodosius into the Church. Finally, Augustine, justifiably recognizable as an African by his dark complexion, presents not his book *The City of God*, but that on the Trinity, the *Liber Trinitatis*, and on the three seals of this book is written: *Vere tres sunt unus* ("Truly, three are one").

Venice was the first center of painting in which canvas became established as a support for paintings. Wood, in this area mostly poplar, was not abandoned until about 1500; and this change rapidly brought about an alteration of the painting's surface. While Giorgione in his *Three Philosophers* (pages 288–289) was still executing careful preliminary drawings on white, younger painters such as Titian went considerably further, using a brownish-red primer, a dark ground which represented a decisive obstacle to preparatory drawing on the surface to be used for painting.

A change such as this does not come about suddenly. The use of textile grounds had been known for a long time in the case of wood carvings, which were often covered by a fabric soaked in plaster and glue before painting; this was occasionally also done with paintings. The most frequent experiments with canvas were carried out in northern Europe from about 1400, mostly in small formats and on delicate fabrics, known in German as *Tüchlein* (clothlets). With a few exceptions—Botticelli worked on black surfaces—in the 15th century the white ground known from wall and panel paintings continued to be used.

While in the north of Europe the clothlets were painted with special binding materials, still a long way from true oil painting, it was in Venice that the technique was developed that was practiced everywhere, above all since the Baroque. Binders were restricted to oils, and heavy-duty canvases were used, which—as Caravaggio shows in his Florentine *Bacchus* (page 509)—were also suitable as mattress covers. So we need not be surprised that the earliest, very handsome canvas painting was created in Venice in a stretcher frame and, already, with the use of oil paints.

Precisely the two painters, Antonio Vivarini and Giovanni d'Alemagna, who in the early 1440s had executed the altars for San Tarasio (page 55) in stark contrast to Andrea del Castagno (page 54) painted their *Altarpiece of the Church Fathers*, signed and dated by them 1446 (page 56), at least partially in varnishes with oil on canvas. For this, they used for the costly materials the technique of gilded relief textiles known as *Pressbrokat*, widespread only in Germany, whereby a model fabric pattern could be repeated. They did this to a height of 3.44 meters (11 feet), the central panel of barely more than 2 meters (6.6 feet) in width being flanked by side panels that, at 1.37 meters (4.4 feet), did not serve as movable wings, but were fixed in place. Canvas was unsuitable as a support for hinged altars; for retables it was favored only in areas where one was restricted to a single view.

The division into three fields of images in the *Altarpiece of the Church Fathers*, as with the only slightly older retables in San Tarasio (page 55), is explained by the framing architecture; it is worked with similar vegetable foliage. That it was removed, presumably when the altar was converted in the 19th century, may be attributable to Antonio Vivarini and Giovanni d'Alemagna's revolutionary concept of the three canvases as a spatial unit.

Thus we come to the third remarkable and daring step made by the two artists with this epoch-making work. Not only did they use canvas, until then not used for monumental paintings, as a ground, and in a boldly revolutionary gesture use oil as a binder, but they also perceived the space as a unit from the point of view of perspective. While they competed in their first approaches to oil painting with Early Netherlandish masters such as Jan van Eyck, who died in 1441, in their composition they followed the Florentine model, as exemplified by Andrea del Castagno. To understand this, the work of the Florentine in Venice is not sufficient; for in the vaults of San Tarasio, Castagno had to treat the figures individually (page 54), and for the mosaic in San Marco he decided to depict the *Death of the Virgin* under a triumphal arch (Volume I, page 321). The convincing analogy is that with Castagno's *Last Supper* in Sant'Apollonia in Florence (Volume I, page 318). Despite the difference between the interior of a monastic refectory and the choir stalls under an open sky, and despite the epochal contrast between Castagno's Renaissance forms and the persisting Gothic-Venetian decorative architecture, the space unfolds in a similar way in the two pictures. At the same time, the perspective, occasionally correctly constructed, appears equally unlikely in both the Florentine and the two painters in Venice, with the steep line of the side walls.

A fourth aspect makes this work by Antonio Vivarini and Giovanni d'Alemagna into a milestone in art history, for the arrangement of the painting is also revolutionary from the point of view of content. The painters no longer add a bewildering number of individual unrelated saints in separate panels surrounding an image of the Virgin, but in the altar painting for the Scuola della Carità they add a thematic unity to the spatial one, which is based on renunciation of the world and the doctrine of the Trinity. The four Fathers of the Church do not appear as isolated individuals; they do not even carry those books and attributes which enable them to be recognized at first glance. Parallel to Jan van Eyck's painting in Bruges for Canon van der Paele of 1436 and to the Florentine retables of Fra Angelico and Domenico Veneziano (Volume I, pages 268–273, 311), they form the basis for Mantegna's altarpiece of San Zeno, less than ten years later (page 75) and for the *sacra conversazione* in Venice in general (pages 22, 23, 124).

Thus, in a painting jointly by Antonio Vivarini and Giovanni d'Alemagna, whose inscription names the painter from Germany in first place, the basis is prepared for a new art in Venice, which could be characterized as follows: in a workshop in Murano, run jointly by a German and a native painter, the first monumental canvas painting for a *scuola* in Venice is created with varnishes in oil, as developed by the Early Netherlandish artists, and in this painting content and space become a unity which is to be attributed to the Early Renaissance in Florence.

Eberhard König

Andrea Mantegna

1430/31–1506

Mantegna's Early Career in Padua

Andrea Mantegna
The Presentation at the Temple (detail page 72)

The man with the serious expression is presumed to be a self-portrait of Mantegna.

Mantegna is among the earliest painters who clearly had a sense of their own appearance in pictures. The most impressive portrait of him, however, shows him in bronze above his tomb (page 123).

Andrea Mantegna was probably born in Isola di Carturo, a village between Vicenza and Padua, in 1430 or 1431. In northern Italy during the 14th and 15th centuries, Padua was a cultural center second only to the politically and economically more powerful city of Venice. Padua had a long history, and isolated traces of the ancient Roman town of Patavium are still visible today. The university, already in existence by the early 13th century, had a reputation for excellence that went far beyond the city itself.

It was in this enlightened and humanist city that Mantegna grew up. At the age of about eleven he was accepted into the workshop of Francesco Squarcione (1394/97–1468), a painter of only moderate significance. In contemporary reports, Squarcione was described as a tailor and embroiderer, though he had clearly also turned to art; one of his few surviving works is the altarpiece the *Madonna and Child* (ca. 1460, now in the Gemäldegalerie, Staatliche Museen, Berlin). Squarcione's real significance lies in the fact that he owned a large number of classical sculptures and casts, as well as an extensive collection of copies and sketches of works by the major artists of the age. At this time, the study of the works of the masters was an essential part of an artist's training, and on the basis of his collection Squarcione built up a busy training workshop that was enormously popular: over the years, 137 students came to him. However, he made it his practice to adopt his students so that he could put them to work without paying wages, and once trained most of them escaped from this exploitative dependency as quickly as they could. Mantegna was no exception. He was soon sufficiently self-assured to make the break, and his "apprenticeship" ended in a lawsuit that won him his freedom in 1448. Just seventeen years of age, he completed his first independent work in the same year: an altarpiece (now lost) for the church of Santa Sofia in

Padua. Though the work of a very young artist, it was greatly admired and his gifts were extolled in poems of praise.

His earliest surviving works are his frescoes in a chapel belonging to the Ovetari family in the Chiesa degli Eremitani in Padua (pages 60–63 above, 64–65). This church (in English, the Church of the Hermits of St. Augustine) was built in the 13th century and is adjacent to the Arena Chapel, whose interior is the masterwork of Giotto (ca. 1267–1337). The greater part of the Church of the Hermits was destroyed during World War II, so today we can gain an impression of the Ovetari Chapel only with the help of photographs and old descriptions. There are also, however, a few fragments of the frescoes that were preserved after being removed in the 19th century to prevent deterioration on the damp walls.

The patron for the frescoes was the notary Antonio Ovetari, who, in a will dated 5 January 1443, provided that immediately after his death 700 gold ducats was to be spent on decorating his family's funerary chapel, which was to the right of the main choir. The exact date of the notary's death is not known, but he must have died before 16 May 1448 as this is the date the heirs drew up the initial contracts for a series of frescoes. There were two contracts. The first commissioned works from the artists Giovanni d'Alemagna (died 1450) and Antonio da Murano, known as Vivarini (1415–1476/84). These two artists were to be responsible for the wall on the right-hand side of the chapel, the main vault, and the front wall. The second contract, also dated 16 May 1448, commissioned Mantegna and Niccolò Pizzolo (died 1453) to execute the frescoes for the second half of the chapel. According to the art writer Giorgio Vasari (1511–1574) in his famous *Lives*, the abilities of Pizzolo, a little-known former assistant of the sculptor Donatello (1386–1466), were already equaled by that of the young

Mantegna. In addition to his work on the frescoes, Pizzolo was also responsible for painting the altar reliefs sculpted by Giovanni da Pisa (died ca. 1460). As Giovanni d'Alemagna died in 1450 and Vivarini worked on the frescoes till 1451, the painters Bono da Ferrara (died 1452) and Ansuino da Forlì (active in 1450s) were brought in for the as yet untouched right-hand wall in 1451. All the frescoes were completed by 1457.

Because so many artists were involved, one of them must have developed an integrated overall concept for the cycle of frescoes, and there is some indication that Mantegna (young as he was) may have been the originator of both the overall formal composition, and also the structural device of painted frames. The coordinated composition of the scenes also looks like his work.

In his will, Antonio Ovetari had provided an outline for the content of the pictures. The side walls of the

chapel area were dedicated to scenes from the lives of St. James and St. Christopher, and the apse wall, with its window apertures, was to depict the Assumption of the Virgin, in the center behind the altar. In the now destroyed vaults, there were portrayals of the four Evangelists, and the four Fathers of the Church and other saints, with God the Father enthroned in the center, above the Virgin Mary. As dictated by custom, the ceiling frescoes were the first to be painted. Mantegna and Pizzolo painted the frescoes in the apse vault, and Vivarini and Giovanni d'Alemagna were responsible for the vault over the body of the chapel. The *Legenda Aurea*, a collection of saints' lives compiled by Jacobus de Voragine (1230–1298), was used as the source for the stories of the saints depicted on the side walls of the chapel. Mantegna probably painted the left wall, which has been almost completely lost (pages 60, 61). The surface is divided by means of a painted

Above and opposite page:
Andrea Mantegna
Scenes from the Life of St. James, 1448–1457
Fresco, dimensions of the wall unknown,
chapel area 875 x 700 cm
Cappella Ovetari, Chiesa degli Eremitani, Padua

The photographs were taken before the chapel was destroyed on 11 March 1944; today only fragments of the lower wall area remain. The left-hand wall showed scenes from the story of the Apostle James. They were, from left to right: the *Calling of St. James and St. John* (above left) and the *Preaching of St. James* (above right); *St. James Baptizing Hermogenes* (opposite, above left) and the *Trial of St. James* (opposite, above right); *St. James Led to Execution* (opposite, below left) and the *Martyrdom of St. James* (opposite, below right).

Above:
The Martyrdom of St. James (detail page 61)

This badly damaged fresco was transferred to canvas in 1886–1891, and thus combined with a copy of the original. The Apostle James is seen lying along the bottom edge of the painting, a device to draw us into the scenes unfolding immediately before us. The moment depicted is the instant before the martyrdom takes place.

Opposite page, above: Andrea Mantegna
The Martyrdom of St. Christopher and *The Removal of His Body*,
Fresco, Capella Ovetari, Chiesa degli Eremitani, Padua

This section of the fresco was detached from the wall in about 1880 because of its deteriorating condition, and is therefore still preserved, though only in a fragmentary state. According to the legend, the giant Christopher wanted to serve only the most powerful of kings, and so finally came to Jesus. He was called upon to carry an infant across a river, and as he almost drowned under this burden, he recognized the child as the Infant Jesus. Christopher was martyred during the Roman persecution of the Christians.

Opposite page, below:
The Martyrdom of St. Christopher and *The Removal of His Body*,
1457–1500
Tempera on wood, transferred to canvas, each 51 x 51 cm
Musée Jacquemart-André, Paris

This copy of the lower section of the story of St. Christopher was probably made shortly after the frescoes were completed. To the left can be seen the huge figure of St. Christopher, almost completely lost in the original. He and the small boy to the right are standing partially outside the decorative framework of the fresco, intermediaries between the viewer's space and the narrative of the fresco.

ornamental frame on which a realistic garland of fruit is hanging, giving the impression that it is standing out from the wall. In the center, two of the acrobatic putti inside the frame are holding up the patron's coat-of-arms. The scenes from the legend of St. James are set within this painted architectural framework dividing up the wall, which is now no longer treated as a uniform whole but as several independent units for self-contained episodes. At first it seems that in each scene the classical unities of time, place, and action have been respected.

In the top register, the left-hand scene depicts the calling of the brothers James and John to be Disciples of Christ (page 60). The background shows a craggy cliff face, a landscape typical of Mantegna. To the right, next to this, James is preaching from a pulpit. The walled square on which the pulpit stands bears no relation at all to the previous landscape.

In the left-hand scene of the central register, the baptism of the magician Hermogenes is depicted (page 61, above left): St. James is freeing him from demons and converting him to Christianity. In the adjacent scene, the trial (page 60, above right), Herod Agrippa is condemning St. James to death. These two scenes are depicted at the same level, as shown by the floor paving, the lines of which converge on a single point, and also a common horizon, which is at about the eye-level of someone standing in front of the fresco. However, the architectural setting does not represent a single, unified space. The row of arches in the baptism scene breaks off abruptly at the edge of the painting and its line is not continued into the right-hand scene. These events occurred in two different places, and in both scenes the action and attention focus on the central figures:

Hermogenes, being baptized, and St. James in conversation with Herod Agrippa. The two scenes are separated by an empty space where an isolated soldier stands looking skeptically out of the frame.

In the bottom register, the scene to the left (page 61, below left) is dominated by a lively crowd. The procession that was supposed to be leading St. James to his execution has come to a standstill. A lame man is kneeling in front of James, who is healing him. Beside St. James, the soldier who is still leading the saint with a rope stands by unperturbed; but facing St. James, another soldier raises his arms in amazement. The figures behind do not seem to have noticed the miracle. At the lower edge of the scene, as a compositional counterbalance to the miraculous cure, a soldier repulses a standard bearer driven by his curiosity to see what is happening. The last scene depicts St. James' execution. These two bottom scenes also share a common perspective, though it is quite different to the one shared by the two pictures in the middle register. The action is pushed forward right up to the front edge of the painting, with a toe and a heel even protruding beyond the boundary of the scene. A range of different emotional reactions is depicted, particularly through stance and gestures, though, as is typical of Mantegna, without exaggerated dramatics: the drama of the narrative is underlined by the enormous depth of the setting. The vanishing point for both of these episodes is situated beneath the base line of the picture, so that the main figures are seen from immediately below and the feet of the characters standing further back are not visible. The scenes are in effect shown from the viewpoint of a viewer inside the chapel and appear to

Above left:
The Martyrdom of St. Christopher (detail page 63)

The arrows shot at the saint were miraculously deflected. The tyrant responsible for the saint's martyrdom was struck in the eye by one of them, at which Christopher said to him, "Tomorrow, when I'm dead, take some of my blood, mix it with some earth, put it on your eye, and you will be healed." When the king followed this advice and found he could see again, he converted to Christianity.

Above right:
The Removal of the Body of St. Christopher (detail page 63)

In this scene, the architecture combines set pieces from classical reliefs and buildings with city palaces of the Quattrocento to create a setting that in no way resembles an actual city. Vasari thought he could identify some of the people in the picture, who were therefore contemporaries from the 15th century rather than figures taken from the classical world.

Opposite page:
Andrea Mantegna
The Assumption of the Virgin (Assunta), 1454–1457
Fresco, base 238 cm
Cappella Ovetari, Chiesa degli Eremitani, Padua

Surrounded by angels, Mary floats towards God the Father, who was originally sitting above her in an oval picture. Presumably the empty space surrounded by the Apostles was intended for Mary's sarcophagus, which Mantegna probably left out because the shape of the apse wall meant that the space available was too narrow.

extend the viewer's space. In the bottom right-hand landscape scene (page 61), Mantegna depicts a rising terrain and in this way circumvents the disappearance of the ground level. Here the action is closed off from the front by the use of a solid-seeming trompe-l'œil barrier that appears to be secured out of frame at the left. One of the soldiers is leaning over the barrier into the chapel.

Of the paintings on the opposite wall, dedicated to scenes from the life of St. Christopher, the four upper scenes are presumably by Bono da Ferrara and Ansuino da Forlì, since the two in the center are signed by them. The two scenes at the bottom, however, are by Mantegna (page 63). Here he was able to create a synthesis of his artistic experience so far. The vanishing point seems to lie in the middle ground of the opposite wall, at the eye level of the figures depicted at the very front of the scene. The ornamental system of painted frames structuring the wall space is interrupted here: a column separates the two scenes of narrative, though they are, nevertheless, played out in the same place and are therefore closely linked. This link is indicated by the soldier standing to the right of the column looking towards the earlier events in the left-hand scene. In this left-hand scene, Mantegna depicts the unsuccessful attempt to martyr the saint. The arrows have failed to strike the saint (one of them striking the man shown in the upper window: page 64, left), and the executioner has resorted to his sword. In the right-hand scenes, the beheaded corpse of the giant is carried from the town.

Finally, between the walls portraying the legends of the saints, the altar wall of the chapel illustrates the *Assumption of the Virgin* (right). This is for the most part the work of Mantegna. Here the synthesis of the actual architectural setting and illusory architectural effects is completely successful. On the left, one of the Apostles is holding on to one of the pillars that frame the scene. The Apostles are standing between and even in front of this architectural framework, close to and on a level with visitors to the chapel, who gaze up at Mary with them. In 1457 the *Assumption of the Virgin* became the subject of a dispute. The widow of the patron complained that four of the Apostles were missing. The judge in the case challenged this purely numerical argument by referring her to the exceptional artistic result. But Mantegna's former master, Squarcione, who had taken sides with the widow, replied that Mantegna should have made the Apostles smaller in order to fit in all twelve of them.

In the Eremitani frescoes, Mantegna was trying out the different possibilities for constructing space through perspective. In doing so, he was not following any one dogmatic concept: for Mantegna, practice was far more important than theory. The upper scenes in the legend of St. James, depicted as if seen from slightly above, seem to be turned towards the viewer; the frescoes of the middle register, which give a direct, frontal view of the scenes, draw the viewer into the action; while the lower scenes, depicted with a low viewpoint, give the viewer a sense of confronting real space.

These novel experiments with space, allied with their almost sculptural visualization of antiquity, meant

that the frescoes had a great impact on later artists. Nevertheless, Mantegna received some criticism for his "all too classical" style: a charge made by Squarcione, for instance, who envied the success of his former student and who (according to Vasari) observed that Mantegna could have just left the color out, since his figures were more like the marble statues of antiquity than living people. It is true that few buildings or details in Mantegna's work can be connected with concrete models: for Mantegna, classical antiquity provided a general rather than specific inspiration. However, he had been educated in classical literature and archeology and had an accurate eye for detail. He had gained a knowledge of Greek art through coins, jewelry, and small bronzes, and of Roman architecture mainly from nearby Verona, where the classical remains included a renowned arena, among other things. Although not an exact representation of the arch in Verona, the triumphal arch shown in the fresco *St. James Led to Execution*

(page 61, below left) bears the inscription: *L.VITRUVIUS [IL] CERDO ARCHITE[C]TUS*, taken from the Arco dei Gavi, which names the famous Roman architect Vitruvius as its creator.

Classical buildings, particularly triumphal arches, appear often in Mantegna's works, and are endowed with a much greater significance than simple background features would normally merit. Except for the lower area of the St. Christopher frescoes, where the figures appear in contemporary dress, Mantegna prefers costumes in a classical style. Like Donatello, Mantegna had studied Roman reliefs in detail and could portray Roman armor with great precision. In 1443, Donatello had gone to Padua to complete reliefs for the altar in the church of St. Anthony, known as the Santo (page 74). Donatello's work there provided an impetus for the artists of Padua, Mantegna too being inspired by the sculptor's creative energy. Several aspects of Mantegna's work clearly show a direct influence on the statuesque attitudes of Mantegna's figures, the chiseled appearance

Andrea Mantegna
St. Luke Polyptych, 1453–1455
Tempera on wood, 230 x 177 cm
Pinacoteca di Brera, Milan

The original frame for these paintings has been lost, but a reasonable reconstruction of the format is possible. St. Luke and the group with Christ were almost without exception flanked by saints local to the city of Padua. Here, in the top left-hand corner we can see St. Daniel, with a model of the city, and next to him the penitent St. Jerome. The half-length figures in the upper section appear to be standing behind a balustrade and fill nearly all the space in the narrow field with their monumental dimensions.

St Luke Polyptych (detail page 67)

St. Luke the Evangelist is enthroned behind a scribe's desk in such a way that his physical presence almost threatens to break the boundaries of the old-fashioned panel. Above him is a *Pietà,* a close-knit group representing Christ in his suffering: his narrow, finely proportioned body, still bound by the Gothic concept of physicality, lies between Mary and John, who are tending him.

Andrea Mantegna
St. Euphemia, 1454
Tempera on canvas, 171 x 78 cm
Museo e Galleria Nazionali di Capodimonte, Naples

St. Euphemia was subjected to various forms of torture during the persecution of the Christians under Emperor Diocletian. These are symbolized by a sword that has pierced her side and a lion biting her arm. The painting was damaged by fire in the late 18th century, so that the detail of the folds of her robe are no longer apparent.

Opposite page:
Andrea Mantegna
St Mark, ca. 1448/49
Casein (?) on canvas, 82 x 63.5 cm
Städel Museum, Frankfurt am Main

Mantegna's first painting on canvas is a key work in his development. For the first time, the artist tried out the effect of the painted frame here, representing Mark in a thoughtful mood. This work was long considered to be from his studio, since there was some doubt about the genuineness of the signature and also, therefore, the early date. The doubts are reinforced by the fact that neither the patron nor the place it was painted is known.

Andrea Mantegna
The Adoration of the Shepherds, ca. 1450/51
Tempera, transferred from wood to canvas,
40 x 55.5 cm
The Metropolitan Museum of Art, New York

In this scene, the realistic portrayal of the two shepherds in ragged clothing betrays Flemish influences. Mantegna was able to study the work of Rogier van der Weyden at the Ferrara court, for which this painting was created. This transposition of literary interpretations of the holy story to a pictorial representation (with the degree of detail favored by miniaturists) was very popular. Mary is surrounded by little angels, their colors representing the fire of divine love (red) and the light of eternity (gold).

of the folds in their clothes, and his experimentation with the construction of space though perspective defined by architecture were all previously seen in Donatello's work. The carved figures on the altar of the Santo clearly influenced the positioning of the individual figures in the frescoes, as well as their physical attitudes. Mantegna must also have been aware of Donatello's work in Florence, either from Donatello himself or through the collection of drawings in Squarcione's workshop. In the lower frescoes of the St. James story, for example, the legionnaire leaning on his diamond-shaped shield (page 61) is reminiscent of Donatello's sculpture *St. George* in the Museo Nazionale del Bargello in Florence.

On the whole, Mantegna stressed the particular. In his *Trial of St. James* (page 61), the triumphal arch has two medallions on which the heads of classical rulers are shown. According to the German art historian Ilse Blum, one of these is Nero, the cruel and unpredictable emperor of pagan Rome; while the other is Augustus, the wise ruler and a witness to Sibylline prophecies, making him one of those who foresaw the coming of Christianity. During the Quattrocento, such classical elements were increasingly used to reinforce Christian teaching. But there was also, independent of any religious intention, a growing interest in classical images and a desire to include details that reflected secular themes. The traditional range of purely religious subjects handed down from the Middle Ages was gradually being expanded to include classical themes: a process in which Mantegna occupied a prominent position.

Andrea Mantegna
St. George, 1460–1470
Tempera on wood, 66 x 32 cm
Gallerie dell'Accademia, Venice

In its spatial organization, this painting is closely related
to Mantegna's *San Zeno Altarpiece* (page 75). The saint
stands in a confident and victorious pose in front of the
dragon he has just slain. The artificiality of the scenery is
stressed by the window-like stone frame that provides the
hero with a very theatrical setting and a view of the
landscape that looks almost like a theater backdrop. The
reflection of the back of the hero's head in his bright halo
is a sign that Mantegna may have seen the work of the
Florentine artist Andrea del Castagno, who was also
working in Venice.

Andrea Mantegna
Presentation at the Temple, ca. 1453–1460
Tempera on canvas, 67 x 86 cm
Gemäldegalerie, Staatliche Museen, Berlin

In the foreground, Mary is handing the Christ Child to Simeon the High Priest. Between them, Joseph is seen watching thoughtfully. The two background figures closest to the outside edges of the painting are presumed to be a self-portrait of the artist and a portrait of his wife, Nicolosia. Mantegna had married the daughter of the Venetian painter Jacopo Bellini in 1453 or 1454.

The illustration shows the nails fastening the cloth, covered by the frame when the painting is displayed in the gallery.

While working on the Ovetari frescoes, Mantegna took on other commissions, including the *St. Luke Polyptych* (pages 66, 67) for the chapel dedicated to St. Luke in the church of Santa Giustina in Padua. The very traditional conception of this altarpiece, which is designed along Gothic lines, reflects a patron with conservative tastes in art. Here the importance of the saints is reflected in their size, scaled down according to their place in the hierarchy. Like similar images in Byzantine art, they stand isolated against a golden background that symbolizes the all-embracing presence of God.

However, a modern element has been introduced with the lower group of saints, where the foreground tapers in sharp perspective, ignoring the boundaries of the painting's fictive space. In addition to this, the solidity of the figures themselves makes them stand out strongly from the uniform background.

Two other paintings from the same period are *St. Euphemia* (page 68) and *St. Mark* (page 69). Like St. Mark, St. Euphemia has been placed in a stone arch decorated with garlands of fruit and leaves. The two saints have been portrayed in the immediate foreground, bringing them close to the viewer. With her direct gaze, the life-size figure of Euphemia, accompanied by a lion, is open to dialogue with the viewer standing in front of her. In contrast, Mark the Evangelist is sitting at a window and looking past the

Giovanni Bellini
The Presentation at the Temple, ca. 1460
Oil on wood, trimmed left and right, 80 x 105 cm
Gallerie Querini Stampalia, Venice

Bellini's version of this subject is clearly connected with the painting by his brother-in-law, Mantegna (page 72); it is not clear, however, which of these paintings was executed first. Typical Venetian elements such as the warm colors and soft outlines are a distinctive feature of this painting. In contrast, Mantegna's figures are modelled with stronger tones of light and shade, and his colors are altogether cooler. The change in coloration is also the result of technique, as Mantegna worked in tempera on cloth and not in oil on wood.

viewer, though his arm and book seem to reach out over the barrier of the balustrade into the viewer's space. This type of composition was derived from Flemish antecedents. Rogier van der Weyden (1399/1400–1464) and Jan van Eyck (ca. 1390–1441) often placed their subjects behind stone balustrades or frames: a well-known example is van Eyck's *Portrait of a Man (Tymotheus Leal Souvenir)* painted in 1432 (National Gallery, London). Through this visual device, subjects are given a stamp of authenticity and actuality: they appear to be sitting, fully alive, just a short distance from the viewer.

Although more restrained, the main figures in Mantegna's *Presentation at the Temple* (page 72) are able to overcome the barrier between the picture's fictive space and the viewer's real space in the same way, since the point of contact is defined by a stone frame encircling the picture. The figures emerge from the dark background with a three-dimensional effect similar to that of a sculpted relief. Yet in spite of this strong physical presence, the figures seem private and remote; none of the figures is looking out of the picture at the viewer. In comparison, Mantegna's Venetian father-in-law, Giovanni Bellini (ca. 1430–1516), maintained a degree of physical distance from the viewer in his version of the *Presentation at the Temple* (above). To bridge this distance, however, he used the young man portrayed to the right, who stares out at us with a complicit gaze. Bellini's composition is less urgent than Mantegna's. The witnesses on either side are spatially at the same level as Joseph and frame the action. The Italian art historian

Ettore Camesasca presumed this was a devotional image of the Bellini family, probably painted for some special occasion such as the birth of a child, or a wedding. On this interpretation, the old man in the center is Jacopo Bellini, the two young men to the right his sons Gentile and Giovanni, and to the left are their mother and their sister, Nicolosia (Mantegna's wife), who is in the same position as in Mantegna's picture.

Two further works are an indication of the artistic influence that operated mutually between Mantegna and Giovanni Bellini. Mantegna's version of *Christ on the Mount of Olives* (page 24) has a very intense effect, each element appearing with equal emphasis: in spite of its distance, the city seems near enough to touch. In the foreground the sleeping disciples Peter, James, and John are lying close together. Christ is kneeling on a rocky outcrop above them, in agonized prayer. Five angels have appeared with a horrifying image of the instruments of Christ's torment. In contrast to Mantegna, who painted a polished and intensely detailed composition focused on the figure of Christ, Bellini (page 25) distributed his figures more loosely across a wide landscape. In the foreground, the disciples sleep on a clean sweep of sand, while in the background an extensive landscape dotted with woods and villages unfolds. The head of Christ, who is in dialogue with God the Father, is outlined above the whole scene in the rays of the setting sun. Here, Bellini has stressed the atmospheric mood of the evening rather than the drama to come. Bellini, it has to be noted, was far more interested in color than form.

THE *SAN ZENO ALTARPIECE*

Donatello
Altar for the Santo in Padua
(reconstruction by H. W. Janson)

In 1443, Donatello was commissioned to complete a high altar that was dedicated in 1450. The altar was a combination of bronze reliefs in the predella with freestanding, fully three-dimensional figures above. The structural device of the columns inspired Mantegna's treatment of space in the *San Zeno Altarpiece.*

Opposite page:
Andrea Mantegna
San Zeno Altarpiece, 1457–1460
Tempera (and other paints) on wood, 480 x 450 cm
San Zeno, Verona

The framework for this devotional painting of Mary is mostly original, though the three predella paintings were replaced by canvas copies during the 19th century. The original wooden panels are now to be found in Paris (page 78, above) and Tours (pages 76, 78 below), legacies of Napoleon's appropriation of works of art as war booty. In the left-hand panel stand St. Peter and St. Paul, St. John the Evangelist, and St. Zeno, who gave the church and the altar his name. To the right, St. Benedict, St. Lawrence, St. Gregory, and St. John the Baptist are depicted.

Mantegna's twin themes of the representation of space and the use of painting as an illusionistic medium—themes already hinted at in the Ovetari frescoes—were taken further with the altar in the church of San Zeno in Verona (page 75). The patron for this commission was Giorgio Correr (1409–1464), who was a notary to the papal Curia and the Abbott of San Zeno. The format was modeled on Donatello's altar for the Santo in Padua (above), which is no longer in its original form, however, because of later alterations. Donatello had used two columns to separate Mary from the saints around her and had provided her with her own, very compact, space. Similarly, Mantegna retained the separation into three parts as in the design for a paneled altarpiece, but now made the individual sections equal in size, and linked them by having them depict the same space.

Mantegna's altarpiece can be compared with an altarpiece by Domenico Veneziano (ca. 1400–1461) for the church of Santa Lucia dei Magnoli in Florence (Volume I, page 311). Here too the architecture of the scene is divided into three sections: a continuing reference to the Gothic design for a polyptych that can also be seen in Mantegna's *St. Luke Polyptych* (pages 66, 67). In Veneziano's picture, pillars are used to separate the area round the Madonna from the saints accompanying her, though they share the same overall space. However, Veneziano's structure contains an optical distraction: Mary is sitting in the center of a three-arched loggia that is situated behind the saints. However, because the tops of the arches coincide with the upper edge of the picture, they extend over the heads of the saints and seem to occupy the upper foreground of the painting. Moreover, the architectural setting behind Mary has no firm anchor from a spatial point of view. The central niche frames Mary and seems to provide the backrest for her throne, but the precise alignment of the architecture changes according to where the viewer looks. Nevertheless, the correctly portrayed architectural perspective provides both a structure for the painting and also an ornamental framework for the scene. In addition to this imaginative spatial organization, another innovative feature of Veneziano's picture is that the architecture behind Mary opens to the heavens, the light falling onto the scene being transformed into the picture's light, delicate tones.

In his altarpiece (page 75), painted about ten years later, Mantegna went even further. The Madonna and saints are in a box-shaped space on a platform open from all sides. The three-dimensional half-columns of the wooden frame are backed by painted pilasters indicating where the picture's fictive space begins. This space, a stage created by illusionistic devices, provides a framework for a *sacra conversazione*. In paintings representing a *sacra conversazione*, the saints are there to intercede for the pious worshipper: they offer themselves to the faithful as intermediaries who can be addressed directly.

On the medallions of the piers are painted flat gray-on-gray reliefs of mythological scenes symbolizing pagan antiquity. Below the coffered ceiling runs a frieze decorated with putti, horns of plenty, and palms. According to the Book of Ezekiel in the Old Testament, the palm motif between two angels was a decoration used in Solomon's temple; here, therefore, it is to be read as a reference to the covenant of the Old Testament. The frieze, then, acts as a link between the pagan world as represented on the piers and the Christian world of the New Testament vividly represented in the painting. The

representatives of the New Testament, life-size and resplendent in bright colors, stand before the two stages of existence preceding them in the history of human development, the world of the Old Testament and the classical world. These earlier stages are represented by works of art. In comparison, Mary and the gathering of saints seem real and animated: they alone can lay claim to the living truth. They appear to occupy the same level of reality as the viewer: it is easy to imagine that we can hear the angels singing. On the steps of Mary's throne (page 75) the contrast is quite clear: near the classical stone putti half-hidden by a rug sit little angels making music, a corner of their robes falling out into the viewer's space.

At the same time, the scene within the picture's fictive space is one of spiritual exaltation, an image of the hope of acceptance into this holy circle on the distant day of the Last Judgment. The figures seem almost within reach and yet far removed from us in their heavenly sphere. This paradox was reflected in the very execution of the painting: Mantegna presents painting itself as an instrument of illusion. In this altarpiece he is commenting on the power of painting to illustrate both earthly and heavenly reality at one and the same time; and, therefore, to represent art itself.

In contrast with the *Madonna and Child Enthroned* on the main panel of the *San Zeno Altarpiece*, the predella shows scenes from the Passion (pages 76, 78). Here too there is a concrete point of reference for the viewer. In the central panel, which shows the Crucifixion (page 78), two men intrude into the lower part of the painting, as though they were just about to move from the viewer's space outside the picture and climb the steps up to the level of Golgotha. They are cut off cleanly by the frame: the head of the man on the right is just coming into view, while the soldier on the left, who can be identified as Longinus, can be seen clad in Roman armor and holding a lance. Longinus, after piercing Christ's side as he hung on the Cross, was converted when holy blood ran down his lance. Here he is depicted acknowledging the divinity of the Son of Man to his companion, who thus assumes the role of a viewer standing between the two worlds. This witness is the intermediary between the living experience of the Crucifixion and a believer's identification with the story of the Passion every time it is told or illustrated.

Andrea Mantegna
The Agony in the Garden (Christ on the Mount of Olives),
1457–1460
From the predella of the *San Zeno Altarpiece* (page 75)
Tempera on wood covered with canvas, 71.5 x 94 cm
Musée des Beaux-Arts, Tours

The composition of this picture is similar to the version of the same subject in the National Gallery in London (page 24). Gethsemane is better described as an orchard than as a garden. As in Bellini's version of the Mount of Olives scene (page 25), an angel is floating on high with the cup that symbolizes the inexorable fate reserved for Christ. This detail demonstrates the lively exchange of ideas between the two artists.

Opposite page:
The Madonna and Child Enthroned (detail page 75)

The Madonna's throne is covered by a decorative Anatolian rug that testifies to Italy's trading connections with the Orient. The horizontal S-shape on the outside border is the first letter of the Armenian expression for "God the Almighty." Where possible, a place of worship would also be furnished with rugs having Christian symbols.

Andrea Mantegna
The Crucifixion, 1457–1460
From the predella of the *San Zeno Altarpiece* (page 75)
Tempera on wood, 67 x 93 cm
Musée du Louvre, Paris

This scene takes place on a cracked rocky plateau on Golgotha. The place of execution is marked by holes in the rock that had already been used for other crosses. At the foot of Christ's Cross lies the skull of Adam, the first man. According to legend, Adam's grave was on Calvary and was exposed by earthquake when Christ died.

Andrea Mantegna
The Resurrection, 1457–1460
From the predella of the *San Zeno Altarpiece* (page 75)
Tempera on wood, 71 x 94 cm
Musée des Beaux-Arts, Tours

In the center of this painting, the bright apparition of Christ stands out, emphasized by the darkness of the rocky grotto. The faces of the guards show a range of reactions to the miracle of the Resurrection, from a still sleepy figure gazing in front of him to a soldier rising to his feet in amazement.

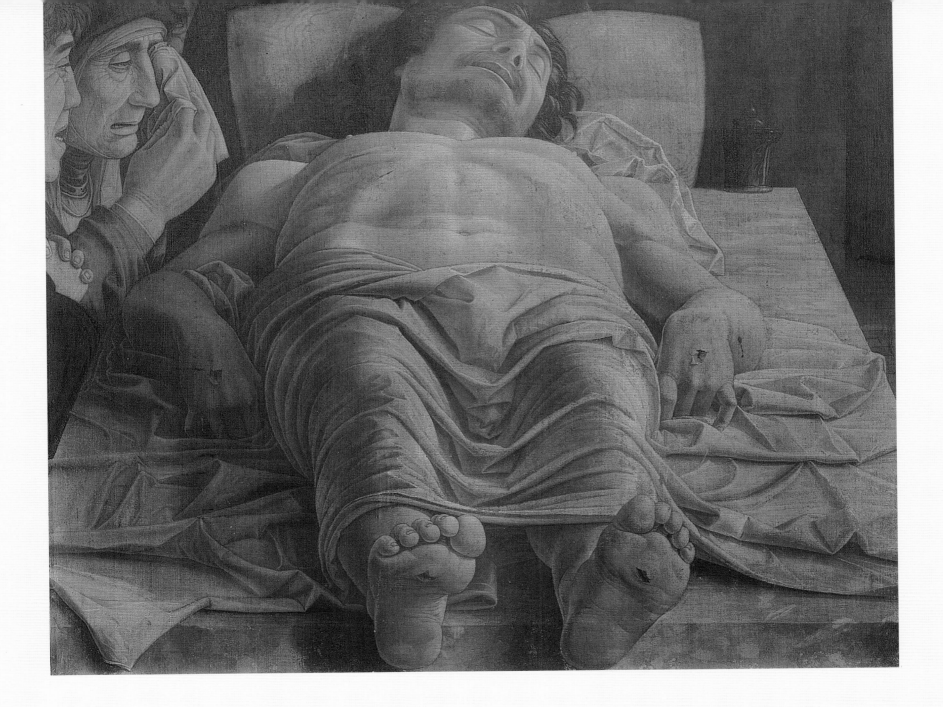

Andrea Mantegna
The Lamentation Over the Dead Christ (Cristo morto),
1464–1500
Tempera on canvas, 66 x 81 cm
Pinacoteca di Brera, Milan

This picture was in Mantegna's studio when he died.
The Italian title in the inventory of the estate was *Cristo in scurto* ("foreshortened Christ"), a prosaic studio expression that describes not the subject but how it is presented.

We do not know who the patron was, where it was meant for, or exactly when it was painted. Perhaps the artist had painted this picture, with its very unusual color scheme and composition, for himself.

THE SHOCK OF MANTEGNA'S BODY OF CHRIST

As heavy as lead, the body of Christ lies on a stone slab, the cloth clinging to his body and the slab as though it were wet. In unprecedented fashion, the observer sees the soles of Christ's feet pointing up over the edge of the stone. The body is strongly foreshortened by perspective, and the head is supported by a firm pillow, so that it is slightly raised above the torso. The vanishing point lies above the format of the image; the observer looks down on Christ, but not beyond him, since the edge of the image above his head prevents any wandering of the gaze. This perspective and the proximity of the body to the edge of the picture seemed to undermine the dignity of the dead man and his divine distance. He is brought quite close to the observer, secularized and thus makes a provocative statement.

Like the treatment, the coloration too is reduced and moves the event even further away from reality. The ashen body lies on the reddish stone as though the latter had drawn all the blood out of it. The stone is spotted with blood, tears, and ointment. Thus the dead material has taken on the elements of the action in order to become a concentrated symbol of the Passion.

Having been taken down from the Cross, the body of Christ, in accordance with Jewish burial rituals, was washed, anointed with aromatic oils, and finally wrapped in clean linen. This ritual was performed on a stone on which Mary's tears "have left indelible traces up to the present day." The anointing stone, at that time preserved in Constantinople, was considered one of the most important relics to have been lost after the invasion of the Turks in 1453.

Mantegna's painting is by no means a purely artistic diversion or a merely illusionistic piece of bravura demonstrating the possibilities of perspective. The fact that the observer gazes down upon the Savior with eyes lowered suggests a reverential approach. It is a devotional image that evokes a compassionate empathy.

IN THE SERVICE OF THE GONZAGA

Andrea Mantegna
St. Sebastian, 1459
Tempera on wood, 68 x 30 cm
Kunsthistorisches Museum, Vienna

A bearded horseman can be seen in the cloud to the left. Images in the clouds like this can also be seen in other paintings by Mantegna, for instance in the third scene of *Triumphs of Caesar* (Hampton Court Palace, London) and the painting the *Triumph of Virtue* (page 110). Already described in classical art theory and adopted by Alberti and Leonardo da Vinci, these were ascribed to the genius of nature, which could stimulate artists and inspire them to improve on nature through their art.

In 1456, Ludovico III Gonzaga (1414–1478), Marquis of Mantua, invited Mantegna to be his court artist. Mantegna did not take up this invitation until three years later, after the Marquis had improved his conditions of employment several times. He promised Mantegna and his family a monthly salary of fifteen ducats, adequate supplies of corn and wood, accommodation, and the cost of moving from Padua to Mantua. In addition to this, Ludovico also gave Mantegna the right to bear the Gonzaga coat-of-arms and gave him fine materials in the Gonzaga colors so that he could have his court costume made. Yet in spite of all these privileges, Mantegna continued working in Padua after 1456, particularly on the altarpiece for San Zeno in Verona, and at the end of 1458 he even bought a house in Padua. He was clearly undecided about whether he should place himself under the authority of a ruling family, since that would mean he had to work exclusively for the Gonzaga court. Commissions, after all, were plentiful in Padua, where he worked for influential personalities such as Giacoma della Leonessa, the widow of the renowned commander Gattamelata (1370–1443), in whose palace Mantegna decorated a room with scenes from the life of her husband (works destroyed by fire in 1760).

The small, exquisite painting of *St. Sebastian* (page 81) dates from this period, possibly commissioned by Jacopo Antonio Marcello, governor of Padua and a confidant of the Gonzaga. Images of the saints were extremely popular. As a handsome young Roman officer in the service of the Emperor Diocletian, St. Sebastian chose to stand by his fellow Christians in the prisons of Rome during the violent persecutions of the Early Church. Because he survived the first martyrdom of being shot by the arrows of Numidian archers, and only met his end through a second torment, by being cudgeled to death, he was seen as having conquered death, and was therefore chosen as the patron saint of

plague victims. In 15th-century Italian art, portrayals of St. Sebastian offered the opportunity of depicting an idealized nude figure in a classical setting. Mantegna tied the saint to the column of a triumphal arch both to emphasize his heroism and at the same time to stress the precise historic setting. Yet the atmosphere is less authentic than it might seem at first glance. The triumphal arch stands in a courtyard closed off by a wall: he would certainly never have found a setting like this in antiquity. Debris from statues and a fragment of a bacchanalian relief lie around, indicating the fall of the pagans and the victory of Christianity. Even this is to be understood more as a symbolic reference, since, from the historical point of view, paganism was far from being overthrown in Sebastian's time. The nude figure of the saint appears more sensual than agonized. The clergy could not be absolutely sure that the believers praying before this depiction of the saint, whose softly lit body twists in unnatural contrapposto, were filled only with chaste thoughts.

Mantegna proudly signed this work, in Greek letters, on the left-hand side of the triumphal arch, as though he wanted to assume the mantel of the great Greek painters. However, this is not simply the expression of an excessive degree of self-confidence, because even his contemporaries acknowledged him as "the new Apelles," equating him with the famous painter of classical Greece.

While he was completing these works, Mantegna was repeatedly allowed to defer taking up his post by the patient Ludovico III Gonzaga. Finally, however, in 1460, Mantegna let his house in Padua and on 7 August moved house to Mantua. As Mantua had no strong artistic tradition of its own, Mantegna—not yet thirty years old and with his reputation as one of the leading moderns—was a great coup for the court. Ludovico wanted his residence, the Castello San Giorgio, built 1390–1406, transformed into a palace.

The conversion work was also to include the royal chapel, the decoration of which became one of Mantegna's first duties. This too was destroyed, this time in the second half of the 16th century.

Today, three paintings from this chapel are mounted as a triptych in the Uffizi in Florence (pages 82–83), though they were probably given this format as recently as 1827, when the frame was made. The differing sizes of the paintings, and the inconsistencies in both composition and iconography indicate that these are individual works rather than parts of a uniformly planned altarpiece. Nevertheless, these paintings (pages 82–83) could have been created for the same chapel. If so, then the decoration must have been based on a simple scheme of incidents from the holy story, from the birth of Christ to Mary's death. Since it was a court chapel, the *Adoration of the Magi* (pages 82–83) was the main image and was presumably placed in the altar niche (which accounts for the concave format of the panel). We can assume that it was flanked by two vertical paintings that have not been preserved. All the panels are exceptional for their rich colors and the use of gold. Mantegna did not use real gold, but a color simulating gold, as recommended by Leon Battista Alberti (1404–1472) in his famous treatise *De Pictura* (On Painting). Patrons often wanted gold leaf, as this meant that they could make a public display of their wealth while also demonstrating God's splendor. But this type of gilding always seemed flat and artificial, and disturbed the unity of the composition, whereas a paint that looked like gold could achieve a finer effect. Mantegna used this gold paint for haloes and for angels, for ornamentation on buildings, sumptuous materials, vessels, candelabra, for candle flames, and even for the reflections of light on garments. In this way, instead of stressing the use of a precious metal, he was able to place more emphasis on its decorative effects and on the reflection of light. The detailed portrayal of the vessels and various other objects in interiors demonstrated Mantegna's inventive gifts, which the Marquis was able to exploit to the full. His court artist had to design bronze vessels and tableware, statues, and tapestries. He collaborated with architects in the conversion of rooms and internal courtyards, and was responsible for the decorations for festivals, and for stage sets and costumes, which have since been lost.

Major commissions included devotional paintings in private apartments, and also portraits of members of the family. Portraits (page 85) were important as a record for later generations, and also made it possible to exchange likenesses with allies and future marriage partners. This type of work was to some extent problematic since the sitters tried to avoid the boring task of sitting as a model. The portraits therefore often had to be completed from sketches or from memory, one of Mantegna's skills that was highly appreciated. Mantegna was not completely happy and in his letters he complained about his working conditions. But the patrons were not always satisfied either. Isabella d'Este, for example, sent her portrait back immediately, probably because the naturalism of the painting did not flatter her enough.

Andrea Mantegna
The Ascension, ca. 1460
Tempera on wood, 86 x 42 cm
Galleria degli Uffizi, Florence

Above the saints, who gaze upwards, Christ floats
somewhat stiffly, surrounded by a mandorla of angels.
Immediately below him stands the Virgin Mary,
occupying a special place in the lower section, the only
figure facing forwards and slightly raised on a ledge of
rock. Compared with the imaginatively decorated depiction
of the *Circumcision of Christ* (page 83), this painting,
executed for the same chapel, seems fairly uninspired.

Andrea Mantegna
The Adoration of the Magi, ca. 1460
Tempera on wood, 76 x 76.5 cm
Galleria degli Uffizi, Florence

The Three Magi symbolize both the three ages of man and
also the three continents known at that time, Asia, Europe,
and Africa. The adherents of different cultures among the
followers of the kings are depicted realistically—they were
familiar because of the activities of cosmopolitan Venice, a
major trading center and slave market. The Magi pay
three-fold homage to Christ: they bring gold for the King
of Man, frankincense for the Son of God, and myrrh, an
allusion to Christ's sacrificial death to redeem mankind.

Andrea Mantegna
The Circumcision of Christ, ca. 1460
Tempera on wood, 86 x 42 cm
Galleria degli Uffizi, Florence

The subject of this painting is the circumcision of Christ eight
days after birth, therefore on New Year's Day. Since the late Middle
Ages, New Year's Day had often been connected with images of the
presentation at the temple forty days later, as prescribed by the law
of Moses (Luke 2: 21–38). Joseph is carrying a sacrifice of two
doves in a basket. The setting is very richly decorated. In the
lunettes, two related scenes from the Old Testament are depicted:
left, Abraham's sacrifice; right, Moses' presentation of the stone
tablets on which the Ten Commandments were written.

Andrea Mantegna
The Death of the Virgin, ca. 1460
Tempera on wood, 54 x 42 cm
Museo Nacional del Prado, Madrid

This scene takes place in a hall viewed in perspective.
The Virgin Mary is on a bier at a distance from the
viewer, with the eleven Apostles around her, each with his
own part to play in the sacrament of death. The view
from the window is spectacular. It shows Mantua with the
long bridge over the River Mincio.

Andrea Mantegna
Christ with the Virgin's Soul, ca. 1460
Tempera on wood, 27 x 17 cm
Collezione Baldi, Ferrara

As a vision perceptible to the viewer, but not to the
disciples, Christ is floating in an aureole in the vault.

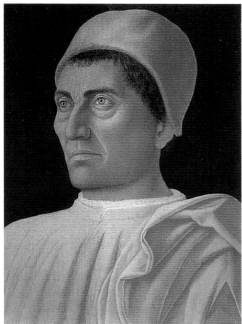

Andrea Mantegna
Portrait of Cardinal Carlo de' Medici,
1460–1470
Tempera on wood, 41.5 x 29.5 cm
Galleria degli Uffizi, Florence

Carlo de' Medici (1428–1492) was an illegitimate son
of Cosimo de' Medici, who was highly influential in
Florence. His robe identifies him as a prelate; his seat
was Prato Cathedral. In 1466, Mantegna was working
in Florence for Ludovico Gonzaga and may have painted
the Cardinal at this time. However, recent research has
thrown doubt on the identity of the sitter.

Andrea Mantegna
Portrait of Cardinal Lodovico Mezzarota, 1459/60
Tempera on wood, 44 x 33 cm
Gemäldegalerie, Staatliche Museen, Berlin

The sketches for this portrait were completed during the
Church Council convened by Pope Pius II in 1459/60,
which was to have united Europe against the Ottoman
Turks. Cardinal Ludovico Mezzarota (1401–1465) was a
warlike prince of the Church, fully conscious of his
power, and a close friend of Ludovico III Gonzaga. The
portrait is one of the earliest examples of the use of the
three-quarter profile in Italian art, a format that had been
developed in the Netherlands during the first half of the
15th century.

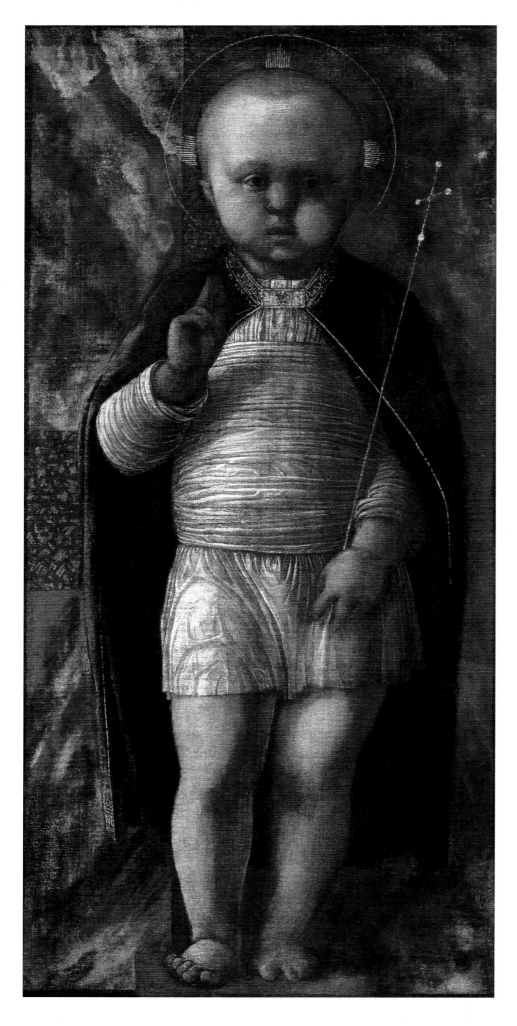

During his early years in Mantua, on 22 September 1464, Mantegna traveled to Lake Garda with his fellow artists Felice Feliciano, Giovanni Marcanuova, and Samuele da Tradate. The companions addressed one another with classical names and titles such as Imperator and Consul, wore laurel wreaths on their heads, and rowed across Lake Garda singing to the sound of lutes, clearly feeling as though they had transported themselves to the realms of Arcadia. Their interest in classical art led them to visit ancient sites such as Toscolano, mainly to copy the inscriptions there. During the Quattrocento, knowledge of inscriptions was particularly significant and often replaced direct contact with classical works of art. Feliciano and Marcanuova filled books with copies and imitations, and carved their own inscriptions on the stones and also on new work in the classical style. At this time a spirit of research was intermingled with a general enthusiasm for antiquity that had no qualms about adding to authentic material.

Andrea Mantegna
The Infant Redeemer, 1485–1495
Tempera on unprepared canvas, 70 x 35 cm
National Gallery of Art, Washington

This is the equivalent in painting of the devotional statues of the Christ Child, used mainly in the Franciscan ritual. The Christ Child is depicted as Imperator Mundi (Ruler of the World), his right hand raised in blessing. In his left hand he holds a wand on which there is a cross; this wand is at once a regal scepter and a symbol of the Passion to come. The picture was presumably hung over a doorway so that Christ gave a blessing to all those coming in and going out.

Opposite page:
Andrea Mantegna
The Virgin and Child, ca. 1465–1470
Tempera on canvas, 42 x 32 cm
Gemäldegalerie, Staatliche Museen, Berlin

Cloaked in a brocade robe, the Virgin Mary is holding the sleeping Christ Child tenderly in her arms. In their close embrace, the two figures merge into a single silhouette. Mary's melancholy gaze forewarns of the Passion of Christ in the distant future. Mantegna's treatment of color here is very reminiscent of the devotional painting of the *Lamentation Over the Dead Christ* (page 79) and the *St. Sebastian* in Paris (page 103). The composition also betrays the influence of Donatello.

THE CAMERA DEGLI SPOSI

Castello San Giorgio in Mantua, 1390–1406
View from the north

The Camera degli Sposi is on the first floor of the northeast tower of the Castello San Giorgio in Mantua, a tower distinctive because of its off-center windows. The castle was built between 1390 and 1406 in what was even then a consciously historical style: though it is clear that *all'antica* did not mean simply an historically correct classical style, it also covered the style of the Romanesque Middle Ages. From about 1456, Ludovico Gonzaga had the walls extended to make an impressive residence; the courtyards had loggias added, and sweeping spiral staircases giving riders (and their horses) access led to the upper floors, which were decorated with frescoes.

Opposite page:
Andrea Mantegna
Camera degli Sposi, 1465–1474
Room area 808 x 808 cm
Castello San Giorgio, Palazzo Ducale, Mantua

The frescoes were already seriously damaged in 1630, during the occupation of Mantua by Imperial troops, and they were allowed to deteriorate until the end of the 19th century. The painting was then "restored" and over-painted a number of times, until, in 1987, extensive restoration work cleared all this away. Missing patches were carefully restored so that it is now possible to have a good idea of how the frescoes originally looked.

Mantegna's main work in Mantua, a work that was to form the basis of his reputation and that of his patron, was the Camera degli Sposi, as it is known (page 89), the only completely preserved room of frescoes by Mantegna. The name "Room of the Bride and Groom" was given in the 17th century, probably because weddings were celebrated there and because the frescoes represent the Marquis and his wife. The earliest name we have is the *camera picta*, simply the "painted room." The Camera degli Sposi occupies an intermediate position between the private and public apartments of the Marquis. It was furnished with a monumental bed and used as reception room: a room for family gatherings and a place where contracts were sealed, including marriage contracts.

The smooth walls of this square room have almost no architectural features apart from two windows and two doors. The flat ceiling vault has apertures for lunettes. The only projecting features are the fireplace, the door frames, and the capital-like corbels that seem to be supporting the vault. The architectural elements on the walls—the bases, columns, and wall arches—are in fact painted. In addition, from one capital to the next Mantegna picturesquely simulated poles from which heavy, gold-embossed curtains with colored linings appear to be attached all the way round the

room. At some points these hangings are thrown back to reveal a scene, and at others they are left down, dividing or closing off the room and covering two of the walls like tapestries. The bed stood in the corner by these curtained walls. This left enough space in front of the hearth for guests, and so the narrative of the frescoes was fully open to view.

The ceiling is a marvel of illusionistic trompe l'œil (page 91): a deep vault is simulated, its fake beams having rosettes at the junctions and gold mosaic cells between. This gives the room a classical atmosphere, with grisaille painting used to simulate marble reliefs. In the eight large caissons, putti are used as caryatids, bearing medallions from which Roman emperors look down. Mythological scenes from the lives of Hercules, Orpheus, and Arion are depicted in the triangular cells between these (page 93). This ceiling decoration was intended as a hymn of praise to the Marquis, who allowed himself to be presented here—with aspirations far in excess of those of a ruler of a small Italian dukedom—as a prince in the tradition of the Caesars. The heroes of the mythological scenes symbolize the determination to succeed through strength, courage, skill, and intelligence. In addition to all this, the stories of Orpheus and Arion are centered on music, the favorite art of Ludovico's long-serving tutor, the humanist Vittorino da Feltre (1378–1446). The central section of the ceiling fresco opens onto the sky, where the allegorical praise of the Duke is subtly continued. Playfully toying with the traditional insignia of rank, a small putto is holding a laurel wreath above his own head, while another putto is holding an apple to symbolize the orb of a ruler, and a third is holding a baton in his hand in place of a scepter. This free interplay of symbols is a demonstration both of an unpretentious court régime and of the burlesque humor of the age.

Mantegna's ceiling fresco was completely novel, something never previously seen in painting. The architectural prototype was the Pantheon in Rome (page 94), with its central vault open to light, air, and rain—though it is not used as a climbing frame for angels, people, and animals, as Mantegna's is! In the Camera degli Sposi, a foreshortened balustrade frames

a view dominated by the blue of the heavens, from which various figures look down (pages 91, 95). Three women standing together in a friendly group smile at the observer. Near them, a maid turns towards a woman whose head-dress identifies her as a woman of noble birth. An orange tree has been precariously balanced on the rim of the balustrade and a peacock is stretching towards it from the opposite side. The whole effect is bright and lively.

The scenes on the walls, on the other hand, are much more sober. The Court occupies the north wall (page 79). The Gonzaga family is gathered with its intimate friends on a high terrace that seems to sit on the room's real fireplace. The space in the scene is bounded at the back by a wall with round marble insets. To the left, dressed in a robe, and with a hat that identifies him as the *condottiere*, the commander-in-chief of the army, Ludovico is shown sitting in an almost domestic setting. A dog has settled down under his seat. Like his successors, Ludovico was an enthusiastic breeder of dogs and horses: breeding such animals was seen as a suitable occupation for a nobleman, and was at the same time a lucrative source of income. In addition, Ludovico's well-paid post as commander-in-chief for the Sforza allowed him his ostentatious lifestyle and his artistic projects. Because of Mantua's geographical position, he had to maintain good relations with his two powerful neighbors, Milan and Venice. These states had an interest in Mantua since they wanted to extend their boundaries to control either the trade routes going north, or the shipping routes on the other side of the river Po. Ludovico skillfully maintained his position through diplomatic finesse and his opportunistic tendency to serve those from whom he expected most advantage.

By 1459 Ludovico had brought himself to the notice of Pope Pius II by offering a meeting place for the Ecumenical Council, which was to call for a crusade against the Ottoman Turks. The costs this incurred for Ludovico pushed him into debt for many years. At the time, Pope Pius was scathing about the unsuitability of the location, in marshland where nothing was to be heard but the croaking of frogs. But decades later, Ludovico's drive as builder and patron had so transformed his capital that several princes, including Pope Julius II in 1506, chose to make a detour to Mantua to visit this brilliant center of the arts. The Florentine architect and art theorist Leon Battista Alberti, who had been in the Pope's entourage in 1459, made an important contribution to this brilliance. Over the next few years he designed the churches of Sant' Andrea and San Sebastiano in Mantua. Mantegna, who had met Alberti during the Council, also certainly met him later, as Mantegna's house was situated close to the site of San Sebastiano.

By 1476, the year inscribed on a stone stele standing on the site, the artist's family home had been built on a plot given to him by the Marquis. Work on it probably began that same year. The building was based on a very original design, probably by Mantegna himself, with advice from Alberti and Luca Fancelli (1430–1495), architect to the Gonzaga. It has a plain, square, three-story exterior that surrounds a circular inner court of only two stories, a design that produces a clear contrast of geometric shapes. The courtyard may well have had a dome: a space of this type could only have been lit by an opening above. Just as in the Camera degli Sposi, so even in Mantegna's own home the eye is drawn upwards: whether the courtyard was covered or open, the effect was the same, a contrast between a solid structure and the airy view of the heavens.

In 1466, on the deaths of his brothers, Ludovico became sole ruler of the now united state of Mantua, which gave him a welcome opportunity to style himself head of state in all confidence. On the fresco depicting the ducal household he had himself portrayed as a busy man of affairs, surrounded by his family and with streams of visitors flocking to see him. His secretary has just approached him to give him a letter (page 97). The heads of these two figures are at about the same level. If he were standing, the Marquis would be far taller than his secretary. Since it would not be right for a person of low status to overshadow a higher-ranking individual, the physical size of the secretary has been scaled down; here a remnant of the medieval concept of rank is still apparent.

On Ludovico's left his wife, Barbara of Brandenburg, is seated amid their children. It was the custom of the Gonzagas to form alliances with ruling houses north of the Alps in order to ensure they had allies over an extensive area. Between the golden yellow dresses of Barbara and her daughter Barbarina, and the dark clothing of the older woman in the background, a female dwarf introduces a touch of red. In this court, a dwarf could not be regarded a bizarre contrast from whom one could expect entertainment, nor as someone to be condescendingly put down. Surrounded as they were by their marshy lands, the Gonzaga themselves were prone to malaria and rickets and were sometimes hunchbacked and obese. This was the reason that one young scion of the Sforzas of Milan rejected his proposed bride, Ludovico's daughter Dorotea. The family portrait does not show deformities of this kind.

Though he made the faces naturalistic, Mantegna was obliged to idealize the overall figure, and he achieved this mainly through a geometrical approach to depicting bodies that provided added dignity. Nevertheless, the rules of anatomy were strictly applied. It is possible that a school of anatomy was founded in Mantua in Mantegna's time; certainly his approach to

Andrea Mantegna
Camera degli Sposi (detail)
Ceiling fresco

The ceiling is divided into areas by painted bands and ornamentation, the areas differing in their degrees of realism. The realistic view of the sky in the center is separated from the modulated gray-gold tones of the ceiling by means of a colorful garland of fruit and leaves around simulated reliefs. Just as with the *San Zeno Altarpiece* (page 75), here Mantegna is operating on different levels of reality.

Andrea Mantegna
Camera degli Sposi (detail)
Ceiling fresco

Here we see two classical scenes: the death of Orpheus,
and Arion being threatened by pirates as he crosses from
Sicily to Corinth. The caissons represent the classical
emperors Augustus and Tiberius, while the wall lunette
is decorated with a Gonzaga seal with a young doe.

Below:
Andrea Mantegna
Camera degli Sposi (detail)
Ceiling fresco

In a further section we see part of the story of the poet
and musician Arion. A dolphin that heard Arion's song
saves him from pirates. Next to this the caesars Tiberius
and Caligula are depicted. The lunette contains a garland
of plants set against a background of blue sky, a motif
repeated in the center of each wall.

Opposite page:
Andrea Mantegna
Camera degli Sposi (detail)
Servants with horse and dogs

There is now no indication of what the small hand on the
far left is pointing at, or who is doing the pointing.
Presumably there was once another figure standing in
front of a curtain drawn back over this pilaster (traces of a
curtain can be seen in the top corner of the scene).

The Pantheon, AD 118–125
Dome with circular opening
Santa Maria ad Martyres/Santa Maria Rotonda, Rome

This temple, dedicated to "all the gods," was the most
spectacular circular building of antiquity, its finely
balanced proportions influencing the domed buildings of
the Renaissance. In the center of the hemispherical vault,
a circular opening of nine meters was left open to the sky
to allow daylight into the interior. This circular building
was built by Emperor Hadrian in AD 118–125 to replace
an older temple that had been destroyed by fire.

Camera degli Sposi (detail page 91)

Here the viewer looks up towards the figures from a ground-level perspective. The bulging thighs of the putto balancing in front of the balustrade clearly shows that Mantegna has divided up the physical structure of the little putto's body into cylindrical sections.

painting figures seems to indicate a knowledge of dissected corpses. More evident, however, is his study of classical sculpture, for his figures clearly possess a sculptural solidity. Their statuesque qualities recall Donatello, whose robed figures, fashioned with classical discipline, Mantegna had already seen in Padua.

A white-haired man dressed in black stands out between two sons of the Marquis. This is possibly Vittorino da Feltre, who was long dead by the time Mantegna came to paint this fresco. He was the court librarian and also tutor to Ludovico and his brothers and sisters, and Ludovico owed his extensive education to this man. Vittorino had also taught the ten-year-old Barbara of Brandenburg when she came to Mantua, bringing her up to be a princess capable of handling government business while her husband was on military campaigns as commander-in-chief. To the right of the royal family stand several men who, judging by their red, white, and gold livery, work for the Gonzaga court (page 97). A flight of steps leads down to a passageway where the curtain has been pulled back to reveal a small section of landscape. Visitors crowd around, welcomed by a nobleman standing on the steps. This gives the impression that the scene on the chimney wall portrays a specific event to which visitors are flocking.

All the frescoes have one characteristic in common: the protagonists are self-assured and composed. In the foreground they are depicted with monumental proportions, a fact which intensifies their already heightened presence. This effect is emphasized even further by the fact that, apart from at the edges of the fresco, hardly any conversation or interaction is taking place between those present, and each figure occupies a space of its own. On the other hand, in spite of the lack of drama, these frescoes do portray an event. The episode depicted on the west wall (pages 98–99), adjacent to the court scene, may help to clarify what is happening. In the right-hand section of this wall, people congregate in front of an extensive landscape (page 101). This scene portrays a meeting between Ludovico III and his son, Francesco, who has been made a cardinal. Francesco is holding Protonotary Ludovico, the youngest son of Ludovico III, by the hand, and he in turn is holding out his left hand to little Sigismondo, Ludovico's grandson (the son of Federico I, who is standing to the right in the picture). This careful arrangement of figures is mainly an expression of the hope that the successors will provide future dignitaries of the Church. In his right hand the cardinal is holding a letter. Although nothing other than Mantegna's signature can be read on this piece of paper, it may indicate a link between the scenes depicted on the two walls.

In fact it is not easy to decipher the narrative content of these frescoes, as there is a complete lack of any

dramatic development. However, the Italian art historian Rodolfo Signorini developed an interpretation in 1985 that we can briefly outline. Despite their differences, the two episodes, it can be argued, are dealing with two closely connected historic events. On 1 January 1462, Ludovico III received a letter that is now in the Mantua archives. This letter was a call from Bianca Maria Visconti to Ludovico Gonzaga, commander-in-chief of the Milan armies, to come to the support of her husband, Francesco Sforza. This letter is being handed to Ludovico in the court scene (page 97). At the same time, festivities were to be held in Mantua on the elevation of Francesco Gonzaga to the rank of cardinal. On his way to Milan in the pursuit of his duty, Ludovico meets his son outside the city (page 101). However, the city in the background does not look like Mantua; some of the classical structures are more reminiscent of Rome. But why should the Eternal City be portrayed like a mirage on the flood plains of the Po? One possible explanation lies in the complex range of references contained in the frescoes. Some very important individuals are traveling with Francesco's retinue: these have been identified as Christian I of Denmark and Frederick III of Hapsburg, who are presumably going to participate in the festivities. Their presence testifies to the influence of the Gonzaga and to their policy of alliances. In this context, Rome would stand for the power of the Pope, whose goodwill had been guaranteed by the 1459 Council and within whose immediate sphere of influence Ludovico had now entered, since a member of his family had assumed an important position in the Church hierarchy as a cardinal.

In addition, on the hill to the left, over the horses (page 92), a faint group of three men with camels can be seen, painted *a secco* (that is, on the dry plaster) and now flaking. They suggest the Three Magi, and so indicate the time of year this scene took place. The oranges on the trees are also an indication of the time of year: winter, which could imply January 1462. However, this group could just as well be an example of Mantegna's exotic imagination. The meeting before the city gates could have taken place on one of Francesco's innumerable later visits, for instance in August 1472, when he became titular cardinal of the church of Sant' Andrea in Mantua. Ludovico is dressed for riding out, as indicated by the enormous spurs on his shoes. The left side of the fresco shows servants with dogs holding ready a horse whose saddle and reins are decorated with the Gonzaga insignia, a sun in an encircling crescent moon. Instead of going to Milan, Ludovico could therefore simply be intending to ride out to the hunt.

Even the application of a detective's skills to art history has not been able to resolve the puzzle of the fresco's meaning. Some of the members of the family were not

Following double pages:
Camera degli Sposi (detail)
View of the west wall

On this side of the chamber, green and above all blue tones predominate, creating a fresh, airy atmosphere. The mountains fade away on the blue horizon. This was the first time Mantegna had obviously used aerial perspective, a compositional device he was not to use again until much later, in *Parnassus* (page 109).

The Court (detail page 97),
Identification of the figures

1 Marsilio Andreasi (?), secretary of Ludovico III
Gonzaga; 2 Ludovico III Gonzaga; 3 Gianfrancesco, third
son of Ludovico III; 4 Ludovico, the youngest son of
Ludovico III; 5 Paola, the youngest daughter of the
Marquis (?); 6 Rodolfo, the fourth son of the Marquis; 7
Barbara of Brandenburg; 8 Barberina Gonzaga (?); 9 the
tutor Vittorino da Feltre (?).

Andrea Mantegna
Camera degli Sposi (detail)
Family and court of Ludovico III Gonzaga

Ludovico Gonzaga maintained a lavish lifestyle and at
times had up to 800 people at his court. Here, we see his
family with their closest confidants. To demonstrate their
affluence, they are dressed in brocades threaded with gold.
Mantegna's interest in antiquity can be seen in the linear
sequences of figures, reminiscent of the reliefs on classical
sarcophagi.

old enough to be portrayed in 1462. For instance, Sigismondo was not born until 1469. He is represented as being about five years old, which would have been his age about the time the frescoes were completed. Bearing in mind that the Quattrocento was not necessarily interested in a strict representation of reality, the concept of these frescoes was more likely an idealized gathering of family members, friends, and allies rather than the depiction of the event in 1462. If this had been a portrayal of a contemporary event, why were the Sforzas themselves not shown at a moment when their power was so significant for the Gonzaga, rather than simply represented by a piece of paper? The relationship with the Sforzas was difficult at times, among other things because of the failed marriage plans mentioned above. But to refer to this influential family and at the same time banish it from the painting would seem too cryptic as a vehicle for any imaginable double meanings. Moreover, there is not the slightest hint as to who wrote the letter. It is improbable that any single incident from the changing fortunes of the Gonzaga family was to be recorded for eternity. An impressive official family portrait of three generations containing general references to their relationships, for example with the Pope, would be much nearer the mark. In addition, the frescoes illustrate events that took place daily in this room: the conveyance and signing of documents.

Over the lintel of the door that breaks up the narrative on the west wall, putti with butterfly and bird wings are holding up a large tablet that gives the date of completion for the frescoes as 1474 (pages 98–99). The dates for the beginning and end of the work on the frescoes of the Camera degli Sposi are also known in other ways; for instance, through orders for materials: on 26 April 1465 Ludovico placed a personal order for two cartloads of lime for the preparation of the walls, and in March 1474 he ordered gold and azurite (blue pigment). It was customary for work with these fine and costly materials to be carried out last.

All in all, Mantegna followed a well thought out color scheme: from festive gold on majestic red, to natural green and airy blue. The varying intensity of the colors is partly a result of Mantegna's experiments with different techniques in fresco painting. The ceiling, curtained walls, and the scene illustrating the meeting were painted *a fresco* (that is, painted on to the damp plaster). Details like the garlands of fruit around the ceiling occula are *a secco* (painted on to dry plaster). For the portrayal of the court, Mantegna used thick tempera on the dry plaster, a technique copied from antiquity and described in the 1st century AD by the writer Pliny the Elder (AD 23/24-79) and the architect Vitruvius. During the Renaissance, experiments with technique were part of a painter's vocation.

Opposite page:
Andrea Mantegna
The Meeting of Ludovico and Cardinal Francesco
Camera degli Sposi (detail)

Surrounded by members of their family and their allies, Ludovico and his son Francesco meet at the city gates. The men are standing close together, though they all appear isolated, as though posing. The ceremonial nature of the scene is underlined by the strictly hierarchical structure. Most of the heads are seen in profile, as on commemorative coins. Paintings like this, using portraits, were intended as a memorial of the individuals portrayed.

THE CLASSICAL WORLD AS A SETTING

Ludovico III Gonzaga died of the plague in 1478 and
for six years his son Federico held the reins of power.
He did not want to lose his father's renowned court
artist, and Mantegna continued to work at the court,
but unfortunately very little of his work from this
period has survived.

By 1484, the eighteen-year-old Francesco II had
come to power in Mantua. To begin with he was
indecisive about whether to follow the tradition of his
two predecessors in relation to the principal artist at his
court. Mantegna therefore approached Lorenzo de'
Medici in Florence, sending by way of recommendation
a picture (possibly a portrayal of the biblical Judith in
miniature), and asking for financial assistance. Since
1476, Mantegna had been occupied with the
construction of his town house and needed money for
this very slow-moving building project. The artist had
previously lived outside the city with his family, and
then, during the extended construction period, had
taken rented accommodation in various parts of the
city. The house must have been completed soon after
1494. But Mantegna was able to enjoy his new home
for only a few years, for in 1501 the Marquis claimed
the building, wanting to incorporate it into his new
Palazzo di San Sebastiano.

The first works from this period were probably the
large *St. Sebastian* (page 103), and the *Lamentation
Over the Dead Christ* (*Christo morto*), which is
discussed on page 79. Both pictures were painted on
canvas, the paint so thin that the texture of the material
is apparent. The restrained, chalky, gray-toned color
also gives the impression that these pictures are linked.
The large *St. Sebastian* was intended as an altarpiece. It
has been shown that during the 17th century it was in
the Sainte Chapelle at Aigueperse, a castle in the
Auvergne in France, and recent research has assumed
that this was where it was originally hung. The painting
may have been executed for the marriage of Chiara
Gonzaga and Gilbert de Bourbon-Monpensier in 1481.
It is naturalistic to the last detail. The figure of the saint
is straighter than in the smaller portrayal of
St. Sebastian (page 81) that can be seen in the

Kunsthistorisches Museum in Vienna. Here again,
Mantegna introduced an indication of the rivalry
between the arts of painting and sculpture: to one side
of Sebastian's feet is a fragment of a marble statue, a foot
in a Roman sandal.

This rivalry between Quattrocento painters and
sculptors was based on a dispute about which of these
arts was the more important. Sculptors argued that
sculpture was superior for they could represent a figure
as a whole, so that it could be viewed from every side.
Compared with this, painting was able only to offer
one view at any one time. The painter Giorgione
(1477/78–1510) represented the opposing view in this
paragone (dispute). According to Vasari's account, this
student of Giovanni Bellini declared that the advantage
of painting was precisely that it could represent
different gestures and poses at one and the same time.
In a painting now lost, Giorgione depicted a male nude
with his back to the viewer. A front view was reflected
in a clear spring at his feet, and side views in highly
polished armor to one side and a mirror to the other.
Mantegna, who also supplied sketches for sculptures
and worked as an architect, took up this challenge in a
different way. His painting aimed to represent the
contrast between life and art, and he consciously
compared the rich variety of colors in images of the
living with the monochrome tones of stone. According
to Alberti, painting, as the most intellectual medium
with the greatest difficulties to overcome, was superior
not only to sculpture, but also to poetry, since both the
eyes and mind of viewers were brought into play.
Mantegna was the prime example of such an artist. He
was one of the most important humanist painters of his
day, and his interests in archeology and literature gave
him the grounding for an art directed at the educated
upper classes.

One of Mantegna's finest illustrations of this ability is
a work for the young Francesco Gonzaga: the *Triumphs
of Caesar* (pages 104–105). Nine paintings, all of the
same size, show a train of followers bearing looted
trophies of war past the viewer; the procession reaches
its high point in the ninth picture with a portrayal of

Caesar on a triumphal chariot. Like his ancestors, Francesco was both a successful army commander and a cultured humanist, and closely identified himself with the great Caesar. The cycle of paintings was intended to honor Francesco's victories as well as those of the Roman commander. But this reference was obviously not direct enough for him, for seven of Mantegna's canvases were brought to the Palazzo San Sebastian in 1506 and complemented by the *Triumphs of Francesco* painted by Lorenzo Costa (ca. 1460–1535).

The individual paintings are grouped together in sequence. The first three paintings (page 105) have no background details: the backdrop to the trophies and ensigns is simply the sky. This concentrates our attention on the objects being carried along, which are depicted in the upper half of the painting. In the fourth painting, the background is formed by a wooded hill, dotted with ruins, which becomes a rocky slope just behind the figures. The sixth scene (above) is dominated by a high bridge. Only here and in the next painting (page 104), which is unequivocally closed off by a massive building, do spectators appear to watch the procession pass by: in the first instance from the bridge, and in the second from behind barred windows.

Colorful costumes, a panoply of booty, elephants, oxen, horses, and sheep provide both everyday and exotic details in a procession in which figures from the widest diversity of races are taking part. There is little subsidiary narrative, though there are a few anecdotal elements, such as the conversation between soldier and officer in the second painting. The objects represented contain multiple references to the emperor's all-embracing drive for power. In several scenes, sculpted

busts and heads of men and women are being carried along on poles, some of them wearing the city crown. This could be in honor of Cybele, the goddess of fertility from Asia Minor, who had been adopted as Magna Mater in Rome in 204 BC. Later, Mantegna portrayed her again in his *Introduction of the Cult of Cybele to Rome* (pages 118–119). The busts may also very possibly represent another Roman goddess, or perhaps the province of Gaul, since most of them are positioned directly below the inscription referring to Gaul.

The figures in these nine canvases of the *Triumphs* are different in style from those in the Camera degli Sposi. Their movement appears more natural, they are no longer constructed from geometrical shapes, and their clothing is less stiff and heavy. Nor are there any identifiable portraits here, but rather types, notably the ideal figure of a blond, curly headed youth typified by the boy leading the oxen. With this cycle, Mantegna was entering on a much more classically oriented phase of his work.

On 2 March 1494, the frescoes in the Camera degli Sposi and the canvases of the *Triumphs* were proudly shown to Giovanni de' Medici, who later became Pope Leo X. At this time, the *Triumphs* series was probably almost complete. Copperplate engravings and woodcuts, as well as painted copies, quickly spread its reputation; as early as 1500 there were engravings by Antonio da Brescia and others. Since the original paintings are not well preserved and have been heavily restored, an exact impression of the detail of the *Triumphs* is available today only from the woodcuts completed from 1598 onwards by Andrea Andreani (active between 1584–1610).

Andrea Mantegna
The Triumphs of Caesar (Scene 6)
Bearers of Coins and Plate, Trophies of Royal Armor

Richly worked royal weapons and body armor are energetically hoisted on poles by the bearers. The use of contrasting red-green coloring gives the scene a luminous glow.

Andrea Mantegna
The Triumphs of Caesar (Scene 7)
Prisoners and Standard Bearers, Buffoons and Soldiers

Even as prisoners, the buffoons play the fool and entertain the procession. In his description of this scene, Vasari was particularly impressed by the small boy who turns to his mother in pain because he has a thorn in his foot. This badly damaged canvas was completely over-painted during the 18th century.

Andrea Mantegna
The Triumphs of Caesar, 1484– ca. 1494
Tempera on canvas, each scene 267 x 278 cm
Hampton Court Palace, London

The Gonzaga domains fell into decay in the 17th century, and in 1629 the nine paintings of the *Triumphs of Caesar* were sold to Charles I of England, and were on exhibition in England from 1649. Since then they have been subjected to over-painting and restoration on several occasions; their condition today is, for the most part, extremely poor. Nevertheless, the series still illustrates Mantegna's highly inventive conception of Caesar's triumphant entry into Rome.

Andrea Mantegna
The Triumphs of Caesar (Scene 1)
Trumpets, Bearers of Standards and Banners

The soldiers are carrying boards with paintings of battles and views of conquered cities. These boards give Mantegna's vision of lost classical painting, of which little was known in the 15th century compared with the knowledge of architecture and sculpture. Pompeii and Heraculaneum, with their extensive house frescoes, were not excavated until the 18th and 19th centuries.

Andrea Mantegna
Bacchanalia with a Wine Vat, ca. 1470
Copperplate engraving, 33.5 x 45.5 cm
Staatliche Kunstsammlungen, Dresden

Drunkenness, sloth, and depravity are the consequences
of the bacchanalia. Even the idealized figure of Bacchus,
which may have been copied from the figure of the god
Mars on a Roman sarcophagus, raises doubts about his
dignity. He is leaning on a horn of plenty and reaching
for a grape. Bacchus, or Dionysus, the god of fertility and
wine, was the model of immoderation, the counterpart to
Apollo.

Mantegna was the first major painter in Italy to involve himself in printing techniques. Copperplate engraving, which had been developed in southern Germany around 1430 (therefore at about the time of Mantegna's birth) made it possible to produce finer reproductions than with woodcuts, which had been used until then. In the second half of the 15th century, engraved reproductions of the major altarpieces were being sold to pilgrims; devotional inserts for prayer books were also being printed, as were playing cards and calendars. Another important aspect of this development was the use of decorative engravings and major individual works as teaching materials for artists' workshops. This was how innovations in art spread throughout Europe.

Vasari, in the first edition of his *Lives*, published in 1550, described Mantegna as the decisive influence in the development of copperplate engraving in Italy. In the second edition, published in 1568, he described the Florentine artist Maso Finiguerra (1426–1464) in this way; certainly Finiguerra's skills as a leading niello artist helped him to create finely worked engravings consisting of light motifs on a dark background. These derived from the metal plates used in his niello workshop, on which silvered motifs contrast with a black background. Mantegna also used printing to achieve chiaroscuro effects, the interplay of light and shade with which he achieved results similar to those in his grisaille painting and simulated reliefs. Nevertheless, he did not view engraving as one of his main achievements. Although he was happy to experiment with the new medium, he left the reproduction of his works to professional engravers, of whose work he was highly critical. Printing enabled Mantegna to earn extra money, and to disseminate his *invenzioni*, his creative insights.

Drawing and printing were also an area where new ideas could be tried out. Because of the unusual size of the plates used by Mantegna, the *Battle of the Sea Gods* (page 107) should be regarded more as a work of art in its own right than a reproduction after an existing painting. Nevertheless, the engravings *Bacchanalia with a Wine Vat* (page 106) and *Battle of the Sea Gods* were frequently linked with Mantegna's early works: with the decoration of the Gonzaga's summer palace, painted during the 1560s. These paintings have not been preserved, though they appear to have been copied in engravings.

The German artist Albrecht Dürer (1471–1528), who was to be the most important graphic artist of the early 16th century, was particularly interested in Mantegna's engravings. He became acquainted with graphic works by Mantegna during both of his journeys to Italy, in 1494/95 and 1505–1507, and during his second visit tried to visit Mantegna himself in Mantua, though this was prevented by Mantegna's death in 1506. In 1494, Dürer copied two of Mantegna's engravings: the right half of the *Battle of the Sea Gods* and the *Bacchanalia with a Wine Vat*. These fine drawings (in the Albertina, Vienna) are proof of the great respect the young German had for the older master, as well

Above:
Albrecht Dürer
The Death of Orpheus, 1494
Pen drawing, 28.9 x 22.5 cm
Kupferstichkabinett, Hamburg

There is a description of this scene in Ovid's
Metamorphoses. It takes place on a high plateau with
no shade, on which all nature's creatures have gathered
around, charmed by the power of music. Grief at the
death of his wife Eurydice had caused Orpheus to turn
to pederasty, a fact symbolized by the boy in flight.
Thracian Maenads murder Orpheus in revenge for
his rejection of women.

Andrea Mantegna
The Battle of the Sea Gods, ca. 1470
Copperplate engraving, two parts, each 34 x 44.5 cm
Kupferstichkabinett, Staatliche Museen, Berlin

The battle is an allegory on the theme of Invidia (Envy),
who is standing top left as an old woman on a sea
monster. Neptune is turning away from the scene: he
does not want to see the bitter struggle between the sea
monsters, not even as a reflection in the mirror.
Apparently this scene was based on a classical description
of the competition between members of a family of
sculptors living on the island of Rhodes. Comparable
battle scenes can, however, be seen on classical reliefs that
were known through sketchbook drawings; Ludovico III
Gonzaga owned such a sketchbook.

as testimony to the success of Mantegna's engravings. In
addition to this, there is another drawing by Dürer for
which a missing work by Mantegna was presumably the
prototype. This is the *Death of Orpheus* (above, right). The
inscription on the tree reads *Orpheus der erst puseran*
("Orpheus, the first defiler of boys"), which plays on the
Italian word *buggerone* (Venetian *buzerone*, and changed
by Dürer to *puseran*). This theme would have fitted in well
with Mantegna's moralistic series on "women's wiles," to
which *Samson and Delilah* (page 117) also belongs.

MANTEGNA'S LATE WORKS

Andrea Mantegna
Parnassus, 1497
Tempera on canvas, 160 x 192 cm
Musée du Louvre, Paris

The title of this painting goes back to the 17th century. The scene in fact takes place in the Helicon Mountains, with Parnassus, the mountain sacred to Apollo and the Muses, visible in the background. The divine lovers Mars and Venus, standing on an elevation in the center of the painting, may represent the union of the houses of d'Este and Gonzaga: the successful military commander Francesco Gonzaga in the role of the god of war and Isabella as the goddess of love: the d'Este family tree was descended, it was believed, from the Trojans, whose patron was Venus.

After the sixty-year-old Mantegna had returned from Rome to Mantua, he made a point of obtaining a recommendation to the recently married Isabella d'Este, who came to the court in 1490 as Francesco's wife. The frescoes in the Camera degli Sposi had been completed for Ludovico III Gonzaga in the year of Isabella's birth. Now, two generations of rulers later, the young countess wanted a *studiolo* in the palace, and to have this decorated to her taste, with complicated mythological themes. Parnassus, the seat of Apollo and the Muses, was a favorite subject for Renaissance painting. Isabella's impulse in selecting this theme was influenced by the Tempietto delle Muse (small temple of the Muses) situated directly beneath the Christian chapel in Federico da Montefeltre's palace in Urbino. Mantegna's small painting for Isabella d'Este's *studiolo* portrays the divine couple, Mars and Venus, standing on a rock arch (page 109). At the feet of Mars a small putto, most probably Eros, is directing his blowpipe at Venus' husband, the furiously gesticulating Vulcan, who stands before his smithy fire in a cavern to the left. In the foreground, below Mars and Venus, the nine Muses are dancing to the sound of the cithara played by Apollo, who is sitting on the far left.

According to the court poet Battista Spagnoli, the "new Virgil of Mantua," Apollo was the sole ruler of Parnassus. But the division of the heavenly mountain into two peaks, seen at the right-hand edge of the picture, is also a reference to Apollo's antithesis, Dionysus. In front of these peaks, Mercury, the Gods' messenger and the guardian of Parnassus, is leaning against Pegasus, the flying horse. Mercury's staff, with snakes winding round it, symbolizes the principle of conflict amidst peaceful concord, thus drawing attention to the contrasting couple of Mars (god of war) and Venus (goddess of love), from whom harmony is born. The Dionysian impetus for the scene is repressed in the main, but becomes clear through the blowpipe directed at Vulcan's genitals, and in the finger gestures of the two Muses on the right. According to teaching on Platonic love, the union between Vulcan and Venus produced Eros, the god of sexual love, and the union between Venus and Mars produced Anteros, the heavenly love that leads to divine understanding. As the emphasis here is placed on the latter union, the

rule of *convenienza,* regarding decorum in a woman's apartments, was preserved.

Mantegna's second work for Isabella's *studiolo* is more puzzling, even though it bears several inscriptions. There is as much uncertainty about who thought out the content for the *Triumph of Virtue* (page 109), as there is about who developed the ideas represented in *Parnassus.* Paride da Ceresara, a humanist active at court, may have been responsible. However, Isabella could also have taken the relevant passages from Spagnoli's poetry and developed ideas for the paintings from these.

From the left, Minerva, undisputedly the personification of virtue, storms into the garden with its topiary arcades. She is looking up to the heavens, where the three cardinal virtues of Justice, Fortitude, and Moderation are floating down surrounded by a halo of clouds. Confronted by this attack, the vices are fleeing towards a swamp. To the left, a woman in rags embodying Inercia (Sloth) is leading the mutilated figure of Otium (Idleness) with a cord. To the right we see the crowned figure of Ignorancia (Ignorance) being carried away by Avaricia (Avarice) and Ingratitudo (Ingratitude).

In the center of the painting, Venus is balanced on the back of a centaur. This is a sensuous Venus, doubling as the voluptuous Luxuria, queen of the vices, who leads us to lust and laziness. Her pose is a warning of the inconstancy of Fortuna (Fortune). Minerva's spear is broken, though this is not necessarily a sign of failure since it could also indicate that she has already engaged the enemy. Perhaps she is still capable of driving the seductive vices to flight through her moral determination, and to rescue the virtues, the font of the arts and sciences, from their prison in the rocks on the right. But Fortuna Luxuria seems indifferent. She goes along with what is happening, as constant change is a feature of her nature: she distributes her gifts here today, there tomorrow. Never taken, never troubled, she always manages to escape.

When Mantegna had completed the *Triumph of Caesar,* he was soon commissioned to paint two large altarpieces. The first was the *Madonna of Victory* (page 112), which was for a church in Mantua dedicated to the Virgin Mary. The painting was supposed to mark Francesco Gonzaga's victory at

Andrea Mantegna
The Triumph of Virtue, 1502
Tempera on canvas, 160 x 192 cm
Musée du Louvre, Paris

To the left, a scroll explaining the picture's theme is entwined round Daphne, who is turning into a tree. It contains the following entreaty in Latin, Greek, and Hebrew: *AGITE PELLITE SEDIBUS NOSTRIS FOEDA HAEC VICIORUM MONSTRA VIRTUTUM COELITUS AD NOS REDEUNTIUM* DIVAE COMITES ("Come thou divine companions of the Virtues, returned to us from heaven and drive these monstrous vices from our realm").

Fornovo on 6 July 1495, and his miraculous escape from death. As the general of an Italian army unit during this bloody battle, Francesco had defeated the French troops of King Charles VIII. The Marquis then styled himself the liberator of Italy, though in fact the enemy troops had not been finally defeated. He chose the Virgin to be his special patron and had several churches built in her name throughout his lands.

During his absence from Mantua, while his brother Sigismondo dealt with the affairs of state, a remarkable event had occurred. A Jewish householder removed an image of the Madonna that had decorated the front of his house. Jews were given sanctuary in Mantua and were protected by the Gonzaga, though they had to pay a high price for this privilege. The removal of a Christian image from a public space was not acceptable and this incident gave the populace a welcome opportunity to attack the owner of the house. This led to an official demand from the Gonzaga that the house owner should restore the image: otherwise he, and not the image, would hang outside his house. Naturally, he gave in to the threats, though it was now too late to prevent further consequences. Soon the whole affair was further intensified when two men from the city, considered to be god-fearing individuals, independently had visions in which, at this very spot, they saw the church dedicated to Mary that had previously stood there. It was not long before the house of the Jew occupying supposed hallowed ground had been torn down and the chapel of Santa Maria della Vittoria built.

Mantegna was also believed to be responsible for the design of this simple building. It was consecrated on 6 July 1496, the anniversary of the victory of Fornovo.

To start off the festivities planned for this day by Francesco and Isabella, the *Madonna of Victory* was placed on a richly decorated stand in front of the church of San Sebastiano. Costumed men grouped themselves around the painting and placed the image of Mary within a living tableau: secured by scaffolding, God the Father hovered overhead, flanked to left and right by a prophet and three singing angels, and the twelve Apostles stood in front. Here the interplay of the different levels of reality, involving artistic representation, earthly mortality, and divine presence, was graphically demonstrated. Then the painting was carried in a procession to the chapel of Santa Maria della Vittoria, where, after a banquet and a Mass, it was installed over the high altar.

Contrary to Sigismondo's wishes, Mantegna's picture does not show any other members of the family apart from Francesco. Mary is enthroned in the center. Her robe is protectively spread by St. Michael and St. George over Francesco Gonzaga, kneeling on the left, and the infant John the Baptist standing to the right on the base of the throne. Through his gesture and the inscription on his cross-like staff, the infant John is pointing to Jesus. John's mother, Elizabeth, is kneeling beside him. In the background, the heads of the patron saints of Mantua, Andrew and Longinus, are recognizable. They are both closely connected with the cult of the Holy

School of Mantegna
Occasio and Poenitentia, ca. 1500
Fresco transferred to canvas, 168 x 146 cm
Palazzo Ducale, Mantua

Balancing precariously on a ball with one of her winged feet is Occasio (Transience). Her hair is blowing into her face, blinding her. If the occasion passes ungrasped, Poenitentia (Regret) remains behind. But Vera Eruditio (True Learning), on the other hand, is standing on a solid base. The wisdom that can be achieved through True Learning protects against the need to be subject to fickle fortune.

Following pages, left:
The Madonna of Victory, 1496
Tempera on canvas, 280 x 166 cm
Musée du Louvre, Paris

By the end of the 15th century, large single paintings were being used as altarpieces, a form that reached its apogee in the works of Titian and Paolo Veronese. The stiffly hierarchical composition of the traditional *sacra conversazione* was also discarded. Mantegna's Virgin Mary is turning slightly away from the central axis, which runs from the Tree of Knowledge on the throne pedestal up through the Christ Child to the branch of coral hanging on a chain. Mary and the idealized, over life-size figures of the saints Michael and George form a majestic group.

Following pages, right:
Trivulzio Madonna, 1494–1497
Tempera on canvas, 287 x 214 cm
Civico Museo d'Arte Antica, Castello Sforzesco, Milan

At the lower edge of this painting, an angel is playing the organ, accompanied by two singing companions. The emblem of the church of Santa Maria Organo includes an image of an organ, since the monks assumed that the name of their church was derived from the musical instrument, though it was probably taken from the nearby Porta Organa. The saints, the organ, and the floating Mary represent elements of a composition that has strong local links.

Blood, the most important relic in the city (a drop of Christ's blood). This relic was kept in the church of St. Andrew, specially built for the many pilgrims who came to see it from plans by Alberti. Longinus, the centurion who had pierced the side of Christ with his lance, was said to have brought this relic to Mantua.

The position of St Elizabeth, to the right of the throne, is unique. In fact, in a votive painting of this type, this place would normally have been occupied by the wife of the male patron, symmetrically opposite him. Elizabeth was the chosen patron of Isabella, as the Italian name Isabella translates into Elizabeth. In this way, the Marquise could be represented indirectly. But then it is unusual that Francesco was not similarly represented by St. Francis, although this perhaps would have made the painting too cryptic. Francesco wanted to give lasting expression to his success. Mary and the Christ Child and the two saints beside her are turning to Francesco alone, as is Elizabeth. The armed saints underline the message of the painting as a tribute to victory that alludes to the triumph of both body and soul.

More crucial to this painting's content, however, is a reference to the sad story of how the church in which the painting hangs came to be built. A panel in the base of the throne reproduces the moment when Original Sin came into the world. Eve was the mother of the first race of mankind, and it was through the mothers Mary and Elizabeth that a new era in human history was introduced. John represented the sacrament of baptism, an essential ritual that separated Christians from Jews. Christ was the Redeemer, marking the end of the old way and the beginning of the new. Thus, this grouping of figures symbolizes the victory of Christianity over Judaism: the picture links the propaganda against the Jews with a triumph (military and spiritual) over the enemy.

Right up to the 18th century, the day of the annual harvest festival procession to the chapel of Santa Maria della Vittoria was 2 July, the day of the Visitation, the meeting of Elizabeth and Mary before their sons were born. Mantegna's *dolcezza,* the softness of his figures, their festive setting beneath a richly decorated pergola, and the harmonious use of the scintillating range of colors betray nothing of the bellicose background to the painting. Proclaimed Queen of Heaven by the medallion on her footstool, Mary is the center of a majestic group that includes the monumental and idealized figures of St. Michael and St. George. They embody the harmony of heavenly beauty and the "cultivated religious sensibilities of the High Renaissance," as the art historian Ronald Lightbown observed. The role of art was now to imitate the perfection of the divine.

The second large altarpiece Mantegna painted after he had completed the *Triumph of Caesar* was the *Trivulzio*

Opposite page:
Andrea Mantegna
Judith, 1491
Drawing, 38.8 x 25.8 cm
Gabinetto dei Designi e delle Stampe, Galleria degli
Uffizi, Florence

During the Renaissance, the great biblical figures were
also counted among the heroes and heroines of antiquity.
Judith, the pious and beautiful widow from the besieged
town of Bethulia, an outpost of Jerusalem, saved the city
by outwitting Holofernes, Nebuchadnezzar's military
commander. Having charmed him and made him drunk,
she cut off his head. The leaderless Assyrians fled when
they saw the bloody head hanging on the city walls the
next morning.

Andrea Mantegna
Judith, ca. 1490 (?)
Tempera on wood, 30.5 x 18 cm
Widener Collection, National Gallery of Art, Washington

Among Mantegna's works there are several representations
of Judith that, without exception, show a comparatively
peaceful scene in which Judith is placing the severed head
in a bag. During the Baroque, in contrast, the dramatic
central moment of the action was preferred, as Judith,
often with great effort, decapitates Holofernes. The dates
suggested for this work range from 1464 to 1495.

Far left:
Andrea Mantegna
Sophonisba, after 1490
Tempera on wood, originally 72.5 x 23 cm (right side cut)
The National Gallery, London

Sophonisba, the daughter of the Carthaginian statesman Hasdrubal (3rd century BC), was for reasons of state married to various men one after the other. When the Roman leader Scipio demanded that Sophonisba be handed over after her husband had been taken prisoner, she drank a cup of poison rather than be taken by the enemy.

Left:
Andrea Mantegna
Tuccia, post-1490
Tempera on wood, 72.5 x 23 cm
The National Gallery, London

Tuccia, a Vestal Virgin accused of incest, proved her innocence by a feat that was proverbially impossible. After appealing to her goddess for help, she carried water home from the river Tiber in a sieve, and so was rehabilitated through a divine pronouncement. The chiaroscuro tones suggest a classical relief, although Mantegna painted this grisaille without a specific model.

Opposite page:
Samson and Delilah, 1495–1506
Tempera on canvas, 47 x 37 cm
The National Gallery, London

Samson is the heroic figure with superhuman strength whose story is told in the Old Testament Book of Judges. His wife Delilah was to find the secret of his strength. After he told her that the secret lay in his hair, Delilah cut his hair off and the Philistines were able to capture Samson and blind him. The grapevine entwined round the tree is a symbol of Samson's drunken stupor.

Andrea Mantegna
The Introduction of the Cult of Cybele to Rome, 1505/06
Tempera on canvas, 73 x 268 cm
The National Gallery, London

From the left the priests in their flowing robes are
approaching with a bust of Cybele. A young follower
falls on his knees in reverence, his position in the center
of the picture emphasizing the unusually wide format
of this work. Behind him, Scipio leads out the group of
Romans who have been awaiting the arrival of this image
of the goddess, which has been brought from Asia Minor.
The family of the patron of the picture, Francesco
Cornaro, had elected Cornelius Scipio as their legendary
ancestor.

Madonna (page 112) for the Olivetan monks of the
monastery of Santa Maria Organo, in Verona. The
Olivetan monks are a reformed order of white
Benedictines, which is why the founder of the order, St.
Benedict, is shown on the right-hand side of the
painting. Standing next to him, St. Jerome is holding a
model of a church: the monks had ordered this painting
for their newly renovated and extended church. To the
left, Gregory the Great can be seen, and at his side
stands John the Baptist, who is pointing to the center of
the painting, directing our gaze to the Madonna and
Child. Holding the Christ Child on her lap, Mary is
hovering in a mandorla of angels, a suitable motif, as
the church is dedicated to the Assumption of the
Virgin. No ground or floor is depicted, and the location
of the event is unclear. The Virgin is seen directly from
the front, though the saints are seen from below, an
apparent disregard for the rules of perspective that in
fact heightens the visionary nature of this luminous
apparition from another plane of reality.

From 1490 onwards, Mantegna produced a series of
illusionistic works representing sculptural reliefs in
marble or bronze. These are in grisaille, light and dark

tones of a single color creating figures that stand
against a background simulating boldly patterned
marble. In Italy, pictures like this, which appear to be
carved in stone, were first seen in the bases of Giotto's
frescoes in the Arena Chapel in Padua, where he
illustrated the Seven Virtues and Seven Vices.
Mantegna certainly knew these frescoes. It was Flemish
painters, however, who provided a new stimulus for
this type of painting in 15th-century Italy. Vasari
described how grisaille was used in Italy for palace
façades, stage sets, and ephemeral structures for
festivals and triumphal processions. Mantegna had
already used this technique for details in his early
painting, the *Circumcision of Christ* (page 83) and for
the ceiling in the Camera degli Sposi (page 91). At the
end of the 15th century, grisaille work was in great
demand, and Mantegna painted a number of pictures
in this technique. The demand for such works was
linked to the limited availability of classical art
treasures, which meant that people were willing to
accept bronzes, sculptures, reliefs, medallions, and
other objects made in the classical style. In
consequence, even the *marmi finti*, imitations of

marble reliefs, found a market. Mantegna's workshop became a center for these works. Since there was a scarcity of sculptors with the relevant skills in Mantua, mock classical reliefs were particularly well represented here. Both the rivalry between painting and sculpture, and the concept of the blending of various levels of reality, meant that Mantegna and his students were here given an opportunity to display their virtuosity.

Such monochrome paintings found a place in small galleries or studies. For example, two of these hung over the door of Isabella's *studiolo*, though both have been lost. Today, we have precise information about only one, *Occasio and Poenitenta* (page 111): this is a fresco by one of Mantegna's students and was later heavily restored. It was intended for the canopy over a hearth in the Biondi Palace in Mantua. The theme had been handed down in a description of the sculpture *Occasio and Poenitentia* by Phidias (the renowned sculptor of ancient Greece) by the 4th-century BC poet Ausonius.

Other paintings in this style follow the traditional medieval cult of the hero, which was continued during the Renaissance with both biblical and mythological subjects. Two of Mantegna's female figures, *Sophonisba*

and *Tuccia* (page 116), representing two heroines of purity and constancy, presumably formed part of a larger series. *Samson and Delilah* (page 117) is a small masterpiece from a series illustrating the theme of "women's wiles." This was a series of stories that had been re-told in images since antiquity, stories that supposedly illustrated women's cunning. The inscription carved in the tree trunk warns that women are wickeder than even the Devil.

The *Introduction of the Cult of Cybele to Rome* (pages 118–119) was one of a series of four long, narrow paintings ordered from Mantegna by Francesco Cornaro at the beginning of 1505, with the approval of the Gonzaga. Mantegna was able to complete only this one painting before his death. However, sketches for the others still exist and the rest of the series was completed on this basis, in Venice; among these is the *Continence of Scipio* by Giovanni Bellini (now in Washington). We have already come across the bust of the goddess Cybele in the *Triumphs of Caesar*. At the end of the Second Punic War, a Sibylline oracle predicted that a Roman victory would be hastened if they brought this foreign goddess to Rome. So in 204

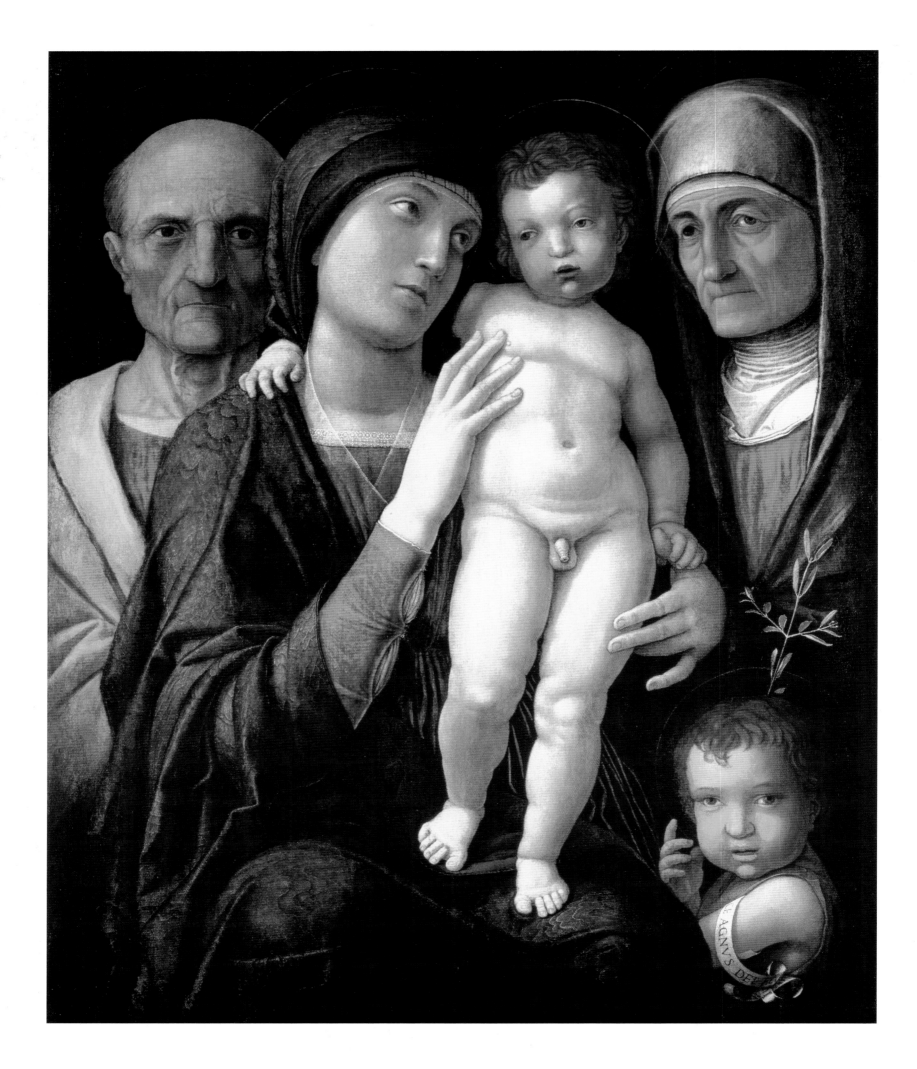

Andrea Mantegna
The Adoration of the Magi, 1497–1500
Oil and tempera on canvas, 54.5 x 71 cm
The J. Paul Getty Museum, Los Angeles

This is one of the most frequently copied of Mantegna's works. The straightforward composition is similar to that of the *Presentation at the Temple* in Berlin (page 72). The posture of the figures is now more natural and more distinctive. The magi are holding fine containers of porcelain, jasper set in gold, and agate.

Opposite page:
Andrea Mantegna
The Holy Family with the Infant St. John the Baptist,
1495–1505
Tempera on canvas, 75.5 x 61.5 cm
Gemäldegalerie, Staatliche Kunstsammlungen, Dresden

The striking face of the man on the left may possibly combine the patron's features and the representation of St. Joseph, who is shown here, contrary to traditional iconography, with no beard. The infant St. John is addressing us directly and directing our gaze to Christ. The softly modeled faces of Mary and the two boys contrast with the two realistically portrayed old people.

BC, the Roman Senate decided that as the most distinguished of all the Romans, the still youthful patrician Publius Cornelius Scipio (235–183 BC) should receive the goddess and give her shelter in his house until a temple had been built. On the right of the painting, a private house is depicted, on the steps of which a musician in oriental dress is standing, playing a pipe and a drum. A band attached to his ruff bears the letters SPQR, the Latin abbreviation for the Roman senate. This symbolizes official acceptance of the cult of this goddess, originally from Mount Ida, near Troy in Phrygia in Asia Minor. The trumpet of a second musician is projecting from the entrance to the house, a compositional device indicating that the action is continuing beyond the picture frame. This implies that the picture frame does not mark the boundary of the fictive space.

At the center of this picture, which has an unusually wide format, flowing movement and statuesque dignity are closely juxtaposed. A young man, a eunuch in the service of the goddess, falls to his knees, thereby bringing the rapidly approaching procession to a halt. The Romans are standing in unperturbed expectation. The gathering of Roman notables contrasts with the vital foreign cult that they have formally decided to adopt. Over Scipio's head the color and form of the background are starting to break up: on the side of the Phrygian followers of the goddess it is glowing like fire, and on the side of the Romans it seems to be set in a blistered yellowish gray. The strong differentiation between light and shade, and the sweep of light across the foreground, shining on the clothes, create a life-like impression. Because the figures stand out boldly in this way, the events unfold as if on a stage parallel to the painting and do not have the appearance of a rigid relief.

Between 1490 and 1506, the year he died, Mantegna painted several more devotional paintings in which the main figures are represented as reliefs standing out against a mostly dark background (pages 120–121).

CRVCIFIGE EVM
TOLLE EVM

CRVCIFIGE CRVC

CRVCIFIGE EVM
CRVCIFIGE TOLLE
EV CRVCIFIGE

Opposite page:
Andrea Mantegna
Ecce Homo, ca. 1500
Tempera on canvas, 54 x 42 cm
Musée Jacquemart-André, Paris

The portrayal of the flagellated Christ combines the timeless devotional image with a historic reference to a real event. The figure of Christ is displayed covered in weals from the flagellation, and with the crown of thorns on his head. The words "What a man is this!" can be read. Of the two men holding him, one is wearing a paper headband with an inscription in pseudo-Hebrew. Two other figures are barely visible in the background. The unfolded sheet of paper in the top corner bears the proclamation of the crucifixion.

Andrea Mantegna
Self-Portrait, ca. 1504–1506
Bronze, height 47 cm
Cappella di Giovanni Battista, Sant'Andrea, Mantua

The bust is a very natural portrait of Mantegna with his head encircled by a laurel wreath, following the tradition of the portraits of Roman patricians. The bronze cast was created by a medallion-maker after a clay model made by Mantegna himself.

Inspired by reliefs on classical tombs, these figures are shown partially hidden behind stone balustrades or a frame. In the last two years of his life, Mantegna painted his own funerary chapel of Sant' Andrea, the largest church in Mantua. He had it decorated with trompe-l'œil monochrome frescoes showing the four Evangelists, and a pergola with garlands of fruit and leaves in the cupola.

Other paintings also intended for this space are rather modest. They are still in the chapel to this day, with a bronze bust of himself (page 123) he designed for his tomb. At court, Mantegna had had several commissions to design sculptures, and after 1490, at the behest of Isabella d'Este, he created a now lost statue of Virgil, Mantua's most famous son, which was to stand in the city's main square. However, apart from the busts, none of the statues still extant can be proved to be his.

A multi-talented artist, Mantegna was a prime example of the *uomo universale,* the Renaissance man with an all-round education. His works were sought by the royal houses of France, Germany, and Spain. His innovations in painting reached artists' workshops throughout Europe through engravings, and masters as different as Dürer (1471–1528), Rubens (1577–1640), and, much later, Degas (1834–1917), copied his works. With bold and original conceptions of spatial design, as demonstrated in the Camera degli Sposi, he provided the stimulus for the profuse and illusionistic symbolism of Mannerist and Baroque art. His representations of nature, correct in every detail, together with his keen feeling for the classical world, demonstrate that he was a widely cultivated humanist whose works were governed by a constant challenge to the boundary between art and life. Even in his own day he was considered one of the Great Masters, his reputation extending far beyond Mantua.

Nike Bätzner

PAINTERS IN MANTEGNA'S CIRCLE

Andrea Mantegna was certainly among the most influential painters of the Italian Renaissance. The studio in Padua where he received his training was already undertaking exchanges that resulted in a richness of perspectives. The leader of the workshop, Squarcione, did everything he could to make talented young people dependent on him. Among them was Marco di Antonio Ruggieri (1433–1478), known as "the lame one" as a result of his physical disability, who therefore went down in history as "Il Zoppo." In 1452 he entered Squarcione's service, even had himself adopted by him, like Mantegna, and just as rapidly dissolved the relationship, working from 1455 occasionally in Venice, from 1462 in Bologna, and in 1471 again in Venice, where he died as early as 1478.

Zoppo's most important work is a *sacra conversazione* from Venice (page 125), which, in the Venetian style, he signed on a *cartellino* and dated 1471. That in doing so he called himself Zoppo proves how strong already was the urge to self-dramatize: a formerly derogatory nickname became the trademark of a master not indigenous to Venice.

The painting dates back to the time before Antonello da Messina and the new technique of oil painting. From the horizontal format that was characteristic of Florentine paintings, we move to an almost square format. It is not only the illusion of the image, as in the *Altarpiece of the Church Fathers* of 1446 (page 56) and Mantegna's altarpiece in San Zeno (page 75), that is unified; with Zoppo, all the figures are shown on one common panel.

The longitudinal extension typical of Venetian Madonnas in the 1470s on the other hand seems exaggerated in a painting (page 124) by another follower of Mantegna's, Cosimo Tura (before 1431–1495), which he created in the 1470s, at the same time as Antonello's altarpiece for San Cassiano and Bellini's panel for San Giobbe (page 140). But this impression is deceptive, for this is the central panel of a polyptych for Luigi Roverella. Certainly this image is in the tradition of the similar upright formats of Madonnas of the 13th and 14th centuries (Volume I, pages 88, 120, 121). But with Tura, as with some of these, the saints standing beside the Mother of God on separate panels were shown at a lesser height. In view of Mantegna's altarpiece in San Zeno (page 75), this sort of gradation represents a backward step. The main image with the Madonna, however, demonstrates an acute sense of architecture. An arch is spanned over the throne, and in strict perspective one looks up to Mary from below. The angels help one to find one's way in the space, for they are seated, each in his own way, on the steps leading up to the throne.

Opposite page: Cosimo Tura
The Madonna with Angels, ca. 1475
Mixed media on wood, 239 x 101.6 cm
National Gallery, London

For Luigi Roverella, Cosimo Tura created his undisputed masterpiece; it was intended for the church of San Giorgio fuori le Mura, that is, "outside the walls" of Ferrara, and is preserved only in fragments. The main section of it is the *Madonna with Angels*, strongly characterized by impressive perspective and vivid colors. It was flanked by two shorter panels, each with two standing saints.

Marco di Antonio Ruggieri, called Zoppo
Sacra Conversazione, 1471
Oil on wood, 268 x 258 cm
Gemäldegalerie, Staatliche Museen, Berlin

This bold arrangement of throne and saints in a landscape, and bearing the inscription *Marco Zoppo da Bologna Pinsit MCCCCLXXI in Venezia* ("Marco the Lame from Bologna painted it in 1471 in Venice"), is still removed from a conclusive understanding of perspective construction; for while the saints–John the Baptist, Francis, Paul, and Jerome–are seen logically in foreshortening perspective, the landscape backdrop is disturbing in its excessive steepness. Nevertheless, the unification of the image space here is a bold step.

Fra Carnevale (Bartolomeo di Giovanni Corradini)
The Annunciation, ca. 1450
Tempera on wood, 87.6 x 62.8 cm
Samuel H. Kress Collection, National Gallery of Art, Washington

A makeshift name was devised from panels from the Barberini collection, in New York and Boston, for this master who stands between Fra Filippo Lippi and Piero della Francesca. Today he has been convincingly identified as a painter monk, above all active in Urbino, who in his own way exemplifies the dissemination of Florentine artistic theories well beyond Tuscany.

The school of Ferrara begins with Cosimo Tura; it flourished under the patron of the arts Borso d'Este (born 1413, Duke of Ferrara and Modena 1452–1471) and his successors. It found its main task, as everywhere in the Italian Renaissance, in the decoration of churches; in addition, however, it was a question of princely self-promotion, which meant a great challenge above all for book illustration, and culminated in the frescoes of the Palazzo Schifanoia (pages 128/129). In both the sacred and secular areas, Tura and his pupils, who could be considered, as it were, grandchildren of the pupils of Mantegna, developed a quite astonishing visual imagination. Like the court of Este, these artists were characterized by humanism and fascinated by the scientifically based art of perspective; and this links both clients and artists with the Florence of the Medici, in particular under Lorenzo the Magnificent (1449–1492).

From the artistic point of view, the painters in question do not quite fit into the concept of a "triumph of color." But even so, in the draftsmanlike tradition deriving from Mantegna, they produce strong color effects, which still respect the outlines and the relief-like modeling, and are distinguished by the positively lurid juxtaposition of local colors, particularly garish green. Only gradually was the strict separation of colored surfaces abandoned in Ferrara, in favor of uniform tones with chiaroscuro effects.

The *Madonna with Angels* from the Roverella altarpiece (page 124) is certainly Cosimo Tura's main work, and the gaudiest in coloring. The architectural perspective there cannot do without Florentine models. Even if one has to realize when looking at the isolated panel that it is actually part of a broken-up ensemble, the mighty arch that is stretched over the figures is also reminiscent of Masaccio's *Trinity* fresco of the 1420s (Volume I, page 17).

Mantegna had transmitted to his pupils the knowledge and high regard for Florentine art of the Early Renaissance; perhaps he sent them to Venice to observe with shock and fascination the frescoes of Andrea del Castagno in the vaults of San Tarasio (page 54) and to admire his design for the *Death of the Virgin Mary* in San Marco (Volume I, page 321). In Padua, these painters could also have seen Donatello (Volume I, pages 220–227), with whom one or other of them may have become personally acquainted. Mantegna had allowed himself to be most intensively influenced by the Florentine Early Renaissance; thus at the beginning of his career he had become a virtuoso of drawing and draftsmanship. But while he himself had with increasing age devoted himself to color, most of the artists in his circle remained true to the ideal of drawing.

Developments run parallel in strange ways, as the boundaries dissolve between individual schools. Those artists above all who found no fixed place in the town where they grew up or studied play a particular role in this context. In the first volume (Volume I, pages 322–375) we have already discussed Piero della

Francesca from Sansepolcro, in whose work much that was initiated by Florentine painters gains new maturity; we have still to discuss Antonello da Messina (pages 130–133). Carlo Crivelli (1430/1436–before 1500) belongs in this group; born in Venice, presumably trained in the Paduan circle of Squarcione and Mantegna, this curious painter is presumed to have died in Ascoli Piceno in the Marches, after a wild and turbulent life, spent partly in fleeing from justice.

His most famous painting depicts the *Annunciation* (right). This panel is primarily determined by aspects of ecclesiastical politics, being based on an inscription that invokes the freedom of the Church (*LIBERTAS ECCLESIASTICA*). Particular surprise was caused by the public scene in which the event takes place: the Archangel Gabriel, in the company of the local saint Emidius, comes out of a street which leads from the background on the left to the magnificent house of Mary; they stop by the window behind which Mary is praying, and the impression is that the archangel is being asked about his intentions.

In fact, it is precisely the public nature of the scene that comes from Florentine tradition. From preliminary stages in the work of Fra Angelico, book illustrators such as Francesco Rosselli transferred the Annunciation from the garden to a city street, while Piero Pollaiuolo (Volume I, page 454) developed a concept in which he moves the event into a kind of palace, but spatially separates Gabriel and Mary, and behind the angel shows the city of Florence in striking perspective. In this way the Florentine painter links the scene from the story of Salvation with the location, as Crivelli did, showing the local patron saint next to Gabriel, holding a model of the town of Ascoli Piceno. The two paintings are alike in the sumptuousness of the decoration and the splendor of the coloration, while both painters have clearly made it their business to keep pace with the new multiplicity of colors from Netherlandish painting.

Let us at this point cast a glance back to a minor master from Urbino, who was based in Florence for a short time during 1445–1446; the *Annunciation* (page 126) by Fra Carnevale incorporates the stage that was the starting point for both Crivelli and Pollaiuolo. This enigmatic painter, who as Bartolomeo di Giovanni Corradini (active from ca. 1445–died 1484) learned to paint in Urbino, was with the Carmelite Fra Filippo Lippi in Florence in 1445–1446, and subsequently entered the Dominican monastery in Urbino in 1449. Urbino itself is in the Marches, but attracted artists from far and wide; Piero della Francesca, whose manner of working can be confused with the style of Fra Carnevale, was among the characteristic figures there before, in the period around 1470, Justus van Ghent, Pedro Berruguete, and Melozzo da Forlì made the ducal court there into a sort of international meeting place (pages 10, 11). Panels such as Fra Carnevale's *Annunciation* still embody the moment of sobriety before a man such as Crivelli discovered color as a token of sumptuousness.

Carlo Crivelli
The Annunciation, 1486
Mixed media, transferred from wood to canvas,
207 x 147 cm
National Gallery, London

Painted for the Franciscan church in Ascoli Piceno, a town in the Marches that belonged to the Church State, this work may allude to papal privileges that had been celebrated since 1482 on the feast of the Annunciation, the 25 March. This is why the Archangel Gabriel is accompanied by the local patron saint, St. Emidius, who holds a model of the town in his hands.

The spirit of humanism in Ferrara is proclaimed most vividly in the frescoes in the Palazzo Schifanoia; this building, a sort of villa, whose name comes from the Italian *schiva la noia* ("drive away boredom"), lay outside the walls of Ferrara. Around 1470, several major parts of the building were renovated; in the course of this progress, a cycle of wall paintings was created for Borso d'Este. In three registers, depictions of three worlds are placed one above another. In the lower zone, which is unfortunately severely damaged, life at the Este court is depicted in a manner very similar to Mantegna's Camera degli Sposi in the Palazzo Ducale in Mantua

(pages 88–101), with life-size figures, and thus with a sort of trompe-l'œil effect. Above this, on a dark-blue ground, astrological figures appear, which pose riddles for interpreters. The topmost section of the wall is devoted to the triumph of the gods of the planets, and to a description of life under their signs.

The cycle is linked with the papal confirmation of privileges, until then only imperial, for the Duke of Ferrara and Modena. This was a time when astrology flourished above all in Ferrara: Pietro Bono Avogaro (recorded in 1467–1506) was active in the city, and there was a professor of astronomy, Pellegrino Prisciani

Opposite page:
Francesco del Cossa
The Months of the Year: April, with the Triumph of Venus,
ca. 1471 (?)
Wall painting
Palazzo Schifanoia, Ferrara

Between impressive trompe-l'œil columns, an area of wall in the Palazzo Schifanoia was allocated to each month. Here the two upper registers of April are shown; below them is a view of Borso d'Este preparing to go hunting. Around the zodiac sign of Taurus, the bull which bears a man with the key of spring, are arranged images of motherly love and the dissolution of all relationships, *dissolutezza*. In a tradition going back to classical triumphal processions, the Triumph of Venus is placed in the center. Independently of Petrarch, who had revived the theme with his *Trionfi* in the third quarter of the 14th century, Venus is here venerated by a kneeling man (Mars?).

Francesco del Cossa
The Planet Children of Venus (detail page 128)

Planet children were a source of fascination to artists at the beginning of the modern age. Here, with the Three Graces in the background, youth is portrayed with loving affection, while spring is also part of the image. In a quite different way from Botticelli, who shows the Three Graces dancing at the front (Volume I, pages 484–485), Francesco del Cossa repeats, with the group of three quietly standing still, a motif that was handed down through the evidence of classical images and would in turn inspire Raphael (page 213).

(1435–1510). Both were credited with the concept of the images of the months. But for the painters, above all Francesco del Cossa (ca. 1435–1477), the opportunity arose to open up a whole cornucopia of world experience, classical imagination, and astronomy.

For centuries these frescoes were covered up. The successful reclamation of what is still to be seen in the Palazzo Schifanoia took place in the years between 1820 and 1840. Like few other cycles, the wall paintings in Ferrara represent a view of the world that was determined by the course of the year and the planets. They transmit into a new era a tradition inherited from the Middle Ages, most finely represented, more than two generations earlier, by the cycle of the months in the Eagle Tower of Trento. For this reason, this cycle, preserved only in fragments, inspired the great Renaissance scholar Aby Warburg (1866–1929) to undertake his finest scientific research. The portrayal of the gods of the planets and their children, above all, captured the scientific interest of Warburg and his colleagues; nowhere else did it take such monumental form as with Francesco del Cossa in the service of Borso d'Este.

Eberhard König

Antonello da Messina and the New Painting in Venice

ANTONELLO DA MESSINA
CA. 1430–1479

Undoubtedly the most significant artist of the south of Italy during the 15th century was the Sicilian Antonello da Messina, who is traditionally credited with having popularized in Italy, in particular in Venice, the technique of oil painting supposedly developed by Jan van Eyck in Flanders at the beginning of the century. Recent research into painting techniques has, however, repeatedly shown that the classic distinction between tempera and oil can be only conditionally applied to European painting of the late Middle Ages and Early Renaissance. Rather, many artists, incidentally including Antonello himself, both north and south of the Alps—and clearly very much earlier than had for a long time been assumed—had experimented with various binders and often worked with mixed media. The Bellini brothers, for example, were familiar with oil painting, and moreover with Early Netherlandish art, in Venice as early as the mid-15th century, and therefore clearly before Antonello's documented stay in that city.

Nevertheless, it is undisputed that the painter from Messina was influenced during his training in Naples in the early 1450s by the art of Jan van Eyck and Rogier van der Weyden, whose paintings were also much appreciated and collected at the courts of both René d'Anjou and Alfonso I of Aragon. This is noticeable primarily in his extremely finely painted portraits, mostly with neutral dark backgrounds. But the Netherlandish influence is certainly still recognizable in two small Crucifixion panels (page 132), created during Antonello's stay in Venice around the mid-1470s and thus part of his later period. This is true for example of the precisely rendered stones, skulls, and bones at the feet of the Crosses, arranged almost in the manner of a still-life, as well as the noticeable localization of the event on a hill, from which in each case one looks down to the valley landscape of the background. In the London panel, the tiny figures of the three Marys can be made out immediately to the left of the Cross, while on the right two men are already striding up the hill with a ladder to take the body of Christ down from the Cross.

Other details, however, appear much less directly influenced by northern models. The Virgin Mary and

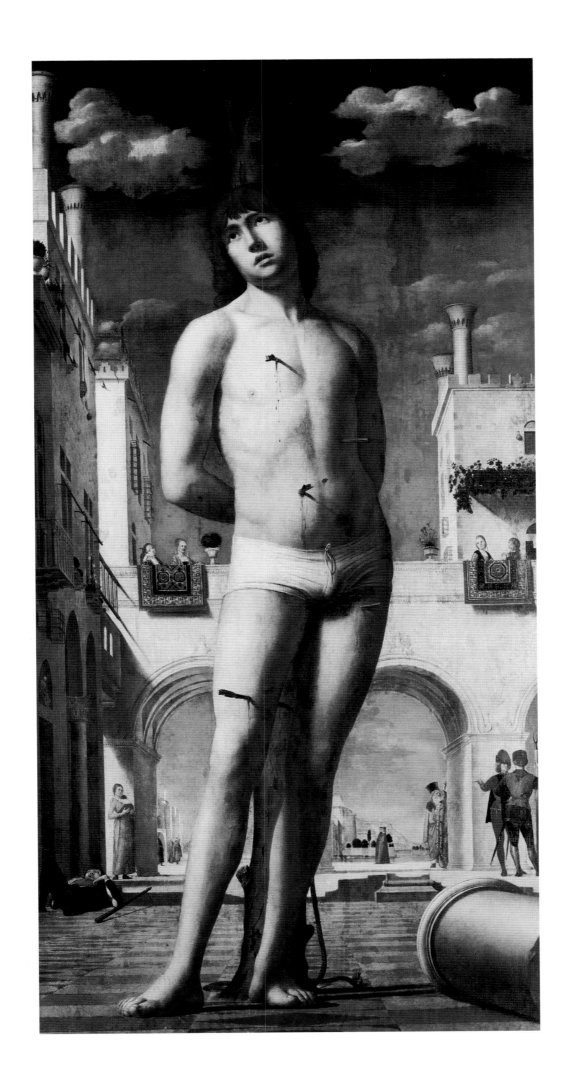

the Apostle John, for example, are portrayed by Antonello as strikingly calm, almost devotional seated figures. In the Crucifixion panels of the Netherlandish painters mentioned, on the other hand, which are often richer in figures and much more dramatic, the mourners mostly stand below the Cross with faces contorted with grief, and with emotive gestures. (Admittedly this can also be observed in many Italian portrayals of the theme, so that Antonello's paintings in any case occupy rather a special position.) Moreover, the Mediterranean-looking buildings in the background, as well as the occasional cypresses towering up in the landscape, clearly announce that both paintings come from the workshop of a painter from the southern Alpine region.

When, in 1478, Venice was once again afflicted by a devastating epidemic of the plague, the Scuola di San

Rocco, founded in response to this, commissioned an altarpiece in several parts with depictions of various saints associated with the plague. Of this polyptych, in whose center stood the figure, carved in wood, of St. Roch (Rocco), the titular saint of the charitable brotherhood, only one side panel of *St. Sebastian*, painted by Antonello da Messina (page 131), has been preserved. It is impossible to say whether this was executed in Venice or after Antonello's return to his home. This only recently restored masterpiece in the Dresden art gallery, unusual in several respects, shows the martyrdom of the Roman soldier Sebastian. According to medieval legend, he was sentenced to death not only because of his Christian faith, but also because of his conversion of a number of pagans and his destruction of idolatrous images. He survived being shot at with arrows, and was therefore finally beaten to

Opposite page, left:
Antonello da Messina
The Crucifixion, 1475
Oil on panel, 52.5 x 42.5 cm
Koninklijk Museum voor Schone Kunsten, Antwerp

This painting, dated and signed (*1475/Antonellus/ messaneus/me … pinxit*) on a painted slip of paper at the foot of the cross, captivates the observer with its precisely depicted anatomy and the convincing lighting of the two thieves. The right-hand figure in particular is shown in an extremely stooping attitude and with a highly foreshortened and bent right leg.

Opposite page, right:
Antonello da Messina
The Crucifixion, 1475–1477
Oil on panel, 41.9 x 25.4 cm
National Gallery, London

Not only the small format of this panel, but also the strikingly calm attitude of the figures of Mary and the young St. John, sitting almost meditatively at the foot of the cross, suggest that this is an image painted for private devotions.

Antonello da Messina
Pietà, ca. 1476/77
Oil on panel, 74 x 51 cm
Museo Nacional del Prado, Madrid

Beside the arm of the weeping angel supporting the dead Christ, two of the three crosses of Mount Calvary are to be seen in the landscape that fades to pale blue at the horizon, while in the right-hand half of the image a church towers up from a walled city, a largely accurate depiction of Messina Cathedral. Not least because of this detail, it is presumed that this *Pietà* was executed after 1476, when the painter returned to his Sicilian home.

death. Diverging from the textual as well as the pictorial tradition (Volume I, page 24), Antonello shows the martyr bound to a tree, gazing up to heaven with a transfigured expression, wearing, instead of the usual loincloth, a short, close-fitting nether garment, and not in the middle of a landscape, but in front of an urban backdrop. From the canal in the background, and above all the strikingly formed conical chimneys on the roofs of the palaces surrounding the square, the city is easily identified as Venice.

The decidedly "artful" character of the image is primarily evident in the contrasts in the lighting, as well as in the perfectly staged perspective, highly evocative as a result of the pronounced low-angle view and extreme foreshortening. At the same time, the pillar (a symbol of the strong faith of the martyrs) that leads the gaze into the distance, as well as the figure of the soldier lying on the ground, placed precisely on the vanishing line, is reminiscent of the battle paintings of Paolo Uccello of two decades or so earlier, which Antonello may have seen in Florence on his way to Venice (Volume I, pages 312, 313).

Also dating from the mid-1470s, Antonello's superbly preserved *Pietà* in Madrid (above) is presumed to have been executed with the help of his son, Jacobello. This work is related on the one hand to a *Pietà* created about the same time by Giovanni Bellini for the *Pesaro Altarpiece* (page 137), and on the other hand, again, to Early Netherlandish art. This is true particularly of its impressive painterly precision and pronounced detailed realism, for example in the skull at bottom left, the right hand of Christ, which is bent backwards, and the puffy red eyes of the distraught little angel.

Giovanni Bellini, *The Transfiguration*, ca. 1455–1460
Oil on panel, 134 x 68 cm
Museo Correr, Venice

No definite knowledge exists about the original function of this painting, formerly attributed to Mantegna. Presumably it was part of a polyptych, perhaps one of the side wings of the silver shrine on the high altar of San Salvatore in Venice. On the other hand, because of the inscription taken from the book of Job, *MISEREMINI MEI SALTEM/VOS AMICI MEI* ("Have pity on me, my friends"), the monastery church of San Giobbe has also been considered as a location. Furthermore, it cannot be stated with certainty what would have been seen in the upper zone of the originally apparently semicircular panel, which was trimmed at an unknown time. Because of the red tip of a garment that can just be seen, a depiction of God the Father, surrounded by cherubim, can be assumed. In favor of this is, not least, the text of Matthew's Gospel: "and suddenly a voice came out of the cloud, saying, This is my beloved son, in whom I am well pleased. Hear him!"

GIOVANNI BELLINI
CA. 1430–1516

The dominant artistic personality in Venice in the second half of the Quattrocento was Giovanni Bellini. Together with his brother Gentile (1429–1507) he received his first training in the workshop of his father Jacopo (1400–1470/71), only a few of whose paintings, unfortunately, survive. Nevertheless, he can be given the credit for contributing substantially to our knowledge of the achievement of the Florentine Early Renaissance in Venice. His sketchbooks, preserved today in London and Paris, give evidence of a pronounced interest in the rules of central perspective (Volume I, page 364).

Lastingly impressed by his brother-in-law of the same age, Andrea Mantegna, as well as later by Antonello da Messina, Giovanni Bellini during his long life created not only an impressive number of paintings, but also contributed decisively to the development of the "Venetian culture of color." Apart from large-format altar panels, his Madonnas, often set against atmospheric, light-flooded landscapes, as well as his many variant depictions of the mourning of the dead Christ, established the fame of this painter, from whose great workshop there emerged important artists such as Giorgione and Titian.

One of his early works shows the Transfiguration of Christ, which became an official Church festival only in 1457, in a landscape foreshortened in a still positively formulaic manner (left). The view of the horizon is largely barred by a mountain reduced to a rocky massif, on which Jesus, according to the three Synoptic Evangelists Matthew, Mark, and Luke, was transfigured in the presence of the Apostles Peter, John, and James. Matthew writes: "… and He was transfigured before them. His face shone like the sun, and His clothes became as white as the light. And, behold, there appeared unto them Moses and Elijah talking with him."

Giovanni Bellini
The Transfiguration, ca. 1480–1485
Wood, 115 x 154 cm
Galleria Nazionale di Capodimonte, Naples

On the railing made from branches in the foreground is a piece of paper painted illusionistically in the manner characteristic of Venetian painting of the Quattrocento, on which the artist has signed his painting: *IOANNES BELLI[NVS]*. It was probably executed for the family chapel of the archdeacon Alberto Fioccardo in the cathedral of Vicenza. In this respect, a detail in the background of the landscape, not yet definitely interpreted, may be surprising. Between Christ and Elijah, two famous buildings in Ravenna can be made out: Theodoric's mausoleum and the bell tower of Sant'Apollinare in Classe. The explanation might be the circumstance that the apse mosaic of the church in front of the gates of Ravenna, dedicated to Bishop St. Apollinaris in 549, contains the oldest known depiction of the Transfiguration of Christ.

Although Bellini clearly distinguishes the figure of Christ by its height and light-colored clothing from the prophets flanking him, in this early work, with its rather clumsy figures, one can hardly speak as yet of the much praised light of Venetian painting. This is also true of the comparatively dull and dry coloration of the rock at the foot of the hill, which is bounded by a stream in the left foreground. Nevertheless, it is precisely in this part of the picture that we can observe evidence of the artist's early encounter with the art of Mantegna, who had been married since 1453 to Giovanni Bellini's sister, Nicolosia. There too we find many instances of rock formations built up in individual layers, traversed by many cracks and sharp edges (page 70).

Some two and a half decades later, Bellini was working on details of this kind in another version of the same theme, in even more meticulous fashion, as though from a positively geological viewpoint (above). Corresponding to the change from vertical to horizontal format, the abbreviation of Mount Tabor has now totally given way to the gently curving landscape of a plateau, in which the gaze can wander almost unhindered along a path leading into the distance toward the horizon and the hills ranged in rows behind each other. While this work has not yet attained the dramatic quality to be observed in Raphael three and a half decades later (page 271), the artist already convinces with a very much more differentiated management of light, seen particularly in the figures of the two prophets and the Savior, brightly lit from the left. The right hand of Jesus throws a precise shadow on the immaculate white garment with its noticeably softer

Giovanni Bellini
Pietà, ca. 1470
Wood, 86 x 107 cm
Pinacoteca di Brera, Milan

In the Gospels, the Mourning of Christ, between the Deposition from the Cross and the Burial, is not described. The source for this theme, popular since the 14th century at first only north of the Alps, but in Italy also from the middle of the Quattrocento, is rather the mystical literature of the Middle Ages.

and more natural folds, and the more pronounced chiaroscuro contrasts, compared with the older version in the Museo Correr (page 134).

Giovanni Bellini made several versions of a subject also new to Italian art in the 15th century, previously depicted almost exclusively north of the Alps—the Mourning of the Dead Christ. Probably his best-known *Pietà* is the horizontal rectangular panel preserved in Milan (above). Opinions differ about its original function: small altarpiece or large devotional picture? Between the marble parapet at the front edge and the sarcophagus, also arranged in parallel to the picture plane, Mary and the Apostle John hold the dead body of Christ in their arms, expressing their grief in their different ways. While the Mother of God clings closely to her dead son in silent mourning, the beloved disciple turns away, looks toward the right edge of the image and seems to be lamenting aloud. Out of this field of tension between closeness and distance, calm and restrained movement, the lifeless arm of Christ is held out toward the direction of the observer. In the gentle light of the evening of Good Friday, his hand rests upon the stone parapet.

The slip of paper painted immediately below it deserves particular attention. The inscription includes not only the artist's name: *HAEC FERE QVVM GEMITVS TVRGENTIA LVMINA PROMANTI-BELLINI POTERAT FLERE IOANNIS OPVS* ("As soon as the swollen eyes [from weeping] allowed a lament to break out, / the work of Giovanni Bellini was

able to weep"). The first part of this couplet is a version of a verse from an elegy by the Roman poet Propertius (50–15 BC), the inscription on a cenotaph mentioned there for a friend fallen in war, which prompted the suggestion that Bellini was alluding to a Christian soldier who lost his life during the Turkish conquest of Constantinople in 1453. Apart from this, the signature inscription has also been interpreted in connection with the artistic theory of the Quattrocento. While there can be no doubt in the case of the classical model that the observer or reader of the inscription is being addressed as the mourner ("Why do you turn your swollen eyelids away from my lament?"), in the case of Bellini's painting it cannot be unequivocally determined whose eyes and laments are meant. Does the inscription refer to the observer, who is, or is intended to be, moved to pity by the depiction of the dead Savior and the mourners? Or does it refer to the figures in the painting and thus—as the second line suggests—to the painting? It could equally be the creator of the painting himself who is meant, who wanted his work to be understood as an expression of his own Christian sympathy and profound piety.

There is general agreement, however, that the Milan *Pietà* with its "extended" signature seems like a reaction to Leon Battista Alberti's treatise on painting of 1435, in which he writes: "The *istoria* will move the soul of the beholder when each man painted there clearly shows the movement of his own soul. It

Giovanni Bellini
Pesaro Altarpiece: Pietà (Anointing of Christ), 1470s
Oil on panel, 106 x 84 cm
Pinacoteca Vaticana, Vatican, Rome

This painting, traditionally called a *Pietà*, apart from the fact that in Italian this concept is used in an extended sense, shows not precisely the mourning of Christ, but another moment in the story of the Passion, described in the Bible in most detail by John the Evangelist: that of the anointing immediately before the burial of Christ. Instead of Mary and John, here it is Joseph of Arimathea, Nicodemus, and Mary Magdalene who surround the body; the bearded Nicodemus holds the container of ointment ready for the young woman.

happens in nature that nothing more than herself is capable of things like herself: we weep with the weeping, laugh with the laughing, and grieve with the grieving." The text paraphrased in the painting, as well as the overt reference to Alberti, who for his part looks back to classical theories of rhetoric and poetry, suggest the conclusion that Bellini's painting is to be perceived not merely as a pious work, but also and above all as a subtle demonstration of the equal status of "modern" painting and classical literature in the spirit of Horace's *ut pictura poesis* ("a poem is like a painting"), and thus ultimately as a document of artistic self-confidence.

Against this background, it must also be taken into account that the painting may have been intended for a humanistically educated collector rather than for an altar or devotional chamber.

In the case of the *Pietà* executed a full ten years later and now in the Vatican Museums (above), on the other hand, it is known that it formed the upper conclusion of a splendid Coronation of the Virgin Mary that once adorned the high altar of San Francesco in the Adriatic port of Pesaro (page 138). Such a heightened and exposed display of the painting in the space of the church corresponds to the skillfully staged

Opposite page:
Giovanni Bellini
Madonna and Child Enthroned, with Angels Playing Instruments, and Four Saints (Frari Triptych), 1488
Oil on panel, central panel 184 x 79 cm,
side panels 115 x 46 cm each
Santa Maria Gloriosa dei Frari, Venice

This triptych, signed and dated below the Madonna on the base of the throne, a pictorial form still very popular in Venice in the late 15th century, captivates us above all through the illusionistic architecture of the frame, probably designed by Bellini himself, which unifies the space of the image. The four standing saints (Nicholas of Bari, Peter, Mark, and Benedict) are the patron saints of the clients from the Pesaro family. Perhaps Albrecht Dürer (1471–1528), who was a friend of Giovanni Bellini, remembered these figures of saints when he painted his so-called *Four Apostles* (now in the Alte Pinakothek in Munich) in 1526, two decades after his first visit to Venice.

Giovanni Bellini
Pesaro Altarpiece: Coronation of the Virgin Mary, 1470s
Oil on panel, 262 x 240 cm
Museo Civico, Pesaro

The theory that the castle to be seen in the background of the "picture within a picture" is a depiction of the Rocca di Gradara near Pesaro has led to various conjectures about the immediate political circumstances of the creation of this painting. Putting these aside, most contemporary observers at the sight of such a fortress, and precisely in connection with the theme of the coronation of Mary as Queen of Heaven, would have first thought of the Heavenly Jerusalem or of the "strong fortress" of Psalms 31 and 46, and thus of the figure of God the Father himself, often present in the same place in comparable depictions.

view from below of the four figures lit from the left, which appear highly sculptural. Meanwhile it is details such as the turning of Christ's body from a frontal to a three-quarter view and thus the vanishing line leading over his shoulders to the area below right of the image, and the head of the dead Christ slightly inclined backward and thus seen all the more as though from below, that Bellini used to construct such an evocative perspective.

In the almost square main panel of the altar (above), St. Paul, St. Peter, St. Jerome and finally, at the extreme right, St. Francis, the titular saint of the church at Pesaro, flank the central scene of the Coronation of the Virgin Mary as in a *sacra conversazione*. The arrangement of the figures corresponds to the order of the five small predella panels at the lower edge of the magnificently framed painting. Thus, below the Prince of the Apostles, Paul, who leans on his sword, his

conversion on the road to Damascus is to be seen. Dazzled by the heavenly apparition, Saul, who has fallen from his horse, covers his eyes with his hand. Peter in the central panel to the right, behind him, is matched in the predella by the martyrdom scene of his crucifixion, while St. Jerome is allotted his penance in the wilderness and St. Francis his stigmatization. The striking rocky landscapes in the latter two scenes once again recall Mantegna. Finally, Bellini has depicted the Nativity in the center of the predella, and thus below the Coronation of the Virgin Mary, and the upper part of the altar with the Anointing of Christ.

The special attraction of this complex painting also consists in the fact that the richly ornamented framing architecture is taken up again in altered form within the main image. On the throne, Christ places the crown of Heaven on the head of Mary, which is humbly bowed, almost as if in an Annunciation scene. Through the high back of the throne, for its part giving the impression of a frame, on whose step the artist has put his signature, one looks as through a window onto a hilly evening landscape. At the same time, however, as in Cosimo Rosselli's *Last Supper* in the Sistine Chapel (Volume I, page 592), the impression is created of a picture within a picture, and it seems as though Bellini actually intended to give this impression, particularly since Alberti in his treatise on painting specifically compares a painting with the view out of a window to illustrate the basic rules of perspective.

Giovanni Bellini
San Giobbe Altarpiece (*The Madonna and Child Enthroned, with St. Francis, John the Baptist, Job, St. Dominic, St. Sebastian, and St. Louis of Toulouse*), late 1470s
Wood, 471 x 258 cm
Gallerie dell'Accademia, Venice

Like Antonello da Messina's *St. Sebastian* (page 131), this altar painting, one of the few works in which Bellini did not include a landscape as background, was presumably commissioned on the occasion of the plague epidemic of 1478. This would explain the prominent position of two saints particularly popular in Venice as protectors from the plague, Job and Sebastian. While Sebastian, pierced by arrows, stands in front of Dominic and Louis of Toulouse in the foreground of the group of three on the right, the painter has particularly singled out Job, who was never canonized but was revered as a saint in Venice, by placing him immediately next to the Christ Child.

The artist presents a similarly unusual view of landscape in an altarpiece dated 1513, that is, during the last years of his life, and possibly executed with the help of Titian (page 282). It is in a side chapel of the church of San Giovanni Crisostomo, rebuilt around 1500 after a devastating fire, and thus still in its original location in the center of Venice, near the Rialto Bridge. The giving of the commission to the leading painter of the city, as he still was at that time, was probably connected with his membership of the Scuola Grande di San Marco, the patrons of the chapel that was to be decorated.

Under a barrel vault or arch stand St. Christopher and St. Louis of Toulouse in front of a parapet adorned with classical grotesque ornamentation. With their staffs, held upright, they look almost like lance-carrying guardians of a portal that allows the view of a high mountainous landscape. Immediately behind the parapet, a rocky massif towers up, which serves St. Jerome as a kind of throne. In this way Bellini skillfully combines two traditional pictorial motifs: the saint's wild natural surroundings, as well as his undergarment opened at the chest, are reminiscent of depictions of penitent hermits in the wilderness, while the books and the strangely crooked fig tree that acts as a lectern allude to his study and his fame as translator of the Bible from Greek into Latin. In this respect it is not surprising that the Greek version of the 13th Psalm is written on the soffit of the arch. On the other hand,

Cima da Conegliano
The Madonna and Child Enthroned, with St. Peter, St. Romuald, St. Benedict, and St. Paul, ca. 1495–1497
Oil on poplar, 206 x 135 cm
Gemäldegalerie, Staatliche Museen, Berlin

The Prince of the Apostles, Paul, standing at the outer right-hand edge of the image and gazing at the observer, can be identified not only by his usual attribute, the sword, and because he faces Peter on the opposite side, but also because of the book in his left hand, which he has opened at his Epistle to the Philippians (EPISTULA AD PHILIPPOS). But what may have induced the painter to choose this particular Epistle of Paul is not known.

this may also be a reference to the titular saint of the church (which significantly is built on a ground plan in the form of a Greek cross), the Greek Church Father John Chrysostom.

The final image, probably originally semicircular, at the top edge was presumably set in a frame that continued the painted architecture, thus heightening the impression of depth of space. According to this principle of illusionistic combination of painted and real space, one of Bellini's greatest altarpieces, the *San Giobbe Altarpiece*, now in the Accademia in Venice (page 140), is documented as having been framed up to the 19th century. The frame of this painting, resembling a triumphal arch, is still in its original place in the church of San Giobbe and its soffit displays the same pattern of rosettes as the painted barrel vault, reminiscent of Masaccio's *Trinity* fresco in Florence (Volume I, page 17), above the sacred space, in front of whose mosaic apse the Madonna sits with the Christ Child on a high throne, surrounded by six saints and three angels playing instruments. This, with the figures shown almost lifesize, additionally enhances the fiction of the continued church space, structured in perfect perspective.

This type of the *sacra conversazione*, popular above all in Venice, is also frequently to be found in the work of a painter possibly trained by Giovanni Bellini, Cima da Conegliano (ca. 1459/60–1517/18). One of his works preserved in the Berlin Gemäldegalerie (page 141), for example, shows the Madonna once again sitting on a high throne under a dome also covered with mosaics. The Venetian character of the work is shown in exactly this detail, for the painted mosaic is a largely faithful reproduction of the dome mosaics executed in the early 13th century in one of the porticoes of San Marco. It shows a scene from the life of the young Joseph, who was sold to the Ishmaelites by his jealous brothers and finally reached Egypt. In the center, and thus directly above the enthroned Madonna with the Christ Child, we recognize the stream into which Joseph was thrown earlier.

This painting was executed in the final years of the Quattrocento for the sacristy of the Camaldolese church of San Michele on the island of the same name between Venice and Murano, which explains the choice of the two saints flanking the throne, standing between Peter and Paul. On the left we recognize

Benedict, while on the right is St. Romuald reading a book. He was the founder of the Camaldolese order that emerged from the Benedictines.

One of Giovanni Bellini's iconographically most unusual and thus controversial paintings shows St. Francis of Assisi in a rocky landscape, once again Mantegnesque, at least in the foreground (page 143). Here the vine-covered cell with its scanty furnishings —lectern, skull, cross, crown of thorns, and a walking stick leaning against the trellis—is rather reminiscent of depictions of hermits and penitents such as Antony Abbot and Jerome. This pictorial tradition also corresponds to the opposition between city and wilderness as a reference to the contrast between a worldly life and ascetic seclusion. In view of the simple brown garment and the threefold knotted girdle there can be no doubt that the monk gazing up to heaven with arms outspread is Francis. It is not clear, however, what period of his life is represented. If, as most researchers presume, it is his reception of the stigmata, the painter has withheld two essential elements, namely his fellow-monk and witness Leo, and above all the crucifix surrounded by seraphim. On the other hand, this may have been visible at the top edge of the picture, which has probably been trimmed.

Disregarding further suggestions for the interpretation of the scene (for example that the saint is singing his famous Canticle of the Sun), various elements of the picture can be understood in connection with the *Imitatio Christi*, which is manifested in the *Life of St. Francis*, such as the donkey to be discerned in the center area, which can be associated both with the path to Mount La Verna, where the saint from Assisi is said to have received the stigmata, and with the entry of Jesus into Jerusalem.

Apart from his great altar paintings Giovanni Bellini also created a number of small-format Madonna paintings, intended for private devotion. Among these, the so-called *Madonna degli alberetti* (in other words the "Madonna of the Little Trees") in the Accademia is the oldest known work of this genre to be dated by the artist himself (page 144). On the piece of paper attached to the slender stone parapet is the signature of the artist (*IOANNES BELLINVS P.*) and also the date, 1487. Apart from the crossed feet of the Christ Child standing immediately above this, which have recently been interpreted as a reference to the

Giovanni Bellini
St. Francis in Ecstasy, 1470s
Oil and tempera on wood, 120 x 137 cm
The Frick Collection, New York

Since this painting was probably trimmed at the upper
edge at an unknown time, it has been assumed that a
crucifix surrounded by seraphim was originally to be seen
there, as is the case with many other depictions of St.
Francis receiving the stigmata. On the other hand, Bellini
may have quite consciously, for whatever reason, replaced
it with the sunlight breaking through the clouds.

Giovanni Bellini
Madonna degli alberetti (*The Madonna of the Little Trees*),
1487
Poplar, 71 x 58 cm
Gallerie dell'Accademia, Venice

The two small trees to left and right in the background
are similar to those to be found in many of the paintings
of Pietro Perugino. However, the motif could just as easily
have been inspired by Early Netherlandish painting,
which incidentally also applies to the green cloth of honor
behind the Madonna.

Crucifixion, the trees towering up to left and right of
the green curtain presumably also have a symbolic
significance. While some scholars see them as an
allusion to the Old and New Testaments, others prefer
to link them with the Song of Songs and the Virgin
Mary. Regardless of the question of significance of the
content, various references have been made to the
stylistic link between this motif and the art of Pietro
Perugino. But to derive from this a relationship of
dependency between the two painters, of whatever
kind, proves problematic, since Perugino, from
Umbria, as far as we know today did not travel to
Venice until the early 1490s.

A somewhat unusual depiction of the Madonna and
Child (page 145), compared with the generally quite
traditional *Madonna degli alberetti*, was created by
Bellini about a decade and a half later for an as yet
unidentified client. This painting, known as the
Madonna with the Sleeping Child (*Madonna del prato*)
exhibited in the National Gallery in London since the
mid-19th century, seems at first glance to be merely a
further variant of the very popular pictorial theme of
Madonna and Child. Forming an isosceles triangle
with her widely spread blue mantle, the young Mother
of God is seated at the front edge of the image, in a
meadow. Her hands folded, she gazes raptly down at

Giovanni Bellini
The Madonna with the Sleeping Child (Madonna del prato),
ca. 1500–1505
Oil and tempera, transferred from wood, 67.3 x 86.4 cm
National Gallery, London

When this painting was acquired in Faenza in 1858 for
the London Gallery, it was at first attributed to various
other Venetian Renaissance artists such as Vincenzo
Catena. Only in the late 1920s was it attributed, as it is
unanimously today, to Giovanni Bellini.

her child, who in contrast to many older treatments of
this subject does not stand or sit on her lap, but is
asleep. The painter, in the spirit of the old saying that
sleep is the younger brother of death, clearly alludes to
the Passion and Mourning of the Dead Christ.

In this connection we are driven to the presumption
that the plants and animals in the spring landscape
behind the Madonna likewise have a symbolic
significance. The bare or dead trees at the left edge of
the image, for example, in view of the hardly accidental
contrast to the other trees, which are already in leaf,
can be seen as a reference to the Passion of Jesus. This
may possibly also be true of the black bird of prey,
looking like a vulture, which, however, can also be seen
as a symbol of the triumph of Christ over death, like
the one in Bellini's *Resurrection* from the 1470s, now

in the Berlin Gemäldegalerie. Finally, the same
interpretation could be placed on the battle to be seen
directly next to the trees between a bird, presumably
intended as an ibis, and a snake.

Moreover, this motif, as well as the almost genre-like
scene in the background of a cowherd leaning on a
fence, has been linked with Virgil's *Georgics*, his "Song
of Farming." Such a connection between the religious
theme of the painting and a pastoral poem of the
heathen classical era may at first seem far-fetched, but
proves to be entirely plausible if one knows that the
classical poet Virgil was revered as a prophet of Christ
in the Middle Ages and Renaissance. The basis for this
was primarily his fourth Eclogue, in which he speaks of
a virgin and a divine male child whose birth in the
future would usher in a new golden age.

In Western painting of the early modern period, it was usual to transfer biblical or legendary events that had taken place in the Holy Land or other distant regions into a setting familiar to the observer. This is the case with Cima's painting for the church of Santa Maria dei Crociferi in Venice. Although the healing of the cobbler Anianus is supposed to have taken place in Alexandria in Egypt, the building flanking the square on the left is typically Venetian (something that strikes us only on second glance because of the extreme foreshortening). In contrast to Florentine and Roman Renaissance palaces with their generally uniformly harmonized façades, here on the first upper floor the central column arrangement of a loggia is to be seen standing off from the massive wall areas.

Cima da Conegliano
Christ with Doubting Thomas and Bishop St. Magnus of Oderzo, ca. 1504/05
Oil on wood, 210 x 141 cm
Gallerie dell'Accademia, Venice

This altar painting, executed for the Scuola dei Mureri (the usual expression in Venetian dialect for *muratori*, that is, masons) in San Samuele, shows the two patrons of this brotherhood standing beside Christ. On the right is Bishop St. Magnus of Oderzo, on the left the Apostle Thomas, who doubted the resurrection of Christ and was therefore challenged by him to touch the wound in his side. Thomas's fiery red cloak, as in many older depictions of this scene, is presumably a reference to the legend of his martyrdom, according to which he had to stand barefoot on burning-hot sheets of iron.

CIMA DA CONEGLIANO AND VITTORE CARPACCIO

Among the most important representatives of the Venetian generation of artists after the Bellini brothers are two painters who at the beginning of the 16th century remained largely indebted to the style of the Early Renaissance: Cima da Conegliano (properly Giovanni Battista Cima, ca. 1459/60–1517/18) and Vittore Carpaccio (ca. 1460–1525/26). While Cima, coming from a family of cloth-cutters (Italian *cimatori*) and named after his birthplace, Conegliano, north of

Venice, left a substantial number of altarpieces and devotional pictures, Carpaccio is primarily known for his detailed cycles of narrative paintings with scenes from the New Testament and legends of the saints, which were commissioned by the lay brotherhoods known in Venice as *scuole*.

Whether Cima received his artistic training in his home town from an unknown master, or was taught by Giovanni Bellini only on his move to Venice in the early 1490s, is still disputed today. Be that as it

Vittore Carpaccio
St. George and the Dragon, 1502–1508
Oil on canvas, 141 x 360 cm
Scuola di San Giorgio degli Schiavoni, Venice

Almost more sinister than the dragon himself are the remains of his gruesome meals. This realistically rendered motif, as disturbing as it is fascinating, of the many fragments of corpses, skulls, and bones is also found in other works by Carpaccio. In addition, the extremely foreshortened depiction of the mutilated male corpse lying on his back behind George's horse almost recalls Mantegna's dead Christ in the Brera in Milan (page 79). Mantegna's painting, later influential even beyond the borders of Italy, was still in his workshop at the time of his death. Whether it was known to Carpaccio and could thus have served him as a source of inspiration is, on the other hand, uncertain.

may, the influence of Bellini, at that time the leading artist in the city, on his sensitive treatment of light, and the rich, warm coloration of his compositions, can hardly be overlooked. This is expressed particularly in an altar panel of the meeting between the risen Christ and Doubting Thomas (page 146). In contrast to his rendering of the same subject now preserved in London, in which the scene, following the Gospel of John, takes place in an interior, Cima here presents the figures in a loggia flooded with bright light in front of a broad landscape. Apart from the convincingly rendered effects of light and shade, it is above all the strictly symmetrical positioning of the arch of this loggia, adjusted to the format of the painting, that reminds us of Bellini's work.

Perhaps, however, the most impressive evidence of his masterly treatment of the rules of perspective, then already long established in Venice, is Cima's painting of a rarely illustrated scene from the life of the patron saint of the Venetian republic (page 147). As the *Legenda Aurea* (*The Golden Legend*) claims, in Alexandria the Evangelist Mark healed the cobbler and later bishop Anianus, who had injured his hand while mending the saint's shoe. Cima shows this event, in a similar way to Antonello with his *St. Sebastian* (page 131), in a lively square, structured as a corner motif. Apart from the curious glances of the men in Oriental clothing, it is above all the vanishing lines of the palace façade bordering the scene on the left, and shown in extreme foreshortening, that come together between the hands of the two protagonists and thus direct the observer's attention to the point where the miraculous healing takes place.

Disregarding the discussion, equally prolonged in the case of Vittore Carpaccio, on conjectural teachers

such as Gentile Bellini, Antonello da Messina and others, it can scarcely be denied that this painter too could hardly escape the influence of the Bellini. As has been mentioned, he predominantly worked for the charitable lay brotherhoods in Venice, who had their assembly rooms adorned with scenes from the lives of their individual patrons. Since the fresco technique usually preferred elsewhere in Italy had not established itself in the damp climate of Venice, the walls were clad with panel or canvas paintings, a procedure that continued to be used up to the second half of the 16th century—one need only think of Tintoretto.

For the Scuola di San Giorgio degli Schiavoni, Carpaccio created a wide-ranging cycle, still preserved in its entirety today and to be seen in its original location, in which among others the legends of St. George and St. Jerome are depicted. The latter enjoyed particular appreciation in Venice because of his taming of a lion, as with St. Mark. Probably the best known of these paintings shows the battle of the patron saint of the brotherhood, St. George, with a dragon, who, as the *Golden Legend* reports, was threatening the Libyan city of Silena (above). After first sacrificing sheep, the citizens were soon forced to supply the beast with humans to eat, in order to keep it away from the city. On the day when even the king's daughter was to be sacrificed, the knight George appeared to put an end to the terror, and after completing his act of heroism to convert the inhabitants of Silena to Christianity.

However much the battle scene arranged parallel to the image in the front area may remind us of late medieval knightly epics or tournaments, and thus lend the painting an almost nostalgic character, it must be remembered that such a theme would remind the

Vittore Carpaccio
St. Augustine in an Interior (*The Vision of St. Augustine*),
1502–1508
Oil on canvas, 141 x 211 cm
Scuola di San Giorgio degli Schiavoni, Venice

This figure of the Church Father Augustine may
possibly be an idealized portrait of Cardinal Bessarion
(1403–1472). The Cardinal, a humanist from
Constantinople who promoted the reunification of the
Greek and Latin Churches, was an honorary member of
the Scuola di San Giorgio and bequeathed to the
Republic of Venice a wide-ranging collection of books,
which was to form the basis of the Biblioteca Marciana,
built from 1537 under the direction of Jacopo Sansovino.

Venetians of the threat to Christian Europe, which had again become severe around 1500, from the Ottomans, advancing through the Balkans. This was particularly true of the *schiavoni*, who resided in Venice but came predominantly from Slavonia, Croatia, and Dalmatia, and thus particularly affected by the Ottoman advance. It is hardly surprising then that a centrally built church rises beyond the bay, behind the king's daughter rescued by George, while the roofs and domes in the city on the dragon's side are occasionally adorned with half-moons.

That Carpaccio too had supremely mastered the rules of central perspective is shown by a glance at his *Vision of St. Augustine* (page 149). In a study lit from the right, in which, apart from many books, sheets of music, a miter and crosier (Augustine was Bishop of Hippo in North Africa in the early 5th century), and an astrolabe as a reference to the scientific education of the saint are to be recognized, the Church Father sits at his desk. The painting captures the moment when the author of *De Civitate Dei* (*The City of God*) pauses while writing a letter to Jerome (the second patron of the *schiavoni*) and looks out of the window, hearing the voice of the saint who has just died. Apart from the hand that he raises from his work, at whose height, hardly by accident, the central vanishing point of the picture's composition lies, the hourglass on the shelf below the window should be noted. Beyond the general symbolism of the transitory nature of life, the hourglass whose sand has run its course is probably also a direct reference to the death of St. Jerome.

Precision of perspective and richness of narrative detail also characterize the cycle of paintings from the Scuola di Sant'Orsola (page 151). According to legend, the King of England wanted to marry the beautiful Ursula, the daughter of a pious king of Brittany, to his son. Because of threats of violence in the event of her refusal, the young woman imposed conditions on her marriage to the heathen prince. He was to have himself baptized and instructed in the Christian faith during her three-year pilgrimage to Rome by ship via Cologne and Basel, accompanied by eleven thousand virgins. Carpaccio's comprehensive cycle describes in minute detail all the events up to Ursula's martyrdom during her return journey via Cologne, meanwhile besieged by the Huns. Like Cima in *St. Mark Healing the Cobbler Anianus*, the painter has placed a great number of the scenes in a Venetian setting.

The first painting shows the reception of the English envoys and in the neighboring bedroom Ursula, listing her conditions for the marriage to her anxious father. The opening of the throne room both on the observer's side and to the harbor in the background may appear not very "realistic." Nevertheless, such a stage-like spatial structure proves to be thoroughly characteristic of the painting of the Quattrocento and is reminiscent, as is the positioning of the figures, of a Florentine work only about ten years older, Domenico Ghirlandaio's *Confirmation of the Rule* (Volume I, page 433).

Henrik Engel

Vittore Carpaccio
Ursula's Father Receives the Envoys of the English King,
1490–1500
Oil on canvas, 275 x 589 cm
Gallerie dell'Accademia, Venice

While the central octagonal church building beyond the canal running parallel to the image reminds us of works by Perugino or Raphael (Volume I, pages 584, 585), all the other buildings in the background appear typically Venetian. This is true of the structure of the palace façades as well as for the clock tower, which recalls the Torre dell'Orologio, built in the 1490s next to the church of San Marco. Beyond this, at the extreme left-hand edge, the island of San Giorgio, off the coast of Venice, can be recognized.

Vittore Carpaccio
The Return of the Envoys (detail), 1490–1500
Oil on canvas, 297 x 527 cm
Gallerie dell'Accademia, Venice

In most of the paintings of the wide-ranging cycle on
the legend of St. Ursula, the painter transfers the events
occurring in Brittany and England to Venice, or to a port
with unmistakably Venetian features. Here the English
king, seated in an octagonal loggia, receives his returning
envoys, who are reporting to him the conditions under
which the pious Ursula would be prepared to marry his
son.

Leonardo da Vinci 1452–1519

LIFE AND INFLUENCE

Leonardo da Vinci
Self-Portrait, ca. 1515 (?)
Red chalk on paper, 33.3 x 21.3 cm
Biblioteca Reale, Turin

A hand-written note from the 16th century titles the drawing "Leonardus Vincius [in red chalk] self-portrait at an advanced age [in charcoal]," so that its interpretation as Leonardo's self-portrait during the last years of his life is generally accepted nowadays. It is reminiscent of Gianpaolo Lomazzo's words from the late 16th century: "Leonardo's hair and beard were so long, and his eyebrows were so bushy, that he appeared to be the sheer idea of noble wisdom." In stylistic terms, however, including the use of parallel hatchings, the drawing could date from before 1500, which would mean that this could not be a self-portrait.

Opposite page:
Leonardo da Vinci
Vitruvian Man, ca. 1490
Pen, ink, and metalpoint on paper, 34.3 x 24.5 cm
Gallerie dell'Accademia, Venice, inv. 228

"The greatest gifts are often seen, in the course of nature, rained by celestial influences on human creatures; and sometimes, in supernatural fashion, beauty, grace, and talent are united beyond measure in one single person, in a manner that to whatever such an one turns his attention, his every action is so divine, that [it surpasses] all other men …" Thus wrote Vasari in 1550/1568 on Leonardo da Vinci.

Leonardo is an ideal representative of Renaissance man, because he distinguished himself in almost all the arts and sciences—physics, mechanics and engineering, mathematics and geometry, anatomy, geology, botany and geography, as well as music, architecture and sculpture—in order to become famous as an artist. He summarizes all his abilities in a letter of 1482 to Ludovico Sforza, offering to serve the Duke above all as a constructor of war machines and as an architect of buildings as well as water mains. Only at the end of the letter does he comment on art: "I can carry out sculpture in marble, bronze, and clay; and in painting can do any kind of work as well as any man, whoever he be."

In his treatise on painting, Leonardo demands knowledge of the character of nature. The painter must first understand the object before he can execute it with his hand and brush; for he should not simply depict nature like a "stupid" mirror. He must translate the three-dimensional world into the two-dimensional in such a way that it again appears to be three-dimensional. To this end, he must study nature and optics like a naturalist.

Leonardo was born on 15 April 1452, the illegitimate son of the notary Ser Piero di Antonio and a peasant girl, Catarina. He spent his childhood and youth in Vinci near Empoli, before being apprenticed around 1469 to Verrocchio (1435/36–1488). Although he was accepted as a member of the painters' guild in 1472, he remained with his teacher for at least a further four years. In 1482, he went to Milan, probably in order to create an equestrian statue. He worked on military and architectural projects for Ludovico Sforza as well as on urban planning, the mechanization of work processes,

and the efficiency of weapons of war. He designed sets for the stage and for celebrations. He became a scientist, who extended his knowledge by the study of books and ancient treatises and took up the pen himself. Natural observations, the growth of plants, and the origins of the earth were topics that fascinated him. In defiance of ecclesiastical prohibitions, he dissected corpses, and the anatomical knowledge he thus gained was applied to his paintings.

In 1499, Leonardo left Milan, to go via Mantua and Venice to the now republican city of Florence. In the summer of 1502, he entered the service of Cesare Borgia. In 1503, back in Florence, he undertook the painting of the *Battle of Anghiari* in the Palazzo Vecchio. The seven years from 1506 that he then spent mainly in Milan were dedicated primarily to anatomy. In 1513, he followed Giuliano de' Medici, the brother of the newly elected Pope Leo X (in office 1513–1521), to Rome, and after Giuliano's death in 1516 he went to serve the French king Francis I (1494–1547). He died in the latter's chateau of Clos-Lucé near Amboise in 1519.

Leonardo's personality remains a riddle. Physical beauty, strength, skillfulness, intelligence, eloquence, generosity, and open-handedness were accompanied by capriciousness and eccentricity. Since he failed to complete many projects, Leo X is said to have exclaimed about him: "Alas! This man will never do anything, for he begins by thinking of the end of the work, before the beginning."

In his *Self-Portrait* (left) he depicted himself with a long beard and a melancholy expression, as befitted the ideal picture of a philosopher. The painter Lomazzo (1538–1600) commented: "Leonardo's hair and beard were so long, and his eyebrows were so bushy, that he appeared to be the sheer idea of noble wisdom." On Leonardo's figures, the French poet Théophile Gautier wrote in 1857: "They seem to know what men do not know … their glances are as mysterious as they are deep, penetrating, wise, so that while they enchant, they disturb and give birth at once to fear and love."

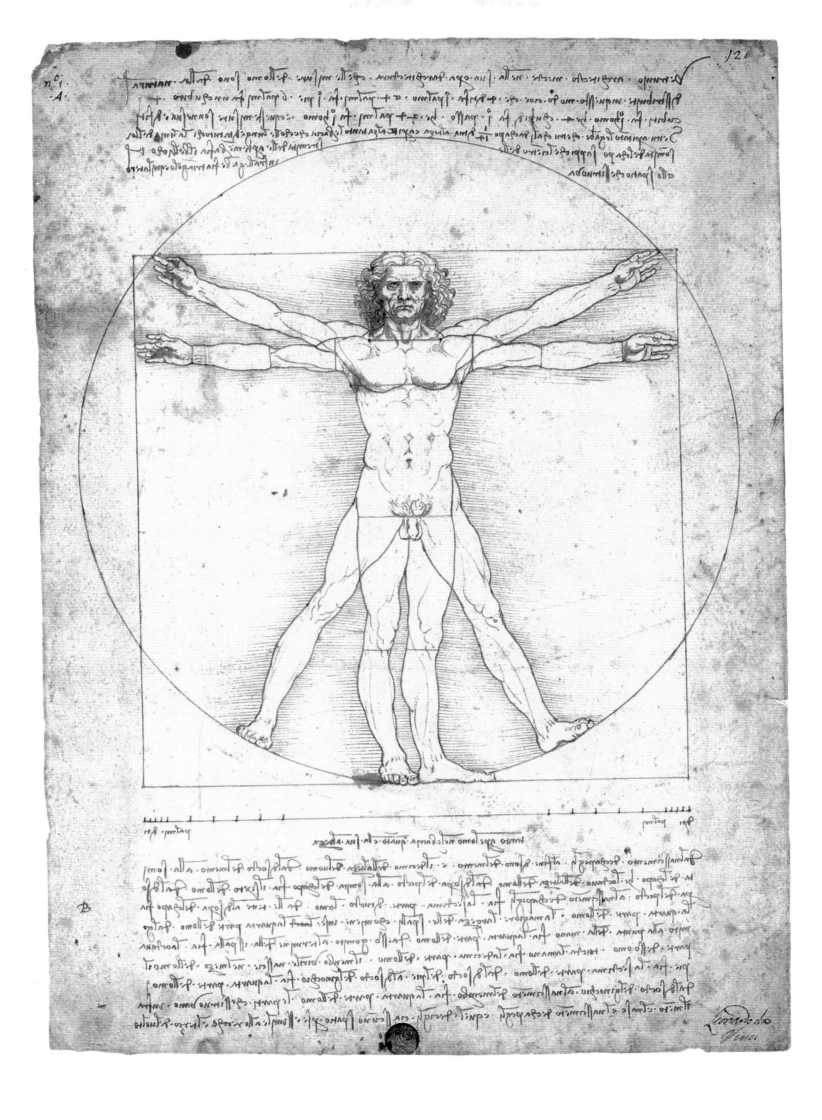

Beginnings in the Florence of the Medici: 1469–1481

Leonardo da Vinci
Landscape Drawing for Santa Maria delle Neve
on 5 August 1473
Pen and ink, 19 x 28.5 cm
Gabinetto dei Disegni e delle Stampe, Galleria degli
Uffizi, Florence, inv. 8 P

The landscape drawing probably shows the view from
Montalbano onto the Valdinievole area and the swamps
of Fucecchio. It is the first artistic work of Leonardo's that
is dated and can definitely be attributed to him, and is at
the same time a real rarity: it appears to be the first
known depiction of a landscape in Italian art that
reproduces an actually existing section of a landscape in
an original drawing.

The depiction of the tongue of hills with the fortress,
the lines of which partially cover the previously drawn
landscape, is a later addition on the part of Leonardo. It
was not drawn at the original location. There are also
weaknesses in the way the fortress is connected to the
scene perspectively, for it is not standing horizontally on
the ground. The striking waterfall also appears to be a
later addition. It is produced using plain yet powerful
strokes, making it unlikely that this was based on actual
observation. The water is falling into a pond, the extent
of which is undefined.

THE WORKSHOP OF
ANDREA DEL VERROCCHIO

The first significant note in Leonardo's artistic biography
is an entry on the occasion of his admission to the
Florentine guild of painters. According to this, Lionardo
di Ser Piero da Vinci, his full name, was allowed to
accept commissions as an independent Florentine
master from June 1472. His apprenticeship, which is
generally poorly documented in the case of Renaissance
artists, a rule to which Leonardo is no exception, had
been completed by this time. In about 1469, he had
commenced his apprenticeship with the sculptor and
goldsmith Andrea del Verrocchio (1435–1488) in
Florence. The city, which had been strongly influenced
by the Medici since 1434, had enjoyed an enormous
economic and cultural upturn since the Trecento. It had
been an artistic capital for two centuries and had risen to
become the greatest center of humanism, in which new
ideas and artistic developments fell on fertile ground.
One of the most renowned artists' workshops in the city

was that of Verrocchio. The range of commissions it
took on covered almost all artistic techniques: sculpture
and jewelry making as well as painting and architecture.
The range of activities and requirements of the
workshop meant that the apprentices received a varied
education that always, however, stressed the
importance of the drawn design (page 159). It was the
basis for a work produced in stone, marble, bronze,
clay, paint, or precious metal. Trained craftsmen who
were familiar with the artistic techniques and various
materials then appear to have been entrusted to
monitor the execution of these designs. Leonardo
himself was later to support the view that drawing was
the most important prerequisite in the training of an
artist, and his first biographer, Paolo Giovio, noted
that: "Until they [the students] were twenty years old,
he [Leonardo] utterly forbade them to work with
brushes and colors and only allowed them to practice
with a slate pencil …"

The first project involving Leonardo in Verrocchio's
workshop was the production of the dome lantern for
the Florentine cathedral of Santa Maria del Fiore. The
Florentine architect Brunelleschi (1377–1446) had
created a technical sensation in the form of the largest
self-supporting dome since antiquity. This was not
merely an achievement in terms of the statics and
structure; it also required new equipment to be
developed to enable the actual building process to be
carried out. After Brunelleschi's death, the
commission for the production and erection of the
unfinished top of the dome was awarded to the
Verrocchio workshop in about 1468. We know that
Leonardo was involved in this project from a note that
he wrote in about 1515, in which he remembers the
special welding technique used for the copper sphere
on the Cathedral's lantern. Leonardo was able to learn
the important fact that the artistic design was only a
stage in the realization of a project. Without taking
the necessary steps such as developing the right
welding process, testing it out on trial pieces,
managing transportation up to the roof of the dome,
ensuring there was a storm-proof anchoring, and
building a work scaffold, the successful outcome of
the project would have been in doubt. This early
familiarity with the running of extensive projects was
surely the prerequisite for his own later pleasure in
experimentation. In addition, it is likely that
Leonardo had already been allowed to see technical
drawings by Brunelleschi during the course of this
project, and these evidently inspired him when

making his own first designs for machines. Thus, for example, in order to create the large wall painting of the *Battle of Anghiari*, he designed a moving scaffold that allowed him to work quickly at any point on the entire surface of the painting. In 1478, Verrocchio's workshop was commissioned to produce a bronze equestrian monument. Leonardo was able to work on the project until about 1482, in the process learning the technical requirements for the production of such a monumental work in bronze. The experiences gathered in this way benefited him later when designing the equestrian monument for the duke of Milan, Ludovico Sforza. No independent works by Leonardo are known from his period of apprenticeship. This is why, in the search for his earliest work, a landscape drawing kept in the Uffizi (page 154) is all the more significant as he dated it, writing left-handed in his extraordinary mirror writing: "Today, on the day of Santa Maria delle Neve, 5 August 1473."

Leonardo's work as an artist starts with a sensation, for pure depictions of landscape, in other words of depicting directly observed nature, were a complete novelty during his time. While imitating nature was the central task of artists at the time, none of them had until then been so rigorous as to go out into the open and draw an actual landscape. Instead, it was customary to create a landscape in the workshop with the aid of sketches or elements copied from models. The landscape was seen as an accessory designed to support the central subject in compositions of the time, the human figure. Simple strokes are used to mark tree trunks and rapidly produced horizontal hatchings mark the crowns. If one compares this with depictions of trees from the Verrocchio workshop, it is noticeable that Leonardo was keeping to his conventions of depiction here. But already he was attempting to depict direct observations and perceptions such as the shimmering of the air in the glistening light. This effect does not, however, appear to have been deliberately aimed for, but rather to have been a chance product of his enthusiastic interpretation of the method of depicting trees. It can be considered certain that Leonardo produced this drawing in front of a real landscape. Thus, for example, the ensemble of the gorge that has been hollowed out by water and the differentiated treatment of the rocks and layers of stone in front of the broad landscape view are surely the result of a concrete observation which he executed using a range

of artistic devices. He used tapering hatchings and the opportunities for variation provided by the pen and ink to give the landscape a convincing sense of depth. He pressed firmly with the pen to create highlights, and used lighter strokes in the background of the picture. He used hatchings to follow the form and model the landscape; others run parallel and determine the light and dark sections. By including a fortress and placing an accent by means of an invented waterfall, Leonardo was able to raise the drawing to the level of an independent work and wrote on it at a point where the landscape achieves its ideal effect of depth. Precisely at that point, where the landscape is creating its greatest sense of depth, his writing emphasizes the contrast between the flat surface of the paper and the illusion of depth.

Andrea del Verrocchio and Leonardo da Vinci
The Baptism of Christ, ca. 1475–1478
Tempera and oil on wood, 177 x 151 cm
Galleria degli Uffizi, Florence

St. John the Baptist baptizes Jesus by pouring water over his head. The extended arms of God, the golden rays, the dove with outstretched wings, and the cruciform nimbus show that Jesus is the Son of God and part of the Trinity. Two angels on the riverbank are holding Jesus' garment. The composition is attributed to Verrocchio, although there can be no definite answer as to which artist produced it. The angel seen from behind and large sections of the landscape are now considered to be by Leonardo.

Leonardo da Vinci
The Madonna and Child with a Pomegranate, ca. 1470
Oil on wood, 15.7 x 12.8 cm
National Gallery of Art, Washington

The Madonna and Christ Child appear in a window,
the child standing on the balustrade below it. Mary
is holding a pomegranate that has been cut open, and
Christ has taken some of it, for he is showing Mary red
pearls of fruit that he is holding in his clumsy child's
hand. Mary appears melancholy, as if she knows about the
future Passion of her son, symbolized by the
pomegranate.

Opposite page:
Leonardo da Vinci (?)
The Madonna of the Carnation, ca. 1473–1476
Oil on wood, 62 x 47.5 cm
Alte Pinakothek, Bayerische Staatsgemäldesammlungen,
Munich

The authorship of this variation on the Madonna and
Child theme was disputed for a long time. The work was
attributed to both an unknown Flemish artist as well as
to Verrocchio and Leonardo. Mary is holding a red
carnation out to the Christ Child, who is attempting to
grasp it. The vividness of the boy, and his well-observed,
childishly clumsy movement does, however, suggest that
it was Leonardo's work. The convincing plastic quality of
the child indicates that during his early years Leonardo
may have worked in three dimensions, using either clay
or other sculptural techniques.

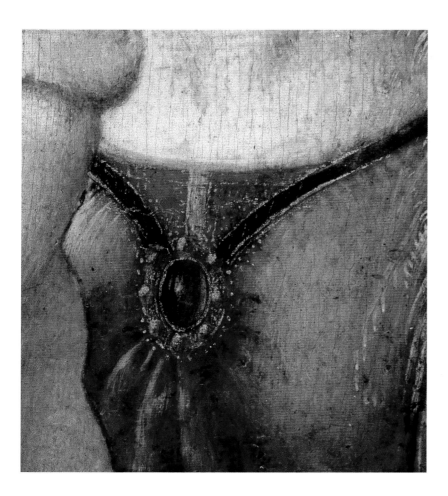

THE BEGINNINGS OF FLORENTINE OIL PAINTING

It is difficult for researchers to reconstruct the definite beginnings of Leonardo the painter. As a result of his membership of the Verrocchio workshop, he took part in pictures produced by the master together with his workshop. In the *Baptism of Christ* (page 155), for example, the angel seen from behind is thought to be Leonardo's contribution. Vasari writes about this painting to the effect that Verrocchio said he "would never touch colors again" after he had seen the grace of the figure created by Leonardo. But from what point Leonardo started to appear as an independent artist cannot be stated categorically. No more is known about his first independent commission other than that sources show it dates from 1478 and was for an altar in the Chapel of San Bernardo in the Florentine Palazzo Vecchio. On a drawing that also dates from 1478, Leonardo noted that he was in the process of working on two pictures of the Madonna. It is not until 1481, however, that we can reasonably confidently connect a commission to a painting that has been preserved: the unfinished panel of the *Adoration of the Magi* (page 172), which is now in the Uffizi in Florence.

The early work of Leonardo is a difficult field of research in more ways than just this because none of his paintings is signed and there are also no longer any sources for the earliest pictures now attributed to Leonardo. The only way of identifying them is by making stylistic comparisons between pictures, based on the art-historical principle that the works of a student are stylistically related to the works of the master. The paintings of the school of Verrocchio can be distinguished mainly by two characteristics: first of all, they demonstrate a closeness to Florentine models such as Filippo Lippi (ca. 1406–1469), and, secondly, they are characterized by an interest in the achievements of painting north of the Alps.

One of these was the use of oil as a paint medium for color pigments, a technique that first appeared in northern painting in the first half of the 15th century, and spread rapidly there. Italian art adopted this technique later. One of the first Florentine panel paintings known today to have been produced with a paint medium containing oil appears to have been the Washington *Madonna and Child with a Pomegranate* (page 156), which is assumed to have been created in about 1470. The panel, at 15.7 x 12.8 cm, is very small by Florentine standards, yet not at all an unusual format in Flemish painting. The Christ Child as well, with his fat tummy, overlong torso, and skinny little arms, differs from the widespread, generally more rounded Florentine type. For this reason it is still disputed whether the painting was created by an Italian painter, or by an artist from north of the Alps.

A drawing of the composition still in existence in Dresden is also not able to shed any light on the matter, as it is presumably a copy of the painting. This and a second picture, the *Madonna of the Carnation*

Above, left:
The Madonna and Child with a Pomegranate (detail page 156) Brooch

The painter of this work knew how to paint the varying reflections of light on the brooch in a striking manner. The material properties are depicted here with a brilliance unusual in Italy.

Above, right:
The Madonna of the Carnation (detail page 157) Brooch

The garment worn by Mary is similar at the neck and breast to the one worn by the *Madonna and Child with a Pomegranate* (page 156). The almost identical petticoat and similar brooch also prove the proximity of the two panels and make it more than likely that Leonardo was familiar with the *Madonna and Child with a Pomegranate* when composing his *Madonna of the Carnation*, irrespective of whether the work was produced by Leonardo himself or Verrocchio's workshop.

Opposite page:
Leonardo da Vinci (?)
Garment Study for a Seated Figure, ca. 1470–1484
Oil on canvas, 26.5 x 25.3 cm
Cabinet des Dessins, Musée du Louvre, Paris, inv. 2255

Garment studies were part of the training of every painter. It is likely that prepared materials were used for this in the workshops in Florence. On them, the students were above all able to study the depiction of light and shade, which is why these works appear to have been carried out primarily in one color. Several such garment studies at different levels of artistic ability survive, though their attribution is disputed. It is above all the fineness of this study that has led to its being attributed to Leonardo.

(page 157) in the Alte Pinakothek, Munich, whose attribution to Leonardo is broadly accepted nowadays, do at least demonstrate that the Verrocchio workshop was familiar with the *Madonna and Child with a Pomegranate.*

The type of head of the Munich Madonna corresponds to the works of the Verrocchio workshop, but the slightly more disorderly and, at the same time, more powerful depiction of the folds and the flowers enables the picture to stand out from those produced by other painters in the workshop and suggests that Leonardo's hand was at work (pages 164 above, and 165 below). For the first time, the rocky hills so typical of Leonardo's later landscapes appear in the background, but here they are probably derived from Florentine models such as the painting of the *Madonna and Child with Angels* by Filippo Lippi in the Uffizi.

The attribution to Leonardo of the *Annunciation* (page 162–163) in the Uffizi seems to be assured by a study of a sleeve that he made of the angel's garment, at least where that one figure is concerned. The painting is considered by various researchers to be a group work produced by several artists. This theory is, however, less convincing, and the panel rather appears to have been conceived by Leonardo, and executed by him as well. The unusual impression that the *Annunciation* panel makes, clearly showing the artist's passion for experimentation, demonstrates to us the attempt being made to characterize the figures, the place, the time, and the events in such a way that the observer is able to understand them visually. The characterization of the place, for example, conspicuously displays this attempt. According to tradition, Mary was visited at home by the angel. Usually in depictions of the Annunciation, she was placed in a building or shown in her room. The angel was a visitor, so he was placed in a garden, on a path, by a door or window, in order to show that he had just arrived. Leonardo moved the entire scene completely into the open, as a result of which he had to create a visual relationship between Mary and the building. In order to achieve this, he was not satisfied with merely assigning a building to Mary, but evidently also wanted to show that this was her home, because through the door we can make out the outlines of a bed. In order to create a visual link between the Virgin Mary and her bedchamber, the painter also draped Mary's blue cloak in three vertical folds, a rhythm that directs our gaze to the door and her red bed. The solution probably seemed so satisfactory to him that he was prepared to accept that, at first sight, Mary appears to have three legs. The noticeable attempt to determine the figures and the event more closely by means of "accessories" and assign these to the figures in a visually comprehensible manner is an important individual feature of this early work.

The conspicuous way in which Mary's garment is draped across her stomach suggests that the panel was produced at an early date. The Annunciation scene narrates the moment at which Mary learns of her pregnancy from the Archangel Gabriel. According to a long-held tradition, God was depicted as a half-length figure sending golden rays of light and the dove of the Holy Spirit down to Mary from heaven. In Florence, depictions started to appear in which only the dove and golden rays were shown. Filippo Lippi introduced a further innovation in his Florentine *Annunciation* in the Martelli Chapel in San Lorenzo, by depicting a conspicuous draping across Mary's stomach that was probably designed to make her pregnant state recognizable. Leonardo adopted this representational concept, but in addition to omitting God the Father, also for the first time omitted the dove, and represented the golden light by means of the golden color of the garment draped across her stomach. Leonardo applied this method of illustrating of the Immaculate Conception to several of his Madonna depictions, such as the later *Madonna of the Carnation* (page 157) and the *Madonna of the Rocks* (page 178). For this reason, the theory that several hands were at work on the *Annunciation* (pages 162–163) appears rather improbable. In this painting, rather, Leonardo created a first original example of the possibilities of pictorial language in painting.

The attribution of the *Portrait of Ginevra de' Benci* (page 166) to Leonardo has generally been accepted. This painting also has the special feature that on the one hand it reflects Flemish models and on the other hand symbolically characterizes the portrayed woman in an unusual manner: Leonardo places a juniper tree behind Ginevra de' Benci, which is a visual representation of her name (*ginepro* meaning "juniper" in Italian).

The portrait used to be dated to 1474, the year when Ginevra was married. A few years ago, it was possible to identify an emblem on the rear side of the panel as that belonging to the humanist Pietro Bembo (1470–1547), and this makes a later date more likely. Bembo had presumably commissioned the portrait between 1475 and 1476, the period during which he lived in Florence, for there are sources showing that he had an intellectual friendship with Ginevra.

The portrait of Ginevra de' Benci has been subjected to a technical examination, which helped to identify tracing marks and fingerprints. The latter indicate that Leonardo used the ball of the thumb or fingers to blur the damp oil colors in order to try to create more gentle transitions than he could achieve with the brush. Similar methods have in the meantime also been found on other paintings by Leonardo.

The painting of the *Benois Madonna* (page 167) surprises us because of the clear tectonics of the compositional structure and the powerful corporeality of the figures. The picture depicts Mary and the Christ Child in a hitherto unfamiliar degree of vividness. Mary is playfully, and with obvious pleasure holding

Leonardo da Vinci
Woman's Head, 1470–1476
Pen, ink, and white pigment on paper, 28.2 x 19.9 cm
Gabinetto dei Disegni e delle Stampe, Galleria degli Uffizi, Florence

The detailed drawing of a girl's head contains elements typical of the school of Verrocchio, such as the diagonally placed eyes with the considerably rounded pupils and hair painted in meticulous detail. A relationship between this drawing and the *Annunciation* predella (pages 164–165) in the Louvre has quite rightly been established. The attribution of the drawing to Leonardo is now just as disputed as its dating.

Leonardo da Vinci
The Annunciation, ca. 1470–1473
Oil and tempera on wood, 98 x 217 cm
Galleria degli Uffizi, Florence

The Archangel Gabriel is kneeling as a dignified profile figure and raising his right hand in greeting to Mary, indicating her divine pregnancy. The Virgin has stopped reading and reacts to the Annunciation with an expression of deep respect indicated by the gesture made with her left hand. There is a conspicuous mistake in her depiction: her right arm had to be painted too long proportionally, so that, despite her seated position, it would still be able to depict the impressive position of her hand over the *prie-dieu*. Leonardo depicted Mary in a three-quarter profile in front of the corner of a room. All three spatial co-ordinates—height, width, and depth—converge on this point, thus creating a sense of depth in the picture as well as enhancing the importance of Mary. Her head clearly contrasts with the dark wall and her body is emphatically framed by the cornerstones whose parallel lines are converging on her.

Leonardo da Vinci or Lorenzo di Credi
The Annunciation, ca. 1478–1482
Oil on wood, 16 x 60 cm
Musée du Louvre, Paris

This Annunciation predella was originally part of the
altar of the Madonna di Piazza in the cathedral of Pistoia,
commissioned from Verrocchio and produced between
1475 and 1485 with the assistance of Lorenzo di Credi
in Verrocchio's workshop. Leonardo's participation in
the work on the altar is the subject of debate. While the
predella panel is reminiscent of Leonardo's great
Annunciation (pages 162–163), it does, however, display
what by Leonardo's standards is an atypical weakness in
the control of the surface, for the angel has been moved
too close to Mary.

The Annunciation (detail pages 162–163) Flowers

In the Christian calendar, the Annunciation is celebrated on
25 March. This time of year is indicated in the way the earth is
covered with grasses and flowers. The leaves stylistically match the
flowers in the painting of the *Madonna of the Carnation* (page 157).

The Annunciation (detail pages 162–163) Festoon

The festoon on Mary's stone *prie-dieu*, with its plants painted in grisaille, is striving for the same vividness as the natural flowers on the panel. The competition between painting and sculpture also becomes obvious if one looks at the little band with which the posy is fastened to the volute; it would be difficult for a sculptor to realize such delicacy.

The Madonna of the Carnation (detail page 157) Flowers

In this detail, the lively rhythm of the foliage, and the modeling by means of edges of light such as those on the leaf halves, testify to the painter's mastery.

Leonardo da Vinci
Portrait of Ginevra de' Benci, ca. 1475/76
Oil on wood, 38.8 x 36.7 cm, trimmed at the bottom edge
National Gallery of Art, Washington

The portrait of the Florentine Ginevra de' Benci was first suggested to be a work of Leonardo's by Gustav von Waagen in 1866, and Wilhelm von Bode was later able to identify the woman depicted as a Florentine lady called Ginevra de' Benci, whose portrait Vasari had already mentioned. About 12–15 centimeters (5–6 inches) of the panel have been cut off at the bottom. The majority of researchers assume that hands were originally painted there, though a convincing reconstruction has yet to be produced. The pale color of her face is conspicuous, and it is possibly meant to reflect the poor state of health that sources tell us Ginevra de' Benci was in. The strict symmetry of her hair which frames her face, and above all the strong contrast with the dark background of the juniper tree, causes the face to look hard and linear, though also particularly fascinating.

out a flower to the naked, rounded baby. He is gazing at it in concentration and attempts to grasp it with his still awkward baby hands. The child's concentrated effort, as well as his proportions, strongly suggest that Leonardo was using his direct observations of a child, which was unusual for this subject matter. That Leonardo made studies using living models on the theme of the Madonna and Child is proven by a beautiful series of sketches for the *Madonna and Child with a Cat*, which attempts to capture a variety of moments in the child's game with the animal. These studies found their expression in the painting of the *Benois Madonna*. The figures are more natural, their actions are more convincing and lifelike. In terms of quality, the picture is already so original that no Florentine painter other than Leonardo could conceivably be its author.

ALBERTI'S INFLUENCE: HISTORY PAINTING AND PERSPECTIVE

In 1436, Leon Battista Alberti (1404–1472) completed his Italian edition of the three books of *De Pictura (On Painting),* the contents of which were soon to find their way into the general knowledge of Florentine artists. As there was no predecessor on which Alberti could base his theoretical undertaking, he made use of a classical work on the principles of rhetoric when formulating his theory of painting: the *Training of an Orator* by the Roman writer Quintilian (ca. AD 35–95). While on the one hand Quintilian explained the high art of rhetorical investigation of a topic, the work on the other hand also contained direct comparisons with painting. According to Alberti, the central task of both rhetoric and painting was to convince the public to perceive something that was not really there. One medium achieved this by means of words, facial expressions, and gestures, and the other with figures in pictures.

Another classical text, the *Historia Naturalis* or encyclopedia of nature by Pliny the Elder (ca. AD 24–79), had an effect on Alberti and the Renaissance that cannot be rated too highly. Pliny, who also wrote about painting and sculpture, considered the highest goal of painting to be to produce an illusory imitation of reality. This was to have a determining influence on the Renaissance and, to a particular degree, on Leonardo. In connection with this, Pliny wrote about a competition in which the two painters Parrhasius and Zeuxis agreed to take part. Zeuxis painted grapes that were so deceptively realistic that birds flew down to peck at them; Parrhasius, however, set up a curtain that was painted so realistically that Zeuxis, who was so proud of the judgment of the birds, demanded that the curtain should finally be removed and the picture behind it revealed. When he realized his error, he awarded the prize to Parrhasius in sincere admiration and embarrassment, saying that he may have been able

to deceive birds, but the other had managed to deceive him, an artist. Later on, Pliny narrates another event involving Zeuxis, who is supposed to have said about a painting that: "I painted the grapes better than the boy because if he had also been a perfect creation of mine, the birds would have had cause to be afraid."

What Zeuxis had not succeeded in doing in Pliny's second example was to form the main object of painting during the Renaissance: the human figure. It was depicted either in altar paintings or in history

Leonardo da Vinci
The Madonna and Child (*Benois Madonna*), ca. 1478–1480
Oil on wood, transferred to canvas, 48 x 31 cm
Hermitage, St. Petersburg

Mary and her child are naturally engrossed in their game, and their gazes make them appear lifelike to a degree that can be found in no contemporary Italian painting of the Madonna. Leonardo achieved this quality by means of nature studies. In 1478, he noted that he was working on two Madonnas. The *Benois Madonna* can be dated to that period. The painting has in its present condition been overpainted in some places and has lost some of the paint layer.

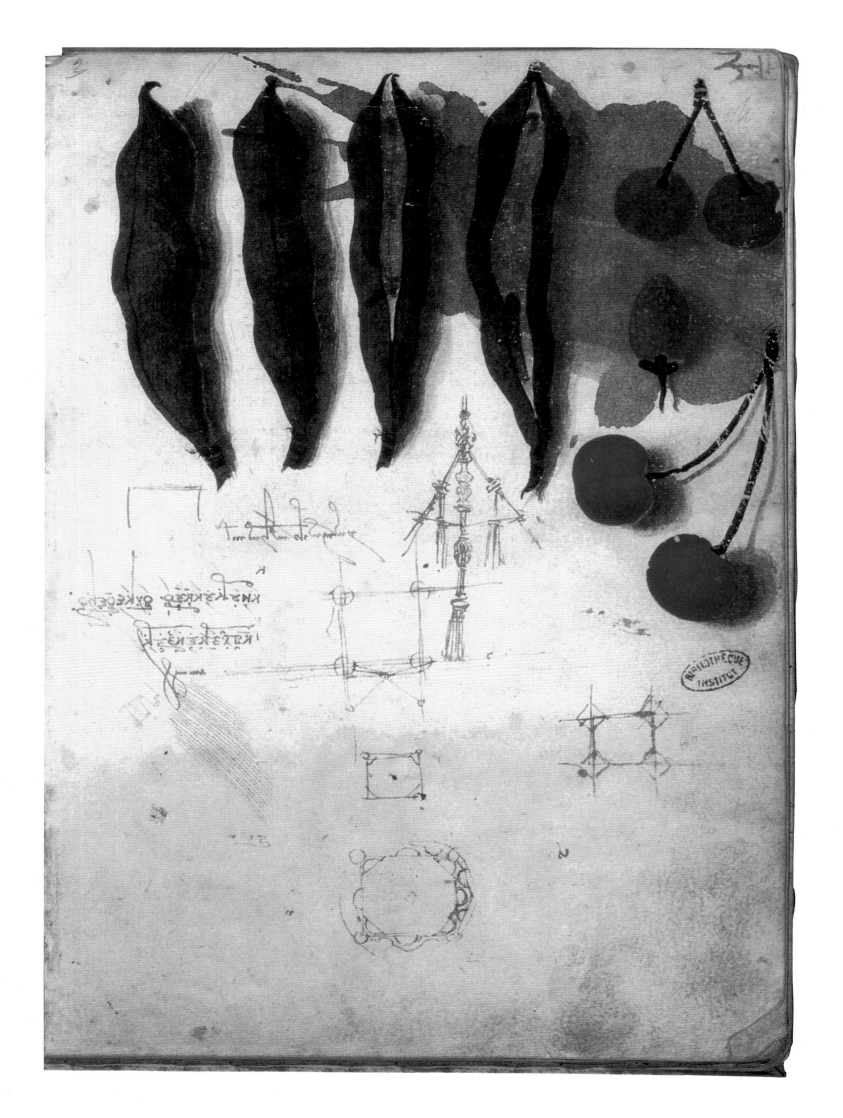

paintings whose themes included historical events, in episodes from the Bible, in stories from classical mythology, and in portraits.

Alberti considered the history painting to be the most venerable genre in painting. Portraits should be similar to those depicted and the person portrayed should appear lifelike. He rejected the conception of the picture as held by the Byzantine or Greek traditions, the painting of icons, which was remote from nature. Leonardo made the following comment: "That painting which comes closest to the object it is imitating deserves the most praise. I state this to the bewilderment of those painters who want to correct the works of nature, such as those who paint a one-year-old child whose head is in actual fact a fifth the size of the entire body, while they paint it as if it were an eighth the size of it … and they have made this mistake so frequently and seen others make it, that it has become something of a custom with them, which has forced its way into their odd judgment and taken root there to such a degree that they are now themselves convinced that nature, and those who imitate nature, are making a great mistake by not doing as they do." Leonardo's criticism shows that Alberti's conception of painting as an imitation of nature was not immediately accepted by artists of the period. Above all, this new formulation was slow in entering the main field of painting, the area of religious art, as these were works that did not merely have to obey aesthetic points of view but primarily had to correspond to the requirements of religious teachings and liturgy.

Alberti incorporated a variety of classical ideas into his treatise. But he personally held the distinction of presenting for the first time a newly developed method of depiction which created a new quality in the imitation of nature, and which was not even known in the classical age that he so greatly admired: central perspective.

While central perspective played an important role for Leonardo, it would increasingly make way for his own developments. The early religious paintings, above all the *Adoration of the Magi* (page 172) in the Uffizi in Florence, are based on perspectival constructions, but what connects *St. Jerome* (page 170) to the *Adoration of the Magi* is less a matter of perspective than of their comparable condition: neither painting was finished, except for an under-painting in shades of brown.

Leonardo's depiction of St. Jerome is impressive largely because of the two-dimensional ornamental arrangement of the figures as well as the enormous perspectival depth of the landscape. The under-painting establishes the levels of brightness of the composition. The dark surface of the rock formations and landscape in the foreground cuts St. Jerome and the lion out like silhouettes. The light surfaces next to them contrast greatly, and afford views onto the landscape lying beyond. The artist relieved the figure of the saint of the manner of representation that had been conventional until then and which depicted him as a small penitent figure on both knees at the edge of the picture. Leonardo also decided not to give Jerome his usual attributes of cardinal's hat and book. The lion, necessary in order for the saint to be identified, has lost its exclusively symbolic function in order to become a more natural-seeming animal. Leonardo thereby distanced himself from the traditional iconography, though nonetheless managing to execute the required theme with a hitherto unknown intensity by depicting St. Jerome not as a Holy Father of the Church but as a beardless emaciated penitent.

It is not known who commissioned the panel, nor why it remained unfinished. Equally, the picture of St. Jerome has not been definitely dated, as is the case with so many of Leonardo's paintings. On the one hand, due to the similar painting technique, it is reminiscent of the *Adoration of the Magi* (page 172), also an unfinished under-painting, but on the other hand the convincing anatomical depiction of the figures suggests that it might be a work dating from the 1490s.

Leonard da Vinci
Fruit, Vegetables, and Other Studies, ca. 1487-1489
Pen, ink, and coloring on paper, 23.5 x 17.6 cm
Institut de France, Paris, Ms. B, fol. 2r

The pods and fruit are painted in color over a large ink blot. This "watercolor" is unique amongst Leonardo's surviving works on paper and can, together with the lunettes of the *Last Supper* (pages 190–191), be considered a precursor of the still-life genre. The sheet is part of the oldest remaining manuscript by Leonardo. In addition to architectural studies, the codex also contains designs for military equipment and flying machines.

Leonardo da Vinci
St. Jerome, ca. 1480
Oil on wood, 103 x 75 cm
Pinacoteca Apostolica Vaticana, Vatican, Rome

In about 370, St. Jerome, later a Father of the Church, is said to have
withdrawn to live as a hermit in the desert of Chalcis near Antioch, in
order to produce a translation of the Bible and live as an ascetic. Leonardo
depicts him as a penitent, not a scholar. St. Jerome is kneeling in a humble
posture that arouses our sympathy, in front of the sketched cross of Christ
on the right, and before him lies the lion, his key attribute. In his right
hand he is holding a stone with which he is striking his breast. The section
around the head was sawn out in the 18th century and not replaced and
restored until the 19th century.

The unfinished *Adoration of the Magi*, commissioned in 1481, combines the three-dimensionality of the figures with a perspectival construction in the background. Mary and the Child, and the middle and youngest magi in the foreground, form a triangle whose peak is Mary's head; for the first time, figures in Leonardo's work come together in the form of a *figura piramidale*. Mary and the two magi are not under-painted, but indicated in only gentle light and shade. It is possible that they were left out so that they could be executed using particularly pure, magnificent colors. This procedure is unthinkable in Leonardo's late work. In his writings, he later criticized this technique: "That which is beautiful is not always best; and I say this about painters who are so very concerned with the beauty of colors that they apply them, not without care, creating very weak and almost imperceptible shadows, not appearing to care about the three-dimensional appearance. And this mistake makes them smooth-talkers without any substance."

Even though the panel remained unfinished, the *Adoration of the Magi*, with its symmetrically composed main group that differs from the traditional linear composition, is now considered one of the most progressive works in Florentine painting. It puts into practice the demands Alberti made of history paintings in a way no other work in its era does. All the figures are involved in the events in the picture. The distinguished magi display their emotions in a more dignified manner than the accompanying figures around them, and the overall number of participants is kept within moderation. The figures are grouped in a circle around Mary and are expressing, with more or less vigorous gestures, their emotion at the first demonstration of divinity of the Christ Child.

Several drawings are considered to be potential preparatory studies for the *Adoration of the Magi*. In addition to a central perspective study of the ruined building in the background, which was given a roof carried by supports in order to clarify the proportions

Leonardo da Vinci
War Chariot, ca. 1485
Silverpoint, pen, and ink on paper, 21 x 29.2 cm
Biblioteca Reale, Turin, inv. 15583

The careful composition of the page suggests that Leonardo intended to present this drawing to someone. It is possible that it was included in the letter of introduction to Ludovico "il Moro" de' Medici, to whom Leonardo described himself as being mainly a military engineer and military architect. The page is convincing not so much as a result of the technical solutions of the chariot as by the convincing visualization. It is uncertain whether the actual technology sketched here was Leonardo's own invention. He would undoubtedly have been familiar with such classical chariots, fitted with scythes, from treatises.

Leonardo da Vinci
The Adoration of the Magi, ca. 1481/1482
Oil on panel, 243 x 246 cm
Galleria degli Uffizi, Florence

Since the Early Christian era, the 6 January has been celebrated as the feast of Epiphany, the appearance of God amongst men in the form of Jesus Christ. Mankind is represented by the Three Magi, who are paying homage to the Messiah. The fall of the pagan world began

at the same time as his appearance. Leonardo appears to have depicted this moment, so dramatic in human history, in his panel. It remained unfinished because Leonardo left Florence and moved to Milan, though we do not know why he did so. Chemical reactions and soiling mean it is now difficult to read this fascinating panel in detail.

Leonardo does not depict the stable with the ox and ass, but takes the account of the Evangelist Matthew more

seriously than most other painters; for contrary to custom the Wise Men from the East lack all signs of royal dignity. An adoration by several individuals was imagined as a ceremonial, which naturally gave precedence to the eldest person. Leonardo's individuality now shows itself in the choice of the moment depicted: the eldest Magus, after paying tribute, remains, deeply moved, on the ground to the right of the Madonna, that is, to her left in the image, while the Christ Child turns toward the middle one.

Filippino Lippi
The Adoration of the Magi, 1496
Oil on panel, 258 x 243 cm
Galleria degli Uffizi, Florence

Although Leonardo broke off his work on his *Adoration of the Magi* (page 172), his design remained authoritative for Filippino Lippi, who was only slightly younger. Filippino retains the composition around the central group of Mary with the Child, but he also follows pictorial tradition in including the ox and ass as well as the stable, which has become a sheltering roof. In the same spirit, he shows Joseph's new role and the turning of the Christ Child toward the eldest magus.

(page 175), a variety of studies of the postures of individual figures exist. This large number of differing types of drawings leads us to conclude that the composition of the panel was worked out very thoroughly.

The painting also differs from the traditional way of depicting the Adoration in Florence by means of the puzzling scenes in the background, the equestrian battles, and an unfinished staircase. This led to the assumption that the Augustinian convent of San Donato in Scopeto, which had commissioned the picture, wanted to use this picture composition in order to convey its own theological interpretation of the Adoration theme. But irrespective of such a theologically learned interpretation, the picture develops its peculiar fascination in its narration of the most varied frames of mind and the compositional connection of the individual groups. This power of attraction is, of course, further intensified by its unfinished state—just as is the case with the picture of St. Jerome. It is certain that there would have been

unfinished paintings produced by other Renaissance painters that did not survive the intervening years. The mastery of Leonardo's works, however, was recognized at an early stage, and they were preserved even though, judged purely by criteria of craftsmanship, they were abandoned works.

The first undisputed work by Leonardo da Vinci, which according to the contract had to be delivered within 30 months, was probably unfinished because Leonardo left Florence in 1481/82 and went to Milan. It is not known what caused him to leave. Vasari's account that he personally conveyed a musical instrument which he had himself designed as a gift from Lorenzo de' Medici (1449–1492) to Ludovico Sforza also fails to explain his move. Amongst Leonardo's papers there exists a draft letter of application to the duke of Milan in which he extols his universal abilities as an engineer, architect, sculptor, and painter. It is, however, disputed whether this letter might not have been written later in Milan, once he had already settled there.

BREAKTHROUGH IN THE MILAN OF THE SFORZA: 1482–1499

Leonardo da Vinci
Head of a Young Woman, ca. 1483
Silverpoint and white heightening on prepared paper,
18.1 x 15.9 cm
Biblioteca Reale, Turin, inv. 15572r

The eminent art expert Bernhard Berenson called this sheet "the most beautiful drawing in the world." It is thought to be a study for the angel in the *Madonna of the Rocks* (page 178).

After the murder of his older brother Galeazzo Maria Sforza (1444–1476) in 1480, Ludovico Sforza (1452–1508), called "il Moro" (the "Moor"), had taken over the guardianship of his brother's son and in doing so seized power in Milan. Galeazzo Maria had already had an equestrian monument put up to his father Francesco Sforza; Leonardo received from Ludovico the commission for a new monument, and worked on it from 1485 until the French invasion in 1499. His first sketch shows a rearing horse, under whose front hooves lies a vanquished warrior; this motif was an allusion to the name Sforza, meaning "strength."

The rearing horse represented such challenges in terms of statics and bronze casting that its execution was repeatedly postponed. In 1489 there were fruitless attempts to engage a specialist from Florence. On 23 April 1490 the artist noted: "Began again on the horse." In June he traveled to Pavia with the architect and engineer Francesco di Giorgio Martini (1439–1502); there he viewed the classical equestrian monument of the Regisole, now destroyed.

Leonardo was so impressed by the skillfully rendered movement of the trotting horse that he gave up following the models of contemporary works such as Verrocchio's *Colleoni* (in the Campo di Santi Giovanni e Pado, Venice). Compared with monuments such as the *Marcus Aurelius* on the Roman Capitol, this bronze appears as stiff, excessively tense, and inhibited as Leonardo's own first design. Back in Milan, he gave up this idea, and now began to study the anatomy and proportions of living horses.

In 1493, on the occasion of the engagement of Ludovico's niece Bianca Maria to Maximilian I (1463–1519), the life-size model of the horse in "earthen material" was unveiled. It was more than 7 meters (23 feet) tall and surpassed everything known until then. Whether the rider was already in place is still uncertain; his casting was perhaps to be carried out later. In the praise of his ruler, but even more in artistry, monumentality, and lively portrayal at the same time, Leonardo was striking out on new paths.

However, in 1494 the 158,000 pounds of bronze that had been collected for the casting was melted down for weapons. In 1499, the French destroyed the model. As late as 1504 casting moulds still existed, in the possession of the French king. During his second stay in Milan, in 1510, Leonardo was once again planning an equestrian monument, this time for Gian Giacomo Trivulzio. Some drawings of horses, all with French watermarks and perhaps dating from the last three years of Leonardo's life, suggest that he was also working on an equestrian monument for Francis I.

The Milan years brought about an important change in Leonardo's character. There he started to read books selectively in his endeavor to raise his experiments, investigations, and observations to a scientific level, and systematized his methods of research. His intensive studies of nature, and the corresponding concentration on the theory of painting, soon made him a recognized member of the circle of scholars at the Milan court. Until this time, his paintings had been influenced by his investigation of traditional methods of depiction. In the process he had already been attempting to produce a more lifelike expression by producing new inner links between the figures in pictures and their surroundings.

The *Madonna of the Rocks* (page 178) in the Louvre was the first picture that Leonardo produced in Milan. The painting is the central panel of a larger altar that the convent of San Francesco Grande had commissioned from Leonardo and two of his pupils, the brothers Ambrogio and Evangelista De Predis (ca. 1455–ca. 1508) and the sculptor Giacomo del Maino (provably active 1469–1502) for its Chapel of the Immaculate Conception. There is no documentation relating to the structure of the altar and its figural program, as the chapel was torn down in the 18th century and the structure of the altar can only be reconstructed in a sketchy manner from the confraternity's documents.

The contract for the *Madonna of the Rocks*, which dates from 25 April 1483, also lists the figural program. According to this, Leonardo was required to paint two prophets and angels on the main panel showing Mary

Leonardo da Vinci
The Madonna of the Rocks, ca. 1483–1486
Oil on panel, transferred to canvas,
199 x 122 cm
Musée du Louvre, Paris

The painting is an early example of the later
more frequent depiction of the dogma relating
to the Immaculate Conception of Mary. The
name of the picture reflects an iconographical
peculiarity: the religious figures are depicted in
a rocky grotto and sitting on a stone ground.
The figures are subjected to a strict spatial
arrangement called a pyramidal composition.
The painting had a considerable influence on
Leonardo's artistic colleagues in Lombardy.

Leonardo and his Workshop
The Madonna of the Rocks, ca. 1495–1508
Oil on panel, 189.5 x 120 cm
The National Gallery, London

The second version of the *Madonna of the Rocks* was produced with the assistance of Leonardo's workshop. It was in the Milan church of San Francesco Grande until bought by an Englishman in 1785. It must therefore have replaced the Louvre version (page 178) in the church at some unspecified point in time. The function of this version is disputed to this day. The side panels with figures of angels by Boltraffio that once belonged to this picture are also in London.

and the Christ Child, but the painting in the Louvre only has one angel, the young St. John, and Mary and the Child. It is therefore assumed that the length of the negotiations between the Franciscans and Leonardo about the altar, which lasted until 1508, were caused by a breach of contract by the artist.

Apart from the panel in the Louvre, two further versions of the painting exist; one is in the National Gallery in London (page 179) and is attributed to Leonardo with the collaboration of his assistants and dated to around 1508. The second is in a private collection. The fact that both versions differ only minimally from the painting in the Louvre, and that the reasons behind these repetitions are not known, is a further unsolved aspect connected to this project.

In this commission, Leonardo was not able to make use of any traditional means of depiction, even though something in the manner of a *sacra conversazione* would have been conceivable. As in the structure of his

Annunciation (pages 162–163), he developed pictorial relationships regarding the interaction of the figures that continue to be very difficult to interpret. While the work is generally connected with the theme of the Immaculate Conception, so far it has not been possible to devise any convincing way of reading the picture.

The figures are woven together in a pyramidal composition by means of gestures and gazes, and the angel gazing out of the picture enables the observer to participate in the events in the painting. The figures are given a three-dimensional modeling through light and shade, and, in a manner comparable to his early Madonnas, placed in front of a dark background from which, on either side, one can gaze into the distance. Thus in this painting Leonardo achieved a backlit effect which by far exceeds his sensitivity before this date in the depiction of surface, space, and light, and this alone makes the Paris *Madonna of the Rocks* (page 178) one of his great masterpieces.

The Madonna of the Rocks (detail page 178)

In the background, the dark rocky grotto extends into a monumental rocky landscape that merges into the diffuse light, its numerous vistas giving the painting an enormous sense of perspectival depth.

Opposite page:
The Madonna of the Rocks (detail page 178)
Christ Child and Angel

In contrast with traditional iconography, Leonardo has not conceived Mary and the Christ Child as a closely united group, but has placed Jesus beneath his mother's hand next to an angel on the right side of the picture. In accordance with the composition of the group of figures which are connected to each other by means of glances and gestures, the angel has embraced him; his finger, however, is pointing at the small St. John in the Mother of God's arms who is adoring the Christ Child, whose hand is raised in blessing, entirely in the traditional manner.

THE FLORENTINE APELLES AND THE DEPICTION OF MAN

The so-called *Portrait of a Musician* in the Milan Pinacoteca Ambrosiana is the only remaining male portrait by Leonardo. Its attribution is now generally accepted. The picture shows a young man with a cap in a three-quarter view facing towards the right. Only his raised right hand is depicted, holding an unfolded sheet of music. The results of an examination of the painting have proven that the hand and the sheet of music were produced using a different technique from the rest of the figure, which suggests that it was reworked at a later date. Whether Leonardo or another artist was responsible for this, and when it occurred, is something we can only speculate about.

The dating of the painting to Leonardo's first years in Milan is suggested by a particular type of Flemish portrait that was derived from the work of Jan van Eyck (ca. 1390–1441) and would probably have been known at the Milan court because of the painter Zanetto Bugatto, who was trained in Flanders. A dark background, a strong three-dimensional character of the head, as well as a vivid gaze and the depiction of both hands were typical features of this type of portrait. Antonello da Messina (ca. 1430–1479), another Italian painter who was committed to the Flemish style, could also have been a possible model for the client and via him for Leonardo himself. Antonello probably spent a short period in Milan during 1475. His portraits are placed against a dark background, do not normally show the hands, and are captivating due to a particular vitality about the eyes.

Leonardo's client appears to have wanted his portrait to be carried out in this or a similar style, for the musician certainly has a concentrated and alert expression, though where he is looking remains concealed from the observer. His tightly curled hair is brightened by delicate heightening. But there is an important difference between this and portraits by Flemish masters and Antonello: the head is modeled more powerfully by light and shade. Leonardo was endeavoring to achieve a pronounced *rilievo* and as a result, on the finely glazed flesh tones, he achieved a play of light more sophisticated than any other painter in Milan at the time could have been expected to achieve.

The later addition of the hand with the sheet of music, which is the device that makes it possible to identify the subject matter of the portrait, could have been inspired by the works of another Flemish artist. Hans Memling (1433–1494), who lived in Bruges, painted several portraits that show only one of the portrayed person's hands. Occasionally, the person is holding an object such as a letter, as in the male portrait in the Uffizi. It is possible that Leonardo did not find out about this type of Flemish portrait until after he finished his painting, and was as a result inspired to rework his picture. The concentrated gaze and the position of the hand focus the portrait on one moment, as if the musician is waiting for his entry.

In the early 1490s, Leonardo formulated his conception of painting for the first time. It was probably one of the customs at the Milan court for the scholars to represent their own disciplines in discussion groups. According to Alberti's beliefs, painting was also one of the sciences, as it was based on mathematical principles. Due to his familiarity with architectural treatises, Leonardo had already received an initial theoretical grounding, but it appears that he did not study Alberti's writings on painting in more detail until he had the idea of writing his own treatise on the subject.

In Alberti's writings, a point is the simplest principle in the science of painting, and can be used to construct a line, which in turn produces the surface that is the

Leonardo da Vinci
Portrait of a Musician, ca. 1485
Oil on wood, 43 x 31 cm
Biblioteca Pinacoteca Ambrosiana, Milan

It was not until 1904 that the hand and sheet of music were discovered underneath over-paintings, and it is these that have given the painting its present title. Since this discovery, efforts have also been made to identify the person depicted. The names of two important court musicians in Milan during that period are known: Franchino Gaffurio (1451–1522) and Josquin des Prés (ca. 1450–1521). But there is no clear indication enabling us to identify either of these two in this portrait.

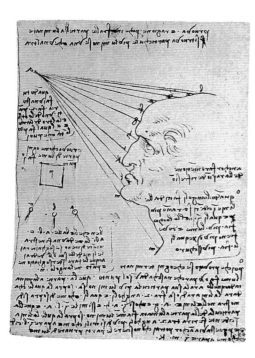

Leonardo da Vinci
Study of the Effect of Light on a Profile, 1487–1490
Black chalk, pen, and ink on paper, 20.3 x 14.3 cm
Gabinetto dei Disegni e delle Stampe, Galleria degli
Uffizi, Florence

"*Rilievo* is the soul and the highest goal of painting," it
says in his book on painting. Leonardo made a very
precise study of the distribution of light and shade. In the
drawing he shows clearly the gradation of light on the
face when it comes from a single source above. This page
is considered to be an early indication of the preparation
of a theoretical treatise on painting.

Right:
Leonardo da Vinci
Male Head in Profile with Proportions, ca. 1490
Pen and ink on paper, 28 x 22.2 cm
Gallerie dell'Accademia, Venice, inv. 236v

This profile head contains notes on proportion such as
"the size of the figure is eight heads." Above the notes on
the left is a circle with a line through it, meaning that the
text was included by Melzi in the treatise on painting.
Leonardo produced not only studies of the proportions of
the human head, but also a table in which he recorded all
possible types of noses. In addition, he combined various
forms of foreheads and chins as well as different types of
noses and mouths.

Opposite page:
Leonardo da Vinci
Group with Five Heads, ca. 1494
Pen and ink on paper, 26 x 20.5 cm
Gabinetto dei Disegni e delle Stampe, Galleria degli
Uffizi, Florence

It has not so far been possible to come up with a
convincing interpretation of these five types. The figure
wearing the laurel wreath is thought to be a portrait. At
any rate, it is the main figure in the group, because with
its profile view it is occupying the most dignified
position, and the others are arranged about this figure.
Leonardo recognized that the moving parts of the face,
such as the eyebrows, eyes, and mouth, were a
prerequisite for the expression of various emotions such as
laughing and crying, anger and fear.

actual medium of painting. The visible part of bodies is
made up of surfaces. If painting wants to imitate
nature, the corporeal or three-dimensional world, it
has to use surfaces to produce the illusion of bodies.
Surfaces are colors and their appearance depends on
the quantity and type of light. "He [Leonardo] felt
nothing to be more important than the rules of optics,
and on it he founded the principles of the distribution
of light and shade," Paolo Giovio wrote in about 1527.

It was principally on the distinction between it and
other imitative arts such as poetry, music, and
sculpture that Leonardo based his conception that
painting was superior to all other arts, above all poetry,
which was highly regarded. First of all, painting was
dependent upon the most important of the senses:
sight. Further, it could narrate a story just as well as a
poem, but surpassed the latter in three respects: first of
all, painting is not tied to any language and is therefore
universally understandable; secondly, it is able to
present an entire story in an instant, whereas poetry
can only string pieces of information together; thirdly,
it shows everything as if it were real. The result is that
the observer is directly affected by it.

Painting surpasses music because music dies away,
but painting is beauty preserved for eternity. It
surpasses sculpture as the sculptor cannot control all
the elements himself, for his works exist in real space
and depend on real lighting conditions. The fact that
the painter can and must depict all dimensions of
nature that can be perceived by the eye makes him an
almost divine creator. In his paintings, he can create a
nature that is so realistic that nature itself is deceived,
such as the birds fooled by the painted grapes in the
episode narrated by Pliny. But he can also create things
that do not exist in nature, such as a fabulous creature,
by creating a hybrid of known parts of animals that
then looks like a possible creature.

Even caricatures of people in the sense of an exaggerated characterization of a person's outward
appearance can be depicted. They are, in the end, based
on studies of nature in which individual sections of expressive heads are exaggerated. In addition to this,
Leonardo stylized individual shapes of noses, eyes, and
mouths and studied their expression with regard to the
appearance of a figure. He used the individual forms of
a face, which reveal a certain type of character, to
investigate people. The puzzling grouping of five heads
on a sheet (page 185) shows how strongly the movable
section of the face around the mouth and chin
determine the expression. Apart from the dignified
profile figure in the foreground, it is the view of the
wide-open mouth in the background that is particularly
impressive.

Leonardo formulated the superiority of the painter
compared to the other artistic genres in the following
words, which also describe the divine act of creation: "In
fact whatever exists in the universe, in essence, in
appearance, in the imagination, the painter has first in his
mind and then in his hand; and these are of such
excellence that they can present a proportioned and
harmonious view of the whole, that can be seen

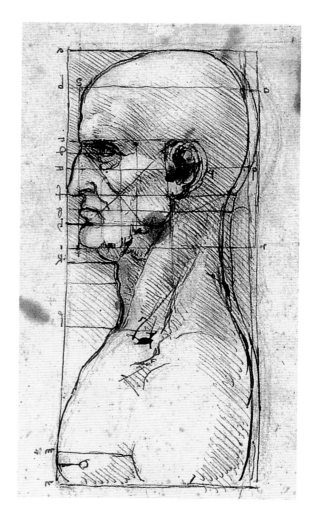

simultaneously, at one glance, just as things in nature."
This phrasing places particular emphasis on an artist's
hands, to which both painters and sculptors had attached
considerable importance since the High Renaissance.

Leonardo's main definition of painting concerned
man: "A good painter has two chief objects to paint,
man and the intention of his soul; the former is easy,
the latter hard, because he has to represent it by the
attitudes and movements of the limbs. The knowledge
of these should be acquired by observing the dumb
because their movements are more natural than those
of any other class of persons."

It is possible that Leonardo was familiar with the
definition of all the imitative arts that the Greek
philosopher Aristotle (ca. 387–322 BC) had written on
in his treatise on poetry. For the first printed book in the
Greek language had appeared in Milan, and evidence
exists that there was a circle of scholars who were familiar
with classical Greek texts. Aristotle's view was that the
object of imitation in art was "men in action" whose
destiny lay between the opposites of worthy and lowly. It
was possible for the classical philosopher to portray the
human character within this scale.

The *Portrait of Cecilia Gallerani* (page 187), known
as the *Lady with the Ermine*, is an important turning
point in Leonardo's painting, first suggested in the reworked version of the *Musician* (page 182). Leonardo
did not interpret man as an outer shape to be imitated,

Leonardo da Vinci
Isabella d'Este, 1500
Black chalk, red chalk, and yellow pastel chalk on paper,
63 x 46 cm
Cabinet des Dessins, Musée du Louvre, Paris,
inv. M. I. 753

This drawing shows Isabella d'Este. Holes were
made in it so that it could be transferred to a painting
surface, but these perforations do not match all the
details of the drawing precisely, in some places correcting
them with great sensitivity. Leonardo probably produced
these perforations himself. The cartoon has clearly been
trimmed and is in a poor state of preservation, so that it
is no longer possible to state with any certainty whether
the unusual coloring with colored chalks was produced
by Leonardo himself.

Opposite page:
Leonardo da Vinci
Portrait of Cecilia Gallerani (*Lady with the Ermine*),
ca. 1490
Oil on panel, 54.8 x 40.3 cm
Czartoryski Museum, Cracow

Cecilia Gallerani is holding the heraldic animal of
Ludovico "il Moro" in her arms. She was his favorite and
gave birth to his child in the same year as he married
Beatrice d'Este. The charming and vivid impression
Cecilia makes gained Leonardo the reputation of being a
talented portrait painter.

but instead viewed him as a speaking individual with a specific emotional constitution. Here, too, something that is not identified has attracted the attention of the portrayed woman; she has turned and is looking over her shoulder, and the ermine across her arm appears to be following the same urge. The observer is attracted by the woman's behavior, wants to know what she is curious about, and in so doing imitates her mental state. In this, Leonardo made use of a phenomenon of painting that Aristotle had already mentioned in his *Poetics*: the inborn tendency to imitate.

In both genres of painting, the portrait and the history painting, it was Leonardo's opinion that giving a figure a soul was a vital factor in the credibility of what was depicted. In this respect Leonardo exceeds the requirements of Alberti, who had only imagined men of action in connection with history paintings. "If they [painted figures] are not endowed by their creator with lively actions according to the intention that you imagine to be in such a figure, [it] will be judged twice dead; dead because it is not alive, and dead in its action," Leonardo noted.

In his *Portrait of Cecilia Gallerani*, the artist is incorporating the observer into a work, building up tension in him without easing it. In his curiosity, the observer is repeatedly referred back to the depicted woman. In Leonardo's words, a painting presented in such perfection would cause "lovers to speak to the portrait of the thing loved as if it were alive."

The *Portrait of Cecilia Gallerani* (page 187), together with the *Portrait of Ginevra de' Benci* (page 166) has been scientifically investigated. The proof of smears caused by the same hand on both works supports their attribution to Leonardo. During the course of this examination, it was also determined that the plain background behind Cecilia Gallerani never included a window, as was thought for so long.

Leonardo used the unusual portrait of Cecilia Gallerani as a proof of his skillfulness when Isabella d'Este of Mantua became interested in having a portrait done. She was an important patron of the arts in Italy and the sister-in-law of Ludovico "il Moro," and in 1498 requested the picture in order to be able to see for herself just how high the quality of Leonardo's portraits was. In an accompanying letter, Cecilia Gallerani remarked that there was little similarity with her present appearance, as she was still young at the time the portrait was produced. This comment is an important clue as to the dating of the painting.

The fashion of the clothes of the portrayed woman was introduced to Milan by Isabella d'Aragon, who married a Sforza in 1489. For that reason, the portrait can scarcely have been produced before 1490. Because old sources show that Cecilia Gallerani was already twenty-five years old at that time, her identification with the portrayed young woman was long treated with reservation, despite the fact that the Greek word *galè* means "ermine," and the valuable furred animal on the woman's arm was hence a visual pictorial embodiment of her name. Only recently have archives been discovered that prove that the dates of Gallerani's life were copied incorrectly, and that Cecilia Gallerani was just seventeen years old in 1490.

Leonardo left Milan towards the end of 1499 and stopped off in Mantua before traveling on to Venice, where he was probably commissioned by the city to produce a defensive structure in Friuli to counter an imminent Turkish invasion. In Mantua before this, he made one or several drawings portraying Isabella d'Este, and it was probably there that he produced a cartoon. In March 1500, the portrait of Isabella was with Leonardo in Venice, as reported by an eyewitness. In 1501, Isabella d'Este asked for another copy of her portrait.

In the Louvre in Paris there exists a cartoon of a female portrait that has been linked to this commission (page 186). Comparisons of the woman depicted there with a medal have confirmed her identity as Isabella d'Este. The cartoon is, however, in an exceptionally poor state of preservation, but is artistically superior to two other surviving paintings in Florence and Windsor Castle, making the attribution of the Paris portrait to Leonardo appear likely. The portrait suggests that

Isabella d'Este made two requests of Leonardo: first of all to be depicted in the profile view, which was considered to be particularly dignified, and at the same time to appear as vivid as the young Cecilia Gallerani in her portrait.

Leonardo succeeded in combining these two elements by once again having the figure react to some stimulus that is not visible to the observer. Despite her almost frontal posture, Isabella has turned her head so far to one side that it appears as if by chance in a precise profile. This vigorous quality can be clearly perceived despite the poor condition of the cartoon in the Louvre. But one of the copies is useful for reconstructing the incomplete lower section in the Paris portrait. At the lower edge one can see the woman's right hand, and one can only guess at the position of the left arm. The right hand is already reminiscent of the *Mona Lisa* (page 201), but the index finger is, as if by chance, pointing to a book lying on the balustrade on the right. This is how Leonardo characterized Isabella d'Este as an educated woman, which is how she is also described in contemporary sources.

IMAGES WITH THE POWER OF SPEECH: THE *LAST SUPPER* IN MILAN

After Ludovico "il Moro" was made duke of Milan in 1494, he decided to make the monastery of Santa Maria delle Grazie his family's burial place. This is the context within which Leonardo was probably commissioned to decorate the monks' dining room, the refectory, with a depiction of the Last Supper.

Leonardo's *Last Supper* (pages 190–191) is not the only wall painting in the refectory. On the opposite wall is a large Crucifixion by the local painter Donato Montorfano, which was completed in 1495 according to an inscription. Both themes were frequently depicted in monastic dining halls in Tuscany. The commission from the Dominican monks for the Crucifixion appears to have gone out before that for the Last Supper, for Ludovico "il Moro" would surely have made use of a more important painter once he had decided that the monastery of Santa Maria delle Grazie was to be his family mausoleum.

Leonardo's *Last Supper* is indisputably one of the most famous and important works in the history of painting. The quality of the wall painting was recognized within a very short space of time after its completion; copies were produced of it and its praises were sung in contemporary sources. After conquering Milan in 1499, the French king is even said to have expressed the desire to bring it to France, but his advisors were apparently able to dissuade him on the grounds that, given the technology of the time, transporting the painting would have been tantamount to destroying it.

Scarcely twenty years after the completion of the work, the traveler Antonio de Beatis reported that,

while the wall painting was *excellentissima*, it was already starting to come to pieces, possibly because the wall had absorbed water. Ever since, every generation has worried and made efforts to a greater or lesser degree to preserve this work. In 1943, during an air raid, a bomb exploded in the refectory of the monastery of Santa Maria delle Grazie and destroyed the roof and the wall to the right of the *Last Supper* right down to the foundations; the work of art, protected by sand bags, fortunately survived this catastrophe largely unscathed.

From 1980, and for a period of twenty years, work was carried out away from the public view on the mural, which had been severely damaged by air pollution and the stream of visitors in all weathers. Today, only a few tourists are admitted for a short time behind a protective screen. The technically demanding restoration by Professor Brambilla and her team was determined by the problematic decision to expose faulty areas, to remove over-paintings, and to preserve only the original condition. The sole exception to this are the wall hangings, where large parts of the over-paintings have been left intact. This measure has uncovered an extremely large number of missing sections, though on the other hand for the first time in centuries it is possible to make out the quality of the work. Colorful reflections of the Apostles' garments on the metal containers have been revealed, as has an extremely subtle depiction of light and shade. The restoration did not merely bring the original colors to light, it also made it possible to examine the construction of the paint layers and the methods of painting used. They confirm a contemporary account according to which Leonardo worked very slowly at the painting and occasionally only painted a few strokes during the course of a day. So slow a method of working would not have been possible if the usual fresco technique had been used for the wall painting, as the paint pigments had to be applied to a moist layer of plaster allowing them to bond with it as it dried.

As in all his major undertakings, Leonardo had thought through the conditions of production and sought a new technical solution for the process of painting. He decided in favor of mixed media and painted over two ground layers using oil and tempera paints, as was done in panel painting. Pietro C. Marani, the Milan curator responsible for the *Last Supper*, feels this particular technique is partially responsible for the fact that the disintegration of the work set in so early, given the unfavorable climatic conditions.

It cannot be determined exactly when the commission went to Leonardo. The completion of the painting in 1498, in contrast, is documented by a reference to it by the monk and mathematician Luca Pacioli in his book *De divina proportione*.

There are differing opinions amongst art researchers as to which episode from the Gospels is depicted in the *Last Supper*. Some consider it to portray the moment at which Jesus has announced the presence of a traitor and the Apostles are all reacting with astonishment; others feel that it also represents the introduction of the celebration of the Eucharist by Jesus, who is pointing

to the bread and wine with his hands. And yet others feel it depicts the moment when Judas, by reaching for the bread at the same moment as Jesus as related in the Gospel of St. Luke (22: 21), reveals himself to be the traitor. In the end, none of the interpretations is convincing, as none of them takes into account Leonardo's conception of painting.

From the time of the Gallerani portrait (page 187), Leonardo developed his paintings by basing his designs on "men in action." As he wrote in his treatise on painting: "A picture, or rather the figures therein, should be represented in such a way that the spectator may easily recognize the purpose in their minds by their attitudes"—as if they had the power of speech.

Once the event had been selected, the least important part of the work of a painter according to Leonardo's own account, he first sketched a rough overall composition in which the figures already made a recognizable contribution to the overall events in terms of posture and gestures (pages 194, 195). If the figures were depicted engaged in a conversation, the emotional state of the speaker, and what was being conveyed, had to be clear from posture, gesture, and facial expression. So he had to start by developing this pictorial plan before he could start working out the individual figures in more detail (page 193), tightening the composition and turning it into a vivid, yet harmonic overall arrangement.

The existing structure of the picture shows that Leonardo's painting of the *Last Supper* was constructed symmetrically according to the laws of central perspective, with a main figure in the center. According to this pictorial logic, as well as the theme upon which the painting is based, Jesus is the main figure in the picture. He is physically and psychologically isolated

Leonardo da Vinci
Apostle's Head and Architectural Study,
ca. 1494–1498
Red chalk, pen, and ink on paper
Gabinetto dei Disegni e delle Stampe, Galleria degli Uffizi, Florence

This head is a study for St. James the Great in which Leonardo was concerned mainly with investigating the expression of the figure. The open mouth and widened gaze create the impression of astonishment. In addition, the sheet includes an architectural study in ink, a design for an aesthetic solution to the corner of a fortress wall, probably representing Leonardo the architect rather than Leonardo the builder of fortresses.

Opposite page:
The Last Supper (detail pages 190–191)
Jesus Christ

The central scene shows Jesus—easily recognized by the gesture of his hand—preparing the Eucharist. Goethe did not make a correct interpretation of this scene as he wrote his description based on an engraving that omitted an important detail: the wine glass to which Jesus is pointing with his right hand.

from the other figures and with his hands is pointing to the bread and wine, making the introduction of the Eucharist the central event (page 192). In Leonardo's conception, the other figures are reacting directly to Jesus, and at the same time, some of them are coming into contact with each other.

James the Great, whose mouth is opened in astonishment, is sitting on the right next to Jesus, and spreading out his arms as if trying to say to the two disciples behind him, who are attempting to command the attention of Jesus with their eloquent gestures and the way they are pushing forward, that they should be quiet and listen.

James the Less, the second from the left, places his hand on Peter's back, while Andrew next to him is still holding his hands before him and speaking, but his eyes are already seeking out Jesus. Peter and John are facing each other deep in conversation, just like the group of three on the far right who still seem to be animatedly discussing the previous announcement of the existence of a traitor.

That this announcement has indeed already taken place is proven by the behavior of John and Peter. In contrast with the usual manner of depiction, in which John is lying against Christ's chest, here Leonardo refers to the Gospel of St. John (13: 24): "Simon Peter therefore beckoned to him, that he should ask who it should be of whom he spake."

By combining these two apostles into a group with Judas in this manner, Leonardo was distancing himself from the traditional scheme of depiction used for Last Suppers, according to which Peter and John sat to the right and left of Jesus. In contrast to the other Apostles, however, he characterized them so clearly that they are

easily identified. He identified Peter by means of the threatening dagger that he would, at dawn, use to cut off the ear of Malchus, one of the soldiers arresting Jesus. John, the favorite disciple, is wearing red and blue garments as is Jesus, and is seated at his right hand, the most honorable place. But Judas above all was clearly characterized by Leonardo, for he was not, as was customary, placed in the center of the picture in front of the table, but placed amongst the row of disciples. He is identified by means of several motifs, such as his reaching for the bread, the purse containing the reward for his treachery, and the knocking over of a saltcellar, a sign of misfortune. Leonardo even formally expressed his isolation from the group by depicting him as the only one whose upper body is leaning against the table, shrinking back from Jesus.

Hence, Leonardo's Last Supper is not a depiction of a simple or sequential action, but interweaves the individual events narrated in the Gospels—from the announcement of the presence of a traitor to the introduction of the Eucharist—to such an extent that the moment depicted is a meeting of the two events. As a result, the disciples' reactions relate both to the past and subsequent events. At the same time, however, the introduction of the Eucharist clearly remains the central event.

Everyone who has personally stood in the refectory in Milan before the Last Supper can confirm that the painting is experienced as an illusory continuation of the real space. That Leonardo created this effect entirely deliberately is shown by the fact that the lighting in the picture corresponds to the light entering through the real windows in the lunettes on the left refectory wall. Researchers have, however, discovered

Leonardo da Vinci
Study for the Last Supper (detail), ca. 1494/1495
Pen and ink on paper, 26.6 x 21.4 cm
Royal Library, Windsor, RL 12542r

The sketched design of the *Last Supper* shows that Leonardo at first planned to simply show the moment at which the presence of a traitor is announced. He enlarged this scene somewhat to the right, depicting it in more detail. Next to Jesus, John is sitting leaning on the table. Judas is, in keeping with tradition, depicted in front of the table and is rising in order to take the bread, thereby identifying himself as the traitor.

that at no point where the observer stands is the pretended continuation of the hall into the pictorial space entirely successful, which would have had to be the case if Leonardo had attempted to achieve this effect using a central perspective construction.

A small observation can, perhaps, qualify this objection. If one stands on the right and looks at the *Last Supper,* the painted space continues almost without a break on the left wall of the refectory; and if one stands on the left, the illusion on the right works. However, if one stands directly in front of the picture, it is the ceiling that determines the main impression and creates the illusion that the refectory continues into the pictorial space. The ideal position for an observer appears to have been avoided out of knowledge of the real use of the refectory, for the monks sat on benches along the long walls. The table of the prior, which might have been considered the worthy position for the ideal viewpoint, does not at first appear to have stood opposite the *Last Supper,* but directly beneath it, for Leonardo's wall painting starts at the precise height of the furniture at the time, a wooden pew. The Crucifixion scene on the opposite wall, in contrast, extends almost to the floor. Not until

later was the seat removed from beneath the *Last Supper,* a doorway made in the middle of the wall and the prior's table placed opposite the painting, just as the German poet Goethe was to find the tables arranged years later when he visited Milan.

Avoiding the ideal viewpoint can possibly only be explained in that, if the laws of perspective had been properly applied, the observer would have to be looking at the underside of the Last Supper table, for he stands significantly lower than the lower edge of the wall painting. Leonardo himself made the following comment on this problem: "A painted figure, if one is looking down at it from above, will always appear as if one is looking down at it from above, even when the eye of the observer is lower than the picture."

So Leonardo's pictorial composition was not determined by geometry; his goal was the visual coherence of the scene. For the first time, the *Last Supper* clearly showed the paradox that characterized Leonardo's painting: "Those who want to produce a deceptively real imitation of nature must not copy nature but deceive the observer. The latter can only, however, be achieved by someone who is familiar with nature and the laws of perception."

Leonardo's Workshop
Study for the Last Supper, ca. 1494/1495
Red chalk on paper, 26 x 39.2 cm
Gallerie dell'Accademia, Venice, inv. 254

This sheet is one of the most remarkable drawings to have been connected with Leonardo. The composition is strongly reminiscent of the *Last Supper.* One thing there is total agreement about, however, is that the stiff figures were not drawn by Leonardo. But it is possible that he produced preliminary sketches of some of them and that they were drawn by a pupil. Whatever the case, the mirror writing is a sign that Leonardo used this piece of paper.

COMMISSIONS IN THE REPUBLIC OF FLORENCE: 1500–1506

Leonardo da Vinci
*Study of St. Anne, the Virgin Mary, the Christ Child,
and the Infant St. John*, ca. 1501–1506
Pencil, pen, and ink on paper
Gallerie dell'Accademia, Venice, inv. 230

The first idea of this composition featuring St. Anne
was that the Christ Child and St. Anne would both be
bending down to the lamb. Leonardo also conceived
Anne in a second position, with her head leaning towards
Mary, though her hand is still resting on the neck of the
lamb. Behind the group he placed a landscape that does
not yet have the form of that in the Louvre painting.
The compositional sketch precedes the sheet with the
compositional sketches for the *Burlington House
Cartoon* (page 197).

Opposite page:
Leonardo da Vinci
Burlington House Cartoon, ca. 1503–1510
Black chalk, white lead on paper, 141.5 x 104 cm
The National Gallery, London, inv. 6337

The cartoon of the *Virgin and Child with St. Anne
and the Infant St. John* is one of the principal works in
the National Gallery in London. In 1986, a vandal shot
at the cartoon and severely damaged it around the area
of Mary's chest. Restorers had an opportunity to examine
the cartoon while repairing it. They could discover no
sign on it that it was used either by Leonardo or any other
artist at a later date for transferring the design to another
medium. In the Pinacoteca Ambrosiana there is a Holy
Family attributed to Bernardino Luini. It corresponds
precisely to the figural composition of the London
cartoon, with the exception that Joseph is added in the
background on the right.

During the years Leonardo was working on the *Last
Supper,* he was also commissioned by Ludovico Sforza
to decorate some halls in the Castello Sforzesco. After
completing them, he noted with resignation that under
the circumstances there could be no more talk of the
"horse." For when Milan fell to the French in battle,
Leonardo moved to Florence again. Before the move to
Florence, it is possible that after staying in Venice he
spent a short time in Rome, which can be deduced
from a note in which the villa of Hadrian in Tivoli is
mentioned. That would have been the first occasion on
which Leonardo encountered a large quantity of
classical works of art. In contrast to many of his
colleagues, however, Leonardo cannot be proven to
have adopted ideas directly from classical models,
although he studied them and was very well acquainted
with their qualities such as grace, movement, and
vividness. This, together with an over-interpretation of
a note that he wrote, until very recently led to the
incorrect conception that Leonardo had rejected the
classical era, which is considered the most important
source of knowledge for the Renaissance artist.
However, one can reach a different conclusion by
remembering the entry concerning the equestrian
monument of the Regisole in Pavia.

A further note written by Leonardo can possibly shed
some light on his attitude to models: "It is a sorry pupil
who cannot outdo his teacher [in this case classical
art]." Here Leonardo was formulating an artistic
standard that derives from orientation to a model.
Appropriating knowledge by copying or repeating is the
basis for recognizing stylistic qualities in the works of
art that have been handed down. Proficiency is
expressed not in the supreme mastery of formal and
craftsman-like methods, but in the interpretation in
which one's own visual language is expressed. The
quotation, in addition to this, reveals a scientifically
working Renaissance artist who believed that extending
one's level of knowledge would produce a continual
improvement of art.

In Florence, Leonardo was given accommodation by
the Servite monks, who according to Vasari,
commissioned him to produce a high altar painting
showing a Virgin of the Annunciation. The theme of
the picture is not completely clear. According to Vasari,
he presented a cartoon of St. Anne, the Virgin Mary, the
Christ Child, the infant St. John, and the lamb, that is
said to have created a sensation. Whether the
composition is identical to the commissioned altarpiece
is, however, not clear from Vasari's writing.

In addition, no drawn plan by Leonardo survives
which contains both the young St. John and the lamb.
Therefore one must assume that Vasari made up a
cartoon based on oral traditions, which he admitted
never having seen as the cartoon was allegedly in
France at the time. It is likely that Vasari is referring to
a group of Leonardo's works which he created showing
the Virgin and St. Anne

WAYS OF NARRATING RELIGION: THE VIRGIN AND ST. ANNE COMPOSITIONS

The worship of St. Anne, which did not begin until the
late Middle Ages, does not derive from any biblical
sources regarding Mary's mother. During the course of
the increasingly important worship of the Virgin,
however, the parents of the Mother of God, Anne and
Joachim, continued to grow in importance, though
Joachim, like Christ's foster-father Joseph, played a
subordinate role. This is the background against which
the development of the theme of depictions of St. Anne
needs to be viewed. In Italy, it was mainly the Byzantine
tradition that was formally followed, by depicting the
Christ Child on Mary's lap, who in turn is seated on the
lap of her mother Anne. At the beginning of the 15th
century, the icon-like stylization of the Byzantine
pictorial form was broken up in Florentine art by
Masaccio (1401–1428), who used a method of
depiction that was based more strongly on observation.
The problem of characterizing two equally large women
as mother and daughter, and at the same time
representing the allusion to the sequence of generations
in an obvious manner, was solved by Masaccio by
placing Mary at Anne's feet (Volume I, page 229).

In the last quarter of the 15th century, the worship of
St. Anne was given an additional boost by the Church
when Sixtus IV (1414–1484, pope from 1471)
would—which was unusual—only grant an
indulgence if the simple prayer had been spoken in
front of a picture of *Anna metterza* (St. Anne with the
Madonna and Child). Alexander VI (1430–1503,
pope from 1492), even combined a prayer to St. Anne
with 10,000 years of indulgences for mortal sins and
20,000 years for venial sins.

This is the context within which Leonardo's interest
in the theme of depictions of St. Anne needs to be seen.

In 1501, the vicar-general of the Carmelites, Fra Pietro da Novellara, noted in a letter to Isabella d'Este, whose Florentine art agent he was, that Leonardo was working on a cartoon including St. Anne. He also described the iconography and included an interpretation of the picture: "On it, a Christ Child is depicted, about one year old, who seems to be wriggling free of his mother's arms and climbing on top of a lamb, apparently in order to throw his arms around its neck. The mother, however, seems to want to move from the lap of St. Anne, where she is sitting, in order to grasp hold of the child and pull it away from the lamb, the sacrificial animal which is a sign of his Passion. St. Anne for her part is rising a little from her seat in order, as it seems, to prevent her daughter from pulling the child away from the lamb; this is possibly meant to represent the Church, which would not wish the sufferings of Christ to be prevented. These figures, although they are depicted in full, fit into a small cartoon as they are all either sitting or leaning forward and each of them is more or less standing in front of the other, in a row to the left; this design is not yet finished, though."

A drawing discovered some years ago in a private collection in Geneva, made by someone in Leonardo's circle, shows a composition that matches Novellara's description. At the beginning of our century, a painting in Berlin (destroyed by fire during World War II), which was considered to be the work of an artist working in Florence at the beginning of the 16th century, was linked with Novellara's description. The picture evidently had the same composition. Two other versions of this painting do, however, still exist in Paris and Madrid.

Leonardo worked on compositions with St. Anne until the end of his life. The painting in the Louvre (page 199) is the last work in the series for which, shortly before his death, he produced detailed studies for Mary's garments (page 189). The composition convincingly reflects the elements that Leonardo had acquired during these years in Florence. Balanced bodies making extensive movements, a clear rhythm, and inspired figures combined to form a painting of classic dimensions. The plasticity of the forms and the depth of space in the picture, with the mountains merging into the fog, are exemplary. The conception of the work dates to the time when he once more moved from Florence to Milan.

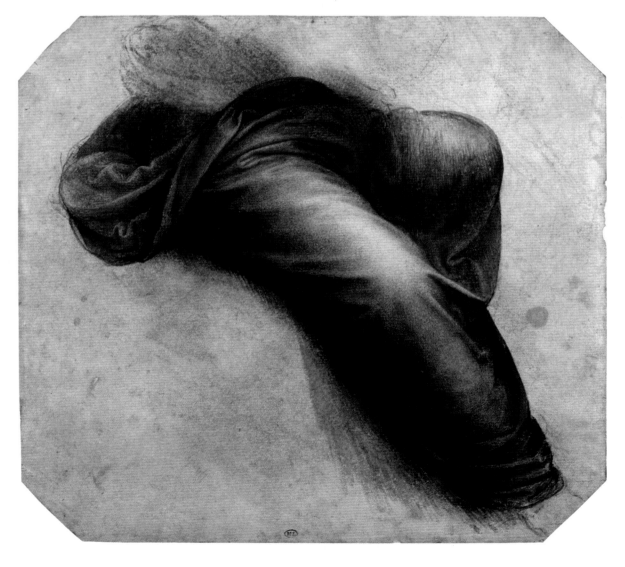

Leonardo da Vinci
Study for the Virgin and Child with St. Anne,
ca. 1503–1517
Black chalk, wash, and white heightening on paper,
23 x 24.5 cm
Cabinet des Dessins, Musée du Louvre, Paris, inv. 2257

The study of Mary's garment has been produced very sensitively. Leonardo used blue and brown washes to give the black garment an impressive delicateness. A second, similarly skillful study in Windsor makes it clear just how carefully he prepared this painting.

Opposite page:
Leonardo da Vinci
The Virgin and Child with St. Anne,
ca. 1508–1518
Oil on panel, 168 x 130 cm
Musée du Louvre, Paris

Mary's gaze is melancholy. She has recognized that her son must suffer his future fate. Her body still seems to be showing the tension of the previous moment when she wanted to pull her child away from the lamb, the symbol of his future suffering. St. Anne is watching the events benevolently. The pyramidal composition is dynamic, yet harmoniously balanced. The colossal sense of depth created by the mountainous landscape gives the painting a perceptible peacefulness and greatness.

MILAN AND ROME 1506–1516/17: THE *MONA LISA* AND *THE LAST SUPPER*

Leonardo da Vinci
Mona Lisa, ca. 1510–1515
Oil on wood, 77 x 53 cm
Musée du Louvre, Paris

From the darkness of the foreground, the bust of a woman in a dark garment emerges, culminating in a gentle face that is turned towards the observer. A smile flits across her face, but her gaze suggests a more serious mood. A slight twisting of her neck, compared to the three-quarter profile of her bust, gives a certain tension to the outline of her neck, and her head is just a little more in profile and almost imperceptibly more vertical. A plain garment swirls about her body, but the fall of the material shows its value. The light is flashing gently across transparent veils. Her only ornaments are a decorative border at her low neckline, which is accompanied by a plaited ornament—one of Leonardo's favorite patterns— and the delicate pleats of the valuable material. The woman needs no jewelry, necklace or rings to emphasize her exceptional quality, her natural elegance is enough. Behind her a low wall with two carved columns accentuates the middle distance in order to enable one to gaze into a peculiarly low lying quiet landscape. Only a road on the left and a bridge on the right show that people have had a formative effect on this inhospitable mountain range.

The woman is sitting on a chair, leaning forward slightly so that her weight when sitting is also spread onto her left lower arm, which is resting heavily on the back of the chair. Her right arm emerges from the depths of the picture, passes through the space, and its hand rests elegantly on top of her left arm. Its little finger is pressed down by the weight of the relaxed hand, and one can directly sense the gentle tactile experience of the outer fingertip of her ring finger touching the wooden chair arm (page 202). Her left hand, in contrast, is active and her fingers are grasping the chair, each finger in a different manner; the little finger has a special role, it is elegantly extended. Gentle light plays on the skin sections and models them so three-dimensionally that they appear alive, surrounded by an atmosphere that deepens increasingly towards the depths of the landscape.

No other picture in the history of European painting is as well known or has proved so fascinating as Leonardo da Vinci's *Mona Lisa* (opposite page). Her enigmatic smile has repeatedly given rise to speculation and during the course of the years has become a topos for the magical dimension of a work of art. The exceptional status of the painting has been achieved not least by its technical mastery, which is as admired as its polished composition. But it is also the case that no other work of art has been exploited to such a degree to further a certain conception of art, and nowadays the original seems almost to disappear behind the countless reproductions. After World War I, Marcel Duchamp was still able to increase people's awareness of the work of art by declaring a Mona Lisa with a mustache to be his work of art. And in 1963 Andy Warhol in his own way criticized the urge to duplicate the Mona Lisa by his silk-screened image of her with countless reproduction, and thus in his way once again posed questions about the original. While it was possible for a Florentine craftsman to steal the panel from the Louvre in 1911 for patriotic reasons, it is now protected from attacks behind armored glass.

The expression of the unknown woman is depicted as softly and sensitively as the flowing of her garment. The naturalness and sensuousness with which her hands are lying on the arm of the chair, and their subdued color, create a peculiar and yet harmonious atmosphere that contrasts with the unusual landscape. Beyond this, in this painting Leonardo was attempting to produce something unique: he was simulating binocular or "two-eyed vision." It is not only the mysterious smile of the portrayed woman that makes this one of the most famous paintings in the world.

An attentive observer will find the most diverse peculiarities in this painting. First of all, the figural composition is reminiscent of the pyramidal form that was noticeable in both the *Adoration of the Magi* (page 172) and the *Madonna of the Rocks* (page 178). Here, however, it is produced by just one single figure, and the arms and hands define the base of this pyramid. The three-dimensional appearance of the figure is linked in several ways with the contrastingly flat seeming background. On the one hand, Leonardo continues the arch-like rise of the veil across the left shoulder into the landscape emphasizing the bridge. On the other hand, the curving path on the left is an ornamental pattern that is emphasized in the cloth on both sleeves as a border of light, thus subtly connecting the flat and three-dimensional structures. However, it is really

Leonardo's famous *sfumato* that unites the plastic convex figure with the enormous perspective depth of the mountainous landscape, creating a harmonious whole picture. The unusual rise in the height of the horizon between the left and right sides intensifies the puzzling character of the landscape, which gradually fades into the diffuse light. Leonardo is a long way from simply painting nature. The refinement and special features of the composition once again show that a painter who wants to present nature as deceptively as possible does not have to depict it in an identical manner, but has to deceive viewers into regarding what they see as being identical with nature.

The very first question asked when attempting to decipher the painting, regarding the identity of the portrayed young woman, cannot be answered. In his description of the picture, Giorgio Vasari said that the portrayed woman was Mona Lisa, the wife of Francesco Giocondo. However, he cannot have ever seen the picture himself. An anonymous predecessor of Vasari's, in his biography of Leonardo, referred to a portrait of Francesco Giocondo, who was a relatively unimportant silk merchant living in Florence, and whose third wife was Lisa. There are, however, various arguments against the painting having been produced during Leonardo's time in Florence, one being that while he was working on the *Battle of Anghiari* he even turned down a commission from Isabella d'Este, and for that reason it is scarcely likely that he was working for an ordinary merchant. Another is that the depiction of the unusual landscape in the background suggests the work has a later date.

The optical studies, which mainly take on tangible form in *Manuscript D* kept in the Paris Institut de France and which cannot have dated from before 1508, are linked to the unusual manner in which the woman in the picture is presented. Leonardo's studies of biopic or "two-eyed" vision would not have progressed far enough for the creation of such a portrait to be feasible until he had returned to Milan. This eliminates the possibility that the portrayed woman can be identified as Mona Lisa del Giocondo. It equally rules out the identification as an androgynous being or a disguised self-portrait of Leonardo himself, as has been suggested. It is not certain whether identifying the person involved would indeed be of any assistance in understanding the painting and its visual references any better, for Leonardo's requirements in this painting seem to have gone beyond creating an individual portrait. It is

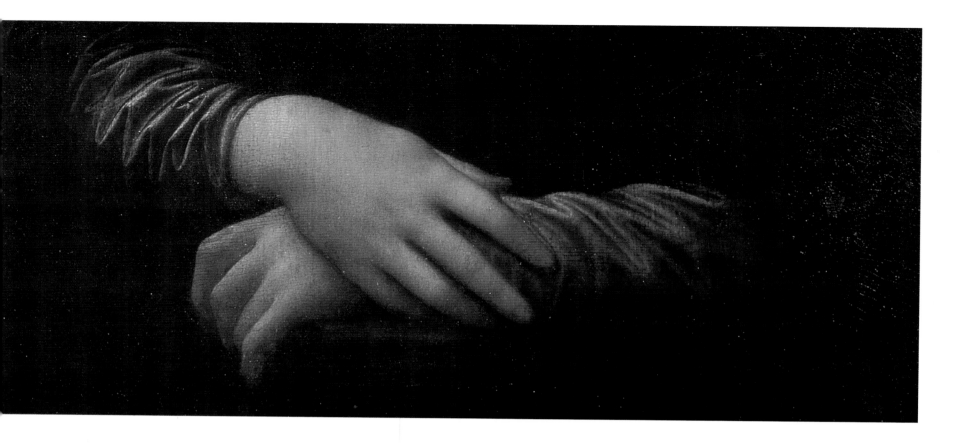

Mona Lisa (detail page 201) Hands

The sensuous quality of the picture is shown particularly well by the hands. The right is resting relaxed on the left, which is gently gripping the chair arm. In his description of the *Mona Lisa*, Giorgio Vasari also praised its vividness, saying that "one could swear that the pulses were beating."

Opposite page:
Leonardo da Vinci
St. John the Baptist, ca. 1510–1515
Oil on wood, 69 x 57 cm
Musée du Louvre, Paris

St. John the Baptist is looking at the observer directly, declaring his identity by means of gestures and gaze. The picture is probably one of the three works that Antonio de Beatis saw in Leonardo's studio in Clos-Lucé in 1517. It is the last painting to be produced by Leonardo himself, and was probably already completed in Rome. The Pinacoteca Ambrosiana in Milan owns a further version that depicts St. John in a landscape, which is related to the painting of the Virgin and Child with St. Anne in the Louvre (page 199).

probably the most demanding conception of an imitative portrait in the history of painting.

The technique of creating an object from a combination of the views of the right and left eyes is, for practical reasons, limited to objects that are constructed symmetrically, so that both views can be depicted on the symmetrical axis without creating particularly great displacements. Man is constructed almost symmetrically, and his rounded head is particularly suited to simulating the phenomenon of "two-eyed" sight. The portrait of the Mona Lisa was the first occasion on which Leonardo made use of this technique in order to achieve a heightened level of *rilievo*. He first portrayed the lady with his right eye and decided that this view should be the main one, or in other words, he did not place the line of intersection along the center of the nose, but used the entire view of the nose. The shortened left view of the Mona Lisa had, therefore, to be trimmed at the center before being added. The distortion thus created can be recognized at the point of transition from the nose to her right eyebrow, and also on the right side of her mouth that, when looking at the right half of her head in isolation, appears to be foreshortened.

In addition, both the dating of the painting and the place it was created are open to debate; it may have been started from 1508 on in Milan, or from 1513 in Rome. The picture certainly never left the artist's workshop during his lifetime. In France it was seen in Leonardo's studio by a traveler who thought it depicted a Florentine friend of Giuliano de' Medici. Giuliano's sudden death would explain why the portrait remained with the artist.

After Leonardo's death, the picture disappeared from written records; it may have passed into the ownership of Francis I or, less likely, gone to Milan with Leonardo's servant Salai as an heirloom. There are, however, Italian sources indicating that Francis I owned the picture. The only query is whether he bought it directly from Leonardo or whether it was purchased for him at a later date in Milan.

Vasari was evidently mistaken in his identification of the young woman and the dating this suggested. But his explanation of the enigmatic smile of the Mona Lisa has at least a striking and ingenious persuasive power where its play on words is concerned. The art historian wrote that Leonardo "employed singers and musicians or jesters to keep her full of merriment." In a sophisticated literary manner, this amusing anecdote ties in with the name that he gave the portrayed woman, for "la Gioconda" means "the merry one."

Irrespective of whether this major work was produced during his time in Milan or later in Rome, the work situation in Milan was definitely very bad for Leonardo. The unstable political situation would certainly have contributed to this to an extent. On a sheet dated 18 December 1511, showing the surroundings of the villa belonging to the Melzi family, the drifts of smoke caused by war are visible in the background. They refer to the retreat of the Swiss troops after attacking Milan on 14 December 1511, and another drawing of a fire on the same sheet relates to a battle that took place two days later.

In 1513, Leonardo turned his back on these uncertain conditions and obeyed the call of his new patron, Giuliano de' Medici, to come to Rome, where the powerful Florentine family of bankers had gained a foothold and from 1513 had provided a pope in the form of Leo X. There is also no evidence of paintings dating from this time, though the artistic climate of the city, and above all the presence of Raphael, will doubtless have kept Leonardo's interest in painting alive. At least one painting by his workshop would have been produced during his time in Rome, *St. John in the Wilderness* (Musée de Louvre, Paris). A youth is sitting on a rock and, with his right hand, is pointing to the spring bubbling up next to him. In his left hand he is holding a staff. The spring can be interpreted as an allusion to baptism, the shepherd's staff identifies St. John the Baptist as a hermit. As in the earlier *Leda*, this is a combination of designs on classical and Christian themes, as the Christian hermit St. John the Baptist is presenting himself naked like the classical god of wine, Bacchus.

The friendly expression of *St. John the Baptist* (right) is not quite as puzzling as the smile of the *Mona Lisa*, though the history of its creation is just as shrouded in mystery. Like the *St. John in the Wilderness* painted in his workshop, Leonardo's own painting is linked to the commission by a Florentine brotherhood of St. John, but like the *Mona Lisa* (page 201) it never left the artist's workshop.

St. John is depicted as a half-length figure, turning his upper body to the left while his head is pointing straight at the observer. His face, shoulders, and right arm are lit, and his raised hand is pointing to the staff with the cross. His left hand is coming from the darkness behind the entire figure into the foreground of the picture, creating an impression of spatial depth. The diagonal line of the picture is formally emphasized by the left hand, where only the fingertips are lit up; this is joined by the way his head is leaning, and at the same time, the fingers are increasing the tactile nature of the leopard skin that the Baptist is wearing in an unusual manner. The figure is not determined by any clear, sharp line; it dissolves into its dark background, and the varnish increases this impression of soft focus. The shoulder-length hair of St. John probably comes closest to demonstrating drawing ability; the treatment of the highlights on his curls is reminiscent of the whirlpools in his studies of water. He is connected to the *Mona Lisa* both by his smile and his gaze, without the same expression having been striven for.

The opportunity of depicting several views in a picture, something that the eye is not capable of achieving simultaneously in the real world, is something that Leonardo began to make use of in characterizing the figures in his paintings. This becomes clear in the picture of St. John the Baptist. His right eye is looking at and addressing the observer directly, attracting his attention to him. If, however, one concentrates on his left eye, one gets the impression that this eye is looking diagonally upwards. This gaze is perplexing, for St. John appears to have a squint. The figure explains itself to the observer by means of its gazes and gestures.

Visual references guide the observer through the painting. All the things one needs a sequence of words

to describe are shown in an instant: "I am St. John the Baptist, God's prophet, who has heralded the coming of Jesus Christ." Thus, the gesture pointing to his chest relates to the eye fixed on the observer, meaning: "I am talking to you." The attribute of the staff with the cross clearly identifies the figure as St. John. The other eye corresponds to the way his finger is pointing upwards, implying that: "He who will save mankind by dying on the Cross will come from heaven."

The Final Years in Amboise: 1517–1519

Francesco Melzi (1492–ca. 1570)
Flora, ca. 1517–1521
Oil on wood, transferred to canvas, 76 x 63 cm
Hermitage, St. Petersburg

The painting of the Roman goddess of flowers, Flora, is directly connected to the Berlin painting of *Pomona and Vertumnus* (page 205). Both reflect the same model by Leonardo, namely the figure of Mary in the *Burlington House Cartoon* (page 197). The painting appears to have remained in the royal collection in France, at least until the mid-16th century. It is possible that a cartoon of the half-length figure also existed, for in addition to some copies at least two almost identical versions of the painting still exist.

When Leonardo was made "first painter, engineer, and architect" by the French King Francis I, he was already sixty-five years old, a considerable age at the time. Like so much in the artist's life, it is not known how he came to be appointed. He had been in direct contact with the French royal family since his second stay in Milan at least—Francis I had reconquered the duchy of Milan in 1515 when he was victorious over the Swiss army at Marignano—he probably met the king for the first time in 1515 in Bologna. Whatever the case, from 1517 Leonardo stayed in the castle of Clos-Lucé with his servant Salai and Francesco Melzi, who was to become particularly important.

Deeply admired by the king, towards the end of his life Leonardo once more performed the function of an artist and engineer in the service of a royal court. As he had done for the Sforzas in Milan, he designed costumes for a masked ball, but his principal activities were as the king's architect. He drew architectural designs for the castle of the queen's mother in Romorantin, which despite their sketchiness already anticipate the great palaces of the absolute monarchs. As in so many of his projects, Leonardo attempted to start by understanding the problem thoroughly so that he could then develop comprehensive measures for improvement. In this case also, Leonardo not only planned the extension of the residence, but also included observations on town planning in order to make sure that the infrastructure of the new residence to be built was suited to the requirements. Thus he planned not merely to border the castle with an artistic network of canals, but to link it with the Loire via a navigable canal so that the town would be connected with the existing trade and travel routes.

No doubt the French king would also have desired the famous artist to produce paintings, but Leonardo was suffering from paralysis. The illness was probably so advanced that he was no longer able to use his brush himself: "And it is true that no more good can be expected of him [Leonardo], because his right side is paralyzed. He has enlisted the aid of a student from Milan who works quite well, and although Master Leonardo can no longer paint with the delicacy one expects of him, he still draws and teachers others," wrote Antonio de Beatis after visiting Leonardo's studio in Clos-Lucé, in an entry dated 10 October 1517 in his journal. This student of Leonardo's was Francesco Melzi, who was his companion during the last stage of his life. He was also the one who completed Leonardo's treatise on painting after his death. Melzi appears to have shared the master's knowledge, and Leonardo developed his last works together with him. He made him his main heir and left him his workshop together with all his notebooks and drawings. An ambassador from Ferrara wrote the following about Melzi in 1523: "[Melzi] was the student and is the heir of Leonardo da Vinci, and possesses many of his secrets, and all his opinions, and also paints very well, as far as I can judge, and in his thoughts he shows discernment and is a very friendly young man."

It was very probably the paralyzed Leonardo who composed the painting of *Pomona and Vertumnus* which Francesco Melzi produced (page 205) and which in a certain sense can be considered the artist's painted legacy. It narrates an episode from Ovid's *Metamorphoses*: Vertumnus enters Pomona's grove in order to convince her of his love. Because she had always run away on previous occasions when he came, he has cunningly dressed as an old woman on this occasion. By telling her about the allegory of the grapevine and elm, he is able to convince her of the importance of togetherness, for the grapevine needs something it can climb up and the elm, when considered on its own, is useless. Persuaded, Pomona gives in to love and her innermost longings and they become a couple.

Vertumnus is a composite figure that represents various moments in time and historical elements in his various parts. His face is that of an old man; only the bonnet identifies him as an old woman. The feet and hands are those of a young person. This makes his transformation visible. The motif of his gait, due to which his garments are still fluttering, shows that he has just arrived. At the point where his right wrist is bent, the grapevine is entwined around the elm. The gentle touch of her shoulder with his youthful hand depicts the moment at which he reveals himself to her. Pomona's eyes are still lowered longingly while he is already gazing at her passionately.

Leonardo had developed a form of pictorial narrative that differed from that in the *Last Supper* (page 190–191) in that every element in the picture now played an independent role in the narrative, while in the *Last Supper* the production was tuned to the effect of entire figures and staged in a more theatrical manner. At first glance, the painting appears to narrate only a single moment in time, but when one looks at the picture more closely the various temporal planes within which the individual figures operate unfold.

Little attention has been paid to the portrait of Francis I (in a private collection in the USA), which the king must surely have commissioned his first court painter and his workshop to produce. Melzi seems to have also produced this portrait that displays both the "divided" vision of *St. John* and Leonardo's own general idiosyncrasy of characterizing figures by means of visual references. If the later inscription is to be believed, it was created in about 1518.

It was probably at the request of Francis I that Leonardo continued working on drawings for the painting the *Virgin and Child with St. Anne* in the Louvre (page 199). He produced wonderful detail studies, but the painting was never completed by him. As in the picture of Pomona and Vertumnus, the pictorial narrative played a central role in his ideas for the painting of St. Anne.

His last drawings from the period in France are almost entirely executed using black chalk, pen, and ink; he no longer appears to have used red chalk. The surviving drawings are characterized by an astonishing ease in the use of lines. In addition to drawings of horses and designs for costumes, there also remains the *Deluge* series, chalk drawings of the cosmic destruction of the world. They are amongst the most impressive drawings to have ever been produced in this technique. These drawings were probably inspired by a real catastrophe that took place in 1515 in Bellinzona, when there was an enormous landslide that engulfed several villages. But they were created at the end of the artist's life, which means that it is feasible to interpret them in the sense of an apocalyptic view of the world in Leonardo's later years. Vasari, though without the benefit of more precise information about the artist, also spoke of a resignation towards the end of Leonardo's life. In accordance with Leonardo's scientific orientation, it ended not with the Christological iconography of the last days, but with a deluge unleashing the forces of nature, which in turn should be given a moral value. The symbolic landscapes could with equal right be seen without a moral background as scientific drawings in which the forces that come into play during a natural catastrophe are clearly shown. It is possible that they were planned as illustrations for a book. At any rate, the remaining sketches and workshop pieces indicate that his creative urges continued without interruption until shortly before his death.

According to a legend that once again derives from Vasari, Leonardo is said to have died in a dignified

manner on 2 May 1519, in the arms of the French King Francis I, though the latter, according to contemporary sources, was staying far away from Amboise in the castle of Saint-Germain-en-Laye at the time. Francesco Melzi informed Leonardo's oldest brother Giuliano and his relatives in his homeland of the death of their relative with the following words: "I believe you already know about the death of your brother, Master Leonardo, who was like the best of fathers to me, and for whose death it would be impossible for me to express the grief I have felt …"

Peter Hohenstatt

Francesco Melzi
Pomona and Vertumnus, ca. 1517–1520
Oil on wood, 185 x 134 cm
Gemäldegalerie, Staatliche Museen, Berlin

Pomona, the classical goddess of fruit, and Vertumnus, the god of transformation, are the main figures in an episode in Ovid's *Metamorphoses*. Until very recently, the attribution of the painting was disputed. This changed in 1995, when the author was able to prove the existence of a documented signature by Melzi, which an art dealer removed in the 18th century in order to be able to sell the picture as a work of Leonardo's.
Due to its poor condition, the painting was not taken seriously for a long time. It was only once it was restored that its similarity to Leonardo's works became evident.

PAINTING BECOMES A SCIENCE

Perhaps there is throughout the world no second example of such a comprehensive, inventive genius that, incapable of being satisfied, longed so greatly for infinity, was so naturally sophisticated and so advanced beyond his own century and the following ones.

Hippolyte Taine, *Travels in Italy*, 1866

The sixty-seven years of Leonardo's life corresponded to one of the most varying and, at the same time, most creative eras in history. During the course of these years, supported by the intellectual current of humanism, many fundamental principles were created from which the modern age was to develop. The invention of the printing press and the discovery of the New World and the sea route to the East coincided with the life and work of Leonardo, whose exploratory urge was limitless—no matter whether he was trying out new techniques in painting, testing new principles of composition or new possibilities presented by the visual idiom or the characterization of a portrait's subject, whether he was conducting anatomical studies, studying the laws of optics, investigating sculpture and the techniques of the work process, or developing hydraulic installations and designing machines.

Even Leonardo's own contemporaries felt his universality to be so unusual that the writer and painter Benedetto Varchi (1502–1566), on the occasion of his public funeral oration (1564) for Michelangelo, Leonardo's younger rival, went so far as to list Leonardo's varied talents, an extremely unusual act given the circumstances. He honored him as the founder and completer of the third and highest method of painting, the *maniera moderna*, and as an arithmetician, musician, geometrician, cosmographer, astrologer and astronomer, as a writer of verses and poetry, philosopher and metaphysician, who had also excelled in anatomy, medicine, botany, mineralogy, and many other fields.

The roughly twenty known paintings—about another twenty are suggested by various sources—and hundreds of drawings demonstrate in a most impressive manner that Leonardo did not consider science and art to be two different things, but felt that they were linked to each other in the most fruitful manner. It was his conviction that the artist had to use the methods of the scientist, and the scientist the tools of art. A scientist who could not draw lacked the means of conveying his knowledge in a vivid manner. An artist, in contrast, had to master the laws of geometry in order to be able to construct a system of perspective or establish the proportions of humans and animals. For him, painting occupied the highest position amongst the sciences as it possessed a significance and power of communication that went beyond all the other sciences. For it did not need to be translated into other languages, like literature for example, and did not fade away the moment it was created as music did. As he wrote in his *Treatise on Painting*: "With its principle, in other words drawing, painting instructs the architect to make his building pleasant to the eye; it teaches the makers of the most diverse vases; the goldsmiths, weavers, embroiderers; it has found the letters with which the various languages are expressed; it has given the arithmetician numbers; it has taught geometry to depict figures; it teaches painters in perspective, astrologers, mechanical engineers and master builders."

Although Leonardo's works were frequently stigmatized because unfinished, they turned his name into a legend. His *Last Supper* (pages 190–191) and *Mona Lisa* (page 201) are two of the most famous pictures in the history of painting. It was Leonardo who brought about a decisive advance in painting. During his stay in Florence he matured into an artist who showed signs of considerable promise, and Leonardo internalized the Albertian tradition according to which painting, in imitation of classical rhetoric, was seen as a means of communication.

According to Alberti, history painting was the most worthy genre in painting and should be staged in such a way, as a readable pictorial narrative, that the observer could visualize a story in the way it had artistically been put into practice. To achieve this, the painter should use both traditional methods of visual language and newly developed attributes and symbols as well as characteristic accessories, which the observers of the time were able to read like words.

A further task that Alberti posed artists was also drawn from the classical body of thought, namely the idea of painting as a deceptive imitation of reality. He considered the greatest achievement to be to create a work that depicted painted persons or objects in such a way as if they were alive or real. Leonardo accepted these challenges as no other painter and in his paintings achieved what he had since the 1490s been attempting to define, in his *Treatise on Painting*, as the fundamental purposes of painting. For Leonardo, the highest artistic goal of painting was to imitate reality. In the painter's opinion, though, this could not be achieved solely by copying nature, but by outwitting the observer. But if it was his task to deceive an observer, then spatiality, three-dimensionality, and people acting in a psychologically accurate manner had to be depicted.

Leonardo achieved the first through his studies of perspective, specifically aerial perspective. In order to realize the second requirement, he investigated the influence of light and shade in the production of *rilievo*, and his anatomical and physiognomic studies relate to the third point. In addition to this, he recognized the importance of the process of perception on the part of the observer for creating an illusionary effect, and his painting by definition strove to achieve this. The attempt to simulate binocular vision was to be one of the last great challenges for Leonardo the painter.

His methodical awareness that the clearly defined nature of a science determines its goal and this in turn decides the method used to reach that goal, and that the results achieved at any stage have to be measured against the defined goal, turned painting, which had long been regarded as a craft, into a true science. This made Leonardo one of the first rationalists in a modern sense, though only a few of his contemporaries absorbed and understood his concepts. It is not, therefore, surprising that his achievements in the history of ideas are only gradually being recognized today, especially as the complications connected with gathering his writings for a long time made it impossible to gain an overall perspective of the entire work of this fascinating person. A history of the influences of his writings has yet to be written.

With regard to his paintings, the debate over the authorship, attribution, and dating is not over yet. In contrast, Leonardo the artist is held in universal respect. This feeling is probably not expressed better anywhere than in the writings of Vasari, where he cites the words of praise of Giovanbatista Strozzi:

Vince costui pur solo
Tutti altri, e vince Fidia, e vince Apelle
Et tutto il lor vittorioso stuolo

"Da Vinci alone vanquished all others,
He vanquished Phidias and Apelles,
And all their victorious followers."

Brigitte Hintzen-Bohlen   *Peter Hohenstatt*

Raphael 1483–1520

RAPHAEL'S EARLY YEARS IN URBINO

Raphael, *The Vision of the Prophet Ezekiel*,
ca. 1518, Wood, 40 x 30 cm
Galleria Palatina, Palazzo Pitti, Florence

The balance of this composition impressed Vasari.
Ezekiel is so small he can scarcely be recognized in the
bottom left of the background, the scenes being
completely dominated by his vision. The "likeness of the
Glory of God" is bursting through the heavenly clouds,
surrounded by the animals that represent the four
Evangelists and by two cherubs. Leonardo's drawing of
Neptune had presented a similar problem of portraying
the figure bursting dramatically into a picture.

Opposite page:
Raphael
Study for the Baronci Altarpiece, ca. 1500/01
Black chalk and metal point, squared, 39.4 x 24.8 cm
Cabinet des Dessins, Musée des Beaux-Arts, Lille,
Inv. Pl. 474

This is the original design for Raphael's first documented
altarpiece, only fragments of which now remain. Up
above, the Virgin Mary, God the Father, and St.
Augustine are crowning St. Nicholas of Tolentino, who
stands below, trampling on the Devil. The models for the
figures were the *garzone*, young apprentices, who in this
study have been drawn wearing everyday Florentine dress.

When Raphael died at the age of thirty-seven, on Good
Friday, 1520, even the Pope wept. We learn of this extraordinary reaction in Giorgio Vasari's *Lives*, published in
1550, in which Vasari calls Raphael a "mortal god."
Raphael of Urbino achieved everything an Italian
Renaissance artist could hope to accomplish: the artist
most in demand for the decoration of the Vatican, where
he created monumental fresco cycles, he also painted
altarpieces, devotional images, and portraits for many of
the most important Italian dignitaries of his age, some of
whom were the greatest art patrons in Europe; and, as
chief architect, he supervised the construction of St.
Peter's in Rome, the most important building project in
Christendom. In addition, he undertook to list and
preserve the ancient monuments of Rome, for he can
be credited as one of the very earliest of the modern
conservators of ancient monuments.

Raphael's meteoric career first began not in Rome but
in Urbino. It was an ideal setting in which to distinguish
himself. He was born there on Good Friday 6 April 1483,
the son of Màgia di Battista di Nicola Ciarla and
Giovanni Santi di Pietro. His father was a painter and
poet at the court of Federico da Montefeltre, one of the
most famous princes and art patrons of Early Renaissance
Italy. When the Duke died in 1482, he was succeeded by
his son, Guidobaldo, under whom Giovanni Santi
continued to enjoy a steadily increasing reputation as
court painter until his death in 1494. According to
Vasari, Raphael's father was not an outstanding painter,
though he was a "man of good sense." Vasari also claims
that Raphael started helping out in Santi's studio at a very
early age. Though Vasari's account tends to be episodic,
so that the documentary value of his *Lives* is sometimes
questionable, it is reasonable to assume that Raphael did
in fact learn the fundamentals of art in his father's studio.
This assumption is supported by the fact that his first
recorded commission (for an altarpiece in 1500)
mentions that his collaborator was Evangelista da Pian di
Meleto, who in 1483 was a *famulus* (assistant) in Santi's
studio. Evangelista is also recorded as being one of the
witnesses when Giovanni Santi's will was read on 29 July
1494.

What is still unclear is where Raphael received his
training after this early period in his father's workshop.

According to Vasari, Giovanni Santi apprenticed his
gifted son to Pietro Perugino. However, there is evidence
from several sources to show that Raphael remained in
Urbino until 1499, a period during which Perugino was
managing a workshop in Perugia, as well as carrying out
commissions in Florence and Rome. By 1500, Raphael,
now seventeen, was presumably no longer an assistant.
The contract mentioned above, for an altarpiece in
Andrea Baronci's chapel in the church of Sant'Agostino
in Città di Castello, a small town near Urbino, is
dated 10 December 1500. Here Raphael is already
described as a *magister*, a "master." Furthermore, stylistic
comparisons that have tried to find signs of Raphael's
hand in Perugino's works remain inconclusive. It is not
until we reach the period around 1502/03 onwards that
Raphael's works show clear links with Perugino. It
therefore seems reasonable to assume that Raphael's
association with Perugino did not begin until after 1500.

In comparison with other early works by Raphael,
we are well informed about the *Baronci Altarpiece*,
since we have not only the contract but also a record of
payment, dated 13 September 1501. The altarpiece is
dedicated to Nicholas of Tolentino, a 13th-century
Augustinian hermit who was not canonized until
1446, though his cult reached an early highpoint of
popularity, especially in Città di Castello, around
1500. The altarpiece was badly damaged in an
earthquake in 1789, and from 1849 onwards the
surviving sections have been kept in various
collections. Raphael's preparatory drawing (page 209)
gives us a general idea of the whole composition,
divided horizontally into two zones. Raphael
repeatedly returned to this form of pictorial structure:
the *Madonna di Foligno* (page 252), for example,
painted while he was in Rome, is just one of several
later versions. In this early altarpiece the figures are still
rather isolated: pictorial space as a continuous entity is
not yet a subject in its own right.

After the *Baronci Altarpiece*, Raphael painted a
number of pictures that confirm the popular view of
him as the painter of charming Madonnas. We do not
know who commissioned them, though their small
scale suggests they were meant for private devotion.
The subject is the familiar one of Mother and Child

reflecting on the Passion and calmly accepting their predestined fate. The figure types are derived from Perugino's studio: in the Madonna we see the same finely proportioned oval face with a small, cherry-shaped mouth, and in the Christ Child the same swollen belly of an infant and shoulders that are proportionally much too narrow. The figures in these early Raphael paintings, though, are closely in contact with one another through looks and gesture. The interest of both the figures and of the viewer is always clearly focused on the picture's central subject.

All Raphael's surviving works from the years 1502 to 1504 show how close his relationship with Perugino was. This is not surprising, since Perugino was one of the most famous artists of the period and was greatly in demand. Patrons commissioning paintings from Raphael—who, though already a gifted artist, was barely twenty years old—probably preferred him to paint in the style of the well-established older artist. Occasionally, indeed, patrons would demand repetitions of a successful composition. In 1505, for example, the Poor Clares at Monteluce commissioned Raphael to paint the *Coronation of the Virgin Mary*, which was to be based closely on Domenico Ghirlandaio's altarpiece in the church of San Girolamo, in Narni. In Raphael's day, unlike our own, imitation was not scorned; Vasari commented approvingly that Raphael, after studying Perugino's paintings closely, "emulated them so exactly and so completely that his copies could not be distinguished from the master's originals." What is striking, however, is that Raphael, having studied this influential forebear attentively, was then able to free himself of the influence in order to develop his own artistic objectives more single-mindedly. These objectives included setting anatomically correct figures in an accurately depicted space constructed according to the principles of central perspective; creating fully rounded, solid-seeming bodies in their full three-dimensionality; and matching gesture and facial expression so exactly that they seem to be integral elements of the composition. A study of Raphael's works shows him making progress towards all of these artistic goals.

These developments are taken a step further in the *Coronation of the Virgin* (left), which, according to Vasari, Maddalena Oddi commissioned for the family funerary chapel in the church of San Francesco, in Perugia. The probable date for the commission is 1503.

Here Raphael solves the problem of pictorial space in the lower section by placing a stone sarcophagus end-on, and standing the figures of the Apostles around it. Almost all of them are gazing up in amazement at the scene of the Virgin's Coronation, so that their intensely characterized faces can be shown, from below, in a range that clearly exemplifies the Renaissance concept of *varietà*. Compared with the angels of the *Baronci Altarpiece* in the Louvre, the Apostles' faces here are even more strongly and emphatically shadowed. Light falls uniformly from the right, so that the Apostle in the right foreground casts a dramatic shadow across the sarcophagus. It is this sarcophagus that determines the

Raphael, *The Coronation of the Virgin*, ca. 1503/04
Wood transferred to canvas, 267 x 163 cm
Pinacoteca Apostolica Vaticana, Vatican, Rome

Raphael combined several themes in this composition. The sarcophagus from which flowers are blooming is a symbol of the Assumption of the Virgin. The upper half of the picture shows the Coronation of the Virgin by Christ, and in the lower half the theme of the so-called Gift of the Girdle is illustrated—St. Thomas, the central figure in the group of the Apostles, is holding the Virgin's girdle, which she has dropped on her way to heaven.

Raphael
The Annunciation (from the predella of the *Coronation of the Virgin*), ca. 1503/04
Wood transferred to canvas, 27 x 50 cm
Pinacoteca Apostolica Vaticana, Vatican, Rome

In a vast and empty loggia, the Angel Gabriel is announcing the birth of Christ to the Virgin. The angel has entered taking great strides, but he is waiting in front of the left row of columns while the Virgin calmly receives his message without rising from her seat. God the Father floats on a cloud in heaven and sends down the Holy Ghost in the form of a dove.

Raphael
The Adoration of the Magi (from the predella of the *Coronation of the Virgin*), ca. 1503/04
Wood transferred to canvas, 27 x 50 cm
Pinacoteca Apostolica Vaticana, Vatican, Rome

The Three Magi arrive with a great retinue to pay homage to the Christ Child with precious gifts. The shepherds, too, who were the first to worship Him, are still standing around the Virgin at a respectful distance. Raphael shows the very different animals that the visitors have brought with them: an aristocratic greyhound on one side, a sheep on the other.

Raphael
The Presentation in the Temple (from the predella of the *Coronation of the Virgin*), ca. 1503/04
Wood transferred to canvas, 27 x 50 cm
Pinacoteca Apostolica Vaticana, Vatican, Rome

This version of the Presentation in the Temple, an important event in the history of the childhood of Jesus, sets the scene in an arcade in front of the temple. The Virgin is holding up her son towards the aged Simeon and the Child is struggling and turning back to his mother. Joseph is standing on the left watching the scene, while a maid on the far right is holding two doves in readiness as a sacrifice.

Raphael
St. George, ca. 1504
Wood, 30.7 x 26.8 cm
Musée du Louvre, Paris

St. George's lance has been broken in the struggle, but
the proud knight is about to vanquish the dragon with
his sword and so free the princess, who is fleeing on the
right. By the middle of the 16th century, this panel
formed a pair with Raphael's *St. Michael* (below). Even
though the latter was painted somewhat earlier, the fact
that they are the same size and have a comparable
iconography implies that Raphael intended that the saints
should belong together.

Raphael
St. Michael ca. 1503/04
Wood, 30.9 x 26.5 cm
Musée du Louvre, Paris

In a bleak landscape with the silhouette of a burning
city in the distance, Michael has just forced the Devil to
the ground and is about to kill him with a blow from
his sword. The monsters crawling out from all sides are
reminiscent of those created by Hieronymus Bosch, while
the figures in the center recall those from the Inferno of
Dante's epic poem the *Divine Comedy*. On the left are
the hypocrites in leaden coats, condemned to follow their
tortuous path, while on the right are the thieves being
tormented by serpents.

depth of this lower pictorial zone. The landscape, rather than being integrated into the composition, is spread out behind the figures like a beautiful tapestry. Discontinuity is again the keynote of the overall composition, which is once more divided horizontally into two sections.

Raphael's exceptional skill in depicting traditional subjects in a new way is especially evident in the predella panels of the *Coronation of the Virgin* (page 211). Because of a predella's subordinate position in an altarpiece, its panels allowed artists more scope for experiment. In the *Adoration of the Magi*, Raphael for the first time employed a compositional principle that was to serve him well many times later when he wished to organize several figures in a lively manner within a confined space. The principle was to arrange groups of people around the central figures in a semicircle, or on segments of part of a circle. This structure enabled him to clarify each figure's exact spatial position, while at the same time avoiding the impression of figures simply lined up in a row, which would quickly become monotonous.

The figures in the foreground of the *Marriage of the Virgin* (Volume I, page 585) are grouped in this way. The success of the composition makes this painting, which is sometimes known by the Italian title of *Sposalizio*, a milestone in Raphael's early works. It was commissioned—probably with Perugino's *Marriage of the Virgin* (Volume I, page 584) in mind—for the Albizzini Chapel, dedicated to St. Joseph, in the church of San Francesco in Città di Castello. In Perugino's picture, the figures are arranged in a broad immobile block in the foreground, and are lacking the fluid grace that their formal gestures, the graceful positioning of

their feet, and their decorative and elaborate hats and head bands lead one to expect. Raphael's figures, by contrast, stand in contrapposto poses, with the soles of their feet firmly on the ground, and yet their well-formed bodies still display a graceful vitality. Raphael was also able, through the vividness of close observation, to depict the expectant tension of those present. The marriage is being completed by the giving of the ring, and Virgin's companions are shown reacting to the event: a woman in the second row is craning her neck so as to get a better view, and the woman in the left foreground—who starts the composition by leading the viewer towards the pictorial center—is gripping her own finger, on which there is no ring as yet, lost in thought.

Raphael's *Marriage of the Virgin* is also famous for its architecturally developed space, which is created by the use of a central perspective whose focus is the Tempietto in the distance. Here, too, motifs from the work of Perugino served as models—taken not only from his *Marriage of the Virgin* but also from the *Giving of the Keys to St. Peter*, of 1481/82, a fresco in the Sistine Chapel (Volume I, page 589).

Raphael, however, increases the illusion that we are looking into a deep space by making the receding rectangular slabs of the floor-pattern become progressively smaller. He has also made a clear tonal distinction between them and a series of broad white stripes, which then emerge all the more clearly as lines converging on the central vanishing point. This gives the pictorial space a continuous rhythm that the viewer can follow without difficulty. In keeping with the laws of central perspective, the figures become smaller as they recede, and so define the distance between the

Above left:
Raphael
The Three Graces, ca. 1503/04
Wood, 17 x 17 cm
Musée Condé, Chantilly

This is Raphael's first study of the female nude in both front and back views. It was probably not based on living models, however, but on the classical sculpture group of the *Three Graces* in Siena. The *Three Graces* and the *Allegory* (*The Knight's Dream*) (above right) probably belong together because they are identical in size. The disparity in the sizes of the figures, however, makes it difficult to believe that they were intended to form a diptych.

Above right:
Raphael
Allegory (*The Knight's Dream*)
ca. 1503/04
Wood, 17 x 17 cm
The National Gallery, London

A young knight is asleep in front of a laurel tree that divides the picture into two equal parts. There is a figure of a beautiful young woman in each half: on the left the personification of Virtue is holding a book and a sword above the sleeping figure, while the figure on the right is presenting a flower as a symbol of sensual pleasure. The probable meaning of the allegory is that the young man's task is to bring both sides of life into harmony.

Raphael
The Embarkation for Basel of Aenea Silvio Piccolomini,
ca. 1502
Pen and ink wash, heightened in white chalk, squared,
70.5 x 41.5 cm
Gabinetto dei Disegni e delle Stampe, Galleria degli
Uffizi, Florence, inv. 520E

This *modello* by Raphael was drawn in preparation for
the first in a series of frescoes illustrating the life of Pope
Pius II (Aenea Silvio Piccolomini), which Pinturicchio
was painting in the Piccolomini Library in the cathedral
in Siena (Volume I, page 575). Raphael's drawing shows
Aenea Silvio when he was only twenty-six years old: he is
on horseback in the center, and, as secretary to Cardinal
Capranica, is just leaving for a session of the Council
of Basel.

Opposite page:
Raphael
Ansidei Madonna, ca. 1505
Wood, 210 x 149 cm
The National Gallery, London

In this *sacra conversazione*, St. John the Baptist stands
on the left, and St. Nicholas of Bari on the right; the
Madonna sits on a canopied throne in the center, the
Christ Child on her lap. While St. John is pointing with
his right index finger to the Redeemer, St. Nicholas is
lost in his book and is taking as little notice of the other,
as self-absorbed as the Virgin and Child are.

foreground and the building in the background. The monumental size of this circular building is indicated by the size of the tiny figures in the colonnade surrounding it, the peristyle. In this painting Raphael succeeded in making the transitions between the different pictorial planes clear and continuous. The connection with the landscape, however, is still unclear.

The problem of integrating figures into landscape convincingly remained a much-debated issue until well into the 16th century. As figures were the key elements, since they conveyed the action, they were shown prominently in the foreground. The landscape played a subordinate role and often served as mere background, or even as something to fill an empty space. So Raphael's treatment of landscape in two small pictures probably painted shortly before his *Marriage of the Virgin*—one of St. George and one of St. Michael (page 212)—is therefore all the more remarkable. These two panels were probably meant to be fitted together as a diptych, and, as they are small and light, they could be easily transported. In both the central figure comes thrusting forwards out of the depths of the pictorial space. The broad, apocalyptic landscape in which St. Michael battles against the Devil under a sky still glowing despite having darkened, sets the whole mood for the picture, and so can in no way be considered mere background.

Small pictures often have unusual subjects and often solve pictorial problems in surprising ways. One example is a panel, measuring only 17 x 17 cm, that depicts the naked three Graces in front of a landscape which looks like that of Umbria (page 213). Another is its companion piece: *Allegory* (*The Knight's Dream*) (page 213), which has the same dimensions, and whose precise subject matter is still debated. Like the panels depicting St. George and St. Michael, these two small paintings were presumably painted for the court of Urbino. This is suggested both by the exquisite execution and also by the subject matter of the *Allegory*. The painting probably depicts Scipio Africanus, whose story is recounted by the classical author Silius Italicus. Having fallen asleep under a laurel tree, Scipio dreamt that two female figures, Virtue and Pleasure, challenged him to choose between them; Virtue pointed out the stony path that leads to her castle. Scipio, like Hercules before him, does not allow himself to be led astray, but follows Virtue. Raphael slightly modified the iconography, in that he gave both female figures symbols not mentioned in the text. Sword, book, and flower indicate qualities that a young courtly knight needed to distinguish himself as a soldier, as someone educated in the humanities, and as a tender lover. This description of the ideal courtier is given in the book *The Courtier* by Baldassare Castiglione, whom Raphael had met in Rome. Presumably, therefore, the *Allegory* presents us with a contemporary variant of the Scipio theme, exhorting us to merge and assimilate the various differing aspects of life. This view is supported by the landscape, which, as in the picture St. Michael, underscores the main theme. On the left-hand side, which is devoted to Virtue, an inaccessible fortress towers up on a steep hillside; whereas on the right, a bridge

stretches invitingly over a river. The two halves of the picture are not strictly divided from one another, however, for the hills behind the tree, as well as the cloudy sky, form part of a background that unites both sides. The contradictions suggested by the landscape motifs are thus resolved in the picture as a whole.

Early in his career Raphael was confronted by another theme very popular with Italian patrons: that of the *sacra conversazione*. This picture type shows the Madonna enthroned centrally, with saints on both sides, all the figures being contained within a single, unified space. Saints from many different periods could be grouped in various iconographic combinations. The donors' patron saints could be combined with local saints or those with an importance that reached beyond just one region, and the throne could be set in a room or in front of a landscape. An example of this picture type is the *Ansidei Madonna* (page 214). According to Vasari, Raphael painted it for Bernardino Ansidei's Chapel in the Servite church of San Fiorenzo in Perugia, which was dedicated to St. Nicholas of Bari. This picture illustrates a problem which applies to the *Colonna Altarpiece* in New York, Raphael's first *sacra conversazione*, and which art historians are also discussing in relation to the *Coronation of the Virgin* (page 210). These two works appear to have been painted in two stages with intervals in between, which makes the exact date of completion uncertain. A date in Roman numerals appears on the hem of the Virgin's mantel in the *Ansidei Madonna*, but it is not certain what that date is. MDV, in other words 1505, is clearly visible; but then the V is followed by one or two further strokes, which could form part of the date, so that 1506 or 1507 are also possible dates of completion. However, the style of the painting suggests the first date is the most likely. At all events, the painting was started earlier, for the Virgin and Christ Child still show Perugino's influence. Moreover, the perspective foreshortening of the throne, which is not deep enough for the Madonna, is unsuccessful. We can therefore assume that the artist began work on this painting even before he painted his *Marriage of the Virgin*. Nevertheless, the figure of Nicholas of Bari dominates the space and is so "present" as a rounded, three-dimensional body that we can assume that Raphael was beginning to respond to new influences when painting the *Ansidei Madonna*.

These influences were largely the result of the time Raphael spent in Florence from late 1504 or early 1505. This was probably not the first time that Raphael had visited the cradle and citadel of the Early Renaissance, but this stay marked an important stage in his development. He began enthusiastically to explore works by Leonardo and the young Michelangelo, whereas previously Perugino, Pinturicchio, Luca Signorelli, and Flemish artists such as Hans Memling had been important to him. This response to the works of other artists reveals a significant aspect of his own creative development: that he learnt as much from studying the art of others as he did from directly observing nature. What is important, however, is that he always endeavored not merely to imitate these models, but to surpass them.

THE CHALLENGE OF FLORENCE

Raphael
St. George and the Dragon, ca. 1505/06
Wood, 28.5 x 21.5 cm
National Gallery of Art, Washington

St. George's struggle with the dragon is now over and the drama ended: the dragon has just been struck a fatal blow with the young knight's lance. The firm pyramidal composition, of which the white horse is a major part, also has a calming effect. The look of indifference on St. George's face is a result of the eyes having been painted over: originally he was looking straight at the monster.

Following pages, left:
Raphael
Portrait of Agnolo Doni, ca. 1506
Wood, 65 x 45.7 cm
Galleria Palatina, Palazzo Pitti, Florence

In 1504, Agnolo Doni, a rich cloth merchant, married Maddalena Strozzi (opposite). These two portraits, which Vasari mentions, were originally in a hinged frame so that they could be opened and closed like a book. In a portrait diptych like this, a form very popular in the Renaissance, the man's portrait was usually on the left, the more important side heraldically.

Following pages, right:
Raphael
Portrait of Maddalena Doni, ca. 1506
Wood, 65 x 45.8 cm
Galleria Palatina, Palazzo Pitti, Florence

This portrait is more noticeably covered with a marked craquelure than its counterpart (opposite). These hairline cracks in the paint, which appear as the paint ages, particularly affect Maddalena's even features and full décolleté.

Raphael must have decided to go to Florence because he was convinced he could learn from other masters. He must also have heard of the artistic rivalry between Leonardo and Michelangelo, who were in the process of designing large-scale battle scenes for the Palazzo Vecchio—according to Vasari, this was the real reason why Raphael moved to Florence. Without doubt, however, he was attracted by the city itself, for it offered a wide range of the very best in new painting. Florence at this time, rather like the great museums of today, acted as a major art center, where students had the opportunity to train hand and eye by copying important paintings, deepening their understanding of composition. This is exactly what Raphael did when, according to Vasari, he studied not only Leonardo and Michelangelo, but also Masaccio. In Florence, Raphael became part of a stimulating artistic milieu, and made friends with artists such as Aristotile da Sangallo, Ridolfo Ghirlandaio, and Fra Bartolommeo. Presumably it was also important to him to have the opportunity of gaining new, wealthy patrons.

It is not clear how long he planned to spend in Florence. According to Vasari, he soon interrupted his stay there in order to deal with his neglected affairs in Urbino, though there is no documentary record of when that actually happened. It is possible that it was during this visit to Urbino that he was commissioned to paint his *St. George and the Dragon* (page 217), which was completed 1505/06. The English Order of the Garter—a high distinction with which Henry VII of England had honored Guidobaldo da Montefeltre in 1504—adorns the saint's left knee: the small panel may well have been meant as a gift for the King of England. A later visit to Urbino, for several months in 1507, is documented.

Raphael also seems to have returned to Perugia quite soon (immediately after his first visit to Urbino, according to Vasari), and it was probably at this time that he completed the *Ansidei Madonna* (page 214) and the *Colonna Altarpiece*. Raphael owed the Borghese *Entombment* (page 227) of 1507, the most famous commission of his time in Florence, to the Baglioni, the same Perugia family who had driven the Oddi into exile. Both families had a chapel in the church of San Francesco al Prato in Perugia. The *Coronation of the*

Virgin (page 210) adorned the Oddi Chapel, and the *Entombment* the Baglioni Chapel. These two clans, which had been warring for decades, and whom Julius II tried to reconcile by means of a joint Mass said in San Francesco on 20 September 1506, probably continued their rivalry on the cultural front.

The clearest indication that Raphael had not permanently settled in Florence comes from a contract that he concluded on 12 December 1505 with the Poor Clares of Monteluce for a Coronation of the Virgin. It states that in the event of any legal disputes he could be found in Perugia, Assisi, Gubbio, Rome, Siena, Florence, Urbino, Venice, and "any other place"—an impressive list.

Perhaps Raphael planned to create an organization of workshops, in the style of Perugino's, which would make it possible for him to work in several different locations. But it is not clear whether he actually built up a studio in Florence with this in mind; whether, in other words, he was working with assistants. At all events, the painter Berto di Giovanni, who came from Perugia, is documented as a collaborator in the contract with the Poor Clares for the Monteluce *Coronation of the Virgin*, a work not in fact completed until after Raphael's death.

It is clear, however, that Raphael did not go to Florence as an unknown. On 1 October 1504, no less a person than Giovanna Feltria della Rovere, the sister of Guidobaldo da Montefeltre, had written a letter of recommendation to Pier Soderini, the *gonfaloniere della giustizia* of Florence, explicitly saying that the young artist wanted to "spend some time in Florence in order to learn," and asking for him to be given every assistance. In other words, Raphael was very well equipped for new challenges and must have entertained high hopes of gaining important patrons in Florence.

He obviously succeeded in this very promptly, for before his move to Rome in 1508 he had completed a number of altarpieces and devotional pictures. Vasari tells us who commissioned them. For a lawyer, Taddeo Taddei, Raphael painted the *Madonna of the Meadow* (page 222); for a friend, the draper Lorenzo Nasi, he painted the *Madonna with the Goldfinch* (Galleria degli Uffizi, Florence); for Domenico Canigiani, who was also a member of the Drapers' Guild, the

Raphael
Portrait of a Pregnant Woman, ca. 1506
Wood, 66.8 x 52.7 cm
Palazzo Pitti, Galleria Palatina, Florence

There are very few examples of portraits of a pregnant woman in Renaissance painting. Raphael shows great sensitivity for the special situation of the mother-to-be by showing both her fragility and her calm pride. Her left hand, resting protectively, gently emphasizes the swell of her stomach, while her gaze rests directly on the onlooker.

Canigiani Holy Family (page 225); and, finally, for the Dei family, who were also active in the silk and wool trade, the *Madonna with the Baldachino* (page 229).

Raphael was able to prove his skill as a portrait painter when, probably in 1506, he painted Agnolo Doni and his wife, Maddalena (pages 218, 219). As with the *Portrait of a Man with an Apple* (Galleria degli Uffizi, Florence), Raphael chose a landscape as the background. In the earlier portrait, however, there is still some uncertainty as to the man's exact spatial relationship with the balustrade (or table) on which his hands are resting. In the Doni double portrait, by contrast, the broader view of the two figures makes it completely clear that the figures are sitting, with their arms resting on a balustrade. The well-manicured hands do not need to be artificially occupied by holding something. They are now put to better use as a counterpoint to the heads, which are held self-confidently erect. The hands are clearly displayed, the subjects showing unmistakable pride in their precious rings. The two figures exude an air of calm confidence. The fact that both subjects are turning towards one another, and the continuing horizontal line formed by a cloud, half of which is in the left-hand picture and the other half in the right-hand one, make it clear that the portraits belong together as a pair. For a moment this apparent harmony conceals the fact that the sections of balustrade are not linked and so do not make sense architecturally, jutting into the picture as they do. This small inconsistency, however, is compensated by the boldness of the composition as a whole, and also by some of the wonderful details, such as the buttons and buckles, Maddalena's transparent shawl, beneath which shines her flawless skin, and Agnolo's white shirt, with its fine frill. These details are not painted pedantically: like everything else, they are blended together in a magnificent richness of color. Maddalena's salmon-pink dress, whose material, like watered silk, is shot through with a cloudy white, prefigures that freedom of brushwork found in Raphael's late Roman portraits.

Raphael's feeling for psychological nuance is shown in the subtle differences between the man and the woman. Agnolo Doni's head is turned more firmly into a three-quarter profile, so that the averted half of his face is in shadow, giving a sharpness to his features. On the other hand, the full, harmonious face of his wife, which is turned almost en face, is evenly lit, making it seem all the softer. In addition, the man is looking straight at the viewer, insisting on a direct encounter, whereas Maddalena's eyes are gently turned to the right, her whole figure appearing more restrained by comparison with her husband's. The delicately shaped tree on the left adds a gentle air to her portrait. By contrast, Doni's head stands out strikingly against the sky. The level clouds frame his head and so strengthen the pictorial structure; as does Doni's arm,

Below:
Raphael
Madonna Connestabile, ca. 1503/04
Wood transferred to canvas, dia. 17.5 cm
Hermitage, St. Petersburg

Raphael met the challenge of creating a round
composition when he painted this delicate Madonna.
He provides a stable structure for the round picture by
means of the vertical figure of the Madonna and the
horizontal lines of the landscape. The Madonna's head
is gently inclined and the contour of her left hand flows
rhythmically into the outline of the Christ Child's body,
thus responding to the circular form.

Right: Raphael
Madonna del Granduca, ca. 1505
Wood, 84 x 55 cm
Galleria Palatina, Palazzo Pitti, Florence

The Virgin is holding her son with a look of great
solemnity. Both are looking at the observer, which
creates the impression that the observer too is redeemed
by Christ's death. Raphael had originally planned an
architectural background, which he later painted over.
The resulting dark ground creates a sense of meaningful
stillness and ensures that the observer's attention rests
on the figures.

which, lying parallel to the picture, acts as a kind of pedestal for the figure and holds the viewer at a respectful distance. Maddalena, on the other hand, turns to us in a much more open manner.

Raphael also valued a monochrome background, as in his *Portrait of a Pregnant Woman* (page 220), which he painted at about the same time as the Doni double portrait. Here, nothing distracts attention from the figure, which, by the very nature of the subject, has a strong physical presence, emphasized by the sitter's gaze and her gesture.

The *Madonna del Granduca* (page 221), one of Raphael's earliest half-length Madonnas from his period in Florence, also stands against a dark background, and is therefore not within a specific space. In this portrait, Raphael had now moved away from Perugino's figure type, which was still evident in his *Madonna Connestabile* (page 221), painted only a year earlier. The Madonna's face has become fuller, and the muscular Christ Child weighs heavily on her arm. As in the portraits, the bodies are now more three-dimensional, with the shadows, no longer confined to the subject's outlines, enveloping the figures. Accessories are not now needed to occupy the Virgin or the Christ Child. These changes result in the figures gaining inner dignity, which makes their solemnity all the more credible.

Raphael
The Madonna of the Meadow, 1505 or 1506
Wood, 113 x 88 cm
Kunsthistorisches Museum, Vienna

The *Madonna of the Meadow* is the first of a series of full-length figure compositions that portray the apocryphal encounter between the boy Jesus and the boy Baptist. The boy Baptist is supposed to have recognized and worshipped Christ as the Redeemer even in their childhood. Raphael makes this clear by letting Christ take the cross from John.

Opposite page:
Raphael
La Belle Jardinière, 1507 or 1508
Wood, 122 x 80 cm
Musée du Louvre, Paris

This painting is the highpoint of all Raphael's Florentine Madonnas. The bodies occupy the space with great freedom, while the figures interact with deep feeling. The arch formed by the frame completes the composition harmoniously. Raphael put the date of the picture into the hem of the Virgin's mantle, as he often did, but it is not clear if the Roman numerals are meant to be read as 1507 or 1508.

Raphael
The Holy Family with Lamb, 1507 (?)
Wood, 29 x 21 cm
Museo Nacional del Prado, Madrid

There are several versions of this picture, which all show the Virgin holding Christ riding on a lamb while the elderly Joseph presides over the family. This version, in Madrid, was later marked with the words *RAPHAEL URBINAS MDVII* on the Virgin's décolleté. As Pedretti has pointed out, the version in Vaduz is dated 1504, and signed, so that it may be considered the original.

Opposite page:
Raphael
Canigiani Holy Family, ca. 1507
Wood, 131 x 107 cm
Alte Pinakothek, Bayerische Staatsgemäldesammlungen, Munich

This is an example of Raphael's favorite form of group composition during his Florentine period, the monumental pyramid. The Virgin and Elizabeth are sitting on the grass with their children, and Joseph is standing over them: this shows the importance of Jesus' adoptive father, and gives expression to the increase in the worship of Joseph after 1500. In 1982 the German conservator Hubert von Sonnenburg undertook a careful restoration of this picture and removed a distorting blue over-painting, dating from the 18th century, from the sky area. Raphael's original concept, with the putti on the upper left and right, can now be admired anew.

In the case of the *Madonna del Granduca*, art historians have rightly emphasized the important influence of Fra Bartolommeo, whose heavy figures are enveloped by voluminous garments. Raphael was striving to achieve monumentality, and he obviously found this in the works of the Dominican monk, who had become a friend.

However, the most important influences on Raphael's creative development during his stay in Florence were Leonardo and Michelangelo, who now took the place of Perugino. His *Portrait of Maddalena Doni* (page 219) seems to be related to Leonardo's *Mona Lisa* (page 201), and Raphael's full-length landscape Madonnas would be inconceivable without the example of Leonardo's innovations. In Raphael's *Madonna of the Meadow* (page 222) and *La Belle Jardinière* (page 223), the mother-child group has been extended to include the boy Baptist. In the *Holy Family with Lamb* (left), Joseph also appears, and the *Canigiani Holy Family* (page 225) includes Elizabeth, the mother of St. John the Baptist. As with the *Madonna Ansidei* (page 214), here, too, it is difficult to decipher the dates in the picture. It is not clear whether the *Madonna of the Meadow* is dated 1505 or 1506, and whether 1507 or 1508 is the correct date for *La Belle Jardinière*. The chronology of these pictures is important, however, for they show Raphael's growing confidence in adapting Leonardo's formulas in his own individual way in both the form and the content of his works. During the same period, Raphael was also responding to Michelangelo's early sculptures, the second great challenge to which Raphael responded with ever more convincing solutions.

As early as the Vienna *Madonna of the Meadow* (page 222), Raphael had employed the basic compositional structure of a pyramid: he recognized in it the magic ingredient in Leonardo's works, for it was a means of arranging figures spatially in a compact group. He saw examples of it in Leonardo's *Madonna of the Rocks* (page 178), and also his *Virgin and Child with St. Anne* (page 199). In these works the figures are connected by looks and gestures in so complex a way that in this early attempt Raphael could not live up to the original composition. The Virgin's foot in particular, which marks the lower right-hand corner of the triangle, extends rather too conspicuously from under her robe. The upper body seems flat, though her head is powerfully accentuated and her shoulders are shown to advantage as the blue mantle no longer covers her head. The boy Baptist is a direct quotation from Leonardo's *Madonna of the Rocks*, and the Virgin's long right arm is taken from the *Virgin and Child with St. Anne*. However, these motifs are not fully integrated. The way the Virgin Mary is holding her arms separates Jesus from St. John, so that the playful handing over of the cross, despite its great importance, seems a little forced.

The various motifs in Raphael's *La Belle Jardinière* (page 223) blend together with remarkable success. Here, a staff and a book function as the symbols of the Passion, but they are of secondary interest. The figures

gaze intently at each other and touch, the result being a denser psychological texture. Here the boy Baptist is now no longer as fully integrated into the scene as he was in the *Madonna with the Goldfinch*. Instead, he is given a role he had already fulfilled in the *Colonna Altarpiece* and the *Ansidei Madonna* (page 214). That is, he is a figure with which the viewer, who is being urged to worship the Redeemer, can closely identify, safe in the knowledge of the Virgin Mary's loving intercession. In *La Belle Jardinière*, Raphael borrowed the Christ Child from Michelangelo's *Bruges Madonna*. Raphael, however, shows the Child turning towards his mother, who is calmly sitting on a rock without having to turn her body, as she does in the *Madonna in the Meadow*. A voluminous mantle gives the figure great fullness, especially as the physical forms have become even more three-dimensional and majestic. Furthermore, showing the figure of the Virgin Mary in three-quarter profile allowed Raphael to integrate it more fully into the surrounding space. This integration is most fully realized, however, through the use of Leonardo's technique of *sfumato*, which allows a painter to model color tones through gentle gradations rather than harsh transitions. Raphael's study of Leonardo's aerial perspective also helped him to depict the broad landscape as a continuous whole: the mountains and the city lose their clarity as they recede into the distance.

One special challenge for Raphael during this period must have been Atalanta Baglioni's commission for a scene from the Passion of Christ (page 227), which he painted in Perugia and which is now in the Galleria Borghese in Rome. In 1500, Atalanta's son, Grifonetto, was murdered by Gianpaolo Baglioni and his associates; in other words, by a member of his own family. This was hardly surprising, for not long before Grifonetto had attempted to kill all the other Baglioni. Gianpaolo was able to escape, and he avenged himself on Grifonetto, who had in the meanwhile repented. Grifonetto died in his mother's arms after she had begged him to forgive his killers.

It is not clear when Raphael received this commission, though the painting is dated 1507, the year it was completed. A long process of design preceded the final work. Raphael frequently changed his mind, and even altered the pictorial theme. Initially, he planned to paint a Lamentation of Christ modeled on one by Perugino, dated 1495, for the church of Santa Chiara in Florence, a painting now in the Palazzo Pitti. A Raphael drawing in Oxford (Ashmolean Museum of Art and Archaeology) is exactly like Perugino's painting, and shows a calm, undramatic composition intended for a thoughtful, sorrowing viewer. Christ's body lies in the foremost pictorial plane. His head and upper body are resting on the knees of his mother, who seems about to sink backwards into the arms of two women who are supporting her. Christ's legs are lying on the lap of Mary Magdalene, who is gazing at Christ with her hands folded in prayer. St. John, mourning silently and immersed in his own thoughts, is standing among a group of other men on the right. The mood matches that of Perugino's picture, and it is conceivable that

Raphael
The Entombment, 1507
Pen and ink over traces of lead point, in stylus, pen and ink, and red chalk, squared, 28.9 x 29.7 cm
Gabinetto dei Disegni e delle Stampe, Galleria degli Uffizi, Florence, inv. 538E

This drawing has preserved the actual *modello* for the group on the left in the *Entombment* (page 227). It is the last study, in which the final composition is for the most part established. Squaring enabled the drawing, which was on a smaller scale, to be transferred easily to the larger format of the painting.

Opposite page:
Raphael
The Entombment, 1507
Wood, 184 x 176 cm
Museo Galleria Borghese, Rome

Atalanta Baglioni ordered this altarpiece for her family chapel in the church of San Francesco al Prato in Perugia. It remains pure speculation whether it was really meant to commemorate her son Grifonetto, murdered in 1500, but the subject of the picture would then be quite understandable, since Atalanta may have identified with the pain of the swooning Virgin as her son is carried to his grave.

Atalanta Baglioni, who like Perugino came from Perugia, asked for a composition in the style of the older master. If that is the case, Raphael succeeded in convincing her to accept a different conception with more dramatic power.

In the picture he delivered (page 227), the heavy body of Christ is carried to the tomb by two strong men who clearly show the physical strain they are under. This means that action, not silent mourning, is in the forefront of the picture. Mary Magdalene has accompanied the dead Christ and is holding his lifeless hand. Boundless pain is reflected in her facial expression: her mouth is open in lamentation, and deep furrows are etched into her smooth forehead. The whole scene is conceived in dramatic terms: the tunic of the man carrying on the right is blowing to one side, as is Mary Magdalene's hair. The group on the right around the Virgin Mary is separated from the main scene, and she has collapsed, as if dead, into the arms of the women holding her. Here, instead of gracefulness, the artist has depicted an infinite suffering that is totally convincing in its naturalness.

A compositional problem Raphael faced here was how to show both groups as independent pictorial centers without allowing them to become two unrelated sections. He developed various solutions in several figure and group studies. In the course of this painting's development, the group around the Virgin moved to the right and became increasingly isolated. The result was that this group formed a kind of devotional picture within the main narrative, where the focus was on action. This creates a contrast between an active and a passive group, with the figures of the swooning Virgin and the dead Christ having a formal function as mirror images of one another, the Virgin supported and Christ carried.

In the squared-up *modello* (above) we can still see, between Mary Magdalene and the man on the right carrying Christ, a woman who thematically belongs to the group around the Virgin. Raphael eventually moved her to the right: her gaze towards the dead Christ now establishes the link between the two groups.

By changing the subject of his picture from a Lamentation of Christ to an Entombment, Raphael created the only large-scale narrative composition of his Florentine period. It represents an aspect of his art he was later to develop superbly in his Vatican frescoes.

As in the painting of his great Madonna pictures, in the development of the Borghese *Entombment* Raphael

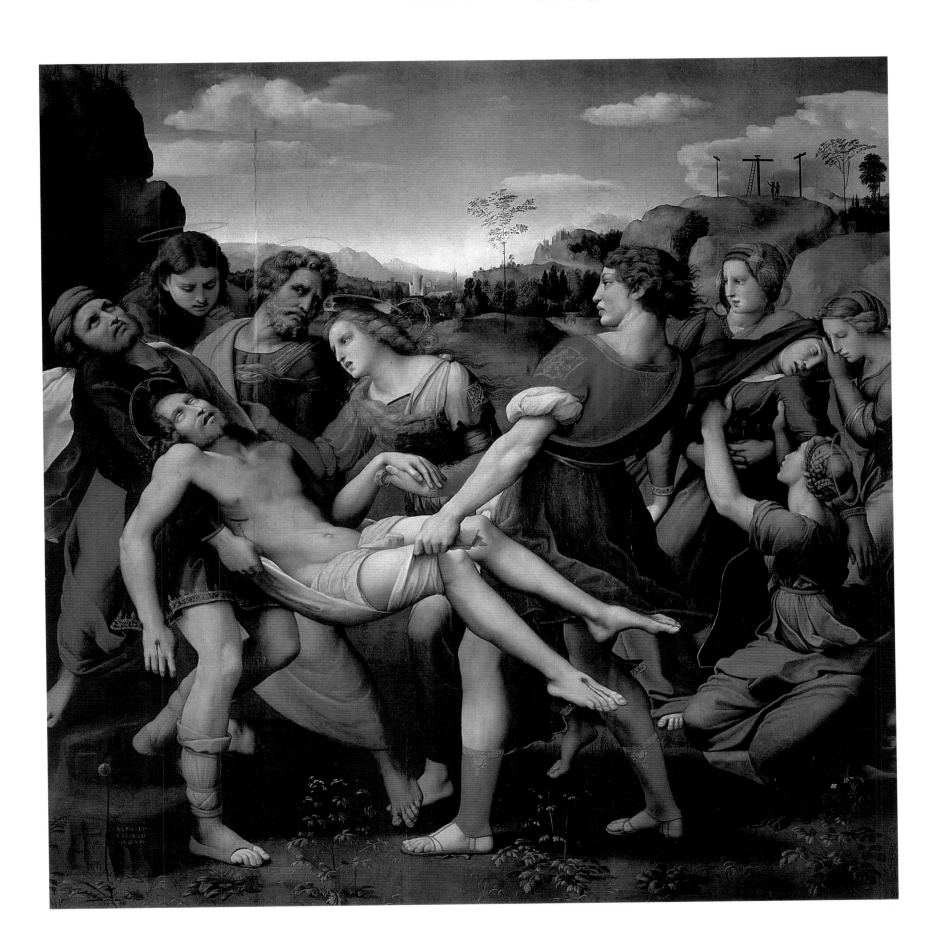

learnt a great deal by studying a wide range of works by other artists. The division of the composition into two sections can be found in a famous engraving, the *Entombment of Christ*, by Andrea Mantegna, in which both the man carrying on the left and the motif of the swooning Virgin can also be seen. Another source of inspiration, presumably, was a classical sarcophagus depicting the burial of Meleager, now in the Vatican. Michelangelo, too, played an important role once again. The muscular woman who turns to face the Virgin and supports her with outstretched arms quotes the figure of the Virgin Mary in his *Doni Tondo* (Volume I, page 611). In this figure we can already detect the monumentality that would later characterize Raphael's four seated figures on the ceiling of the Stanza della Segnatura (page 231), and also the last works he painted in Florence, around 1508.

In a letter dated 21 April 1508 to his uncle, Simone Ciarla, in Urbino, Raphael mentions a painting for which, by Easter, he had already completed a cartoon. This is generally thought to be his *Madonna with the Baldachino* (page 229). It was intended for the chapel of the Dei family in the church of Santo Spirito, in Florence, though it had still not been completed when Raphael moved to Rome. In his will of 20 July 1506, Rinieri di Bernardo Dei had expressed his wish to have the altarpiece painted, and gave detailed instructions about what it should contain. Thus, St. Bernard, his patron saint, was to appear in the picture: he is standing behind St. Peter. The Dei family did not, in fact, accept the uncompleted altarpiece. They preferred to commission a replacement from Rosso, a Madonna that is dated 1522 and that, like the *Madonna with the Baldachino*, is now hanging in the Palazzo Pitti. The unfinished work remained in Raphael's possession, and after his death his executor, Baldassare Turrini, purchased it for his own chapel in Pescia Cathedral.

In the light of this complicated history, it is not surprising that for a long time it was unclear which parts Raphael had painted himself, and which might have been painted by another artist later. The most recent restoration work, however, has removed all doubts about the picture's authorship. Apart from a horizontal strip along the top edge, which was added later, Raphael painted the whole picture himself. Even

Raphael
The Madonna with the Baldachino, 1507/08
Wood, 276 x 224 cm
Galleria Palatina, Palazzo Pitti, Florence

When Raphael went from Florence to Rome in 1508, this picture remained behind unfinished. The Virgin is enthroned beneath a baldachino. St. Peter and St. Bernard are on the left, while St. Augustine, and probably St. James the Elder, stand on the right. The restoration carried out in 1991 proved that all parts of the painting were by Raphael's hand, except the strip above the columns, which was added in 1697.

the angels, whose coloration and figurative vitality seem astonishingly modern, were also his work.

When compared with his earlier *sacra conversazione*, this painting is impressive by virtue of the freedom and authority of its use of space. The throne has been placed in a large semi-circular apse and leaves plenty of room for the saints, who turn to one another in lively conversation or point towards the Virgin Mary. Against the concave background of the imitation classical architecture, the baldachino projects forward in a convex shape, balancing the spatial relationships. The models cited for this superb composition include Venetian paintings, as well as works by Fra Bartolommeo, whose monumental figures in Florence fascinated Raphael.

It is difficult to confirm what exactly his models were, but by 1508 Raphael was certainly ready for a further step in his career, and entirely equal to the challenges he was to meet in Rome.

Raphael's Career in Rome 1508–1513: The Pontificate of Julius II

Raphael
Ceiling of the Stanza della Segnatura, ca. 1508–1511
Stanza della Segnatura, Vatican, Rome
The ceiling design is attributed to Sodoma, but he painted only the central octagon and the small spaces between the tondi. Raphael painted the personifications of Philosophy, Poetry, Theology, and Justice, as well as the four large panels in the corners, whose subjects refer to the two adjacent personifications. The architectural frames and their decorations are thought to be the work of a German painter, Jan Ruysch.

The remarkable career that awaited Raphael in Rome was meteoric. It was also to be brief. The credit for having recognized and fostered his talent is shared by two popes: Julius II, of the della Rovere family, and his immediate successor, Leo X, a Medici. Neither acted unselfishly in this: they both saw in Raphael a congenial collaborator in their struggle to create a humanistically colored vision of the papacy. The two popes differed in character, taste, culture, and political program. Yet the Restauratio Romae gave them a common goal: to restore ancient Rome's cultural and political importance under papal leadership.

As early as 1453, Nicholas V had begun reconstructing and extending a 13th-century building in the Vatican. Later, the Borgia pope, Alexander VI, used some of the apartments on the first floor of the north wing, and it was here that his successor, Julius II, resided at the beginning of his pontificate. Towards the end of 1507, Julius decided to refurbish the second floor, the so-called Stanze, because he no longer wished to live in the apartments occupied by his predecessor, whom he detested. He was annoyed by the frescoes Pinturicchio had painted for Alexander: less for any artistic statement they made than because they displayed Alexander's insignia everywhere. The artists whom Julius II commissioned to paint frescoes in the new apartments included Perugino and Sodoma, an artist who lived in Siena. Raphael took over this work on his arrival in Rome.

On 21 April 1508, Raphael wrote a letter from Florence to his uncle in Urbino asking him to procure him a letter of recommendation: he intended applying to the *signoria* in Florence to decorate one of their chambers (about which nothing further is recorded). In Florence, Raphael's career prospects had improved dramatically, for Michelangelo had left the city and was busy working on the frescoes in the Sistine Chapel in Rome, and Leonardo had moved back to Milan. In the circumstances, Raphael himself seemed surprised to be summoned to Rome. We do not know for certain whether it was in late 1508 or early 1509 that he joined the other artists in the Stanze. At all events, he was certainly there by 13 January 1509, as an entry in the ledger of the Papal Exchequer confirms. He must have established himself within a very short time, for as early as 8 October 1509 he was accorded the ecclesiastical honorary title of "Brief Writer," which was a sign of his acceptance at the Papal Court and, at the same time, a guarantee of a regular income.

Sodoma had made a successful start to the refurbishment of the Stanza della Segnatura (page 231). Hovering cupids hold the keystone of the whole vault with the coat-of-arms of Nicholas V, who built the Stanza, over an octagonal opening in the roof, which allows a clear view of the sky. In order to reinforce this illusion, he selected imitation gold-mosaic for the other pictorial backgrounds on the ceiling. Sodoma received the contract for the ceiling fresco on 13 October 1508.

Raphael
The School of Athens, 1509
Fresco, width at the base 770 cm
Stanza della Segnatura, Vatican, Rome

The School of Athens is a depiction of philosophy.
The scene takes place in classical times, as both the
architecture and the garments indicate. Figures
representing each subject that must be mastered in
order to hold a true philosophic debate—astronomy,
geometry, arithmetic, and solid geometry—are
depicted in concrete form. The two main figures,
Plato and Aristotle, are shown in the center, engaged
in such a dialogue.

Segnatura means "signature," and so denotes the
room's function in the mid-16th century, when the
pope used to sign and seal Papal Bulls and Briefs here.
Julius II wanted to use it as a private library.

The traditional way of decorating libraries went back
to the Middle Ages. Each of the four wall-surfaces was
allocated one faculty from the spectrum of knowledge
then available: Theology, Philosophy, Jurisprudence,
and Medicine. Since the late 15th century, Medicine
had been replaced by Poetry.

The decorative work on the Stanza della Segnatura
follows the usual pattern, whereby Theology,
Philosophy, Jurisprudence (as Justice), and Poetry were
presented as female figures. They all appear in four large
tondi on the ceiling. Along the walls are allocated to
them the appropriate *uomini famosi*, men and women
from history who had won fame in each of these fields.

When Raphael began working on the refurbishment
of the Stanza della Segnatura, this program of
decoration had already been decided. Possibly there

were plans for the entire room. Raphael's plans did not
alter the overall pattern at all, and yet his new ideas
drove all the other artists—including the highly
regarded old master, Perugino—out of the Stanze.

We can understand why his work was so successful
with the pope if we compare the traditional way in
which the *uomini famosi* were depicted in a fresco by
Perugino, completed around 1500, with Raphael's
famous philosophers, depicted in the *School of Athens*.
In Perugino's picture, the figures are all standing in a
line; Raphael, by contrast, portrayed not a row of
figures but an event, setting the figures in a context that
probably aptly depicts his humanist contemporaries'
view of the ancient world (below).

We do not know if the pope summoned Raphael
because he was hoping for an alternative design to the
stylistically traditional solution offered by Perugino,
though it is quite likely. According to Vasari, it was
Donato Bramante who had drawn the pope's attention to
Raphael. He and Raphael may well have been related.

Raphael
Disputa, ca. 1510/11
Fresco, width at the base 770 cm
Stanza della Segnatura, Vatican, Rome

The fresco can be seen as a portrayal of the Church
Militant below, and the Church Triumphant above. A
change in content between a study and the final fresco
shows that the *Disputa* and the *School of Athens* (opposite
page) can be seen as having a common theme: the
revealed truth of the origin of all things, in other words
the Trinity. This cannot be apprehended by intellect alone
(philosophy), but is made manifest in the Eucharist.

Furthermore, Bramante was on very good terms with Leonardo da Vinci, whose *Last Supper* (pages 190–191) in Santa Maria delle Grazie in Milan had established a completely new pictorial concept; in the 1490s Leonardo was working on his fresco at exactly the same time as Bramante was extending the church. So Bramante was familiar with the latest trends in painting, trends now being practiced by Raphael, and was aware that Perugino's more tender but less dramatic style was a thing of the past.

Leonardo's starting-point was the assumption that all the figures in a painting should play a role in the pictorial event. First of all, he would sketch out the outline composition, in which he depicted the figures as "stick people" to show what they could contribute to the action. If the main figure was telling a story, for example, the story's content should be apparent from the figure's pose, gestures, and facial expressions.

Moreover, Leonardo insisted, the reactions of those listening should also match the words of the storyteller. Only when this overall arrangement was sketched out would he paint the individual figures in greater detail, tighten up the composition, and fashion a harmonious picture. By this means Leonardo made his figures not only physically present but also—and above all—involved emotionally. Raphael had learnt this approach to painting during the years both artists had worked in Florence. His preliminary sketches from this period are much freer than his earlier works.

Even today there is still controversy over the order in which Raphael completed the frescoes in the Stanza della Segnatura. It seems reasonable to assume that first he finished the compositional sketches for all four walls, as well as the remaining ceiling pictures. He probably painted the four female personifications in the ceiling tondi first. Their monumental appearance

Raphael
Parnassus, ca. 1509/10
Fresco, width at the base 670 cm
Stanza della Segnatura, Vatican, Rome

Mount Parnassus, the home of Apollo, is, like the hill on which the Vatican is built, a place where in ancient times there was a shrine to Apollo dedicated to the arts. This has a direct bearing on the picture because through the window on the wall where the fresco is painted there is a view of the Cortile del Belvedere and the hill of the Vatican. There were newly discovered classical sculptures in the Cortile, such as the *Ariadne* that Raphael used as a model for the muse to the left of Apollo.

Above left:
Parnassus (detail page 234) Dante Alighieri

The Florentine poet Dante Alighieri (1265–1321), author of the *Divine Comedy*, is here depicted standing behind the classical Greek poet Homer. A preparatory study, now in Windsor, shows the detailed working out of the portraits. For Homer's face, Raphael used as a model a classical sculpture, the *Laocoön*, that had been discovered just a few years before. It is not known which model he used for Dante.

Above right:
Disputa (detail page 233) Dante Alighieri

Dante was one of the first humanists and one of the originators of the Early Renaissance. His *Divine Comedy*, a verse epic from 1320, was regarded as a theological work in Raphael's time, which is why in the Stanza della Segnatura the poet is included among the famous men of the Church.

Right:
Philosophy (detail page 231)
Fresco, dia. 180 cm
Stanza della Segnatura, Vatican, Rome

The woman enthroned is enveloped in a garment that has four colors, each of which represents one of the four elements, which in turn are symbolized by their pattern. Blue is for the stars (air), red is for the tongues of flame (fire), green is for the fish (water), and golden brown is for the flora (earth). Philosophy holds two books with the titles *Morals* and *Nature*, while two genii hold texts with Cicero's words *Causarum Cognitio* ("Know the Causes"). This picture is situated above the *School of Athens* (page 232).

suggests the influence of Fra Bartolommeo's work in Florence, and their body rotation that of Leonardo and Michelangelo. The unusual way in which Poetry (page 231) is supporting her book on her upper thigh is prefigured by the figure of St. Peter in the *Madonna with the Baldachino* (page 229). Later, Raphael completed three of the four rectangular picture areas on the ceiling; the fourth appears to have been painted by an unknown master.

"Know the causes" is the Latin inscription on the two tablets held by genii on either side of *Philosophy* (page 235). This is also the theme of the fresco on the wall immediately below *Philosophy*: the fresco to which, in the 17th-century, the writer on art Bellori gave the now famous title of the *School of Athens* (page 232). In the center stand Plato and Aristotle, the two most illustrious philosophers of classical times (page 29), immersed in a dialectical discourse. Only this form of discourse can lead to knowledge of causes, since it reveals contradictions and allows arguments for and against a proposition to be expressed. We can identify Aristotle from his book *Ethica (Ethics),* whose subject is the proper way for a person to behave in this world. Under his arm Plato is carrying the book *Timaios (Timaeus),* the dialogue in which he reflected on the nature and the creator of the cosmos. In his *Parmenides*, he speculated about the origin of numbers and defined the dialectical "triad" as their fundamental prerequisite: "I can only grasp the one if there is a second, which is different from the first. This difference between one and two constitutes the third." Plato saw a divine principle in this "triad," which is why Raphael depicts him (page 29) pointing upwards.

In the ceiling fresco above the *School of Athens*, *Philosophy* (page 235) is looking towards Poetry, under which Apollo, the classical god of music and poetry, on Mount *Parnassus* (page 234), is sitting by the stream flowing from Mount Helicon, the sacred residence of the Muses that is dedicated to the arts. He is surrounded by the nine Muses as well as nine ancient and nine modern poets (page 235). Playing a *lira da braccio*, Apollo is gazing upwards, indicating that his arts, music and poetry, are divinely inspired.

The motto accompanying the ceiling figure of Poetry is "Inspired by the Spirit." Her gaze directs the viewer to the figure of Theology, whose right hand is pointing towards the fresco beneath her, on which we can see the most important fresco in the Stanza, which Vasari called the *Disputa* (page 233). Here we are shown something that the ancient world could not know before the birth of Christ: the truth as revealed in the form of the Holy Trinity. The composition divides into two scenes, one above the other. In the lower scene the *uomini famosi* of the Church are in conversation. The central motif here is the Host on the altar, the truth as revealed in our living world. Positioned vertically above the Host (in the upper scene) we can see the dove, the symbol of the Holy Ghost, then Jesus Christ, and above Him God the Father—in other words, the Holy Trinity. Christ is the center of a form known as a deësis, in which the Virgin Mary on his right and St. John the Baptist on his left are interceding for humanity. Sitting on a semi-circular bank of cloud are those saints who directly witnessed the divine revelation, and from whose successors the Church was founded. As we have seen, Plato had anticipated the notion of the Trinity: the Christian doctrine of Salvation, in other words, had a precursor in classical philosophy. At this point the whole meaning of the room becomes clear: as Vasari observed, here the ancient world and Christianity are brought together in harmony.

The personification of Justice leads us into the period following the Incarnation of Jesus. She is looking down towards the lunette where there are three other personifications who, together with her, represent the four Cardinal Virtues, namely Fortitude, Wisdom, and Temperance. On the wall allocated to Justice we see only two *uomini famosi*, each of whom appears in a scene of his own. These scenes depict the handing over of important documents relating to the history of Civil and Canon (Church) Law. Emperor Justinian, a temporal ruler, presents the Pandects (a compilation of Roman laws) to the jurist Trebonianus, whilst Pope Gregory IX accepts the Decretals (a codification of Church law) from St. Raymond of Penaforte (page 236). This form of depiction had some compositional advantages, for here the wall space was broken up by a large off-center window.

In order to realize the basic concept of his program for the Stanza della Segnatura, which was to show the *uomini famosi* in conversation, Raphael needed to know more about these people than simply their names and symbols. To achieve this he had to consult a humanist who could not only answer his questions clearly but who also had a feeling for what was relevant to a painting. We now believe that this person was the poet and librarian Tommaso Inghirami. At the very

least, he played a role in developing the program of the
Disputa. We find Inghirami's portrait in the *School of
Athens*: he is on the left, where, crowned with a laurel
wreath, he stands writing behind a broken column.

The *School of Athens* (page 232), the theme of which
is dialectical discourse, is aptly named. The Athenian
philosopher Socrates, who was Plato's teacher, speaks of
the four steps that a pupil must climb in order to
conduct a philosophical discussion. They are: geometry,
astronomy, arithmetic, and solid geometry. With this in
mind, Raphael has depicted four steps leading to a
monumental hall. Socrates, who is standing next to
Plato on the left, with some other pupils, is counting
what we may assume are those four steps on his fingers.
Holding a celestial globe, the astronomer, Zoroaster, is
standing at the bottom right, talking to the astronomer
Ptolemy, who is holding a disc of the earth. Alongside
him, geometrician Euclid is explaining a star-shaped
geometrical figure to his pupils. On the left sits
Pythagoras, the arithmetician; he appears to be copying
something about the theory of musical harmony from a
tablet that a pupil is holding in front of him. Only solid
geometry cannot be linked to any named individual.
The man who is resting his elbow on the large block of
stone was added later, after the fresco was completed.
Art historians like to identify him as Michelangelo.
Here, it is supposed, Raphael was paying homage to the
master of the Sistine Ceiling, whose style this figure
reflects. The art historian Matthias Winner, however,
has suggested a much more plausible explanation for
this later addition. For Winner, the stone block
representing solid geometry can be interpreted
differently.

Pope Julius II seems to have been fond of the
metaphor of "living rock" as the origin of the Church.
This goes back to the First Epistle of Peter, in the New
Testament. There, Christ is described as the "chief
cornerstone" who is "elect, precious unto you ..." but
"a stone of stumbling, and a rock of offence, even to
them which stumble at the word." Raphael did indeed
depict a cornerstone, as we can clearly see from its fine
moldings.

Raphael built up his compositions in the Stanza della
Segnatura symmetrically. This allowed him (in the
School of Athens, for instance) to arrange groups to the
left and the right of the central figures as independent
units, as a kind of *sacra coversazione*. Intermediate
figures link these groups by means of gestures,
movements, and glances, so that the impression of a
large, lively school of philosophy is created.

An architectural backdrop, which prefigures future set
designs, provides the background. Vasari believed this
had been designed by Bramante, and it is certainly true
that such an architectural backdrop is scarcely
conceivable without his influence. However, Raphael
could well have designed it, for even in his earlier
works he had displayed a thorough knowledge of the
principles of pictorial architecture. Figures are pressing
into the picture from right and left, creating the
convincing impression of an inhabited architectural
space; some figures are leaning against the walls. With
a minimum of motifs, Raphael succeeds in blending
the background architecture harmoniously into the
pictorial whole.

Deep in debate, Plato and Aristotle are striding
towards us from the depths of a majestic hall. Both
figures, though, have been composed like standing
sculptures, and only Plato's hesitant step and Aristotle's
forward-pointing gesture give any indication of
movement. It is in fact the architecture that gives
the figures a sense of movement. The semi-circle of
the archway in the far distance, which frames the
two figures, is echoed rhythmically in semi-circles of
ever increasing size, creating a sense of movement that
is transferred to these two main characters. It was
compositions of this kind that convinced the pope of
Raphael's abilities. According to Vasari, the pope
decided to dispense with frescoes by other artists in order
to allow Raphael full scope to develop his program.

Even so, Raphael did not rest on the laurels he had
won from his work on the Stanza della Segnatura. On
the contrary, he remained just as willing to learn, took
up new subjects, and developed old ones further.
Nevertheless, he retained his clear symmetrical layout,
which had been so successful, as a compositional
principle. This form allowed him to achieve a
monumental overall effect that was easy to grasp, and
also created an ideal framework for his style of
composition, which was based on contrasts.

The commission for the Pope had alerted all Rome to
the young artist, and notably a wealthy banker, Agostino
Chigi, a friend of Julius II. Chigi commissioned Raphael
to decorate the ground floor of his newly built villa with
a mural featuring the sea-nymph Galatea (page 239).
This nymph was the first classical subject Raphael had
painted since his *Three Graces* (page 213).

The basic design is both simple and ambitious.
Galatea is the main figure. For her, Raphael once again
employed the *figura serpentinata*, depicting her amid
a turbulent mass of bodies twisting and turning in

Raphael
Portrait of a Cardinal, ca. 1510/11
Panel, 79 x 62 cm
Museo Nacional del Prado, Madrid

The red cape and hat identify the figure as a cardinal, but his identity has remained unknown. It might be Cardinal Francesco Alidosi, whom the humanist Bembo described with the cutting words, "Faith meant nothing to him, nor religion, nor trustworthiness, nor shame, and there was nothing in him that was holy."

Opposite page:
Raphael
Portrait of Pope Julius II, ca. 1512
Panel, 108 x 80 cm
The National Gallery, London

Pope Julius II gave this painting to the church of Santa Maria del Popolo, where after his death it was displayed on important feast days. In 1591 Cardinal Sfondorato sold it to Scipione Borghese. Its provenance until its acquisition by The National Gallery in 1824 is also documented, so that it can be said with certainty that the London picture is authentic, despite the many other existing versions.

the water, a few elegant cupids hovering above. The overall composition is dominated by an exciting rhythm, created by movement and counter-movement, with Galatea's red robe its triumphant focus.

Galatea is surrounded by a storm of physical temptation: naked bodies, passion, noise, tumult, and lust. She is indifferent to it all, her tender gaze seeing only the Cupid of Platonic love, who is sitting up above, his arrows still in his quiver. Standing in a shell, Galatea races through the water, remarkably calm considering the violent movement of the dolphins pulling her. Despite this inconsistency, Raphael created a harmonious and at the same time lively painting of incredible charm.

"We have to admit that Raphael was the superior artist in the painting of eyes and capturing the liveliness of a look." So concluded a comparison between Raphael and Michelangelo written in 1625 by Cardinal Federico Borromeo, founder of the Biblioteca Ambrosiana in Milan. The Madrid *Portrait of a Cardinal* (above) appears to bear out Borromeo's words. We see the dignitary seated in three-quarter profile against a dark background. His upper body is not turned towards us, though his eyes gaze at us all the more directly. The Cardinal's right eye is particularly striking in its rhythmic line, its three-dimensional modeling, and its clear expression. The convex shape of the eyeball is clearly defined in its socket, the eyelid coming down at a slight angle over the moistly gleaming pupil. The sitter's gaze is so direct it is difficult to meet it. This unknown figure was probably one of the more important people in the papal court, for his portrait (with the same penetrating look) is to be found on the left-hand side of the *Disputa* (page 233).

In this portrait, with its captivating colors, Raphael was once again trying to achieve a design rich in contrasts. The finely folded material of the sleeve, painted in broken white, forms the base on which the portrait bust is set. In its fluid softness this material forms a stark contrast to the stiff, heavy *mozzetta*, the cape worn by high dignitaries of the Church, and emphasizes its heaviness. This red fabric rises like a pyramid, and, together with the glowing red of the cap, frames the pale, cool skin of the gaunt subject.

The detail of Raphael's depiction directly recalls the Doni portraits (pages 218, 219), though now the conception is freer, the light softer. This portrait also reveals his increasing skill in rendering detail in a life-like way.

At about the same time as he painted this early Roman portrait, Raphael also completed the portrait of Tommaso Inghirami (Galleria Palatina, Palazzo Pitti, Florence). This scholar and poet was appointed Prefect of the Papal Library in 1510, and it is presumably from this period that the portrait, now in Florence, dates. It is assumed that Inghirami developed the program for decorating the Stanza della Segnatura jointly with Raphael.

As a close examination of the panel has shown, a green curtain originally formed the background. Raphael appears to have abandoned this in favor of the same kind of dark background he used for the portrait of the unknown cardinal (page 241). Despite this similarity between the two paintings, Raphael used a completely different approach in the Inghirami portrait. He portrayed the poet in a small pictorial narrative, depicting the intimate moment at which the scholar, sitting at his desk, is awaiting divine inspiration. His right hand holds his pen expectantly, while his left hand rests on a blank sheet of paper. An open book confirms that he is a scholar.

The idea of showing an author being divinely inspired dates back to classical times. In his interpretation of this theme, Raphael once again focused on the subject's eyes. In the process, he achieved a real feat, for Inghirami had a severe squint. Raphael depicted this defect honestly, and yet it is not in the least disturbing because the scholar's look, directed upwards and to the left, can be seen positively, as his search for inspiration. This subterfuge doubtless assured Raphael of his patron's approval, and that of the scholar's humanistic friends. It would also have earned the approval of Pliny the Elder, the classical writer whom humanists were fond of quoting. Pliny had praised the ancient Greek painter Apelles for inventing a technique that enabled an artist to conceal any physical defects in the subject of a portrait. Apelles painted King Antigonus in such a way that it was not possible to see that he had only one eye.

In his picture, Raphael made it more difficult for himself by showing both his subject's eyes, yet he was able to avoid any hint of a disturbing impression by ingeniously making the subject look for inspiration.

Here, too, Raphael developed a convincing pictorial space for the figure. Inghirami's stout body occupies its place behind the table in an imposing way. His right arm and hand are foreshortened to brilliant effect, and cover the full depth of the pictorial space in the foreground. The figure's sculptural three-dimensionality and the varied play of light and shade in the skin tones establish a direct link with the earlier *Portrait of a Cardinal*. A delicate glazing technique distinguishes both portraits, and this suggests that Raphael painted both immediately after his Florentine portraits, in other words during his first years in Rome.

When Julius II commissioned Raphael to paint his portrait, it must have been both an honor and a burden. How could he possibly surpass the portraits of the cardinal and Inghirami, both of which the pope undoubtedly admired? Raphael solved this problem by combining the two aspects of these portraits he had developed to such advantage: a clear emphasis on both expression and action (page 240).

A private audience provides the portrait's context. Raphael has shown us to a standing place, as protocol would demand, while the pope remains seated. The papal chair, whose backrest finials are crowned by the acorns from the della Rovere coat-of-arms, is presumably standing on a small pedestal; and behind the chair are emerald-green hangings bearing the papal coat-of-arms, crossed keys. Julius is calm and dignified. Audience means "listening," and that is exactly what the pope appears to be doing. He is looking at someone whom we cannot see, but who seems to be kneeling in front of him, his gaze open but critical, as if reflecting on what he has just heard. This makes his strong grip around the left-hand armrest look all the more powerful, while in complete contrast his right hand is holding a soft piece of cloth almost playfully. As in other Raphael paintings, a window is reflected in this picture, this time in the golden acorns of the finials. Even in his portraits, Raphael's central concern was with a picture's artistic effect, as another detail confirms: he has quite clearly moved the chair finial to the right to ensure that the pope's face is clearly delineated.

In a subtle interplay of look and gesture, Raphael communicates the contrast between the venerable pope's age and his historically documented energy. This, together with Raphael's depiction of precious materials, and his magnificent color harmonies, created by the velvet red, emerald green, and variations of white with gold highlights, make this a portrait worthy of a pope. Even though nowadays photography has made us familiar with realistic portraits, we can still agree with Vasari when he says that Raphael portrayed the pope "with so much realism and truth to life that when standing before the picture you have the strange feeling it might be alive."

The frescoes in the Stanza della Segnatura had established Raphael as a court painter. His next

commission, the decoration of the Stanza di Eliodoro, on which he worked from 1511 to 1514, confirmed his reputation in a very impressive way. The name of this room is derived from the fresco that Raphael painted first: the *Expulsion of Heliodorus* (above). The program for this room was not a traditional one: the subjects were developed specifically for this room and for Julius II personally. The general theme is that of God's intervention in human destiny, and it is presented through four stories, two from the Acts of the Apostles and the Apocrypha, and two from Church history. The room's ceiling was painted by Peruzzi and his assistants (possibly to designs by Raphael), about 1514. Here, four thematically corresponding scenes from the Old Testament are presented. The subjects of the previous frescoes have not come down to us.

The Pope intended to use this room as a private audience chamber. Accordingly, the frescoes were meant to illustrate the power of the Church and its representatives. The subjects are the Church's four enemies: those who affront the dignity of the Church,

those who threaten the Church and the whole of Christendom, those rulers who do violence to the Church's representatives, and finally those within the Church whose faith is weakened by doubt. The program was so general that a contemporary onlooker could well have recognized ecclesiastical opponents of the day, especially when Julius II himself appears in the scenes.

The opening scene, the *Expulsion of Heliodorus* (above), shows how the prayer of Onias, the High Priest, is heard, and Heliodorus, the Syrian occupier of Jerusalem, intent on plunder, is driven from the Temple by divine intervention. This scene could be interpreted as the pope's warning to the French forces who formerly occupied parts of the Vatican State.

For Raphael, these scenes represented a new artistic challenge. The task was to depict historical scenes of events that followed each other chronologically, even though a painting can show only one event at a time. Raphael's solution was to use the technique of simultaneous narration, which allows an artist to

Raphael
The Expulsion of Heliodorus, ca. 1512
Fresco, width at the base 750 cm
Stanza di Eliodoro, Vatican, Rome

In his depiction of the rider and the two hovering youths who expel the Syrian invader Heliodorus from the Temple, Raphael follows the text from Maccabees in the Apocrypha exactly. The horse owes a debt to Leonardo's design for the *Battle of Anghiari* in the Palazzo Vecchio in Florence.

depict several successive events in a single picture. So in the *Expulsion of Heliodorus* we see both the prayer of High Priest Onias, and, alongside that, the expulsion of Heliodorus.

Julius II appears as a witness to the events. By directing his gaze towards the High Priest in the pictorial center, he helps the viewer to follow the events in the correct chronological sequence, and at the same time draws the viewer's attention to the power of his office, represented here by an Old Testament High Priest. Chronologically, the scenes follow one another in the familiar "reading direction" of left to right. This makes Julius II seem like a viewer within the picture, the kind of figure the art theorist Alberti, in his famous treatise on painting, demanded for historical pictures. Once the viewer had been introduced to the scenes in this way, Heliodorus' highly dramatic punishment by a rider in golden armor and the two hovering youths in the right-hand half of the picture hardly needed further explanation.

Raphael placed the altar with the praying High Priest in the pictorial center, the vanishing point towards which the perspective lines of the spatial structure converge. The dramatically lit domes and the octagonal floor-slabs, which match the shape of the altar base, recede rhythmically towards the priest and create a counter-weight both to the dramatic scene on the right and to Pope Julius II on the left.

Here, for the first time, Raphael separated the historical figures who actually took part in the event from those figures of another period who witness its re-enactment: taken together, they depict two different planes of reality in one and the same setting. Traditionally, artists had often brought together people from different epochs in the same spot at the same time. The *sacra conversazione* is based on this principle, and Raphael's *Disputa* (page 233) follows the same pattern. In the *Expulsion of Heliodorus*, in contrast, those who participated in the past events belong to a different sphere from the pope with his retinue, the present-tense witnesses of those past events. Portraits, figures grouped in pyramid form, heavy fabrics and strong colors all distinguish the pope's retinue from the historical figures, who, painted in pastel tones, are swathed in flowing garments and performing dramatic gestures.

Raphael
The Mass at Bolsena, 1512
Fresco, width at the base 660 cm
Stanza di Eliodoro, Vatican, Rome

In 1263, a Bohemian priest, troubled by doubts about the doctrine of transubstantiation (the belief that the body and blood of Christ are present in the Eucharist), started on a pilgrimage to Rome. On his way he celebrated mass at Bolsena, and during the consecration the Eucharist began, miraculously, to bleed. Each time he wiped the blood away with a cloth a cross of blood would reappear, a miracle that swept away the priest's doubts. The cloth became a venerated relic and was later kept at Orvieto Cathedral.

Opposite page:
The Mass at Bolsena (detail page 244)
Pope Julius II

As in the *Expulsion of Heliodorus*, Raphael here made Julius II a witness of a miracle that took place in the past. On 7 September 1506 Julius had stopped at the cathedral at Orvieto to see the relic of the cloth that was used to wipe the blood from the Eucharist, and thereby to demonstrate his personal connection with the miracle for which Urban IV had instituted the Feast of Corpus Christi.

An off-center window opening made the second scene, the *Mass at Bolsena*, difficult to design. Raphael's ingenious solution was to paint a flight of steps leading up to a high platform, thereby incorporating the window opening into the picture and creating a symmetrical composition. On this platform, towards which we look up as if it were a real architectural detail, stands, in the very center of the picture, the altar on which the miracle of the Mass at Bolsena takes place (page 244).

To Julius II, the veneration of the Host was a personal concern. In order to make this clear, he himself takes part in the event he is witnessing, kneeling bare-headed at the altar, his hands clasped in prayer (page 245). A Bohemian priest, also kneeling at the altar, looks in astonishment at the Host in his left hand, whilst in his right hand he holds a cloth on which several blood-red crosses can be seen. A semi-circular wooden parclose stands behind the altar, creating an intimate space for this scene of worship. In the background a magnificent piece of architecture, in the style of Bramante, towers above, opening up to give a view of the sky.

Once again Raphael separated the historical figures on the left (the ones who actually attended the Mass at Bolsena) from the papal retinue on the right, a compositional principle also used in the earlier scene, the *Expulsion of Heliodorus* (page 243).

The third wall, on which Raphael painted the *Freeing of St. Peter* (page 247), is also broken up by a window, though centrally this time. Here Raphael employed a similar solution to the one he adopted in the *Mass at Bolsena*. Once again, the picture has a symmetrical, three-part architectural structure. On the left and the right, steps lead up into the scene, whilst the dungeon in the center lies just above the window opening. An angel frees St. Peter from his chains, then, holding him by the hand, leads him out of the dungeon. The choice of subject can again be explained from the biography of Julius II, whose titular church was called San Pietro in Vincoli, St. Peter in Chains. The most important relics preserved there were the chains with which St. Peter had (it was believed) been bound in prison. Julius withdrew to this church to give a prayer of thanks when, in 1512, he heard of a victory over the French forces threatening the Papal State.

When Julius II died, on 21 February 1513, Raphael had probably not started work on the fresco. Nevertheless, he had already decided on the overall design, as we can see from a sketch that was probably made when the pope was still alive (page 247). In the drawing, the architecture and the figures are already sketched out as they will appear in the fresco; in other words even at this early stage Raphael was clear about the narrative structure of the work. In the left foreground we see a soldier who is aware of the light issuing from an angel who has appeared in St. Peter's prison cell. Two guards standing further back are blinded by the brightness of this figure and hold their hands in front of their eyes; on the right, soldiers lie asleep.

In the fresco Raphael reduced the number of figures on the left, and instead emphasized both the monumentality of the individual figures and the expressiveness of their gestures. In comparison with the sketch, the torchlight in the painting greatly enhances the drama of the scene on the left.

In the fresco Raphael also solved a problem that had remained unresolved in the drawing. In the drawing the central room is not immediately recognizable as a prison. It was not until he completed the painting that Raphael put bars over the cell, creating one of the most remarkable examples of *contre-jour* painting in the history of art. Light appears in the picture in several different forms. Dawn is already breaking on the horizon, whilst the moon is still shining in the night sky. The torch held by the soldier on the left lights the action on the steps dramatically, and the unearthly brilliance of the angel illuminates both the prison and the right-hand side of the picture. This glowing light radiating from the angel, which bathes him in pastel tones, places him on a different level of reality. This was the first time that Raphael used light, as well as color, to distinguish between human and heavenly figures. He continued to use this technique, which he displayed to magnificent effect in the *Sistine Madonna* (page 253).

Although Raphael's main task was to decorate the Stanze, he still found time for a subject that had preoccupied him for a long time: the Madonna and Christ Child with the boy Baptist. A drawing in Lille documents the compositional considerations that Raphael developed in three Madonna pictures. In the center of the drawing we see the sketch for the *Madonna Alba* (page 248), which more or less matches the painting. In the upper left-hand corner of the picture, Raphael drew two other figure studies (page 249), preparatory sketches in which he explores the relationship between the Virgin Mary, the Christ Child, and the boy Baptist. The drawing in the center has also been linked with the *Madonna della Tenda* (page 249), but in this drawing Raphael appears to be toying with the idea of a circular composition, for the Madonna's back is bent in such a way that the figure might be fitted into a tondo. This suggests that the sketch is more closely linked with the *Madonna della Sedia* (page 250).

Sigismondo Conti must have commissioned Raphael to complete the Madonna di Foligno (page 252) by 1511 at the latest, for by 18 February 1512 Conti, the Papal Secretary and Prefect of the Stonemasons' Lodge of St. Peter, was already dead. Until 1565, the panel adorned the High Altar of the church of Santa Maria in Aracoeli, where Conti is buried. Thereafter it was transferred to the Franciscan church of Foligno (which explains its present name), where it remained for over 230 years.

Here the picture type Raphael chose was again that of the *sacra conversazione*. The donor is included in the picture, and is kneeling on the right, with St. Jerome recommending him to the Virgin Mary, who, in turn,

Raphael
The Freeing of St. Peter, 1514
Fresco, width at the base 660 cm
Stanza di Eliodoro, Vatican, Rome

The story in the New Testament says that King Herod
took Peter prisoner and intended to have him killed. In
prison, the Apostle was chained to two guards, but an
angel of the Lord freed him despite the close watch. The
fresco is dated 1514 on two painted tablets in the picture.

Right:
Raphael
Study for The Freeing of St. Peter, ca. 1512
Pen and ink wash, heightened with white chalk over
stylus and charcoal underdrawing, 25.7 x 41.7 cm
Gabinetto dei Disegni e delle Stampe,
Galleria degli Uffizi, Florence, inv. 536E

In spite of the heavy damage on the upper edge, the
drawing reveals how Raphael developed the *Freeing of
St. Peter*. At this stage he was concerned with indicating
the main areas of light and shadow in order to create the
desired light effect in the fresco.

is interceding between the saint and Christ. The viewer is also involved, for St. John the Baptist stands on the left, looks straight at us, and points (in a traditional gesture) to the Madonna. In front of him kneels St. Francis, fervently interceding for all those who are praying before the picture. His slightly inclined head, his beatific expression, the firm grip he has on his crucifix, and his relaxed gesture, made towards the viewer, all anticipate Baroque motifs. Raphael had mastered a pictorial language that allocate a specific role to each figure (a role conveyed through pose, look, and gesture) before he painted his Roman works. What is new is the visionary concept, which presents the Madonna and Christ Child enthroned on clouds, with a yellow light behind them. Here, Raphael was drawing on an old tradition: the Roman emperor Augustus is supposed to have had a vision in which the Virgin Mary with the Tiburtine Sibyl appeared against a burst of light—a vision that was said to have taken place where the church of Santa Maria in Aracoeli, the church for which Raphael's picture was intended, was built.

Once again Raphael was faced with the problem of having to depict various levels of reality in a single picture. The three saints really do see the vision before them: St. Jerome is looking directly at the Virgin Mary and with his right hand is pointing out the meteorite that is falling in the depths of the picture. Conti, on the other hand, has a blank expression: he appears not to see the vision; as far as his prayer of thanksgiving to the Virgin Mary is concerned, he is dependent on his intercessor, St. Jerome.

The *Sistine Madonna* (page 253) is probably Raphael's most famous Madonna. What is the source of its appeal? Behind a drawn-back curtain we see an apparition bathed in golden light, a heavenly vision. Walking on clouds, the Madonna moves towards us, the hem of her robe fluttering, her shawl blown out by the wind. An elegant rhythm characterizes the entire figure. She holds the Christ Child up to be seen, but protectively; her sad expression indicates that she is already aware of her son's fate. He sits confidently in her arms, which makes his shyly inclined head seem all the more gentle, just as the uncertainty in his eyes makes

Raphael
Madonna Alba, 1511–1513
Panel transferred to canvas, dia. 95 cm
National Gallery of Art, Washington

Paolo Giovio, Raphael's first biographer, commissioned this Madonna. Jesus has taken the cross from the boy Baptist, thus indicating the symbol of his Passion. The older boy is looking at him full of understanding, and visibly saddened. The Virgin has put her hand on his shoulder as if to comfort him.

Left: Raphael
Madonna Studies, ca. 1511–1513
Red chalk, pen and ink, heightened with white chalk,
42.2 x 27.3 cm
Cabinets des Dessins, Musée des Beaux-Arts, Lille,
inv. pl. 456

The subject of the Madonna and Child presented Raphael
with the constant challenge of finding new variations on the
theme. Some of the studies were not used as a basis for his
paintings until years later. This drawing in red chalk shows
several variations on the same page. In the center is the study
for the *Madonna Alba* (page 248), while the sketch above
was used later for the *Madonna della Sedia* (page 250).

Right: Raphael
Madonna della Tenda, ca. 1512–1514
Panel, 68 x 55 cm
Alte Pinakothek, Bayerische Staatsgemäldesammlungen,
Munich

The Virgin and Child are sitting in front of a green curtain
that has been drawn to one side. The boy Baptist is pressing
close to the two figures, and Jesus is trying to look over his
shoulder as if to see who is there. The authenticity of the
painting is no longer in question. What remains controversial
is whether it was executed before or after the *Madonna della
Sedia* (page 250), which is closely related stylistically.

the way He is holding his mother's shawl all the more
expressive. Like the Virgin Mary, he is majestic, yet
responds in a very human way to the fate that awaits
him.

The saints on the left and right form part of the vision.
We can recognize St. Barbara by her attribute, a tower.
The kneeling pope has been given a tiara on which there
is an acorn from the della Rovere coat-of-arms. His
features are those of Julius II; the halo, however, means
this is meant to be Pope Sixtus, the patron saint of the
della Rovere family. This interpretation is supported by
Vasari, who states in his *Lives* of 1550 that this picture
was to be found on the high altar of the abbey church of
St. Sixtus in Piacenza. This church owned some relics of
St. Barbara, which explains why she appears in the
picture together with St. Sixtus. Julius II had a personal
connection with this abbey, and during his period as a
cardinal he gave financial support to various building
projects there. What is not yet clear, however, is whether
the picture was simply sent to Piacenza, or whether it
was in fact intended for this location from the very
beginning.

This is the only altarpiece Raphael painted on
canvas rather than wood panel. This has led to the
suggestion that it formed part of the temporary
feature adorning the tomb of Julius II. According to
this interpretation, the deceased Julius II appears as
St. Sixtus, professing the following as he intercedes in
heaven for humanity, together with the Virgin Mary:
"I, Julius, am bringing my influence to bear on behalf
of the world." His gesture could well be interpreted in
this way.

In his *St. Cecilia with Saints* (page 255), which
dates from around the same time as the *Sistine
Madonna*, Raphael painted another large-scale
altarpiece. Elena Duglioli dall'Olio, who was later
sanctified, commissioned the painting for her family
chapel in the church of San Giovanni in Monte,
Bologna, which was completed in 1516, after some
rebuilding work.

Her head inclined to the side and her eyes gazing
upwards, the saint, who has just stopped playing her
organ, is listening to the singing of an angelic choir.
Raphael had used this pose in an earlier picture,

RAFFAELLO SANZIO
N. AD VRBINO 6 APRILE 1183
M. IN ROMA 6 APRILE 1520
MADONNA DELLA SEGGIOLA

151

Raphael's Workshop
The Madonna with the Fish, ca. 1513–1515
Panel, transferred to canvas, 215 x 158 cm
Museo Nacional del Prado, Madrid

The Archangel Raphael is presenting the young Tobias to the Virgin enthroned in the center. Tobias is holding a shining fish, with whose gall bladder he has, according to the story in the Old Testament, cured his father's blindness. St. Jerome is on the right with a lion (his main attribute) and a magnificent book. The panel is believed to be by workshop assistants, including Francesco Penni and Guilio Romano.

Opposite page:
Raphael
Madonna della Sedia, 1512–1514
Panel, dia. 71 cm
Galleria Palatina, Palazzo Pitti, Florence

The bodies of the Virgin, Christ, and the boy Baptist fill the whole picture. The tender, natural looking embrace of the Mother and Child, and the harmonious grouping of the figures in the round, have made this one of Raphael's most popular Madonnas. The isolated chair leg is reminiscent of papal furniture, which has led to the assumption that Leo X himself commissioned the painting.

Parnassus, when depicting blind Homer receiving divine inspiration. St. Paul, St. John the Evangelist, St. Augustine, and Mary Magdalene stand about her like pillars, with calm gestures and restrained movements; only St. Cecilia can hear the music. The directions in which the figures are looking guide the viewer through the picture. Mary Magdalene's gaze, directly at the viewer, draws us into the picture, her arm then leading us to the pictorial center. Behind St. Cecilia, St. Augustine and St. John exchange meaningful looks and seem to be communing silently about the saint;

next to her, St. Paul looks quizzically at the instruments lying on the ground (page 254). At first, it is surprising that these are damaged and unplayable; in fact, this is a way of showing the limits of earthly music, which cannot equal divine harmonies. As the art historian Anna Maria Brizo has recognized, Raphael made the divine accessible through the figures of saints fulfilled by the vision: God's presence becomes tangible in the mystical experience of human beings. Worship itself has become the picture's subject, for only worship can lead to a vision of the divine.

Raphael
Madonna di Foligno, ca. 1511/12
Panel, 320 x 194 cm
Pinacoteca Apostolica Vaticana, Vatican, Rome

The papal secretary Sigismondo de' Conti donated this
ex voto altarpiece in 1511. A meteorite had fallen on
Conti's house, a catastrophe Conti himself survived.
Raphael portrays this event in the background. Conti
is kneeling in the foreground and St. Jerome is
recommending him to the Madonna, while John the
Baptist and St. Francis are on the left.

Opposite page:
Raphael
Sistine Madonna, ca. 1513/14
Canvas, 265 x 196 cm
Gemäldegalerie Alte Meister,
Staatliche Kunstsammlungen, Dresden

Generations of visitors to the Gemäldegalerie Alte Meister
in Dresden have been deeply impressed by the way in
which Raphael portrayed the Madonna in this painting.
It has been reproduced over and over again, and almost
everyone is familiar with the putti leaning on the
balustrade. The Madonna appears from behind a curtain,
confident and yet hesitant. The curtain gives the illusion
of hiding her figure from the eyes of the onlooker and at
the same time of being able to protect Raphael's painting.

St. Cecilia with Saints (detail page 255)
Musical Instruments

Vasari attributed this wonderful still-life to Raphael's assistant, Giovanni da Udine. A close examination has shown, however, that the instruments are by the same hand as the rest of the painting, namely by Raphael.

Opposite page:
Raphael
St. Cecilia with Saints, ca. 1514–1516
Panel, transferred to canvas, 238 x 150 cm
Pinacoteca Nazionale, Bologna

This altarpiece was commissioned by Elena Duglioli dall'Olio of Bologna. She was famous for having visions and ecstatic fits in which music played a great part, which is probably why she asked for a picture of St. Cecilia, the patron saint of music. Raphael decided on a painting in the style of a *sacra conversazione*, with St. Cecilia in the center surrounded by St. Paul, St. John, St. Augustine, and Mary Magdalene.

MASTERY ACHIEVED, 1513–1520: THE PONTIFICATE OF LEO X

When Julius II died in 1513, Raphael had to interrupt his work on the Stanze only briefly, for very soon Giovanni de' Medici, who took the papal name of Leo X, was elected as his successor. He was expected to inaugurate a period of peace, and there were hopes for a new unity between Church and Christendom. People understood the name Medici, meaning "doctor," as a reference to Leo's task: to heal the wounds of the Christian world. His temperament was very different from that of his warlike predecessor, and he did indeed use his diplomatic skills to make the Papal State stronger. When Leo X made his triumphant entry into Rome, the banker Agostino Chigi, made an apt observation: warlike Mars was being followed by Pallas Athene, the goddess not only of war, but also of wisdom and the arts. Like his predecessors, Leo saw it as his duty to re-establish the glory of ancient Rome under papal leadership. He very nearly achieved this aim, though he was to go down in history as the pope under whom the Western Church finally split apart. He also left his successors a mountain of debts.

This cultivated pope found in Raphael a man who could realize ambitious cultural objectives, and he greatly extended the artist's range of tasks. First he was to complete the frescoes in the Stanza di Eliodoro. In the case of the *Freeing of St. Peter* no change seemed necessary, for by sheer coincidence the scene alluded to one of Leo's personal experiences: when he was a cardinal, the French had temporarily made him a prisoner-of-war in Ravenna.

For the fourth wall, Julius II had foreseen a painting of the meeting between Leo I and Attila, King of the Huns, in 452; by another coincidence, this was an incident in which a patron saint of the new pope was the main figure. In the Renaissance, a person's name was considered very important, since it was seen as determining its owner's character and personal destiny. Like his predecessor, Leo X saw himself confronted by a Turkish threat to the West. Indeed, it is possible that Giovanni de' Medici chose the name Leo solely for the reason that, following the example of Leo I, he wanted to avert a Turkish threat. Accordingly, Raphael was able to retain the projected subject under the new pope, even though he reworked the composition in certain key respects.

In a drawing in the Louvre from the time of Julius II, the Apostles, St. Peter and St. Paul, halt Attila and his warriors in the foreground, whilst the papal retinue appears in the background. In the fresco, however, the pope is in the foreground, riding in from the left and with a view of Rome behind him. With just a gesture of his hand Leo succeeds in halting the advance of the attacking Huns. God has intervened at his request. St.

Peter and St. Paul, who hover above Leo armed with swords, represent the divine, but they are acting only at the instigation of the pope—a pope who has the features of his later successor, Leo X (pages right).

The narrative is presented more dramatically here, so new compositional solutions were called for. Raphael found them by exploring classical relief sculptures; those on Trajan's Column in Rome, for instance, whose elaborate gestural language fascinated him. He replaced his much-admired symmetrical composition with a balanced interplay between different masses and forces, though his compositions were still full of contrasts. Whilst the papal retinue on the left looks authoritative and is virtually static, the figures in pastel colors on the right-hand side of the picture are violently agitated.

In mid 1514 Raphael began decorating another room, now known as the Stanza dell'Incendio. The plan was to show four different scenes, in each of which a pope called Leo took part. They are: the *Burning of the Borgo* (pages 258–259), the *Battle of Ostia*, the *Coronation of Charlemagne*, and the *Justification of Leo III*. For the *Burning of the Borgo*, Raphael used the basic idea of the Attila scene. Once again it was the pope who, with merely a movement of his hand, called a halt to the blazing inferno that threatened to destroy a whole district of the city.

The start of the work on this project coincided with the death of Bramante, who had, up to then, supervised the rebuilding of St. Peter's. To fill the vacant post, Leo X organized a competition. Much to his own surprise, as he explains in a letter, Raphael won and Leo X appointed him the new architectural supervisor of the rebuilding work on St. Peter's.

He also appointed two experienced collaborators—Fra Giocondo from Verona, and Giuliano da Sangallo the Elder, the Medici's architect—to help Raphael, who had no architectural experience. Within a very short time, they had helped him to develop his own expert knowledge. They made him familiar with the classical textbook on architecture by Vitruvius, and in 1514 Raphael commissioned the scholar Fabio Calvo to translate this into Italian, a translation he then studied intensively. This manuscript, complete with Raphael's handwritten comments, is now in the Staatsbibliothek, Munich. Following the death of Fra Giocondo in 1515 and of Sangallo in 1516, Raphael was appointed to be in sole charge of the colossal project.

Raphael's new duties had two decisive effects on his work. First, he had scarcely any time left for individual works of his own, so that his workshop became increasingly involved in completing projects (pages 260, 261), as had happened already with the frescoes in the Stanza dell'Incendio. The second effect was to deepen

Raphael
The Repulse of Attila, ca. 1513/14
Fresco, width at base 750 cm
Stanza di Eliodoro, Vatican, Rome

In 452, Pope Leo I managed to halt Attila the Hun,
on his way to invade Rome, at the River Mincio near
Mantua. The Eternal City was thus saved from
destruction. In the fresco, Leo X, in the figure of his
namesake, is riding with great dignity in the
company of his retinue towards the Huns, who are
galloping into the picture from the right. A mere
wave of Leo's hand is enough to repel them.

Following double pages:
Raphael
The Burning of the Borgo, 1514
Fresco, width at base 670 cm
Stanza dell'Incendio, Vatican, Rome

The event depicted happened in 847 and is documented
in the *Liber Pontificalis* (a collection of early papal
biographies). Pope Leo IV managed miraculously to halt
the raging fire, which was threatening an area of the city,
by his benediction from the loggia of Old St. Peter's.
While those in the foreground are desperately trying to
put out the fire, the female figure in yellow with her back
to us is begging them to look at the only effective source
of help, the Pope.

Raphael's Workshop
The Hill of Calvary, ca. 1515
Canvas, 318 x 229 cm
Museo Nacional del Prado, Madrid

The religious community the Olivetani of Santa Maria
dello Spasimo in Palermo commissioned this picture from
Raphael. When it was being transported by sea to Sicily, it
is supposed to have gone down with the ship, and to have
drifted into the port of Genoa. Monks found it there and
thought its appearance a miracle.

Raphael's Workshop
The Boy Baptist in the Desert, ca. 1517
Canvas, 163 x 147 cm
Galleria degli Uffizi, Florence

This painting was carried out to Raphael's design by
workshop assistants. The brown rocky background and
the modeling of the figure show the strong influence of
Leonardo. The quality of the light is not typical of
Leonardo, though; it does not surround the forms
softly but models them sharply.

Raphael's interest in the ancient world. In August 1515,
Leo X appointed him Director of Antiquities, his role
being to take care of Rome's ancient monuments. This
post required a wide-ranging knowledge of classical
architecture, sculpture, and painting. It also reaped
artistic rewards, for Raphael in his future work on room
decoration. He had a map prepared on which all the
city's ancient buildings were to be marked. By the time
of his death only a small fraction of this map had been
completed, and even that has not survived.

The Sistine Chapel was the official private chapel of
the popes, where the Conclave, the body which elected
a new pope, also met. The rebuilding of St. Peter's
made it necessary for other high-level ceremonies to be
held in the Chapel. Pope Sixtus IV della Rovere, the
uncle of Julius II, had had the Sistine Chapel built, and
had commissioned the leading artists in Florence in
the late 15th century to adorn it with episodes from the
lives of Christ and Moses. He also had imitation
tapestries showing the della Rovere coat-of-arms
painted.

On important Church feast days venerable wall-
hangings were hung in front of these simulated
tapestries. The hangings depicted scenes of Christ's
Passion, and, according to one legend, they came
originally from Jerusalem. In Leo X's opinion these had
become too worn and unsightly and had therefore to
be replaced. The timing was clearly right, for this
replacement gave Leo an opportunity to leave behind a
visible sign of his own papacy in the most important
chapel in Christendom. The coat-of-arms of Leo X,
commissioned from Raphael, unmistakably adorns the
borders of the new tapestries.

Initially a scholar (no name has come down to us)
was presumably commissioned to provide a program
for the cycle of tapestries, and was instructed to select
the scenes that would accord with the key features of
the new pope's ecclesiastical policy while remaining in

Raphael (Workshop?)
St. Michael and Satan, 1518
Panel, transferred to canvas, 268 x 160 cm
Musée du Louvre, Paris

The painting was a gift from the Pope to the French king,
Francis I. It is now debated whether the work, long
thought to be by workshop assistants, may not in fact be
by Raphael after all, the stylistic anomalies being
attributable to poor restoration techniques.

keeping with the decoration already there. Leo
expected Raphael to interpret these themes artistically.
Presumably, Raphael was commissioned to do this in
late 1514 or early 1515; by June 1515 he had received
an advance payment. The designs were completed by
late 1516, since we have documentary evidence that
the final payment was made on 20 December.

The tapestries were woven in the finest tapestry
workshop of the day, that of Pieter van Aelst in
Brussels. One tapestry was completed by 1517, and
seven tapestries were ready to be hung in the Sistine
Chapel for the Christmas festivities of 1519. Three
others must have arrived shortly before Leo's death in
1521, for the inventory made just after his death lists a
total of ten tapestries. During the Sack of Rome in
1527, these works were stolen, and were not returned
until the 1550s. Seven of the cartoons, designs drawn
to scale, are in the Victoria and Albert Museum,
London. The tapestries themselves, all woven by Pieter
van Aelst, are now in the Vatican Museums.

The tapestries recount stories from the Acts of the
Apostles. Four of them depict scenes from the life of
St. Peter. These are: *Christ's Charging of Peter*; the
Miraculous Draught of Fishes; the *Healing of the Lame
Man*; and the *Death of Ananias*. The other six
tapestries illustrate scenes from the life of St. Paul. They
are: the *Stoning of St. Stephen*, which depicts an event
St. Paul ordered; the *Conversion of St. Paul*; the
Blinding of the Sorcerer, Elymas; the *Sacrifices in Lystra*;
St. Paul in Prison; and *St. Paul Preaching in Athens*
(page 262).

St. Peter and St. Paul were both martyred in Rome, a
fact that substantiated and legitimated the choice of
this city as the seat of the papacy. Leo X was using the
program of the tapestries to demonstrate this, and thus
to assert that ecclesiastically his immediate predecessors
had been right to return to Rome after the so-called
Babylonian Captivity in Avignon.

Raphael's designs revolutionized the tradition of
tapestry weaving, for they required a faithful rendering
of atmosphere, light, textures, and pictorial form that
had never been seen in this medium before. Here, for
the first time, the usual monochrome background, or
one depicting flowers and small ornaments, was
abandoned in favor of a genuine pictorial space in
which the figures could move about.

In the task he had set himself Raphael was facing a
double challenge. First, he was well aware how
important this project was to Leo X. Secondly, he felt

Raphael
Cartoon for *St. Paul Preaching in Athens*, ca. 1514/15
Mixed media on paper, mounted on canvas,
343 x 442 cm
Victoria and Albert Museum, London

The Acts of the Apostles say that Paul was enraged when he saw how many images of pagan gods there were in Athens. A group of philosophers asked him to explain his position in the Areopagus, the ancient debating site in Athens. In the cartoon, Paul is lending emphasis to his talk with dramatic gestures, while those listening are all reacting in very different ways. The man on the right at the front, with the ecstatic look on his face, is probably Dionysius Areopagita, who is said to have been converted to the Christian faith by this sermon.

overshadowed by Michelangelo's Sistine ceiling, by which he knew he would be measured as an artist. Michelangelo had achieved impressive and in some cases extreme color effects.

Raphael remembered his own pictorial effects, as demonstrated in the frescoes of the Stanza di Eliodoro. In his designs, he staked everything on the atmospheric effects of the light and color, enlivened by contrasts and delicate nuances. In this respect, however, the final outcome was a failure, in that he had over-estimated the technical potential of tapestry weaving. All the same, the tapestries were an enormous success when shown in the Sistine Chapel in 1519.

At the same time, Raphael again succeeded brilliantly in his historical depictions. As earlier in the *School of Athens* (page 232), he developed a pictorial language that made the ancient world alive and tangible. The compositions are full of tension and the narrative style dramatic. The figures' facial expressions can be easily read, their grand gestures are eloquent, and they elicit varied and unmistakable reactions from the onlookers. In *St. Paul Preaching in Athens* (pages 262, 263), the viewers become the listeners, joining the circle of those people the Apostle is addressing. In this scene, Raphael succeeded in creating a classical mood by integrating into the composition motifs from Roman reliefs and classical figures, buildings, and statues.

By the time his work in the Stanza di Eliodoro was almost finished Raphael had achieved total mastery of the use of light and color. We can also see this in his portraits of *Baldassare Castiglione* (page 265) and *La Donna Velata* (page 264), which he painted about 1516. By this time harsh color contrasts have disappeared from the pictures. Light plays on the fabrics and enlivens the compositions.

Raphael
Study for *St. Paul Preaching in Athens*, ca. 1514/15
Red chalk over stylus underdrawing, 27.8 x 41.8 cm
Gabinetto dei Disegni e delle Stampe,
Galleria degli Uffizi, Florence, inv. 540E

Raphael made drawings for his tapestry cartoons, just as
he did for his paintings. The figure of St. Paul was
adopted into the final version almost unchanged, but the
positions of the figures to right and left in the cartoon
were changed markedly. The man in the center with his
finger laid reflectively on his lips was abandoned entirely.
It is possible that assistants in Raphael's workshop posed
for this drawing.

In the portrait of Castiglione, the coloration seems to
be reduced to one main color effect, the limpid blue of
the sitter. In the woman's portrait, however, the interest
lies in the contrast between her restrained appearance
and the billowing material of her dress. Unusually free
brushstrokes here achieve the most delicate effects,
creating highlights and making the material's texture
more tangible. Raphael crops the hands of both
subjects, which has the effect of bringing the sitters
closer to the viewer. The faces of the two sitters look at
the viewer from eye-level and with an air of being an
equal.

Raphael must have completed Castiglione's portrait
before the end of 1516, for around that time
Castiglione, who was ambassador of the court of
Urbino, was recalled to Mantua from Rome, and, now
married with a child, he was not able to return to his
ambassadorial duties in Rome before 1519. His portrait
stayed with his family, as a letter from the writer Pietro
Bembo, dated 19 April 1516, makes clear. It is also
confirmed by Castiglione himself, who wrote an elegy
that expresses the feelings of his wife, who stayed at
home: "Only your portrait, painted by Raphael, can
almost alleviate my sorrow when it makes your features
present for me." The notion of attributing enough
power to a painted portrait to make the subject seem
present is an expression of artistic praise that goes back
to classical times.

Another portrait type can be traced back to a literary
tradition of classical times: that of the double portrait
that commemorates the sitters' friendship. Mantegna
was the first artist to paint this kind of double portrait,
in 1480. A portrait of this kind by Mantegna, now lost,
portrayed two writers who were separated because one
of them had to go back to Hungary from Mantua. A

similar situation led to Raphael's *Double Portrait of
Andrea Navagero and Agostino Beazzano* (page 266). In
this case three friends were involved, for Pietro Bembo
probably commissioned the picture from Raphael. A
letter that mentions a joint excursion the friends made
(together with Castiglione and Raphael) to Tivoli in
the spring of 1516 talks about the circle these men had
established. Moreover, because we are aware that
Navagero was recalled to Venice in late 1516, we know
why this double portrait was commissioned. We also
know who owned it: in 1530 the portrait was hanging
in Bembo's house in Padua. Navagero and Beazzano
seem to have just been interrupted in mid-
conversation, and they are turning spontaneously
towards the viewer. The magnificent lighting makes
the heads look very three-dimensional, and the way
they are looking from moistly glistening eyes endows
both expressions with great immediacy. The rich but
restrained coloration and the subtle highlights on the
subjects' skin and garments relate the picture
stylistically to the portraits of Castiglione and *La
Donna Velata* (pages 264, 265), painted shortly before.

Raphael's later portraits are painted on canvas,
possibly because this is easier to transport than heavy
wood panels. Also on canvas is a double portrait
showing the artist himself standing behind a man on
whose shoulder his hand rests familiarly (page 267).
Raphael painted it only a short while after the double
portrait of Navagero and Beazzano, and it is stylistically
related to it. Further, the expressiveness of this gesture
links it to the designs for the tapestries and to Raphael's
last altarpiece, the *Transfiguration* (page 271), works in
which Raphael had developed a powerful and eloquent
language of gesture. The unknown man is pointing out
of the picture, but at the same time has turned towards

Raphael
La Donna Velata, ca. 1514–1516
Canvas, 82 x 60.5 cm
Galleria Palatina, Palazzo Pitti, Florence

The features of this woman, who has never been decisively identified, can be seen in the *Sistine Madonna* (page 253); the unknown woman seems to represent Raphael's ideal of beauty at this time, a fact that helps to date the painting. The style is reminiscent of that of Raphael's portrait of Castiglione (opposite page), particularly in its reduced range of colors, and this too supports the dating.

Raphael and is looking at him. Exactly what he is pointing at is just as keenly debated as his identity. Was this unknown man one of Raphael's friends, and was the gesture of turning intended for the person commissioning the picture? If so, we should interpret this double portrait as a souvenir picture. It is also possible, however, that Raphael and the unknown man are standing in front of a mirror.

Raphael also painted a very personal portrait in the so-called *La Fornarina* (page 268). Turning to her left, a half-naked woman is sitting against a background of dense foliage in the pose of the classical *Venus pudica*. As in that figure type, she is holding one hand modestly over her breast, while the other is lying on her lap. In fact, of course, these gestures only make the viewer more aware of the beautiful subject's charms. At the same time, the index finger of her right hand points unobtrusively, yet unmistakably, to a bangle on her upper arm, bearing the inscription: *RAPHAEL URBINAS*.

Unlike the double portraits, this picture has been painted in delicate glazes on wood. Radiographic examination has revealed that the background was initially laid out as a landscape view. The inscription on the arm-bangle was also changed from its original form, RAPHAEL URBS. Today, there is some doubt about the authenticity of this painting on stylistic grounds.

Raphael
Portrait of Baldassare Castiglione, ca. 1514–1516
Canvas, mounted on panel, 82 x 67 cm
Musée du Louvre, Paris

Baldassare Castiglione, a humanist and a writer, was one of the most important men of the Italian Renaissance. His popular book *Il Cortegiano, The Courtier*, gives insights into the thinking and culture at the court of Urbino at the turn of the 16th century, and is written in a style that is delightfully clear and precise. Rubens admired Raphael's portrait of Castiglione so much that he copied it.

Nevertheless, the transparent veil with a few powerfully touched-in highlights, the delicate gradation of the soft skin, and the superbly painted turban-like head-dress are all worthy of Raphael. He may well have completed the painting around 1515.

What is doubtful is whether Raphael would have signed the work so conspicuously if it had been intended for him or his lover. His other friendship portraits are not signed, and in his late works signatures generally appear only if the pictures had left Rome or if his studio had been involved in a painting's execution. But in that case, it is not at all clear for which collector the portrait was intended.

Raphael also immortalized his patron, Leo X, in an imposing portrait. It depicts him together with his nephews, Cardinal Giulio de'Medici, the future Pope Clement VII, and Cardinal Luigi de' Rossi (page 269). Initially, Raphael was planning to paint a portrait of the pope on his own. The artist must have extended the composition after 1517, for only then was de' Rossi made a Cardinal. By 1 September 1518 the painting was already on its way from Rome to Florence. In its first phase the composition was strongly reminiscent of his *Portrait of Pope Julius II* (page 240). Whilst Pope Julius is seated, the onlooker is standing on one side, a silent and deferential observer. In his portrait of

Raphael
Double Portrait of Andrea Navagero and
Agostino Beazzano, ca. 1516
Canvas, 76 x 107 cm
Galleria Doria Pamphilj, Rome

These two humanist writers were friends of Raphael's
in Rome. They had, like him, come from elsewhere.
Navagero came from Venice and just before he returned
to Venice from Rome the two poets had themselves
commemorated in this portrait.

Julius II, Raphael had concentrated primarily on
depicting the pope's character; in this portrait of
Leo X he placed an antique column behind the pope
and showed him reading a priceless 14th-century
illuminated manuscript. The Church dignitary looks
up pensively, obviously struck by the beauty of the
book, which he has been examining with a magnifying
glass. Raphael did not reproduce the manuscript in
exact detail, but with sufficient precision for it to be
identified as a typical Neapolitan Bible, of which one
example, the Hamilton Bible, is in Berlin. Beside the
book stands an elaborately worked golden bell, ready
to summon Leo's servants. Here Raphael has portrayed
a lover of the arts, not a potentate.

Raphael devoted all his skill to making this portrait
have an immediate impact. To help achieve this it was
vital that the pope was depicted at a precisely
determined moment. He has just been examining the
miniatures in the manuscript. Now, deep in thought,
he is staring straight ahead. The pope dominates the
picture monumentally, relegating the two cardinals to
subordinate roles. To the right of Leo X (that is, on the
privileged side) stands his nephew, Giulio, who is
turning towards the pope and, like him, is ignoring the
viewer. Cardinal Rossi, however, who is demonstrating
his closeness to the pope by holding his chair firmly, is
looking directly at the viewer. The index finger of his
left hand is unobtrusively pointing to the main figure,

Raphael
Double Portrait, ca. 1517–1519
Canvas, 99 x 83 cm
Musée du Louvre, Paris

This portrait of Raphael was not one of the artist at work but a self-portrait with a friend. He stands calmly behind the unknown man, looking out of the picture with a serious expression. The friend's gesture is not meant for the onlooker, but seems more directed at Raphael, as if he were showing him something—himself, perhaps, in a mirror.

as if he wished to point out the pope to us, though with fitting reticence. With minimal means Raphael has succeeded in clarifying the hierarchical relationships of all three people depicted, and at the same time in involving the viewer in his scenario.

In the early 16th century, the discovery of the buried ruins of the Domus Aurea, a building that dated back to Nero's time, helped stimulate interest in classical decoration. On Raphael's behalf, Giovanni da Udine studied the wall-decorations and their production methods. The subterranean building was colloquially known as the "grotto." As a result, during the 16th century this kind of decoration, which rapidly became popular, was called "grotesque." Raphael and his studio

emulated this decorative style for the first time when Cardinal Dovizi Bibbiena gave Raphael a commission for the decoration of his bathroom and his Loggetta in the Vatican Palace. We know from a letter that this work was completed on 20 June 1516.

At the same time, between 1514 and 1519 Raphael was at work on another large-scale project in the Vatican Palace, the completion and decoration of the loggias. At his death, Bramante left this architecture unfinished, so that first Raphael needed to complete the building before he could start on the decoration work. For the loggia on the second floor, which had not yet been built, Raphael moved away from Bramante's formal architectural language and based

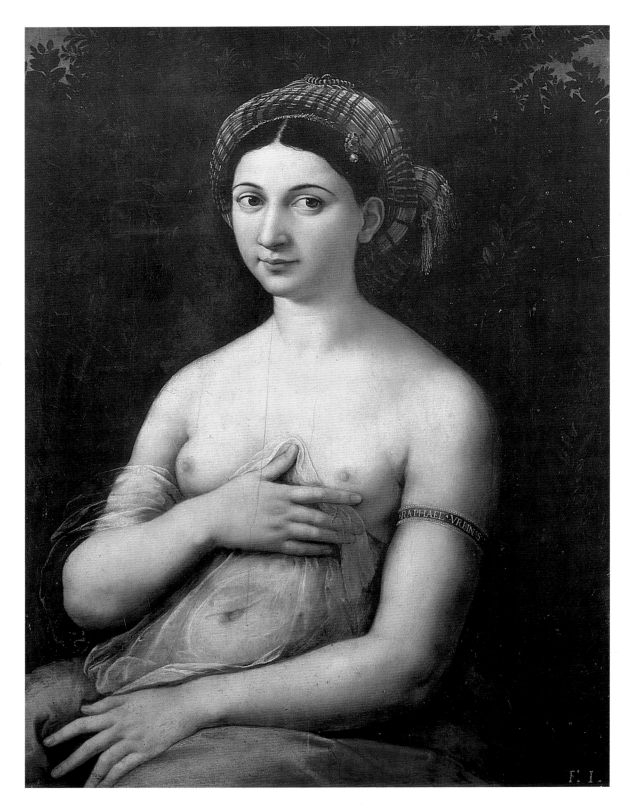

Raphael
La Fornarina, ca. 1518/19
Panel, 85 x 60 cm
Galleria Nazionale d'Arte Antica, Rome

Raphael signed the portrait on the bracelet and, because it is positioned so suggestively next to her naked breast, she has been identified as Margherita, the woman with whom Raphael is supposed to have been passionately in love.

Opposite page:
Raphael
Portrait of Leo X with Cardinals Giulio de' Medici and Luigi de' Rossi, 1513–1519
Panel, 155.2 x 118.9 cm
Galleria degli Uffizi, Florence

Here Pope Leo X had himself painted as a lover of the arts, with a splendidly illuminated Bible open on the table before him. His relatives, the Cardinals Guilio de' Medici and Luigi de' Rossi, surround Leo X in the picture, making a family portrait that was sent from Rome to Florence on 1 September. As the indisputable sign of the power of the house of Medici, it was hung on the occasion of Lorenzo de' Medici's wedding to Madeleine de la Tour d' Auvergne.

himself instead on the style of a classical gallery, inspired by the so-called Tabularium, an ancient Roman building overlooking Forum Romanum from the Capitoline Hill. The gallery's unrestricted view over the city (a prospect the loggia also enjoyed until the late 16th century) was especially captivating. Under Pope Sixtus V, extensions to the Papal Residence obscured this view.

Between 1511 and 1519, Raphael was also kept busy by a series of commissions from the banker Agostino Chigi. Chigi wanted the chapel in the church of Santa Maria del Popolo in Rome converted into a family mausoleum. Raphael designed the architecture as well as the decoration. On a square ground plan, four columns, based on Bramante's designs for St. Peter's, were to support a cupola lit by windows, which was meant to be reminiscent of the Pantheon. The whole project made great play with complex perspective and precious materials, which makes the mausoleum seem larger and more ornate than it really is.

The most elaborate project to occupy Raphael during the last years of his life was an architectural one: planning the Medici residence, now known as the Villa Madama, on the slope of the Monte Mario in northern Rome. His plan was ambitious, for he was to design a villa worthy of classical antiquity. As well as the ruins of ancient buildings like Hadrian's Villa in Tivoli, Raphael studied classical descriptions of villas, such as those in Pliny the Younger and in Vitruvius's architectural textbook. He also had ruins surveyed, including the Marcellus Theater in Rome. Raphael worked with a team of architects that included, among others, Antonio da Sangallo the Younger, whose now deceased uncle had taken charge, together with Raphael, of the rebuilding work on St. Peter's in 1514. Raphael's design for the Villa Madama promised to fulfill the high expectations it had raised. He began work on the sketches in 1517, and they were finished by 1519. By the time he died a year later, parts of the villa had already been built. Giovanni da Udine and Giulio Romano had already started work on decorating the rooms.

The *Transfiguration* was the last work Raphael painted himself, and more often than not it has been described as his artistic legacy. It was commissioned by Cardinal Giulio de' Medici, who was given the Archbishopric of Narbonne in February 1515. On this account, Giulio, the future Pope Clement VII, donated two monumental altarpieces to the cathedral there. By the end of 1516 at the latest he had commissioned the *Transfiguration* from Raphael; he also commissioned the Venetian artist, Sebastiano del Piombo, to paint the *Raising of Lazarus* (page 371), which is now in the National Gallery, London. This double commission resulted in an artistic contest, in which Sebastiano's friend, Michelangelo, also became embroiled, when Sebastiano sent the preparatory drawings to him in Florence.

Del Piombo's subject, the Raising of Lazarus, was suitable for a dramatic historical painting in the monumental style of Michelangelo. Raphael's task, by contrast, was to depict the revelation of Christ's double nature as a human and divine, a Christological subject which did not lend itself to a dramatic portrayal. He solved this problem by means of an iconographic innovation. In a single pictorial event he was able to combine two unrelated Bible stories, which, considering Christ's "double nature," was entirely apt. The first was Christ's Transfiguration, which he depicted as a vision, an approach often used before. The second was the story (related in Matthew 17: 15) of the "lunatic" boy who was healed by Jesus: here Raphael was able to use his skills in dramatic portrayal to the full.

The painting's various levels of meaning, as interpreted by the art historian Rudolf Preimesberger, can only be touched upon here. The healing of the sick boy should be read as a tribute to the donors, the Medici, whose name means "doctors." Christ is in fact the boy's healer, so here a direct link with the painting's

donor is created. The name Medici also stood for deliverance from the Turks, who threatened all Christendom. The reflection of a small crescent moon in the bottom left-hand corner of the picture is not merely an allusion to the child's lunacy, but is also a symbol of the Ottomans. Raphael introduced another specific reference to the commission by depicting Justus and Pastor, the most important patron saints of Narbonne Cathedral, who can be interpreted as witnesses of the Transfiguration.

As soon as they entered the church, believers were meant to see the vision from afar and understand it as an ever-recurring event. With this in view, Raphael conceived the upper half of the composition as a light-filled, brilliantly illuminated space in which the wind is dramatically blowing the figures' garments. He emphasized the everlasting nature of the scene by placing the main figure at the center of a circular composition.

Only the person who was able to step right up to the picture (in other words the priest celebrating the Mass) would directly confront the second scene, below. The gesture of the figure sitting in the bottom left-hand corner is there for the benefit of the viewer and demands his or her whole attention. The direction in which characters are looking and gesturing lead the eye through a scene bathed in cool moonlight and made dramatic by strong chiaroscuro. At the center of this asymmetrical composition stands the boy, who has just been seized by terrible convulsions. Even though the boy is unattractive, Raphael was able to make even his figure fascinating. He is pointing towards Jesus Christ, who redeems everyone from suffering.

Raphael died unexpectedly on Good Friday, 6 April 1520. Apart from a few touches, the *Transfiguration* was complete. Vasari wrote: "He was laid out in the room where he last worked, and at his head hung his painting of the transfigured Christ, which he had completed for Cardinal de' Medici. The contrast between the picture, which was so full of life, and the dead body filled everyone who saw it with bitter pain." This scene has undoubtedly persuaded people to celebrate the painting as Raphael's legacy. Giulio de' Medici did not send the panel to Narbonne, but kept it in Rome and donated it to the church of San Pietro in Montorio. There it could serve to instruct other artists, and it was admired by both Mannerists as well as Roman painters of the Baroque. Later generations of artists not only admired this work but saw in most of Raphael's compositions promising models for the future, from which they could imitate, vary, or borrow motifs. It was as if they all agreed with Vasari when he said: "And thus, those who follow Raphael will win fame in this world, and, if they follow his exemplary mode of life, will be rewarded in heaven."

Stephanie Buck   *Peter Hohenstatt*

Raphael
The Transfiguration,
ca. 1519/20
Panel, 405 x 278 cm
Pinacoteca Apostolica Vaticana, Vatican, Rome

Two scenes are incorporated into this altarpiece, which was the last work painted entirely by Raphael himself. The upper zone shows Christ's Transfiguration on Mount Tabor. The prophets Moses and Elijah are hovering next to him, while the Apostles who witnessed the event are lying on the ground dazzled by the radiant figure. Below there is a scene from Jesus' life, the healing of the possessed lunatic boy.

Florence in 1500

FRA BARTOLOMEO (1472–1517)

Fra Bartolomeo and Andrea del Sarto belong to those Florentine painters of the dawning High Renaissance whose posthumous fame does not match that of Leonardo, Michelangelo, or Raphael, but who were nevertheless among the artists most in demand in Florence during their lifetimes. And it was precisely the compositions of Fra Bartolomeo (also known as Bartolommeo and Baccio della Porta), who was an apprentice in the workshop of Cosimo Rosselli, that for their part significantly influenced the then young Raphael.

As was the case with Sandro Botticelli and numerous other Florentine artists of the late Quattrocento, Fra Bartolomeo, affected by the penitential sermons of the Dominican priest Girolamo Savonarola, who was excommunicated by Pope Alexander VI in 1497 and publicly executed the following year, experienced a deep religious crisis during which he burned many of his works, in particular the nude drawings. According to Giorgio Vasari, he is even said to have decided to give up painting altogether following his consecration in 1500 as a Dominican friar at the San Domenico monastery in Prato and his move shortly afterwards to the Florentine monastery of San Marco. His first major painting after overcoming this crisis is considered to be the altar panel depicting the Vision of St. Bernard painted between 1504 and 1507 and already mentioned in conjunction with Filippino Lippi (Volume I, page 550).

After a lengthy period of working in Venice and Lucca, near Florence, Fra Bartolomeo received perhaps the most significant and prestigious commission of his artistic career in the autumn of 1510—that is, still during the time of the republic under Pierio Soderini, characterized by the spirit of Savonarola and the exile of the Medici, who were banished in 1494. However, intended for the altar of the Sala del Consiglio Maggiore in the Palazzo Vecchio, his *Madonna and Child with St. Anne and the Patron Saints of Florence* (page 273) was not completed, for the hall initially served as soldiers' quarters when the Medici triumphantly returned to Florence in 1512. It was only shortly before his death that Fra Bartolomeo again began producing a large-scale work and was therefore unable to complete it, which has proved to be a particular stroke of luck for art historians, since the already well-advanced underdrawing provides us with an intimate insight into the painter's working methods. Following almost four centuries of being kept at ever new locations in Florence, including periods of display at the Palazzo Pitti and in the Uffizi, it finally reached the Museo di San Marco in 1922.

Despite its incomplete condition, this work, also known as the *Pala della Signoria* after the location originally intended for its display, captivates through the underdrawing's already pronounced plasticity and tremendous vitality of the figures, distinctly lighted from above left, their precisely captured physiognomy, as well as the competent structure of the perspective. In this, the painter has succeeded in integrating the staggered and animated figures grouped around the Madonna into a harmonious spatial order, something that can also be found in the works of Raphael.

A further exceptional work in Fra Bartolomeo's œuvre are the two small-scale paintings in the Uffizi depicting

Fra Bartolomeo
The Madonna and Child with St. Anne and the Patron Saints of Florence (Pala della Signoria), 1510–1512
Poplar, 465 x 308 cm
Museo di San Marco, Florence

Although several of the saints cannot be identified for certain because of the incomplete nature of the work, and because their traditional attributes are either lacking or not yet shown in detail, Giorgio Vasari asserts that all the patron saints of Florence are assembled here. By contrast, however, there can be no doubt that the Virgin Mary, on whose lap the Christ Child sits facing the figure of St. John as a child, is shielded from behind by her mother, Anne, who is raising her gaze upward to the three-faced head of the Holy Trinity.

the Annunciation (above), which, according to Vasari, were commissioned by Piero del Pugliese to frame a marble relief of the Madonna by Donatello in his possession. However, at the time that Vasari viewed the small tabernacle it was already a part of Grand Duke Cosimo I de' Medici's (1519–1574) collection. For whatever reason, the work was dismembered into its individual parts during the late Cinquecento. The right-hand panel was thereby trimmed along the bottom edge, as is clearly shown by the wooden strip added later. But a narrow strip on the right-hand edge of the left panel is obviously also missing, for it is hardly conceivable that the painter would have forgone depicting the hands of the Angel of the Annunciation—raised in greeting and holding a lily.

Whereas the depictions of the Birth of Jesus and the Presentation in the Temple on the reverse of the panels have been executed completely in color, the divided Annunciation to Mary depicted here on the front or outside panel has been kept monochrome. This no doubt reflects the interrelation with Donatello's marble relief, which today can no longer be identified with certainty, and provides evidence that influence from north of the Alps on Italian Renaissance art was still

unbroken at the turn of the 16th century. The simulation of sculpture through the medium of painting enjoyed great popularity in the art of the Old Netherlandish Masters in particular—for example in the works of Jan van Eyck, Rogier van der Weyden, and Hugo van der Goes, which were also highly regarded and collected in Italy.

By contrast, a further work Fra Bartolomeo (page 275) probably drafted and perhaps even began shortly before his crisis of faith but which then, however, was completed by Mariotto Albertinelli (1474–1515), his close colleague over many years, shows the influence of the Umbrian painter Pietro Perugino who was to spend several, at times lengthy, periods in Florence. The *Visitation*, painted for the Compagnia della Visitazione and since the late 18th century on display in the Uffizi, portrays, on a narrow section of grass with flowers in front of a cross-arch vaulted loggia that could just as well be by Perugino (Volume I, pages 550, 582), the encounter between the Virgin Mary and Elizabeth directly after the Annunciation mentioned in St. Luke's Gospel. The same is true of the narrow views of landscape containing two conspicuously thin trees with sparse foliage that can be seen on the outer edges of the picture.

Fra Bartolomeo (Bartolomeo della Porta)
The Annunciation (*Tabernacolo del Pugliese*),
ca. 1498
Oil on wood, 19.6 x 8.7 cm (left panel) and
17.8 x 9.2 cm (right panel)
Galleria degli Uffizi, Florence

The special appeal of these two panels dating from before the painter's long creative crisis lies primarily in the monochrome imitation of stone rather than the somewhat traditional composition. As in numerous other depictions of the Annunciation, especially popular in Florence during the Early Renaissance, the scene takes place in an unadorned, clearly structured space. Therein, in accordance to the customary direction of reading, the archangel kneels on the left holding a lily, while on the right the Virgin Mary stands at her lectern, raising her gaze from her book.

Fra Bartolomeo and Mariotto Albertinelli
The Visitation, 1503
Oil on wood, 232.5 x 146.5 cm
Galleria degli Uffizi, Florence

This altar painting, dated by the inscription MDIII between the pseudo-antique "grotesque" ornamentation on both front pillars of the loggia, shows the influence of Perugino. On the other hand, however, the more meticulously arranged lighting with its pronounced light-and-shade effect already appears to display the inspiration of Leonardo da Vinci.

Andrea del Sarto (1486–1530):
A "Painter without Flaw"

"And so, after dealing with the lives of many artists, with the one excelled in coloring, the other in drawing, and yet another in inventive skill, we now come to the most admirable Andrea del Sarto, through whom nature and art have shown with one single individual everything that painting might create through drawing, coloring, and inventive skill." With these words, Giorgio Vasari begins his description of the life of one of the most significant Florentine artists of the early 16th century, who was a "painter without flaw" (*pittore senza errori*) and from whose workshop emerged such outstanding proponents of Mannerism as Rosso Fiorentino, Jacopo da Pontormo, Francesco Salviati, and finally—and not surprisingly—the author of the praise quoted here. Andrea del Sarto (actually Andrea d'Agnolo) was, as his name reveals, the son of a tailor (Italian *sarto*), and at the age of six he initially began an apprenticeship with a

goldsmith before being trained as a painter in the workshop of Piero di Cosimo, a pupil of Rosselli.

The work of this artist, who was already highly regarded during his lifetime, encompasses, apart from numerous altar and devotional pictures, a dozen portraits as well as various murals created over a period of many years, in particular those in the two cloisters of the Florentine church of Santissima Annunziata. Among these is a lunette fresco (above) in the Chiostro dei morti above a side entrance to the church, which, with its skillfully staged and pronounced perspectival view from below, already seems to herald the illusionist mural and ceiling frescoes of the 17th and early 18th centuries and, according to Francesco Bocchi (*Le Bellezze della Città di Firenze*, 1591) is said to have been especially admired by such dissimilar and antithetical artists as Michelangelo (representing

Andrea del Sarto
The Holy Family (*Madonna del Sacco*), 1525
Fresco, 191 x 403 cm
Chiostro dei morti, Santissima Annunziata, Florence

Andrea del Sarto was already being praised in the art literature of the second half of the 16th century for his skill in portraying robes in a particularly convincing way, and this obviously is in part an allusion to his name and thereby his father's occupation (Italian *sarto*, tailor). For example, in Francesco Bocchi's *Discorso sopra l'eccellenza dell'opere d'Andrea del Sarto, pittore fiorentino* of 1567, the painter is said to have finished the robes of his figures "as the best tailor would."

Andrea del Sarto
*The Madonna and Child with St. Francis of Assisi and
St. John the Evangelist* (*The Madonna of the Harpies*),
1517
Oil on wood, 207 x 178 cm
Galleria degli Uffizi, Florence

In this altarpiece, too, it is also the portrayal of the robes
that was already singled out in the 16th century as being
especially successful, this time by Giorgio Vasari: "The
feet are also very beautiful and above all the robes, since
Andrea always outlined his figures with copious folds and
gently curving recesses in such a way that the naked body
underneath could be seen."

disegno) and Titian (representing *colore*). Vasari, too,
says: "The execution of this work proves that in respect
of *disegno*, grace, quality of coloring, and vitality and
three-dimensionality [*rilievo*], he has overtaken all
painters who have until now been active, and left them
far behind."

The fresco from 1525 that has become known as the
Madonna del Sacco portrays the Virgin Mary turned
toward the viewer and seated with the infant Jesus on an
asymmetrically depicted marble step, over which her
garments flow. Similar to depictions of the Holy Family
resting during their flight from Egypt, Joseph is placed
on the Mother of God's right, reading a book and
supported by a large white sack that has provided the
fresco with its name. In this, the figure of the elderly
Joseph is reminiscent of the antique or pseudo-antique
portrayals of a river god that were extremely popular

during the Renaissance, and, on the other hand, attests
to Andrea del Sarto's struggle with Michelangelo's
monumental figures in the frescoes of the Sistine
Chapel—as does the infant Jesus sitting on Mary's lap
with widely splayed legs—which has contributed to
speculation over a reputed sojourn in Rome in the years
around 1510.

As far as gaining inspiration from other artists of his
time is concerned, a connection with Leonardo da Vinci
has been repeatedly pointed out in the so-called
Madonna of the Harpies in the Uffizi (page 271).
Influenced by Leonardo's *sfumato*, Andrea del Sarto gave
the faces of the six figures of the painting conspicuously
soft and even blurry features, almost devoid of firm,
defined contours. The same is true of the pronounced
contrast effect between light and shade, employed with
great nuance through which the painter lends his

convincingly spatially integrated figures their enormous plasticity. The altarpiece painted for the Florentine convent of San Francesco de' Macci near Santa Croce depicts the Virgin Mary in front of an alcove, standing in a balanced contrapposto pose on an octagonal pedestal with an already large Christ Child on her arm. While the two smalls angels at her feet appear to be supporting the Madonna, the two saints placed at her side are turning toward the viewer: on the left, the convent's patron saint, in the process of elegantly turning with cross in hand to gaze over his shoulder; and on the right, the figure of St. John the Evangelist draped in a luminous red cloak and with an opened book in his hands.

At the corner of the octagonal stone pedestal, on which, apart from the signature of the painter (AND[REA DEL] SAR[TO] FLO[RENTINUS] FA[CIE]B[AT]) and the date (1517), the beginning of a 14th-century Marian hymn in abbreviated form can be read, four winged chimera-like beasts can be seen. Vasari called these figures "harpies apparently in the posture of adoration," thus coining the title under which the painting is most commonly known today. However, these peculiar creatures lack the bird-like bodies characteristic of harpies, which led to their interpretation as sphinxes, to be understood as an allusion to the lions decorating the Throne of Solomon and thereby also to Mary as the seat of divine wisdom. By contrast, in more recent times the "chimeras" have been considered to refer to the locusts mentioned in the ninth chapter of the Book of Revelation (Apocalypse) that at the end of time, immediately prior to the last judgment, arrive on earth with the smoke rising from the "well of the abyss" opened by the fifth angel. And indeed, Vasari also pointed out the smoke-like veil of transparent cloud that surrounds the figures in the upper section of the painting, even though it is difficult to spot at first glance. With this background, the *Madonna of the Harpies*, significantly accompanied by St. John, can also be interpreted as the "Apocalyptic Woman," also from the Book of Revelation, even when such attributes as the crescent moon under her feet or the crown of twelve stars are missing.

Although the Madonna is standing almost sculpture-like on a pedestal instead of sitting as the Mother of God on a throne flanked by saints as in numerous other depictions, the painting follows in its overall composition the type known as a *sacra conversazione* that was widespread in Italy from the middle of the Quattrocento. And the strictly symmetrical composition with its figures forming an equilateral triangle is completely in accordance with 15th-century painting tradition. On the other hand, the sophisticated treatment of light and shade already mentioned, as well as its Leonardesque *sfumato*, show the painting to be just as much a work of the early 16th century, while the subtle pose of the turning figure of St. Francis already displays Mannerist tendencies that can be increasingly observed in the painter's later works.

After completion of the *Madonna of the Harpies* and his marriage in the spring of 1518, Andrea del Sarto spent a little more than a year at the court of the French King, Francis I, in Fontainebleau. He would probably have enjoyed a longer, more glittering career there, had he not—as Giorgio Vasari describes in detail with a clearly critical undertone despite his respect for his mentor—loved to the point of folly his young wife, Lucrezia, described as being exceptionally beautiful, and so had been drawn back to Florence.

About ten years after his return to his homeland, Andrea painted the *Sacrifice of Isaac* (opposite page), which is today in the Gemäldegalerie in Dresden. The painting was originally intended for Francis I, but on the death of the artist and the imprisonment of Giovanni Battista della Palla, the art dealer acting for the king, it was initially sold through the mediation of Filippo Strozzi to the Margrave of Guasto, Alfonso d'Avalos, and finally reached Dresden in the mid-18th century.

With a spacious hilly landscape in the background, the almost life-size and (despite his great age) strikingly sturdy figure of the patriarch Abraham is portrayed only slightly to the left of the painting's vertical middle axis as he is about to sacrifice the only son, Isaac. In the process, he turns his head toward the small angel hovering above him, who is calling out to him: "Lay not thine hand upon the lad, neither do thou anything unto him: for now I know that thou fearest God, seeing thou hast not withheld thy son, thine only son for me." Vasari was impressed by the dramatic scene and remarked about the figure of the youth, "…that one sees the beautiful and tender youth Isaac, completely naked, shivering with fear of death and almost dying, without being harmed at all. And not just that his neck had been tanned by the heat of the sun—the parts of the body that were covered by clothing during the three-day journey present themselves in the purest white." Abraham's resting servant in the middle ground to the right and the grazing pack-ass beside him provide a reference to the journey to God's chosen place of sacrifice in the Land of Moriah also mentioned in biblical sources. By contrast, on the left can be seen the ram that Abraham will soon sacrifice to the Lord in place of his son. The painter has deviated from the biblical account only in as far as he has not depicted the bundle of firewood that Isaac himself has carried with him as lying on the altar, but behind it to the right.

Apart from the convincingly portrayed expression of despair on the youth's face and the precise modeling of his body, it is primarily his bent pose that provides evidence of the influence of Mannerism on Andrea del Sarto's art. In this respect, the relationship between the figure of Isaac and one of the two sons of Laocoön, writhing in their death struggle with two sea serpents in the famous antique group sculpture, is repeatedly pointed out. This Hellenistic sculpture, today on display in the Vatican Museum, was excavated in Rome in January 1506 and the pronounced muscularity of its figures and above all the dramatic movement they express inspired generations of artists and contributed significantly to the development of what is known as typically Mannerist *figura serpentinata*.

Henrik Engel

Andrea del Sarto
The Sacrifice of Isaac, ca. 1527/28
Oil on poplar, 213 x 159 cm
Gemäldegalerie Alte Meister, Staatliche Kunstsammlungen, Dresden

Despite being commonly known by the name of Andrea del Sarto during his lifetime, the Florentine artist signed most of his paintings with the monogram consisting of the two intertwined capital As (AA for his correct name Andrea d'Agnolo) that can be seen here on a stone in the foreground.

Giorgione 1477/78–1510

As is the case with several other great Venetian painters, Giorgione originally came from the Terraferma, the mainland; the landscape, wildness, and foreignness of which had a special appeal for the inhabitants of the lagoon. Born 1477 or 1478 in Castelfranco, for Vasari he takes on the roll of the artist from a humble background whose forename is more than enough to identify him, albeit in the expanded form that changes a common George into the "Big George." His family name was not investigated due to the poorly substantiated assumption that Giorgione was called Barbarelli because the painter was an extraordinarily amiable foreigner (*barbaro*) to Venice.

Giorgione first surfaces in Venice, at least according to contemporary sources, somewhat later. First mention of him concerns a payment in 1507 from the city tribunal (Consiglio dei Dieci: the Council of Ten); and the painter worked for the Doge's Palace again in the following year. He is mentioned once more in 1508, this time in connection with the painting of the façade

of the German trade depot, the Fondaco dei Tedeschi. That he is already dead by 1510 is evident from a letter by Isabella d'Este, Marchesa of Mantua, dated 25 October, in which she instructs an agent to buy up paintings by the dead artist. Giorgione's art had evidently rapidly become recognized at the courts of the ruling class.

Giorgione maintained his ties to Castelfranco, where he painted a mural frieze in the Casa Pelizzari featuring still-life motifs. His only altarpiece, a *sacra conversazione* (page 283) painted either as early as 1500 or later in 1504, is preserved in the cathedral. He probably learnt his trade with Vincenzo Catena (ca. 1470–1531) in Venice; his self-portrait (page 284) is painted on a piece of canvas from this workshop. Catena is considered a sound, if not particularly conspicuous, pupil of Giovanni Bellini.

Giorgione's beginnings are also associated with Bellini himself, whereby it is not forgotten that the young painter from Castelfranco posed a late challenge for the

Giovanni Bellini
Sacred Allegory, ca. 1487–1505
Oil on wood, 73 x 119 cm
Galleria degli Uffizi, Florence

One of the characteristics of Venetian painting around 1500 was not only the new oil and tempera technique, but also several excellent paintings that break completely with tradition: neither the title nor the content of some important paintings are known, for they were beyond every iconographic tradition. Among them is a work by Giovanni Bellini that provides just as much ground for argumentation over the date of its painting as over the precise definition of its meaning. Mary's throne stands on a terrace in a landscape; it is joined by the Apostles Paul (recognizable by the sword) and Peter; St. Jerome and St. Sebastian, a confessor and a martyr, approach from the right to join them. But the women beside the throne are not as easy to identify, and the search for a text on which the depiction might be based is dispiriting. When the figures are seen from the right, the impression could arise that they are just beginning to position themselves to form a *sacra conversazione*, while still allowing the Christ Child to romp about with the other small naked children.

Above left:
Giorgione
Moses' Trial by Fire, ca. 1505
Oil on wood, 89 x 72 cm
Galleria degli Uffizi, Florence

Giorgione painted a pair of pictures depicting two Old Testament events in very similar landscapes and at roughly the same time as Bellini completed his *Sacred Allegory* (page 280)—most experts are convinced the paintings are by the artists' own hands. He shows a rarely depicted scene from Moses' childhood: the Pharaoh's young daughter brings the little boy to her father after finding him in a small rush basket, and the baby must undergo the trial by fire.

Above right:
Giorgione
The Judgment of Solomon, ca. 1505
Oil on wood, 89 x 72 cm
Galleria degli Uffizi, Florence

The story of the Judgment of Solomon is much better known that Moses' Trial by Fire: after the death of an infant boy, two women claim the surviving child is their son. Wise King Solomon decides the mothers' argument by apparently ordering the child to be cut in two in order to give each of the women a share. The child is returned to the woman who prefers to give up the child completely, because she has thereby proved herself to be the true mother. Giorgione sets the scene as a mirror image of *Moses' Trial by Fire*; he shows the one child lying dead on the ground as well as the mother of the other, who is willing to give up her child and therefore begs Solomon to spare her son's life.

established master. The new direction could well have resulted from criticism of Vincenzo Catena, who atmospherically enlivened space in a similar way to Giorgione, primarily, however, in the painting of interiors; one thinks of his paintings of *St. Jerome* in the National Gallery, London, and in the Städel Museum, Frankfurt. Giorgione, by contrast, proved himself primarily as a landscape painter—his most famous painting is that of a thunderstorm, *La Tempesta* (page 291).

Bellini's ability to change, already shown in relation to his brother-in-law Andrea Mantegna and to Antonello da Messina, a Sicilian proponent of Netherlandish painting, can also be seen in the further development in his work that occurs with the appearance of the younger Giorgione. At times, the two artists' paintings are very similar, as if Giorgione had worked in Bellini's workshop: splendid rocky crags and trees serve to open up the wide scenic views known from the Terraferma. In this, both painters define the eye level in the same way: in several paintings (pages 280, 281) small figures form a loose relief in front of a backdrop that again rises to a height that is precisely the same as theirs. There then follows a view of the brightly emerging sky above a colorfully vivid mountain silhouette.

Whereas Giovanni Bellini already stood in the solid tradition of his father Jacopo, Giorgione acts as if he cares nothing for all the accepted customs of the day.

Interpreters designate his most significant paintings as "riddles" because their themes elude a simple interpretation and can best be understood as "painted poetry." But the older masters also loved cryptic subject matter; Bellini's *Sacred Allegory* is a variation on the idea of the *sacra conversazione* (page 280): the familiar figures, the Apostles, a Church Father, a martyr, and two further female saints, are gathering around the Virgin Mary's throne. The Christ Child will have to be called, for he is playing with a small tree, an allusion to the Tree of Knowledge under which Eve once yielded to temptation. Perhaps Bellini was thinking about models he would have to muster to paint a Madonna with saints. But the dignity of the scenery turns this into a poetic portrayal of the tacit agreement of those who have actually ascended into heaven to a landscape, the beauty of which is in itself praise of god's creation.

Giorgione set two scenes from the Old Testament (above) in a very similar setting. These pendants belong to his early works, for unlike in the rest of his work, the subjects are clear. Like Bellini, he uses a throne as a focal point for his relief-like composition, but has to accommodate more figures: the figure of a monarch is depicted on the left in one painting and on the right in the other. In the trial by fire of the infant Moses, and in the fate of the unknown child who can be returned to its true mother following Solomon's

Giovanni Bellini
St. Jerome with St. Christopher and St. Augustine
(*San Giovanni Crisostomo Altarpiece*), 1513
Oil on wood, 300 x 185 cm
San Giovanni Crisostomo, Venice

Altarpieces primarily serve as a focus for the eye during
the sacrament. That is why a manifestation of God,
usually as the infant Jesus on Mary's lap, is often to be
found at the center, preferably somewhat raised. To
depict a central figure who is taking absolutely no notice
of the viewer is rare. The figures in question in the
splendid *San Giovanni Crisostomo Altarpiece* are the two
accompanying figures: St. Christopher and the Church
Father St. Augustine as an amazingly young man; while
the hermit St. Jerome in profile is turning toward the
high altar of the small Venetian church for which the
painting was created. The architecture plays an important
role here: the two life-size saints stand at the bottom, in
front of a waist-high wall and beneath an arch that lends
the two the appearance of belonging to the church
building itself. Behind them, a rocky crag rises up; it
belongs to the view outside, which then leads upward in
the mild evening light to the main figure above.
Giorgione had already been the first to take in earnest
the radical step of opening up the wall above the altar
in his *Madonna of Castelfranco* (opposite page). The
question of whether a lost work of the older artist
preceded the panel in Castelfranco cannot be answered
with certainty.

Opposite page:
Giorgione
The Madonna of Castelfranco, ca. 1500 or 1504
Oil on wood, 200 x 152 cm
Duomo, Castelfranco Veneto

The *sacra conversazione* in Giorgione's hometown
Castelfranco is his only work intended for ecclesiastical
cult purposes that still exists. This panel from the church
of San Liberale is often associated with the funerary cult
of the Costanzo family of Castelfranco, in whose chapel
it was erected. Tuzio Costanzo was an admiral and
Viceroy of Cyprus and had lived in Castelfranco; his son,
Matteo, who died in 1504, was interred in the chapel.
Giorgione's panel is usually associated with this date; but
it may have already been painted earlier, around 1500.
The main patron saint of the church, St. Liberale, stands
like a figure of St. George to the right of the throne,
St. Francis to the left. As in Bellini's *San Giovanni
Crisostomo Altarpiece* (left), both figures seem to be a part
of the space within the church, while Mary, not appearing
to be quite so engrossed as Bellini's St. Jerome, is
embedded in the upper scene of sky and landscape.
The peculiar "emptiness" between the figures is foreign
to Bellini and his Venetian contemporaries. When
considering the relationship between this work and
Bellini's *San Giovanni Crisostomo Altarpiece* complex,
questions about dating are irrelevant; for the older artist's
work was painted in 1513, three years after the death of
the younger master. Since only one of the few works that
can be attributed to Giorgione with certainty, the *Portrait
of a Woman* (*Laura*) from 1506, to be found in the
Kunsthistorischen Museum in Vienna, is dated, but can
hardly serve to determine the date of the other, this work
should in fact only be dated "before 1510," the year of
the artist's death.

Opposite page:
Giorgione
Portrait of a Young Man, pre-1510
Canvas, 58 x 46 cm
Gemäldegalerie, Staatliche Museen, Berlin

In many respects, this painting, generally accepted as being by the artist's own hand, is a metaphor of both the Renaissance in general and the early deceased Giorgione. Despite the VV monogram, the person portrayed has remained nameless to this very day; in tune with the fact that the artist's paintings can still assert themselves even when no expert can successfully entitle and interpret them. The man is young, on the threshold of maturity; he has not tied his garment properly, which like the painting gives the impression of not being completely finished. The figure surfaces from the surrounding darkness and turns slightly to face the viewer. In doing so, the fingers grasp a peculiarly stepped wall. The Renaissance is here a condition that still awaits completion, a moment of youth that is becoming aware of its existence; and much of which is still indeterminate, as is Giorgione's method of painting itself. The viewer needs confidence and fantasy to see the young man, maybe based on the V of the monogram and the possible semantic context of the word *victoria* (victory), as a Vittore or Vincenzo, or the letters as a play on the idea of a victory that has been gained in a humanitarian context rather than in the art of warfare.

Giorgione
Self-Portrait as David, pre-1510
Oil on canvas, 52 x 43 cm (cut down)
Herzog Anton Ulrich-Museum, Brunswick

This painting is usually perceived to be a truncated self-portrait of Giorgione, whose original appearance is conveyed, as a mirror image, by a copper engraving by Wenzel Hollar from 1650: the painter intended to portray himself as David with Goliath's decapitated head, and used an already painted canvas for this. X-ray examination reveals the fragment of a Madonna and Child in the style of Vincenzo Catena, with whom Giorgione had worked. Questions arise not only regarding the poor state of preservation, but also the work's relationship to other versions that are closer to the engraving, but in contrast to the Brunswick work cannot claim in their painting technique to be by the artist's own hand. For art historians, Giorgione's physiognomy was defined as that of David's in the woodcut based on this painting that appeared in the 1568 edition of Vasari's *Lives*.

judgment, Giorgione has been inspired by the juxtaposition of king and helpless infant, something that lends itself well to visual representation. A deeper meaning can scarcely arise here, for both infants are shown at a harrowing moment—Moses grasps the coals in the brazier and the living child is about to be cut in two. The artist conveys nothing about the rescue of Moses, for he survives the test, nor does he convey anything of Solomon's wisdom (the child is saved).

For altarpieces (page 283), Giorgione changes the height of the horizon and abandons the relief character just as Bellini does (page 282): in the lower register stand the saints above whom the landscape rises. Above the horizon and landscape backdrop, the main figures rise up, remarkably reduced in their proportions, as if they are part of the spiritual rather than temporal realms. Giorgione achieves this effect in Castelfranco, although spatially the Madonna belongs completely to

the foreground. Bellini outlived the younger artist and possibly developed his ideas further (if one does not accept the idea that it was Giorgione who followed on from paintings of the older artist that no longer exist). In 1513, three years after Giorgione's death, Giovanni Bellini takes a further decisive step forward in his most beautiful "Giorgionesque" painting by integrating the hermit St. Jerome completely into the landscape.

Nothing is known about the effect of the panel in Castelfranco on Giorgione's contemporaries. The painting is rather small in format, but so spaciously laid out that the space created between the figures is more characteristic of Catena than Bellini. Nevertheless, it is hard to avoid a comparison with the *sacra conversazione* in San Zaccaria (page 23) that Bellini painted more or less ten years later: in both cases the flanking saints are similarly arranged in relation to the viewer. Bellini had painted his *San Giovanni Crisostomo Altarpiece* (page 282) only shortly before.

With Giorgione, a new kind of painter emerges; one who has to assert himself in a center, such as Venice around 1500, which is already occupied by other masters. The young painter from Castelfranco was probably the first to realize that the newcomer therefore had to be given a face. He chose a role that stands for youth, strength, and the surprise victory of the little man over the great and powerful; for he portrayed himself as David (left), and not as the bloody head of Goliath (page 491), as did Caravaggio later. In doing so, in the psychological penetration of the young victor, he at the same time allows that same disturbing indeterminacy to emerge that is attributed to the melancholic and the creative artist.

However, Giorgione left behind a far more intensive impression of his own skill with another portrait: in the

Titian (?)
Il Bravo, ca. 1510–1520
Oil on canvas, 77 x 66.5 cm
Kunsthistorisches Museum, Vienna

Themes surfaced in Giorgione's paintings that play with the indeterminate, including lurking danger. Half-figures emerge from the darkness; they may allude to concrete figures from literature and real life, but they quickly lose their names; for they embody forces that free themselves from the anecdotal to become visual poetry: the young man with his glowing complexion and wreath bound in his blond hair is being stopped by an unsavory character; he does not yet see the knife awaiting him. Such paintings were formerly attributed to Giorgione, but an increasingly large number have in the meantime been credited to the young Titian.

light of works such as the *Portrait of a Young Man* (page 285) in Berlin, Bernard Berenson (1865–1959) was of the opinion that the Renaissance represents in history a moment of innocence; in another passage he says that such paintings reminded him of a time in his own life when all paths still lay open to him. No other figure embodies Giorgione's departure into a new kind of art more intensively than this unknown person, who, with the tie to his garment casually open and his right hand touching the step of a small wall, gazes at the viewer with a youthfulness that still awaits a full growth of beard.

Luck really must have lent portraiture a helping hand, for it is primarily in its reception that such a commission became a work of art that, stripped of name and anecdotal characteristics, can be read as documentary evidence of the dawn of a new era. Today, the question of the identity of the person behind the VV monogram on the Berlin painting is scarcely of interest. The gaze of this character head, symbolic of an entire era, seems to convey a desire to become a part of the viewer's consciousness, and possibly even his life.

From the 17th century onward, a work painted without the intention of being a portrait was termed a "tronie," a French term only recently readopted in the field of art history to refer to an out-of-the-ordinary face. Tronies differ from fantasy portraits such as those in the *studiolo* of Federigo da Montefeltro (Volume I, page 367) or Andrea del Castagno's Legnaia frescoes (Volume I, page 320), and are equally at variance with allegorical personifications. They are solely concerned with the essence of a person; when they have been painted from life, the model was chosen according to the artistic merit of the countenance alone, and not because of rank or status.

Painting character heads was a part of art before the idea of portraiture was conceived; for generations before Giorgione, painters had already occupied themselves with it. But with his large portrait—today known as *La Vecchia* (opposite page)—he may well have been the first to have made a person without a name the subject of an autonomous work of art: out of the darkness, an old women gazes at the viewer over a parapet like that bearing the bust of Bellini's *Doge Loredan* (Volume I,

page 15). Her body does not occupy the middle of the picture; rather, bent by time, she has shuffled in from the right. A scroll in her hand announces that with time (*COL TEMPO*) she has become what we see: her hair is sparse, her skin wrinkled; she shows the burden of old age. She addresses the viewer by pointing to her heart.

In her clean garments, which she cannot arrange tightly, she is not the ugly, disheveled old woman or the matchmaker of the comedies already known around 1500, and no comparison can be made with Dürer's half-naked old woman in the Kunsthistorische Museum in Vienna. And yet Giorgione's old woman has neither wealth nor rank, which, for example, could be expressed through a piece of jewelry. This picture conveys nothing except the harrowing tiredness of age, as the attempt of a painter to express through his own observation the portrayal of age to be found in the last chapter of Solomon's Ecclesiastes.

An especially interesting twist is provided by the nevertheless mistaken notion that it is possible to see Giorgione's own mother in the old woman. The painter

Opposite page:
Giorgione
La Vecchia, pre-1510
Tempera and nut oil on canvas, transferred from flax to hemp canvas, 68 x 59 cm
Gallerie dell'Accademia, Venice

COL TEMPO stands written on the scroll the old woman holds in her hand. Anecdotal accounts have even led to the person portrayed being seen as the painter's mother. This idea may well have surfaced in the time shortly after his premature death; for an artist like Giorgione, who surfaces as a young man, transforms art wonderfully, only to die before his time, simply demands the personalization of his works. A portrait of the artist's mother is mentioned in Gabriele Vendramin's inventory of 1569. The painting should probably be displayed alongside the *Young Man* (page 285) from Berlin: it displays a new understanding of people, in a painting that requires neither a concrete name nor the justification of being dependent on an allegory. This nameless painting is perhaps the first work of its kind in European painting: a character head full of expression that is admired as the work of a famous master.

from the turn of the 16th century is thereby put on a par with artists such as Rembrandt who, in his penchant for self-dramatization, made his own family the subject of his art. Dürer's austere charcoal drawings in the Berliner Kupferstichkabinett would here be a contemporary parallel; but, in contrast to the Nuremberg artist, Giorgione would, however, have divested the elderly woman of her identity in the elaborate format and turned her into a character head, a true tronie.

The personal interpretation began at an early stage; for a portrait of his mother by Giorgione's hand was already listed in 1569, for which *La Vecchia* may have been mistaken. Giorgione accrued themes such as this from the surroundings of his life and not from the tradition of his art. In this respect, he paved the way for another painter from a later time: Caravaggio. From Giorgione's circle stem the first genre paintings portraying such scenes of violence between young people as were happening during Caravaggio's early time in Rome. None of the paintings that still exist can be attributed to Giorgione for sure; paintings thought today to be more likely by Titian and now dated to the years after 1510 (page 286), were attributed to him in older inventories. Had experiences of the young artist—even when only imaginary experiences—been reflected in paintings in which the dark figure of a journeyman, a bravo, attacks a youth, then this would speak just as much of self-dramatization as of the new artistic leeway opened up by Giogione's short life.

To the amazement of his contemporaries, Giorgione dared to seek out new themes, although it was obvious that only a small circle of potential buyers existed for such works.

For later times, Giorgione's major works opened the way to a new perception of the painting; they also attracted an astonishing degree of erudition. The best example of this is provided by a Viennese painting known as the *Three Philosophers* (right). One usually assumes that a painter has followed a concrete subject; however, the opinion of interpreters concerning everything he has captured in the painting would perhaps have pleased Giorgione: precedence is given today to an interpretation from Salvatore Setti, according to which the three can be understood to be philosophers and, at the same time, the Three Magi,

meeting above the cave in which Adam and Eve once lived, to locate the Star of Bethlehem. The rejection of any symbols of royalty that is not textually substantiated speaks of a philological stringency that is, however, in contradiction to a Giorgionesque devotional painting in National Gallery in London, in which the three wear the regal emblems.

Since, in the Viennese painting, the youngest of the three is a young man with a mass of curly hair, some people like to consider him to be a self-portrait in the sophisticated formula of a profile—something that Filippo Lippi had already achieved in Florence in the 1440s, but in Venice is typical only of the elderly Titian and Veronese (Volume I, pages 9, 440; Volume II, page 31). Then the two also painted portraits of painters, Vittore Carpaccio as well as the aged Giovanni Bellini, that are equally reminiscent of Leonardo's self-portraits as Raphael's Aristotle (page 29).

The cave evokes thoughts of Plato's cave analogy (in Book 7 of the *Republic*); it is supposedly being measured by the young man, beside whom maturity and old age appear as personifications of Arab philosophy and mathematics. But basically the way is open for almost anything in antiquity and more recent spiritual history understood as a trinity: in the most varied of interpretations, the figures represent the three Religions of the Book; most important support for this idea is provided by X-ray pictures that in an earlier version reveal the old man with rays above his forehead (or a peculiar headdress). If Moses with his radiant countenance represents Judaism, then Muhammad symbolizes Islam; however, the beardless young man cannot be intended to represent Christ, so he becomes the Antichrist—thereby clearly proving the fragility of the entire interpretation.

No one can identify the suggested philosophers for sure, something that can be done with ease in Raphael's *School of Athens* (page 232). For this reason, the theories involved are more of interest from the perspective of cultural history: the interpreters go beyond the scope of pagan antiquity; one recognizes Aristotle and his successors in Arab Averoism and in the humanism of the Renaissance, or Aristotle, Ptolemy, and the almost contemporary figure of Regiomontanus, the astronomer Johannes Müller of Königsberg (1436–1476). The

Giorgione
The Three Philosophers, pre-1510
Canvas, 123.5 x 144.5 cm
Kunsthistorisches Museum, Vienna

The simultaneous personification of the three ages in life by three men can primarily be seen in the depictions of the Three Wise Men from the East at Christ's birth. Although initially believed to be a depiction of three philosophers, they were soon considered to be the Three Wise Men, here seen as astrologers (magi) rather than kings. The painter may well depict them assessing the Star of Bethlehem, but he then intentionally makes things more difficult for the viewer by not actually showing the object of their attention. In doing so, Giorgione adopts an unusually modern position; for the painting proffers an almost philological critique of the insouciance with which all other painters of the day have turned the Wise Men into kings. But before any critical examination of the meaning, Giorgione's share in the work must be clarified, for Marcantonio Michiel believed that Sebastiano del Piombo actually completed it. Despite the many unanswered questions—and that, too, is a characteristic of Giorgione's work—this painting is certainly one of the most beautiful of the Renaissance. Technically interesting is the fact that infrared examination has disproved the earlier belief that the painting was at least partially created on the easel without detailed preparatory sketching; the preparatory drawing is in part actually extremely precise.

proponents of hermetic philosophy also have their say, transplanting their fresh shoots from the Florence of Lorenzo 'il Magnifico' de' Medici to Venice. Doubts about all this already begin with the turban: when illumination painters such as Leonardo Bellini, a younger brother of Giovanni, painted the ancient philosopher in Venetian prints of Aldus Manutius' Aristotelian writings around 1480, they placed a turban on his head. For Christian Venice, antiquity and the Orient were bound together by their paganism; both were known as *saraceni*, Saracens. Representatives of classical philosophy were therefore portrayed in Venice like the Orientals known from their trading colonies.

Interpreters have also forgotten the role of looking and the play with meaning: the landscape is only of interest to the interpreters because they believe they recognize the cave from Plato's cave allegory or the legends surrounding Adam and Eve. That the scene takes place on the edge of a wood, which up until the *Weltgeschichtliche Betrachtungen (Reflections on History)* of 1905 by Jakob Burckhardt is considered a metaphor for the transition from wildness to culture, is overlooked. The painting portrays the awakening of man's awareness, the tranquility cannot prevent its fulfillment with Christian, pagan, or, more recently, also philo-semitic thought. In analogy to Lessing's play *Nathan the Wise*, the *Three Philosophers* is thereby a kind of "ring parable" of modern painting.

Giorgione's most beautiful work poses similar problems: under a flash of lightening in the sky above, it combines a landscape with ruins in the foreground and a view of a city in the middle distance (page 291). The picture, together with the *Concert Champêtre* in the Louvre, which was formerly considered to be a work by Giorgione but is today attributed to Titian (pages 294–295), is one of those scandalous works in which the woman is naked but the man fully dressed. Because no one has been able to suggest a conclusive textual source, interpretation of the scene has been going round in circles for more than half a century; as early as 1952, Creighton Gilbert suggested considering whether the painting has a subject theme at all. The immense vigor the work possesses stems precisely from its "indefinability." A conclusive interpretation would serve only to shackle the imagination the painter has aroused. For what is really gained when a painting that sets a force of nature and people in a sophisticated relationship of suspense suddenly becomes the illustration of a text that no one knows and that not even the painting can bring back to life?

The associations have varied wildly, even in the early past, ranging from the suggestion of "Soldier and Gipsy Woman" (Marcantonio Michiel, 1530) to the artist's own family (Lord Byron, 1817; Burckhardt's *Cicerone*, 1855). The fact that the man's clothes are more those of a shepherd of the time speaks against the notion of a soldier; which has lead to the field of

options being narrowed to the theme of Paris on Mount Ida with a completely misleading prediction of Troy's fall through the lightning bolt above the city.

The interpretation of the scene as a depiction of the artist's own family, which is certainly just as false, fits in with the tradition that sees Giorgione's mother in his portrayal of an old woman (page 287). In this case, however, the painter is standing in a garden while his lover, Cecilia, breastfeeds a child. Passages of text that have been associated with the composition can consistently be found in writings such as Francesco Colonna's *Hypnerotomachia Poliphili*, published by Aldus Manutius in 1499, or Jacopo Sannazaro's *Arcadia*. Such reference would have been understood by a small community of insiders. Today, weary of the search for a textual basis, interpreters are for the most part content to see this entrancing painting as an example of a landscape with arbitrarily inserted figures.

But to capitulate completely does not seem sensible: one approach may promise to be more successful, challenging the synchronism of the picture: technical examination has revealed that a second naked woman was initially portrayed in the foreground on the left; she has given way to the clothed young man. The fact that the mother with her suckling child has remained the same shows that the artist divided the periphery from the core of the depiction and regarded only the woman under the grove of trees as the painting's theme. In accordance with the customary layout for book pages, the man on the left, with the ruins behind him falling away abruptly to the right, fills the margin, and therefore belongs more to the "margin" than to the picture.

However, margins mediate between viewer and main scene. One cannot simply bound out of the margin into the picture as if jumping over the small stream; that is shown by the man, who, with his body turned toward us, is not only looking at the woman, but at the picture itself, ready to defend the intimacy against any intruder. The woman can just as well be an anonymous mother as a figure from a myth or a novel; in her creatural situation she is being guarded by the man on the margin of the picture. To me, this appears to be the key to understanding the painting, in the center of which the lightening bolt's force of nature against motherly care and tenderness stands in a sphere that is being shielded from interference from the world, and thereby also the viewer, by a shepherd rather than a soldier.

That later times have erroneously turned this into a depiction of Giorgione and his lover, even the name of whom is fantasy, is for me not without charm; for one would prefer to have such a unique, consummate artist, who in addition died before his time, conveyed not only through his works, but actually have him, in his paintings, before one's very eyes.

Eberhard König

Giorgione
The Tempest (*La Tempesta*), pre-1510
Tempera and nut oil on canvas, 82 x 73 cm
Gallerie dell'Accademia, Venice

Giorgione's *Tempest* is one of the most enigmatic paintings in the history of art. The first person to write about it, Marcantonio Michiel, made it a banal depiction by talking of "a soldier and a gypsy woman." Contemporaries found the parallel of the dressed man and the naked woman scandalous. Interpretations try to establish a textual source based on traditional lore from antiquity, ranging from the stories about Deucalion and Pyrrha to Mercury and Io, to Adam and Eve. According to one of the most recent attempted explanations (Jürgen Rapp, 2004) "the scene depicts the departure of Paris, who is bidding farewell to the nymph Oinone and her children at the source of the Kebren in the Ida Mountains." The thunderbolt is striking the city of Troy, which appears directly behind the main scene. In opposition to this interpretation, with which only expert insiders could be familiar, the same author recognizes another modern interpretation that sees the initially two naked women as a pictorial elegy, in which their undefined hapless fates confront each other. Both competing concepts for reading Giorgione's paintings thereby conflict sharply with each other, for it is disputed whether the artist had a concrete subject in mind at all.

Titian 1488/90–1576

The Beginnings:
Titian, Bellini, and Giorgione

Titian
Self-Portrait, ca. 1550–1562
Oil on canvas, 96 x 75 cm
Gemäldegalerie, Staatliche Museen, Berlin

This painting has been given a variety of dates ranging
from the early 1550s to the 1560s. The manner in which
the white is applied as a thick mass of paint in irregular
and occasionally very large sections is reminiscent of
Titian's style in about 1560, but the painting was not
completed. There is only a suggestion of where his left
hand is. It is interesting that he omitted any reference to
his occupation. The only biographical allusion is the
golden chain, the sign of his knighthood.

Although there were already biographies devoted to
Titian during his lifetime, we do not know the precise
date of his birth. We owe one of the descriptions of his
life to his close friend, the author Lodovico Dolce
(1508–1568). In 1557, in his *Dialogue on Painting*
(*L'Aretino*), he says Titian was about twenty years of age
during his work on the Fondaco dei Tedeschi in 1507.
Giorgio Vasari also dates Titian birth at around 1488 or
1490. Nevertheless, it was long believed that Titian was
actually born considerably earlier, around 1476. For, in a
letter to the Spanish king in 1571, he himself says he is
ninety-five years of age, presumably to speed up
payment of amounts of money for which he had long
been waiting. This would make him about 100 years old
when he died in 1576. Even if born as late as 1490, and
this is more than likely on the basis of the chronology of
his works, the result would be an extraordinarily long
lifespan and creative career. Over a period of almost
seventy years, Titian succeeded as few artists either
before or after him have in continually renewing and
developing his skill.

Sometime during the late days of the 15th century, at
nine or ten years of age, Tiziano Vecellio and his older
brother Francesco, who also became a painter, came to
Venice to begin an apprenticeship in the workshop of
the mosaicist Sebastiano Zuccato (d. 1527). They came
from the small alpine village of Pieve di Cadore. Their
parents were respected, modestly well-off citizens. The

reason why Titian's father sent his sons to an uncle in
Venice to begin training as artist is unknown. But that
he recognized and fostered the talents of his sons is
undisputedly to his credit.

The city to which the brothers came was one of the
most densely inhabited cities in Europe at the turn of
the 16th century. The Venetians proudly described their
city-state, which at the time held a great deal of territory
on the mainland, in Istria, and around the southeastern
Mediterranean, as a republic. It was ruled by aristocrats,
from whose ranks the senate and the Doge—the head
of state who primarily fulfilled representative duties—
were chosen. In addition, there was also a tier of
wealthy citizens and a broad mass of more or less
poor people, who formed the bulk of the population.
They too, however, were also integrated into the city
administration through certain civil service posts that
were not allowed be allocated to aristocrats, in order
to prevent an excessive concentration of power among
their ranks, and above all through religious brotherhoods, the *scuole*.

At the beginning of the 16th century, Venice was
badly affected by the military struggles between the
emperor, the pope, and the king of France that took
place on Italian soil. For a while it was even threatened
with the loss of all its territory on the mainland.
However, the island state itself was hardly ever attacked
and never conquered. Its defensive wall of water was

Giorgione
Sleeping Venus, ca. 1508–1515
Oil (?) on canvas, 108.5 x 175 cm
Gemäldegalerie Alte Meister, Staatliche
Kunstsammlungen, Dresden

This is the painting that the Venetian Marco Antonio
Michiel saw in 1525 in the house of Jeronimo Marcello in
Venice. He commented that Titian added the landscape
and a putto to Giorgione's painting, and this has indeed
been confirmed by X-rays. The position of the sleeping
Venus was to become characteristic of Titian's depictions
of Venus.

Titian (?)
Concert Champêtre, ca. 1510–1511
Oil on canvas, 110 x 138 cm
Musée du Louvre, Paris

The significance of the dressed young men and two naked
women is as yet uncertain. Though the painting is now
generally given the title *Concert Champêtre* or country
concert, there continues to be just as much dispute about
its theme as there is about who painted it. It used to be
attributed either to Giorgione alone or to Titian and
Giorgione together. Because of a re-evaluation of Titian's
early style, it is now considered to be his work alone,
though not all authors agree.

too secure. Peace reigned within the state itself. The
wealth acquired through trade, the stable government,
and a cleverly devised system of administration made
Venice perhaps the most secure city in Europe.

As Lodovico Dolce reports, the young Titian soon
left the workshop of the mosaicist Zuccato and turned
to painting. He entered Venice's leading workshop
for painters, which at the time was run by Gentile
Bellini (1429–1507); his father Jacopo Bellini (ca.
1400–1470) had founded its fame. Gentile's younger
brother Giovanni (ca. 1430–1516) was considered
throughout northern Italy to be one of the most
progressive artists; but as far as honors are concerned, it
was Gentile who was significantly more successful. By
1469, the Emperor had already made him a member of
the nobility; and in 1479, the republic officially sent
him to Turkey to paint the Sultan. Titian soon also left
Gentile and turned to Giovanni Bellini, whose style
dominated the Venetian art of the late 15th and early
16th centuries. Early works definitely attributable to
Titian clearly show Bellini's influence, in particular in
their treatment of light and color.

Besides Bellini, another, significantly younger, artist
also determined the style of Venetian painting shortly
after 1500: Giorgio da Castelfranco, known as
Giorgione (1477/78–1510). His main clients were
young noblemen rather as opposed to the old elite.
Most of his works were created for a close circle of
customers. He knew how to adapt traditional themes to
suit his clients' high level of learning and sophisticated
taste. Or he devised new topics, full of mythological,
literary, and astrological allusions, according to their
preferences and requirements. The form and content of

Titian
Gypsy Madonna, ca. 1512
Oil on wood, 65.8 x 83.8 cm
Kunsthistorisches Museum, Vienna

This painting got its name from the black hair and pale
face of the Madonna, as well as the charming contrast of
colors. This type of Madonna, with very dark eyes, is not
found in Titian's later works.

his picture motifs are often so encrypted that, to this
day, it has not been possible to interpret them. Titian's
relationship to the ten-year-older Giorgione, who also
emerged from Bellini's workshop, was different from
that of his relationship to Bellini. Titian's works, which
clearly show Bellini's influence, can always be clearly
distinguished from those of the master. For a long time
this did not apply to Giorgione. Many works today
considered to be by him were formerly attributed to
Titian, and vice versa.

An X-ray examination in 1931 provided evidence
that there was once a small putto to the left of the
Sleeping Venus (page 294). This confirms an old report
that Titian added the landscape and a putto to
Giorgione's figure. Speculation that both artists also
cooperated on other works, such as, for example, the

Concert Champêtre (pages 294–295), and that Titian
adopted the older artist's style completely, seems to be
confirmed. Their relationship to one another was
redefined, however, for the occasion of the major Titian
exhibitions in Venice and Washington in 1990, and in
Paris in 1993. Numerous technical examinations of the
paintings had been undertaken prior to the 1990
exhibition. Now Titian's more spontaneous, wide
brushwork were distinguishable from the fine, gently
stroking style of Giorgione. This provided the basis for
a clearer picture of Titian's early work. It shows him to
be an artist, who, like other young painters, followed
Giorgione in his choice of theme, but who owed just as
much to Giovanni Bellini and his own inventive talent
for the coloring and figure composition as to the young
master from Castelfranco. Their relationship is today

interpreted as one of interaction, as an intensive examination of the other's artistic skill. Titian is no longer considered to be merely the receiving partner in this relationship, but also as the contributing one.

The orientation for Titian's earliest works came from both Bellini and Giorgione. His half-figure Madonnas, such as the *Gypsy Madonna* (page 296) and the *Madonna of the Cherries* (above), are completely dependent on Bellini's type of Madonna. But Titian's own mastery is already apparent in the *Gypsy Madonna*. Due to the unusual and delicate color combination of light blue, white, and dark red, and the dreamy, forlorn gaze of the Madonna and Child, many researchers have also felt themselves reminded of Giorgione, to whom the painting was attributed at one time. The landscape surrounding the Madonna is closely related to the

background of the *Sleeping Venus* (page 294). The, in this context, peculiar appearance of the folds of the precisely observed veneration shawl, and the equally well observed play of light on the materials, bear testimony to Titian's authorship. For these are precisely the aspects of Bellini's artistry that Titian most made his own and developed further in the years that followed.

After the fire of 1505, Titian and Giorgione were commissioned to decorate the façade of the Fondaco dei Tedeschi, the German commercial exchange, in Venice. The commission did not initially seem to promise the kudos that both painters would gain through the frescoes. But as Lodovico Dolce reports, especially for the barely twenty-year-old Titian, these murals, highly visible from afar, were to become the prelude to an almost unprecedented career.

Titian
Madonna of the Cherries, ca. 1515
Oil on wood, transferred to canvas, 81 x 99.5 cm
Kunsthistorisches Museum, Vienna

In this half-length picture of the Madonna, Titian was still keeping entirely to a pictorial idiom typical of Giovanni Bellini. St. Joseph is on the left, and Zacharias, the father of John the Baptist, on the right. Christ, depicted as a naked child, is giving the Madonna the cherries that give the painting its name.

First Successes:
Titian's First Commissions,
His Own Workshop, and the *Sensaria*

Titian
The Miracle of the Newborn Child, 1511
Fresco, 340 x 355 cm
Scuola del Santo, Padua

St. Anthony worked a miracle in which a newly born child spoke in defense of his mother, who had been accused of adultery. The closely observed, very individual faces show Titian's mastery of his craft, even at this early stage of his career.

The frescoes on the Fondaco dei Tedeschi were completed by 1508/1509. While Giorgione worked on the more important façade facing the Grand Canal, the younger, less well-known Titian had to make do with the façade on the side street. It is now no longer certain that Titian was a member of Giorgione's workshop at this time, something which had long been accepted as a matter of course. The meager remnants that still exist of the Fondaco frescoes confirm that two quite different artistic personalities were at work. A standing female nude by Giorgione has the same delicacy and daintiness as his *Sleeping Venus* (page 294). The stylized elegance of the softly modeled forms belong in a poetic dream world, while Titian's *Judith* (Galleria Franchetti, Ca' d'oro, Venice), despite its ruinous condition, radiates the same powerful physical presence as the frescoes in the Scuola del Santo (page 299) in Padua, created a year later. The same physical presence is visible in the nudes in the disputed and mysterious *Concert Champêtre* (pages 294–295). It has not yet been possible, however, to provide a conclusive interpretation for the presence of men from various social levels together with naked women in a landscape. The attribution of the painting to Titian has also not yet been accepted by all authors. Nonetheless, this painting conveys to the modern observer a strong visual concept of the yearning for Arcadia that prevailed when it was painted. As is the case here, this yearning becomes tangible in numerous Venetian paintings painted under the influence of Giorgione, though it is not possible to express it in a conclusive interpretation.

Giorgione's influence on Titian is clearest in his choice of motifs. Yet even in the first works that can be attributed to him with some certainty, Titian emerges as an independent artistic personality. Even though the motifs he adopted from Giorgione and Bellini are obvious, he manages to incorporate them into a new, independent form. In addition, he discovered the graphic arts at a very early stage. In 1508 he produced his first large woodcut, the *Triumph of Christ*. Working with various graphic techniques, and producing drafts for paintings in the form of drawings, were features of his entire career. As his fame spread, other artists emerged who distributed his paintings as graphic works, notably the Netherlands artist Cornelis Cort (1533–1578).

In 1510 Titian was commissioned to produce some frescoes in the Scuola del Santo in Padua (page 299), the place where the Brotherhood of St. Anthony met. The grave of this important saint is just a few steps away in the Santo, the church of St. Anthony. Padua had only recently become part of the Venetian state again, after having briefly fallen into the hands of the League of Cambrai, Venice's enemies.

Venice's battles against the League, to which France, the Holy Roman Empire, and the Pope had at times belonged, had brought the Republic to the brink of collapse. The end of hostilities did not, however, bring immediate relief to the city. For during 1509 and 1510 there was an outbreak of plague in Venice, one of its victims being Giorgione. It is likely that it was not easy for a young artist to win commissions under these conditions. However, the Augustinians of Santo Spirito in Isola commissioned a votive picture showing St. Mark and the plague saints Roch and Sebastian together with Cosmas and Damian, the patron saints

Titian
Portrait of a Man, ca. 1512
Oil on canvas, 81.2 x 66.3 cm
The National Gallery, London

The very affected posture of the sitter is characteristic
of Titian's early portraits, which were still painted under
the influence of Giorgione. The blue sleeve displays a
masterly use of color. It is proof both of Titian's ability
to depict materials, and also of his mastery of color as a
means of conveying a picture's meaning.

of doctors (Santa Maria della Salute, Venice). This
painting once again shows a close connection with
Giorgione, for he first used a similar composition for
his *Castelfranco Madonna* (page 283), and the
expression on the face of St. Sebastian is reminiscent
of the melancholy appearances of his figures. At the
same time, the treatment of the other figures and
garments shows the influence of Bellini. The
directness with which the figures are related to the
subject of the picture—an example being the saintly
doctor who is pointing to the wound that St. Roch is
displaying on his leg—distinguishes this work from
those of Titian's models. Nonetheless, his dependency
on Bellini and Giorgione that can still be seen in the
painting is a strong argument in favor of dating the
work to about 1510, as is the fact that this was the year
the plague ended, which would have been the reason
for commissioning the work. As a result it is, together
with the firmly dated frescoes in Padua, one of Titian's
earliest independent works.

In about 1510, Titian painted *Noli me tangere*
(opposite page) and the *Concert* (below). Despite the
somewhat formless bodies, there is a captivating
quality about the depiction of Christ and Magdalene,
a result of his use of color, and in particular his
treatment of the white materials, which show Titian to
be a master of light and color. He is able to give tactile
qualities, light and luster, to colorless material. The
white undergarment worn by the clergyman in the
Concert displays the same use of color.

At the same time, however, the *Concert* has an
additional portrait-like dimension. This is another area
where both Giorgione and Titian are greatly indebted

to Giovanni Bellini. Taking Netherlandish works as a
starting point (Hans Memling (ca. 1440–1494) was his
most important model) Bellini succeeded in creating
portraits that did not depend solely on great realism, as
many Netherlandish portraits did. Even though he is
depicting only the face and shoulders, he succeeds,
mainly by means of color, in successfully capturing the
character of his subject. His combination of colors
enables Bellini to use just a few shades to produce an
impression of spiritual anxiety or weariness, festive
magnificence or moral humility.

So far it has not been possible clearly to differentiate
Titian's and Giorgione's early portraits. Only Titian's
broader brushstrokes and greater interest in fabrics that
reflect light enable us to attempt carefully to distinguish
them. Both Giorgione and Titian chose to depict a larger
section of their subjects than Bellini did. This provided
them with the opportunity to characterize their sitters by
their posture, movements, and dress. They replaced the
colorful background that had played such an important
role in Bellini's works with mainly neutral black or gray
ones. Later, Titian introduced curtains or an occasional
view opening onto a landscape.

In about 1510, Titian began to win independent
commissions and to establish himself as a painter in
Venice. In 1513, he opened his own workshop, in
which he employed two assistants, one of whom had
worked for Giovanni Bellini. During the same year, he
wrote a petition asking to be allowed to produce a
painting for the Sala del Gran Consiglio, the Senate's
large assembly hall in the Doge's Palace. His
submission to the Consiglio dei Dieci, the Council of
Ten, provides us with a fascinating insight into both

Titian
The Concert, ca. 1510
Oil on canvas, 86.5 x 123.5 cm
Galleria Palatina, Palazzo Pitti, Florence

This painting has been considered a work by the young
Titian only since it was last restored in 1976. The faces
of the figures at the sides are badly damaged. Only the
center figure and the garment of the figure on the right
display his skillful use of color. Pictures of musicians were
frequently painted in the 16th century. However, it was
very rare for such an intimate relationship between the
musicians to be depicted. The youth on the left draws the
observer into the scene, thus including him in the web of
glances and touches.

Opposite page:
Titian
Noli me tangere, 1511–1512
Oil on canvas, 109 x 91 cm
The National Gallery, London

"Noli me tangere," do not touch me, is what Christ said
to Mary Magdalene in the Gospel of John (20: 14–18),
when he met her on the morning of his Resurrection.
Despite some awkwardness in the construction of the
figures, Christ and Magdalene fit in harmoniously into
the wonderful landscape that takes up most of the
picture.

Titian
Sacred and Profane Love, 1514
Oil on canvas, 118 x 279 cm
Galleria Borghese, Rome

During the course of the 20th century numerous authors have attempted to determine the meaning of this painting. The two most accepted theories agree in interpreting the nude woman as Venus. The first theory sees her as a personification of sacred or heavenly love, and the clothed figure, also Venus, as a personification of profane earthly love, fertility, and nature. The second theory is that the clothed figure is Polia, a character in a Renaissance novel, who at first vows to live a chaste life but ends up being won over to love.

his artistic self-confidence and also his precise ideas on the way his art should be practiced.

From the 1470s onwards, the leading Venetian painters had been restoring the old frescoes in the Sala del Gran Consiglio and, when this attempt failed, replacing them with paintings on canvas. The Bellini workshop carried out the major part of this work. Other painters employed on this major state commission were Alvise Vivarini (ca. 1445– ca. 1505) and Vittore Carpaccio (1455/65–1526). In 1577, all these paintings were destroyed during a fire in the Doge's Palace. In his petition, Titian makes a specific reference to the fact that he would be willing to turn down numerous invitations to work at Italian courts,

even in Rome, if he was sure of having an opportunity to prove his abilities in Venice. He says that when he started training in Venice his aim was not to become rich, but to make his art famous. He offers to work at the most difficult location, a wall full of windows. The only reward he wants for his work is to get the next free *sensaria* on the Fondaco dei Tedeschi. As was shown by the historian Charles Hope at the Titian Congress in Venice in 1976, this position did not mean that the painter who held the title was also the official state painter, as was believed for so long. Rather, the *sensaria* was simply the payment made for a state commission worthy of a trading republic. The Venetian government handed out thirty of these more

or less honorary titles, some of them to artists. The *sensaria* was an office held for life. If no position was available, the painter was put on the waiting list or, in cases of particular honor, was moved to the top of the list. The office paid about 120 ducats a year, the holder did not need to pay taxes, but if the offer which led to him being given the office of *sensaria* was not carried out, the title could be revoked. If a position quickly became vacant, an artist who lived a long life would earn more from it than from being paid only once for his paintings. On the other hand, there were financial advantages for the republic if the painter had to wait a long time for a free *sensaria* or died young.

Even though this commission did not have the same status as that of the official position as state painter, the work on the Doge's Palace nonetheless greatly enhanced his exceptional reputation as an artist. That Titian, scarcely twenty-five, should have applied for and been given such a commission is proof of his considerable artistic self-confidence and the high regard in which he was already held, even though he was not given a *sensaria* until the death of Giovanni Bellini in 1516. However, Titian was extremely slow getting around to painting the work that had gained him this much-desired title.

It is possible that his success in gaining that position played a major part in his being commissioned to

Titian
Flora, ca. 1515–1520
Oil on canvas, 79 x 63 cm
Galleria degli Uffizi, Florence

The beautiful woman carrying flowers is thought to be Flora, the classical goddess of flowers and spring. She is one of the first of a series of portraits of ideal female beauty that Titian painted. The sheen of her reddish golden hair, the soft hue of her skin, and the just visible breast whose bareness is skillfully emphasized by her hand and the pink brocade, display Titian's abilities as a subtle colorist and his sure feeling for sensuality.

produce one of his greatest masterpieces, *Sacred and Profane Love* (pages 302–303). The man who commissioned the work, Niccolò Aurelio, was at the time a secretary to the Council of Ten to which Titian had written. Aurelio ordered the picture in 1514, on the occasion of his wedding to Laura Bagarotto. It has not yet been possible to decipher the subject of the picture. It is certain, however, that the theme is connected to love and marriage. The reason for commissioning such a magnificent painting of high intellectual demands might have been the scandal caused by the wedding. Aurelio was a respected state official, but the bride was already widowed and the daughter of a man executed

for high treason. The sensation caused by the marriage was even noted by the city's official historian, Marin Sanudo (1466–1533).

The private allusions in the subject, the theme of love, the references to the classical age, and the beautiful landscape all convey the aura of a distant, lost world of shepherds and gods that was to preoccupy "new" Venetian art, even after Giorgione's death. The movement of materials, which emphasizes the volume of the bodies, the play of light and shadow, the softness, delicacy, and colorful beauty of the flesh tones, the harmony of the color composition, the figures in the background, depicted with just a few brushstrokes,

Titian
Venus Anadyomene, ca. 1520
Oil on canvas, 76 x 57 cm
National Gallery of Scotland (on loan from the Duke of Sutherland), Edinburgh

The word "Anadyomene," which means "one who has surfaced," is a reference to the birth of Venus. According to classical mythology and the poetry of Hesiod (ca. 700 BC), Venus rose fully formed from the ocean in Paphos on Cyprus (or Cythera). This is the moment depicted by Titian. The relatively small painting shows one of his women's figures typical of the 1510s and 1520s. This painting should be seen not as a portrait of an individual but as a depiction of female beauty.

Titian
Salome, ca. 1515
Oil on canvas, 90 x 72 cm
Galleria Doria Pamphilj, Rome

The main focus is on neither the horrific events nor the religious significance of the scene. It is not even clear if this is Salome with the head of the Baptist, or Judith with the head of Holofernes. The former is suggested by the displaying of the head on a platter, the latter by the presence of the female servant who is a feature of the traditional iconography of the Judith story. The painting, with its wonderful color contrasts of red, green, and white, and its delightful female figures, is one of Titian's depictions of an ideal of female beauty. This is why it was frequently copied.

Titian
Portrait of a Young Woman, ca. 1515
Chalk on brown paper, 41.9 x 26.5 cm
Gabinetto dei Disegni e delle Stampe, Galleria degli Uffizi, Florence

It is very difficult to date this drawing. It seems, however, that Titian mainly portrayed women of this type in his early works, such as the frescoes in the Scuola del Santo (page 299). The tilted position of her head is also reminiscent of portraits painted during the same period.

the precisely observed buildings gently disappearing into the distant mist—all these factors show that Titian deserves a special position among his contemporaries. The painting continues to fascinate viewers to this day. Titian achieved all this through his virtuoso use of color. Technical examinations of his paintings show how revolutionary was the artist's use of the new medium of oil painting. Every detail, in particular the flesh tones and materials, is built up using numerous pigments that were constantly being remixed. This was the way in which he was finally able to achieve his refined use of color, in particular his inimitably delicate changes of color. Especially worthy of note are

the carefully harmonized shades of red, purple, yellow, white, and blue on the face of the naked Venus, contrasted with her strands of golden hair, which is tied back with a ribbon of delicate purple. Any of the uncertainty that might have been evident in his depiction of figures in *Noli me tangere* (page 300) and the Padua frescoes (page 299) has now completely disappeared. Paintings such as *Salome* (above) and *Flora* (page 304) are closely related to the *Sacred and Profane Love*. The type of woman which Titian now preferred to depict no longer derived from Bellini or Giorgione. Titian himself would now become a model for other artists.

Venetian Commissions and Works for North Italian Princes. Titian Revolutionizes Venetian Art

Titian
Assumption of the Virgin (Assunta), 1516–1518
Oil on wood, 690 x 360 cm
Santa Maria Gloriosa dei Frari, Venice

The Italian name "Assunta," by which this painting is also commonly known, derives from the Latin word *assumptio*, which means "to accept," and therefore has a direct bearing on Mary's ascension into heaven. The *Assumption of the Virgin* was the first major official commission that Titian received for an oil painting in Venice. That is probably why he so proudly painted his signature on the right, beneath the seated figure of St. Peter. He seldom signed later paintings that remained in Venice.

On 29 November 1516, Giovanni Bellini died at the age of 84. For as long as he had been alive and in full possession of his creative powers, neither Giorgione nor Titian had ever been able to obtain a public commission for a large-scale oil painting. But now, in 1516, Titian was approached by Germano da Caiole, the prior of the large Franciscan monastery in Venice. He commissioned him to paint a new work for the high altar in the Franciscan church of Santa Maria Gloriosa dei Frari, the *Assumption of the Virgin* (page 307). Together with the Dominican church of Santi Giovanni e Paolo, this enormous church was one of the two important churches of the mendicant orders in Venice, and it played an important role in the public life of the city, being used, among other things, as a burial site for the Doges. As Lodovico Dolce records, the unveiling of the *Assumption of the Virgin*, which took place on 19 May 1518, was a shock for the Venetians, and in particular for the other artists in the city. Until then, they had been used to seeing more or less static individual figures that, in older works, even had an entire panel devoted to them. The vivid movements of the figures and the great dramatic quality of the scene broke all Venetian traditions. Only gradually, Dolce wrote, did the initial rejection change to a boundless admiration. He himself praised the altar and made his great admiration for the work clear by comparing it with works by Raphael and Michelangelo. At a time when central Italian writers such as Vasari were debating who the leading artist of the age was, and narrowing the list of candidates down to Raphael and Michelangelo, Dolce secured Titian a place among the great. At the same time, Dolce's comparison suggests an explanation of Titian's fundamental break with the traditional altarpieces of Venice that has lost none of its validity to this day. Because of the vivid movements of the powerful figures in the *Assumption of the Virgin*, Roman works have repeatedly been cited as the source of Titian's ability to create a greater sense of movement and energy than was usual in Venice up to that time. But the works of Raphael and Michelangelo that are used as comparisons are certainly not direct models. Raphael's Vatican *Transfiguration* (page 271), whose dramatic movements are very similar, was not

painted until after the *Assumption of the Virgin*. The same is true of a fresco on the same theme that, according to Vasari, was created by the Venetian artist Sebastiano del Piombo (ca. 1485–1547) after a design by Michelangelo, for the Borgherini Chapel in San Pietro in Montorio in Rome. Titian himself had not been to Rome yet, though it is possible that he could have received reports about, and possibly even drawings of, the works of Raphael and Michelangelo in the Vatican and the Sistine Chapel.

It must be said, however, that even Titian's earliest works such as the frescoes in Padua (page 299) show that he is attempting to depict voluminous figures with complex movements. The spectators who are facing one another, or the young man who is approaching in the scene with the talking newborn child, as well as the twisted and complexly foreshortened body of the wife who has been stabbed to death, all show the same sense of pictorial drama, though the more pronounced gestures of the *Assumption of the Virgin* do suggest there was some Roman influence. In the *Assumption of the Virgin*, Titian also retained the traditional practice of arranging the heads so that they are all at the same level, a device he had already used in Padua. Here, however, the device no longer seems awkward and static. The entire effect of the painting is dominated by the upward movement. Titian achieves this compositionally by means of a triangle of red hues, created by the red garments worn by the Apostles and the Madonna's red dress. The broadening reddish black shape formed by God the Father's cloak seems to open to receive the upward movement. The form and content of the painting coincide completely.

This altarpiece made Titian the most celebrated painter in Venice. At the same time, it drew him to the attention of Bellini's old patrons in the northern Italian ruling houses. From January to March 1516, Titian stayed in Ferrara with Duke Alfonso d'Este, for whose private study, his Alabaster Room, Bellini had painted a Banquet of the Gods in 1514. The background of this painting was later overpainted by Titian, though technical examinations have shown that before he did so another artist had already been at work on it. The

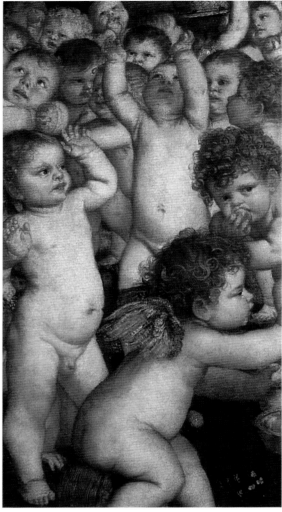

Titian
The Worship of Venus, 1518
Oil on canvas, 172 x 175 cm
Museo Nacional del Prado, Madrid

The composition of the work is modeled on a classical painting on the same theme, described by the Greek writer Philostratus (beginning of the 3rd century AD) in his *Eikones*, in which he writes about the paintings in a classical collection. Nowadays it is disputed whether he was writing about real works or ones he had invented. During the Renaissance, numerous artists attempted to produce paintings that matched the classical models described by Philostratus.

The Worship of Venus (detail page 308)

In classical times, Cupids were considered to be the children of nymphs, who were the female nature spirits closely linked to Venus. Titian depicted every one with a precise eye for the enchanting freshness and comic gestures of small children.

overpainting was not, as used to be assumed, carried out during Titian's first stay in 1516. From 1517 until about 1525, Titian was to produce three large mythological paintings for the duke, all of which were hung in his private work and study room. Such a *studiolo* was one of the most important rooms in a Renaissance palace. The place where collections of art works and books were kept, it was a demonstration of one's education and personal taste. Alfonso's sister Isabella d'Este, who was married to the Margrave of Mantua, Francesco II Gonzaga, was very proud of the famous art collection in her *studiolo*. It is perfectly conceivable that Alfonso was attempting to create something similar. He commissioned works from Giovanni Bellini and Raphael. However, because of the early death of Raphael in 1520, his paintings for Alfonso were unfinished. If that had not been the case, Titian would have been working in direct competition with him.

The first painting, which Titian completed in 1518, was the *Worship of Venus* (above). This commission had originally been awarded to a central Italian artist, Fra Bartolomeo (1475–1517), but he died in 1517. We know from one of Titian's letters to the duke that he was given precise instructions as to the painting's subject. His interpretation of the subject, however, must have been a

surprise, particularly in view of Fra Bartolomeo's very conventional design, which is now in the Uffizi. In addition to the masterly depiction of the landscape and materials, which is equally apparent in the enchanting putti and the shining silk fabrics, Titian uses the art of perspective to give the painting a sense of dynamism that the theme does not actually require. The eyes of the observer are led from the bottom left, along the broad path filled with countless playing putti, diagonally across and into the background. On the left, the ground rises gently, so that we cannot see right into the background. On the right, the statue of Venus, the actual focus of the festivities, blocks our view into the distance.

In December 1522, Titian finished the second painting, *Bacchus and Ariadne* (opposite page). It is likely that the third painting, the *Bacchanal* (pages 310–311), was finished by 1525. In both cases, Titian's feeling for color and the breathtaking energy of the movements are particularly impressive. In the first painting, Ariadne is waving despairingly at the ship disappearing in the distance, on board which is Theseus, who left her behind while she was sleeping. But as she waves, she is already looking at her new lover, Bacchus, who is approaching from the right with a retinue of satyrs and nymphs. While his train does not appear to have come to a standstill yet, Bacchus himself is just about to get down

Titian
Bacchus and Ariadne, 1520–1522
Oil on canvas, 175 x 190 cm
The National Gallery, London

This painting is probably based on a variety of classical texts, all of
them concerning Ariadne, the daughter of the king of Crete. Because
of her love for Theseus, she helped him escape her father's labyrinth
by means of a ball of thread. However, Theseus deserted her on Naxos
while they were returning to Athens. There, she became the lover of
the god Bacchus. Above her, already visible, is a crown of stars
representing the Corona Borealis, into which she (or, according to a
different tradition, her bridal head-dress) is eventually transformed.

Right:
Titian
Bacchanal, 1523–1525, or earlier
Oil on canvas, 175 x 193 cm
Museo Nacional del Prado, Madrid

Like the two previous pictures, this painting was destined to be hung in the Alabaster Room in Ferrara Palace. Like *The Worship of Venus*, it derives from a description written by Philostratus. The inhabitants of the island of Andros are shown taking part in a bacchanal, an orgy for Bacchus, the Roman god of wine. According to classical mythology, Andros was the god's favorite island, where rivers ran with wine instead of water.

Bacchanal (detail page 310– 311)

Titian was not afraid to depict humorously the more basic aspects of the bacchanal.

from his chariot. The broad sweeping movement of the length of reddish pink silk—his only clothing apart from a wreath of leaves—underlines the force of his movement. There are no apparent dramatic spatial effects in the third painting in the series, the *Bacchanal*. The elaborate method by which the imaginary space is created, by means of the complex way in which the figures overlap, does not become clear until the painting is looked at more attentively. Much the same is true of the marvelous *Entombment of Christ* (page 312), painted at roughly the same time and now in the Louvre.

In his works painted between 1515 and 1530, Titian worked intensively on ways of creating a sense of space. At the same time, he focused the narrative of his pictures on a very precise moment. The figures appear to have been captured at a moment of movement, so that in the very next instant they will change to a new course of action. By means of these two concerns—unexpected spatial compositions and a dramatic sense of change—Titian frequently succeeded in producing entirely new interpretations of traditional themes.

The *Annunciation* (Cappella di Malchiostro, Cathedral, Treviso) was painted for the altar in the Malchiostro Chapel in Treviso Cathedral about 1519. As in the *Worship of Venus* (page 308), Titian made use of an unusual perspective. The Archangel Gabriel is rapidly approaching from the back of the picture. Mary is turning her head back. Titian depicted her shock at her heavenly visitor in an inimitable manner: all the Virgin is doing is wrapping her ample garment, full of folds, more tightly around her body as if to protect herself from the swift approach of the angel. In an

Annunciation scene, one would traditionally have expected to see the angel approaching Mary on the same picture plane. None of Titian's contemporaries can have been prepared to see such a familiar theme depicted using such a revolutionary spatial composition.

Titian achieved a similar effect in his second large commission for the Frari church, the *Pesaro Altarpiece* (page 313) painted for the Pesaro family. The painting is a *sacra conversazione*. This term applies to depictions of the Madonna with various saints, who would be called upon at this altar to intercede on a worshipper's behalf. The central position was normally reserved for the Madonna. Titian, however, moves her from the center to the right of the painting. This means that a visitor to the church, approaching the high altar from the western entrance, would see the Madonna from a long way off. And this indeed makes it possible to show the donor, who is portrayed in profile in the traditional manner, kneeling in front of her instead of beside her. His family, in contrast, kneel on the right and do not meet the eyes of the Madonna or saints. It was very unusual for the donors to appear in a painting for a Venetian altar. However, the painting has a votive character as it is a commemoration of the victory won against the Ottomans by Jacopo Pesaro, the commander of the papal fleet, together with the Venetians.

By having the Madonna placed to one side, the painting gains a degree of movement that until then would scarcely have seemed possible. Titian's work became the prototype for an unending series of altarpieces, which repeatedly make use of its dynamic force.

Titian
The Entombment of Christ, ca. 1523–1526
Oil on canvas, 148 x 205 cm
Musée du Louvre, Paris

Here Titian skillfully uses the direction of the light to support the dynamics of movement that permeate the entire painting. The greatest contrast of light and shade is present on the body of Christ. The observer's eyes are first drawn to his winding sheet and legs, before moving to his upper body, which is lying in darkness. The shadow in this area treats the subject of Christ's death and entombment in an unusual way, using purely formal means of expression.

The fresco of St. Christopher in the Doge's Palace (Palazzo Ducale, Venice) also dates from the early 1520s. Despite the limitations of fresco painting, which requires the artist to work rapidly and confidently because he is painting on wet plaster, Titian succeeded in producing a figure with a monumental physical presence. He used hatching to produce light and shadow, giving an extraordinary three-dimensionality to the saint's muscles. His experience in creating designs for woodcuts was probably of prime importance in helping him to develop this method of representing light and shade.

Between 1520 and 1522, Titian painted the *Polyptych of the Resurrection* (pages 314–315) for Venice's papal legate, Altobello Averoldi, who was born in Brescia. The figure of St. Sebastian, on one of the altar's side panels, has much the same physical presence and muscularity as his St. Christopher. Titian does not portray the saint as a delicate, slim youth as the previous generation of Venetian painters had. Instead, his Sebastian corresponds to the new ideal body as characterized in Rome by Michelangelo. This Sebastian is often compared to Michelangelo's Slave for the unfinished tomb of Pope Julius II, now in the Louvre.

In the *Polyptych of the Resurrection*, Titian employs the traditional structure of a polyptych altarpiece that depicts principle subjects on a central panel and less important ones on the side and top panels, a type rarely used in the 16th century. The composition of the Averoldi altarpiece clashes with the dramatic effect of the traditional form of altarpiece. The left panel, showing the kneeling donor and saints Nazaro and Celso, is clearly related to the center panel, showing the Resurrection, by means of the gestures and gazes of the figures. In contrast, and despite the ground being at the same level, the right side panel showing St. Sebastian seems to distract from the main panel because of the much lighter, shining blue sky and the muscular body of the naked saint. In an age that was completely shaped by Christianity, it would have been obvious that the two top panels, showing Mary on the right and an angel on the left, belonged together as an Annunciation. This was also an arrangement found in many other polyptychs. Without knowing this, however, it would be quite conceivable to see both scenes as part of the central scenes, the Resurrection of Christ.

Though the panels do not fit particularly well within a traditional polyptych, the exceptional quality of the individual panels once again clearly shows just how far Titian had moved away from traditional forms by the mid 1520s.

Shortly before the Pesaro altarpiece, Titian painted the altarpiece the *Madonna in Glory with the Christ Child and St. Francis and St. Alvise with the Donor Alvise Gozzi* (Museo Civico, Ancona). This panel, which had been commissioned by Alvise Gozzi, shows the Madonna with a number of saints who lived at different times. We can see Venice behind the figure of the donor. Though the conjunction of these figures with a Venetian background is anything but realistic, Titian effortlessly succeeds in creating a much more believable narrative space on a single panel than he does in the *Averoldi Polyptych* (pages 314–315).

Opposite page:
Titian
Pesaro Altarpiece, 1519–1526
Oil on canvas, 385 x 270 cm
Santa Maria Gloriosa dei Frari, Venice

Until this painting appeared, it was customary to depict the Madonna in the center of an altarpiece. The way Titian moved her from the center of the picture to the edge was a revolutionary modification of the traditional pictorial composition that was frequently copied, especially during the Baroque. The Venetians of the time must also have felt that the prominent position taken up in the painting by the donor of the altarpiece was equally unusual. The most important member of the Pesaro family, Jacopo, the Bishop of Paphos, is kneeling directly in front of the Madonna, and his brothers and their sons are opposite him. While pictures of donors were usual in other places, they were normally avoided on altars in Venice, probably for political reasons.

Titian
Polyptych of the Resurrection (Averoldi Polyptych),
1520–1522
Oil on wood, 278 x 122 cm
Santi Nazaro e Celso, Brescia

Titian's impulse to capture bold bodily movements is not
easily accommodated within the traditional structure of a
polyptych, which necessitated depicting different pictorial
elements on a number of panels. It is certain that this
antiquated form was used at the request of the client, the
papal legate Altobello Averoldi. He is depicted (bottom
left panel) with the patron saints of the church, St.
Nazaro and St. Celso, to whom he donated the altar.

The Archangel Gabriel (top left panel) appears to be
rushing in from the left, his garments streaming behind
him. He spreads his greeting out on a banderole, which
he is holding out to Mary on the opposite panel. His
right hand, part of the banderole, his wings and the
fluttering ends of his belt are all cut off by the edge of the
picture. This creates the impression that the almost square
panel is much too small to contain the magnificent figure
of the angel. This artistic trick enables Titian to intensify
the sense of tension and dynamics of the painting.

The bright figure of the ascending Christ (center panel) is
surrounded by clouds that are lit up by the red rays of the
early morning sun. The light in the upper part of the
painting forms a vivid contrast to the darkness of the
tomb, where the only flashes of light are reflections from
the guards' armor. This dramatic effect of the light
supports the theological message of the Resurrection.

The panel showing St. Sebastian (bottom right) was
finished by 1520. Jacopo Tebaldi, the representative of
the Duke of Ferrara, was so impressed by the painting
when he saw it in Titian's workshop that he urged his
master to buy it. Tebaldi offered to pay Titian 60 ducats
for this single panel: Averoldi was paying him only 200
ducats for the entire altarpiece. In the end, however, the
Duke of Ferrara shied away from making the purchase,
probably afraid of annoying the powerful legate Averoldi.

TITIAN BETWEEN THE REPUBLIC AND EMPEROR. LANDSCAPE AS NARRATIVE

The artistically lit clouds of the *Averoldi Polyptych* (pages 314 -315) and the threatening clouds, shot through with sharp yellow bolts of lightning, of the *Entombment of Christ* (page 312) are indicators of an aspect of Titian's work to which he increasingly devoted his attention from about 1530—the use of landscape not just as the scene of the events, but as a feature that plays a role in determining the picture's meaning. The most important example of this new conception, the *Martyrdom of St. Peter Martyr*, has since been lost. Titian painted it between 1526 and 1530 for the Dominican church of Santi Giovanni e Paolo in Venice. Vasari wrote of the painting that "of all the pictures painted so far by Titian this is the most finished, the most celebrated, the greatest and the best conceived and executed." Countless copies were made of the altarpiece, which was destroyed by fire in 1867. The painting was the summation of a series of pictorial solutions Titian reached in the 1520s. Powerful, monumental figures making dramatic, emotional gestures focused the story on its climax. The saint is lying on the ground. The murderer is swinging his sword in order to kill him in the next instant. Two angels are already on their way from Heaven with a martyr's palm. St. Peter Martyr appears to have already seen them, for he is looking towards them, not his attacker. His fleeing companion is also looking back towards the angels. The climax of the story will take place in the next instant. The attacker will split Peter's skull, making him a martyr for which he receives the palm. The continuation of the scene would be clear to anyone who knew the story of this saint. That the events

Titian
Madonna and Child with the Young St. John the Baptist and St. Catherine, ca. 1530
Oil on canvas, 101 x 142 cm
The National Gallery, London

In his pictures of the Madonna dating from the early 1530s, Titian avoided large, emphatic gestures. The figures are nonetheless interconnected by a series of complicated overlapping movements that form a compositional whole. For example, St. Catherine is carefully holding the Christ Child above Mary's lap, clearly about to either lift him up or lay him down. Thanks to Titian's superb mastery of such difficult movement motifs, the observer becomes aware of this only when analyzing the work more closely. We can only guess at the original color composition of the painting as it was detrimentally affected by a cleaning procedure that was too harsh.

Titian
Man with a Glove, ca. 1520–1522
Oil on canvas, 100 x 89 cm
Musée du Louvre, Paris

Here the muted grays, blacks, and whites make individual
highlights of color—such as the sitter's blue eyes, red lips,
and flushed ear lobes, and the chain around his neck—all
the more prominent. The casual though clearly contrived
pose, emphasized by the signet ring on his right hand,
together with the unified use of color, clearly differentiate
this portrait from Titian's portraits of rulers, which are
characterized by stiff poses and a colorful splendor.

Titian
The Young Englishman, ca. 1540–1545
Oil on canvas, 111 x 93 cm
Galleria Palatina, Palazzo Pitti, Florence

The light color of the portrayed man's hair and eyes, and
the elegance of his pose, led earlier interpreters to think
he was a young Englishman, though there is no evidence
to confirm this suggestion. The portrait is, however,
undisputedly one of Titian's most masterly portraits.

Titian
Portrait of Francis I, 1539
Oil on canvas, 109 x 89 cm
Musée du Louvre, Paris

Titian never saw Francis I, the king of France (1494–1547). He nonetheless succeeded in painting an impressive portrait of the ruler. The model for his portrait was a medal made by Benvenuto Cellini (1500–1571), showing the king in profile. The erect posture, broad torso, and magnificent garments give the portrait a regal air. The flat hat with its delicate feathers, together with his fine hair, which is brushed across his face in a similarly feathery way, give a certain lightness to the otherwise very proud royal portrait.

are not depicted, that instead they take place in the observer's mind, creates the particular tension of this altarpiece. A sense of mounting tension is created in much the same way in numerous works painted before this one, such as the *Assumption of the Virgin* (page 307), and the *Annunciation* in Treviso. However, Titian achieves a new quality in this painting by linking more of the landscape, and not just the light, to the dramatic events that are unfolding. The trees appear to be sharing the movements of the protagonists: they are effectively a paraphrase of the main lines of movement of the figures.

A comparable interest in movement can be observed in the Madonna paintings of the 1530s, though they are much more reserved in their gestures and action. Instead of stirring drama, they convey quiet contemplation, the harmony of the colors playing an important role in this. An impressive example is the *Madonna and Child with the Young St. John the Baptist*

and St. Catherine (pages 316–317). Titian makes technically difficult aspects, such as the intertwined movements, appear easy, and here too the action, though it has been captured on canvas, is clearly about to continue. The colors in the foreground are repeated in the background, giving an impression of harmonious unity. The same can be said of the *Madonna and Child with St. Catherine and a Rabbit* (page 34), which Titian probably painted for Federico II Gonzaga (1500–1540), the young marquis who became the Duke of Mantua.

The court of Mantua was the nearest place where many Venetians could study the new directions that art was taking in Rome. Works by Raphael could be found here, and since 1524 Raphael's most important student Giulio Romano (ca. 1499–1546) had been working here. Federico II Gonzaga was the nephew of Alfonso d'Este, Titian's most important patron during the 1520s. It is likely that Alfonso had brought Titian to Federico's attention. But from 1527 there was another herald spreading Titian's fame throughout Italy, the writer Pietro Aretino (1492–1556), who was also in close contact with Federico. It was Federico II Gonzaga who would finally introduce Titian to his most important client during the following decades. It was in the winter of 1529 that Titian met Emperor Charles V for the first time, in Parma, and in 1530 he painted his first portrait of him, which has since been lost. The earliest of his surviving portraits of the emperor is the *Portrait of Charles V* (Museo Nacional del Prado, Madrid), which was painted either in 1532 or, more likely, in 1533. In the autumn of 1529, Charles had come to Italy in order to resume the custom, which had lapsed since the mid-14th century, of being crowned emperor by the pope. It was no more than a symbolic act aimed at bringing a temporary halt to the hostilities between the emperor and pope. The emperor did not travel as far as Rome, but was crowned by Pope Clement VII in Bologna in February 1530. An entire range of diplomatic activities went hand in hand with the coronation. The representatives of a number of Italian aristocratic families went to Bologna in order to wait upon the emperor, make new contacts, or even acquire new titles or properties for their families.

The commission which Federico II Gonzaga gave to Titian must also be seen in this context. Federico, whose family enjoyed a long-standing relationship with the German emperors, was made the Duke of Mantua. His portrait (Museo Nacional del Prado, Madrid), which Titian may have painted as early as 1523, or not until 1529, is considered—along with his *Portrait of Ippolito de' Medici* (Galleria Palatina, Palazzo Pitti, Florence) and the *Young Englishman* (page 319)—to be one of the finest male portraits he painted.

Works such as the *Knight of Malta* (page 318), the *Man with a Glove* (Galleria degli Uffizi, Florence) and the *Portrait of Vincenzo Mosti* (Galleria Palatina, Palazzo Pitti, Florence) illustrate Titian's style of portraiture. In contrast with his earlier portraits, Titian was now faced with the task of portraying an important dignitary. Federico's proud, erect posture contrasts with his dreamy gaze; his face is framed by thick, short curls and he is gently laying his hand on a small dog who is pawing at him for attention. Titian succeeds in simultaneously conveying an impression of strength, eagerness, and a sensitive, self-confident calmness, corresponding to the Renaissance's ideal courtier as described in Il Cortegiano, *The Courtier*, by Baldassare Castiglione (1478–1529). However, the clothing, the velvety bluish-purple jerkin with gold trim, the magnificent sword and jewels, create a delicate, festive character in keeping with the duke's particular position. Titian had learnt Giovanni Bellini's lessons: his portraits create an impression through posture, color, and the play of light, all of which clearly reflect the position and personality of the sitter.

During Titian's lifetime, he was mainly admired for the verisimilitude of his portraits. But on closer observation it becomes apparent that he did not attempt to depict every feature or aspects of a person. He restricted himself to essentials, which he expressed not merely through depiction, but also through his choice of colors and forms, and his ability to convey

the tactile properties of the clothing. It is precisely this skillful concentration on essentials, rather than an exact realism, that make his portraits so easy for the observer to understand. Titian succeeded brilliantly in capturing certain aspects of a personality, ranging from a sitter's social status to his individual characteristics. In some cases it is to be doubted whether they were always historically accurate: social conventions and expectations will probably have played an equally important, if not greater, part.

In the 1530s, Titian reached the pinnacle of his career. He was working for Venetian patrons, for the most important northern Italian princely houses, and for the Emperor. In contrast to his friend Giulio Romano, though, he had always carefully avoided becoming the court painter for just one patron. Titian always remained an independent artist.

Left: Titian
Portrait of Eleonora Gonzaga, Duchess of Urbino,
ca. 1536–1538
Oil on canvas, 114 x 103 cm
Galleria degli Uffizi, Florence

In 1509, aged sixteen, Eleonora Gonzaga (1493–1555) married the Duke of Urbino, Francesco Maria della Rovere. The portrait corresponds completely to the Renaissance ideal of virtue. It displays nothing of Eleonora's powerful personality, which came to the fore when she actively supported her husband in his attempt to regain his territory, repeatedly ruling in his stead when he was away on campaigns.

Titian
La Bella, 1536
Oil on canvas, 89 x 75.5 cm
Galleria Palatina, Palazzo Pitti, Florence

Like so many of Titian's other works, it is likely that this portrait is an idealized portrait of female beauty, and not a precise depiction of any one person. This is corroborated by the Duke of Urbino, who, in a letter he wrote on 2 May 1536, simply described it as the "lady in the blue dress." The painting gains its opulent, sensuous appeal mainly from its masterful combination of color values, from the blue dress with red sleeves, through to the flesh tones and the golden brown, skillfully plaited hair.

Though he was awarded the title of Count Palatine and Knight of the Golden Spur by Charles V in 1533, and was repeatedly invited to visit his court in Spain, Titian left Venice only for short trips. Some may feel it to be astonishing that he preferred the comparatively modest position of a Venetian craftsman to the role of artist at a brilliant court. But even if his foreign title meant nothing in Venice, this was where he was sure to have both a regular income and the security and freedom that no court could offer him. As an adroit businessman, he will also have been quite happy to be able to play various clients off against each other.

The rising number of important commissions enabled him to move into a new house on the edge of Venice in 1531. It was both his workshop and dwelling. While it was no palace, it was large enough to be known as the Ca' Grande, the Grand House.

Apart from the Emperor and various Venetian clients, Titian painted the finest works of the 1530s for the ducal della Rovere family in Urbino.

In 1536 he painted the mysterious *La Bella* (page 321), a portrait of a beautiful young woman that was also ordered by Duke Francesco Maria della Rovere (1490–1538). It is very likely that this painting, as well as *Flora* (page 304) and other paintings of this sort, was not a simple portrait but the depiction of an ideal of female beauty, though many authors have pointed out the subject's similarity to Eleonora Gonzaga. Its interpretation as a portrait is based on inventories that always name the painting together with a portrait of Eleonora's mother Isabella d'Este (1474–1539). The latter painting is an idealized portrait of the young Isabella, painted by Titian when the margravine of Mantua was already more than sixty years old. It is possible that her daughter had the same idea, to have a

Titian
Venus of Urbino, 1538
Oil on canvas, 120 x 165 cm
Galleria degli Uffizi, Florence

The motif of the reclining figure is reminiscent of Giorgione's *Sleeping Venus* (page 294) in Dresden. Nowadays, the painting is normally interpreted as an allegory of marital love and fidelity; there have been some suggestions that there might be a connection with the wedding of Guidobaldo della Rovere and Giuliana Varano in 1534. There is an inimitable mastery in the way Titian modeled the skin tones of the naked woman, using a variety of colors from yellow through blue to dark red, all of which blend to form a soft, peach-colored hue.

youthful portrait of herself painted when she was already in her forties. It is more likely, however, that Titian also applied a certain ideal type to the portrait of Eleonora (page 321) that was painted between 1536 and 1538, and that it was simply possible to express this type in a purer form in the *La Bella* than in the portrait of a real person.

In the portrait, Eleonora is wearing a magnificent dress in the colors of the house of Montefeltre, the rulers of Urbino until Francesco Maria della Rovere, who was made the heir of the last Montefeltre. She is sitting in front of an open window. We see out onto one of the most beautiful landscapes that Titian ever created. Today the top layer of color has been destroyed in some places, but it is still possible to make out the wonderful blue shades in the distance and the golden flashes of the trees, fields, and rooftops in the sunlight. It is mainly the opulent dress and valuable jewelry that give the rather gentle woman an air of grandeur. Her lowered eyes and fine narrow mouth, in contrast, convey an impression of modesty. Only the firm chin, softened by the hint of a double chin and firmly pressed lips, suggests something of the power and determination that were indeed characteristic of Eleonora. The entire intention of the portrait is to depict a beautiful, demure, and modest Renaissance lady. It is lavishly praised as such by Pietro Aretino in one of his letters. Ten years later Titian painted a similar female portrait that conveys the character of the subject solely by means of her modest expression and her sumptuous clothes, which he makes all too obvious. This is his *Portrait of Isabella of Portugal* (Museo Nacional del Prado, Madrid), which he painted without ever seeing her.

The counterpart to the portrait of Eleonora was that of her husband Francesco Maria della Rovere (Galleria degli Uffizi, Florence). He is characterized predominantly as a military leader. As if the magnificent shining armor and gleaming helmet were not enough, he is also leaning on the command staff of the Republic of Venice, and on the velvet cloth behind him we see the command staffs awarded to him by Florence and the Pope. Between them is an oak branch with his personal motto. He is gazing directly at us with pride and determination. Nonetheless, one cannot help feeling that a small delicate man is being crushed by the burden of his duties, for Francesco does not fill the entire picture.

As in his other portraits, Titian depicted only a few aspects clearly. He still managed, however, to convey the impression of an individual personality. In contrast to his earlier portraits, it is mainly the air of authority that is being expressed here in the stiff posture of the subject and the splendor of his armor. This masterly ability to combine the expression of authority with an individual likeness meant that he was very much in demand as a portrait painter for the ruling classes.

He painted another masterpiece of the 1530s for the son of Eleonora Gonzaga and Francesco Maria della Rovere, Guidobaldo della Rovere (1514–1574), who succeeded to his father's title in 1538: his *Venus of Urbino* (page 322–323). In a letter to his agent in Venice, Guidobaldo simply described the subject as "the naked woman." The strong erotic aura and portrait-like character of the painting led many early art historians to consider it to be a portrait of a courtesan. Though this interpretation is no longer considered very plausible, no satisfactory explanation of the subject has yet been

Titian
Pardo Venus (Jupiter and Antiope), 1535–1540, reworked ca. 1560
Oil on canvas, 196 x 385 cm
Musée du Louvre, Paris

In 1574, Titian described this painting in a letter to the secretary of Philip II as being "the naked woman with the landscape and satyr." Its present name, *Pardo Venus*, derived from the Spanish palace of El Pardo, where the painting was for a long time kept. The reclining naked figure was interpreted as a Venus. In fact, the painting depicts the moment when Jupiter, in the form of a satyr, approached Antiope, a king's daughter, who will give birth to twins.

offered. It is very clear in all the paintings of this type, from the *Flora* (page 304) and *La Bella* (page 321) to the later pictures of Danaë and Venus, and even to the *St. Mary Magdalene* (Galleria Palatina, Plazzo Pitti, Florence) commissioned by Federico Maria della Rovere, that the main objective was the depiction of feminine beauty. Moreover, Titian, like his client, frequently described such a female nude simply as "the naked woman." This, for example, was the term he used for the *Pardo Venus* (page 324) in a late letter to Philip II. The highly erotic depiction of the female body and the unexpected similarity to many other figures of women is very confusing for modern viewers. Scholars have only just begun to examine this aspect of Renaissance art seriously. Titian provides many examples of artistically challenging works that explore this erotic tension. While early research on these works was frequently characterized by prudishness or male voyeurism, the very different position of women in the Renaissance is now an integral part of scholarly attention. It is precisely in this 'field that the most interesting developments are to be expected during the next few years.

However, Titian did not work only for the court of Urbino during the 1530s. Federico II Gonzaga also continued to feature as one of his patrons. One of his commissions for his palace in Mantua was for a series of portraits of twelve Roman emperors for the palace in Mantua. These works have been lost.

At the same time, the Venetians were insisting that Titian should keep the promise he made in 1513 and produce the large battle painting for the Sala del Gran Consiglio for which he had been awarded the *sensaria*. In 1537 the Great Council underlined its demands by threatening to ask for the return of all the funds he had received until then. Titian fulfilled his obligation, but this large painting was destroyed in 1577 by a fire in the Doge's Palace.

Another work which was commissioned in Venice between 1534 and 1538 still exists: the *Presentation of the Virgin at the Temple* (pages 326–327) in the assembly hall of the Scuola Grande di Santa Maria della Carità. The Scuola's building is now part of the Venetian art gallery, the Gallerie dell' Accademia, so it is still possible to admire Titian's masterpiece in its original setting.

This is an incomparable combination of large group portrait and religious painting. All the leading members of the Scuola are depicted in the large group of onlookers. Behind them there extends a marvelous alpine landscape. In contrast, there is a wall behind Mary and she stands completely alone on the steps of the temple. It is an important part of the legend that Mary climbs the steps on her own, without help. Titian emphasizes her solitude, in contrast to the group of onlookers, by setting her against a different background and by painting her dress in the same color as the sky. So he creates two pictorial zones: that of the group portrait and that of the religious picture, which, though closely interrelated, can be contemplated either together or individually.

As in all Titian's paintings of the late 1530s, the special characteristics of this picture are its quieter

Titian
Alfonso d'Avalos Addressing His Troops, 1539–1541
Oil on canvas, 223 x 165 cm
Museo Nacional del Prado, Madrid

A military commander addressing his troops is a classical motif that was revived during the Renaissance. There is a specific model for the painting when, in the war against the Turks in Hungary in 1532, Avalos spurred on his faltering troops with an address. However, it is likely that there is a more general allegorical meaning beyond that. For the small boy carrying the duke's helmet is his son Francesco Ferrante, who would have been only one year old in 1532.

Titian
The Presentation of the Virgin at the Temple, 1534–1538
Oil on canvas, 335 x 775 cm
Gallerie dell'Accademia, Venice

The various architectural elements, the portraits, the
beautiful landscape in the background, and the variety
of realistically painted details make this painting look as
if it is the precise reflection of a very diverse reality. In
fact, these are individual set pieces in which Titian was
attempting to demonstrate the virtuosity of his painting
technique and prove his ability to depict the world more
precisely than any writer or sculptor could. This
competition with other arts, known as the *paragone*,
was a central feature in Renaissance art theory.

composition and the great realism of its details. Even
though the protagonists appear to be connected to each
other by glances and gestures, these are in fact less
complicated, dramatic, and contrived than those of the
pictures from the 1520s and early 1530s. The egg
basket in the foreground, the hens and the little black
pig, the veined marble columns behind Mary and the
mossy front edge of the steps—all these are depicted in
a more lifelike manner than at any other point in
Titian's creative work. Something similar is true of
many pictures created during the 1530s, such as the
enchanting fruit basket in the *Madonna and Child with
St. Catherine and a Rabbit* (page 34), the valuable clock
on the Duchess of Urbino's table (page 321), and the
Duke's shining armor (Galleria degli Uffizi, Florence).

This method of depiction continued to characterize
some of his paintings into the early 1540s, including
the *Pardo Venus* (page 324), *St. John the Baptist*
(Gallerie dell'Accademia, Venic) and *Alfonso d'Avalos
Addressing His Troops* (page 325). By this time,
however, there are already signs of a change in Titian's
manner of painting, a change that in art history has
come be known as the period of his "Mannerist crisis."

EMPEROR AND POPE:
THE "MANNERIST CRISIS."
TITIAN'S TRIP TO ROME

Titian, *The Last Supper*, 1542–1544
Oil on canvas, 163 x 104 cm, Palazzo Ducale, Urbino

Titian's workshop carried out less of the work on this section of the processional banner than on its companion piece. Although it is clear that Titian did not take any great pains over the painting and left parts of it for his workshop to do, we can accept that the particularly skillful, rapidly painted areas of color, such as the bottle of wine on the table, were painted by the Titian himself. Typical of Titian is the confident and adroit organization of a composition that would normally require a horizontal format into an upright one.

Opposite page:
Titian, *The Resurrection*, 1542–1544
Oil on canvas, 163 x 104 cm, Palazzo Ducale, Urbino

Like the *Last Supper* above, this painting was originally part of a single processional banner for the Corpus Domini Brotherhood in Urbino. Documents relating to payments made in 1542 and 1544 still exist. As early as 1546, the banner was split. Here, Titian is repeating the composition of the *Polyptych of the Resurrection* (pages 314–315). The greater range of colors, however, is typical of his work shortly after 1540, even though both sections of the banner would have been produced with the assistance of his workshop.

The term "Mannerism" is used in very different ways in art history. By now, just as much space has been devoted to its definition as to the question of whether (and when) one should use it in order to define a style. The common denominator of the various interpretations is that Mannerism refers to a turning away from a precise depiction of reality in favor of an artificial style that is clearly based on the artist's own personality and concerns. From one case to the next, Mannerist works are characterized by an intriguing artificiality. The leading exponents of Mannerism included artistic personalities as differing as Michelangelo, Giulio Romano (and other pupils of Raphael), Correggio (1494–1534), and Parmigianino (1503–1540).

During the course of the 1530s, a powerful competitor for Titian's Venetian clients emerged in the form of Giovanni Antonio Pordenone (1484–1539), who outdid Titian both by selling his works at a lower price and by painting mighty figures modeled on those of Michelangelo and Giulio Romano, much to the delight of his patrons. Even Titian's friend Pietro Aretino once described him as the only one who could equal Michelangelo.

At the end of the 1530s, Cardinal Giovanni Grimani invited the Roman artists Francesco Salviati (1510–1563), Giovanni da Udine (1487–1564), and Giuseppe Porta (ca. 1520–1575) to Venice in order to decorate his palace near Santa Maria Formosa in the Roman manner. In 1541, Giorgio Vasari also arrived at the invitation of his fellow Tuscan Pietro Aretino (they were both from Arezzo) in order to produce the stage scenery for Aretino's comedy *La Talanta*. All these artists introduced Mannerist ideas to Venice. One of the artists working in Venice itself was Andrea Schiavone (ca. 1510/15–1563), who modeled himself on artists from northern Italy, such as Parmigianino (1503–1540) and Correggio (ca. 1494–1534) rather than Roman ones. Works by all these artists, as well as the many engravings of works by Raphael, Michelangelo, and Correggio, must have made an impact on Titian's art. He again began to experiment with color and space. In this sense one can certainly talk of a creative crisis in his life; during this time, there was little uniformity in his works. But it was a creative crisis in which he was trying out new means of depiction, and from which he was to emerge, now almost sixty years old, with an entirely new style.

He needed numerous assistants to carry out the countless commissions of those years. His works are not always the ones that have survived. Many of the works we now possess are merely adaptations of his designs by more or less talented assistants, some of whom worked for him for a very short period. He occasionally added a few brushstrokes to works produced by his assistants in order to make them his own. That is why many of the paintings which left his workshop from the 1540s onwards are much more difficult to classify and date than his early works. This is reflects in the literature on the subject, with a wide range of dates being suggested for some works.

His processional banner for the Brotherhood of Corpus Domini in Urbino (pages 328, 329) displays stylistic characteristics of both the 1530s and the 1540s, as well as those of his workshop. As in the *Presentation of the Virgin at the Temple* (pages 326–327), he now shows a greater interest in architectural motifs. He frequently pays far less attention to the recording of the subject than to working out color values. Alongside this, however, there are passages that are almost still-lifes, such as the bottle of wine on the supper table. He did not achieve these perfectly convincing illusions through a painstaking skill in painting details, as did the Netherlandish artists of the 15th century, but solely through a knowledge of the effects of colors. For example, in the case of the wine bottle, he creates the illusion of a transparent glass bottle filled with wine by means of a patch of red that deepens towards the left, and a couple of white lines.

The ceiling paintings for the Augustinians in Santo Spirito in Isola clearly show the way in which Titian approached the new forms created by the Mannerists (pages 330, 331). Both Pordenone and Vasari, as well as the artists working for Cardinal Grimani, had created ceiling paintings before him. But Titian's ceiling paintings were like a thunderbolt. Their monumentality and foreshortened view from below (the so-called *sotto in sù*) went beyond anything that had existed in Venice until then, even though some of the forms he used are modeled on Correggio and the frescoes by Pordenone in the cloister of Santo Stefano in Venice. Vasari, who may originally have been commissioned to produce the work by the Augustinians, emphatically praised Titian's mastery of *sotto in sù*. In the powerful, muscular figures with

Titian
Cain and Abel, 1542–1544
Oil on canvas, 292 x 280 cm
Santa Maria della Salute, Venice

This painting, like the *Sacrifice of Isaac* (page 330), was originally part of a ceiling decoration for the monastery of Santo Spirito in Isola. The carved ceiling into which the paintings were set, and which no longer exists, was designed by Jacopo Sansovino. In 1656, the paintings were transferred to the church of Santa Maria della Salute. The powerful muscular bodies and the clouds streaked with bright light are elements that can be seen in Titian's art since the 1520s. By now, however, he is no longer interested in rendering space and the different textures of objects—skin, fur, clouds, and stone appear primarily as color.

Opposite page:
Titian
The Sacrifice of Isaac, 1542–1544
Oil on canvas, 328 x 282 cm
Santa Maria della Salute, Venice

This, the largest of the paintings for Santo Spirito, was painted for the central section of the ceiling. The entire picture surface is dominated by the heavily foreshortened, muscular figure of Abraham, whose outstretched arms link the dramatic centers of the painting. At the bottom right, he is firmly bending down the head of Isaac, his only son and heir. To prove his faith, Abraham is prepared to sacrifice his son in accordance with God's will. At the top left, the angel of God appears, seizing the sword in order to save faithful Abraham's son.

incredibly strong, confident movements, Titian proved that he was far superior to Pordenone and Vasari. This once again confirmed his leading artistic position in Venice. He did, though, increasingly turn to more important patrons outside Venice. The 1540s, even more than the previous decade, are characterized by works painted for the emperor and his immediate entourage. Even Pope Paul III, whose predecessor had made a vain attempt to lure Titian to Rome, also received some paintings.

In about 1540, Titian painted two works for the imperial governor of Milan, Alfonso di Avalos, the Duke of Vasto (page 325). In 1978, it was possible to prove that Titian received a further commission in connection with this Milan task, to paint his *Christ Crowned with Thorns* (page 332) for the Milan church of Santa Maria della Grazie, a work that displays his reaction to the works of Giulio Romano.

Shortly afterwards, he created the enchanting portrait of the Pope's twelve-year-old grandson,

Ranuccio Farnese (page 333). It is the first of a series of pictures that Titian painted for the Pope's Farnese family from then until 1546. At the same time he painted another charming child's portrait, that of *Clarissa Strozzi* (page 334). In these two portraits Titian shows himself a master in depicting childhood in all its freshness, adding a light sheen to the eyes and lips, reproducing the play of the light on hair, and conveying a sense of imminent movement. In the portrait of Clarissa Strozzi, he added attributes such as the little dog and the putti playing in the relief. In that of Ranuccio Farnese, he relied solely on formal means, such as the fresh coloring of his cheeks, the reflections in his eyes, and his shining lips. Titian's portraits of children always seem particularly authentic, while his portraits of adults always seem to be modified by various contemporary ideals. A direct comparison with the works of his contemporaries reveals Titian's mastery in both areas. His copy of Raphael's 1512 portrait of Pope Julius II (page 240) also dates from

Titian
Christ Crowned with Thorns, 1540
Oil on wood, 303 x 180 cm
Musée du Louvre, Paris

The muscular bodies and the heavy rustication in the
background of this painting clearly show Titian's interest
in the vocabulary of forms developed by Giulio Romano
in Mantua. The varied arrangement of colors, with areas
of powerful, almost cornflower blue contrasting with
yellow, green, and pink is typical of Titian's palette in the
early 1540s and harmonizes much more delicately than
the colors in the Urbino processional banner (pages 328,
329). Despite this new use of color, there are still
exceptionally realistic details in the painting, such as the
crown of thorns, the tormentors' sticks, and the chain
mail of the tormentor in the foreground.

Opposite page:
Titian
Portrait of Ranuccio Farnese, 1542
Oil on canvas, 89.7 x 73.6 cm
National Gallery of Art, Kress Collection, Washington

Ranuccio Farnese (1530–1565) was the son of Pier Luigi
Farnese, the son of Pope Paul III. He came to Venice in
1542 to be the prior of San Giovanni dei Forlani, which
belonged to the Knights of Malta. The white cross on his
cloak clearly shows that he is a member of the order. The
way he is looking out to the left of the picture, and the
slight turning of his body, makes him look as if he is
about to move from the place where the artist has
captured him on canvas. This movement contributes
considerably to the impression of childlike freshness that
the painting radiates.

the 1540s (Galleria Palatina, Palazzo Pitti). So far it is unknown whether Titian copied that picture, or a replica of it which might have been in Urbino at the time, or perhaps a third version of the same prototype. A comparison with Raphael's portrait of Julius shows Titian's impressive ability to create an idealized yet completely accurate image of a sitter (Galleria Palatina, Palazzo Pitti). In Raphael's version, the Pope is sitting in the corner of a room in front of a green silk wall covering. Though Titian depicts Julius in the same setting, he chose a closer viewpoint. He does not bother to depict the room, instead concentrating solely on the figure of the Pope. He treats the garments in a much more summary manner than Raphael, while overemphasizing the effects of light on the fabrics. The sum of these changes is a portrait with greater presence. Though Titian copied the old man's face down to the last wrinkle, the Pope's face appears to be more powerful and less melancholy than in Raphael's original. Titian achieved this by means of a little trick that had a decisive influence on the entire expression of the painting. While the corners of Leo's mouth are drawn down in Raphael's painting and his lips are scarcely visible, in Titian's version the lips are soft and slightly curved. The corners of his mouth have been softened to form wrinkles that defined the edges of his cheeks. He also gives the Pope an almost unnoticeably more erect sitting posture. These changes may seem trivial, but they are actually made with a clear awareness of the effect of minor details, and give the portrait a more powerful personality.

The *Portrait of Ranuccio Farnese* (page 333) was the first occasion on which Titian made contact with Pope Paul III Farnese. Though Cardinal Pietro Bembo and others had repeatedly invited him to Rome, Titian had refused every invitation. In 1543, when the Pope came to northern Italy in order to negotiate with the emperor, Titian finally agreed to paint his portrait. He not only painted the famous *Portrait of Pope Paul III* (page 340), which has frequently been copied. Titian also painted a version in which the Pope does wear a cap, perhaps painted for the Pope's grandson, Cardinal Alessandro Farnese (page 335). The latter introduced Titian to the Farnese family and, as an important patron of the arts, had commissioned other paintings from Titian.

It is possible that at this stage Titian had already been promised a church living for his son Pomponio, who had decided to become a clergyman, as a reward for his portraits; his other son, Orazio, worked in his workshop. Titian asked that Pomponio be given the wealthy abbey of San Pietro in Colle, whose properties bordered those owned by the artist himself in Ceneda.

The promise that his son would be given this living was what finally persuaded Titian to visit the Eternal City. On 20 September 1544, the papal ambassador in Venice wrote to tell Cardinal Alessandro Farnese that the artist was prepared to come to Rome to "paint Your Honor's illustrious household down to the last cat."

But Titian did not get to Rome until October 1545, accompanied by an escort which Guidobaldo della Rovere had placed at his disposal. He was given quarters in the Belvedere, which was frequently used to accommodate guests of the Pope. Here, as he wrote in a letter to Charles V, he started studying those classical works he had never seen. Vasari claims to have guided Titian on these trips, although he was not even in the city during the first part of Titian's stay in Rome. It is certain that Titian will have seen the great works of Raphael and Michelangelo and other contemporary Roman artists, just as, in turn, his workshop in the Belvedere became an attraction for Roman painters. In the same letter in which he wrote that Titian would be coming to Rome, the papal ambassador also wrote of a "naked woman" that the artist had started work on at Alessandro's request, and which he would be bringing to Rome. This nude, the ambassador wrote, would make the *Venus of Urbino* (pages 332–333) look like a nun, if only Titian finally got the living he wanted for his son. The painting that Titian brought to Rome was the *Danaë and Cupid* (pages 336–337). According to Vasari's report, even the great Michelangelo saw this painting in Titian's studio in the Belvedere. He took obvious pleasure in pronouncing his verdict, though it is not certain that Michelangelo expressed himself in those terms; it is possible that Vasari put words in his mouth. Michelangelo apparently commended it highly, saying that his coloring and his style pleased him very much "but that it was a shame that in Venice they did not learn to draw well from the beginning and that those painters did not pursue their studies [of ancient and modern works] with more method. One could not learn from nature alone." Whether this is really what Michelangelo said, or an invention of Vasari's, it nonetheless reflects the debate on art that raged in the mid-16th century. Vasari and Michelangelo represented the Tuscan and Roman view, which valued the inventive powers of the artist, and also his knowledge of other art, in particular classical and contemporary works, far more highly than his simple ability to imitate nature. Venetian theorists, such as Lodovico Dolce, influenced by Titian's style, felt that color and the ability to imitate nature were just as important. From Dolce's point of view, the perfect artist, indeed the god amongst artists, would be the painter who was able to combine Michelangelo's drawing with Titian's color.

In 1546, Titian abruptly stopped working for the Pope, leaving the painting of him together with his grandsons unfinished, even though the artist wrote to assure the Farneses that he would soon be returning to Rome. While he was given an honorary citizenship by the Romans, he had not received the desired living for his son. Indeed, Aretino had warned his friend before he left not to expect too much of the papal court.

Most scholars nowadays agree that his *Portrait of Doge Andrea Gritti* (page 341) was painted shortly

Titian
Portrait of Cardinal Alessandro Farnese, 1545–1546
Oil on canvas, 99 x 79 cm
Museo Nazionale di Capodimonte, Naples

Alessandro Farnese (1520–1589) was the son of Pier Luigi Farnese and the grandson of Pope Paul III. Though he was showered with ecclesiastical honors by his grandfather, he did not succeed in becoming pope when Paul died in 1549. Nonetheless, he continued to exert considerable influence on Roman politics until his death, and was, in addition, a particularly important patron of the arts.

Opposite page:
Titian
Portrait of Clarissa Strozzi, 1542
Oil on canvas, 115 x 98 cm
Gemäldegalerie, Staatliche Museen, Berlin

Clarissa Strozzi was the daughter of Roberto Strozzi and Maddalena de' Medici, who lived in exile in Venice from 1540 to 1542. Along with the portrait of Ranuccio Farnese (page 333), this painting is the second enchanting child's portrait Titian painted in 1542. Clarissa is feeding her little dog, but, like Ranuccio, is looking at something taking place outside the picture. This again creates a vivid sense of movement. The putti on the relief emphasize Clarissa's childlike vitality.

Titian
Danaë and Cupid, 1544–1546
Oil on canvas, 120 x 172 cm
Museo Nazionale di Capodimonte, Naples

The story of Danaë deals with one of the amorous escapades of Jupiter, the most powerful god in classical mythology. He visited Danaë, the daughter of the king of Argos, in the form of a golden shower because her father, Acrisius, had locked her up in a bronze tower after it was prophesied that a son of Danaë would kill him.

The most important work that Titian created for the papal family in Rome was the *Portrait of Pope Paul III and His Grandsons Ottavio and Cardinal Alessandro Farnese* (page 339). It was not, however, completed, and disappeared into the Farnese family's palace. The triple portrait, which mirrors the dramatic and conflict-ridden story of the Farnese family and the pope's artful tactics, is now considered to be a masterpiece of psychological art.

Before he stayed in Rome, Titian had produced two other portraits of Paul III. In the *Portrait of Pope Paul III* (page 340), Titian presents us with an image of an old but still powerful pope. This impression is created by the fact that the figure is shown looking down on us slightly. The dark red of the chair and robes blends with the white of his pleated surplice to produce a magnificent mountain of color, at the top of which sits the old man's small head. In contrast to the robes, which are painted in broad brushstrokes, his head appears framed by finely painted hairs. The dark eyes that are gazing at the beholder piercingly are given additional vitality by means of gentle highlights. Just as fine, and extremely unusual in Titian's works, are the hands with the conspicuous Ring of the Fisherman. The painting is the complete expression of papal power and greatness, even though the Pope himself is a very old man. In this portrait, all the viewer might know about the pope's sinful life has to be set aside. The portrait with his grandsons, however, is frequently interpreted as a clear psychological profile that would be worthy of a Shakespeare—that, at any rate, is the view of Rodolfo Pallucchini and Harold Wethey in their monographs on Titian. In complete contrast to the two previous portraits, it positively invites one to include everything one knows about the enigmatic character of the Pope and the power struggles among his successors.

Whatever the case, this triple portrait was surely one of the most difficult tasks Titian was faced with during his career, as he had to take matters of protocol and politics into account. The very fact that the Farnese family chose Titian, the emperor's favorite portrait painter, was a political signal. The presence in the painting of only two of the pope's five male descendants is also part of the context of the contemporary political events.

It was possible for the newly elected pope to give two of his relations, normally nephews, the positions of cardinals, and they carried out the important business of papal government. In the case of Paul III, however, they were his actual direct grandsons, the sons of his son Pier Luigi, Alessandro and Ranuccio. But in this portrait Cardinal Alessandro appears with his secular brother, Ottavio. The latter had been married to Margaret of Austria, a natural daughter of Charles V, since 1538. During the period in which the portrait was begun, the emperor was in close diplomatic contact with the pope, and Cardinal Alessandro, who frequently spent time at the imperial court as the papal legate, was their intermediary. Charles' main goal was financial support for a war against the Protestant princes in Germany. In return, the emperor let the pope, who was always keen to increase his family's properties and gain important titles for members of his family, know that he would be prepared to hand over the duchies of Parma and Piacenza to his son-in-law Ottavio. Both territories had fallen to Charles V with Milan. On 26 August 1545, the pope gave these duchies to his son Pier Luigi although the emperor had made it quite clear through diplomatic channels that he would be happy to see them ruled by Ottavio and Margaret, but not by Pier Luigi. Surprisingly, Charles did not react immediately.

It was at this rather awkward moment during the winter of 1545/46 that the pope, who no doubt felt it to be a quite hopeful political situation, had himself portrayed by the emperor's favorite artist together with those grandsons of his with whom the emperor had the most contact.

Cardinal Alessandro is standing behind the pope's chair and is holding the knob on the backrest, a sure sign of his future ambitions. Clement VII, Paul III's predecessor, makes the same gesture in the portrait of Leo X and his nephews (page 269) that was painted by Raphael. Paul III, who is bent by age, is however turning with a friendly look on his face towards his secular grandson Ottavio, the emperor's son-in-law. His left hand is tightly gripping the armrest of his chair. It creates the impression that he is having to make a great effort in order to turn his stiff upper body. His evident age contrasts vividly with the erect, upright posture of Alessandro behind him, and this too may be a subtle reference to his plans of succession.

Ottavio, in contrast, is about to bow to the Pope. This is a formal part of the ceremony of greeting a pope. It starts with three bows and ends with the pope's foot being kissed as a sign of total submission. Titian moved Paul III's shoe, embroidered with a golden cross, clearly into the picture as a sign of Ottavio's next movement. Every visitor to the pope, even members of the clergy, were obliged to bow in this way. Titian, however, depicts only Ottavio in this posture, while Alessandro (perhaps aspiring to be the next pope) is standing erect behind his grandfather. Only the emperor's own relative has to carry out the ceremonial greeting; every aspect of the picture indicates his

Titian
Pope Paul III and His Grandsons Ottavio and Cardinal Alessandro Farnese, 1545–1546
Oil on canvas, 200 x 173 cm
Museo Nazionale di Capodimonte, Naples

Paul III was born Alessandro Farnese in 1468 and became pope in 1534. He began his career in the ecclesiastical hierarchy under Pope Alexander VI. Despite this, he fathered four children. His only surviving son, Pier Luigi, in turn had four sons, Alessandro, Orazio, Ottavio, and Ranuccio. Two of his grandsons, Cardinal Alessandro and Ottavio, appear with their grandfather in this painting.

submissive attitude. Though it must remain speculation, it is difficult to imagine who apart from the Emperor or his representative in Rome this painting could be addressing.

The claim to power of the pope and his hopes for the continuing rise to power of his family are laid bare in this painting in a most extraordinary manner, and Titian as usual presented these aspects in a masterly manner. It is extremely unlikely that it was Titian's intention in this portrait, as has so frequently been written, to make a silent criticism of the pope's way of life. Though Martin Luther may have called the pope an Epicurean pig or devil, squandering the Church's possessions for the benefit of himself and his successors, one cannot attribute the same opinion to Titian. As an Italian, he would have considered these practices to be entirely normal. Moreover, he himself was in Rome in order to obtain an abbey for his son Pomponio.

The pope's confidence that he would be able to prevail against the emperor turned out to be false. At the time when the painting was begun, it must still have seemed that the emperor was not going to react. But in March 1546 the imperial governor of Milan, the Duke of Vasto, died. The successor that Charles V chose was not Ottavio, as the pope had possibly hoped, but Ferrante Gonzaga. That made his intention to take Parma and Piacenza back from the Farnese family very clear. A short while later, Pier Luigi Farnese was murdered and Piacenza was retaken by imperial troops. Paul III now placed his hopes on support from France, where he had arranged a marriage between his fourth nephew, Orazio, and a natural daughter of the French heir to the throne, just in case his imperial card did not take the trick. While Ottavio was able to hold Parma for the Farnese family, the magnificent prestigious picture of papal might that Titian had been in the process of painting no longer served any purpose. It vanished into the Farnese Palace, unfinished.

Opposite page:
Portrait of Pope Paul III, 1543
Oil on canvas, 106 x 85 cm
Museo Nazionale di Capodimonte, Naples

Painted in Bologna in 1543, this portrait was the first work Titian painted for Paul III. Paul III was typical of those Renaissance popes who aroused the fury of the Protestants. Neither chaste nor poor, he used the political and financial power of his office to act as the third power between the Hapsburgs and France. For political rather than religious reasons, however, he recognized the need to renew the Catholic Church. In 1545, he convened the Council of Trent, which played a decisive role in introducing reforms.

after his return to Venice. This would mean that the portrait was painted after the Doge died. It nonetheless succeeds in capturing his powerful personality. Color is just as important here as in the portrait of Pope Paul III (page 340) and that of Pietro Aretino (page 18), which was also painted about 1545.

Titian used broad brushstrokes to apply the highlights to the red garment in Aretino's portrait. With the exception of the face, the painting appears to have been dashed off with a few powerful brushstrokes. It is no surprise that Aretino commented in a letter to Cosimo de' Medici, to whom he gave the painting, that his portrait would have been far clearer if he had been prepared to pay more money. This expresses more than just the dissatisfaction of a client. Parallels

Titian
Portrait of Doge Andrea Gritti, ca. 1545
Oil on canvas, 133 x 103 cm
Kress Collection, National Gallery of Art, Washington

The fine harmony of the reds and golds, and the upward sweep from the bottom left of the open brocade cloak, whose strong lines end at the top of the Doge's hat, give this painting a sense of power and glory. The Doge's severe gaze, signaling his strength and determination, deepen this impression. For stylistic reasons (compare the application of the colors in the portrait of Pope Paul III, page 340) it is nowadays assumed that this portrait was not painted until about 1545, long after Gritti's death in 1538.

with Venetian art theory come to mind. In the 1530s, Aretino had praised Titian as an artist whose painted reality was far superior to the real world. Looking out of his window at a sunset above the Grand Canal, he remarked that only Titian was capable of capturing the colors of this moment. The more liberal use of paint, which became increasingly important to Titian from the 1540s onwards, was initially met with a lack of appreciation on the part of Aretino.

During the winter of 1547/48, Titian was invited by the emperor to attend the imperial Diet in Augsburg. Following his victory over the Protestant League at Mühlberg in 1547, Charles V had summoned the leading representatives of the two sides to Augsburg. Titian, who had undertaken the arduous journey over

Titian
Portrait of Charles V Seated, 1548
Oil on canvas, 205 x 122 cm
Alte Pinakothek, Bayerische Staatsgemäldesammlungen, Munich

Like his portrait of Charles V at Mühlberg (opposite page), this portrait was painted during the imperial Diet of Augsburg in 1548. It is, however, thought that Titian did not create the work single-handedly. There is, most noticeable, an awkwardness in the foreshortening of the perspective of the chair, and the red carpet is an isolated color contrast, very unusual in Titian's work. But there are also areas of high quality. The face, above all, demonstrates a fine power of observation. The deformation of Charles' lower jaw has been skillfully concealed. The intimate atmosphere of the painting, which contains no regal affectations, is unusual in Titian's portraits of rulers.

Opposite page:
Titian
Portrait of Emperor Charles V at Mühlberg, 1548
Oil on canvas, 332 x 279 cm
Museo Nacional del Prado, Madrid

The painting commemorates the emperor's victory over the Protestant princes at the Battle of Mühlberg on 24 April 1547. The dominant red in the foreground, visible on Charles' helmet decorations, his sash, and the horse's trim, was the color of the Catholic faction in the many religious wars of the 16th and 17th centuries.

Venus and Cupid with an Organist, ca. 1548
Oil on canvas, 148 x 217 cm
Museo Nacional del Prado, Madrid

In the 1540s and early 1550s, numerous versions of this theme were painted. All of them are repetitions, with some slight alterations, of a painting for Emperor Charles V that Titian began in 1545 and delivered in Augsburg in 1548. Some scholars consider this painting to be the work that Titian brought to the Diet of Augsburg. However, given that it was over-painted on numerous occasions, doubts have repeatedly been expressed as to whether this can be an original by Titian.

the snowy Alps to Germany despite his advanced age, was inundated with commissions. He painted numerous portraits, of which the most important is the *Portrait of Emperor Charles V at Mühlberg* (page 343). With this painting, Titian established an entirely new type of portrait in European painting, similar to an equestrian statue but with a greater sense of movement. The charging horse, the emperor's long lance, and the open landscape on the right give the picture a great dynamic force. This forward momentum is quite naturally identified with the emperor. As a stance, it is the perfect expression that he is powerful, authoritative, and confident of victory. Even Charles V's deformed

jaw (his lower jaw jutted out further than his upper jaw) is reinterpreted by Titian as a sign of determination. The shining armor and glittering horse's harness are a return to the realism of Titian's earlier years. The landscape, in contrast, consists of broad areas of color.

Another portrait of the emperor (page 342) dating from this period continues to puzzle researchers. It is quite certain that it was not produced entirely by Titian alone. However, individual sections are so high in quality that one scarcely feels able to attribute them to any painter other than the great Venetian. For a long time it was assumed that Lambert Sustris (?- after

Titian
Adam and Eve, ca. 1550
Oil on canvas, 240 x 186 cm
Museo Nacional del Prado, Madrid

The combination of blue, dark green, and broken reds make this painting particularly charming. The background dissolves in uncertain forms. The painting seems to be comprised solely of a foreground. Here, all the picture elements are related to each other by means of skillful overlapping and contacts. There is considerable sensuous charm in the position of Adam's hand on Eve's right shoulder, just above her beautiful, full breast, as she reaches for the apple with her left hand.

Titian
St. John the Alms-Giver, 1545–1550
Oil on canvas, 229 x 156 cm
San Giovanni Elemosinario, Venice

This painting is the main altarpiece in the church of San Giovanni Elemosinario in Venice. It shows the saint as an alms-giver. The altar frame bears the date 1533, and there are also various sources suggesting an early date. For stylistic reasons, however, this date has been disputed by scholars since the 1930s. Nowadays, it is generally accepted that the painting was created after 1545, and probably in about 1550. Sections such as the saint's white surplice, where the color and movement of the fine material have been created with broad brushstrokes in various shades of white, are characteristic of Titian's manner of painting at the beginning of the 1550s.

1565) was the second artist who worked on this portrait and that he completed a design by Titian. The Duch painter worked in Padua and Venice and, as his works show, was in close contact with Titian. As it is known that Sustris was also in Augsburg, it was naturally assumed that he came to Germany as Titian's colleague. Since the discovery of an important source which Vincenzo Mancini published in his book about Sustris in 1993, it does, however, appear possible that Sustris came to Augsburg entirely independently of Titian.

On his return to Venice, Titian painted many other works for the Hapsburgs, most of which he had been commissioned to produce in Augsburg. The altarpiece for the Venetian church of San Giovanni Elemosinario, showing the church's patron saint, *St. John the Alms-Giver* (page 345), was painted during the same period. Art historian Francesco Valcanover wrote a comment on this painting, and two other paintings for Queen Mary of Hungary, sister of Charles V, in the catalogue for the 1990 Titian exhibitions. He claimed that with these paintings Titian made real what Venetian art theorists had been asserting in their argument with the Florentines: that color was superior to drawing, painting superior to sculpture, and Venice superior to Rome.

TITIAN'S LATE WORK:
THE DYNAMICS OF COLOR

At the beginning of the 1550s, Titian was faced in his native city by two young artists whose careers, begun at the end of the 1540s, were developing rapidly: Jacopo Tintoretto (1518–1594) and Paolo Veronese (ca. 1528–1588). Whatever the artistic legend, however, it is not likely that Titian faced direct competition from them. The status of their clients was different, and his position as the leading artist in Europe was too secure. Moreover, there is evidence to show that Titian did not rate Tintoretto very highly as an artist.

Titian continued to work for the Hapsburg emperors throughout the 1550s and 1560s; at first for Charles V, and later for his son Philip II, the successor to the Spanish throne. Despite the fact that payments from Spain, which had become wealthy by plundering South America's gold treasures, were not very regular and at times did not arrive at all, Titian was paid on a far more generous scale by the Spanish king than by the tight-fisted merchants of Venice. We know that Tintoretto, who gained the majority of Venetian commissions at this time, produced many of his works at cost, or at best for a modest profit only. Titian, on the other hand, was overwhelmed with commissions from all over Europe. However, it would be wrong to conclude from the fact that he now painted fewer works for his native city that there had been a decline of interest in him in Venice. On the contrary, it is further evidence that Titian had long ceased to be a purely Venetian artist. He had become the European prince of painting, and would remain so for posterity.

One of two impressive self-portraits by Titian has survived from the period between 1550 and 1565 (page 292). While some art historians assume that this picture was painted as early as 1550, it is generally dated to the period around 1560–1562. Various writers have attempted to use this portrait to draw conclusions about Titian's state of mind in the 1550s and early 1560s, a time when he suffered a succession of great misfortunes. When Pietro Aretino died in 1556, Titian lost not only one of his closest friends but also an important advisor in artistic matters. In 1559 his brother Francesco, who had been one of his most important assistants, died, followed in 1561 by his daughter Lavinia. Nevertheless, it would be inappropriate to deduce too much about Titian's own fate from this image of an elderly artist, for even in a self-portrait Titian allowed only certain facets of his personality to be seen. He depicts himself as an old but powerful man, an impression largely created by the

fact that his body fills the entire width of the picture. On the right side he is even cut off slightly by the edge of the picture. This artistic device creates the impression that the forceful personality of the sitter is breaking out of the picture. At the same time, the pictorial space around him appears to continue beyond the picture's borders. His clear intention, confirmed by turning his head to the right, is to present the image of a vivid and powerful personality.

Titian effectively emphasizes the mass of his form by means of a voluminous, sleeveless fur coat. The firm positioning of the hands underlines the sense of power, even though the left hand is not fully fleshed out. At first the right hand, resting on a small table, appears to be painted just as sketchily. However, highlights on the narrow, nicely formed fingernails show that this hand must be considered largely completed. Even more than the hands, the garments also are dissolved into areas of color—here far more noticeably than in the portraits he had painted shortly before this. But now there are also fewer bright, luminous passages, a feature that gives the picture a simpler appearance. While the magnificent fur cloak and the golden chain, a sign of his knighthood, indicate his prosperity and raised social position, his painting technique and his use of colors reduce their emphasis. The tactile qualities of the valuable materials are scarcely indicated, so that the impression of modest pride is retained, an impression underlined by the restrained colors. Only the fully lit head, firmly turned to a three quarter profile view, is painted more finely. Bright reflections in his eyes give him an intelligent, alert expression. Direct contact with the observer is achieved by the fact that he is looking to the right, which is Titian's way of avoiding anything provocative in his portrait. At the same time, because he is looking away from the observer, Titian appears withdrawn. This is perhaps why some art historians have used this self-portrait to deduce that Titian lived a more secluded life after the deaths of so many of those close to him.

Late in 1550, Titian was once again invited to an Imperial Diet in Augsburg; and again he was commissioned to paint a large number of works for both Charles V and Philip II. For Charles V (who at the meeting of princes announced his imminent retirement from public office) Titian painted mainly religious pictures during the remaining years until Charles' death in 1558. The majority of them went with him to the

monastery of St. Jerome in Yuste in Spain, to which he retreated in 1556. For this secluded place of retirement, Charles ordered, in addition to devotional pictures, the large altar painting the *Trinity in Glory* (page 347), which depicts the resurrected members of the imperial family before the Holy Trinity on Judgment Day. This work was probably commissioned during the Imperial Diet in 1551. It emerges, from letters both Titian and the Spanish ambassador in Venice wrote to Charles V, that Titian was working on the painting by 1553 at the latest. In 1554, it was taken by sea to Brussels, and from there was sent to Yuste. In his will, Charles V stipulated that a high altar should be built using this painting.

For Philip II, Titian painted several portraits, and also mythological scenes and allegories with a strong erotic element. In his letters to Philip, Titian described these works as *poesie* and *favole*, vague terms that can be roughly translated as "poetic inventions" and "fables" respectively. The use of the word *poesie* to describe paintings touches on an important concept of art during the Renaissance. The expression *ut pictura poesis* ("as in painting, so in poetry")—taken from a poem on the art of poetry written by the Latin poet Horace (65–8 BC)—

was the basis for treating painting and literature as equals; it was also the basis for a rivalry between these two arts that encouraged a theoretical study of painting. This theme—the question of which of the two art forms, poetry or painting, was better able to do justice to a subject—was debated in numerous treatises, including Lodovico Dolce's *Dialogo della Pittura (Dialogue on Painting)*. As early as 1969, the German art historian Harald Keller drew attention to the fact that Titian was not the only Venetian to use the term *poesie* to describe secular painting. We can assume, then, that *poesie* was a specialist term for secular themes in paintings based on literary sources.

Four of the numerous pictures painted for Philip II during the 1550s were intended to furnish one room. This emerges from a letter Titian wrote to Philip II in the summer of 1554. Titian mentions not only two works already completed, *Danaë with Nursemaid* (below) and *Venus and Adonis* (page 350), but also two accompanying paintings, *Perseus and Andromeda* and *Jason and Medea*, which were also destined for the same room. In this commission, Titian faced a task similar to the one he had faced once before, at the beginning of

Titian
Danaë with Nursemaid, 1553/54
Oil on canvas, 129 x 180 cm
Museo Nacional del Prado, Madrid

The cupid in the first version of this subject for Alessandro Farnese (pages 336–337), an allusion to love, is here replaced by an old woman. Such a nursemaid, who was locked up with Danaë, is mentioned in a variant of the Danaë story in various classical texts. Quite apart from this, she is a very useful contrast as the beauty of the naked Danaë becomes even more pronounced when compared with the ugliness of this old woman.

his career, with the paintings for Alfonso d'Este's Alabaster Room. But now Titian was not one artist among many, he was the only artist commissioned and was responsible for the entire program. Whether he received precise instructions from Philip II or Philip II's advisors, or whether he himself was free to choose his themes, is uncertain. What is certain, however, is that he was given complete liberty to execute the individual themes as he saw fit. It also becomes clear from this letter that Titian was principally interested in aspects of form. His comments on the two paintings already completed, *Danaë and Venus* and *Adonis*, deal solely with the fact that he depicts the female nude from both sides in order to provide a "graceful" view for the room for which the paintings were intended. In the same letter, Titian announces his intention to create further interesting views of the body in the painting *Perseus and Andromeda* (in the Wallace Collection, London) and in *Jason and Medea*, which was planned but never completed.

In fact it is not likely that at this point there was a specific room for which these pictures were destined. When Philip II became king of Spain in 1556, on his father's abdication, he did not yet have a permanent residence. During the 1550s and 1560s, both the old castles in Madrid and Toledo, and also the palace of El Pardo and the castle in Aranjuez, were being renovated. The building that is most closely connected with the name of Philip II, the Escorial, was not planned until 1557 onwards; construction work started in 1564. Until the mid 1560s, Philip II lived in the castles of Spanish noblemen. He was accompanied on his travels by the entire royal household and by all his possessions, including his paintings. Perhaps this frequent change

of place explains the changing plans for the cycle of paintings, and also the length of time Titian worked on them. *Jason and Medea* was never painted. Instead, at the beginning of the 1560s, Titian finally completed the *Rape of Europa* (in the Isabella Stewart Gardner Museum in Boston).

The literary source for all these paintings is the *Metamorphoses* of the Roman poet Ovid (43 BC–AD 17/18), a collection of mythological tales featuring the transformations undergone by various men and gods. Numerous scholars have attempted to decipher the entire intellectual conception of this cycle of paintings; certainly an important element in these various interpretations is the fact that since the Middle Ages Ovid's mythological stories had been given varying moral, and also Christian, interpretations, which were handed down with the text. One of the first editions to omit any form of moral interpretation was published by Titian's friend Lodovico Dolce in 1553. In a study published in 1985, the art historian Jane C. Nash collected the majority of the (often contradictory) interpretations of the *poesie* Titian painted for Philip II. One interesting point many of the authors of these interpretations have highlighted is Philip's strict Catholicism, which appears to contradict the sensuality of these *poesie*. However, as Nash and others have shown, it is also possible to attribute religious meanings to the paintings. Such an openness of interpretation must have played an important role during the 16th century and may have contributed to the high regard in which the paintings were held. But in statements made both by Titian and by Lodovico Dolce, who writes about these paintings in a letter dating from 1554, there is no reference of any kind to such matters. Dolce writes

Titian's Workshop
Danaë, ca. 1552–1553
Oil on canvas, 119 x 187 cm
Hermitage, St. Petersburg

This is another version of the highly successful series on the Danaë theme produced by Titian's workshop. When compared to the version he painted himself (page 348), the difference in quality becomes evident. The distorted face of Danaë and her cord-like hair mock any attempt to compare her with the skillfully lit head of the Danaë in Madrid (opposite page).

Titian
Venus and Adonis, 1553/54
Oil on canvas, 186 x 207 cm
Museo Nacional del Prado, Madrid

This painting is also one of the classical mythological works painted for Philip II and which he himself described as *poesie*. Venus, the goddess of love, falls in love with Adonis, a beautiful youth. Her love is not, however, enough to stop him pursuing his favorite pastime, hunting, which will lead to his undoing, for he is gored to death by a boar. There is an interesting letter from Titian to Philip II that deals with this painting. The artist makes a special point of mentioning that he was particularly interested in depicting the human form from both sides.

solely about Titian's skillful reproduction of the body and about the perfection of the depiction—in other words about purely formal aspects of the painting. This linking of faith and sensuality can also be seen in some of Titian's religious paintings of this period, such as depictions of St. Mary Magdalene, of which Titian's workshop produced many variants (page 27), and the richly colored *Adam and Eve* (page 345). His workshop now carried out the majority of the paintings more frequently than had previously been the case. There are countless workshop variants of some of the particularly successful compositions, such as the various pictures of Venus and St. Mary Magdalene, as well as several *Ecce Homo*.

At the beginning of the 1550s, Titian started to use a noticeably lighter palette; many of the pictures he painted now have a characteristic pale gold color. His female ideal also changed. At the beginning of his career he had preferred supple, soft, and elegantly proportioned limbs that, despite their physicality, still had a certain slenderness; now he preferred more mature bodies, more strongly shaded, with broad hips. Instead of dark, reddish hair, he now painted women with pale blonde hair braided with shining pearls. When these works are compared to Veronese's depictions of women, the similarities are immediately evident. The pale and broken pastel tones are also typical of the younger artist, who, unlike Tintoretto, was sponsored by Titian.

By the end of the 1550s at the latest, Titian had come to value the exploration of color above all other aspects of his art. To begin with, his paintings continued to be characterized by larger areas of color that were already more important than either precisely drawn objects or the clear definition of the picture's space. Towards the end of his life, his paintings were covered with webs of vibrant color. Paintings such as the *Martyrdom of St. Lawrence* (page 351), the *Crucifixion* (pages 352, 353), and the *Annunciation* (pages 354, 355) illustrate various stages in this development. Also, it becomes clear, if for example we compare the *Crucifixion* in the Escorial (page 352) with the *Crucifixion* painted just three years later in Ancona (page 353), that Titian was still able to find different ways of painting precisely the same subject. This continuing search for new compositions and pictorial inventions distinguishes him from the majority of other painters, and not only those of his own era. But there are also numerous copies of successful compositions reproduced by his own workshop, probably with touches added by the master himself at the urging of his clients.

Opposite page:
Titian
The Martyrdom of St. Lawrence, ca. 1548–1559
Oil on canvas, 493 x 277 cm
Chiesa dei Gesuiti, Venice

Here Titian chose to depict a night scene so that the light of the fire by which St. Lawrence was being martyred would be particularly effective. Only parts of the architecture are rendered visible through streams of light and this gives the entire painting a tense air of menace.

In the Escorial *Crucifixion* (left), a broad landscape stretches out behind the Cross. In the middle distance, the holy women are returning to Jerusalem; on the left, soldiers are heading towards the city in the background. The Cross has been moved right up to the foreground and is seen from below; the landscape, in contrast, is seen from slightly above. At the bottom of the picture only a narrow strip of ground separates the observer from the foot of the Cross; higher up, the cross bar stretches across the entire width of the picture. In this way the Cross completely dominates the picture. The landscape behind looks like a specific place seen at a definite time; its very expanse, however, conveys an impression of timelessness. While the landscape and figures are depicted in great detail, the sky dissolves into a sea of color that bathes the upper part of the picture, where the body of the dead Christ is, in a dramatic play of color. Formal contrasts—such as the movement of the turbulent sky and the unmoving rigidity of the corpse—reflect the emotional conflicts implicit in the drama of the events.

How different, in contrast, is the *Crucifixion* in Ancona (page 353), painted just a few years later. Here, Titian's main theme is not the tragic isolation of Christ, but the grief of Mary, St. John, and St. Dominic. The image gains its timeless quality not from the landscape, which is almost imperceptible, but from the fact that it depicts a saint who lived in the late 12th and early 13th centuries alongside Mary and John beneath the Cross. Every form of naturalistic narration has disappeared; it is the use of light and color alone that determine the impact of the picture. The only point of comparison between the two Crucifixions is the sky. In his avoidance of details, Titian goes so far as to leave the faces of Christ and Mary unlit, and therefore unclear. The figures of Mary and St. Dominic appear to have no volume. Mary's figure is completely contained within the contours of her blue cloak. The red of her other garment does not create a contrast because, being a plum red, it seems just another shade of the cloak's blue. St. Dominic embraces the foot of the Cross from behind. As a result, he is only partially visible, and appears even more fragmented because of the stark contrast between the white and black in his habit. The shining white of his garment forms a curved line that begins at the bottom left next to the Cross, continues behind the Cross to the right, starts to rise and then continues in the pale hands, twisting itself like foliage around the Cross.

Downcast, Mary is wrapped tightly in her cloak. There are only a few further features, such as the eyes, red with crying, that shine out from the darkness of her face, and her hands, which are turned downwards, characterizing her feelings. In the case of St. Dominic, his despair is conveyed by the movement of the white line of the garment, which achieves an almost abstract life of its own as it twines around the stem of the Cross.

The mythological paintings Titian painted for Philip II from the late 1550s onwards, such as *Diana and Actaeon* (page 357) and *Diana and Callisto* (page 356), are painted in light and, at times, astonishingly varied

Titian
The Crucifixion, 1558
Oil on canvas, 371 x 197 cm
San Domenico, Ancona

Though this was painted only a little later than the
superb Crucifixion in the Escorial (page 352), there are
already clear signs that Titian's style has progressed to the
point where he is painting purely with color. The scene
with the mourners is taking place only in the foreground.
The sky and the figures under the Cross are all painted in
dark colors. Blue and black dominate the scene; white is
used to produce dramatic highlights. Titian succeeds in
representing St. Dominic's sorrow as he embraces the
Cross almost entirely by means of the distribution of
light and the broad sweeping brushstrokes.

Opposite page:
Titian
The Crucifixion, ca. 1555
Oil on canvas, 214 x 109 cm
Sacristia, Monastero di San Lorenzo, Escorial

Particularly impressive in this painting are the wonderful
colors and the modulated lights on the body of Christ, as
well as the carefully painted landscape, which is a rare
feature in Titian's late work. The ruins, the city in the
background, and the marvelous colors of the hills are
reminiscent of Veronese's early landscapes. The cross,
isolated in front of the broad landscape, gives the painting
a timeless quality that emphasizes its devotional function.
The work's theme is not the moment of the crucifixion,
but the loneliness of death.

shades of color. These two Diana pictures painted for Philip II extend the cycle of mythological pictures based on scenes in Ovid's *Metamorphoses*. Their vivid colors clearly distinguish them from the two earlier paintings in this series, *Danaë with Nursemaid* (page 348) and *Venus and Adonis* (page 350). But even in the Diana pictures the depiction of the nude seen from various angles and in various movements continues to be an important aspect of the composition. It is even given priority over creating a faithful depiction of the literary source. In Ovid's description of the scenes in which Actaeon discovers Diana in the wood, her nymphs surround her immediately, so that Actaeon sees only the top half of her body. By contrast, in Titian's depiction of *Diana and Actaeon*, the goddess is not immediately surrounded by a circle of her nymphs; she is shown full length, she and her nymphs illustrating a range of poses. The scene probably depicts the instant at which Actaeon first sees the naked bathers; but it does not look as if the nymphs are about to jump up immediately in order to stand in front of their mistress. Titian has moderated the fright that, according to Ovid, the nymphs received from the sudden appearance of the unknown man. The surprised bathers display a wide range of reactions, from the complete lack of interest shown by the nymph drying Diana's leg, to the open curiosity of the nymph who is hiding behind the column.

The gentle colors of *Danaë with Nursemaid* (page 348) have given way to strong contrasts. Dark emerald green appears next to strong, bright red and blue, completed with delicate purple, sky blue, pink and gold tones. A similarly unusual color composition, one also characterized by strong colors, is that of *Venus Blindfolding Cupid* (Galleria Borghese, Rome), which

Titian
The Annunciation, 1559–1564
Oil on canvas, 403 x 235 cm
San Salvatore, Venice

This painting was commissioned by 1559 at the latest, but probably not finished until 1564. Mary's room is similar to that in the earlier Annunciation in Treviso (Capella di Malchiostro, Cathedral), but is no longer of central importance given the magnificent colors of the scene. Titian conceived the events as a divine vision, swathing everything in a cloud of color. Particularly worthy of note are the flowers at the bottom right, glowing like flames. They are a reference to the burning bush that Moses saw, a symbol of the Virgin Birth.

Opposite page:
Titian
The Annunciation, ca. 1557
Oil on canvas, 280 x 210 cm
San Domenico Maggiore, Naples

In this painting the miracle of the Annunciation is also conceived as a vision. But here the use of colors and the conception of the figures are of an inferior quality to those in the superb version in Venice (page 354).

Titian
Diana and Callisto, 1556–1559
Oil on canvas, 188 x 206 cm
National Gallery of Scotland (on loan from the Duke of Sutherland), Edinburgh

Jupiter, the principal god of Roman mythology, impregnates the nymph Callisto, who is part of the entourage of the chaste goddess of hunting, Diana, and therefore also sworn to chastity. As they bathe together, the goddess discovers that Callisto is pregnant and disowns her. This painting is badly damaged. But the contrast between the lilac sky and the green vegetation ensures that the painting's colors are still as enchanting as ever.

was painted some years later. In *Venus Blindfolding Cupid*, however, the sky, which gleams with shades of red, orange, and peach, picking up on the colors in the foreground, creates a more harmonious effect than that achieved in the pictures of Diana, which have a bold and shimmering colorfulness.

While in these mythological paintings Titian was principally experimenting with unusual combinations of colors and color effects, in the religious paintings of the late 1550s and early 1560s he began more and more to repress pictorial space and the volume of figures in

favor of color. This is true of the *Crucifixion* (page 353) in Ancona as well as for *Christ Crowned with Thorns* (page 365) and the *Annunciations* (pages 354, 355). The *Annunciations* in particular gain their visionary character from a use of color that dissolves the figures and their surroundings. Eventually this use of color, often quite independent of the natural color of objects, came to be applied to the mythological pictures. The *Death of Actaeon* (page 358), in which Titian once more dealt with the Diana myth for his Ovid cycle, acts as a link between the mythological works of the late 1550s

and early 1660s and the religious works of this period. Now the colors of the sky, earth, and trees hardly differ. The picture is dominated by yellow, gold, brown, and gray tones, in places combined with green, blue, and a little red. Only Diana is highlighted by the bright gold and the pink shimmering red of her dress. By using the same red for the garments worn by Actaeon, who is being torn apart by his dogs, Titian emphasizes Actaeon's role as the second main figure. However, the naked parts of Diana's body, together with stag's head of Actaeon, almost merge into the same yellow, brown,

and gray tones that dominate the entire picture. Only in the way he applies the color does Titian distinguish the individual objects. He paints the sky more evenly and softly than he paints the trees, whose leaves he indicates with broad, more or less blurred brush strokes. Diana's skin tones have been standardized to create a smooth surface, and her dress is dissolved into numerous fine shades of color. The left-hand side of the picture, where Diana stands, is characterized by a more even application of color that makes the surface of the picture appear smoother. On the right-hand side of the

Titian
Diana and Actaeon, 1556–1559
Oil on canvas, 188 x 206 cm
National Gallery of Scotland (on loan from the Duke of Sutherland), Edinburgh

Actaeon the hunter comes across Diana, the classical goddess of hunting, and her nymphs as they are bathing. As he has seen the chaste goddess while she is naked, he is turned into a stag and is torn apart by his own dogs, who fail to recognize him. This painting is captivating largely because of its rich and unusual colors; nor does it shy away from using strong colors such as the bright red on Actaeon's turned-down boots.

Titian
The Death of Actaeon, ca. 1559 or 1570–1575
Oil on canvas, 179 x 198 cm
The National Gallery, London

This painting shows Actaeon who, having been changed
into a stag, is hunted by Diana and torn apart by his own
dogs. Letters show that the work was already planned in
1559, in connection with the pictures of Diana bathing
(pages 356, 357). There are, however, stylistic reasons
—such as the forest, which dissolves into patches of color
around Actaeon on the right side—for considering a later
date to be more likely.

Opposite page: Titian
The Flaying of Marsyas, 1575/76
Oil on canvas, 212 x 207 cm
State Museum, Kromeriz

The *Flaying of Marsyas* is the sum of all Titian's experiments
with color during the 1560s and 1570s. In contrast to his
St. Sebastian (page 366), this painting is built up using
countless colors. Marsyas the satyr challenged the god
Apollo to take part in a musical competition. Marsyas lost
and his punishment was to be flayed alive. At first, the
horrific process seems to disappear behind the shimmering
colors. One needs to look more closely in order to see that
Apollo has already begun stripping his skin; a little dog is
licking at the satyr's blood.

Titian (?)
St. Jerome, ca. 1575
Oil on canvas, 184 x 177 cm
Nuevos Museos, Escorial

As in many of Titian's late works, there are justified doubts as to the extent to which Titian worked on this painting. It is indeed extremely difficult to judge whether figures as flat as those in this picture are indeed part of the artist's late work. The same is true of the books and the hourglass on the left.

Preceding pages, left:
Allegory of Time Governed by Prudence, ca. 1565
Oil on canvas, 75.6 x 68.6 cm
The National Gallery, London

This is an exceptional portrait which depicts the aged Titian on the left above a wolf's head, his son Orazio in the center above the head of a lion, and his nephew Marco above a dog's head. They represent time governed by prudence. The Latin inscription also relates to this theme. Though it was common enough during the Renaissance to use three human heads to symbolize the ages of man, and to use three animal heads to symbolize prudence, it was very unusual to use them as the theme of a painting. As Titian used personal motifs, it can be assumed that he chose the subject matter himself.

Preceding pages, right:
Portrait of the Doge Francesco Venier, post-1564
Oil on canvas, 114 x 99 cm
Museo Thyssen-Bornemisza, Madrid

Francesco Venier (1490–1556) was elected Doge on 11 June 1554. He reigned for scarcely two years, until 2 June 1556. This portrait is an excellent example of the way Titian used color during his late period. The picture does not break up into countless colors. Only in the garment is there a fine play of golden hues, underlining the delicacy of the frail Doge. So far, there has been no explanation for the fire in the lagoon, which is visible through the window. In terms of color, the fire provides an important contrast with the blue sky.

picture, where the dramatic death of Actaeon is shown, the colors are applied thickly with a smaller brush, creating an impression of restless movement that intensifies into a whirl of colors around Actaeon. In this way both color, and the way it is applied, play an important role in determining the nature of a picture's content. Another example is the *Flaying of Marsyas* (page 359), a breathtaking late masterpiece; here the colors at first conceal the cruelty of what is taking place, but when looked at more closely emphasize the monstrous nature of the scene depicted. The picture's strange colors, built up tones of gray, green, sand, and dull purple, create an increasingly melancholy and threatening mood.

The artist Jacopo Palma il Giovane (1544–1628) provided a fascinating description of the way in which Titian worked. He started by sketching his subject with just a few strokes using a full, thick brush. He then continued using the same brush, with whatever traces of paint were left in it, to produce the colorful reflections of light. When he had finished for that day, he would lean the canvas against the wall, face down, and let the paint dry before he continued working on it at a later date. During the last phase of his work he used a wide range of colors, frequently applying them with his fingers in order to achieve the desired effect. Vasari, who visited Titian in his workshop in 1566 and described the same technique, was clearly very

Titian, *Religion Succored by Spain*, 1572–1575
Oil on canvas, 168 x 168 cm
Museo Nacional del Prado, Madrid

The kneeling woman, beside which are a fallen cross and chalice, is a personification of Religion being attacked by the serpents of Unbelief. From the left, the personification of Spain is approaching, wearing a fluttering garment, to assist Religion. The painting is alluding to the leading role that Spain played in the wars of religion. At the same time, the background commemorates the victory of the Christian fleet over the Turks in the Battle of Lepanto in 1571.

impressed by these paintings. In his *Life of Titian,* Vasari describes in some detail the effect of these paintings: "They cannot be viewed from near to, but appear perfect at a distance. This method of painting is the reason for the clumsy pictures painted by the many artists who have tried to imitate Titian and show themselves practiced masters; for although Titian's works seem to many to have been created without much effort, this is far from the truth and those who

think so are deceiving themselves." The art historian Theodor Hetzer, who in 1935 published a book on Titian's use of color, summed up his method of painting very aptly: "There is a colorful play of light glimmering and gleaming across the entire picture. The thick application of the paint and the rough grainy canvas that Titian now preferred cause the picture to radiate countless lights and reflections … Every square centimeter has the same intensity of movement as the

Christp Crowned with Thorns, ca. 1570–1576
Oil on canvas, 280 x 181 cm
Alte Pinakothek, Bayerische Staatsgemäldesammlungen,
Munich

This painting uses the same composition as the *Christ Crowned with Thorns* in the Louvre (page 332). Here, however, Titian has omitted any definition of space. The individual picture elements appear to emerge out of the dark masses of color. The sheer wealth of colors is not noticeable until one looks more closely. Mustard yellow and broken reds provide some strong color highlights in the foreground. Large sections of the painting on the right were not completed. Like so many works during his late period, this work also remained unfinished.

entire surface. Nothing is undissolved or dull, nor does anything require a broader context in order to be effective. What we get is something in the nature of a picture that has been broken down into atoms of color; each fleck of color exists independently and is as valid as any other."

Not all of Titian's late paintings, however, show this process taken to such extremes. In some of them certainly, such as *St. Sebastian* (page 366), the figure and landscape seem to emerge from colors that seem to cover the canvas at random and form a thick carpet of color, or, as Palma Giovane put it, a "bed of color." By contrast, in the allegory *Religion Succored by Spain* (page 363), there are much more subtle gradations of color. But here, too, the sheer variety of colors needed to produce the delicate sheen on the red outer garment worn by the personification of Spain is astonishing. From the end of the 1550s, there were no further developments in the style of the works that Titian painted. He developed an individual solution for each of his canvases, some of which, as Palma describes, were painted over several years. Late works such as his *Portrait of Doge Francesco Venier* (page 361) also show such individual solutions. In the painting of the Doge, the magnificence of the robes with the interwoven gold threads—so noticeable a feature in the *Portrait of Doge Andrea Gritti* (page 341)—has been moderated to a delicate shimmering that seems to cover the entire painting with its sheen. By applying the colors gently, Titian succeeded in capturing the character of the Doge, who, though physically extremely weak during his period in office, was very strong-minded. By contrast, in the *Allegory of Time Governed by Prudence* (page 360), which shows Titian with his son Orazio and his nephew Marco, he achieves his effect mainly through his use of light. Titian's self-portrait, personifying the past, is disappearing into the twilight, and even seems to physically dissolve into it. Orazio, the personification of the present, is lit from the side, so that half of his face is in shadow; and the profile of the young Marco, the future, is fully lit.

In Titian's late *Self-Portrait* (Volume I, page 9), his figure almost dissolves into the dark background.

Though this is in part due to the aging of the pigments of a painting that was originally somewhat lighter, the dark effect was quite intentional. His face is accentuated by the almost white highlights on the collar and the hair shining beneath his cap. The background is slightly lighter around his head. He also used highlights on things that were important to him. He emphasizes his golden chain as well as the brush he is holding, which he paints almost black on black as an indication of his artistic skill. His use of dark colors, together with his technical mastery, combine to create an impression of a man of strength and modesty who had no wish to conceal his art and his imperial title. This self-portrait once again gives us an impressive image of his ability and personality.

His final artistic legacy, a *Pietà* (page 367) he began painting for his own tomb, was to remain unfinished, as did many of the paintings of the latter years of his life. Titian had intended this work for the church of Santa Maria Gloriosa dei Frari, in which he wished to be buried. Titian died on 27 August 1576, in his house in Biri Grande. There had been a serious outbreak of plague in Venice and as a result the city authorities, who had advanced ideas in medical matters, forbade funeral ceremonies in order to reduce the risk of infection. But an exception was made for the city's great son, whose art had contributed in so many ways to the Republic's fame. He was buried on 28 August 1576, in Santa Maria Gloriosa dei Frari, after a brief ceremony. The attendance of the canons of San Marco at his funeral officially honored the republic's greatest artist. His monument in the city was not erected until the 19th century. The great artists of the following centuries have repeatedly referred to him. In very different ways, his art influenced painters such as Nicolas Poussin, Peter Paul Rubens, Anthony van Dyck, Diego Velázquez, Rembrandt, Francisco Goya, Eugène Delacroix, Édouard Manet, and Auguste Renoir, to name but a few. An indication of the high regard in which Titian's achievement was held was the fact that in the 17th century the artist Luca Giordano (1634–1705) rose to fame by forging works by Titian.

Marion Kaminski

Titian
St. Sebastian, 1575
Oil on canvas, 210 x 115 cm
Hermitage, St. Petersburg

Together with his *Flaying of Marsyas* (page 359), this
St. Sebastian is one of the greatest masterpieces of Titian's
late work. The painting is built up using only shades of
black, gold, and brown, with a very few touches of red.
The saint's body appears to emerge from the surrounding
colors as an intensification of color. Vasari's enthusiastic
description of Titian's method of painting by creating
patches of color that "cannot be viewed from nearby, but
appear perfect at a distance," is particularly applicable in
this instance.

Opposite page:
Pietà, 1576, completed later
Oil on canvas, 378 x 347 cm
Gallerie dell'Accademia, Venice

Titian planned to donate this painting to the church of
Santa Maria Gloriosa dei Frari in the hope that he would
obtain one of the much-desired burial places there.
During his lifetime, however, he failed to reach an
agreement with the friars. The picture was not finished
and was eventually completed by Palma Giovane. The
painting depicts the dead Christ and his grieving mother,
but also shows Magdalene in an unusually violent
movement, something that has been taken as an allusion
to the terrible plague that raged in Venice while Titian
was working on it.

QVOD TITIANVS INCHOATVM
PALMA REVERENTER ABSOLVIT
DEOQ DICAVIT OPVS

Giorgione's Successors

SEBASTIANO DEL PIOMBO (CA. 1485–1547)

As Giorgio Vasari reports in his celebrated *Lives of the Artists*, the Venetian Sebastiano del Piombo (actually Sebastiano Luciani) initially started learning with the already elderly Giovanni Bellini but then, just like Titian, continued his training in Giorgione's workshop, and also matched the new, accentuated pictorial style of his master so closely that it has often been difficult to differentiate the works of the one from those of the other. According to various older sources, Sebastiano is even said to have completed one of Giorgione's most famous paintings, the *Three Philosophers* in Vienna (pages 288–289), a view still held by some today.

In 1511, a year after Giorgione's premature death, Sebastiano was invited by Agostino Chigi, a powerful banker staying in Venice at the time, to accompany him back to Rome: according in turn to Vasari, it was not just Sebastiano's reputation as an excellent portrait painter that led to the invitation, but also his extraordinary musical talent. Although not trained as a fresco painter, once he reached Rome he took part in the work that had already been begun by Raphael, Giulio Romano, and other artists, of decorating the Villa Farnesina, which Baldassare Peruzzi had just built on the banks of Tiber for Agostino Chigi. Apart from a stay in Venice during the late 1520s, Sebastiano remained based in Rome for the rest of his life. He soon became friends with Michelangelo and repeatedly worked to his drafts, a working relationship that is well documented in the extensive exchange of letters between the two artists.

As a result of his training with the most significant Venetian painters of the early 16th century, and the subsequent heavy influence of Florentine masters such as Raphael on the one hand and Michelangelo

Sebastiano del Piombo
Portrait of a Young Roman Woman, ca. 1512/13
Oil on wood, 78 x 61 cm
Gemäldegalerie, Staatliche Museen, Berlin

This painting displays the Venetian origins of the painter even more strongly than the portrait of Clement VII (page 368), painted almost one and a half decades later, even though the work has occasionally been attributed to Raphael. Apart from the unknown young woman's soft facial features, that do indeed remind one a little of Raphael's style, and the Venetian composition—half-figure in front of a dark interior background with a view out of a window—it is primarily the white highlighting on the bright sleeves and the fur-trimmed cloak, and the visible brushwork inspired by Titian, that lend the painting its Venetian character.

Opposite page:
Sebastiano del Piombo
Portrait of Clement VII, ca. 1526
Oil on canvas, 145 x 100 cm
Galleria Nazionale di Capodimonte, Naples

This portrait of Clement VII is one of the few to portray the Medici pope still without the beard characteristic of his later portraits and was therefore probably painted shortly before the Sacco di Roma (the sack of Rome by the troops of Emperor Charles V), which he—and his portrait painter, Sebastiano del Piombo—only narrowly escaped by fleeing to the Castel Sant'Angelo, near the Vatican.

on the other, it is not easy to classify Sebastiano's comprehensive range of works, today scattered throughout the world, and to assign them to one region or school of painting. In his works, warm Venetian coloring merges with Florentine-Roman *disegno* and Michelangelesque monumentality. Following Raphael's death in 1520, Sebastiano soon rose to become the most sought-after portrait painter in Rome, though it is said that numerous commissions owed more to his elegant appearance, that of a courtier, than to his artistic abilities; at least according to Vasari, whose not always benevolent, at times almost derisive, *Life of Sebastiano* must undeniably be read with a critical eye.

One of the most prestigious commissions the painter received was to paint the portrait of Pope Clement VII (page 368). Sebastiano obviously fulfilled this task to the great satisfaction of the Pontiff, since he received from him further portrait commissions over the following years. Furthermore, he was appointed Keeper of the Papal Seal (*piombo*) in 1531, which led to the name by which the artist is commonly known today. Clement VII, born Giulio de' Medici, was the second of a total of four popes from that powerful Florentine family. As the son of Guiliano de' Medici, murdered in the cathedral of Santa Maria del Fiore in the course of the Pazzi Conspiracy, he was the nephew of Lorenzo the

Magnificent and a cousin of Giovanni, who, for his part, had also sat on the papal throne under the name of Leo X (page 269).

Politically, Clement's eleven-year pontificate (1523–1534) was inauspicious. A whole series of diplomatic errors in association with the struggle between the German Emperor and the King of France for dominance of northern Italy led in the spring of 1527 to the Sacco di Roma, the devastating plunder of the Eternal City by marauding German and Spanish troops. Nevertheless, it was under the rule of this second Medici pope that several of the most significant works of art of the Roman Late Renaissance were created.

Sebastiano del Piombo's portrait in Naples (page 368) is in the still relatively young tradition that began with Melozzo da Forlì's portrait of Sixtus IV (Volume I, page 561), reached its first climax with Raphael's portrait of Julius II (page 240), and was eventually continued by painters such as Titian (page 340). Notwithstanding all obvious formal parallels to the portrait by Raphael, painted approximately fifteen years earlier, Sebastiano's painting expresses both the artist's Venetian training and the influence of Michelangelo. The marked Venetian character of the painting reveals itself particularly in the raised, white reflective highlighting of the red silk with its visible brushwork; while the strong near view, the bulky, picture-filling figure of the pope, as well as the turning of his head away from the axis of the body, show the artistic debt to the style of Michelangelo.

A highpoint among the portraits painted by Sebastiano at the start of his years in Rome is the portrait of a young woman (page 369) that was long considered, due to the remarkably soft facial features of the person portrayed, to be a work by Raphael, to have been inspired by Leonardo da Vinci, and even to be a portrait of the artist's lover. However, the motif of a half-figure in front of a dark architectural background, as well as the window view of an atmospheric evening landscape at the side, unquestionably identifies the painting as the work of a Venetian artist. It has intermittently been listed under the title of *St. Dorothy* due to the fruit basket at the bottom being interpreted as an allusion to the legend of that early Christian martyr, according to which she was taunted by a young man shortly before her death, who asked her to send him a basket of heavenly flowers and fruit from the hereafter. Upon Dorothy's prayer, an angel immediately appeared bearing such a basket, which is then said to have led to the conversion of the unbeliever. However, since neither a halo nor a palm branch as a symbol for the saint's martyrdom are to be found in Sebastiano's painting, the tendency today is to see it as a portrait of an unknown Roman woman who was perhaps actually called Dorothy (Dorotea), in which case the fruit basket can be understood as an allusion to the saint after whom she had been named.

As far as Sebastiano's stylistic development in Rome is concerned, and the position he occupied as an artist in the tense competition between the two great rivals Raphael and Michelangelo, there is hardly any other work of greater significance than his *Raising of Lazarus*

(page 371), painted between 1516 and 1519. The work was commissioned by Cardinal Giulio de' Medici, later to become Pope Clement VII, who had shortly beforehand been appointed archbishop of Narbonne, in southern France, by Leo X, and who had already commissioned Raphael to paint the *Transfiguration of Christ* (page 271) for the cathedral there. The choice of subject for Sebastiano's counterpart, which portrays Christ in his role as *medico divino* (Divine Doctor), may, on the one hand, be a reference to the family name of the client, but may also, on the other hand, be linked to the relics of St. Lazarus venerated in Narbonne.

The only account of the miracle of his resurrection in Bethany, near Jerusalem, is to be found in the Gospel according to St. John: Lazarus had already lain in his grave for four days when Jesus, accompanied by his disciples and numerous inhabitants of the village —including Mary and Martha, the sisters of the deceased—arrived, had the rock in front of the cave tomb removed, and called out "Lazarus, come forth!" Sebastiano's painting depicts the last few minutes of this event. Jesus, dressed in red and blue, is standing on the left and pointing at the already risen Lazarus, who is being freed from the white cloths of his shroud, while, in the middle ground to the left and right, two groups are busy discussing the event—evidently an advance indication on the part of the painter of the events following on from the story of Lazarus, namely the decision of the Pharisees and high priests to kill Jesus.

The many witnesses of the miracle display very different reactions—very much in the terms of the *varietà* already described decades earlier by Alberti in his painting treatise—ranging from the deeply moved Mary kneeling before Jesus and the praying figure also kneeling in the left foreground, who could well be St. Peter, to the disbelieving and curious man in a green garment leaning forward behind Jesus, and to those who, like Martha, frightened by Lazarus turn away or hold the hems of their garments to their faces because of the stench of his corpse. To an extent, the various bodily poses, gestures, and facial expressions bear great resemblance to those in the *Transfiguration of Christ* (page 271) painted by Raphael at the same time.

Whether that painting, also commissioned by Giulio de' Medici for Narbonne, could have served as a direct source of inspiration for Sebastiano del Piombo when he saw it for the first time, is not known. Similar figures and movement motifs can, however, also be found in older works by Raphael. One can, for example, consider the *School of Athens* (page 232) and compare the philosophers on the right, bent over a slate board lying on the floor, with the man in the white shirt standing directly behind Lazarus. In contrast, other details in the Lazarus painting testify to the direct influence of Michelangelo, particularly the muscular build of the protagonist. With his twisted body and his raised and bent right leg, his head turning toward Jesus while his arm moves in the opposite direction, he could also be sitting among the *ignudi* in the main ceiling fresco of the Sistine Chapel (Volume I, pages 618–619). But one does not have to look far, because there also exists, by

Sebastiano del Piombo
The Raising of Lazarus (detail page 588),
ca. 1517–1519
Oil on wood, transferred to canvas, 381 x 287 cm
The National Gallery, London

The painter signed his work on the stonework plinth beneath Christ with an indication of his Venetian origins: *SEBASTIANVS VENETVS FACIEBAT*. Whereas numerous figures of the main scene undoubtedly bear witness through their richly diverse poses and dramatic gestures to the influence of both Raphael and Michelangelo, the background landscape, overhung by dark clouds and with a rich contrast in lighting, clearly proves itself to be Venetian in inspiration. A comparison is provided, for example, by Giorgione's *Tempest* in the Accademia in Venice (page 291).

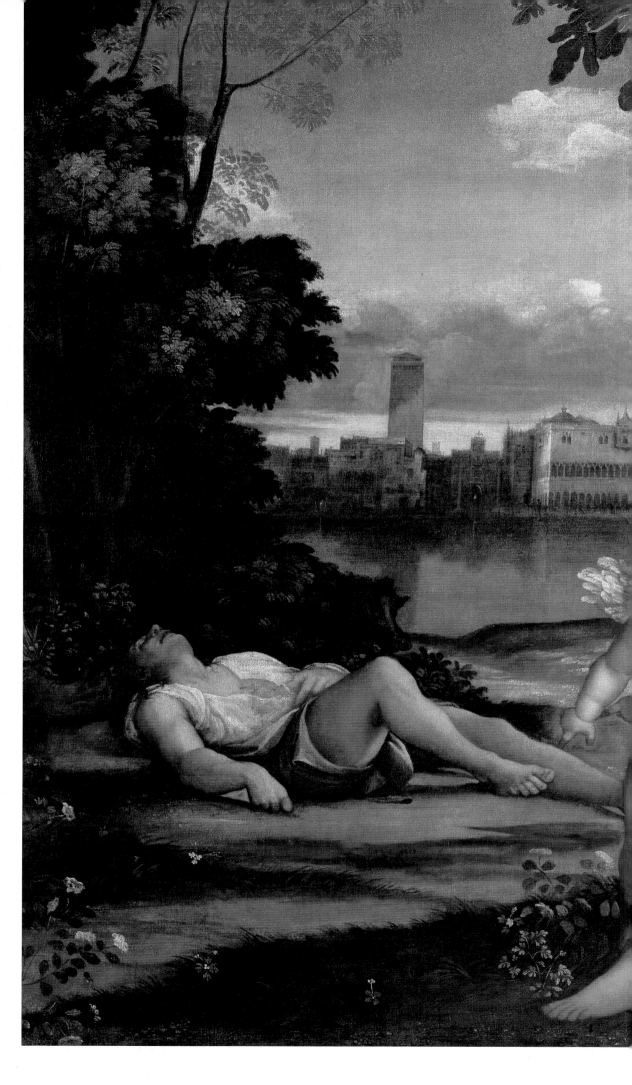

Michelangelo himself, three draft drawings of Sebastiano's Lazarus figure, as well as of the man helping to loosen the shroud cloths.

In contrast to this already very Roman painting, the *Death of Adonis* (right), a work painted only a few years earlier, around 1512, proves itself to be still thoroughly influenced by Sebastiano's time in Venice, and not just because of the *veduta* of the lagoon city to be seen in the background beyond the water and the Giorgionesque landscape. For example, the naked female back on the right is reminiscent of the *Concert Champêtre* (pages 294–295) in the Louvre, alternately attributed to Giorgione or Titian. By contrast, the strong figure of the woman in yellow, leaning forward further to the left, already provides evidence of a Michelangelesque concept of the figure. This Uffizi painting, possibly painted for Agostino Chigi, is one of Sebastiano's few works, apart from the Villa Farnesina frescoes, with a mythological content. Whereas other painters often depict the moment when Venus anxiously tries to deter her lover Adonis from the dangerous hunt (page 350), or the scene in which a wild boar is killed, Sebastiano has chosen to portray the silent mourning of the goddess of love. Only the boar that can be seen emerging from the bushes behind the lying figure of Adonis on the left points to the manner of his death.

Henrik Engel

Sebastiano del Piombo
Death of Adonis, ca. 1512
Oil on canvas, 189 x 285 cm
Galleria degli Uffizi, Florence

A comparatively small but precise view of the city of Venice can be seen in the background, giving the impression that Venus, the goddess of love, is mourning the death of her lover, Adonis, on the Lagoon city's island of San Giorgio. The façade of the Doge's Palace facing the water can clearly be recognized, as can a section of St. Mark's lying behind it and the Torre dell'Orologio. By contrast, the foundation stone for the St. Mark's Library on the Piazzetta opposite the Doge's Palace was not laid until 1537, while the spire erected in 1514 on the campanile that dominates the city skyline is still missing in Sebastiano's painting, facts that have contributed to dating the work.

Lorenzo Lotto
Christ Taking Leave of His Mother, 1521
Oil on canvas, 126 x 99 cm
Gemäldegalerie, Staatliche Museen, Berlin

This painting is perhaps a counterpart to either a copy
or the surviving remnant of the nocturnal depiction of
the *Adoration of the Shepherds* in the Accademia, Venice;
for in 1648 the canvas is mentioned together with a
Christmas painting by Ridolfi in the Tassi household,
Bergamo. For this reason, it was thought as early as 1793
to portray Elisabetta Rota, wife of Domenico de Tassi.
The composition conforms to the classical division of a
book page with border and text area; it would be a verso
page with the broad margin to the left, to which Jesus also
belongs.

LORENZO LOTTO (CA. 1480–1557)

Fierce competition evidently existed between painters
in Venice at the beginning of the 16th century. It
ensured that many of them attempted to gain attention
with a bold process of rethinking. Instead of relying on
the conventional reading of a known biblical story,
Lorenzo Lotto in Recanati, for example, attempted in
his painting of the *Annunciation* (page 375) of 1527 to
grasp almost every aspect in a new way: the angel enters
the scene from the right was indeed already perfectly
well-known at the time; but the space between Mary

and the angel is astounding, as is the wild movement
emanating from the figure of God the Father at the
top right: with his hand outstretched in a blessing he
gives the impression of himself wishing to swing down
to earth in the flesh. The Virgin, fleeing from the
heavenly onslaught, imploringly raises her hands to
the view, while behind her a frightened cat darts across
the room. Incidentally, one can imagine the room with
its view of the garden to be in a palace rather than the
home of a carpenter.

The artist exaggerates the events in his *Christ Taking Leave of His Mother* (page 374) even more decisively: the scene is set in a hall more like that found in northern Italy in a Palazzo della Ragione, the main civic building of a city administration. The round window to the sky seems like the eye of God; the three arches beneath it, opening out onto an enclosed garden as a symbol of Mary, read like an allusion to the Trinity and remind one of Jan van Eyck's *Rolin Madonna* in the Louvre (page 7) as well as Lorenzo di Credi's *Annunciation* (page 15). The bed of the Virgin and the lectern at which she was perhaps praying before the Annunciation adjoin the grand main room, which, despite its princely dimensions, is meant to be her home in Nazareth.

Peter and a second Apostle are patiently waiting for Jesus to leave with them, while he kneels before Mary like an angel of the Annunciation, or as if in prayer on the Mount of Olives. He is wearing the same robes and colors, even including a white veil, as the Mother of God, something quite outrageous in terms of traditional iconography. Mary, for her part, is collapsing, as if she now sees what will happen to her and her son. Her fainting during the farewell prefigures her later collapse under the cross; and, as on Golgotha, the Apostle John and St. Mary Magdalene come to her assistance. A benefactress is present at the scene, while next to the cherry branch at the bottom of the picture an apple reminds the viewer of Eve, turning Mary herself into a second Eve. Lorenzo Lotto, who has portrayed the scene, leaves a small note bearing his name and the year it was painted, 1521, in the bottom frame of the picture.

Lorenzo Lotto
The Annunciation, 1527 or ca. 1534/35
Oil on canvas, 166 x 114 cm
Pinacoteca Civica, Recanati

This painting is first mentioned as hanging in a merchant's chapel in Recanati in 1601. It could have been an altarpiece, but may well have been the left-hand panel of a larger ensemble. The painter has divided the image surface into a main area with margin and then moved the figures to the margin in order to express the incomprehensibility of the Word becoming Flesh through the empty middle of the picture, in which an hourglass is running.

In the face of the competition in Venice already mentioned above, it was more difficult for a talented artist, also perhaps plagued by a restive spirit during a turbulent time, to survive in the city than for less inspired painters. Lorenzo Lotto, born in Venice around 1480, came up against workshops such as those of Bellini in the city or of Vivarini in Murano that had already dominated the market for generations. Besides them, masters like Vincenzo Catena (ca. 1470–1531) and Vittore Carpaccio (ca. 1455–1526) had already captured a market, while young talented artists from outside, such as Giorgione from Castelfranco or Titian from Cadore, crowded into the city.

One of the younger artists, Sebastiano del Piombo (ca. 1485–1547), had left Venice after a grandiose start, in order to work in Michelangelo's Rome. Lorenzo Lotto, on the other hand, was primarily drawn to the Marches between Bergamo and Ancona; he appears to have traveled from commission to commission without ever finding work that would result in sufficient follow-up orders to enable him to settle down permanently. The painter lived without a wife and children; much is known about him because he kept systematic records of his income. The result is a bewildering mosaic of relocations with only a few gaps: in 1503 Lotto is mentioned as a painter in Treviso; in 1505 he completes his first dated and signed work, an allegory, today to be found in Washington. In 1506 he tarries in Recanati, a small town whose present status as an art venue is still due to his paintings (page 375). What Lotto paints in the Vatican in 1509

remains obscure; he does not stay long in the Eternal City dominated by Raphael (1483–1520). By 1511 he is already in Jesi in the Marches, by 1521 in Bergamo, and by 1523 in Jesi again. In 1524 he is working for Trescore and for Bergamo, but by 1526 he is back in Jesi. The portrait of Andrea Odoni (page 381), dated 1527, was painted in Venice; but in 1532 Lotto is living in Bergamo again, although his will from 1527 is made in Venice. In 1538 he is working in Ancona, 1539 in Cingoli and Macerata, and lives alternately in Venice and Treviso from 1540 onward. On 12 December 1545 he makes a second will in Venice, then, seriously ill, finds accommodation in Treviso with the goldsmith Bartolomeo Carpan. However, he recovers and in 1549 again returns to Ancona, and in 1552 to Jesi.

Lorenzo Lotto spends the final years of his life in Loreto, a place of pilgrimage dedicated to the Virgin Mary, which claims to possess the house in which the Virgin experienced the Annunciation. Here the painter finally loses the restlessness that hat made up his whole existence; for in 1554 he enters the sanctuary of Santa Casa di Loreto as a lay-brother; he died, at the latest, three years later in 1557, at the age of almost eighty.

None of Lorenzo Lotto's large-scale works wrote art history, even though his impressive altar panels, which remain in situ, make a journey in his footsteps worthwhile. The distinctive voice of Lotto's art can be heard in the great galleries of the world, where biblical stories, devotional pictures, paintings with figures from mythology, and portraits have found a home.

Lorenzo Lotto
Christ and the Woman Taken in Adultery, 1527–1529 (?)
Oil on canvas, 99 x 126 cm, extended to 124 x 156 cm
Musée du Louvre, Paris

An adulteress about to be stoned is led to Jesus, who says to the angry crowd: "Whosoever among you is without sin, let him cast the first stone" (John 8: 7). By 1581, at the latest, this painting was in the possession of the French Protestant leader, Philippe de Mornay. The canvas later became the property of the crown and was extended on all sides by about 12–13 cm (about 5 inches). Such alterations served to adapt paintings to decoratively fit into galleries (as was the case, for example, with Caravaggio's *Fortune Teller* in the Louvre, page 537).

Lorenzo Lotto
*The Madonna with Angel, St. Catherine of Alexandria,
and the Apostle Thomas,* ca. 1528–1530
Oil on canvas, 113 x 152 cm
Kunsthistorisches Museum, Vienna

When faced with such a picture, it should not be forgotten that in the case of commissioned paintings it is the buyer, and not the artist, who determines the format of the canvas and at the same time decides whether he wishes to have full figures portrayed or whether half figures will suffice. Lotto, who painted his *Christ and the Woman Taken in Adultery* (opposite) with half figures in the same year as he did this painting, this time had to accommodate four large figures in a horizontal rectangle. Almost as if he wanted to increase the complexity of the task (contemporary art theorists of the time spoke of *difficoltà*), he chose a shaded location under a tree, and thereby created a poetic landscape idyll.

Lorenzo Lotto's paintings bear witness to the fame of an astounding painter: he is a master of the portrayal of half-figures with biblical scenes in front of a darkened background that surfaced in various European centers of art around 1500, following its inception by Andrea Mantegna, perhaps with such paintings as the *Presentation at the Temple* (page 72). This new type of painting was most successful in Venice; Giovanni Bellini concerned himself with it, but Dürer (1471–1528) too, during his stay in Venice, wanted to demonstrate with his *Christ Aged Twelve at the Temple* (Museo Thyssen-Bornemisza, Madrid), completed in only a few days, just how well a master from the north had mastered their art. Lotto's most impressive example of this style is his *Christ and the Woman Taken in Adultery* (page 376). According to tradition, Jesus should bend down and write in the sand, "Whosoever among you is without sin, let him cast the first stone." In the case of the half-figures,

however, everything is reduced to the discussion, and the biblical story becomes a kind of genre painting of the time when Christ debated with the Pharisees and the scribes.

Even more astounding is the Viennese Madonna in the tradition of a *sacra conversazione* with St. Catherine and the Christ Child (page 377). Accompanied by an angel that would do justice to the English pre-Raphaelite painters of the 19th century, the Mother of God has sought the shade of the broad overhanging boughs of a tree. The kneeling saints press toward her like benefactors in disguise. The thought automatically occurs that only an artist who, like Lotto, restlessly traveled from place to place could himself appreciate just how much refuge an individual tree along the wayside could provide.

Lotto's poetic fantasies are even more enchanting than his religious paintings; in them, he proves himself to be a worthy heir to Giorgione and the later works of Bellini. Landscapes fascinated him, but he also allows inspiration from north of the Alps to flow into them. He frees himself from the established conventions of an easily readable visual language when he has a putto, which could also be Cupid, the child-like god of love, trickle a rain of gold onto a contemplative girl out of an evening sky, while the wild inhabitants of the forest either lurk behind a tree or play at the water, without us knowing exactly what the scene is intended to say (page 378).

There is also the question of the remit behind the commissioning of this painting; for the puzzle of what can be seen in the picture is not a matter for the painter alone, he is surely also playing on the intentions of its prospective owner. A glance in such a book as Francesco Colonna's *Hynerotomachia Poliphili*, printed with a wide circulation by the Venetian publisher Aldus Manutius in 1499, thwarts any hope of possibly deciphering this play with nature and human being, mythology and atmosphere. The visual fantasy of the wood engravings that accompany the hard-to-read Latin text is inexhaustible; much remains hieroglyphically abstruse, even when literary text is brought into play with visual motif. Sleep is a main theme of this famous book; the themes of sleep and dream, as well as reflection and trance, also permeate the pictorial poetry of the Venetian Renaissance.

The allusions to be found in the scandalously embarrassing *Venus* (page 379) in New York are more

Lorenzo Lotto
Dream of a Girl, or *Allegory of Chastity*, ca. 1506
Oil on wood, 43 x 34 cm
Samuel H. Kress Collection, National Gallery of Art, Washington

This painting may well have formed the outer cover for a portrait; something that has at least been proved for the second allegory in the Kress Collection, it belonged to the portrait of Bernardo de' Rossi. In view of this enigmatic painting's portrayal of a girl dreaming in the landscape, which mistakenly brings to mind Jupiter's shower of gold for Danaë, it has been suggested that the humanist Giovanni Aurelio Augurelli, who was in Treviso between 1503 and 1506, may have conceived the imagery. Another composition can be detected under the present surface, upside-down as is usually the case when a painting is reused: it depicts a naked youth, perhaps Hercules at the crossroads.

Lorenzo Lotto
Venus and Cupid, ca. 1527 (?)
Oil on canvas, 92 x 111 cm
The Metropolitan Museum of Art, New York

Perhaps intended as a portrait, Venus appears with a figure of cupid who is urinating in a wide arch over her body. The painting is supposed to be originally from Venice and was in the past erroneously associated with an entry in Lotto's account book from 1540. The puzzling motif of a boy urinating can sometimes be found on so-called "birth plates" (round panel paintings called *desco di parto* that served as gifts). The scene is therefore thought to be associated with fertility; such a painting would therefore be intended for engagements or as a wedding gift. Mario d'Armano reputedly ordered it for his daughter Armana. The disconcerting notion that there had been a counterpart to it depicting Susanna and the Elders cannot be verified.

precise: the format frees itself from the flat rectangle in which the reclining, at times sleeping, goddess of love is otherwise set (Volume I, page 29). Under some kind of tent, Venus is propping herself up against an ivy-entwined tree trunk, almost as if she is beckoning the viewer to come to her. She stares out of the painting with a mild rather than an alluring gaze, with her left hand clutching her heart and her right hand holding a myrtle wreath with burning incense holder, which the child figure of Cupid is grasping. The small god of love, armed with bow and arrow, aims his stream of urine at the goddess of love, a symbol of fertility that troubles modern sensibilities. A mussel shell hangs beside Venus; a rose lies in front of her, the petals of a second are strewn over her body. A small snake surfaces from underneath her sheet.

In later times, the picture was painted over and given a decisively more banal impression. Until it was cleaned in 1984, the Venus had a nondescript face, now she appears as if in portrait. Around her head she wore a simple circlet, now she wears her Venetian bridal crown again. In addition to the crown, the incense and myrtle also fit in with the picture of a marriage. The snake indicates danger. The mussel perhaps alludes to the female sex, but it is also found as the noisy trumpets of small satyrs in the London picture of Botticelli's *Mars and Venus* (Volume I, page 30); it may well therefore be hung here to emphasize the tranquility of the idiosyncratic tryst that Venus is giving an intimate viewer.

Lotto's influence as a portrait painter has been particularly enduring; his portraits may well lack the splendor of Titian's, but they stay in the memory, if only through their spiritual vibrancy. Several of these paintings expand the dimensions of the European portrait: one of them is the threefold portrait of a man in Vienna (below). It could be the earliest surviving example of a multiple depiction of a head in one picture, only intended to provide a sculptor with so much information about the physiognomy of the person portrayed that he could begin work without ever having seen the subject. Later, Anthony van Dyck (1599–1643) painted King Charles I of England, and Philippe de Champaigne (1602–1642) depicted Cardinal Richelieu, from three angles, while Hyacinthe Rigaud (1659–1743) made do with delivering a portrait of his mother from only two.

After all, Jacopo Sansovino (1486–1570) came to Venice from Florence in 1527, just before the painting was done; he could have made something similar from Lotto's portrait as later happened with the Richelieu portrait, which made two busts possible; the one by Gianlorenzo Bernini (1598–1680) in the Louvre in Paris and the other by Francesco Mocchi (1580–1654) in Niort in Poitou. However, Lotto's artistic skill is so beguiling that we cannot be content with such a servile function. It

is thought to be a portrait of a goldsmith, most often Bartolomeo Carpan in Treviso, the friend who at times provided Lotto with shelter. In addition, one can also play with the name of the town, the next large town on the mainland opposite Venice: *tre visi* means "three views." A parallel is seen in the case of Giorgione; according to Vasari, he is said to have depicted in one common painting a figure from behind, in reflection from the front, and then, through another reflection, in profile.

The *paragone*, the competition between painting and sculpture, was also a part of the rivalry between artists in Venice. Lotto would have stood a chance with the Viennese painting only when it was not primarily intended to serve a portrait bust. That he engaged in the *paragone* is demonstrated by this stately portrait of Andrea Odoni showing ancient marble works (page 381). The scintillating liveliness of Lotto's painting and the sturdy fullness of the figure triumph above the fragments from antiquity; and though the collector is shown as proud of his important antiquarian items, Lotto resolutely binds him to his own era, even if it is only through the small crucifix that Andrea presses to his heart.

Eberhard König

Lorenzo Lotto
Goldsmith (?) in Three Views, ca. 1530
Oil on canvas, 52 x 79 cm
Kunsthistorisches Museum, Vienna

Proven to have been in the possession of Vincenzo II Gonzaga in Mantua in 1627, the painting initially became part of the royal collection of King Charles I of England, after whose execution it was sold to the Spanish ambassador. The small box in the man's hand has inspired attempts at identification: as a game of chance—lottery—it may allude to the painter's name; today, however, it is usually considered to contain the goldsmith's range of finger rings. The painting had even been thought to portray the three Carpan brothers who were all goldsmiths from Treviso, which would explain the three views (*tre visi*). Portraits showing the one and the same head from different viewpoints have otherwise only served the purpose of enabling sculptors to fashion a likeness of a person they have not seen.

Lorenzo Lotto
Portrait of Andrea Odoni, 1527
Oil on canvas, 104.6 x 166.6 cm
The Royal Collection, Her Majesty Queen Elizabeth II

Marcantonio Michiel, who viewed Odoni's collection in 1532, reports that he saw a painting by Lotto in the bedroom that showed Andrea examining marble fragments of works from antiquity. Because of its signature and dating, the painting constitutes a significant fixed point in the artist's work. It portrays an important merchant and collector from a family with origins in Milan, but whose father had settled in Venice. Whether or not the collector is holding a statuette of Diana of Ephesus in his hand, as thought since the time of Jakob Burckhardt, is a matter of contention. What is certain is the figure of Hercules struggling with Antaeus seen in the background to the left; the head in the foreground is thought to be of Hadrian, for there is evidence that Odoni's collection contained such a piece; the other works cannot be identified for sure. Despite all the pagan works, it should not be forgotten that Odoni is holding a tiny crucifix in his left hand.

GIOVANNI GIROLAMO SAVOLDO
(CA. 1480 – AFTER 1548)

Hardly anything is known for sure about the training and early career of the Brescia-born painter Savoldo. Although he is mentioned in Florence in 1508 as a member of the physician and apothecary guild also responsible for artists, the works attributed to him display little evidence of any serious dialogue with early Cinquecento Florentine art. In fact, apart from Lombard and also isolated examples of Dutch influence, his works, consisting almost exclusively of biblical stories and portraits, are characterized above all

by Venetian influences, primarily those of Giorgione, Titian, and Lorenzo Lotto, but also that of Cima da Conegliano. For their part, Savoldo's works, with their often subdued colors and at the same time pronounced light-and-shade contrasts and shiny metallic light effects, no doubt made a considerable contribution to the development of late 16th-century north Italian painting and also inspired the young Caravaggio.

Commissioned by an unknown client in 1530, *Tobias and the Angel* (above) shows, in front of a wooded

Opposite page:
Giovanni Girolamo Savoldo
Portrait of a Man in Armor (*Gaston de Foix*), ca. 1529
Oil on canvas, 91 x 123 cm
Musée du Louvre, Paris

Referred to as a portrait of the French commander Gaston de Foix, who fell in Ravenna in 1512, from the 17th century right up into the 19th century, the painting was later also interpreted as an allegory or even a self-portrait. Since the rediscovery of the artist's signature on the note visible in the background mirror, the attribution as a work by Savoldo can no longer be doubted.

background, the episode, popular since early Christian
times, from the apocryphal Book of Tobit. During his
journey from Nineveh to Ekbatana, Tobias catches a fish
in the Tigris. At the behest of the Archangel Raphael
accompanying him, Tobias grabs the fish and removes its
heart, liver, and gall bladder, whereby, at the end of the
adventurous journey, the gall bladder miraculously heals
the blindness of Tobias' father. First documented in
1910, and initially attributed to Titian, this painting
proves itself to be typical of Savoldo's work, not least
through the extremely fine painting of the silkily shining
and softly flowing garments in comparison to the
atmospherically blurred background.

Painted shortly before, his perhaps most fascinating
Portrait of a Man in Armor (below) shows a man clad in
à shining breastplate who—leaning slightly to the side
and looking at the viewer—is supporting himself on a
table, set parallel to the picture plane, on which further
pieces of armor lie. In doing so, he is presenting himself
in front of two mirrors set at right angles to each other,
providing not only a view of him from three different
perspectives, but also an extended insight into the room
around him. Notwithstanding the often discussed
question regarding the man's identity, research has
consistently highlighted the optical legerdemain
characteristic of the painting and its significance in
relation to the *paragone*, the contest of the Arts. Even
though many of the 16th-century theoretical writings on
art concerning this subject were composed only after this
work was painted, this painting appears to be an almost
programmatic demonstration of the equality if not
superiority of painting over three-dimensional sculpture;
for, with the help of the painted mirrors, it is also possible
for the painter to display a figure from various angles.

DOSSO DOSSI (CA. 1489–1542)

Dosso Dossi
The Sorceress Melissa (Circe?), ca. 1518
Oil on canvas, 176 x 174 cm
Galleria Borghese, Rome

The title *Circe*, first mentioned in 1790, is still preferred by some researchers who associate the painting with the theme of "female trickery" extremely popular in Renaissance art and literature—north and south of the Alps. Additional evidence in favor of the rival opinion that it is more probably a portrayal of the sorceress Melissa from Ludovico Ariosto's *Orlando furioso* is provided by the original figure of a knight discovered underneath the armor and the animals on the left-hand margin of the painting during X-ray examination of the generally well-preserved painting when it was last restored in 1996. This knight and the men resting in the middle ground to the right could well be the hero Ruggiero and his companions, who are being freed by Melissa from the clutches of the evil sorceress Alcina.

The city of Ferrara, located on the plane traversed by the River Po in the north-east of the Emilia-Romagna, experienced its comparatively short, but all the more vibrant, cultural heyday in the 15th and 16th centuries under the Dukes of the House of Este. In accordance with the fashion of the time, sculptures and coins from antiquity were collected at the ruler's court, palaces were furnished with sumptuous tapestries and "paintings in the new style," and vernacular poetry was fostered: here such outstanding works as the unfinished epic *Orlando in Love* (*Orlando inamorato*) by Matteo Maria Boiardo (1441–1494) and its sequel *The Frenzy of Orlando* (*Orlando furioso*) by Ludovico Ariosto (1474–1533) were composed.

In the field of painting, painters from outside the area, such as Pisanello, Jacopo Bellini, and Andrea Mantegna were brought to the court of Ferrara by Lionello d'Este (1407–1450) during the first half of the Quattrocento. It was only from the middle of the century onward that Ferrara developed a school of painting of its own—although constantly in dialogue with neighboring centers of art. Cosimo Tura (ca. 1429–1495), Francesco del Cossa (ca. 1436–1477), and Ercole de' Roberti (pre-1450–1496) decisively shaped this development and created their most significant works in Ferrara. One example is provided by the sadly only partially preserved fresco cycle in the Palazzo Schifanoia (pages 128–129) depicting the months of the year, uncovered again only at the end of the 18th century.

In the days of Alfonso I (1476–1534) and his son Ercole II (1508–1559), the Ferrara School was dominated by Dosso Dossi (actual name Giovanni Luteri), often working together with his brother Battista; and Garofalo (real name Benvenuto Tisi, ca. 1481–1559), named after his presumed place of birth in the north of the city. Whereas Garofalo showed himself to be clearly influenced by Raphael's compositions following a lengthy stay in Rome, Dossi's mature works are more inspired by the great Venetian painters Giorgione and Titian, even though the painter is also said to have traveled to Rome before settling permanently in Ferrara. Today, it is not known whether he was trained by the above-mentioned Francesco del Cossa or in Venice, or perhaps both.

Despite these largely obscure initial years, Dossi spent most of his life as court painter in Ferrara, where his presence is first documented in 1513. His task as official court artist involved far more than just painting. It also involved designing the decorations for feasts and plays, as well as, for example, the painting and gilding of furniture and wall paneling; in short, almost everything associated with the magnificent décor of a Renaissance court.

Dossi's painting proves to be similarly wide-ranging. Apart from the usual court portraits, he painted—also for clients outside the court—altarpieces and devotional pictures, as well as a range of (in part) very unusual, and today still enigmatic, paintings with allegorical, mythological, and literary themes. These include *The Sorceress Melissa* (page 385), a work that probably made its way to Rome at the turn of the 17th century and is first mentioned in 1650 in a description of paintings on display in the Galleria Borghese: "Una Maga che stà facendo incantesimi,"("a sorceress in the act of performing sorcery").

In front of a more or less Giorgionesque landscape, a young woman with a turban-like headdress is sitting in the middle of a flat, stone oval, or possibly somewhat ineptly shortened representation of a circle. On this oval, as on the book lying on the ground and almost completely covered by her lavish dress, several arabesque characters can be seen that even now have not been deciphered and that were possibly never intended to be deciphered, but only serve to identify the stone area as a magic circle. The same is true of the writing and geometric symbols on the board held by the woman in her right hand while lighting a fire in the chalice beside her with the torch in her left hand.

Should the title *The Sorceress Circe*, listed in the 1790 inventory of Galleria Borghese and still often used today, be correct, then the armor visible on the right-hand margin, the two birds, and the dog staring at the viewer remain a mystery, for it is difficult to associate them with the well-known story of the seductive Circe. The 10th part of the *Odyssey* explicitly states that the sorceress transformed the companions of the hero Odysseus into pigs, and not birds or dogs.

An alternative literary source for interpreting the

picture, the *Orlando furioso* by Ludovico Ariosto mentioned above, was suggested by the art historian Julius von Schlosser in 1900. Begun in 1502, and with a first version published in 1516, this epic "for the amusement and recreation of noblemen and high-minded gentry and ladies" retells in numerous interwoven plots the struggle of Charlemagne's trusted followers against the Saracens threatening France. The author overlays the historical events with motifs from epic accounts of medieval chivalry as well as with numerous legends and fables to create a fantastic story featuring a love-sick knight, fairies, magicians, and monsters, as well as adventurous journeys to the far corners of the world. When the hero Ruggiero and his followers are turned into animals, plants, and stones by the evil sorceress Alcina, Ruggiero's lover Bradamante and the sorceress Melissa come to their aid. Melissa successfully restores the captive knights to human form and returns their weapons to them.

Should the woman in Dossi's painting, created just after the book was published and probably intended for Duke Alfonso I, really be Melissa, then the armor, the three animals, as well as the peculiar puppet-like figures on the trees behind them would indeed be considerably less puzzling; and the three men in the middle ground to the right that almost remind the viewer of Titian's *Concert Champêtre* (pages 294–295) could be understood as a reference to the freed knights. However, the question still remains as to why the painter should have chosen the sorceress Melissa to be the picture's main figure. A possible explanation can be found in the third Canto of *Orlando furioso*: in the cave tomb of the magician Merlin, Melissa shows the beautiful Bradamante the future offspring of the House of Este, whereby Bradamante herself and her lover Ruggiero are revealed to be the family's first parents. In the light of this, Dossi's painting—as well as the epic itself— may

be understood as a work exalting the Este family, since it presents the "prophetess" of the ducal line.

Another painting—depicting, as peculiar as it may seem, Jupiter, the father of the gods, painting butterflies (left)—has proven to be a lot more enigmatic and its research accordingly contentious. The figure of Jupiter is easy enough to identify due to the bundled thunderbolts lying in front of him; as is the figure of Mercury with his winged helmet and caduceus, seated beside him and turning toward a woman approaching from the right, urging her to be quiet by pressing a finger to his lips. But, as far as the identity of the flower-crowned female figure and the statement the painting is intended to make are concerned, opinions differs greatly.

Some interpret the painting as a free adaptation of a text by Leon Battista Alberti, in which the personification of Virtue (*virtus*) wants to complain to Jupiter over her unjust treatment at the hand of both gods and humans, but is turned away by Mercury. Others tend to see it as an allegory. According to this latter interpretation, Jupiter represents artistic creativity, and the young woman the virtue of not allowing oneself to be mislead by the fickleness of fate; so that Mercury is to be understood as fulfilling his role as protector of knowledge and art. Furthermore, the painting has also been interpreted from an astrological point of view, and even on the basis of Dossi's horoscope. It is therefore hardly surprising that some believe they recognize a self-portrait of the artist in the figure of the father of the gods, who here appears in the guise of a creative god (*deus artifex*). Although it will be a long time before the last word is spoken about the iconography of this highly distinctive painting, it can hardly be doubted that the art of painting itself is one of its themes.

Henrik Engel

Dosso Dossi
Jupiter, Mercury, and Virtue, 1520s
Oil on canvas, 112 x 150 cm
Karolina Lanckaronska Collection, Wawel Castle, Cracow

Many of Dossi's diverse range of works are considered almost impossible to interpret due to their unusual, and at times almost esoteric, themes. But there can be little doubt that this work, presumably painted for Duke Alfonso I and today to be found in Cracow, takes the art of painting as its theme—at least on a superficial level. It depicts no less a figure than Jupiter, the father of the gods, painting butterflies. However, opinion in respect of the identity of the woman kneeling in a yellow dress on the picture's margin on the right, and of the deeper interpretation of the picture as a whole, is far from unanimous. Traditionally thought to be the personification of virtue (*virtus*), the young woman has also been interpreted as Virgo or Flora.

Florentine Mannerists

Rosso Fiorentino (1494–1540)

Although the concept of Mannerism established itself in art historiography in the course of the 20th century as a largely neutral designation of a style and era, in general it still retains a negative connotation. Thus today anything that appears unnatural, exaggerated, eccentric, or affected is called mannered. As an art-historical term, Mannerism refers to European art during the period between Renaissance and Baroque, that is, the years from about 1520 to 1600. A fine argument could be educed here about the intelligibility of such definitions and boundaries, as with many another concept relating to style or era, particularly since during this period there were artists whose works could be described as "Neoclassical" rather than "Mannerist," and even positively "anti-Mannerist." As a result, it is not surprising that there are occasional references to the "Late Renaissance" in the context of the years following the death of Raphael in 1520, or to "Neoclassicism" when we turn to, for example, the Carracci family of artists in the Bologna of the late 16th century.

When Vasari speaks of *maniera*, then it is usually in the sense of *bella maniera*, and thus implicitly in the sense of the *maniera di Michelangelo*, by which he not only suggests what young painters should take as their models, but also expresses the view that the art of the early Cinquecento reached a quality with Raphael, Leonardo, and the "divine" Michelangelo that was hardly to be surpassed in the future. In the word *maniera* Vasari himself coined a term which a full two hundred years later was to become the, at first derogatory, designation of the art of his own time. It was supposedly an art of decadence after the great flowering, an art on which critics comment that with its elongated, excessively restless and distorted figures, as the art historian Ernst Gombrich aptly formulated it, it imitated the manner rather than the spirit of Michelangelo's work.

Among the earliest and most important representatives of Mannerism is the Florentine painter Giovanni Battista di Jacopo di Guaspare, better known under the nickname referring to his red hair, Rosso or Rosso Fiorentino. As Vasari says about his only scantily documented early years, the painter at first modeled his work on Michelangelo's compositions. At the same time, Vasari creates the picture of a brilliant loner, who would accept no teacher who could not compete with Michelangelo. Today, however, we assume that Rosso received his training together with Pontormo in the workshop of Andrea del Sarto.

After staying for about a year around 1520 in Volterra, southwest of Florence, where he created his superb *Deposition from the Cross* (page 391), the young Rosso was first drawn back to Florence and finally, in 1524, to Rome, where he hoped for commissions from the recently elected Medici Pope Clement VII, who came from his own region. But as early as 1527, the year of the devastating Sack of Rome by the German Emperor Charles V's mercenaries, he was forced to flee the city. In 1530, after a series of stopovers in the smaller centers of art in eastern Tuscany and Umbria, thanks to a recommendation by his friend, the poet Pietro Aretino

Rosso Fiorentino
Moses Defending the Daughters of Jethro, 1523
Oil on canvas, 160 x 117 cm
Galleria degli Uffizi, Florence

Unlike Botticelli (Volume I, pages 600, 601), Rosso Fiorentino depicted the Midianite shepherds and Moses as naked or only very scantily clad athletes. Nude figures in paintings with biblical subjects were by no means a rarity at that time. Nevertheless, Rosso's composition, with the protagonist's naked genitals placed exactly in the center, is exceedingly daring, and it was only a little later that works such as this made feelings run high among the Catholic clergy, and finally led to the decree on images issued by the Council of Trent, as a result of which the genitals of all Michelangelo's figures in the Sistine Chapel were concealed by the notorious painters of the "fig-leaf campaign."

nude figure, the Michelangelesque, muscular Moses, undoubtedly about to emerge as victor. With legs apart, he stands in the center of his opponents, who are already lying on the ground, stretched toward the observer, and bends far forward, his face contorted with rage, raising his arm to deliver a further mighty blow. Behind him, strangely calm, stand the sheep of the seven daughters of the priest Jethro. Of these, the young woman dressed in delicate blue, shrinking back from a final attacker approaching from the left, must clearly be Jethro's daughter Zipporah, the later wife of Moses.

Figures shown in strong foreshortening already appear in paintings of the Early Renaissance, for example in Mantegna's *Lamentation over the Dead Christ* in Milan (page 79). But the tumult depicted by Rosso Fiorentino is not determined by pronounced foreshortening effects alone, but also by extremely contorted bodily postures, violent movements, and strongly expressed emotions. It was not least the debate on the hierarchy of the arts, conducted with increasing energy in the course of the 16th century and increasingly intellectualized, that contributed to the popularity of such poses in the painting of the Mannerists. Against the background of the *paragone*, as the debate was called, severely distorted figures, which could, as it were, be seen from several angles, appear as though a reaction to the arguments of the sculptors or their defenders, who saw their creations as being superior to painting because one could walk around them and look at them from all sides.

The *sacra conversazione* on this page may therefore appear all the more conventional, at least at first glance. Rosso painted it only a few years before the Moses painting, for the hospital director of Santa Maria Nuova, the setting being a funerary chapel in the church of Ognissanti. The basic concept of this early work is still in the tradition of the 15th century, while the two cherubs sitting side by side on a step in front of the throne and reading a book show a certain kinship with Venetian pictures of this type (page 140). However, the usual spacious and magnificent throne building is missing. Instead, the Virgin is positively cramped in the tightly bounded space of the image by the four saints—from left to right, John the Baptist, Anthony Abbot, Stephen, and Jerome—and it is hardly surprising that Rosso's painting was refused, for the reason reported by Vasari, that the figures, decked in lurid colors and with darkly shadowed eyes, looked like devils.

One of Rosso's masterpieces, on the other hand, the previously mentioned *Deposition from the Cross* of 1521 in Volterra (page 391), is an enormously dramatic painting. Here the drama and pathos are the result not only of the sorrowing figures in the lower half of the image and the movements circling around Christ in the upper half, but also the powerful, though only slightly differentiated, chiaroscuro and the resulting clear, two-dimensional forms, particularly of the brightly lit garments. This effect is also due to the fact that not all parts of the painting were completed. Against the background of a sky becoming gradually lighter from the upper edge of the image to the low

(1492–1556), he was summoned by the French King Francis I to the court of Fontainebleau, where he was soon entrusted with directing the decoration of the palace with frescoes and stucco work, and where he spent the last ten years of his life.

Rosso's early and intensive engagement with Michelangelo is expressed in hardly any other work as clearly as in a painting executed in Florence shortly after his stay in Volterra, a painting which is probably identical with the one mentioned by Vasari as a "scene in which Moses slays an Egyptian" (page 389). However, Vasari himself apparently never saw this painting, which soon went to Francis I in France and returned to Florence only toward the end of the 16th century. Otherwise it would probably have struck him that Rosso was not depicting the murder of an Egyptian, but the defense of the daughters of the priest Jethro against the Midianite shepherds, a subject only very rarely portrayed in painting.

One need only compare Rosso's bold composition with the fresco created about four decades earlier by Botticelli of the *Trials of Moses* (Volume I, pages 600, 601) to see how fundamentally the perception of art changed during this relatively short period of time and what is meant by "Mannerism." With Botticelli, dramatic movement of the figures is restricted to the scene at the lower right edge of the mural—and here indeed the moment is depicted when Moses slays the Egyptian overseer of the Israelite laborers. The driving away of the shepherds from the spring, recognizable behind that scene, appears almost innocuous in comparison. Raising a cudgel, but with an expressionless face, Moses, shown in almost statuesque fashion, points the way to the two young men, who seem equally unmoved.

In contrast, Rosso has taken the subject as an opportunity to portray a violent brawl, with the central

Rosso Fiorentino
The Madonna and Child with Four Saints, 1518
Oil on wood, 112 x 141 cm
Galleria degli Uffizi, Florence

Undoubtedly the most unusual figure in this early work by Rosso is John the Baptist, who stands on the left. Contrary to biblical as well as pictorial tradition, instead of the cloak of camel hide specifically mentioned in the gospels of Matthew and Mark, he wears an undergarment of leopard skin. Above all, however, we notice his bright red hair, which suggests that the painter was making a double reference to himself, that is, to his forename, today no longer very common, of Giovanni Battista (John the Baptist), and his nickname Rosso, which referred to his red hair.

Opposite page:
Rosso Fiorentino
The Deposition from the Cross, 1521
Wood, 335 x 198 cm
Pinacoteca, Volterra

This monumental altar painting, executed in Volterra for the Cappella della Croce di Giorno in San Francesco, is signed at the foot of the ladder which leans against the Cross (*RUBEVS FLO. FAC A. S. MDXXI*), but not all parts of it have been completed. This is evident above all where parts of the underdrawing still show through, allowing us to read individual notes by the painter on the colors he intended to use. This incomplete state also explains the chiaroscuro contrasts, which are distinctive, but not worked out in every detail. This is particularly noticeable in the garment of the sorrowing Apostle John, who turns away from the Cross in his grief, burying his face in his hands.

horizon, but entirely cloudless and thus positively insubstantial and abstract in appearance, in which Emil Maurer (2001) saw an "analogy with the former gold ground," rises the tall Cross, from which the body of Christ, smiling because his spirit has been released, is being brought down. Even if it cannot be denied that the skin of humans changes color after death, and although Cennino Cennini in his *Libro dell'arte*, published around 1390, explicitly recommends the use of green pigments when depicting a corpse, the flesh-color of the body of Christ, only a few hours dead at the moment being shown here, is exaggerated, in striking contrast to the brilliant red garment of Mary Magdalene, who kneels in front of the Cross and the Mother of God.

Much less pronounced are similar color contrasts in a *Lamentation over the Dead Christ* (page 393), painted in the following decade, during Rosso's final creative period at the French royal court. Nevertheless, this picture too is not lacking in drama. The painter achieves this by means of a scene lit as though by a shaft of light falling from the left, as well as the related shadow formations, now nuanced in subtle detail, but most of all through the figure of the Virgin Mary mourning her son, spreading her arms across the entire width of the painting, in front of the merely suggested cave of the tomb, and gazing at the observer as though to appeal for sympathy.

The intensity of the already comparatively muted colors is continuously reduced from front to back, so that, despite the severely constricted image space, an impression of great depth and three-dimensionality is created. This effect is additionally enhanced by the figure of Mary Magdalene placed at the front left edge,

Agnolo Bronzino
Pietà, 1529
Oil on wood, 105 x 100 cm
Galleria degli Uffizi, Florence

In front of a hilly landscape seen in perspective, becoming blue in the distance, in which three crosses on the left allude to the Passion that has just been endured, the body of Christ leans against a rock, its pale skin bathed in evening light. The Virgin Mary and Mary Magdalene sit behind him in silent sorrow. Although the figure of the Apostle John, mentioned by Giorgio Vasari and indeed usual in paintings of this subject, is missing, this work —as is confirmed by the payment documents found a few years ago—is identical to one which Rosso, according to Vasari, painted for the convent of Santa Trinità in Florence.

Rosso Fiorentino
The Lamentation over the Dead Christ,
ca. 1530–1540
Oil on wood, 127 x 163 cm
Musée du Louvre, Paris

In front of the Virgin Mary, who spreads her arms across the entire breadth of the image to express her grief, the body of her son is laid by Mary Magdalene and the Apostle John on two cushions, on which the family arms of the commissioning client Anne de Montmorency—small dark blue eagles on an orange ground—can be discerned. De Montmorency, the senior general of the king of France, had commissioned the painting for the chapel of his chateau at Ecouen, north of Paris. It probably remained there until bought by the Louvre in the late 18th century.

since she leans so far forward toward the observer that she seems almost to break through the surface of the painting. As far as the choice of color tones for the clothing of both Mary Magdalene and the despairing Mother of God is concerned, Rosso's painting shows clear parallels to an early work of his younger Florentine colleague Agnolo Bronzino (page 392), who had studied with Rosso's fellow-pupil Jacopo da Pontormo. This almost square painting, probably executed for the convent of Santa Trinità in Florence, was for a time attributed to Rosso, until the payment documents found a few years ago confirmed the authorship of Bronzino as well as the date of 1529.

Unlike Rosso's *Lamentation over the Dead Christ*, recognizable as a Mannerist work not least because of

the torsion of the unusually muscular back of the scantily clad Apostle John at the right-hand edge of the work, the *Pietà* painted only a few years earlier by Bronzino gives a positively classical impression (page 392). Here we can hardly speak of the elongated limbs, distorted proportions, artificial movements, or exaggeratedly emotive gestures of Mannerism. Rather, this painting achieves its emotional effect through the anguished expressions of the two women and the body of Christ, bathed in the evening light. Particularly convincing is the way in which the painter has captured the backward-slumped head and the right hand lying limply on the ground.

Henrik Engel

JACOPO CARRUCCI, CALLED PONTORMO (1494–1557)

Pontormo
The Visitation (detail), 1528/29
Oil on wood, 202 x 256 cm
San Michele, Carmignano

The painting has lost none of its evocative power, with its swirl of glorious colors, captivating gestures, and the entreating glances exchanged by the protagonists. The visionary aspect of the scene is intensified by the magical, glowing quality of Pontormo's painting. Ever since the late Middle Ages, the Visitation has been considered one of the main events depicted in the Life of the Virgin. The Evangelist Luke describes the meeting of the two pregnant women as follows (1: 41–42): "And it came to pass, that, when Elizabeth heard the salutation of Mary, the babe leaped in her womb; and Elizabeth was filled with the Holy Ghost: And she spake out with a loud voice, and said, Blessed art thou among women, and blessed is the fruit of thy womb." Originally painted for the Villa Pinadori in Carmignano, the painting has been in the local parish church since 1740.

The Florentine painter Jacopo Carrucci, called Pontormo after his birthplace in Tuscany, was forgotten by history for more than three centuries. Soon after his death a mantle of silence descended upon him; even his exact date of death is obscure.

With a painter of the quality of Pontormo, who was active in one of the most important centers of the Italian Renaissance, such a disappearance into obscurity must seem somewhat odd. None of Pontormo's Florentine contemporaries experienced a similar fate. Pontormo's teacher, Andrea del Sarto, only eight years older than he, and the painter Fra Bartolomeo, for example, have remained well known across the centuries, not to speak of the great ones of the era, Leonardo, Raphael, and Michelangelo. Apart from a mention in the Florentine chronicle of Francesco Bocchi of 1591, there are hardly any references to Pontormo. None of the connoisseurs of Italian art of the 17th and 18th centuries or the Renaissance specialists of the 19th century pay any attention to him, although his frescoes and paintings for the most part remain in their original locations in and around Florence.

Pontormo is a typical discovery of the early 20th century. Apparently it was only the eyes of those influenced by modern artistic movements such as Impressionism, Expressionism, and Cubism that were able to grasp the outstanding significance of his painting. Soon after 1900, several brief essays herald an awakening interest in Pontormo. In the course of the 20th century, Pontormo's exquisite painting increasingly found recognition and admiration. With Rosso Fiorentino, he is now considered one of the two main representatives of early Florentine Mannerism.

The bold perspectives and severe formalism of his compositions, the stylized gestures far from any idea of naturalism, the artificially bunched-up garments, which seem to allow free rein to the play of color surfaces, the fearful, meditative expression of many faces in Pontormo's paintings—all this in the early 20th century seemed a harbinger of artistic freedom in which the painter's subject is eloquently expressed.

But if we read Giorgio Vasari's account of the life of his contemporary Pontormo, one thing strikes us immediately: all those paintings which seemed so incredibly modern and gave the greatest aesthetic pleasure to the 20th-century observer are more or less severely condemned by Vasari.

This is true of the *Deposition* in Santa Felicità (page 403) as well as of the superb fresco that Pontormo created around 1520 for the Medici villa at Poggio a Caiano. Vasari's life of Pontormo manifests a clearly twofold view of the artist: the extraordinary and highly promising early work of the artist is followed by a lamentable decline in quality in the second half of his life. According to Vasari, Pontormo must have been a sort of infant prodigy in painting. Even Raphael and Michelangelo had recognized the extraordinary gifts of the young painter and forecast a great future for him. Unfortunately, however, Vasari suggests, Pontormo's restless spirit had always searched for novelty and shamefully forsaken the path of good Italian models that he had entered upon. Vasari does not mince his words in criticizing Pontormo, reprimanding all his works after his early period, executed from about 1520, as bizarre, extravagant, and immoderate.

In the *Visitation*, created for the village church in Carmignano (opposite page), the meeting between the two biblical female figures Mary and Elizabeth, Pontormo finds an effective depiction for the approach and greeting of the two women, who both announce their pregnancy. The later significance of their sons, Jesus and John the Baptist, still being carried in the womb at the time of the meeting of Mary and Elizabeth, is translated by Pontormo into an exquisitely picturesque rendering of their garments. The movement of the folds and the brilliant colors, as well as the impressive gesture of greeting, capture all our attention.

The correspondence between the colors and gestures formally links the group of four figures together.

The two female figures behind Mary and Elizabeth in Pontormo's painting are enigmatic, for there is no iconographic justification for them. Possibly these figures, gazing straight ahead out of the picture, can be explained as an artistic duplication of the protagonists, who are seen from the side. As an echo within the image, they embody, on a second level, a variation on the event shown in the foreground. The simultaneous depiction of the same figures in the same painting would at least be a frequently tested method of representation, even if this example represents a highly concentrated version of it.

The four tall female figures, with their formally corresponding postures, look as though arranged around an imaginary axis of symmetry. Their changing positions embody an artistic principle that was called by the Latin term *varietas* (diversity) in the art literature of the period and was regarded as a main criterion for a successful composition. The artistic exaggeration of the depiction of the figures not only gives this altar painting a spiritual character, which may have been Pontormo's intention, but can also be described in postmodern terms such as, for example, fictionality, simultaneity, and immateriality. In addition there are further formal features that give a very modern look to the image: the serial nature of the very arrangement of figures; the correspondence of the figures at front and back, which intensifies into a compact structure; the autonomous-looking color surfaces, their idiosyncratic coloration, and the skilful system of related shades of color.

Meanwhile, not only is there a hint of the modern about Pontormo's painting; his personality too clearly embodies the type of the modern artist. Vasari describes Pontormo as a sensitive intellectual, a reclusive eccentric, a melancholic. References to his homosexuality underline his otherness. Like Michelangelo, Pontormo had no interest in elegant clothing. When he came into some money around 1530, he bought, rather than some imposing mansion in Florence, that dwelling so impressively described by Vasari as a tower-like refuge: "The room where he slept and sometimes worked was approached by a wooden ladder which he drew up after him, so that no one could come up without his knowledge or permission." No wonder that Pontormo, with such bohemian characteristics attributed to him, could lastingly capture the imagination of the 20th century.

A further circumstance that seems positively to highlight Pontormo's modernity: in the last years of his life, Pontormo kept a sort of journal, entering brief notes in a simple notebook daily from January 1554 to October 1556, now published under the title *Il libro mio*. Now, one should not imagine this to be a journal in the modern, post-Romantic sense. On the contrary, the brief notes on the sluggish progress of work on the frescoes in the choir of San Lorenzo in Florence, the stereotypical records of meals eaten, the related entries on his physical health, on bowel movements, weather conditions, and astronomic constellations, reveal disappointingly little about the writer's personality. Pontormo's writings rather illuminate the great gap between the 16th and 20th centuries. An understanding of Pontormo's *Il libro mio* as evidence of a life lived will thus be gained only by someone who undertakes a reconstruction of its content based on the thinking of the time. In the commentaries on the most recent editions of the text, accordingly, there are references to the modern understanding of a total design for living derived from classical sources, which links the microcosm of man with the macrocosm, and recommends self-observation as part of a way of life based on dietetics and spirituality.

It is only the recollection of circumstances and categories of the period of history when Pontormo wrote his journal that allows us to form a lively image of the artist. This procedure is also advisable when studying his painting. A limiting factor here, however, is that the development of the artist's œuvre as well as the course of his life are available to us only in highly fragmentary form. Pontormo spent most of his sixty-two years in Florence, undertook few journeys, and these did not lead him further than the environs of Tuscany. His early work of the 1510s was executed exclusively in Florence. He created his major works in the following decade. The fresco in the Medici villa in Poggio a Caiano was completed in 1521, the frescoes in the Certosa di Galluzzo were painted between 1523 and 1525, and subsequently Pontormo worked until 1528 on the decoration of the Capponi chapel in Santa Felicità.

Relatively little is known about the time from 1530 up to his death. His great decorative works of the 1530s and 1540s in the Medici villas in Careggi and Castello have become as dilapidated as the masterly late work in the choir of San Lorenzo, on which Pontormo worked for more than ten years. Without the loss of these works, Pontormo's importance as an artist would certainly be more visible to us today.

As far as the beginning of his artistic career is concerned, we rely on the partly contradictory information in Vasari's biography of him. Pontormo is said to have moved several times from one teacher's workshop to another. Even Leonardo da Vinci is said to have taught him. In the early summer of 1508, however, Leonardo was already busy again at the court of the Sforzas in Milan, which leads us to conclude that any contacts between him and Pontormo were, if anything, sporadic, but by no means amounted to a formal teaching relationship. Around 1511/12, Pontormo, together with Rosso Fiorentino, was demonstrably an apprentice and co-worker of Andrea del Sarto. Andrea's workshop, after Leonardo, Michelangelo, and Raphael had left Florence, was among the most modern in the city. Andrea del Sarto, who is considered, next to Fra Bartolomeo, the most important master of the Florentine High Renaissance, certainly exercised the greatest influence on the young Pontormo. The glowing colors of Andrea del Sarto's paintings, the monumentality of his figures and the clarity of his composition form the starting point for Pontormo's first works. This is clearly expressed in the great fresco of the *Visitation* (page 397), which Pontormo painted

Pontormo
The Visitation,
1514–1516
Fresco, 392 x 337 cm
Chiostrino dei Voti, Santissima Annunziata, Florence

A lively and animated crowd surrounds Mary and Elizabeth as they greet each other. In contrast to the active movement of the figures, the architectural background with its niches provides a symmetrical organization of the picture space reminiscent of antiquity. Above the niche of the apse, Pontormo's *Sacrifice of Isaac* represents an unusual iconographic feature, functioning as a picture within the picture. The *Visitation* was the first major work commissioned from Pontormo. The fresco is part of a cycle depicting scenes from the Life of the Virgin executed by several Florentine artists in the cloister of the monastery church Santissima Annunziata.

for the forecourt of the church of Santissima Annunziata in Florence between 1514 and 1516.

Here a relationship with Andrea del Sarto in a double sense is evident. Pontormo's early masterpiece manifests borrowings from his former teacher, and not only in terms of the portrayal of the figures and the coloration. This fresco bears witness to the artist's declared intention to compete with the achievements of Andrea del Sarto's painting, to which the location adds considerably. In the cloister-like forecourt of the church, a whole cycle of frescoes showing images of the Life of the Virgin Mary was created, each section of the wall being painted by a different Florentine artist. According to Vasari, the Servite monks who commissioned the work positively banked on Pontormo's ambition, "thinking that the competition with the other masters who had worked there would spur him to produce something extraordinarily fine." In order to judge Pontormo's achievement fully, one must see his fresco in the context of the whole cycle. His *Visitation*, placed in the eastern corner of the forecourt between Franciabigio's *Marriage of the Virgin Mary* and Rosso's *Assumption*, appears decidedly more monumental in structure. With regard to the coloration, however, Pontormo adjusts his picture to the neighboring frescoes. In the opposite corner, Andrea del Sarto had painted his fresco the *Birth of the Virgin* in 1513/14, experimenting with asymmetrical groupings (opposite page).

Asymmetry is also the formal criterion in Pontormo's rhythmically moving group composition that lends tension to the image (page 397). Pontormo uses an isosceles triangle as the basis for the arrangement of the two protagonists Mary and Elizabeth. These two female biblical figures are shown in slight perspective on a series of steps. In placing St. Elizabeth in a kneeling position below Mary, who is standing, Pontormo transfers the motif of the steps to the composition of the figures. As if spontaneously, this results in a rising and a descending line, which provide a formal cohesion in the arrangement of the composition of several figures.

Without resorting to the usual pyramidal scheme, Pontormo depicts the superior position of Mary, which is particularly justifiable in this location, since the church of the Santissima Annunziata is dedicated to Mary, the Queen of Heaven. Thus Pontormo's fresco shows itself to be a work handling the story to be told in accordance with the significance of the location and its supporting environment. A further detail clarifies the reference to the location of the wall painting. The treatment of light within the image corresponds exactly to the light conditions in the forecourt of the monastery, so that the natural local light only enhances the impression of the image. Pontormo's art shows itself at this early stage to be already extremely complex and well thought out. The inclusion of external conditions such as architecture and light and the dialogue with another work of art in the immediate proximity are qualities frequently found in Pontormo.

In 1523, when the plague began to rage in Florence, Pontormo took quarters in a Carthusian monastery to the south of the city. For the cloister of the Certosa di Galluzzo, he painted five lunette frescoes with scenes from the Passion of Christ, which are today in a dilapidated condition despite several restorations. In his detailed commentary on the Carthusian frescoes, Vasari particularly stressed the fact that Pontormo had extensively—and in his view excessively—relied on Albrecht Dürer's graphic reproductions. And indeed several figures in the images are easily recognized as being inspired by Dürer's wood engravings. Vasari complains that from about 1520 Pontormo had diverged from his own good style, which his natural talent and industrious practice had bestowed on him. The blame for this lay with his excessively one-sided study of the prints of the German artist, which at that time had reached Italy in large editions. Vasari's arguments here are unmistakably patriotic. His polemic against the *maniera tedesca* (German style) was part of a long tradition in Italy that goes back to the cathedral of Milan built in the Gothic style in the late 14th century; more than a hundred years later, Raphael held forth on the barbaric ugliness of the Gothic arch. In Vasari's day, Italians felt an even greater sense of superiority over northern Europeans in view of the many recently excavated classical works of art.

To be fair, Vasari's vehement criticism is not directed against Dürer himself, whom he sincerely admired. But he finds it highly improper for an Italian to make use of pictorial languages that are foreign to his nature. For Vasari, it is simply contrary to nature for Pontormo to move so far from his own predispositions. Behind this is the idea that *maniera* or style affects an artist's whole personality and behavior. This attitude is clearly expressed in Vasari's commentary on another work also created by Pontormo for the Carthusian monks. *Supper at Emmaus* (page 401), a large-format painting on canvas, again derives in iconographic and thematic terms from a Dürer engraving. But this time, Vasari's comments are entirely positive: Pontormo had painted this work "without forcing his nature … and, as he followed his genius, it proved a marvelous success." Vasari particularly praises the lifelike portraits of the monks who stand behind Christ and wait on him. Thus it is the lifelike and natural that Vasari prizes most in a painting. He may also have admired in Pontormo's Emmaus painting the realistic depiction of glasses, plates, and bread arranged on the table in the manner of a still-life. The painting originally hung in the refectory of the Carthusians. Housed in a stone frame in such a way that the scene was observed as though through a door, the painting was an invitation to take part in the meal with Christ.

As Vasari stresses, Pontormo decided around 1530 to follow the art of Michelangelo. And in a clear reference to his life of Michelangelo, in what follows Vasari sketches an image of Pontormo that pursues this decision even to the way in which he conducted his life. The struggle of the artist working in isolation in San Lorenzo on his masterpiece, which has not survived to the present day, described by Vasari manifests clear parallels with Michelangelo's self-denying struggle for the ceiling frescoes in the Sistine

Andrea del Sarto
The Birth of the Virgin, 1513/14
Fresco, 413 x 345 cm
Chiostrino dei Voti, Santissima Annunziata, Florence

Pontormo's teacher, Andrea del Sarto, was also involved in the creation of the cycle illustrating the Life of the Virgin in the cloister of the monastery church Santissima Annunziata. His depiction of the Birth of Mary in an elegant interior is characterized by a great wealth of detail, something not found in the work of Pontormo. What both master and pupil share, however, is the use of elaborately dressed female figures that are placed in an irregular pattern throughout the scene and dominate the pictorial space.

Chapel. A tendency toward brooding and self-doubt, loneliness and melancholy, are further characteristics attributed to both artists by Vasari. But in a modern reading of Vasari's *Lives* we can observe, before all the psychological description, a characterization in accordance with the works of the artists, which underlines the uniqueness and special position of the works created by Michelangelo as well as by Pontormo. Pontormo's engagement with Michelangelo is multi-layered and varies according to his different phases of work. Let us therefore turn once again to the 1520s and a high point of Pontormo's art, the altar panel of the *Deposition* in the Capponi Chapel of Santa Felicità (page 403), the picture that gave the impetus to the rediscovery of Pontormo in the 20th century and that is today considered the chief master achievement of Florentine Mannerism.

Pontormo undertook his costly decoration of the Capponi Chapel immediately after his work on the Carthusian frescoes in Galluzzo. In the fall of 1525 he returned to the city from his three-year stay at the monastery outside its bounds. There he received the commission to paint the chapel just acquired by Lodovico Capponi, which Brunelleschi had built in 1410 for the Barbadori family in the southwestern corner of the nave of the church of Santa Felicità. Pontormo's painting of the ceiling rotunda had to give way in 1565 to the rebuilding of the church as a court chapel of the Medici, for the famous Vasari Corridor, a secret passage built for the Medici, which links the Palazzo Vecchio with the Palazzo Pitti; it leads through the church at the upper story level, which meant that the dome of the chapel had to be flattened out. Pontormo's painting was thus lost. The fresco of the *Annunciation* on the west wall of the chapel (pages 404, 405), the tondo paintings with the portraits of the Evangelists in the vault pendentives, and the outstanding altar panel with the *Deposition* (page 403) were preserved.

While in Pontormo's frescoes of the Passion in Galluzzo an increasingly spiritual visual language, almost to be called symbolic, has already developed, with the visionary portrayal of the *Deposition* we are looking at an image in which a multi-layered content is contained in a correspondingly complex composition. This panel, in which Pontormo again proves himself an important iconographer, shows a scene from the Passion of Christ, in which three scenes, the Deposition from the Cross, a *Pietà*, and the Burial, are condensed into one image. The contrived treatment of the biblical story corresponds to the stylized manner of its depiction. With no indications of location, it is composed entirely of the figures of the group around the dead Christ and the fainting figure of Mary. Pontormo's *Deposition* is an image full of movement and at the same time highly moving. Through the manner in which the body of Christ is here presented and offered to our gaze, we as observers are forcefully challenged to participate actively in the events of the Passion, as never again until the 17th century by Caravaggio and Rembrandt. The female figure who hurries toward Mary to comfort her, seen from the back, functions as an identification figure. Sympathy with grief is shown in this painting by means of various emotive gestures; shock at the death of Christ is expressed in a whirlpool of movements. But their graceful lightness reminds us of the merciful salvation of mankind as the center of Christ's sacrificial death. For the almost balletic movements in Pontormo's *Deposition* embody to a high degree what contemporary art literature described as *gracia*, the same term that also characterizes God's grace toward mankind. Pontormo's pictorial invention thus proves to be a visual metaphor for the promise of salvation in the ascension of Jesus, the Son of Man, into the region of the divine and spiritual. For this reason, Salvatore Nigro (1996) has suggested changing the name of the painting to the *Transformation of Christ*.

Pontormo's visual idea in the *Deposition* is substantially supported by the exceptional coloration. Light tones—pink and blue—predominate. To these are added green and orange in various nuances. All these colors seem to shine as though lit by a magic light. This unusual combination of colors suggests a comparison with Michelangelo's tondo the *Holy Family with St. John the Baptist* (Volume I, page 611), which has gone down in history as the *Doni Tondo* after Angelo Doni, who commissioned it. Also comparable is the emphasis that both Michelangelo and Pontormo have placed on the linearity of their compositions. Both artists develop their depictions substantially out of the line that contours the figures, but also, as an internal drawing, ensures a sharp outline for folds in garments, strands of hair, or muscular body parts. With his emphasis on the draftsmanlike in the *Deposition*, Pontormo allies himself to the primacy of *disegno* proclaimed by Michelangelo. In the vocabulary of the day this meant not only drawing, but also the artist's drawing-linked design activity, or, more precisely, his conceptual activity in relation to content.

Iconographically the program of the Capponi Chapel is focused totally on Christ, a rarity, since private chapels in Italy were mostly dedicated to a saint or placed under the patronage of the donor. On the wall to the right of the *Deposition* is the fresco of the *Annunciation* (pages 404, 405). The movements of the archangel and Mary appear as balletic as those observed in the neighboring altar painting. There is a Michelangelesque feeling in the powerful figure of the angel and his dynamically gathered garment. Pontormo, however, transforms it by means of his own softer and more delicate body modeling.

Further references to Christ are seen in the four portraits of the Evangelists in the vault pendentives, who, equipped with quills, act as transmitters of the glad tidings of Jesus. Within the row of four, Pontormo has laid greatest value on the formulation of individual heads, and on the correspondence of gestures and looks. The Capponi Chapel in Santa Felicità has rightly been described as Pontormo's masterpiece. Vasari, however, does not give them his full approval. In the *Deposition* he criticizes the lack of areas of shadow. In addition, the contorted figures of the *Annunciation* fresco showed

Pontormo
Portrait of a Lady with a Dog, ca. 1532/33
Oil on wood, 89 x 70 cm
Städel Museum, Frankfurt am Main

An elegant lady in a bright red dress is shown seated in front of a niche bathed in bright green light and framed by two pilasters. This clash of complementary colors imparts a touch of flamboyance to the representative portrait of the beautiful unknown sitter. The lady's clothes, her jewelry and accessories, as well as the "grotesque" mask decoration of the chair's armrest, all combine to express what at that time must have been a highly modern idiom. The *Portrait of a Lady with a Dog* is further distinguished from Pontormo's early portraits by the artist's use of light. In the former, the sitter is perfectly illuminated. The enamel-like quality of the brushwork is reminiscent of the works of Bronzino, to whom the painting is occasionally attributed.

Pontormo
The Deposition from the Cross, 1525/26–1528
Oil on wood, 313 x 192 cm
Capella Capponi, Santa Felicità, Florence

For the mortuary chapel of the Capponi family in Santa Felicità, Pontormo painted one of his most outstanding works. The composition consists of ten figures interlinked in animated movement and seemingly revolving around an empty central space. They are lamenting the loss of Jesus Christ, who is being carried to his grave held by two angels. In the right-hand corner, another figure (bringing the total to eleven) gazes out of the painting with a face marked by grief: this is Pontormo, who has placed himself amongst the group of the mourners.

"his curious ideas and how he never rested content … his brain was seeking for new fancies and was not content with holding fast to one." Nevertheless, Vasari has to admit that when Pontormo's work in the Capponi Chapel "was finally uncovered … all Florence marveled."

The surmounting of static pictorial patterns by enhancement of the elements of movement, as expressed for example in the Capponi Chapel, characterizes one of the most important artistic achievements in Pontormo's generation. The study of human movement is therefore among the most important abilities of any painter. The observations of the leading art theorist of the Quattrocento, Leon Battista Alberti (1404–1472), had suggested to Renaissance painters the insight that in a "mute" picture, emotions could be conveyed by body movements alone. Only a clearly developed body language was capable of convincing the observer of the event being portrayed and drawing him into the story. In Pontormo's work we can find many examples of emotionally heightened body language, which incidentally goes along with an increasing disregard for narrative accessories, for traditional attributes, and, as in the *Deposition from the Cross*, for indications of space and locality. From the few surviving works of his final years we can conclude that Pontormo's reception of Michelangelo's art was led by interest in various aspects and was more or less intense at various times. The *Portrait of a Lady with a Dog* (above), which is dated to the 1530s, speaks a pictorial language very far from that of Michelangelo. This portrait of a lady, with its cool elegance, from the time of the presumed high phase of Pontormo's Michelangelo studies is therefore also excluded from the work of Pontormo by many scholars and attributed to Bronzino.

The lack of sources makes it difficult to clarify definitively the relationship between Pontormo and Michelangelo. But one thing is certain: Pontormo was a versatile, ambitious, and talented artist, with an unmatched openness to artistic innovation, who could fairly compete with one of the greatest men of his time. The sense of a certain spiritual kinship may have strengthened his choice of model. Like Michelangelo an intellectual artist, as interested in theoretical questions of art as in the practice, Pontormo was able to raise painting to a new level. In 1548, Pontormo replied to Benedetto Varchi's question as to whether sculpture or painting were to be accorded first place with a letter that may be considered his artistic legacy. Of course, painting is a higher art than sculpture for Pontormo, since it demands higher intellectual powers in the artist and does not, like sculpture, require the use of physical effort. Michelangelo too, Pontormo claims, proved the "depth of his *disegno* and the greatness of his divine intellect" not in his "wonderful sculptures," but in the "miracles of his painting." Pontormo's high claims for art here become quite evident. One thing, in his opinion, raised painting into heavenly spheres: the painter's will "to surpass nature, by breathing the spirit of life into his figure, allowing it to appear alive and making it two-dimensional." And if the painter, adds Pontormo in hair-splitting vein, "had considered that God, when he made man, made him not two-dimensional but three-dimensional, as he was so much easier to bring to life, then the painter would not have sought out an object that demands so much art and wonder-working, and is in a way divine."

Doris Krystof

Pontormo
The Annunciation, 1527/28
Fresco, 368 x 168 cm
Capella Capponi, Santa Felicità, Florence

The meeting between Mary and the Angel of the
Annunciation is depicted on the western wall of the
Capponi Chapel. The two figures are separated from
one another by a window. There are almost Baroque
characteristics in the figure of the angel in flight,
his garments billowing out as if from a breeze. The
young Mary responds to the angel's prophecy with
amazement, almost disbelief, as she gracefully turns
to the left towards the source of the glad tidings.

Agnolo Bronzino
Bia, Illegitimate Daughter of Cosimo I de' Medici,
ca. 1542
Oil on wood, 63 x 48 cm
Galleria degli Uffizi, Florence

Bronzino's portraits of the Medici child and the *Portrait of Clarissa Strozzi* painted by Titian about the same time in Venice (page 334) are among the milestones in the history of portrait painting, in so far as they are the oldest known autonomous depictions of children in which the subjects are not posing as "little adults" and representing the pride of their families, but actually captured in all their childishness. If this is more clearly expressed in Titian's painting than with Bronzino, this may be because little Clarissa is only two years old. But even the five- or six-year-old Bia, who may no longer have been alive at the time the picture was executed, can, despite her comparatively stiff posture, hardly disguise the fact that she would rather be otherwise occupied.

AGNOLO BRONZINO (1503–1572)

Agnolo Bronzino (properly Agnolo di Cosimo di Mariano), whose nickname, used by himself in many signatures, as with Rosso Fiorentino presumably refers to his reddish-brown hair color, was born in Monticello, south of the Arno, at that time near Florence, now part of the city area. After an initial period of study with Raffaellino del Garbo (ca. 1466–1524), he became the pupil and finally for many years the co-worker and close friend of Pontormo, who was barely ten years his senior. Important proofs of their productive collaboration are, for example, the cycles of frescoes at the Carthusian monastery in Galluzzo and the Capponi Chapel in Santa Felicità (pages 404, 405). Apart from a long period of activity at the court of Urbino in the early 1530s and short stays in Rome and Pisa, Bronzino lived all his life in Florence. As court painter to the Medici Grand Duke Cosimo I (1519–1574), apart from frescoes, allegorical paintings, and the usual designs for tapestries, theater and festive décor, he created above all a number of exquisite portraits.

But Bronzino was not only a painter and princely decorator. A highly cultured man of letters, according to Benedetto Varchi (1503–1565) Bronzino not only knew by heart the whole *Divine Comedy* by Dante, but was also very familiar with the works of Petrarch; he also wrote a whole series of burlesque and satirical texts, as well as sonnets inspired by Petrarch, including some in honor of his late teacher Pontormo. He was one of the first members of the Accademia Fiorentina, founded under Cosimo I, and in 1563 was a founder member of the Accademia del Disegno. Like Pontormo, Benvenuto Cellini, Vasari, Michelangelo, and others, he took part, with a letter addressed to Varchi, in a debate initiated by the latter on the question of the superiority of painting over sculpture.

Bronzino's brilliant career as court painter to Cosimo I began in the early 1540s with his painting of the private chapel on the second floor of the Palazzo Vecchio of Eleonora of Toledo (1522–1562). Eleonora was the wife of the Grand Duke, and as daughter of the Viceroy of Naples had brought a handsome dowry into the marriage in 1539. At that time, too, Bronzino executed the famous portraits of the many children of the Medici princes, for example the presumably posthumous portrait of Bia, the illegitimate daughter of Cosimo, born in 1536 or 1537 (above). Contrary to the tradition of depicting dead persons in profile, he shows the rosy-faced five- or six-year-old girl, in her costly clothing and jewelry, turned almost entirely toward the observer. Sitting on a chair with curved arms, she looks upright and self-possessed, but also somewhat tired of posing. As though about to leap up from her chair the next minute, she has lifted her left arm from the arm of the chair, while the fingers of her right hand play with her red-gold chain belt, at the end of which hangs a little ball just visible behind her silvery white gown. This is clearly a so-called pomander, a scent ball such as is also to be seen in Titian's *Portrait of Clarissa Strozzi*, painted about the same time in Venice (page 334).

Agnolo Bronzino
The Panciatichi Holy Family, ca. 1540–1548
Oil on wood, 117 x 93 cm
Galleria degli Uffizi, Florence

This memorial picture, painted for the merchant
Bartolomeo Panciatichi, who was also politically active,
is signed *BRONZO FIORE[N]T[INO]* on the stone next
to the feet of the sleeping Christ Child, but not dated.
Most scholars place its execution around 1540, but the
neo-classical or positively anti-Mannerist portions of the
image, such as the balanced composition and the calm
demeanor of all four figures, have given rise to the
presumption that it might equally well have been painted
much later, that is, after Bronzino's stay in Rome in the
late 1540s, and thus under the direct influence of the
works of Michelangelo and Raphael.

The medallion on Bia's necklace, inspired by classical
Roman coins or medals, bears a portrait of her father in
profile, an ingenious picture within a picture. This may
appear odd, since in this way, if the painting was indeed
executed after the girl's death, the dead person would
appear to be living, but the living one would seem to be
already dead. But presumably this initially confusing
effect was intended by the painter, and it may perhaps
be interpreted as expressing the grief of the father, still a
young man himself, over the untimely death of his
daughter. This interpretation of the painting is
supported not least by the lighter circular area of the

ultramarine blue background, resembling a halo,
around Bia's head, and indeed the particular costliness
of the paint itself, obtained from precious lapis lazuli
and thus lending nobility to the subject of the portrait.

Despite his position at the Medici court, Bronzino
found enough time to work for other clients too. He
executed three important paintings for the Florentine
Panciatichi family alone (pages 407, 408, 409), two of
these however, admittedly, shortly before his time as
official court artist.

The merchant and scholar Bartolomeo Panciatichi
(1507–1582), born in France, whose forebears came

Agnolo Bronzino
Bartolomeo Panciatichi, ca. 1540
Oil on wood, 104 x 84 cm
Galleria degli Uffizi, Florence

The old Florentine palazzo of the Panciatichi family, who were originally from Pistoia, lies in the present-day Via Cavour, precisely opposite the Palazzo Medici-Riccardi. The building rising to the right behind the subject of this portrait, with its unmistakable black and white family coat-of-arms, is not however a faithful rendition of this palazzo. Nevertheless, the band of white squares running below the coat-of-arms is a copy of the characteristic decoration of the inner courtyard. In addition, the long curved brackets on the three narrow windows of the palazzo on the left are decorative elements typical of Florentine architecture of the Mannerist period, similar to those to be found in Michelangelo's Medici Library.

from Pistoia, was in his early years a page at the court of Francis I. He had received his humanistic education in Lyon, where he had already come into contact with the various currents of the early Reformation. When he moved to Florence with his wife Lucrezia in the late 1530s, he rapidly developed a political career in addition to his occupation as a merchant. Thus in the mid-1540s he went to France again for a short time as the Grand Duke's envoy. On his return to Florence, he brought back a number of early Reformation writings and was soon part of that comparatively small circle of scholars who were propagating Calvinism there. These activities, however, soon placed him in great difficulties. It was only thanks to the protection of Cosimo that he was able to evade the Inquisition; only his assurance that he

would abandon his involvement with the Reformation enabled him to continue in his various political offices.

The two portraits of Panciatichi and his wife Lucrezia created by Bronzino about 1540 (above, opposite page) may at first hardly seem like companion pieces, despite the approximately matching formats, since the couple, contrary to tradition, do not turn toward each other. However, other elements prove to be highly traditional. Lucrezia, as befits a lady, holds in her hand a prayer book bound in red, matching her dress, and presents herself sitting in an armchair in an indefinable interior setting, in front of a semicircular wall niche. She is flanked by two fluted columns with Ionic and therefore "female" capitals. In contrast, her husband and his dog, the latter at first easily

Agnolo Bronzino
Lucrezia Panciatichi, ca. 1540
Oil on wood, 102 x 85 cm
Galleria degli Uffizi, Florence

At about the same time as Bronzino's Panciatichi portraits were painted, the Florentine humanist Agnolo Firenzuola (1493–1543) was writing his *Dialogo delle bellezze delle donne (Dialogue on the Beauty of Women)* in Prato. Although this was first published in Florence in 1548, one might almost think that the painter had modeled his no doubt idealized portrait of Lucrezia on this text. There the proportions of the female body are compared, in a manner as scholarly as it is amusing, extravagantly and in full detail, with, among other things, classical Roman and Greek vases of the most varied shapes. The ideal picture proposed at the end of a woman beautiful in every respect, as the fictitious partners in the conversation themselves acknowledge, proves a dream hardly to be attained in reality.

overlooked, stands in front of a stone parapet with classicistic ornamentation, behind which the view opens up of a row of various buildings, lit from the left, and of a small area of blue sky. So while the wife is linked with an interior space and thus with domesticity, her husband is placed in the outside world.

Even if the architecture in the portrait of Bartolomeo Panciatichi does not represent a "portrait" of the city of Florence, some details do exemplify characteristics of early Mannerist Florentine architecture. This is true for example of the three windows to be recognized to the left of the subject, whose upper cornices are supported by long curving brackets, very similar to those seen in the two cloisters of the Medici Library, built to plans by Michelangelo a short time earlier.

In addition to these portraits, brilliant in a double sense of the word, Bronzino painted a *Holy Family* for the Panciatichi (page 407), whose precise date still remains contentious. This painting, probably intended for private devotion, shows the Christ Child lying on a costly blue cushion against the background of a cloudy night sky and a castle, above which, to the left, a red banner flies, bearing the family arms of the client. The Virgin Mary, in glowing red clothing, and Joseph, shown contrary to both biblical and pictorial tradition as unusually young, watch lovingly as the boy John the Baptist tenderly approaches the child. According to the old saying about sleep being the little brother of death, the sleep of the holy child is undoubtedly to be understood as a reference to his Passion to come. This interpretation is supported not only by his bodily posture, reminiscent of a *Pietà*, but also by his hardly accidentally crossed feet, and the text of the banderole lying in front of him on the ground, belonging to John, *Ecce agnus dei*, only the word *[A]GNVS*—that is, (sacrificial) lamb—is legible.

As the Bronzino paintings discussed here show, violent motifs of movement, extremely heightened torsion, and strong emotive effects, such as we see for example in Rosso's Moses painting (page 389), which are indeed determined by the subject, are by no means indispensable or exclusive characteristics of Mannerist art. The *Panciatichi Holy Family*, for example, charms us with its positively classical balance of composition and, if we ignore the gloomy clouds above the castle in the background, the notably calm, harmonious atmosphere. Only the neck of the beautiful Madonna may, also because of her slightly inclined head, seem a little too long, and remind us of the *Madonna of the Long Neck* painted by Parmigianino about a decade earlier (pages 30, 415), and thus of one of the earliest works often cited in the context of Mannerism. On the other hand, such over-elongated necks, some even longer—undoubtedly an ideal of female beauty—are certainly to be found in the Quattrocento too. We need only think of Botticelli's *Birth of Venus* (Volume I, pages 494–495).

Apart from the formal criteria already discussed in the context of Rosso Fiorentino, Mannerist painting is sometimes also characterized by an enigmatic quality that is as ingenious as it is confusing. For a humanistic and equally demanding public, a number of intellectually coded paintings were created around the mid-16th century, which positively invited multi-layered and contradictory interpretations. Among Bronzino's most famous and at the same time most enigmatic creations is an allegory acquired in 1860 for the London National Gallery (page 411), which according to Vasari was painted for Cosimo I and sent by him as a diplomatic gift to King Francis I of France.

The dominant figure in the picture is Venus, goddess of love, unmistakably recognized by the pearl jewelry in her hair, the golden ball in her left hand—presumably a reference to the golden apple given to her by Paris as a prize for her beauty—as well as the two billing doves in front at the left. She ardently kisses Cupid, who embraces her, and whose arrow she holds in her raised right hand, almost as a trophy. The amoretto-like boy, running toward her with a little chain of bells on his left ankle, on the point of scattering the pair with rose petals, does not seem to notice that he has stepped on a thorny twig. He clearly incorporates the joys of love, while the other figures have been interpreted in various ways. Thus the old woman screaming and tearing her hair behind Cupid has been interpreted as a personification of lust, jealousy, madness, or even syphilis, which was rife in Europe from the 16th century, and thus the dangers accompanying unchaste love. The female figure to be recognized above, with a mask-like face, has been seen alternately as a personification of night, of betrayal, of foolishness, but also of truth and of oblivion. Meanwhile it is not clear whether she is trying to cover the protagonist with the large blue cloth or to free them from it, or to prevent one or the other action, in conflict with the figure of the Michelangelesque, muscular old man on the opposite side of the image. He is easily identified, on account of his wings and the hourglass seen at his neck, as Kronos (Time) or Saturn.

In accordance with the varying interpretations of individual figures, this painting, which has also been experimentally linked with Bronzino's own writings, has been continually given new titles (*Allegory of Love*; *Luxuria*; *Venus, Cupid, Madness, and Time*; *Truth Unveiled by Time*; the *Unveiling of Lust*; and so on). However, there is agreement—at least to a substantial degree—that the basic theme is love accompanied by multifarious pitfalls and subject to time, in short, transitory earthly love. As a reference to the occasionally deceitful nature of love or, to put it in Petrarchan terms, its equally sweet and bitter taste, in addition to the three theatrical masks at front right, clearly also gazing at the observer, a chimerical figure behind the boy with the roses presents a honeycomb in one hand, while the other holds the end of her scorpion-like spiky tail. She is reminiscent of the monster Geryon described in Dante's *Divine Comedy*, which acts as guardian of the deceivers' eighth circle of hell.

Henrik Engel

Agnolo Bronzino
Allegory of Love (*Venus and Cupid*),
ca. 1540–1545
Oil on wood, 146 x 116 cm
National Gallery, London

This enigmatic picture, painted for Cosimo I de' Medici, was at some unknown point in time trimmed by several centimeters at the lower edge, and has in addition been subjected to a series of over-paintings, intended to conceal portions of the image perceived as offensive or provocative. The buttocks of Cupid, for example, were for a long time covered by a twig of myrtle, and the private parts of Venus by a veil. Only in the course of a restoration carried out in 1958 was the painting, still controversial with regard to its interpretation or even interpretability, freed from such prudish over-paintings.

Parmigianino
Self-Portrait in a Convex Mirror, 1523/24
Wood, dia. 24.4 cm
Kunsthistorisches Museum, Vienna

Many other European Renaissance artists have tackled the multifarious possibilities of the effective use of mirrors in painting. For example, think of the convex mirror in the background of Jan van Eyck's *Arnolfini Wedding* in London, painted as early as 1434, or the so-called *Portrait of Gaston de Foix* by Savoldo (page 383). Parmigianino's exceedingly sophisticated device of not only portraying himself in front of a convex mirror with the resulting distortion, but doing so on a curved surface, and thus giving the impression that the painting itself is a mirror, is unique. It is thus no surprise that the work, as Vasari reports, aroused great amazement and admiration in Pope Clement VII, to whom it was presented by Parmigianino.

Mannerists in Northern Italy and Venice

PARMIGIANINO (1503–1540)

"Inquiring one day into the subtleties of art, he began to draw himself as he appeared in a barber's convex glass, and when he saw all the oddities produced by the curving of the mirror, how the ceiling beams seemed to warp, the doors and all buildings were strangely shortened, he decided to amuse himself by reproducing everything in this way. He had a ball of wood made at a turner's and divided in half, and on this he set himself to paint all that he saw in the glass, including himself, so much like nature that it can be neither appreciated nor believed. … And the work altogether was a happy success, so that the reality was no different from the painting."

With these words of praise, Giorgio Vasari described a truly uniquely subtle self-portrait (page 412), painted by Francesco Mazzola, called Parmigianino from his birthplace, Parma. He had trained in Correggio's workshop, then went to Rome in the summer of 1524 in order to introduce himself as an artist to Pope Clement VII, who had been elected less than a year earlier. As Vasari, who had clearly seen the work himself, further relates, this spectacular painting had a stunning effect and brought the young artist not only the favor of the Pope but also some prestigious commissions and even the reputation of a "second Raphael."

Above left: Parmigianino
Portrait of a Man, ca. 1530–1540
Oil on poplar, 88 x 68.5 cm
Galleria degli Uffizi, Florence

As is suggested by the only partly visible right hand of
the man gazing seriously at the observer, this painting
was trimmed at some unknown time at the lower edge
and sides. For this reason the subject of the relief to be
seen on the right is also not easily determined. A bearded
man can be seen with a young woman kneeling in front
of him and holding an amphora in her hands. If, as has
been variously presumed, the subject is the meeting
between Eliezer of Damascus, sent to Mesopotamia by
Abraham to find a bride for his son, and Isaac's future
wife Rebecca, it would be tempting to imagine that
Parmigianino was commissioned to execute this portrait
on the occasion of a wedding.

Above right: Parmigianino
Portrait of a Woman (Anthea), ca. 1524–1527 or
1535–1537
Oil on canvas, 136 x 86 cm
Galleria Nazionale di Capodimonte, Naples

The white apron, which may seem somewhat unusual
in view of the generally so elegant appearance of this
unknown young woman, has sometimes allowed the
assumption that Parmigianino was here portraying his
maid. However, the study of many other North Italian
portraits of the 16th century has shown that even very
distinguished ladies wore such "aprons."

It is all the more astonishing that the Pope soon passed
on the ingenious little work as a gift to Pietro Aretino,
through whom it was passed on to Venice and, after
some time in the possession of the architect Palladio, to
the court of Emperor Rudolf II in Prague, and finally, in
the 18th century, to the Kunsthistorisches Museum in
Vienna, where it is today still one of the prize exhibits.
The unusually fully documented provenance of the
painting alone allows us to guess at the value that must
have been placed on it from the start. Admittedly,
contrary to Vasari's description, the wooden support is
not a half-ball of wood, and yet the painting is clearly
convex, so that it does indeed convey the impression
of a convex mirror and thus also leaves no room for
doubt that it depicts anyone other than the painter
himself. At the same time, he probably made use of
several mirrors, for otherwise it is hard to explain the
contrast between the extremely distorted-looking space
in which the easel and the painting can only with
difficulty be made out at the right edge, the equally
distorted hand, and the face, which on the other hand
looks as though seen in a flat mirror.

Much less well documented is Parmigianino's
Portrait of a Man (above), presumably created during
the last decade of his life, when, after his successful stay
in Rome had been abruptly curtailed by the sack of the
city in 1527, he was living once again in Northern Italy.
Since the first mention of it in the late 17th century this
painting was for a long time regarded as a further self-
portrait of the artist. This notion however is
contradicted straight away by the hair and eyes,
noticeably darker than in the Vienna picture, of the
bearded man with the strikingly slender, almost
feminine fingers. Various attempts to link him with a
specific individual from Bologna or Parma have so far
not had any convincing results.

The same is true of the splendid *Portrait of a Woman*
in the Museo di Capodimonte in Naples (above). This
three-quarter-length view of a young lady, almost
frontally turned toward the observer with only a slight
turn and a slightly outstretched left leg, wearing a large
marten or sable fur over her shoulder, is in older sources
usually associated with a Roman courtesan known as
Anthea, who is said to have been Parmigianino's
mistress. According to this theory, the painting would
have to be dated to the time of his stay in Rome.
However, the majority of modern scholars see it as a
mature work of the mid-1530s. The identity of the
woman wearing a costly gown of yellow Atlas silk
remains controversial. While some claim her as the
painter's wife, his daughter, or even, because of the white
apron, his maid, others presume that in view of her

Opposite page:
Parmigianino
The Madonna of the Long Neck
(*Madonna dal collo lungo*), 1534–1540
(detail page 30)
Oil on wood, 219 x 135 cm
Galleria degli Uffizi, Florence

The strikingly long neck to which this perfect example of Mannerist painting owes the name by which it is known today, the equally long slender fingers, and the unusually elongated figure of the Madonna (see page 30) correspond to an ideal of female beauty derived from various literary sources. On the other hand the equally marked "Mannerist" proportions of the pillar rising behind the Madonna, with a ratio of about 1:12 between the lower diameter and the height, is contrary not only to any real architecture, but also to most architectural treatises from the classical period (Vitruvius) through the Quattrocento (Alberti) to Serlio and Palladio in the 16th century.

Parmigianino
The Madonna and Child with Mary Magdalene, John the Baptist, and Zechariah (*Madonna di San Zaccaria*), ca. 1530
Oil on poplar, 75.5 x 60 cm
Galleria degli Uffizi, Florence

At first glance one might take the old man in the foreground for Joseph, and thus the whole painting for a depiction of the Holy Family with John the Baptist and Mary Magdalene, particularly since Joseph is certainly sometimes seen with a book, for example in Andrea del Sarto's *Madonna del Sacco* (page 276). The fragmentary writing to be deciphered in the open book, *V PVER.PRO/AN FACE DNI*, can however be completed to form a passage from the song of praise of Zechariah in the Gospel of Luke, which refers to his son John, the later Baptist: *Et tu, puer, propheta altissimi vocaberis; praeibis enim ante faciem Domini parare vias eius* ("And thou, child, shalt be called the prophet of the Highest: for thou shalt go before the face of the Lord to prepare his ways").

striking resemblance to one of the angels in the so-called *Madonna of the Long Neck* (pages 30, 415) she could be a member of the Baiardi family, who commissioned that painting.

Apart from many other fine portraits and wide-ranging fresco cycles, Parmigianino also created a whole series of altar and devotional pictures, such as the *Madonna di San Zaccaria* created around 1530 for the Bolognese Bonifacio Gozzadini (above). In front of a landscape closed off by a range of mountains in the background, the Virgin sits beside Mary Magdalene. On her knee the Christ Child, lost in meditation, is tenderly approached by John the Baptist in his characteristic garment of hides, in a manner reminiscent of Bronzino's *Panciatichi Holy*

Family, painted a good ten years earlier (page 407). Behind the old man Zechariah, sitting at front right, is a classical triumphal arch with an inscription that is difficult to decipher. The word *ZOZIME* in the second line may be a reference to the late classical Egyptian-Greek alchemist Zosimus of Panopolis, which has led to speculation about Parmigianino's alleged passion for alchemy. As Vasari reports in an extremely disapproving tone, in his later years the artist not only severely neglected his painting in favor of these "eccentricities," but also wasted all his money on them, which finally caused his impoverishment and early death. However, the passages in question in Vasari's life of Parmigianino are today generally viewed with great skepticism.

Undoubtedly, Parmigianino's most famous painting next to the Vienna self-portrait, often cited in basic explanations of Mannerism as the perfect example of the style, is the so-called *Madonna of the Long Neck* (pages 30, 415). It was executed only a few years after the *Madonna di San Zaccaria* for the Baiardi family, for the church of Santa Maria dei Servi in the painter's hometown of Parma, but was never completed and has been subjected to the most varied interpretations. The early literature, for example, drew attention to such genuinely conspicuous sensual or erotic elements as the naked leg of the angel approaching with a vase, and the transparent clothing of the Madonna, and cited these as indications of the secularization of religious art by Mannerism. As late as 1928, Nikolaus Pevsner wrote that this image is the "most sophisticated masterpiece of worldly decadence to have been painted in the 16th century."

More recent research, however, has concerned itself on the one hand with the potential literary sources of the ideal of female beauty of the Cinquecento, which is embodied in almost exemplary fashion by this Madonna figure, certainly disproportioned but at the same time charming. Here too the *Dialogo delle bellezze delle donne* by Agnolo Firenzuola, already mentioned in connection with Bronzino, was cited, although it was not written until after Parmigianino's death. On the other hand, the cross on the large vase, mentioned by Vasari but only brought to light again in the last stages of restoration, as well as the vase itself, has diverted attention to the deeply religious content of the painting. The shimmering vase might be an allusion to the Virgin Mary as a pure vessel of the divine conception, or perhaps, because of the cross inscribed on it, also to the Christ Child lying as though crucified on his mother's lap and, significantly, sleeping. The large vase can be seen as a container for ointment and thus in the spirit of the typological interpretations of the Song of Songs ("Thy name is as ointment poured forth"), as a reference to the name of Christ, which means "the Anointed."

Correggio
The Adoration of the Child, ca. 1518–1520
Oil on canvas, 81 x 77 cm
Galleria degli Uffizi, Florence

The mighty column standing on a high pedestal, and pointing heavenward far beyond the border of the image, is a motif frequently used, especially in the Baroque era, to represent emotion. It is found in a very similar form not only in Correggio's great Dresden painting (opposite), but also in Titian's *Pesaro Madonna* (page 313), created about the same time or only a little later, and also anticipating the Baroque.

CORREGGIO (1489/94–1534)

Opposite page:
Correggio
Holy Night, commissioned 1522
Oil on poplar, 256 x 188 cm
Gemäldegalerie Alte Meister, Staatliche
Kunstsammlungen, Dresden

The provenance of this painting, undoubtedly one of Correggio's best, is unusually well documented. Commissioned in 1522 by Alberto Pratoneri, from at least 1530 it adorned his family chapel, dedicated in that year, in the newly built church of San Prospero in Reggio Emilia. From there, in 1640 it became part of the collection of Francesco d'Este in Modena, whose descendants sold it a century later to Augustus III of Saxony.

Parmigianino's most famous pupil was his compatriot from the Emilia, Antonio Allegri, called Correggio after his birthplace near Parma, Reggio, and Modena. In contrast to his teacher, Correggio was among those 16th-century painters whose art can only inadequately be characterized as High or Late Renaissance, Early or pre-Baroque, or above all Mannerist, or can hardly be reduced to one of these concepts alone.

Correggio's work is testimony on the one hand to an intensive engagement with the "classical" Raphael and Michelangelo, as well as with, primarily, the sensitive treatment of light and *sfumato* of Leonardo. Contrary to Vasari's account, it is today presumed that Correggio was actually in Rome about 1518, where he was able to study the ceiling frescoes of the Sistine Chapel and the decoration of the Villa Farnesina. On the other hand, however, some of his works, with their occasionally extremely bold perspectives and evocative fore-shortening effects, as well as the wealth of movement of the figures, already have features that could be called "heralds of the Baroque." And indeed Correggio, about whose own education hardly anything is known for certain, exercised considerable influence both on the Carracci in Bologna and on the next generation of early Baroque painters such as Giovanni Lanfranco from Parma (1582–1647), to name only one.

The eldest of the paintings by Correggio seen here, the small-format *Adoration of the Child* in the Uffizi (page 416), was created around 1518–1520, that is, shortly after the painter's presumed stay in Rome. In the early 17th century, it reached Florence as a gift from the Duke of Mantua, Ferdinando Gonzaga, to Cosimo II de' Medici. In a Neoclassical ruined landscape, the Virgin Mary kneels in a posture as devotional as it is loving before her child, whom she has laid on a stone step on an outspread bundle of hay, placed on the hem of her blue cloak. Apart from the touching intimacy of this scene, its skillfully staged lighting is impressive. While the sun sets behind the hazily blurred hills, which are reminiscent both of Leonardo's landscapes and of Venetian painting, part of the light in the foreground comes from a source to the left outside the image, as is clear from the lower part of the massive column shaft. But more than this, it almost appears as though the Christ Child shines with a light emitted from his own person.

This motif, very popular in European painting from the turn of the 14th century, can be primarily derived from the visions of St. Bridget of Sweden (ca. 1303–1374), in which a celestially bright light is described that is said to have emanated from the Holy Child at his birth. With an unprecedented intensity, hardly attained by later painters, Correggio rendered this overwhelming phenomenon of light in a second painting, in which he makes it the actual theme of the

Correggio
The Rape of Ganymede, 1531
Oil on canvas, 164 x 71 cm
Kunsthistorisches Museum, Vienna

"And to Tros in turn there were born three sons unfaulted, Ilos and Assarakos and godlike Ganymede, who was the loveliest born of the race of mortals, and therefore the gods caught him away to themselves, to be Zeus' wine-pourer, for the sake of his beauty, so he might be among the immortals." In these few words, Homer describes in Book 20 of the *Iliad* the abduction of Ganymede by the Olympian gods. Correggio, however, clearly took as the model for his depiction later sources such as Ovid's *Metamorphoses*, for he shows the father of the gods himself, transformed into an eagle, carrying off the beautiful boy.

nocturnal scene (page 417). This splendid painting, now in Dresden, created for the family chapel of Alberto Pratoneri in Reggio, fascinated Giorgio Vasari. In the second edition of his *Lives*, he expresses himself appreciatively on the figure of the young shepherdess who stands between the crib and a column, which rises up behind the angels floating on clouds and seems to burst through the borders of the image. Dazzled by the bright light, she lifts her hand toward her face, which is almost contorted in pain, while the Madonna, with a calm expression, turns just as lovingly toward her child as in the Uffizi painting, only a few years older.

Apart from many other altarpieces and devotional pictures, in the course of his comparatively short life Correggio also created a series of mythological paintings. From 1530, the year of the coronation of Emperor Charles V, he produced a cycle, still preserved in its entirety today, though scattered between different museums, of depictions of the amorous adventures of Jupiter, the father of the gods (pages 418, 419, 420, 421). This was commissioned by the Duke of Mantua, Federico II, of the Gonzaga family, who came to power in the same year. Whether these pictures were the same as those which according to Vasari were to be presented to the Emperor on his coronation in Bologna is still disputed today, particularly since Vasari mentions only two of the total of four paintings (which moreover he had not even seen himself). Possibly the cycle was also intended for the decoration of the Palazzo del Tè, the

Correggio
Jupiter and Io, ca. 1530
Oil on canvas, 162 x 73.5 cm
Kunsthistorisches Museum, Vienna

The superb figure of Io, who is turning her back to the viewer as she emotionally surrenders herself to Jupiter, the father of the gods, who is hidden in a dark cloud, allows us to guess what fascinated the painters of the Baroque in Correggio's work. It is hardly difficult to imagine how inspiring such a nude must have been to, for example, Peter Paul Rubens (1577–1640), particularly since many engravings of Correggio's works were available at an early stage. It is even possible that Rubens saw this painting himself when he went to Italy in 1600 and was active in Mantua for many years as court painter.

summer residence of the Duke at the edge of the city of Mantua, built at the same time by Giulio Romano, the pupil of Raphael, since it was only years later that the paintings arrived at the court of Philip II in Spain, and finally, by complex routes, at the museums in Vienna, Berlin, and Rome.

These paintings, inspired by Homer, Ovid, Lucan, and other classical authors, show the divine seducer, Jupiter, who repeatedly takes new shapes in order to approach the objects of his desire without being caught by his jealous wife, Juno. Thus Ovid writes in his *Metamorphoses* about the abduction of the Trojan prince Ganymede: "The king of the gods once burned with love for Phrygian Ganymede, and to win him Jupiter chose to be something other than he was. Yet he did not deign to transform himself into any other bird,

than that eagle, that could carry his lightning bolts. Straightaway, he beat the air with deceitful wings, and stole the Trojan boy, who still handles the mixing cups, and against Juno's will pours out Jove's nectar." In Correggio's painting in Vienna (page 418), a certain moralizing undercurrent is unmistakable. For the dog—seen from behind at the lower edge of the image, and conveyed with a comparatively fleeting, elegant brushstroke almost reminiscent of Titian—may be meant as a symbol of fidelity, as he gazes after his master, who has been abducted by the eagle Jupiter. Ganymede, for his part, turns toward the observer with a look expressing skepticism as much as a plea for help.

Paintings such as this explain why the concept of Mannerism is hardly suitable for the characterization of Correggio's art. Despite all the dramatic dynamism

Correggio
Leda and the Swan, ca. 1532
Oil on canvas, 152 x 191 cm
Gemäldegalerie, Staatliche Museen, Berlin

The state of preservation of this painting is not as good as it may appear at first. When, in the early 18th century, it reached the collection of Duke Philippe d'Orléans (1674–1723), the latter's son Louis (1703–1752) found the naked Leda, seduced by Jupiter in the form of a swan, so offensive that he had it cut up into small pieces, and the head of the king's beautiful daughter was completely lost. It was only in the second half of the century that the individual parts were put back together and the head repainted with very much softer features.

Correggio
Danaë, ca. 1531/32
Oil on canvas, 161 x 193 cm
Galleria Borghese, Rome

In a bedchamber with a view from a side window, which is evidence of the Venetian influence on Correggio's late work, the king's daughter, Danaë, receives the golden raindrops that fall on her from the cloud floating above, in which Jupiter, the father of the gods, is hidden. The few drops are easily overlooked, however, at first glance. Perhaps this is why Vasari described the painting as a depiction of the goddess of love Venus with her son Cupid.

and the extreme torsion of the young Ganymede, there is nothing unnatural or affected about the portrayal. The fantastic subject does not entail the crossing of the borders of the comprehensible. The same is true of the second, tall rectangular painting on display in Vienna (page 419), perhaps atmospherically the most impressive of the series. The beautiful Io, daughter of the river god Inachos, was seduced by Jupiter in a valley that he rapidly filled with a cloudy mist. Correggio shows the nymph from behind, turning her raised head into profile and surrendering to the god with a transfigured look. Like the paw of a huge bear, part of the dark cloud curves around her body, and only at a second glance can one detect in it the blurred outlines of a hand, just as Jupiter's face is seen only hazily in the part of the cloud close to Io's cheek.

The third work, *Leda and the Swan*, in the Berlin Gemäldegalerie (page 420), has a special place in the Mantuan cycle, since it is a comparatively traditional narrative painting, which unlike the others is not restricted to capturing a single selected moment of the event, but presents three consecutive scenes in a single spatial arrangement, as was customary above all in the painting of the 14th and also the 15th century. At the extreme right edge, on the banks of the Eurotas, Jupiter, in the form of a white swan, swims toward the king's daughter, Leda, who still rather shyly shrinks away from him. The union of the ill-matched couple, which, according to myth, produced the beautiful Helen as well as the Dioscuri, Castor and Pollux, is seen in the foreground. On the right, Leda is to be seen for a third time, gazing after the swan, which is already flying away, while a maid helps her to dress.

The fourth painting, now on display in the Galleria Borghese (page 421), finally, shows the seduction of Danaë, daughter of the king of Argos. The king, who because of the prophecy of an oracle feared death at the hand of a grandson, had locked up his beautiful daughter in an underground vault to keep her far from the world of men. However, Jupiter, in the form of a shower of golden rain, entered the dungeon and fathered on Danaë the hero Perseus, the story of whose adventures was told in the context of a painting by the Florentine Piero di Cosimo (Volume I, page 554).

Apart from a total of about fifty paintings on panel and canvas still preserved today, it was above all Correggio's frescoes in Parma whose amazing illusionism influenced generations of Baroque painters. Already active as a fresco painter in the early 1520s in the convent of San Paolo and at San Giovanni Evangelista, Correggio received the commission to paint the great crossing dome of the Romanesque cathedral of Santa Maria Assunta (pages 422, 423), a task that was to occupy him until his death in 1534. There had of course been illusionistic ceiling paintings before, such as those in the Camera degli Sposi in Mantua (pages 91, 95) and Michelangelo's frescoes in

the Sistine Chapel (Volume I, pages 618–619). But Correggio's *Assumption of the Virgin*, with its simulated view out of the crossing into the bright spheres of the heavens, surpassed all that had been done before, and Vasari already reports that in the many figures the artist "has marvelously foreshortened the view as seen from below." In the shell-shaped pendentives that link the crossing with the octagonal drum, there appear, in extreme foreshortening, sitting on clouds, the saints John the Baptist, Hilary of Poitiers (a 4th-century bishop whose relics are in Parma), Joseph, and Bernardo degli Uberti (an early 12th-century bishop of Parma). Above them the Apostles, standing between the round windows, lead the gaze toward the dome above. Surrounded by angels making music, the Mother of God floats with outspread arms, gazing past Adam and Eve toward the brightest light and her son, who rushes toward her in a dramatic movement.

Despite all the recognition and admiration already bestowed on Correggio's work in his lifetime, there were also some isolated critical comments in view of the many naked bodies, which were considered offensive. The provost of the cathedral is said to have remarked at the unveiling of the fresco that it reminded him of a "ragout of frogs' legs."

Opposite page:
Correggio
The Assumption of the Virgin, 1526–1534
Fresco
Cathedral of Santa Maria Assunta, Parma

With the impressively evocative dome frescoes in the cathedral of Parma, but also in the church of San Giovanni Evangelista (also in Parma), Correggio went far beyond everything done so far in illusionistic ceiling painting. The view selected here from the crossing in a southeast direction shows, in the pendentive shaped like a large shell, leading to the windowed drum area, St. Hilary, an early Christian from Poitiers, who enjoyed particular veneration in Parma because of his relics preserved there.

Correggio
The Assumption of the Virgin (detail page 423)

In view of the patronage of the cathedral of Parma, Santa Maria Assunta, the Assumption of the Virgin Mary was to be depicted in the great dome. Like no other painter, Correggio succeeded in creating the impression that the church building was actually open to the light-flooded heavens.

On concentrically arranged bands of cloud, and surrounded by many smiling angels and saints, Mary is lifted aloft, with all the figures appearing in extreme foreshortening and appearing to dissolve the closer they approach the intense light.

Jacopo Bassano
Two Hunting Dogs, 1548/49
Oil on canvas, 61 x 79.5 cm
Musée du Louvre, Paris

This painting, traditionally seen as one of the earliest pure genre paintings of Italian art, but today also interpreted in terms of religious symbolism, is among those works by Bassano that brought him praise beyond the borders of the Veneto, and also from posterity. Particularly in the 17th and 18th centuries, the painter was reproached by various writers for having occupied himself too much with such trivial and everyday subjects, remaining satisfied with the mere imitation of nature.

JACOPO BASSANO (1510–1592)

Two hunting dogs with spotted fur, tied to a gnarled tree stump in front of a blue sky, one lying down, the one standing behind him and gazing at the observer with lowered head, dominate a small landscape-format painting by Jacopo Bassano now in the Louvre (above). One might think this was merely a fragment, part of an originally much larger composition, perhaps a hunting scene or a depiction of the myth of Diana and Actaeon. However, traces of trimming which would confirm such an impression are not to be found. Rather, a contract with the Venetian nobleman Antonio Zentani signed by the artist on 5 October 1548, states that *due brachi, cioè cani solo* ("two hunting dogs, that is, only dogs") were to be painted. The particular emphasis on the fact that nothing was to be seen in the picture apart from two dogs shows that the partners to the contract were aware that the nature of the subject was still unusual in the mid-16th century. The assumption that the contract refers to the painting by Bassano today exhibited in the Louvre, and not to his very similar painting in the Uffizi,

which was probably painted some years later, is supported by its dimensions, which approximately agree with the estimate in the contract.

This work has met with particular attention in art-historical research since it has always been seen as one of the earliest pure genre pictures created in Italy. Recently, however, there have also been attempts to interpret the two hunting dogs in symbolic terms, and see the picture as a religious allegory on the human path of life, wavering between virtue and sin. According to these, the dog lying down and appearing somewhat sleepy embodies the sin of sloth (*accidia*), and the one standing, virtue and energy. Be that as it may, the painting has had some influence on other painters. The motif of the dog lying down, for example, is found almost unaltered and in a prominent place in Tintoretto's painting of *Christ Washing the Feet of His Disciples* (pages 432–433).

The painter Jacopo del Ponte, known by the name of his birthplace, Bassano del Grappa, had studied with his

Jacopo Bassano
The Flight into Egypt, 1542
Oil on canvas, 157.5 x 203.2 cm
Toledo Museum of Art, Toledo (Ohio)

In the structure of the landscape, this painting from the church of the Santissima Annunziata in Ancona manifests certain parallels with the so-called "world landscapes" of the Antwerp artist Joachim Patenier (ca. 1485–1524). This is true particularly of the depiction, not quite correct in terms of perspective, of the peasant houses on the low ground of the central area. In view of the very high horizon and the consequently raised point of view of the observer, the rows of roof ridges should be placed much higher, for on an isolated view of the houses one almost gains the impression that one is standing not on elevated ground, but in the middle of the little village in the valley.

father and later with Bonifacio de' Pitati in Venice, but like his colleague Paris Bordone, who was trained by Titian, he was predominantly active in the Veneto province. In many other, primarily religious paintings by Bassano, there are a number of depictions of animals, which often give the works a positively pastoral character. This is true above all of the subject of the Adoration of the Shepherds, frequently treated by Bassano, as well as for a series of paintings of the Flight of the Holy Family into Egypt, including the painting of the early 1540s, today displayed in Toledo, Ohio (page 425). In front of a wide wooded and hilly landscape, whose central area and background may recall the so-called "world landscapes" by Joachim Patenier executed in Antwerp a good two decades earlier, the Holy Family, accompanied by three shepherds, an ox, and two sheep, as well as a dog, moves along a hill from right to left, contrary to the usual "reading direction." Despite the overall compact composition, the figures in

the small group of travelers, painted in strong, clear colors, seem strangely isolated from each other. While the shepherd dressed in green turns toward the oxen he is leading, the Virgin Mary and the Christ Child, as well as the donkey on which they ride, gaze dreamily at the stony road that lies ahead of them, on which Joseph strides ahead, for his part also lost in thought. Only the two other shepherds turn toward each other as they walk.

As with the two hunting dogs in the Louvre, recent research has also detected in this painting a level of moralistic significance, beyond the ostensible subject of the Flight into Egypt. The village scenes of the central area of the image, such as the peasant woman with a goose under her arm, walking beside her husband across a meadow, have been seen in terms of the theme, popular in the Renaissance and the Baroque, of the path of life, narrow and full of privation, but leading to salvation, in contrast to the broad road of earthly pleasures.

Paris Bordone
Mars and Venus Surprised by Vulcan, ca. 1549
Oil on canvas, 168 x 198 cm
Gemäldegalerie, Staatliche Museen, Berlin

The menacing clouds above the mountainous wooded landscape symbolize on the one hand the anger of the deceived blacksmith god Vulcan, but on the other also the disaster that seems to be brewing for the adulterous lovers. With a little effort it is possible to recognize at the top right edge of the painting the Olympian gods, led by Mercury, whom Vulcan will summon as judges of the two deceivers. However, as Homer reports in Book 8 of the *Odyssey*, the story ends in farce, since not only the lovers, caught in Vulcan's net, but also the cuckolded husband are subjected to the mockery of the gods.

PARIS BORDONE (1500–1571)

Apart from a long stay at the French court in Fontainebleau and a supposed journey to Augsburg, the painter Paris Bordone, born in Treviso near Venice and trained in Titian's workshop, was active throughout his life in Northern Italy, where he was also influenced first by Giorgione and later by artists such as Palma il Vecchio (1480–1528) and Pordenone (1484–1539). For his mainly private clients he created many portraits, as well as altar paintings and mythological and allegorical scenes. Two of his paintings from the later 1540s, today preserved in Berlin and Cologne, are already characterized by Mannerism and are probably identical with those mentioned by Vasari in the second edition of his *Lives*, where he claims they were commissioned by the Milanese courtier Carlo da Rhò for his palazzo (above, opposite page).

In spite of their different formats, these pictures could certainly have been planned as pendants, since both deal with the theme of adultery. The Berlin painting (above) shows the blacksmith god Vulcan, who has surprised his wife, Venus, the goddess of love, who looks toward the observer, in a midday tryst with Mars, the god of war. The painter diverges from the classical tradition of the story by placing the event not in the marital bedchamber, but in a mountain landscape under a sky overcast by storm clouds.

With a glance at the so-called *paragone*—the debate, intensively conducted above all in the course of the 16th century, on the hierarchy of the various artistic genres, notably painting and sculpture, but also literature and music—attention should also be drawn to the wide-meshed net of chains in which the cuckolded husband is about to entangle his wife and her

Paris Bordone
Bathsheba Bathing, ca. 1549
Oil on canvas, 234 x 217 cm
Wallraf-Richartz-Museum, Cologne

The urban view in the background of the event is clearly inspired not only by classical buildings and contemporary Renaissance architecture: it also draws on Sebastiano Serlio's treatise on architecture as a model. David's palace on the right-hand side of the image is, hardly by chance, supported by "masculine" Doric columns, while to the left, behind Bathsheba, a circular building surrounded by "feminine" Corinthian columns is to be seen, which resembles the remains of the Temple of the Vestals in Rome.

lover. In the literary sources, Homer's *Odyssey* and Ovid's *Metamorphoses*, Vulcan, intent on revenge, is said to have forged a net, worked more delicately than a spider's web and thus invisible, but at the same time inextricably strong, which in addition he laid as a trap in the marriage bed, rather than, as in Bordone's image, casting it like a gladiator over the two illicit lovers. Here we see the dilemma of the *paragone* and the limits of painting. How can a painter show the invisible? In such a case, literature undoubtedly proves superior, as it can indeed represent the invisible by describing it in words.

As Mannerist in style as the blacksmith god, who is shown hurrying toward the scene in a strongly exaggerated physical posture, are the three female figures in the foreground of the Cologne painting (above), which illustrates the beginning of probably the best-known Old Testament story of adultery. In front of a luxuriant lemon bush sits Bathsheba, bathing at the edge of a stream, turning to her two maids, one of whom leans toward her mistress with an exaggerated movement similar to that of Vulcan toward the two adulterers in the

Berlin painting. Easily missed at first glance, old King David leans out of a window of the palace seen to the right in the central area. David has fallen passionately in love with the beautiful Bathsheba and seduces her, although he has learned that she is married to the Hittite Uriah, a high-ranking officer in his army. As the Second Book of Samuel reports, Bathsheba becomes pregnant by David. When the king fails to attribute paternity to her husband, he sees no other resort but to have him sent to the front in the war against the Ammonites so that he is killed during the enemy's attack. Clearly the painter is alluding to this part of the story in the figure of the rider just to be discerned in the background.

As in many other depictions of the theme, Bathsheba offers herself less to the gaze of the king than to the observer. In this sense it seems as though the observer, male or female—in this case perhaps the wife of the Milanese client—is being asked to adopt the role of the protagonists of the dramatic story, in order to ponder the state of his or her own marital fidelity.

Henrik Engel

Tintoretto
Self-Portrait, ca. 1547, Oil on canvas, 45.7 x 38.1 cm
Philadelphia Museum of Art, Philadelphia

As if responding to a sudden call, the young Tintoretto turns to the viewer, his eyes wide. Amidst his curly hair, his famous musical ear appears open like a stethoscope, on the alert for commissions, picking up intrigues. His forehead, illuminated by light falling on it from the side, together with the inner radiance of his eyes, convey inspiration, his sense of artistic mission, and his confidence in the early maturity of his own skill.

Tintoretto
Self-Portrait, ca. 1588, Oil on canvas, 62.5 x 52 cm
Musée du Louvre, Paris

Marked by the strain of a life full of cares, the old master turns to the viewer *in maestà* (in majesty), that is to say in a particularly dignified full frontal attitude. The asymmetry of composition in Tintoretto's early self-portrait (above) has given way here to physiognomic asymmetry. The hair on the artist's head, still thick, is smoother now, but the bushy beard seems to be windblown as if by the breath of fate. The light, falling almost vertically from above, suggests a metaphysical reference, also reflected in the stillness of the picture: the lips seem to be seated beneath the silvery beard, and the ears are almost invisible too.

Jacopo Robusti, known as Tintoretto 1519–1594

THE "ADOPTIVE SON OF APELLES"

In the fall of 1547, the Venetian painter Tintoretto received a curious letter:

"To the Darling of Nature, the Healing Potion of Aesculapius, the Adoptive son of Apelles, Messer Iacomo Tentoretto, painter.

As a single peppercorn exceeds, outdoes, and counterbalances ten bunches of poppy, thus and not otherwise are you, related by blood to the Muses, and it is very certain that, although only recently arrived in this life, you come equipped with a great spirit. You have a scanty beard and a well-stocked mind, a small figure and a great heart, you are young in years and old in understanding, and in the short time that you spent studying, you learned more than a hundred others who were born masters. … Do you know that you have as fine a manner of depicting gestures, attitudes and human dignity, foreshortenings, profiles, shadows, backgrounds, and perspectives, as another artist, he who rides the modern Pegasus? It may truly be said that, if you were as well provided with hands as you are with heart and knowledge, there would be nothing, no matter how difficult, that you could not master. By the blood of gnats, brother, you are dear to me, for you are an enemy to idleness, since you pass part of your time increasing your reputation, part of it restoring your physical powers, and part of it in the edification of your mind. That is to say, you labor to derive utility and fame from your work, you eat to live, not to indulge the flesh, and you make music, laugh, and sing in order to remain sane, unlike many who become so involved in the creation of a work of art that thereafter, all at once, they lose their minds and their reason."

The man who penned this humorous eulogy was Andrea Calmo (1510/11–1571), the most outstanding author and actor of comedies in 16th-century Venice. On close examination, the letter proves to be a literary portrait equal to Tintoretto's *Self-Portrait* (above), of about the same period, in the sureness of touch with which it sketches in the artist's character.

At the time when he painted this picture, Tintoretto had indeed "only recently arrived in this life." From the registers of deaths of Tintoretto's parish church and the Venetian public health authorities, it can be deduced that he was born in 1519. Unlike most of the other great Venetian Renaissance painters, Tintoretto was a true native of Venice, born and bred there. However, there were many immigrants among the around 150,000 inhabitants that made it one of the largest cities in Europe at the time. It is probable the silk dyer Battista Robusti, Tintoretto's father, who came from Brescia (as did the family of Jacopo's later wife, Faustine Episcopi), had forebears in Lucca, since the textile industry, and particularly the silk trade, had been brought to Venice by craftsmen from Lucca in the 14th century. The Venetians described the people of Lucca as "Toscani," a fact that may have encouraged Tintoretto to adopt Tuscan and Roman artistic models (such as Raphael, Michelangelo, and Giulio Romano).

There is early evidence of his interest in foreign artistic ideals, although it was still indirect, in his full-size copy of Vittore Carpaccio's *Martyrdom of the Ten Thousand* (both Gallerie dell'Accademia, Venice). While the Venetian painters of the High Renaissance (artists such as Giorgione, Titian, Jacopo Palma il Vecchio, and Sebastiano del Piombo) were more inclined to celebrate the female body, Carpaccio's painting contains variations on the male nude. In this the artist is following the example of Michelangelo, who set out a "catalog" of the male anatomy in every possible physical attitude and foreshortening of perspective on the ceiling of the Sistine Chapel in Rome. It is not clear whether Tintoretto's copy of Carpaccio was an exercise carried out for his own interest, or a picture painted as an official masterpiece, or on commission, perhaps for the Venetian Ottobon family. In any case, Tintoretto's study from a distance of Romano-Tuscan art was to continue in the future with the aid, in particular, of graphic prints reproducing works by Raphael and Michelangelo.

Unfortunately, the precise nature of the dyer Battista Robusti's connection with the silk trade is not known, nor do the records show whether he was a craftsman, a dealer, or an entrepreneur. Tintoretto's contemporary Raffaello Borghini and his first biographer Carlo Ridolfi agree in stating that Jacopo's father was a *cittadino*, meaning that within the hierarchical structure of Venetian society he belonged to a high-ranking social class with its own further subdivisions, enjoying trading privileges and qualified to occupy certain official positions. Jacopo's excellent contacts with the élite of his native city—for instance, several of its Grand Chancellors—and the patronage he received early from notable patricians, might also account for Calmo's references to his "great spirit" and "well-stocked mind." There were far more Venetian *cittadini* than patricians who owned books, and they were people of considerable intellectual distinction.

But although Tintoretto may have come from a privileged social class, he had a handicap referred to several times by Calmo: he was of small stature, and that may be one of the reasons for his lifelong and strikingly intense artistic interest in groups of social outsiders such as slaves and the sick (pages 431, 434–435). Seen in the context of his conspicuously small size, moreover, certain aspects of Jacopo's conduct may be explained as compensatory behavior. As Calmo indicates, in spite of that small size he liked to set himself Herculean tasks, literally dyeing gigantic areas of canvas with color, and pitting himself against the greatest in his profession in the process. His unusually concentrated combination of natural talent, knowledge, and wit meant, said Calmo, that he outshone a truly considerable throng of rivals

like "a single peppercorn." He took as his artistic name the nickname Tintoretto, "little dyer," deriving from his origin and his almost dwarflike stature.

Titian was supposedly responsible for what Calmo describes as Jacopo's unusually brief period of training, since after a few days he threw his apprentice out of his studio, out of jealousy of his precocious talent. At any rate, the most important monumental painting to have been completed in Titian's workshop during the time in question, the *Battle of Spoleto*, hung in 1538 in the Sala del Maggior Consiglio and destroyed in the fire at the Doge's Palace in 1577, is clearly echoed in Tintoretto's work. In the *Conversion of Saul* (below) Tintoretto adopts numerous elements from Titian's much admired battle painting.

Tintoretto
The Conversion of Saul
Oil on canvas, 152.4 x 236.2 cm
National Gallery of Art, Washington

This large canvas shows the Conversion of Saul, formerly a persecutor of Christians and later known as Paul, when he was flung to the ground by a bright light on his way to Damascus, blinded, and addressed by the loud voice of

God. Echoes of famous works by Leonardo, Raphael, and Titian demonstrate the young Tintoretto's huge ambition. He is already emulating the great battle paintings of the High Renaissance. His deliberate infringement of the lateral boundaries of the picture by using centrifugal motifs of movement, for instance in the horsemen front left and back right, still seems slightly naïve, not least

because the steeds themselves resemble rocking horses. Horses had been rare in Venice since the middle of the 15th century, and Tintoretto, as an inhabitant of the city, therefore had to rely for his studies on Verrocchio's equestrian statue of captain-general Colleoni (Campo San Giovanni e Paolo, Venice) and perhaps on casts of models of horses by Leonardo.

THE DIGNITY OF CREATION

Tintoretto
The Miracle of the Slave, 1547/48
Oil on canvas, 415 x 541 cm
Gallerie dell'Accademia, Venice

Tintoretto invested all the skill of his early maturity in this canvas, his largest to that date. The cleverly devised composition unobtrusively merges motifs from tapestries by Raphael, paintings by Titian and Lorenzo Lotto, frescoes by Pordenone and Jacopo Bassano, and ideas from graphic prints by Lucas van Leyden and Antonio da Trento. The crowd of onlookers of different nationalities is intended to show that St. Mark, who appears from on high bearing a gospel, was the Apostle of the people. In front of the backdrop of Jacopo Sansovino's Loggetta, shown on the left of the picture, these figures might come straight from the bustle of the Piazza di San Marco.

In 1548, Jacopo Tintoretto became the most important monumental painter of the city of Venice almost overnight when his *Miracle of the Slave* (opposite page) was at last installed early in April in its appointed place, above the committee gallery in the Chapter Hall of the Grand Confraternity of St. Mark (the Scuola Grande di San Marco), and after long disputes, probably over payment. The subject of the picture is the legend of a Provençal heathen lord's slave who went on pilgrimage to the tomb of St. Mark in Venice without his master's permission. On his return he was to be punished—as the painting shows—by having his eyes put out, his feet cut off, and his mouth smashed, but the instruments of torture refused to do their work. The Provençal lord, enthroned in the shadows to the right of Tintoretto's picture, his head suddenly illuminated by a divine shaft of light, was converted by this miracle, and subsequently went on pilgrimage himself with his slave to the tomb of St. Mark.

The Scuola Grande di San Marco, founded in 1260, which commissioned the *Miracle of the Slave*, was one of the most prominent and distinguished confraternities of Venice. The scuola's magnificent building was erected at the end of the 15th century, and its façade confidently quoted the outline of the basilica of St. Mark. It was splendidly adorned with stone carving, paneling, tapestries, and paintings by well-known artists, many of them members of the confraternity themselves. Once the *albergo* (the boardroom and treasury) was completed in 1534, it was decided in 1542 to adorn the Chapter Hall next to it with paintings. There is much to suggest that Tintoretto was already trying to gain a footing in this scuola at the time, but did not succeed; the commission went to painters of interior decoration who could work fast. Not until 1547, when his future father-in-law Marco Episcopi took office on the governing board as the *guardian da matin*, did circumstances again favor Tintoretto, but by now the only place left to be filled by a commissioned painting was on the front wall towards the Campo Santi Giovanni e Paolo, a particularly difficult location for a picture because of the strong light falling into the hall. Tintoretto mastered his task by framing the painting with architectural features so that it looked like a third window between two real

ones, and by using strong local colors and lighting full of contrasts. The light falling in from the right corresponds to the real light as it shone into the hall at the time of evening meetings. In a hastily written eulogy the writer and art critic Aretino praised the picture's great faithfulness to life, and as soon as it was set in its place in the wall paneling (which had corner indentations) of the Chapter Hall, it attracted crowds of eager viewers: "The expressions, attitudes, and appearance of the throng of people surrounding the work are so like those of the figures in the picture itself that it seems to be real rather than simulated." In a letter to a mutual friend, the sculptor and architect Jacopo Sansovino, written the same month, Aretino stated that since he, Sansovino, was *hors concours*, Tintoretto had in effect won the "race" between the artists of Venice. Although he himself now accepted few commissions unless they came from the European aristocracy, Aretino's friend Titian was very angry when he returned from Augsburg and heard of the eulogies written in his absence. Aretino felt obliged to declare that his own assessment of the picture had been "over-hasty," but time has confirmed his original judgment: in future, Tintoretto was to dominate the Venetian market in large-scale "history paintings" (that is, those depicting subjects from history, mythology, the Bible, and Christian legends). His only remaining dangerous rival was Paolo Veronese (1528–1588).

After the *Miracle of the Slave*, Tintoretto supplied a succession of milestones in the history of Venetian art. His next major work was *Christ Washing the Feet of His Disciples* (pages 432–433), which he probably began in 1548, and of which there is another and almost identical version in Newcastle-upon-Tyne. This picture is one of the earliest examples in Tintoretto's oeuvre of the genre of *quadri laterali*, painted in what was often an extreme landscape format, and usually intended to be installed in pairs on the side walls of a chapel or presbyterium, where they would be seen not only from below but, most important of all, at a slanting angle. Through his skillful if unorthodox use of perspective, his imaginative and empathetic approach to religious subjects, and the narrative abilities that he thus developed, Tintoretto became a specialist in this pictorial genre and helped it to

reach a peak in Venice. *Christ Washing the Feet of His Disciples* is intended for a left-hand wall, and consequently Tintoretto has shifted the vanishing point of the perspective to the view of someone approaching the picture from the left. The rest of the panorama unfolds from this point. As in the early *cassoni* paintings, the viewer's eye is first attracted to a figure in the foreground. The elaborate attitude of the Apostle shown putting on his shoes again after his feet have been washed is reminiscent of a soldier in Michelangelo's *Battle of Cascina* (Volume I, page 614), a famous figure shown from the rear that had been circulating in the form of an engraving since 1517. As an extant nude study shows, Tintoretto checked the pose with a living model so that he could depict it not merely as a mirror image but from its other side, which is invisible in Michelangelo's version, thus mastering what art experts regarded as an example of extreme *difficoltà*. The older Apostle, seated on the

ground further back and wearing particularly tight leg coverings, is taken from the same context. A connoisseur would have recognized it as a parody of a figure in the foreground of the *Battle of Cascina*. However, taken together with the New Testament subject, the informal subsidiary scene could equally well be regarded as (literally) a footnote to the subject of charity. Above this scene, the perspective draws the viewer's glance to the distance, where Tintoretto presents his vision of an ideal Venice in the style of classical antiquity, with a canal bounded by a triumphal arch, an obelisk, and a temple. The eye now slides swiftly over the boat floating on the water and the rustic table set on the same axis of perspective, and back to the foreground, to linger, finally, on the main scene being enacted by Christ, St. John, who is assisting him, and St. Peter.

Typical of Tintoretto is the ingenuity he employs, while preserving the Aristotelian unities of time, place,

Tintoretto
Christ Washing the Feet of His Disciples, 1548/49
Oil on canvas, 210 x 533 cm
Museo Nacional del Prado, Madrid

During the Last Supper, Christ rises, wraps a cloth
around himself, and begins washing the feet of the
Apostles. When Peter protests, Christ replies: "What
I do thou knowest not now; but thou shalt know it
hereafter." Tintoretto sets the scene in the interior of a
palazzo with a view of a canal. The example Christ gives
his disciples of humility and charity was ostentatiously
imitated on certain occasions by the upper classes of
Venetian society: the Doge used to wash the feet of
twelve poor people on Maundy Thursday, and twelve
of the *nobili* and their ladies did the same in 1524 at
the Ospedale degl' Incurabili (a hospital for incurable
syphilitics).

and action, in showing various phases of the same act
(in this case the removal of the disciples' footwear, the
washing of their feet, and the covering of their feet
again) by distributing them between different figures.
He thus presents a dramatic version of the incident
described in the New Testament. However, though the
background of the picture may suggest a stage set, it is
far removed from the Passion plays of the medieval
tradition, which were still being performed in Venice in
1515. Instead, Tintoretto takes his guidelines from the
latest developments in the secular theater, which strove
in theory and practice to reconstruct the Vitruvian
drama of antiquity.

A model for the classical buildings in the background
of *Christ Washing the Feet of His Disciples* was the
woodcut depiction of an ideal setting for tragedy in the
second book of Sebastiano Serlio's *On Architecture,*
published in 1545. Tintoretto's colleague and neighbor
Paris Bordone used the same model for the background
of his *Bathsheba Bathing* (page 427). Bordone's picture,

however, unlike *Christ Washing the Feet of His Disciples,*
contains no link between the action and its setting;
indeed, the bathing scene and the view of the
background were painted on two different pieces of
canvas. Tintoretto's ability to provide the more
convincing version may be ascribed in part to his
practical theatrical experience with various *compagnie
della calza.* He was happy to write amusing lines and
devise special effects for these companies of noble
amateur actors, who could be recognized by their
colored hose (calze), for in this way he could make
contact with potential patrons; for instance Marco
Gussoni, for whose new palace on the Canal Grande he
painted frescoes around 1552.

The dog centrally placed in the foreground of the
picture is a striking detail in Tintoretto's *Christ Washing
the Feet of His Disciples.* In religious paintings, a dog
often conveys a negative meaning, and can appear as an
attribute of Judas, or may symbolize the enemies and
persecutors of Christ. However, since the dog in Jacopo's

picture is lying very much at its ease, it seems to incorporate, if anything, the humility Christ has just demonstrated. Although this dog is depicted in a particularly naturalistic manner, Tintoretto did not paint it "from life" but was imitating another painting, Jacopo Bassano's *Two Hounds* (page 424). It was not unusual for Venetian painters like Titian to be commissioned to paint portraits of dogs. Generally, they appeared as companions to their masters, for instance in full-length portraits of princes. Bassano's painting is unusual because, as the patron who commissioned it stipulated, it was to show "only dogs." Like the animal in Tintoretto's *Christ Washing the Feet of His Disciples*, the two hounds could also have an allegorical meaning, perhaps as an exhortation to watchfulness. In Petrarch, a black dog and a white dog symbolize day and night, and thus the rapid passage of time, while Venetian book illustrations contain depictions of the human soul as a white stag ("La Cerva Bianca") pursued by the dogs "Desio" (Desire) and "Pensier" (Care).

Was Tintoretto's exact copy taken from Bassano's double portrait of the two hounds perhaps intended as a tribute to his colleague? It is more likely that Jacopo, who was famous for his ability to adapt like a chameleon to different styles, was anxious to show that he could easily produce similar works of art if he wanted to. As his biographer Ridolfi rather loftily indicates, Jacopo Tintoretto used to suggest that those who wanted portraits "of animal creatures" had better apply to the animal painter Bassano.

After the *Miracle of the Slave*, no more commissions except for minor occasional works could be expected from the Scuola Grande di San Marco for the time being, so Tintoretto now tried his luck with the Scuola Grande di San Rocco, which had similar grand ideas of display. The Confraternity of St. Roch, founded in 1478 and elevated to the status of a Scuola Grande eleven years later, had a magnificent Chapter Hall; building work had begun in 1515. After moving into the new building, the scuola tried, against the will of the

Tintoretto
St. Roch Healing the Plague Stricken, 1549
Oil on canvas, 307 x 673 cm
San Rocco, Venice

The plague was a constant danger in the harbor city of Venice, and the state sought to counter it by taking careful precautionary measures, for instance the building of the Lazzaretto Nuovo as a quarantine hospital around 1470. Tintoretto's painting could equally well show the plague hospital of the Lazzaretto Vecchio, also built on an island in the lagoon as early as 1423. The young women shown here entering from the sides of the picture to wash the sick, bind up their sores, and feed them, are probably unemployed prostitutes, who were pressed into service in the Lazzaretto Vecchio in times of plague.

neighboring Franciscans of Santa Maria Gloriosa dei Frari, to turn the old building opposite into a hospital for old and single *confratelli* (members of the confraternity). It is assumed that Tintoretto's painting *St. Roch Healing the Plague Stricken* (above) not only set out to show the miracles worked by St. Roch in the early 14th century in various plague hospitals, but was also a reference to the scuola's own hospital project.

Like *Christ Washing the Feet of His Disciples* (page 432–433), the picture is a *quadro laterale*. It was commissioned by the Confraternity of St. Roch for the right-hand wall of the interior of the choir of San Rocco—a church that, as the last resting-place of the saint's body, was a major place of pilgrimage, particularly in times of plague. The gloomy lighting of

the picture is intended to convey the oppressive atmosphere of a plague hospital, and also to integrate the picture as impressively as possible into the dimly lit church. The ray of light streaming in from the right foreground is several times interrupted by the figures in the picture, so that they are illuminated only here and there. Viewers have to use their imagination to supplement the details of the dreadful scene, which are difficult to make out in the darkness, and are thus drawn into its horrors themselves. Jacopo probably drew inspiration not only from the illusionistic frescoes in the choir, executed in San Rocco by Giovanni Antonio da Pordenone, but also from the eerie sight of the wax votive offerings displayed in the dim light of the church: it may be deduced from a document of 1573

that many pilgrims left wax figures, some of them life-size, along the walls of the church, hoping to gain the favor of St. Roch (Rocco) to protect them against the plague.

No doubt Tintoretto's concern with social outsiders ought not to be simply taken as a sign of identification with the underprivileged, or social criticism in the modern sense. The beggars and the sick, who after the 1520s and the urban renovation works in Venice were moved out of the city itself to isolated hospitals, some of them even to the galleys, were permitted to feature even in Tintoretto's paintings only as heroic and idealized figures. It has recently been pointed out that their physical suffering is expressed indirectly, through elaborate physical attitudes which the expert can often

recognize as citations from famous Romano-Tuscan examples of painting or sculpture, and that they are thus esthetically ennobled. For instance, Tintoretto painted the young seated patient from a statue executed by the sculptor and architect Bartolomeo Ammanati in 1545/46 for the tomb of the famous Paduan legal scholar Marco Mantova Benavides. Tintoretto boldly adopts the motif of the scroll held by Ammanati's *ignudo* (male nude) in the form of a muslin bandage. The slightly altered physical pose and the life-like depiction of the man's anatomy and skin color suggest that Jacopo Tintoretto had the Paduan sculpture portrayed by a living model, and the painter could have reproduced the attitude of the sick man standing next to him in a similar way.

IMAGES OF WOMEN

Susanna and the Elders (detail pages 438–439)

Tintoretto's pictures often contain still-lifes painted with virtuosic skill. The items he depicted include instruments of torture, weapons, and cooking utensils, and are to be understood as annotations, or commentaries on the main subject of the work. The precious objects sparkling in the dark grass here (a jar of ointment, a mirror, comb, hairpin, pearl necklace, and ring) show that Susanna is a pampered lady used to luxury, lavishing special care and expense on the care and adornment of her body—perhaps for professional reasons.

Women have a special place in Tintoretto's work. The sympathy, intensity, and sustained interest with which he seeks to understand the fundamental situations of feminine life are unique for this period. He paints temptresses and victims of sexual violence, mothers and daughters, heroines and Muses, Horae and whores. It would be rash and probably useless to try building up a uniform picture from these representations of women, which are often contradictory. However, a study in some detail of certain selected works casts a surprisingly revealing and sometimes rather disturbing light on the image of women entertained by Tintoretto and his time. The available documentary records of Jacopo's family history, and some posthumous anecdotes, also help to illuminate certain facets of the subject.

As in the *Miracle of the Slave* (page 431), Tintoretto frequently places female figures in the foreground of his paintings. Whether they are entering from the sides of the picture or turning their backs to the viewer, they are looking at the narrative depicted. They are figures with whom the viewer can identify, and clearly show that Jacopo expected to appeal to women as well as men when he devised his paintings.

This may be one of the reasons, but only one, why Tintoretto's figures of women often appear ambivalent. His large-scale historical paintings, for instance, contain a range of female supernumeraries, from whores to symbolic figures of Caritas (Charity). The same ambivalence occurs in *Susanna and the Elders* (pages 438–439), a subject to which Tintoretto returned several times; it even features in a cartoon of the mosaic for San Marco. Susanna should be the personification of persecuted innocence, but Jacopo's painting contains certain revealing details. First there is the mirror leaning against the hedge, a very popular export item in the Venetian luxury trade, a classic symbol of lust, and an attribute of prostitutes. In front of the mirror, Tintoretto places a still life of items suggesting vanity (page 437): lace-edged underclothes, a velvet gown magnificently embroidered with jewels, a comb, hairpins, gold rings, and a pearl necklace. Foreign visitors to the city regarded the beautifully dressed and groomed Venetian ladies who bleached their hair with sun and salt water on the *altane* (wooden superstructures on rooftops) as one of its chief attractions. Books of beauty hints were bestsellers. In 1562, the Senate made it compulsory to declare ownership of pearls, as a measure to counter excessive public display: all necklaces were stamped with a seal and registered. In 1543, prostitutes had been forbidden to wear pearls, rings, or other items of goldsmith's work (including costume jewelry, which was very popular), since they aroused the envy of chaste ladies. Both painter and patron may have thought of Susanna, who obviously likes jewelry, as a courtesan, for the Murano glass ointment jar in the foreground of the picture suggests not only the transience of the human body but also the sinner Mary Magdalene in the New Testament. It is possible that the picture was intended as a *portrait historié* for the lover of a young lady of doubtful repute. Since the painting was seen and copied remarkably often by Flemish painters (for instance Dirck Barendsz., Paolo Fiammingho, and Lodewijk Toeput), the patron who commissioned it could have been a Flemish merchant living in Venice—a man like Daniel d'Anna, whose family was art-loving, and who could also identify with the name of the biblical Daniel, who saved Susanna's honor.

A work that was to have a strong influence on later artists was his *Presentation of the Virgin* (pages 440–441). It shows the child Mary ("little Mary," or literally "Marietta"), alone but fearlessly climbing a huge staircase to be presented in the temple. Today the two halves of the picture have been stitched vertically together, but they originally adorned the outsides of the wings or folding shutters over an organ that was demolished in the 19th century. It was installed between the central nave and the side aisle on the right in Tintoretto's favorite church of Madonna dell'Orto, near the choir, and was still regarded as the best organ in Europe in 1582. Tintoretto's commission to paint the wings dated from 1548. He finally completed the work in 1555/56, not least, perhaps, because his father-in-law had acquired the site for a tomb in the central nave of Madonna dell'Orto in 1555, almost directly in front of the organ. It was here that Jacopo himself was later interred (1594) together with Marietta, his favorite daughter, who had died early in life (1590), his wife

Faustina (1621), and Domenico (1635), his son and the successor to his workshop.

To assess the composition of the *Presentation of the Virgin* properly, we must imagine the two halves of the picture restored to their original condition as separate canvases. It then becomes clear that unlike the left wing, the right wing is a perfectly self-contained composition. We could almost say perhaps the "dependent" left wing represents the Old Testament, and the "independent" right wing the New Testament. Tintoretto's use of lighting would confirm such a theory: the standing scribes and Pharisees, and the beggars seated as if on the steps of a church, are still surrounded by darkness. Only the violently agitated figure of a prophet in the foreground, stepping out of the shadows, indicates that one day Mary will carry the Light of the World within her.

Tintoretto had obviously worked out that when the organ was opened the left wing would move first, thus briefly showing its internal picture of St. Peter at the same time as the outer right wing. At that point observant viewers would realize why the high priest does not, as in Titian's depiction, wear the usual breastplate with twelve gems symbolizing the twelve tribes of Israel. Instead, Jacopo gives him a stola crossed over his breast—like St. Peter, whose tiara marks him out as the first pope. To counter the Protestant tendencies that had reached Venice at this time, the painter is illustrating the claim of Catholic Rome to be the sole heir and protector of the true faith. The Roman reference continues on the right-hand inner wing, showing the martyrdom of St. Paul, prince of the Apostles, who was executed in Rome in 64 BC at the same time as Peter.

It is possible that Tintoretto, like many other Venetians, was not entirely happy with a program so strongly promoting the papacy. At any rate, he undermined the complex theological and political subject in a curious way that, again, casts some light on his ideas of women. An intriguing detail in the *Presentation of the Virgin* is the curiously rumpled dress of the hesitant little girl in the foreground, which constitutes a "puzzle picture" of an outsize female sexual organ. The left-hand inner wing of the organ, where there is a kind of counterpart in a huge key of heaven dangling between St. Peter's legs, shows that he did this intentionally. It cannot be chance that the two complementary pictorial jokes—worthy of Pietro Aretino, and in the case of St. Peter only slightly more subtle than the polemics of Protestant pamphlets—were simultaneously visible when the left wing was opened, revealing the full ecclesiastical statement of the organ pictures. Later, Tintoretto's satirical references here were thought to require another explanation. In 1751, Johann Georg Keyssler reported the tale told by an imaginative guide showing visitors round Madonna dell'Orto: "The organ was painted by Tintoretto as penance for ruining a maidservant in the house of a nobleman where he was staying." Interestingly, recent research leads to the conclusion that Tintoretto's favorite daughter, Marietta, was possibly either born out of wedlock, or the result of a premarital liaison with a German woman.

Tintoretto
Susanna and the Elders, ca. 1555
Oil on canvas, 146.6 x 193.6 cm
Kunsthistorisches Museum, Vienna

In this picture the Old Testament story of the slander of Susanna, wife of the rich Joachim, by two lecherous old men whose plot is uncovered by the young Daniel, becomes a kind of atmospheric satyr play. Evening light flatters the body of the young woman, who looks more like a pagan nymph or goddess of love than a biblical heroine. Absorbed in the contemplation of her own beauty, Susanna has not yet noticed the two old voyeurs who are about to approach her. Italian Renaissance comedy, following the example of classical antiquity, made the amorous old man a stock character.

Tintoretto
The Presentation of the Virgin,
ca. 1553/1556
Oil on canvas, 429 x 480 cm
Madonna dell'Orto, Venice

This painting, consisting of two vertical halves now stitched together in the middle, once adorned the outsides of two organ wings. The monumental stairway indicates the musical connection; its fifteen steps or "grades" refer to the fifteen graduals, the psalms sung by pilgrims in annual temple processions. The singers' gallery above the organ was also painted by Tintoretto. The dark carving of the breastwork and the frames of the wings were partly gilded, like the stairway in the painting; Tintoretto picked out its undulating ornamentation in gold leaf. This "Byzantine" stylistic element is particularly effective in the shadowy area on the left, where it produces a sense of mystic illumination. The richly decorated steps on Mary's way into the temple are reminiscent of the Scala dei Giganti in the interior courtyard of the Ducal Palace, the lower section of which, like the stairway up to the temple, has fifteen steps. Like the high priest in Tintoretto's picture, the Doge used to receive important guests on this staircase. Jacopo deliberately emphasizes the parallel by showing the high priest's magnificent headdress worn over a *rensa,* the thin white fabric cap with long bands worn by the Doge of Venice beneath his *cornu,* or ducal cap.

Long after his death, according to Tintoretto's biographer Carlo Ridolfi, wild rumors of the way he handled erotic temptations in later life were still current. "He found himself at one point in a villa where he had gone to paint a fresco. The gentleman of the house from time to time left him in the company of one of his beautiful ladies while he went off to Venice on business. He was therefore often importuned by the same lady as to what this or that figure meant. In order to rid himself once and for all of the annoyance he said to her: 'Signora, have dinner prepared; then, if you like, I will come this night to sleep with you and give you five ducats.' The good woman willingly accepted the terms and, having dined, she went to bed with him. But the poor old fellow, exhausted from the labors of the day, could scarcely raise a feeble lance and went to sleep for the rest of the night. Getting up early the next morning, without a word to her he returned to his usual activity. Waking from her sleep, the woman was astonished at not finding her lover, but saw the agreed payment on the table. At this point full of indignation and by now dressed, she quickly went to where he was painting and began to lament about the short stay of her amorous cavalier, and of the disdain he showed in leaving her bed without even saying good-bye. But he, after enduring for a short time the importunity of the woman, finally said to her: 'Be satisfied, Signora, that I did not fail in my word. But if I were to tell the truth, I have at times enjoyed with less expense some poor girl who was better than you are.' Thus he shamed the pretensions of the courtesan, giving her to understand that he had paid for her services and not for her person, as often happens also in painting."

THE GREAT "ENVIRONMENTS"

Moses Receiving the Tables of the Law (detail page 444)

On the peak of cloud-capped Mount Sinai, Moses, his arms outstretched in a Christ-like attitude, receives the two Tables of the Law brought to him by God and ten angels, some of them, as with Michelangelo's angels, without wings. In the blaze of God's aureole, Moses seems to become an astral body in an effect suggesting the transfiguration of Christ on Mount Tabor.

Following pages, left:
Tintoretto
Moses Receiving the Tables of the Law, pre-1562
Oil on canvas, 1450 x 590 cm
Madonna dell'Orto, Venice

The giving of donations to make the Golden Calf is depicted in the lower part of this picture: four strong men carry a wax or clay model of the calf through the Israelite camp, and jewelry and golden vessels are being collected in baskets. Women are helping each other to remove their earrings. Aaron, maker of the idol, is seated in the foreground right. In conversation with the skilled craftsman Belzaleel (with compasses) and his assistant Oholiab, he is giving orders for the placing of the Calf —it is to go on the altar in front of the picture, in the choir of the Madonna dell'Orto itself.

Following pages, right:
The Last Judgment, pre-1562
Oil on canvas, 1450 x 590 cm
Madonna dell'Orto, Venice

Iconographically, this is probably Tintoretto's most complex painting, and it has still not been fully interpreted. The artist shows the Last Judgment as a raging elemental event of cosmic dimensions. If, as is often claimed, Tintoretto ever strove to achieve a synthesis of Titian and Michelangelo, then it was here, where he combines the composition of the Gloria of 1553 for Charles V with the monumentality of the wall painting of the Sistine Chapel. As in late medieval northern panel painting, Christ is shown as Judge of the World, with the lily of mercy and the sword of righteousness, while the Virgin Mary and John the Baptist intercede for resurrected mankind. A particularly unusual feature is the depiction of the Last Judgment as a catastrophe involving flooding, probably not expressing a primeval Venetian fear so much as the typological idea of that other great judgmental act, the Deluge.

In the period of over 400 years that has passed between the present day and the death of Jacopo Tintoretto, many of his works have been destroyed, mutilated by changes to their format, shifted to another position as a result of rebuilding, or transferred to museums and thus removed from their original context entirely. This is particularly unfortunate because Tintoretto matched his large history pictures to their locations with the utmost precision. He used to take unfinished paintings for trial hangings in their intended positions, and would then make quite extensive changes to their composition if necessary. He spared no pains in his wish to manipulate viewers, surrounding them with entire worlds of images and creating his own pictorial universe, and in this his approach was very modern. He preferred to work on large spatial ensembles that, like the modern concept of an "environment," challenged the viewer's capacities of association and reflection on different levels. We can guess at that effect today only in the Scuola Grande di San Rocco, often described as "Tintoretto's Sistine Chapel." Until the 19th century, however, several other large ensembles of works by Tintoretto existed, rivaling the Scuola Grande di San Rocco in magnificence and pictorial abundance, including the "environment" that really was Jacopo's equivalent to the Sistine Chapel.

At about the same time as Jacopo Tintoretto moved from the Campo San Cassan to live near Madonna dell'Orto around 1547, the Augustinian Canons of San Giorgio in Alga embarked on ambitious refurbishments of their church which were eventually to extend from the decoration of the organ (pages 440–441), commissioned in 1548, to the completion of the Capella Contarini. The transformation of Madonna dell'Orto into a total work of art, an achievement destroyed in the 19th century by the passion of that period for neo-Gothic restoration, was probably undertaken in competition with the church of San Sebastiano, built in 1505 to 1548 and then magnificently adorned by Paolo Veronese. In some ways the refurbished Madonna dell'Orto already displayed Baroque features, particularly evident in the trompe-l'oeil painting executed on the flat wooden ceiling around 1556 by two specialists from Brescia, the brothers Cristoforo and Stefano Rosa, who had previously worked under Giulio Romano on the interior decoration of the castle of Mantua. Individual paintings on canvas, mainly of Old Testament scenes, were set into an illusionistic architectural painted setting (*quadratura*), which was designed to be seen from below. Since Tintoretto took no part in the competition of 1566 to design the reading room ceiling in the library built by Sansovino, we may assume that he was occupied with the canvases for the ceiling of Madonna dell'Orto at the time. Cooperation between Tintoretto and the Rosa brothers continued on the walls of the clerestory. The twelve prophets and twelve sibyls depicted between the windows must have been shown standing or sitting in trompe-l'oeil niches. The chiaroscuro medallions on biblical themes placed below the windows were reminiscent of Michelangelo's Sistine frescoes.

The culmination of the church furnishing came in the choir, where architecture, sculpture, paneling, goldsmith's work, frescoes, and oil painting related perfectly to each other. The central section of the wall of the choir was dominated at the time by a colossal wooden statue of St. Christopher, over 5 meters (16 feet) high. The lower part of the wall was lined with wooden choir stalls, and an altar magnificently adorned with six candelabra stood in the middle of it. The gigantic canvases of *Moses Receiving the Tables of the Law* (page 444) on the left interior wall of the choir and the *Last Judgment* (page 445) on the right interior wall are its most important decorative items. To create as great an illusion as possible, Tintoretto made use of the way the real light fell into the choir. He painted the four cardinal virtues of Wisdom, Justice, Temperance, and Courage gazing up to heaven, to be placed above the original four windows of the choir and in the pointed spandrels of the end; a fifth virtue was later added to the cycle, which is still extant. For technical reasons, the vault itself had to be painted al fresco. The lavish architectural painting of the ceiling of the nave was continued here, but was interrupted in an illusionistic manner to provide a view of heaven with angels blowing trumpets descending from it. As messengers of the law or envoys come to raise the dead, these angels were shown flying as if from above into the two wall paintings of *Moses Receiving the Tables of the Law* (page 444) and the *Last Judgment* (page 445). The effect of this vertiginous panorama must have been extraordinary when the famous organ played.

To make sure of staking his claim to cover the huge wall surfaces of Madonna dell'Orto, Tintoretto initially seems to have asked the canons, when he executed the two mighty paintings in the choir, for no more than a payment of 100 ducats toward expenses for materials. At

the usual contemporary rate, charged per square yard for large canvases, the pictures ought to have cost at least five times that sum. It is possible that a patron was subsequently found to pay Jacopo an additional fee. Since the choir of Madonna dell'Orto was not only the presbytery, but was also the funerary chapel of one branch of the Grimani family, it has been thought that the patrician Girolamo Grimani, who died in 1570, commissioned and donated the huge paintings in the choir, and in that capacity had his own portrait included in the *Last Judgment* (Volume I, page 639), directly above St. Jerome (Girolamo). Unlike Tintoretto, Girolamo Grimani had seen the Roman counterpart of the painting at first hand. He could have urged Tintoretto to venture on this breathtaking challenge to Michelangelo's *Last Judgment* on returning from his first period of duty as special envoy to the papal court in 1555. The Netherlandish painter Dirck Barendsz. (1534–1592), who left Amsterdam for Venice in 1555, brought a version of this Venetian answer to Michelangelo, almost to the Roman painter's own door, for in 1561 he painted a Last Judgment (Volume I, page 639) that clearly shows the influence of Tintoretto's painting in its iconography, composition, and coloring. It was commissioned by the Flemish Benedictines of Farfa, northeast of Rome.

With a little imagination, a modern visitor to Madonna dell'Orto can conjure up the original effect of the entire ornamental complex, since important parts of it are still extant. Not so with the Chapter Hall of the Scuola Grande di San Marco, where the walls all around the hall were once adorned with pictures by Tintoretto and later additions by his son Domenico. The carved wooden ceiling has been preserved, but during the Napoleonic period Jacopo's paintings were dispersed; the wall paneling, the committee gallery on the end wall facing the Campo San Giovanni e Paolo, and the benches on the longer walls were all torn out. The scuola was converted into a hospital, and the former Chapter Hall now contains a library of medical history. If we look more closely at the long east wall with the entrance to the Chapter Hall, it is still possible to see traces of the drawing for the paneling design. As on the southern end wall, where the *Miracle of the Slave* (page 431) was installed in April 1548, the paneling here consisted of frames with corner indentations, a shape developed from that of the animal skins which used to be stretched over walls in such places. However, in contrast to the *Miracle of the Slave*, the three pictures by Jacopo (pages 446, 447, 449) that hung on this wall until 1807 show no sign of any matching indentations, evidence that they were not originally intended for this position.

The three-part cycle of paintings here was produced for the prosperous doctor and polymath Tommaso Rangone da Ravenna (1493–1577), who was *guardian grande* (chief officer) of the Grand Confraternity of St. Mark in 1562. Like many of his predecessors in the office, Rangone craved recognition and made use of his position to immortalize himself through a fine work of art calculated to attract attention. At his own expense—and thus with the consent of his *confratelli*— he commissioned Tintoretto to provide the three great canvases showing the miracles worked posthumously by St. Mark, and also a cycle of the seven virtues and seven vices for the long western wall of the Chapter Hall, which contained the windows. Nothing now remains of these wall pictures, executed in ocher chiaroscuro. Nor are the three canvases in their original condition, for they were trimmed, in some places drastically, during the 19th century. Investigation of the back of Tintoretto's canvas *St. Mark Rescuing a Saracen from Shipwreck* (page 446) has shown that the subject was originally to have been another miracle of St. Mark, set not at sea but in an interior. The dramatic shipwreck scene with its "horrible effects" (in the words of Rafaello Borghini, writing in 1584) subsequently depicted on the canvas was intended as a counterpart to the famous *Storm at Sea* in the neighboring *albergo*, which had been executed decades earlier, probably by Palma Vecchio and Paris Bordone. The rejected interior shown on Tintoretto's canvas formed a symmetrical parallel to the architecture in the painting of *St. Mark Working Many Miracles* (page 449).

In planning this cycle, Tintoretto very obviously had in mind a unified composition such as the tripartite designs on the ground floor of the scuola's outer façade, where the main and side doors are each flanked by two symmetrical low reliefs, giving the architectural illusion of receding toward the portals set between them. Rangone and his painter probably first intended to place the group of three paintings, conceived in strictly symmetrical terms, on the northern, narrow side of the Chapter Hall, opposite the *Miracle of the Slave*. In this position the three pictures, placed side by side like tapestries, would have acted as a large screen to conceal the building of the chapel behind them until it was completed. Thus placed, the central painting of the *Removal of the Body of St. Mark* (page 447) would have elongated the perspective of the Chapter Hall: the arcades on the left, which are reminiscent of the Piazza San Marco, would have continued the line of the row of round-arched windows on the west wall, and the wall subdivided into frame-like sections on the right side of

Tintoretto
St. Mark Rescuing a Saracen from Shipwreck,
between 1562 and 1566
Oil on canvas, 398 x 337 cm
Gallerie dell'Accademia, Venice

The picture was originally intended to be the left "wing" of a three-part cycle showing posthumous miracles of St. Mark. The saint's soul, at an earlier stage in the painting shown in flight top left in the central picture, the *Removal of the Body of St. Mark* (page 447), has materialized in this painting top right, where St. Mark is shown as a flying figure coming in haste to rescue a Saracen who has called on him in his hour of need, and conveying him to a lifeboat as a reward for his conversion. The symbol of the power of God's own aid symmetrically balances the figure of the saint, manifesting itself as a mysterious cloud in human form. The lower edge of the picture shows the donor Tommaso Rangone with his golden knightly robe flung back, helping another Muslim into the Christian boat.

Tintoretto
The Removal of the Body of St. Mark,
between 1562 and 1566
Oil on canvas, 398 x 315 cm
Gallerie dell'Accademia, Venice

After the martyrdom of St. Mark in Alexandria, his mortal remains were to have been burnt on a pyre (shown in the center of the picture). However, a great storm broke out, enabling the Christians to take the body of their bishop to safety. Using rapid brushstrokes in lead white, Tintoretto conjures up a ghostly ballet of fleeing pagans in the background of the picture. In the right foreground, Tommaso Rangone, this time in an ermine-lined robe of office, occupies a privileged position near the saint's body as it is carried away. What was originally the central strip-shaped section of the floor shows that a good deal of the painting has been trimmed on the left side. In the process, carried out in 1815–1816, the soul of St. Mark flying to heaven was removed; it had been depicted by Tintoretto, using a brush dipped in lead white and applied to the canvas, as a crystalline male nude top left.

The configuration of the group almost audibly marching over the square, which is flooded with rainwater, is reminiscent of an Entombment of Christ painted by Giovanni Antonio da Pordenone in the cloisters of Santo Stefano. The content of this tribute to a much admired predecessor has a purpose: the formal echoes of an entombment scene enable Tintoretto to endow St. Mark, as patron saint of Venice, with something almost resembling Christ-like status, very much in line with the ideas of the Grand Confraternity of St. Mark for whose Chapter Hall the picture was painted.

the picture would have corresponded to the paneling on the long east wall. Soon, however, plans for the hanging of the three pictures must have changed, and it was decided to place them all on the same long east wall, for they take careful account of the way the light falls in through the two south windows looking out on the Campo. Vasari saw the three pictures on the long east wall as early as 1566, arranged in a sequence that did not correspond at all to the original concept.

At the Scuola Grande di' San Marco the protracted building works and inevitable temporary measures, the annual shift of emphasis to different parts of the refurbishment program as every new board took office, and finally, differences of opinion between the ambitious Rangone and his *confratelli*, eventually prevented the realization of an integrated environment. Even today, the almost intact ensemble of paintings in

the choir of San Cassiano shows how precisely Tintoretto could adjust his paintings not only to their surroundings but to each other if he was given a free hand. In 1563, the sacramental altar of the church was moved to the choir, and the Scuola del Santissimo Sacramento, responsible for serving that altar, was now able to refurbish the choir itself. Two years later the officiating guardian of the scuola, Giampiero Mazzoleni, commissioned Tintoretto to paint an altarpiece showing the resurrection of Christ and Saints Cassian and Cecilia, the patron saints of the church. Relics of the saints were contained in the old *pala* (altarpiece) of the high altar. This *pala*, an icon of embossed and partly gilded rolled silver on a wooden base, was to be retained, like the mosaics in the choir, when the scuola carried out its conversion. To that end, a mechanism was fitted to the altar allowing the old

pala to be lowered beneath the level of the new altarpiece and raised again when necessary, for instance on certain feast days. There was nothing unusual about this: in San Marco, it was possible to fold up the panel painting executed in 1345 by Paolo Veneziano and his sons to protect the *Pala d'Oro* by turning a hand crank, and in 1534 a canvas by Titian, capable of being lowered, was installed to protect the medieval silver-gilt *pala* on the new high altar of San Salvador. However, in the case of San Cassiano it was not the modern picture that had to make way on feast days, but the venerable *pala*, which was lowered out of sight on ordinary days. Even when it was raised on feast days it covered only a part of the new painting.

As the work of renovation progressed, Tintoretto was commissioned in 1568, when Cristoforo de Gozi was guardian of the same scuola, to supply two more large paintings for the side walls of the choir of San Cassiano. Since the main entrance to the church was on the side facing the Campo, the visitor's glance fell first on the left-hand interior wall of the choir, for which Tintoretto painted a Crucifixion. Using this picture as his point of departure, he devised a very sophisticated system of inter-relationships of form and content, which included the picture for the high altar painted earlier and the Descent into Hell placed opposite the Crucifixion.

The composition of the *Crucifixion* is at first glance eccentric in the literal sense: the crosses of Christ and the two thieves are all in the right-hand half of the picture, seen from below. The unusual diagonal position of the crosses shows Tintoretto taking account of the angle of vision of a viewer standing in front of the choir. That viewer is intended to see the crosses on the same axis as the high altar, so that Christ seems to be looking into the nave. On the whole, setting the Cross on a similar slanting angle had previously been a feature mainly of small-scale German paintings, for instance by Albrecht Dürer and Lucas Cranach, and in fact Tintoretto used a graphic print of northern provenance as his model for the crucified Christ. If one compares this relatively small etching by Maerten van Heemskerck, which is full of busy movement, with the large-scale clarity of the painting, it is obvious that Tintoretto's basic design for his composition was his own—created in dialogue, so to speak, with the place where it was to hang—and he used the print only as a practical aid. Perhaps he even placed a grid drawn to scale over the central section of the leaf in order to

transfer Heemskerck's figure of Christ more quickly and accurately to the canvas. Tintoretto's asymmetrical composition, with the crosses placed on the diagonal, was immediately echoed not only by Titian and Veronese but also in Venetian book illustration.

While Maerten van Heemskerck's print shows the soldiers casting dice for Christ's garment, Tintoretto depicts the fixing in place of the titulus, the abbreviated inscription which, according to Roman custom, stated the reason for the condemnation and execution of the crucified man: I.N.R.I. = Jesus Nazarenus Rex Judaeorum (Jesus of Nazareth, King of the Jews). In medieval tradition, the seven-runged ladder so conspicuously placed in the picture is to be understood as the ladder of the virtues leading to heaven: the soul of the viewer is invited to climb step by step, supported by the seven virtues or seven gifts of the Holy Spirit, to a mystical union with Christ. However, the ladder has a function in the composition of the picture too: picking up the gaze of Christ, it leads to the figure of Mary, who has sunk to the ground in grief in the left-hand lower corner of the painting. St. John's consoling gesture points her (and the observer) to the picture of the *Resurrection* on the high altar, or depending on the observer's viewpoint to the *Descent into Hell* opposite the *Crucifixion*. Tintoretto skillfully linked these two pictures by making the figure of Christ in the *Resurrection* appear to be flying across into hell, although in fact the *anastasis* (Christ's descent into Hell to free Man's first parents from Limbo) actually takes place before the Resurrection and after the laying of Christ in the tomb. While in the *Descent into Hell* Christ's athletic body, handsome head surrounded by luxuriant brown locks, and the royal red cloak he wears derive from the *Resurrection*, painted three years earlier, Jacopo Tintoretto makes a small change to the banner of victory. In the *Descent into Hell* it acquires a reddish glow, forming a triumphant counterpart to the Roman military banners in the background of the *Crucifixion*. The eye contact between the crucified Christ and Mary is matched in the *Descent into Hell* by the similar eye contact between Christ and Eve, who occupies a position in the right-hand bottom corner of the picture similar to the Virgin's in the picture opposite. The three-part cycle in San Cassiano thus comes full circle in content as well as form, for in the typological comparison between the Old and New Testaments the Virgin Mary assumes the role of the New Eve.

Tintoretto
St. Mark Working Many Miracles, 1562–1566
Oil on canvas, 396 x 400 cm
Pinacoteca di Brera, Milan

It has recently been shown that this picture does not, as was long assumed, show the rediscovery of the body of St. Mark on 25 June 1094, but various miracles of healing worked by the patron saint of Venice: he is depicted raising a man from the dead, restoring a blind man's sight, and casting out devils. As in the *Miracle of the Slave* (page 431), which he painted for the same location, Tintoretto illustrates the power of St. Mark by placing the invisible guidelines of his construction of the perspective in the saint's outstretched hand. The donor Tommaso Rangone, who claimed great healing powers for himself, thereby making large sums of money, had his own figure painted kneeling humbly, but none the less wearing the magnificent golden robe of a *cavalier aurato*. Doge Girolamo Priuli had only recently bestowed the title of "Golden Knight" on him.

TINTORETTO AT THE
SCUOLA GRANDE DI SAN ROCCO

Tintoretto
The Apotheosis of St. Roch, 1564
Oil on canvas, 240 x 360 cm
Scuola Grande di San Rocco, Venice

The spirit of Michelangelo, who had only recently died, seems to permeate this ceiling picture. While the figure of God the Father is very reminiscent of the Creator in the frescoes of the Sistine Chapel, his encounter with the rising St. Roch suggests Titian's famous *Assunta* (page 307), the epoch-making altarpiece of 1516–1518 in the nearby Frari church, showing the Assumption of the Virgin. The muscular figure of the saint, patron of the victims of the plague, and the attractive representatives of the nine choirs of angels, slightly reminiscent of Gothic cathedral sculpture, seem to stand on the edge of an opening in the roof itself. This extreme and un-Venetian illusionism ultimately derives from the Mantuan ceiling pictures of Andrea Mantegna (see page 91).

In search of large wall surfaces to suit his exuberant imagination, Tintoretto's eye had fallen on the Scuola Grande di San Rocco at quite an early date. The confraternity, founded in 1478, acquired the status of a Scuola Grande only eleven years later. Together with some 200 smaller confraternities, the five Scuole Grandi—a number that rose to six with the elevation of the Scuola di San Teodoro in 1552—made an important contribution to the widely envied social and political stability of the Venetian Republic. While in the Middle Ages there were still scuole which encouraged both men and women members, and a double governing board to run them, the institutions later increasingly became purely male societies. The Scuole offered their members both decent burial and assistance at times of need, for instance if they fell sick or suffered an accident. The benefits could take the form of a monthly pension (*mese*), housing (*casa per amor de dio*), or a minimal dowry (*donzelle*) for daughters who might otherwise remain unmarried and thus, as was the accepted view of the times, in moral danger. In the richest and largest of the Scuole Grandi, a smoothly functioning administrative system was essential to manage the income from foundations and real estate, to examine applications for support, and not least to supervise the confraternity's liturgical and ritual duties. In order to avoid any abuse of their official positions, the board was re-elected annually. The complicated hierarchy of offices and the endless elections were like a copy on a smaller scale of the great machinery of state, particularly in the Grand Confraternities, whose Chapter Halls were smaller versions of the Sala del Maggior Consiglio in the Ducal Palace. Since the state itself was governed by the two thousand or so patricians who made up the Great Council, the Scuole Grandi offered craftsmen, middle-class merchants, and freelance professionals a welcome opportunity to compensate for their lack of real political power. And since the Grand Confraternities were in constant competition with each other for fame and honor, this compensation took the form not only of social commitment but also of outward show. When the jeweler and poet Alessandro Caravia criticized the addiction to splendor shown by the Scuole in a satirical work of 1541, he specifically had in mind the magnificent new Chapter Hall which the Scuola Grande di San Rocco, still quite a new institution, had been

building for itself since 1515. Although at a later date Jacopo Tintoretto painted a portrait of Caravia for the collection of the goldsmith, jeweler, and art dealer Hans Jakob König, he naturally enough tried to profit from the building criticized by the writer, and get his own work displayed there. The pictorial world of the Scuola Grande di San Rocco today probably seems as if it were conceived easily in one smooth process, but it is really the outcome of a dogged struggle, lasting for decades, in which the artist showed almost superhuman patience and persistence.

As in the Scuola di San Marco, he had been preceded by fast-working decorative artists who provided the new Chapter Hall with large and thinly painted fabric hangings and canvas wall coverings for the feast of St. Rocco (Roch) in 1542. In the summer of 1546, pictorial decoration was contemplated for the Sala dell'Albergo (the confraternity's own treasury and boardroom) but no plans were presented to the general membership. The painting of *St. Roch Healing the Plague Stricken* (page 434–435), which Tintoretto executed in 1549 on commission from the Scuola for the neighboring church of St. Rocco, was intended to give the painter entry to the Scuola itself and acceptance by it. Unfortunately, Titian noticed what Tintoretto was doing. In 1551, he renewed his own membership of the Confraternity of St. Rocco, which had lapsed some 18 years earlier, and even, in 1553, surprisingly offered to create a painting for the large *albergo* wall over the committee gallery. Since nothing of the kind materialized in the years that followed, he probably simply wanted to block his younger rival's progress. Not until 1559 was Tintoretto able to resume intensive contact with the Confraternity of St. Roch, when he painted various miraculous cures performed by Christ on the double doors of a huge cupboard where the valuable liturgical vessels of San Rocco were stored. Five years later, on 22 May 1564, 37 members of the full committee (*banca e giunta*) decided to provide money at least for gilding the central oval of the ceiling of the Sala dell'Albergo and a painting for it. The list of donors shows that most had Tintoretto in mind from the first: one member said he would contribute only 15 ducats if the commission went to any other artist. On 31 May it was decided to hold a competition in which "three or four of the most outstanding masters of Venice" were to

participate. However, the competition was never publicly announced, and after coming to a secret agreement with those members who favored him, Tintoretto presented the completed picture (page 451) to the governing board three weeks later, on 22 June 1564. To facilitate its acceptance, he asked no fee at all, and at the same time he promised to supply further ceiling pictures for the Sala too. A week later, when the full membership officially decided against holding the competition and accepted the gift, Tintoretto had his foot in the door.

In its content, the oval showing the *Apotheosis of St. Roch* (page 451) forms the keystone of the *albergo* ceiling. Since the smaller pictures swiftly supplied later, showing allegorical representations of virtues and the other Scuole Grandi, relate to the central picture, it is now thought that a program had been drawn up well in advance. Perhaps the oval picture was even begun before Tintoretto's friends made their first official move on 22 May.

The lightning strike made by Jacopo in conquering the scuola created a sensation and aroused displeasure. Nonetheless, when a vote was taken on his membership on 11 March 1565, he was accepted by the general membership by 85 votes to 19. The new governing board, under Girolamo Rota, immediately commissioned the decoration of the walls of the *albergo*.

The cycle of pictures was to take as its subject the Passion, from Christ Before Pilate to the Ecce Homo, the Carrying of the Cross, and finally the Crucifixion.

The program was carried out in reverse order, for Tintoretto began with the last of these pictures, the *Crucifixion* for the back wall above the committee gallery. Jacopo must have taken his critics' breath away with this monumental work, for in its narrative wealth and pictorial opulence it is a universe in itself. He signed it, both proudly and humbly, as *TINCTORECTVS*, the "upright dyer" (tinctor rectus).

This very characteristic little pun provides us with an insight into Tintoretto's education. Unlike Titian, he must have had some knowledge of Latin. It also offers evidence of many of those qualities that determined Jacopo's character as it is presented in contemporary sources and posthumous anecdotes: honesty, candor, obstinacy, physical and psychological stability, an awareness of the tradition of craftsmanship, and also a ready wit.

PRINTS FROM THE NORTH

In his *Crucifixion* (right), Tintoretto shows not only the Cross of Christ erect, but two preceding phases of the incident in the figures of the two thieves. Similar depictions of the work of the executioners—for instance boring holes ready to take the nails, or nailing Christ to the Cross as it still lies on the ground— are more usual in German and Netherlandish art than Italian painting. In fact, Tintoretto bases his

presentation of the raising of the Cross on a German model, a woodcut by Hans Baldung Grien. The book on the Passion of Christ illustrated by Baldung must have traveled along the busy trade route passing through Augsburg, Mittenwald, Innsbruck, and the Brenner road, thus reaching Venice, where the Germans had a large trading house of their own (the Fondaco dei Tedeschi, today the main post office building). In spite of protectionist guild regulations, the geographical situation and transalpine commercial connections of Venice exposed Venetian artists to the competition and influence of German and Netherlandish painting and graphic art. Flemish paintings were admired and collected in Italy around the middle of the 15th century, particularly for their faithfulness to life. There were already echoes of the compositions, pictorial subjects, and stylistic characteristics of such artists as Jan van Eyck and Rogier van der Weyden in Paduan and Venetian painting, for instance in the work of Andrea Mantegna and his brother-in-law Giovanni Bellini. Later, paintings from the workshops and circles of such Netherlandish painters as Hieronymus Bosch, Jan Gossaert, Herri met de Bles, and Joachim Patinir found their way into the patrician houses of Padua and Venice. Many such painters visited Venice themselves, for instance Dürer (1505/06) and Jan van Scorel (1520/21), and left major works there.

Northern landscapes of small format on religious or fantastic subjects were particularly popular among collectors in the Veneto, and included pictures of conflagrations "in the Flemish manner." They left many echoes in the works of Venetian Renaissance painters born around 1480/90—for instance, the pictures of Savoldo, whose own wife was Flemish. Like Titian, who according to Vasari had "several outstanding German landscape and foliage painters" in his studio, and worked with such artists as Johann Stephan von Calcar and the Amsterdam painter Lambert Sustris, Tintoretto too had assistants from northern regions.

Influence at least as strong as that of painting north of the Alps came from the countless woodcuts, engravings, and etchings from the Netherlands, Germany, and Switzerland that began to reach Venice in the late 15th century. Venetian painters and graphic artists like Titian, Girolamo Romanino, and Giulio Campagnola borrowed from them not only landscape scenery but also figural subjects and indeed whole ideas for compositions. It has even been said of some artists, such as Lorenzo Lotto, that they adopted the ideas of the Reformation along with northern prints. For instance, a translation of the Bible by Antonio Brucioli published in Venice in 1532, and later accused of being heretical, contains woodcuts copied from Hans Holbein's illustrations for Martin Luther's translation of the New Testament.

The most influential prints to make their way across the Alps to Venice and thence to other artistic centers of Italy include the famous woodcut series by Albrecht Dürer: the *Life of the Virgin* (1501–1510), the *Great Passion* (1496–1510), and the *Small Passion* (1509/10), which although it is indeed of smaller format is much

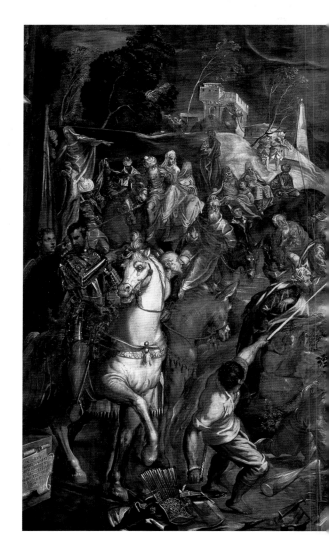

Tintoretto
The Crucifixion, 1565
Oil on canvas, 536 x 1224 cm
Scuola Grande di San Rocco, Venice

The models for this monumental Crucifixion are to be sought outside Venice, in German graphic prints, and in the Paduan frescoes of Altichiero and Giusto de Menabuoi (page 41). In the good and bad thieves to the left and right of Christ, who is already crucified, Tintoretto depicts different phases of the execution. He shows the body of Christ surrounded by a great aureole, so that it seems to have separated from the Cross, thus giving the impression that Tintoretto is bringing the Redeemer out of the area of the picture itself and into the viewer's space. Hovering over the boardroom gallery of the charitable Confraternity of St. Roch (Rocco), Christ speaks as the representative of suffering mankind: "I thirst!"

the more extensive of the two. Even in his early woodcut the *Triumph of Faith* of 1510/11, the young Titian tried to imitate the expressive and dynamic line of Dürer's prints. Five years later, perhaps with the participation of Titian, an Apocalypse was published in Venice with woodcut illustrations heavily dependent on the Nuremberg master. The influence of Dürer's prints art continued into the second half of the 16th century: of the fourty-nine woodcuts contained in a book that appeared in Venice in 1557 on the Life and Passion of Christ, fourteen are copied from the *Life of the Virgin* and twenty-six from the *Small Passion*.

It is not yet certain whether the inspiration for Tintoretto's *Adoration of the Shepherds* (page 454) was the original woodcut from Dürer's *Small Passion* or the copy by Marcantonio Raimondi (page 454). In any case, Tintoretto's monumental, atmospheric, and very individual version represented a qualitative leap that makes the observer forget the model, which was already relatively old at the time. In the dormant stock of ideas stored in Jacopo's private artistic laboratory, Dürer's woodcut (or its copy) would have been only one among many well-worn prints that were hoarded over a long period, stacked and restacked, and might be brought out for use when needed years or even decades later. The age of the models played no part; the only

important consideration was the pictorial ideas that could be gleaned from them. In working on his *Flight into Egypt* (page 35), Tintoretto went to the woodcut on the same subject from Dürer's *Life of the Virgin* (or Marcantonio Raimondi's copy of it) but found only the framing palm tree suitable for his purposes, and moved it from the left to the right of the composition. The free and independent way in which Jacopo treated his models is also evident in the *Annunciation* (page 455). Tintoretto took over the spatial disposition and Mary's attitude of alarm, slightly altered, from an engraving by the Netherlandish artist Maerten van Heemskerck (page 455), but merged them with motifs from other prints and ideas of his own to form an entirely new composition. Soon after Jacopo's death, this picture in its own turn was reproduced and distributed as an engraving by the Fleming Justus Sadeler.

Tintoretto's admirers and patrons at the Scuola di San Rocco included, beside the 1565 *guardian grande* Girolamo Rota, a merchant of Flemish descent called Paolo d'Anna, the treasurer Marino Malipiero, Veronese's patron Alvise Cuccina, and Marco Balbiani, who was chief officer of the confraternity in 1573. Balbiani, whom Jacopo painted in a work long thought to be a self-portrait, wanted to commission a carved wooden ceiling for the church of San Rocco during his

Marcantonio Raimondi
The Adoration of the Shepherds
(after Dürer), after 1515 (?)
Engraving, 124 x 97 cm
Kupferstichkabinett, Staatliche Museen, Berlin

The model for Tintoretto's *Adoration of the Shepherds* may have been not Dürer's original woodcut from the *Small Passion* but this outstanding engraving, copied to the scale of the original.

Marcantonio Raimondi, from Bologna, was the best copyist of Dürer's graphic prints in Italy, and worked faster than any other—he was also the most damaging to Dürer's own business. In all, his workshop produced copies of eight engravings and over sixty woodcuts by the Nuremberg master, and to Dürer's great annoyance they came on the art market as genuine. According to Vasari, Raimondi had acquired his models in the Piazza di San Marco in Venice.

Tintoretto
The Adoration of the Shepherds, 1577–1581
Oil on canvas, 542 x 455 cm
Scuola Grande di San Rocco, Venice

As so often in the works of Tintoretto, it is difficult to decide whether the horizontal seam on the gigantic canvas inspired him to create this unusual composition on two levels, or whether, conversely, he aimed to conceal the seam with the aid of the composition. Despite their poor surroundings, the Holy Family are remote from earthly regions. As in Dürer's composition (page 456), which served as the model, the rafters anticipate the Cross of Christ. Deliberately, and with admonitory intent, Tintoretto contrasts the dilapidated roof above the Holy Family with the magnificent carved and gilded ceiling (page 456) beneath which the full membership of the Scuola Grande di San Rocco used to assemble.

Tintoretto
The Annunciation, between 1582 and 1587
Oil on canvas, 422 x 545 cm
Scuola Grande di San Rocco, Venice

Of the eight phases into which the Venetian Theatine monk Giovanni Marinoni (1490–1562) divided the story of the Annunciation, Tintoretto's painting shows the second, following the angel's greeting: "And when she saw him, she was troubled at his saying, and cast in her mind what manner of salutation this should be" (Luke 1: 29). In late medieval painting north of the Alps, Mary's conception is often shown as a depiction of the infant Christ flying toward the Virgin on a divine ray of light, like a naked putto. As if to follow the path of the heavenly child's flight exactly, Tintoretto multiplies this motif into a whole phallic swarm of putti.

Philipp Galle, after Maerten van Heemskerck
An Angel Appears to St. Philip, 1575
Engraving, 21.3 x 27.5 cm
Graphische Sammlung Albertina, Vienna

The engraving designed by Maerten van Heemskerck provided Tintoretto with an important source for the setting and main figure of his *Annunciation* (above). In some respects this is a process of influence in reverse: as Vasari commented, the many engravings that Heemskerck had made in Haarlem from his own drawings after his return from his stay in Rome (1532–1536/37) were often "very much in the Italian style." Tintoretto may have sensed in them not only a formal language related to his own but, above all, a related artistic temperament driven by as unbounded a delight in narrative as his own.

The Chapter Hall
View of the altar
Scuola Grande di San Rocco, Venice

Between 1575 and 1581, Tintoretto provided the
Chapter Hall of the Grand Confraternity of St. Roch
(Rocco) with a range of gigantic wall and ceiling
paintings. In the course of his work he created a very
complex system of inter-relationships, both of form and
of content, between not only the wall paintings and the
ceiling pictures above them, but also between the pictorial
decoration and the architectural design of the whole hall.
As the principal scene of Tintoretto's activities, the Scuola
Grande di San Rocco has always been a place of
pilgrimage for artists and art-lovers. Recently, Woody
Allen, a great admirer of Tintoretto, set one of the scenes
in his film *Everybody Says I Love You* in this hall.

Opposite page: Tintoretto
The Brazen Serpent, 1575/76
Oil on canvas, 840 x 520 cm
Scuola Grande di San Rocco, Venice

When the Chosen People wandering in the desert were
decimated by a plague of fiery serpents as a punishment
for despising the divine manna (the "bread" that fell from
heaven), Moses set up a brazen serpent: the sight of it was
to cure the Israelites. This incident is the Old Testament's
typological parallel to the crucifixion of Christ, and
Tintoretto also makes it a terrifying image of the plague
epidemic raging in Venice in his own time. Enveloped in
shadow, God the Father hovers over the scene in anger,
like a crucified figure. The dead and dying seem to be
falling out of the lower half of the ceiling picture in the
Chapter Hall of the Confraternity of St. Roch.

Tintoretto
Moses Striking the Rock, 1577
Oil on canvas, 550 x 520 cm
Scuola Grande di San Rocco, Venice

God the Father, borne aloft on a supernatural crystal globe, comes in haste to save his thirsty people. The water struck by Moses from the rock for the Israelites seems to be spurting toward the viewer past the leaves of a fig tree. To care for the health and nourishment of the poor, the common denominator between the three great ceiling paintings, was among the principal social obligations of the Scuola Grande di San Rocco.

Tintoretto
The Massacre of the Innocents, 1582–1587
Oil on canvas, 422 x 546 cm
Scuola Grande di San Rocco, Venice

With intense inner involvement, Tintoretto presents a picture of masculine brutality and feminine courage. As always, he uses not faces but bodies, draperies, lighting, color, and artistic technique to convey expression. The dreadful marks on the ramp of the stairway, for instance, appear as if painted in real blood. The glance of the woman at the lower edge of the picture suggests that her right arm, cut short by the edge of the picture itself, was once stretched out into the viewer's own world in a plea for help. To achieve this literally gripping effect, Tintoretto may have attached an arm made of plaster or stucco to the picture, as many Baroque painters did later.

period in office, and many paintings by Tintoretto would certainly have been installed in it. His successor Alvise Zanochin reassigned the project: since the old and only temporary ceiling decoration of the Chapter Hall was now "very obviously decayed," the carver was to work not on the church ceiling but on that of the Sala Grande (page 456). In April 1575, the heavy, elaborately decorated wooden ceiling was ready to have painted canvases installed. Ideas for the pictorial program had probably been drawn up long ago, but all plans were shelved in the face of the catastrophe that overwhelmed Venice and destroyed its zest for life in the summer of the year 1575: the arrival of the Plague.

By the summer of 1577, over 45,000 Venetians had fallen victim to this terrible epidemic, more than a quarter of the population, who numbered about 180,000 in all. The first cases of plague were diagnosed

on 25 June 1575, in Tintoretto's parish of San Marziale. Only a week later, on 2 July, Jacopo approached the governing board of the Confraternity of St. Roch and offered to paint the central picture of the Chapter Hall ceiling free of charge. In view of this timely coincidence, one may suspect that Tintoretto had struck a pious bargain with St. Roch, patron of the victims of the plague, for his family's protection, secretly promising him the gigantic canvas as a votive gift. In the summer of 1576, work on the painting was so far advanced that plans could be made for its installation. Since Tintoretto had envisaged the ceremonial unveiling of the picture for 16 August, the feast of St. Roch, he suggested to the committee on 22 June, that they might have the surrounding carving on the ceiling gilded, and for the task he named a certain master with whom he intended to negotiate a special price. This apparently trivial detail is good

Tintoretto
St. Mary of Egypt, 1582–1587
Oil on canvas, 425 x 211 cm
Scuola Grande di San Rocco, Venice

Like its counterpart (right), this picture is a religious landscape
painting. The key to its interpretation is in the figure, seen from
behind, of the hermit looking up meditatively from her pious
reading. To give outward expression to Mary's religious ecstasy,
Tintoretto portrays it in terms of the landscape: the trees shoot
up like fireworks, their leaves exploding as if in a shower of sparks
before the dark sky.

Tintoretto
St. Mary Magdalene, 1582–1587
Oil on canvas, 425 x 209 cm
Scuola Grande di San Rocco, Venice

Like the landscape with the figure of St. Mary of Egypt (left), this
work too was influenced by northern models: it suggests the
paintings and prints of the Danube School (for instance by Albrecht
Altdorfer and Wolf Huber), and woodcuts by Hans Baldung Grien,
the Nuremberg graphic artist Virgil Solis, and the mysterious artist,
known only by his monogram of HWG, who depicted St. John the
Evangelist on Patmos, surrounded by a fantastic landscape.

evidence of the careful and comprehensive control Tintoretto had by now acquired over the furnishing of "his" Scuola.

A few days after the unveiling of Tintoretto's extraordinary ceiling painting, on 27 August 1576, Titian died: perhaps, like his son Orazio, of the plague. By now the epidemic had reached its peak. Early in September the Doge made a vow to build the votive church of Il Redentore. In a solemn rogation service in San Marco he tried to encourage the stricken population by speaking of the trials of the children of Israel in the Old Testament, reminding the congregation of two particular miracles whereby God had saved his chosen people in their hour of need: the rain of manna, and the miracle of the water produced when Moses struck the rock. Tintoretto took these two incidents as the subjects of the other two huge pictures he painted for the Chapter Hall ceiling in 1577 (page 458). There was still some opposition to Tintoretto and his art in the Confraternity of St. Roch. With diplomacy and a positively oriental skill in negotiation, Jacopo persuaded the Scuola to comply with its good fortune. In January 1577 his offer was accepted: he had promised that for the time being he would charge only his expenses for materials for the two planned pictures of the miracles of manna and water, leaving payment for the completed works to the Scuola's discretion. Work on the *Rain of Manna* was already in progress when, on Annunciation Day (25 March) 1577, a day of national celebration in Venice, Tintoretto made a solemnly phrased offer to provide all the pictures necessary for the rest of the ceiling on the same conditions. In November 1577, when a large part of this Herculean task had been completed in less than a year, Jacopo Tintoretto finally ventured on his last and decisive coup: "And to show the great love that I bear to this our honorable scuola, out of the devotion I owe to glorious St. Rocco, and in my wish to see this scuola completed and adorned with pictures in every place where they are necessary, I am content to devote the rest of my life to its service, and will pledge myself so to do. I promise that besides the aforesaid ceiling I will make the ten great pictures that are to be placed in the [meeting] hall between the windows, the altarpiece for the high altar, and also, when the time comes, to provide the ceiling of the church of the glorious St. Roch with painting wherever figures painted on canvas in oils are appropriate, and similarly to provide all other necessary history paintings for both the scuola and the church, and that with all my skill and knowledge. And I promise to give three large pictures ready and installed every year on the Feast of St. Rocco—when the paintings in the great hall are finished, in the series of their commissioning. I will bear the costs of colors for all my pictures, and as for payment for the ceiling of the chapter hall, I will be content with the 200 ducats I have received. That additional fee upon which the board might decide, by conscientious assessment and judgment of my work, I donate to the scuola—on condition that, in recognition of my labors and the works named above, to be executed throughout my lifetime, I will be paid a pension of 100 ducats every year on the Feast of St. Roch, when I have installed the three large, completed pictures approved by Your Highnesses [the governing board, and the Doge as a born member]."

In Tintoretto's practical plans for his life, this deal with the Scuola di San Rocco assumed a value similar to that of the stipend granted to Titian from 1550 by Philip of Spain for the regular delivery of mythological or religious paintings. One hundred ducats might be twice the annual wage of a skilled worker in the Venetian wharves and artisans (*arsenale*), but Titian had received at least 500 ducats a year from the coffers of the Habsburgs alone. The main purpose of Tintoretto's bargain, then, is not to be sought in economic calculations. Since he had indeed brought his large family unscathed through the two years of the plague epidemic, it is understandable that he felt an obligation to St. Roch. Up to the completion of the work in 1587, he invested more inventive power and artistic virtuosity in the pictorial ornamentation of the Scuola di San Rocco than in many more prestigious commissions. However, his commitment to the Scuola di San Rocco was a matter not merely of veneration for the saint, but also contained elements of a very modern desire for artistic self-fulfillment. Tintoretto could give his imagination free rein here; something impossible, for instance, in the Ducal Palace, where there was certainly a need for new pictures after the fires of 1574 and 1577, but an artist must work to rigid iconographic guidelines and suffer resentful rivals. Since the legend of St. Roch himself had been depicted in pictorial terms in the neighboring church, he now had a chance to project his personal vision of the great biblical stories on huge canvases in the Scuola's chapter hall. The prospect does not seem to have pleased all the members, since it took several applications before Tintoretto's offer was finally accepted by the governing board and the full membership on 28 February 1578.

Hans Leu the Younger (?)
Meadow Landscape with Watermill, ca. 1520/25
Pen and black ink on paper with red-brown ground, color-washed in gray, and heightened in white, 20.7 x 15.2 cm
Kupferstichkabinett, Staatliche Museen, Berlin

A fairytale atmosphere permeates this drawing, which is influenced by the "Danube style" and may be by Hans Leu the Younger, the most important Zurich painter of the late Middle Ages. Tintoretto possibly had such works as this in mind when he painted the two pictures St. Mary of Egypt and St. Mary Magdalene (page 460). There are relationships not only in the composition and the thematic material, but also in the special use of a red-brown ground bathing these expressive landscapes in a mysterious twilight. The two Venetian canvases are, of course, considerably larger than this drawing, but it is noticeable that Tintoretto in effect drew these almost monochrome pictures with his brush rather than painting them.

THE LATE WORK AND
TINTORETTO'S LEGACY

Tintoretto
Bacchus, Ariadne, and Venus, 1577/78
Oil on canvas, 146 x 167 cm
Palazzo Ducale, Venice

Although this picture has suffered some damage (partly as a result of cleaning and the retouching of large areas of color) it is clear that in it Tintoretto was using a more conservative technique with a higher degree of finish than usual. He was adjusting to the particular situation from which the picture would be seen: the works of art in this room, the Salotto Quadrato, were hung in bright daylight, and could be viewed at close quarters by foreign visitors and envoys to the Ducal Palace. It would have been inadvisable to distract the minds of such a public from the propaganda value of the glorification of the Venetian state by employing an unusually modern style of painting.

It had been almost as difficult for Jacopo to gain entry to the Ducal Palace as to get a footing in the Scuola Grande di San Rocco. He first managed to place a work there in 1553, in the same year as Paolo Veronese, but not only was his future rival Veronese ten years younger, he had only just arrived in Venice. At first Tintoretto defended his recently acquired territory by offering outrageously low prices, which worked to Veronese's detriment as well, but later two devastating fires dampened his enthusiasm for working in the Ducal Palace. After the destruction in May 1574 of the Collegio and the Senate halls, which had contained among other works votive paintings by Tintoretto, the conflagration of December 1577 claimed not only Titian's *Battle of Spoleto*, but also several important pictures by Jacopo in the Sala del Maggior Consiglio and the Sala dello Scrutinio. In order to meet his deadlines, Tintoretto delegated to his workshop many of the allegories, votive pictures and historical paintings later commissioned from him for the Ducal Palace. However, the four allegorical paintings now in the Anticollegio were executed by Tintoretto himself: the *Three Graces and Mercury*, *Minerva Keeping Mars From Peace and Harmony*, *Bacchus, Ariadne, and Venus* (page 463), and the *Forge of Vulcan*. Originally these paintings adorned the walls of the Salotto (or Atrio) Quadrato, a magnificent vestibule between the Scala d'Oro and the Sala delle Quattro Porte. In 1564/65, while his patron Girolamo Priuli was in office as Doge, Jacopo had already painted a handsome ceiling picture for this important central waiting room, a place where there was much coming and going. It showed the Doge kneeling before the allegorical figures of Peace and Justice. The wall paintings executed in 1577/78 are of the same quality. In these works Tintoretto presented an abstract political program, heavy with symbolism, in captivatingly sensual terms.

This is particularly obvious in the *Three Graces and Mercury*. The attributes of the Graces—the dice, the rose, and the myrtle branch—correspond to those in a book entitled *Le imagini dei Dei de gl'antichi* (Images of the Gods of the Ancients), by Vincenzo Cartari, which went through many editions in Venice at this time; after 1571 it also had illustrations, and it was used

by many artists. According to Cartari, Mercury, as companion and leader of the Graces, personifies reason and well-considered speech. As in the sculptural program of Sansovino's Loggetta, where Mercury symbolizes the eloquence of the statesmen of Venice, Tintoretto's painting refers to rhetoric as an important element in Venetian politics. In addition, the presence of Mercury indicates that the ruling class of Venice distributes its favors (*grazie*) and its love (symbolized by the rose) with reason; that is, according to the recipients' merits and worth. The interlinking of the gestures of the Three Graces, and the parallel arrangement of the axes of the bodies, are to be seen as suggesting unity and the harmonious discharge of office, a major virtue to the Venetians and one on which, for instance, the state treasurers prided themselves in the dedicatory inscription of their votive painting. As in the other pictures in the cycle, there are two other levels of meaning: while the Graces, who appear weightless, and the figure of Mercury, which is capable of flight, personify the element of air, the burgeoning plants and graceful flowers show that the season is spring. The cycle of pictures in the Salotto Quadrato derives its really momentous significance from the way it is integrated into the perpetual cycle of the seasons and the all-embracing order of principle embodied by the elements: on the cosmological level, the Venetian state is an image of natural order and divinely ordained harmony. Naturally Jacopo does not miss the chance of showing variations on the female nude according to the rules of art in the figures of the Three Graces. However, the main attraction is really the light: sunlight plays over the women's bodies, filtered through a canopy of leaves that is largely out of sight. These "pre-Impressionist" lighting effects are all the more beguiling because once again, Tintoretto makes use of the way the light really falls into the room, creating the illusion of prolonging it into the pictures.

The four paintings used to hang opposite each other in pairs, as they still hang today in the Anticollegio, at a right angle to the row of windows. While the picture of the Graces is lit from the right, *Bacchus, Ariadne, and Venus* (page 463), opposite it, is lit from the left. As in the Ferraran picture painted by Titian, who had only

just died (page 309), Tintoretto's picture shows the meeting of Bacchus and Ariadne, daughter of the king of Crete, on the shores of the island of Naxos. The ship of Theseus, whom Ariadne had helped to escape from her father's labyrinth, is seen sailing home to Athens in the background. However, Tintoretto depicts not a passionate scene of "love at first sight" on the part of Bacchus, but a solemn wedding ceremony: the flying goddess of love is bringing Ariadne the constellation of the Corona borealis as a golden bridal crown; in Titian's picture, it hangs high above her in the sky. In the painting in the Ducal Palace, the Cretan princess assumes the role of Venice, endowed by divine love with the immortality of a constellation. The marriage of Ariadne, seated on the shore, and Bacchus standing in the sea, reflects the ceremony of the wedding of Venice itself to the sea. This ritual was performed every year on Ascension Day, when the Doge threw a golden ring into the waves from his magnificent state galley, the Bucintoro, restating the partnership between the Queen of the Seas and the protective barrier of the waters that nourished her.

Within the four-part cycle, *Bacchus, Ariadne, and Venus* represents the element of water and the season of fall. Earth and summer are symbolized by the following picture, *Minerva Keeping Mars From Peace and Harmony*. While the allegorical figures of Peace, crowned with an olive branch, and Harmony, holding a cornucopia as a symbol of abundance, turn to each other in a friendly manner, Minerva, as the personification of shrewd Venetian diplomacy, keeps war far from the city. Nonetheless, La Serenissima was at a stage of high technological development, and very well equipped for armed confrontations, as illustrated by the picture opposite, the *Forge of Vulcan*, representing both the element of fire and winter in the form of a snowy landscape in the background.

It was owing to Tintoretto's outstanding abilities as a painter that the program, which is both complex and abstract, did not impair the artistic quality of the pictures themselves. He left it to the authorities concerned to decide on the fee for his work, in the same way as he had recently done at the Scuola Grande di San Rocco. The four pictures for the Ducal Palace were assessed by Tintoretto's colleagues Paolo Veronese and Jacopo Palma il Giovane, who decided on a value of 200 ducats in all: a relatively fair price.

A little later these two expert assessors were themselves in competition with Tintoretto to adorn the most prominent wall surface available in the Ducal Palace after the fire of 1577: the huge front wall of the Sala del Maggior Consiglio. Around 1365 the Paduan artist Guariento had depicted the *Annunciation* and the *Coronation of the Virgin Amidst the Heavenly Hosts* above the wooden gallery where the Doge sat with the Signoria (representatives of the highest authority of the city state of Venice). It may be that even in the 1550s Tintoretto had a new decoration for this wall in mind.

Around 1565 at the latest, when the young painter Federico Zuccari, who had trained in Rome, was applying for the commission to paint the *Paradise*, Jacopo submitted a design of his own, perhaps the model admired by Goethe in Verona in 1786 and taken away to the Louvre in Paris by Napoleon's troops a little later (above). As in Guariento's fresco, which referred, among other themes, to the mythical founding of Venice on Annunciation Day (25 March) in 421, it shows the coronation of the Virgin as Queen of Heaven. The saints and the heavenly hosts sit on concentrically arranged banks of cloud, increasing in size as they come further down the picture, and finally giving the illusion of extending into the viewer's space and including it in the cosmic events. A picture very similar in size and composition (Istituto di Ricovero e

Tintoretto
Paradise, ca. 1565 (?)
Oil on canvas, 143 x 362 cm
Musée du Louvre, Paris

The best description of this picture is by the German poet Johann Wolfgang von Goethe: "A Paradise by Tintoretto, or rather the coronation of Mary as Queen of Heaven in the presence of all the patriarchs, prophets, saints, angels, et al., a nonsensical idea executed with the greatest genius. There is such ease of brushwork, spirit, and wealth of expression here that to admire and enjoy the piece properly one would have to own it, since the work may be said to be infinite, and the least of the angels' heads have character …"

Tintoretto's Workshop
Paradise, 1588–1592
Oil on canvas, 700 x 2200 cm
Palazzo Ducale, Venice

Opinions are divided on the monumental final version of the *Paradise*. Tintoretto's contemporary rival Federico Zuccari said critically that he had depicted the inhabitants of Paradise "like common folk in a market place." Charles Dickens believed the "Assembly of the Blest ... to be, take it all in all, the most wonderful and charming picture ever painted." Jean-Paul Sartre reacted with a mixture of distaste and fascination. To him, Tintoretto's *Paradise* was a rather negative Utopia: "At any rate, angels and men alike are passive, circling in the sky as dying cats drift and circle in the small whirlpools made in the canals by the *vaporetto* passing by."

di Educazione, Venice) was in the possession of the Ottobon family, and from 1559 to 1575 Giovanni Francesco Ottobon held the highest office open to a *cittadino* in Venice, the post of *cancellier grande* (grand chancellor). Since Tintoretto was a close friend of his, it seems quite likely that the painter would have given the influential Chancellor a model for his version of the *Paradise*, as a self-advertisement. However, the project remained in abeyance until the fire of 1577, which did considerable damage to Guariento's fresco. Around 1580 a competition for new designs was announced, and modelli were submitted by Tintoretto, Paolo Veronese, and two painters of a younger generation, Francesco Bassano and Jacopo Palma il Giovane. The jury awarded the commission first to Francesco Bassano and Paolo Veronese, but on Veronese's death in 1588 it went to Tintoretto after all. The final version (below), completed around 1592, was executed under the supervision of Jacopo's son Domenico in the former Chapter Hall of the Scuola Grande della Misericordia, not far from the artist's studio, which itself was far too small for a work of this size. The separate parts of the gigantic canvas were stitched together in the Ducal Palace, and Domenico then completed and retouched the finished painting from scaffolding.

The picture in the Ducal Palace contains considerable iconographic differences from the design in the Louvre, since it no longer shows the coronation of the Virgin, but Christ as Judge and Ruler of the world.

On the right, the Archangel Michael holds the balance for weighing souls and the sword of justice, and on the left the Archangel Gabriel holds a lily, in this context a symbol of both the Annunciation and the Last Judgment. Between Christ and Mary, in the central axis above the ducal throne, hovers the dove of the Holy Ghost, here also symbolizing the divine inspiration of the Venetian head of state. The political message is clear: Christ is a divine Doge, the assembly of the male nobility of Venice meeting below the picture is a reflection of the hierarchy of Heaven, and its decisions are the expression of the divine will.

Despite all the efforts expended by Jacopo and his studio, the master's artistic legacy did not lie in the ornate Doge's Palace, which was built to impress, but in the Benedictine monastery church of San Giorgio Maggiore, which was imbued with spiritual intellect. This had been constructed, from designs by the leading architect Andrea Palladio (1508–1580), in a commanding island location, and was decorated with paintings by Tintoretto and his associates. The complex program, no doubt developed by Jacopo in close consultation with Michele Alabardi, who was elected prior in 1591, reached its culmination in the presbytery. For its side walls, Tintoretto painted the *Israelites in the Desert* (page 466) and the *Last Supper* (page 467)—two pictures on a large scale, in form and content relating both to each other and to the high altar standing between them, a spectacular sculptural design. Its main

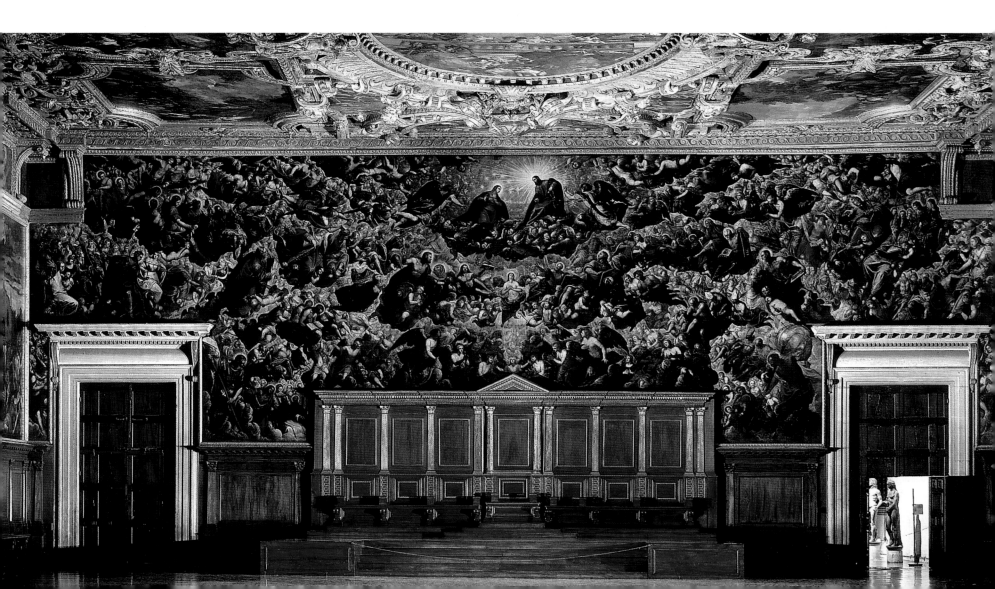

bronze decoration, executed in 1591–1593 by Girolamo Campagna, who had studied with a pupil of Jacopo Sansovino, shows the four Evangelists bearing up the globe, with God the Father standing on it in the attitude of a judge. One of the designs has been ascribed to the painter Aliense (Antonio Vassilacchi, 1556–1629), who sometimes worked with Tintoretto. The bold idea of translating a pictorial motif current in the Middle Ages into a large work of sculpture in the round may have been Jacopo's own since the idea is anticipated in the crowning element of the campanile of his favorite church, completed in 1503.

It was from here, in 1590, that the grief-stricken Tintoretto bore to the grave a workshop assistant particularly dear and precious to him: his daughter Marietta, known as La Tintoretta. Ridolfi tells us that Jacopo Tintoretto gave Marietta, born soon after 1550, an extensive artistic training. He himself taught her drawing and painting, and the noted organist and composer Giulio Zacchino (ca. 1550–1584) gave her lessons in singing and instrumental music.

In 1572, when the painter, who had many children and, unlike Titian, still obtained no permanent income from sinecures, applied for a brokerage bringing in about 120 ducats a year, he hoped to preserve the

benefit for his family after his own death, and mentioned in the official application not only sons but also daughters. Finally, his will contained the express wish "that both my male and my female children be heirs of my entire property." Since Marco Robusti had spurned his father's profession in favor of the theater, after the early death of Jacopo's eldest son Giovanni Battista in 1593 it was obvious that his brother Domenico would have to take over the maintenance of the Robusti family. Domenico himself never married. Jacopo's four remaining daughters after Marietta's death—Perina, Ottavia, Laura, and Altura—felt the pinch of financial difficulties: whereas Tintoretto's colleague Paris Bordone could give his four daughters a dowry of 200 ducats each, Jacopo placed two of his own daughters in a convent and was unable to give the other two, Ottavia and Laura, any dowry.

In the middle of May 1594 Jacopo Tintoretto fell seriously ill, and became bedridden. To the dismay of his family the doctors could not lower his constant high temperature. Although he suffered from insomnia for nights on end, Tintoretto counted to the last on his strong constitution. Not until a few hours before his death was he prepared to dictate his last will to a notary who had been summoned in haste: "[…] I wish all items

Tintoretto
The Israelites in the Desert, ca. 1593
Oil on canvas, 377 x 576 cm
San Giorgio Maggiore, Venice

The unusual iconography of this painting is still not entirely explained. There is much to suggest that Tintoretto—perhaps with a glance at Protestantism— was depicting the Israelites' scorning of the manna that led to the plague of fiery serpents and finally the setting up of the brazen serpent (page 457). Or the picture may combine different themes: the camp of the Israelites in the oasis of Elim, the washing of their clothes at the foot of Mount Sinai, the making of the copper basin for the sanctuary, the cooking of the manna, etc. The figure of Moses right foreground, shown in conversation with Aaron, is intentionally made to resemble Christ. Moses forms a typological link with the painting opposite (page 476).

As so often in Tintoretto, a certain scriptural meaning is concealed behind details that appear to be merely those of genre painting: the donkey driver top right could be Balaam who beat his animal because it was afraid of the angel of the Lord, whom Balaam himself did not see (Numbers 22: 22–35).

Tintoretto
The Last Supper, ca. 1593
Oil on canvas, 365 x 568 cm
San Giorgio Maggiore, Venice

The curious diagonal position of the table for this *Last Supper* is explained by the installation of the painting on the right wall of the presbytery of San Giorgio Maggiore. The table was to be perceived by visitors to the church as an extension in perspective of the high altar, or conversely the high altar was to be seen as a prolongation of the table for the Last Supper. The priestly bearing of Christ and the liturgical utensils on the small side table play on the same connection. The winged apparitions characterize the Eucharist as the "bread of angels" (St. Thomas Aquinas) and in their non-material, otherworldly nature indicate the mystery of transubstantiation (the transformation of bread and wine into the body and blood of Christ).

While the composition of the *Last Supper* as a whole follows a wall hanging by Giulio Romano depicting the Passover, the detail of the eerily flickering candlestick was suggested by the *Crowning with Thorns* by Titian (Alte Pinakothek, Munich), which Tintoretto had acquired from the master's estate when he died.

relating to my profession to go to my son Domenico, but in such a way that they, and in particular the items pertaining to the study of my profession, are to serve him and my son Marco for their common use, so long as they hold peacefully and lovingly together as good brothers. I wish my son Domenico to complete those of my works that may remain unfinished with his own hand, employing the style and care he has always applied to so many of my works. I ask my son Marco to live at peace with his brother, and not to neglect the practice of our common profession, his and mine, but to support our house through virtuous and elevated activity. [...]"

Tintoretto died in his house on the Rio della Sensa on 31 May 1594. Three days later a great funeral procession of his colleagues, friends, and family made its way to Madonna dell'Orto, where Tintoretto was laid to rest in his father-in-law Marco Episcopi's family tomb in front of the great organ.

Under Domenico, the studio lost its domination of the urban Venetian market to the main representative of the early Venetian Baroque, Jacopo Palma il Giovane, himself strongly influenced by Tintoretto. Jacopo's fame was not endangered by the decline of his workshop. Even in the master's lifetime, painters of note took his artistic innovations to many parts of Europe. El Greco,

for instance, who came from Crete to Venice in 1567, and may have paid another visit, coming from Rome before leaving for Spain in 1575/77, was a declared admirer of Tintoretto. As a young man, the Flemish Baroque painter Rubens studied the works of Jacopo in Venice. His Dutch counterpart Rembrandt never visited Italy, but borrowed ideas from the Venetian's compositions from their reproductions in engravings. In France, veneration of Tintoretto was a prominent and constant factor: the outstanding Rococo painter Jean-Honoré Fragonard drew masterpieces by Tintoretto while he was in Venice. The Romantic artist Delacroix found Jacopo's dark pictorial fantasies captivating, and his rival Ingres, like the Impressionist Degas, was inspired by the life story of Tintoretto to produce a historical painting. In the first number of the surrealist art journal Minotaure, published in Paris in 1933, Tintoretto was represented by six reproductions. Works by Ellsworth Kelly, Bob Thompson, Martial Raysse, Ulrike Rosenbach, Ron O'Donnell, and many others are evidence of the continuing fascination that Tintoretto's paintings have had for artists of the 20th century.

Roland Krischel

Veronese 1528–1588

ARTISTIC BEGINNINGS IN VERONA

Giovanni Gregori
Paolo Veronese, pre-1648
Copper engraving from: *Carlo Ridolfi, Le maraviglie
dell'arte ovvero le vite degli illustri pittori veneti e dello stato*
Venice 1648, vol. 1, p. 282
Staats- und Universitätsbibliothek, Göttingen

In 1648, the painter and art historiographer Carlo
Ridolfi published an extensive biography of Veronese.
This portrait introduces the painter's *vita*, and is probably
based on a self-portrait, now lost, then in the possession
of Veronese's descendants in Venice in the second half
of the 17th century.

Paolo Caliari, called Veronese, was born in 1528 in
Verona, the son of the stonemason Gabriele Bazaro and
his wife Caterina. After a period of training in the
workshop of his uncle and later father-in-law Antonio
Badile, a second-rate local master, Paolo seems to have
been taken in as a pupil by Giovanni Caroto. Caroto, as
a draftsman, was a major contributor to the treatise *De
origine et amplitudine civitatis Veronae* (1540) and
during the 1540s may have opened the young painter's
eyes to the unique collection of classical works of art and
architecture which still distinguishes Verona today above
all other North Italian cities. Little is known about
Paolo's early years. Familiar through his teachers with the
pictorial tradition of Venice, Verona, and Brescia, he
belongs to a generation of younger painters who
responded in their different ways to the challenge of
central Italian Mannerism shaped by Raphael and
Michelangelo. His early altar paintings for churches in
Verona include the *Raising of the Daughter of Jairus* for
San Bernardino, preserved in an oil sketch (Musée du
Louvre, Paris, ca. 1546); the *Bevilacqua-Lazise
Altarpiece* (Museo Civico di Castelvecchio, Verona, ca.
1546–48) for San Fermo Maggiore; and the
Lamentation over the Dead Christ (Museo Civico di
Castelvecchio, Verona, ca. 1547) from the sacristy of the
Hieronymites of Santa Maria della Vittoria. All these
bear witness to his productive dialogue with various
models. Cool daylight colors, like those preferred by
Francesco Morone and Caroto, painted architectural
works that give evidence of his study of the classically
oriented buildings by the architect Michele Sanmicheli,
as well as elements of Parmigianino's elegantly gracious
language of forms, are here united in restrained fashion,
and in a manner that must have appeared to his clients
as an alternative to those forces that rejected painterly
perception of color, and any kind of study of nature, in
favor of highly artificial effects. Success and recognition
were not slow to follow. The young painter's
acquaintanceship with Sanmicheli fundamentally
changed his situation. From that time Veronese was also
in demand in aristocratic circles as a portraitist and
fresco painter. While his *Portrait of Isabella Guerrini*

Gonzaga Canossa (Musée du Louvre, Paris, ca. 1547/48)
is convincing precisely because of its rejection of all
external elements, the demand for magnificence
determines the form of the two Da Porto portraits
created around 1551/52 (Galleria Palatinia, Palazzo
Pitti, Florence; The Walters Art Gallery, Baltimore) from
the town mansion of Count Iseppo da Porto in Vicenza,
designed by Andrea Palladio. Executed with technical
brilliance, the full-length portraits of Da Porto, a knight
of the Holy Roman Empire, his wife and their children,
modeled on portraits by the Lombard painter Moretto
da Brescia (ca. 1498–1554), are among the young
Veronese's finest inventions.

As a fresco painter, Paolo not only took part in the
decoration of the Palazzo Porto in Vicenza; in 1551 we
find him in Treville, near Castelfranco. Together with
Anselmo Canera and Giovanni Battista Zelotti he
followed the call of Michele Sanmicheli, the builder of
a villa commissioned by Alvise Soranza, which was to be
decorated with frescoes. Only a few fragments of this
once famous decoration, today preserved among other
works in the cathedral of Castelfranco and in Venice,
have survived the demolition of the villa in 1817. They
allow us at least to surmise what progress was made by
Veronese when he decorated walls and ceilings with
mythological and historical depictions, and extended
whole rooms by artistic means. There is much evidence
that after his activity in the Villa Soranza Paolo
proceeded directly to Venice.

The *Giustinian Altarpiece* (page 471) in the church of
San Francesco della Vigna was commissioned by
Lorenzo (d. 1553) and Antonio Giustinian (d. 1565).
High dignitaries and influential personalities in public
life were among the family circle of these two brothers,
who were related to the doges Andrea Gritti and
Francesco Donà, to Daniele and Marcantonio Barbaro,
and to the Grimani family. The *Holy Family with
St. Antony Abbot, St. Catherine, and John the Baptist*,
Paolo's contribution to one of the most popular themes
of Venetian painting of the Cinquecento, is known to
have been on the model of Titian's *Madonna of the
House of Pesaro* (page 313) of 1519–1526 in the church

Veronese
The Feast in the House of Levi (detail pages 484–485)

With his eloquent gesture, which is remarkably similar to that of Alexander the Great in the painting in the London National Gallery, the elegantly dressed Venetian accompanied by a page links the figures in the left arch with Christ as the focus of the picture, in terms of both form and content. Without being a self-portrait, the portrait-like, characteristic head with a high forehead and distinctive nose does have a certain resemblance to the portraits we have of Veronese himself.

of the Frari. The dialogue with Titian's altarpiece resulted not in some spiritless copy, but a thoroughly original interpretation. At first Paolo rejected the inclusion of the donors; Titian's model did not form a precedent in this case. Instead, Paolo adopted his asymmetrical pyramidal composition as well as elements of pictorial architecture, which suffice for symbolic and narrative demands, without being clearly defined in spatial terms. In his coloration, too, the painter from Verona went his own way. He translates the atmospherically dense, warm colors of Titian into coolly glowing tones: pink, orange, green, and violet in manifold shades are counterbalanced on the right by the dark grey of the cloak of St. Antony Abbot, whose excessively grandiose lengths of fabric seem to conceal what becomes clear at the latest when the relationship between head and body is examined. The anatomy of the figure has caused difficulties for the painter. These and other weaknesses seem to have given Agostino

Carracci occasion for careful corrections when he prepared an engraving of the painting in 1582. However, Agostino's academic criticism cannot disguise the fact that toward the end of the 16th century he was one of the first non-Venetian artists to recognize the particular significance of Veronese and the *Giustinian Altarpiece*.

In 1552, Cardinal Ercole Gonzaga (1505–1563) commissioned four painters from Verona, including Paolo Veronese, to produce altar paintings for the cathedral of San Pietro in Mantua. The *Temptation of St. Anthony* (page 470, left) must have been finished by the end of 1552, since the painters Paolo Farinati, Battista dell'Angelo del Moro, and Domenico Brusasorzi wrote to the cardinal on 11 March 1553 to ask for the collection of their works and for their payment. Paolo himself signed this letter *Paullo spezap[re]da* ("stonemason"), which shows that he adopted the surname Caliari, that of his maternal grandmother, only on his final move to Venice. The *Temptation of St. Anthony*, taken to Paris in 1797 on the instructions of Napoleon, is among the major works of his early period, and aroused the amazement of Vasari, who enthusiastically hailed it as the best of the four altar paintings. Clearly the painting is related to the high-quality drawing (page 470, right) in the Musée du Louvre. If this drawing, with its pictorial design, preceded the painting, one might suppose that the ambivalent character of the depiction prevented its later execution in paint. In contrast to the painted version, the lyrical theme impedes the comprehension of the subject. The seductress looks like a nymph, the devil does not immediately appear to be one, and is at first reminiscent of a faun. As a zealous champion of Catholic reform, who for a time was considered a promising candidate for the highest office of the Church, Ercole Gonzaga may have been displeased with the lyrical undercurrent of the design, so that Paolo was forced to use other artistic means in order to complete the task to the satisfaction of his client. To see the figure of St. Anthony as well as the new lyrical atmosphere of the scene as a reaction to Titian's famous *St. Peter Martyr*, which was burnt in 1867 in the church of Santi Giovanni e Paolo in Venice, is a long shot, but in this drawing the first hesitant step seems to be suggested that came immediately before Paolo's move to Venice, where he finally settled.

Paolo's activity in Venice began with a prestigious commission. Between 1554 and 1556 he was a significant contributor to the decoration of various official rooms in the Doge's Palace. The mythological and allegorical ceiling paintings in the Sala delle Udienze and Sala della Bussula owe their particular attraction to the imaginative choreography of his lively, powerfully structured figures in front of a brilliant blue sky. In fact, Veronese was initially in demand chiefly as a ceiling painter. In 1555, with the *Coronation of the Virgin Mary* in the sacristy of San Sebastiano, he laid the foundation stone for his magnificent decoration of the Renaissance church with paintings and frescoes. Its high point is represented by the three colorful ceiling paintings of the nave with scenes from the story of Esther (1556). Admired by contemporaries, in the 17th century they continued to be considered textbook examples of perspective foreshortening.

In 1556/57, Veronese struck out a new path in his ceiling paintings for the Great Hall of the Libreria Vecchia. The *Allegory of Music*, which won the award of a gold chain, had no need of dramatic effects. The structure of the image is balanced, and forms and colors develop their effect in clear harmony. In the 1550s, Veronese was also active in the province of Veneto, in 1555–1556 in Montagnana as well as in nearby Verona, where he created the *Feast in the House of Simon* (Galleria Sabauda, Turin, 1556–1559/60) in the refectory of the Benedictines of Santi Nazaro e Celso, the first of his great feast paintings. The Benedictine monasteries affiliated to the Cassinese Congregation of Santa Giustina in Padua would soon be among the most important of the painter's clients. His altarpieces and devotional paintings for churches in San Benedetto Po, Praglia, Venice, Parma, and Padua frequently owe their existence to personal links between these monasteries.

The same is true of the patronage of the Hieronymites, which had already made use of Veronese's services in the late 1540s, in the sacristy of the monastery church of Santa Maria della Vittoria in Verona. This was also the monastery of Fra Bernardo Torlioni, who succeeded for some seventeen years in retaining the allegiance of the painter, "his beloved fellow-countryman," to himself and to the church of San Sebastiano in Venice. Through his acquaintanceship with Michele Sanmicheli and Andrea Palladio, his successful work in the Doge's Palace, as well as for private clients in the circle of Titian, Sansovino, and Daniele Barbaro, Veronese matured in the 1550s into a painter much in demand for history paintings both sacred and secular. Among his most impressive portraits is the *Portrait of Daniele Barbaro* (page 473). It was the product of the unerring eye of a careful observer. Unlike Titian, Veronese did not succeed in penetrating the psychology of the individuals he portrayed. Distance, rigor, and objectivity characterize the appearance of the learned Venetian aristocrat and churchman who became Veronese's most important patron in the late 1550s.

Opposite page, left:
Veronese
The Temptation of St. Anthony, 1552
Oil on canvas, 198 x 151 cm
Musée des Beaux-Arts, Caen

Painted in 1552 as a commission by Cardinal Ercole
Gonzaga for the cathedral of San Pietro in Mantua, the
altarpiece illustrates in almost square format an episode
from the life of St. Anthony of Egypt, who from 286 to
306 retired to an isolated fort in the desert near Thebes.
There he was exposed to numerous fearful temptations
by the Devil and his demonic accomplices, in the shape
of seductive women. The artistic resources employed
match the dramatic subject. Foreshortened perspectives
and *torsioni*, carried off with virtuosity, abound in this
pictorial confection. The atmospheric coloration and
employment of warm colors are reminiscent of the
paintings of Correggio, which Veronese may have seen
in Mantua.

Opposite page, right:
Veronese
The Temptation of St. Anthony, 1552
Pen and chalk on paper, 41.4 x 35.6 cm
Département des arts graphiques, Musée du Louvre, Paris

As early as the 17th century, when this drawing was
part of the collection of Everard Jabach in Paris, it was
considered the work of Veronese. We can only guess at
the purpose of the drawing. The often-voiced suspicion
that it was a never implemented *modello* for the painting
in Caen cannot be rejected out of hand, in view of
Cardinal Gonzaga's art policies. As a strict man of the
Church who had spent time in Bologna and Rome,
Ercole was a passionate advocate of the reforms of the
Council of Trent, and indeed from 1561 he was its
presiding cardinal. It was under his patronage that Giulio
Romano renovated the cathedral of San Pietro in the
manner prescribed in the Catholic reforms, and further
churches and monasteries in the diocese of Mantua were
to follow. It is possible that the lyrical, bucolic character
of the scene did not please the Cardinal, so that Veronese
was forced to drop the design and rework the religious
story with a more obvious message.

Right:
Veronese
*The Holy Family with St. Antony Abbot, St. Catherine,
and the Infant John the Baptist* (*Giustinian Altarpiece*),
1551
Oil on canvas, 313 x 190 cm
San Francesco della Vigna, Venice

Clearly contrasting cool colors in the service of precise,
dramatically constructed forms are the main
characteristics of Veronese's first altar painting for a
Venetian church. Infrared reflectography recently brought
to light a surprising technical finding: originally, parts of
the pictorial architecture in the background of the picture
were differently arranged. In an early phase, the column
now behind Mary was roughly in the center of the
picture. As the painting proceeded, it was overpainted
and moved right. Clearly not initially envisaged,
therefore, was the awkward-looking pier fragment with its
engaged half column, whose relationship with the other
architectural motifs produces inconsistencies of
perspective. When Agostino Carracci copied the large
painting around 1582, one of the things that he corrected
was the sharp edge at the top of the pier.

THE MASTER OF SPATIAL ILLUSION

Opposite page:
Veronese
Daniele Barbaro, ca. 1561–1566
Oil on canvas, 121 x 105.5 cm
Rijksmuseum, Amsterdam

Around 1560/61, Veronese was commissioned by
Daniele Barbaro to provide the interior frescoes for
Barbaro's Palladian villa in Maser (detail page 477).
The artist and his client had probably been acquainted
since the early 1550s. A dating of 1556 has been
suggested, based on Barbaro's edition of Vitruvius
published in 1556 and the two volumes of this edition
lying on the table. However, in view of the rather more
aged appearance of the subject, a dating to the first half
of the 1560s looks preferable. The upended book in front
of a globe depicts a small putto on the left pointing with
a rod at a geometrical proportion drawing. As this figure
appears in the corresponding illustration of the Vitruvius
edition sideways on, slightly averted and also wholly
without clothing, it might be presumed that it was
Veronese himself who provided the drawing on which this
illustration is based. Likewise, the volume on the table
—the page open shows parts of the title page of the
Dieci libri—alludes to the cleric's real sphere of activity.
Though he had been appointed Patriarch of Aquileia,
he devoted himself mainly to humanistic studies and
architectural theory. Veronese catches the physiognomy
of the subject and his apparatus in paint with unusual
precision. This was evidently a response to his client,
whose interest lay in precision in his own field of activity.

In the painting *Frederick Barbarossa Kissing the Hand
of the Antipope Victor IV*, Veronese's biographer Carlo
Ridolfi paid homage in 1648 to a work that he himself
had never seen in the original. Nonetheless, this picture
had been described in detail by Vasari and copied on
several occasions by contemporary painters, before it
fell victim to a fire in December 1577 in the Sala del
Maggior Consiglio in the Doge's Palace. Probably just
six meters high and more or less square, this work,
which was commissioned on 7 January 1562, was
Veronese's largest history painting until then. It
contained the portraits of the doge and of numerous
Venetian noblemen and office bearers, including
Lorenzo and Antonio Giustinian, the donors of the
Giustinian Altarpiece (page 471). Ridolfi mentions that
this work owed its creation to the painter's reputation
and the fame of his unique works in Maser.

According to this, Veronese's cycle of frescoes in
the Villa Barbaro must have been completed by the
end of 1561, and it remains surprising that the
painter's extensive work in Maser has left no trace in
either the writings of his client Daniele Barbaro or
the *Quattro libri dell'architettura* written by his
famous colleague, the architect Andrea Palladio.
Palladio, who otherwise did not hesitate to mention
assistants and colleagues and made no exception in
Paolo Veronese's case where the decoration of the
Palazzo Porto in Vicenza was concerned, remained
silent when he wrote about the villa, located in the
fertile Trevisan countryside close to Asolo, in his
treatise in 1570. Only a letter written to Daniele
Barbaro by Giulia da Ponte in 1559 provides vague
clues as to when the painter started work. It
mentions the nymphaeum (*ninfeo*) surrounding the
fountains to the north, which at this time was also

complete and perhaps even already decorated with
allegorical fresco paintings.

Planning of the overall layout had probably started in
1551. It was carried out by Palladio between 1556 and
1558, though certain peculiarities of the complex have
led to the supposition that he was forced to make major
concessions to the taste of his client, the amateur
architect. Thus there are some suggestions that Daniele
Barbaro was responsible for the design of the
nymphaeum, lavishly decorated with small ornaments,
while his brother Marcantonio, who regularly lived in
the villa and occasionally did sculptural work,
contributed some of the conspicuously coarsely
modeled statues. As Norbert Huse has shown, the
collaboration of client and architect also left unusual
traces on the exterior of the manor house. To name just
a few features, there is the round arch of the balcony
door which, in contrast with Palladio's ideas, penetrates
the entablature of the pediment on the first floor; also,
the unusual ground plan of the manor house itself,
which is drawn conspicuously further forward than the
working quarters on either side, evidently in imitation
of the triclinium of the classical Pliny villa in
Laurentinum. Finally, it appears as if inside the central
plan residence there has been a continuation, with
different roles, of features all too evident in the exterior.
Decorative sculptural elements such as door frames,
plain fireplaces, and the entablature that structures
individual rooms have been executed in stucco—a
material not typical of Palladio, and their detail is
contrary to the architect's strict formal language.
Instead, individual forms are re-encountered in the
painted architecture of Veronese, who was perhaps
indeed responsible for the entire interior decoration
under the direction of the architect's client. Was it

Federico Zuccaro
Frederick Barbarossa Kissing the Hand of the Antipope Victor IV, copied from Veronese, ca. 1563–1565
Pen drawing, 33.6 x 22.8 cm
János Scholz Collection, Pierpont Morgan Library, New York

The drawing is based on a picture by Veronese, which, commissioned in January 1562, was destroyed by fire in the Sala del Maggiore Consiglio at the Doge's Palace in 1577. When Federico Zuccaro was honored with the task of replacing the painting during the restoration work, his subject was the Humiliation of the Emperor Barbarossa (Sala del Maggiore Consiglio, Doge's Palace), inspired by Veronese's lost painting. In 1648, Carlo Ridolfi records that it was the fame of the frescoes of the Villa Barbaro that brought Veronese the commission for the history painting.

Opposite page:
Veronese
The Girl in the Doorway (see page 476)

The picture shows a girl, presumably a member of the Barbaro household, apparently entering the Sala almost by chance, but it is in fact one of the painted trompe l'œils that still captivate visitors to the Villa Barbaro in Maser.

consequently the tense relationship between the sculptural and painted decorative forms on the one hand and the constructed architecture on the other that led the architect not to write a single word about the cycle of frescoes in his treatise in 1570? The question remains unanswered. More importantly, the esoteric iconography of the magnificently colored frescoes also appears to derive from the client. To parade their, in part, quite contradictory interpretations would be beyond the scope of this account. The leitmotif of the decorations embodies a concept of harmony that is developed in varying ways and is already discernible in Daniele Barbaro's coat-of-arms. Recorded on an escutcheon that is crowned by a cross, the ring echoes the shape of the circle. The circle is not merely a symbol of unity, perfection and, in this connection, of heaven and the spiritual as opposed to the material world; it is also the expression of an all-embracing concept of order and harmony. In the figural fresco paintings, which decorate a total of five rooms and the central hall in the main building's piano nobile, this concept of harmony is discernible time and time again.

To begin with, illusionistic fantasy landscapes in the central main room (page 476), framed by painted arcades and columns, establish a dialogue with those windows out of which one can see out onto the landscape of the nearer surroundings. These are joined, on the wall surfaces of the transept wing, by eight musicians. Their significance is revealed only when one looks at the frescoes in the Sala dell'Olimpo. Contained within a circular cloud formation, the Muse Thalia, who is riding on a headless snake, forms the center of a painted planetarium. Assigned to her are Saturn, Jupiter, Mars, Apollo, Venus, Mercury, and Diana, the gods of the starry sky with their respective signs of the Zodiac. A possible key to the interpretation of this iconographically unusual constellation is provided by a woodcut which Gafurius used in 1518 as an illustration in his treatise *De harmonia musicorum instrumentorum opus* and which anticipates central elements in Veronese's depiction. Both the music-making Muses in the central main room and the fresco in the Stanza di Bacco (Bacchus Room) appear, according to this, to be alluding to the harmony of the spheres: the cosmic and harmonious sound, inaudible to man, created by the planets and their movements. The theory of the harmony of the spheres, which derives from the teachings of the ancient Greek philosopher Pythagoras (6th century BC) forms a central theme in Daniele Barbaro's edition of Vitruvius, and underlines the scholar's pronounced interest in astronomy. His ancestor, Ermolao Barbaro, had already devoted some treatises to this discipline. Daniele himself studied it intensively within the context of architectural theory.

His portrait (page 473) testifies eloquently to this fact. In it, proportions and the orders of columns appear as fundamental elements of architectural work, next to a sphere, the model of the skies.

Other ceiling paintings by Veronese take the form of allegories in order to allude to love or the virtues of justice, moderation, and strength, or appear as in the case of Bacchus, Vertumnus, and Saturn to be an allegorical reminder of the fertility of nature and the agricultural use of the villa. In general, mythological and secular elements combine quite unexpectedly with each other in many parts of the decorations. In the Sala dell'Olimpo, for example, it is Giustiniana Giustinian (page 477), the lady of the house and wife of Marcantonio Barbaro, who appears with her wet-nurse behind a painted balustrade, while on the other side of the room one of her two sons is studying a book. Right at the end of the row of rooms in the east wing, a nobleman in hunting attire steps out as if by chance through a painted door, while in the central hall an inquisitively sniffing dog before a painted balustrade tempts us, even today, to mistake it for the real thing. Apart from these references to everyday events in the villa's life, scattered religious depictions also form part of the fresco decorations. In the Stanza della Lucerna (Room of the Oil Lamps), the *Madonna della pappa* quite evidently needs to be seen in combination with the allegorical ceiling fresco in the room, in which a personification of the Catholic faith is facing a beggar accompanied by a personification of Mercy. With an eloquent gesture, Religion indicates a snake twisted into a circle that is biting its tail, and in 16th-century iconography this was a symbol of infinity. The moralizing tenor of the scene cannot be ignored. One cannot exclude the possibility that it could be indirectly linked with the Calvinistic tinges in the comments of the patriarch Giovanni Grimani on divine pre-ordination, which had caused concern and became the object of an examination by the Papal Inquisition in Rome in 1561. In contrast to the position of the Calvinists, who considered love of one's neighbor to be solely a service to the glory of God, not to mankind, this iconographically unusual depiction speaks up, like a profession of faith, for the priority of the Catholic religion and a love of one's neighbor permeated by the eternal values of the faith; and once again it appears to confirm to what extent Daniele Barbaro had an overall influence on the creative process and the form of the frescoes.

Supported by his brother Benedetto Caliari (1538–1598), a painter who specialized in depicting architecture, Veronese developed a pictorial world in Maser that is unique in its quality and narrative density. As a fresco painter and master of spatial illusion, he

unquestionably profited from the experiences he had gained in the church of San Sebastiano, for the wall paintings produced from 1558 for the clerestory area, above the gallery, and in the spandrels of the choir arch had also been decorations that negated the pre-existing architectural structures and that formed a comparably imaginative union of ornamental, sculptural, and architectural decorative forms. The actual protagonists in the pictorial world in the Villa Barbaro, ancient gods from classical mythology and allegories exemplifying human virtues, are components in a decorative program that was subject to rational principles of order and harmony, and whose choice of artistic methods corresponded to the demands imposed on contemporary painters by the art theoretician Lodovico Dolce. Thus, individual figures and architectural forms reflect a study of the classical period reformed by Raphael's work in Rome, and suggest that, during his work in Maser, Veronese was profiting from experiences he had gained during a visit to the Eternal City as part of the retinue of the Venetian ambassador, Girolamo Grimani. The question of when this journey took place is very much open to speculation, especially as Grimani was in Rome on several occasions between 1555 and 1565. Nonetheless, if his later explanations

to the Inquisition are to be believed, Veronese appears to have been acquainted with Michelangelo's *Last Judgment* in the Sistine Chapel even before it was overpainted by Daniele da Volterra (ca. 1509–1566), meaning that he must have seen it before 1560. It is more than likely that he would have had an opportunity to study the decorations of classical villas during the course of this journey. The illusionistic quality of the frescoes in Maser, the deceptive power of the painted architecture and figures, were first praised by Carlo Ridolfi in 1648.

Nevertheless, the competition between illusion and reality had already been keeping the contemporary art theoreticians of Venice busy. Hence the conception that painters were capable of achieving illusionistic effects with the aid of color had been passionately discussed in 1557 in the above-mentioned *Dialogo della pittura* by Dolce, using the example of the competition between the classical painters Zeuxis (ca. 425 BC) and Parrhasius (ca. 420 BC). According to Pliny (ca. AD 23–79), Zeuxis succeeded by means of his careful painting technique in reproducing grapes so realistically that birds flew up and began to peck at them. Parrhasius, meanwhile, had painted a curtain. When Zeuxis demanded that he pull the curtain aside so that

View into the cruciform Sala a Crociera of the villa from the southeast
Frescoes and stucco decoration
Villa Barbaro, Maser

Painted Corinthian columns and "arcades," presumably carried out by Veronese's brother and assistant Benedetto Caliari, form a light architectural framework for the extraordinarily delightful trompe-l'œil landscapes with small figures and classical buildings. A continuous stucco cornice provides an upper edge and three-dimensional wall articulation, and was—like the door frames—presumably done to a design by the painter. In 1648, Veronese's biographer Carlo Ridolfi was the first to identify the musicians as muses. A pair of them flanked each of the illusory doors in the "transept" vestibules through which visitors appear to enter the room. The final elements of the decoration are the grisaille equestrian scenes below, which are in the style of cameos.

Veronese
Giustiniana Giustinian and Her Nurse, 1560/61
Fresco
Villa Barbaro, Maser

Dressed in the elegant style of a Venetian noblewoman, the wife of Marcantonio Barbaro is shown alongside her nurse behind a balustrade. Both figures form part of the painted decoration in the Sala dell'Olimpo. Closer inspection of the figures reveals the very vigorous brushstrokes used by the painter. The gown of Giustiniana is made up of white dotted flecks of paint, which, in conjunction with the gleaming blue of the lengths of materials and the highlights, create an extraordinarily dashing effect.

he could see his competitor's picture, he was forced to acknowledge that it was a painted one (*Naturalis historiae*, XXXV, 65–66). For the Venetian Dolce, this anecdote was a metaphor that expounded how color and the way in which it was used could enable painted works to surpass their real-life models. When this concept of the technique of painting was put into practice, it was necessary to pay attention to careful use of foreshortenings and sophisticated nuances in the skin tones, as well as reproducing the human figure in an appropriate manner. Taking another look at the central fresco in the Sala dell'Olimpo, it becomes clear that Veronese would have felt that his work was completely justified by Dolce's treatise. This is, of course, also true

of the *varietà*, which, as Leon Battista Alberti had already pointed out, was one of the most important characteristics of a high-quality pictorial invention. With an eye to Raphael's function as a model, Dolce had updated the law of variety in order to entrust it to contemporary painters as an alternative to the Mannerists' style of painting. Veronese, who revealed that he was very familiar with Dolce's treatise on the occasion of his examination by the Inquisition in 1573, adopted these recommendations in Maser, and more: by turning the successfully tested principle of *varietà* into an artistic program, he made a decisive contribution to the further development and enrichment of Venetian painting.

A PROGRAM OF INVENTIVENESS

The Wedding at Cana (detail pages 480–481)
Bride and Groom

Since the 13th century, the Benedictine convent of San Giorgio Maggiore in Venice has served time and again as a refuge and home to secular and clerical personages of rank and stature. In the 16th century, the monastery was said to be among the most prosperous in the city, and it is therefore no surprise that the young Englishman, Thomas Coryat, touring Europe in 1608 to broaden his intellectual horizons, should see the venerable monastery as the finest and richest in all Venice. Coryat's tour of the monastery included the refectory, which, with its *Wedding at Cana*, was considered one of the principal sights of the city. If we are to believe the monastic chronicle written in 1619 by Don Fortunato Olmo, kings and princes had clamored for copies of the picture. Certainly, it is the festive mood of the picture, set in a world very familiar to contemporary viewers, that must have prompted demands of this kind. On the left of the richly laden table, the bride and groom of the biblical wedding open the gently undulating procession of beautiful, portrait-like heads, whose individual features constantly captured the imagination of viewers in the 18th century, and even occasionally induced romantic visitors to the refectory to see a portrait of the painter's own beloved in the bride.

At the start of the 1560s Paolo Veronese, with Tintoretto and the old master Titian, was among the leading painters in Venice. In the Doge's Palace he had proved his ability to fill even large pictorial surfaces effortlessly with figures and architecture. New standards were set in Venice by the *Wedding at Cana,* intended for the refectory of the Benedictines of San Giorgio Maggiore (pages 479, 480–481). This painting, which fell victim in 1797 to Napoleon's art robberies, was commissioned on 6 June 1562, soon after the completion of Palladio's refectory, and completed a year later. Don Andrea da Asola, previously abbot of the Benedictine abbey San Benedetto Po, had taken up office in 1564 as the new abbot of the monastery of San Giorgio Maggiore and seems to have ensured that his portrait was retrospectively added to the painting. While Ridolfi in 1648 remarked critically that the portraits of clerics that Paolo had had to include purely as a matter of obligation did not harmonize well with the other ideas derived from fantasy, the number of individualized heads has always aroused admiration. Even Vasari was enthusiastic. In 1568, he praised the wealth of figures in the most varied postures as well as the multiplicity of garments. His particular interest was in *varietà*, the wealth of invention of motifs, which on closer examination prove to be part of an overarching, precisely thought-out order. Christ, who gazes straight ahead, takes up the center of the panel, in which the rows of tables of the dining hall once found their fictional conclusion. Symmetrically arranged architectural structures, opening up the depth of the image, and reminiscent in detail of buildings by Palladio and Sansovino as well as stage designs by the architect and theorist Sebastiano Serlio (d. 1554), frame the arena of the event. In their severe verticality they correspond with the figure of the Lord, who forms a calm and still center in the middle of the feast. Along the table and in the region of the terrace at a higher level, an almost unbelievable wealth of detail unfolds. Riches and splendor characterize this interpretation of the biblical story of the miracle of the wine, which the writer Pietro Aretino had transformed in a strikingly similar way into a vision of magnificence, in *L'humanità di Christo* (Venice, 1551).

In view of the multiplicity of inventions, it is not surprising that this monumental painting was considered Veronese's masterpiece in his own lifetime. As the "most beautiful picture in the world," probably by far the most frequently copied painting in Venice, it was for centuries a major destination for visitors to the city. In 1660 and 1674 the Venetian Marco Boschini eloquently laid the foundation stone for a legend with tremendous audience appeal. Boschini believed, for example, that he could recognize in the quartet of musicians the portraits of Titian, Jacopo Bassano, Tintoretto, and Veronese. Undoubtedly this romantically colored interpretation, obstinately circulated up to the present day, was a product of his imagination, a Baroque metaphor, which served to illustrate in symbolic terms Veronese's particular gift for translating colors into a play of forms indebted to the laws of musical harmony. Probably it would hardly have occurred to Veronese himself in his day to immortalize himself in such a superficial way, and, of all things, in the circle of his competitors. Works by contemporary Venetian painters who took up the motif and varied it in imaginative ways, such as a fresco by Veronese's brother Benedetto Caliari in Magnadola, as well as the depictions of the *Wedding at Cana* by Andrea Vicentino (San Trovaso, Venice), Giovanni Battista Bissoni (San Vitale, Ravenna), and Alessandro Maganza (San Barnaba, Mantua), confirm that the musicians were not a motif based on a specific interpretation.

The *Wedding at Cana* represented a great rise in prestige for Veronese as a pictorial architect. Between 1563 and 1573 he produced in Venice, Padua, and Vicenza (page 482) works of comparable size and style, all of which adorned the front walls of monastery refectories. Richness of invention and *varietà*, which were expected and approved by the clients in 1562 in the case of the *Wedding at Cana*, find their high point in the painting known today as the *Feast in the Large House of Levi* (pages 484–485), which was commissioned as a replacement for a *Last Supper* by Titian that was destroyed in the dining hall of the Dominicans of Santi Giovanni e Paolo. On 18 July 1573, this work, which was painted as a Last Supper, resulted in the painter's being summoned before the

Veronese
The Wedding at Cana, 1562/63
Oil on canvas, 677 x 994 cm
Musée du Louvre, Paris

Covering a total area of about 67 square meters (721 square feet),
the painting for the dining room of the Benedictine monastery of
San Giorgio Maggiore in Venice depicts the biblical scene of the
wedding at Cana (John 2: 1–11). When the wine ran out during the
meal, Christ changed water into wine at the request of his mother,
Mary. Veronese moves the scene to a brightly lit terrace in front of
imaginary Venetian palace façades. In the second half of the 16th
century, the increased interest in rich subject matter among painters
and clients in Venice and the Veneto led to the simple core event
(initially just the miracle of the wine) being gradually overlaid with
lavish settings of more and more markedly realistic depictions of
wedding gatherings. Yet in Veronese's painting, the compositional
parallels with depictions of the Last Supper nonetheless manage to
bring out the analogy between the transformation of the water into
wine and sacramental wine into the blood of Christ.

The contract of 6 June 1562 specified both the exact size and the
appropriate number of figures for the subject. As a precaution,
Veronese was instructed to use only the best raw materials for his
paints and not to omit the use of the finest ultramarine. As
ultramarine, made from ground lapis lazuli, was highly expensive,
the intention of this admonition was to circumvent the current
practice whereby painters often short-changed their clients by using
azure blue made from copper ore. The agreed fee for the painting
was 324 ducats. While he was working on the picture on the island
of San Giorgio, the artist had free board, and was promised a barrel
of wine on completion of the picture. The monumental painting
was finished seventeen months later. Veronese probably had
Benedetto Caliari with him as his assistant. Once famed as one of
the principal sights of Venice and admired for centuries both north
and south of the Alps as a masterpiece of Venetian art, the work
remained influential into the 18th century. Looted by Napoleon, in
the 19th century it was studied, copied, and taken as a model by
generations of French, German, and English artists visiting the
Louvre.

A leading part was played in the formation of the legend by the
Venetian Marco Boschini (1660–1674), who thought he recognized
the portraits of Titian, Jacopo Bassano, Tintoretto, and Veronese in
the quartet of musicians. A bare one hundred years later, the
Wedding at Cana was transformed in the eyes of connoisseurs into a
record of a historical event in the form of a group portrait. Above all
in England, copies of a dubious "account" were circulated that
recorded a number of further portraits (of Charles V, Vittoria
Colonna, and others). This tradition is first apparent in a report
of 1769 by the English scholar William Cole about a copy of the
Wedding at Cana in the possession of Thomas Bromley, Lord
Monfort, at Horseheath, Cambridgeshire.

tribunal of the Inquisition. By his refusal to transform his work in progress into a *Feast in the House of Simon*, Veronese had himself set the ball rolling and was now forced to take a stand. Fools, German mercenaries, deformed dwarfs, and other figures caused offence, and were considered by the inquisitors as objectionable and not in keeping with the subject of the Last Supper. The painter's reference to the necessity of *ornamento* to fill the surface was of little use to him. Veronese was ordered to alter the offending depiction within three months at his own expense, to make it suitable for the Last Supper. As is well known, the Venetian painter skillfully avoided reworking the incriminated details. All that was changed was the title of the painting, which in the form of the easily legible Latin inscription *FECIT. D. COVI. MAGNV. LEVI - LUCÆ CAP. V.* documents the apparently effortless transformation from a Last Supper to a Feast in the House of Levi.

In the church of San Sebastiano, Veronese did not need to fear competition. A long-term relationship of trust linked him with the prior of the monastery, who was from Verona, so that the execution of the altarpiece in the Cappella Maggiore seems like a *fait accompli*. In the paintings on both sides of the *Martyrdom of St. Sebastian* and the *Martyrdom of St. Mark and St. Marcellianus* the theme becomes a theatrical event. Brightly lit architectural elements act as decorative backdrops in front of which the depictions, rich in detail, unfold in landscape format. Both these works offer figurative motifs of exquisite beauty. But

weaknesses too are recognizable. The dense well of more or less uninvolved supernumerary figures, as well as isolated heads rather inopportunely inserted into the image, make it clear that Veronese must have taken advantage of the help of collaborators. With the ceiling paintings in the church of San Sebastiano he had already been supported by his brother Benedetto and a certain Antonio. Their contributions are difficult to identify in detail. In view of the wealth of commissions and commitments in the 1560s, it is hardly surprising that Veronese was forced to delegate certain aspects of his work.

With the *Marogna Altarpiece* for the church of San Paolo in Verona and the *San Zaccaria Altarpiece* for the Venetian church of that name, he produced further large-format altar paintings within a few years. The journey to Verona that he undertook in 1566 on the occasion of his marriage to Elena Badile thus offered hardly more than a brief breathing space. He was increasingly approached with requests by private collectors and clients. As early as 1567, the impressive allegories *Omnia Vanitas* (Frick Collection, New York) and *Honor et Virtus post mortem floret* (page 488) were offered for sale in Venice. Probably not long after, Veronese created *The Family of Darius before Alexander the Great* to the commission of a member of the Venetian Pisani family (National Gallery, London). Here his creative contrast with the works of Titian and Tintoretto again becomes particularly noticeable. The beauty of the individual figures, coupled with the

Veronese
The Feast of Gregory the Great, 1572
Oil on canvas, 477 x 862 cm
Basilica di Monte Berico, Vicenza

This is the only one of the monumental Feasts still in the position it was originally intended for, though seriously damaged by Austrian soldiers in the 19th century. Once again, the painter uses great imagination to develop an ideal architectural landscape that acts as a light-filled foil to offset the vivid colors in their dramatic brilliance. A feature of all the Feast pictures by Veronese is that he dispenses with strict central perspective. Instead, the broad format always incorporates several focal points.

stately splendor of light-flooded architecture, set standards and aroused the enthusiasm of the German poet Johann Wolfgang von Goethe (1749–1832), when he visited the Palazzo Pisani-Moretta on the Canal Grande in 1786. Magnanimously, his enthusiasm allowed him to overlook the contemporary clothing that had incurred criticism in France in the second half of the 17th century. The pictorial architecture on the other hand is ideal, varying the motif of the arcade with double half-columns in allusion to the "loggetta" built in 1537–1549 by Sansovino next to the campanile of San Marco. Only exceptionally did Veronese include actually existing buildings in his paintings. In the case of the *Adoration of the Madonna by the Coccina Family* (Gemäldegalerie Alte Meister, Dresden, ca. 1571) this probably happened at the express wish of the client who commissioned this series of four paintings, which, as recent research has shown, were probably first hung in the *portego* or main hall of the palazzo of the Venetian Coccina family of merchants.

In 1574 and 1577, devastating fires in the Doge's Palace destroyed among other things the decorations of the Sala del Collegio, the Sala del Maggior Consiglio, and the Sala dello Scrutino. For Veronese, his collaborators, and many other notable Venetian painters and their workshops the redesign of these spaces provided a rich field of activity for years to come. Under the direction of Andrea da Ponte, and perhaps even with the participation of Palladio and Marcantonio Barbaro, a new program of decoration was immediately initiated for the Sala del Collegio. Payments made to Veronese are evidence of the beginning of work in December 1575. The decoration of the gilded soffit, an entirely separate project, comprises three large paintings set within subsidiary polychrome images and six history paintings executed with marked chiaroscuro. As a painted self-representation, the allegories, accompanied by Latin inscriptions, mirrored the political-religious self-image of the republic of Venice and its virtues. Certainly it is not by chance that sketches and *modelli* have survived for a whole range of projects in the Doge's Palace. The artistic freedom that Veronese had tried to justify in 1573 to the Inquisition was here more narrowly limited from the start by guidelines as to content and the existence of iconographic programs. It is not surprising then that Veronese was again involved with designs for what was probably the most prestigious enterprise of Venice.

The story, as complicated as it was exciting, of the competition to redesign the main wall of the Sala del Maggior Consiglio began around 1560. A decisive factor was the wish to replace the fresco the *Coronation of the Virgin Mary* by the Paduan painter Guariento di Arpo (first documented 1338–ca. 1370) of the 1360s, the so-called *Paradise*, with a new work in keeping with the period. Only after the great fire, probably in 1582, were various painters finally invited to submit *inventioni*. Today we know, on account of the surviving models, that Palma il Giovane, Francesco Bassano, Tintoretto, and Veronese took part in the competition. Veronese prepared the project with a number of drawings as well as an oil sketch. After long deliberation, the commission was given to Veronese and Francesco Bassano, but they were unable to agree. When Veronese died a year later, the choice fell on the aged Tintoretto, who for his part delivered several oil sketches, but finally left it to his son Domenico to complete what is probably the largest painting in the world in 1592 (page 465).

In the early 1580s, with the *Triumph of Venetia*, a painting inset in the heavy gold frame of the ceiling of the Sala del Maggior Consiglio, above the seats of the Doge and his councilors (page 486), Veronese delivered the boldest test of his proficiency as a ceiling painter. Again on the basis of a drawn *modello* (Collection of Lord Harewood, Leeds) he created here a "proto-Baroque" pictorial invention that with its perspectival structure, well-considered compositional arrangement of the three groups of figures, brilliant colors, and skilled division of light and shade was soon admitted to the canon of the city's most famous works.

The pervasive upward view, the *di sotto in sù*, had already been successfully experimented with by Veronese on several occasions, but the work occasionally known as a "machine" in the 18th century released new creative means in the realm of ceiling painting which were influential far beyond Venice, into the regions of southern Germany and the Alps, and which found a rebirth in the work of the Venetian painter Giovanni Battista Tiepolo (1696–1770) in the elegant clothing of Venetian Rococo. As a ceiling painter, Paolo Veronese once again played a decisive part in the Sala del Maggior Consiglio in the formation of a politically motivated, specifically Venetian civic iconography. Like a queen, Venetia, the personification of the state, is enthroned on a band of cloud against a background of triumphal imaginary architecture. With this patriotic program, developed with the decisive participation of the Venetian noblemen Giacomo Marcello and Giacomo Contarini as well as the cleric Girolamo Bardi, the painter was faced with clear guidelines as to content. He was to depict Venetia enthroned, in allusion to the world-ruling Roma, over city and land, crowned by a Victoria, the goddess of victory, in the presence of the seven virtues and the four seasons. Moreover, he was to include a festive crowd in the depiction. Both in the design and in the actual ceiling painting, Veronese omitted the representation of the four seasons. In addition, the oval image included eloquence and strength in the form of the statues of Mercury and Hercules.

Apart from this official activity for La Serenissima, in the course of the 1570s Veronese completed a number of altarpieces and devotional pictures as well as a whole series of portraits. With some exceptions, the personalities depicted in many cases remained anonymous. In addition, there were allegorical and mythological subjects, which at times even became the favored theme of the painter and his workshop. In fact, Veronese's enormous output between 1560 and 1588 resulted not least from his work together with members

Following double pages:
Veronese
The Feast in the House of Levi, 1573
Oil on canvas, 555 x 1,310 cm
Galleria dell'Accademia, Venice

Commissioned by the Dominicans of Santi Giovanni e Paolo in Venice, the painting gets its present title from the painter's interrogation by the Venetian Inquisition. Individual figures and motifs had caused offense, so that accusations of heresy were voiced aloud during the cross-examination. The original subject of the enigmatic picture is controversial. Veronese himself added to the confusion in no small measure by saying that it was "… a picture with the supper that Jesus Christ celebrated with his disciples in the house of Simon."

Veronese
The Triumph of Venetia, ca. 1579–1582
Oil on canvas, 904 x 580 cm
Sala del Maggior Consiglio, Doge's Palace, Venice

As one of the three great pictures for the ceiling of
the Sala del Maggior Consiglio, this crowded scene
glorifies the enthroned personification of Venetia
among the gods of Olympus as a symbol of eternal
rule. Bold foreshortened perspectives catch the
viewer's eye as much as the variety of figures and
splendor of the painted architecture.

Veronese
The Finding of Moses, c. 1580
Oil on canvas, 50 x 30 cm
Museo del Prado, Madrid

This small painting, which probably came from the collection of Charles I of England, is one of the earliest and finest versions of an Old Testament subject inspired by the works of the painter Bonifazio de' Pitati (d. 1553). Several replicas in Veronese's own hand are known, together with a number of variants and sundry derivations carried out with the help of his workshop. The scene is a riverbank in a highly atmospheric landscape. The story tells of an infant boy left out in a basket on the Nile, who is found by the Pharaoh's daughter and brought up by her as her own son, Moses. The bridge and city are reminiscent of Verona. When Marco Boschini repeatedly describes Veronese in the 17th century as the treasurer of painting and compares his works with jewelry, this is the picture that seems to be meant by the metaphor. The delicately nuanced interplay of light and shade, achieved with a fine brush, unfolds to produce the glowing effect of brilliant jewels.

of his family and assistants. Following the model of Titian, Tintoretto, and the Bassanos, he soon managed a well-organized workshop in Venice, where he was joined by his younger brother Benedetto, his sons Gabriele (1568–1631) and Carletto (1570–1596), and his assistants. As "Haeredes Pauli," his sons continued to run the workshop successfully after their father's death, and took over the completion of unfinished paintings; they made personal variations on Veronese's pictorial inventions that were particularly popular among collectors (above); and in the context of new commissions made more or less uninhibited use of his style, motifs, and compositional ideas. In doing so, his artistic heirs were able to fall back on a wide-ranging corpus of ink, chalk, and chiaroscuro drawings, of *ricordi* and *modelli* of the most varied functions, which had served Veronese in his lifetime as working material, and which for the most part remained in the possession of the family until 1682.

Veronese's depictions of biblical themes, but above all his allegories and mythologies, were greatly in demand—and not only in Venice, where a gap in the market had opened through the death of Titian (d. 1576). The *Annunciation* signed and dated 1583, which was executed with the participation of his workshop (Patrimonio Nacional, Real Monasterio de San Lorenzo de El Escorial, Madrid), reached Spain in the same year. The high regard bestowed on this painting, barely 5 meters (16 feet) in height, seems to have persuaded King Philip II in 1585 to summon Veronese to Spain. However, the latter declined, so that the Titianesque *Annunciation* remained for the time being the only painting by Veronese in the royal collection, probably even until Diego Velázquez (1599–1660) succeeded in Venice in acquiring the two colorful mythological paintings of *Venus and Adonis* and the *Death of Procris* for Philip IV (1605–1665).

For Duke Guglielmo Gonzaga (d. 1587) in Mantua, Veronese painted a version of the *Finding of Moses,* very popular with collectors (page 487); Carlo Emanuele I of

Savoy (1562–1630) was a further princely personality in Italy who was particularly pleased with this theme. For his residence, the young duke commissioned four paintings, which were largely executed by helpers and arrived in Turin around 1582. Supposedly, the German emperor already owned two mythological works by Veronese in 1584, *Mars, Venus, and a Weeping Cupid,* as well as *Venus,* but apart from the fact that these works have not been definitively identified to this day, it remains questionable whether the account by Raffaello Borghini refers to Emperor Maximilian II (1527–1576) or his son and successor Rudolph II (1552–1612) in Prague. The latter ascended the imperial throne in 1576. As an ambitious collector, Rudolph II nourished a particular love of complicated allegories and erotic "allusions." Even if his role as a client of Veronese's

Veronese
Honor et Virtus post mortem floret, pre-1567
Oil on canvas, 219 x 169.5 cm
Frick Collection, New York

Marked top left with the inscription *(HO)NOR ET VIRTVS / (P)OST MORTE(M) FLORET,* this picture is also described as *Hercules Between Virtue and Vice,* alluding to the story told in Hesiod of when Hercules meets two beautiful women at a fork in the road. The youthful hero of the allegory is an elegantly clad Venetian in white silk garments, who was taken at the end of the 17th century, when the picture was in the collection of Queen Christina of Sweden in Rome, to be a self-portrait of the artist. Unhesitatingly he turns to Virtue, who is crowned with a laurel wreath. Drops of blood on his ripped leg covering testify to the fruitless attempt by Vice—Lust and Pleasure, in the long run the death-bringing opponent of Virtue—to hold back the man of honor and win him over.

Veronese
The Crucifixion, ca. 1582
Oil on canvas, 102 x 102 cm
Musée du Louvre, Paris

It is debatable whether this picture (which once belonged to the Cologne-born Paris banker Everard Jabach (1610–1695) but by 1683 at the latest was in the possession of the French King Louis XIV) is identical with a picture on the same subject described by Marco Boschini in the Casa Garzoni in Venice in 1660. The arrangement of the crosses links the picture with an incomparably more dramatic Crucifixion painted for the Venetian church of San Nicolò della Lattuga (Gallerie dell' Accademia, Venice). Both works display the same glowing colors and the occasional borrowing from Tintoretto. Particularly memorable is the shrouded figure in the yellow robe, which is often identified as Mary Magdalene, but is more probably Synagoga, the personification of Judaism.

remains unclear, in the early 17th century the Venetian painter was represented in the gallery of the castle in Prague by a number of mythological paintings in the guise of allegorical fables. These included the two impressive paintings *Omnia Vanitas* and *Honor et Virtus post mortem floret* (page 488), which had already been offered for sale around 1567 to Duke Albrecht V of Bavaria and presumably reached the possession of Rudolph II through the good offices of the antiquarian Jacopo Strada.

While Veronese's heroes and heroines of mythology shine out in full light in the 1570s, the religious works of his late period are in many cases characterized by a noticeable reduction of media. Individual landscapes and night scenes gain in importance, as in the case of *Christ in the Garden of Gethsemane* (Pinacoteca di Brera, Milan). Scenes from the story of the Passion, such as the *Crucifixion* in the Louvre (above) bring to life the pain of grief by means of powerful contrasts of light and dark, and require no decorative accessories. Carefully weighted effects of light and dark also characterize the *Miracle of St. Pantaleon* for the church of the same name in Venice, one of the last and most atmospheric works of

the painter, who died on the night of 19 April 1588. Colored half-shadows denote the transitions between individual forms and allow us to understand why Paolo Veronese has been celebrated across the centuries as a colorist par excellence.

While art critics in the course of the 19th century continually reproached him for superficial displays of magnificence and the neglect of the next world in favor of this world, it was almost without exception painters who maintained an unprejudiced view as observers of the work of Veronese. Among them was Paul Cézanne (1839–1906), who went positively into ecstasy on a visit to the Louvre in front of the *Wedding at Cana* (pages 480–481): "That is painting. Every bit, the whole, the physicality, the values, the composition, the shiver, it is all there ... one sees nothing but a great colorful wave, eh? ... That is what a painting should give you first of all, a harmonious warmth, an abyss into which the gaze dives." In stating that Paolo Veronese "paints as we see," Cézanne was naming a central quality of the Venetian master's painting.

Andreas Priever

Michelangelo Merisi da Caravaggio 1571–1610

IN SEARCH OF THE ARTIST

CARAVAGGIO'S SELF-PORTRAITS

Rarely have a painter's life and art contrasted so starkly as is the case with Michelangelo Merisi da Caravaggio. After an eventful life full of violence and conflicts with legal authorities, the artist died—not by another's hand, but certainly "marked by the knife." There have been many attempts to find self-portraits of the artist in his paintings. The beheaded giant, Goliath, in a picture in the Galleria Borghese (opposite page) is supposed to be a self-portrait. Some people have seen a second self-portrait in the face of the youthful David who is offering the blood-soaked head to the viewer, as if Caravaggio was expressing his own contradictory nature in this painting. This presupposes an extraordinary age-difference, though other speculations about Caravaggio's self-portraits also take little notice of facial changes as the artist grew older. Yet a drawing by Ottavio Leoni (1509–1590) of Goliath's head offers posterity the best available picture of how Caravaggio looked (page 497).

At all events, as early as 1672 the biographer, Gian Pietro Bellori (1615–1696), identified the artist with this dead head, thus continuing a tradition started by Michelangelo (1475–1564). His face, distorted even more grotesquely, is depicted upon the skin that the flayed Apostle, Bartholomew, is holding in his hand in the Sistine Chapel fresco of the *Last Judgment* (left). The great Florentine artist flayed, and the artist from Caravaggio in Lombardy beheaded—unless this is all mere coincidence, or the future biographer's whim, this self-portrait in Goliath's hacked-off head proves that there is no truth in the belief that Caravaggio never took anything from the great masters!

Certainly, Caravaggio's possible self-portrait as the slain Goliath goes beyond the painting with the Apostle's flayed skin. Nor should we forget that Michelangelo was already getting on in years and must have felt flayed alive after his Herculean labors on the Sistine Chapel, whereas Caravaggio was still under forty, whatever the precise date of the Borghese *David*.

For many scholars, this painting brings Caravaggio's life to a monumental close. This view makes the Borghese *David* one of the art-works which can be seen as a last will and testament. For Caravaggio to mark his end with a self-portrait in the features of a giant slain by a youthful assailant creates the kind of monument which art history reserves for its greatest heroes.

In the Borghese *David*, Caravaggio commits himself to the noble young hero whose victory over Goliath was understood to herald Christ's triumph over Satan. As such, he became a guiding light not only for the Jewish people but also for Christian states like the Florentine Republic. At first glance Caravaggio appears to be indulging in artistic irony by depicting himself as a slain figure and incorporating a good deal of self-doubt in the self-portrait. Beyond that, however, death at the hands of a handsome youth adds an erotic overtone to the bitterness death inevitably brings. For this reason, Caravaggio's self-portrait in the hacked-off head has encouraged Freudian speculation, insofar as this pictorial subject expresses sexual dependency and surrender.

Paintings from Caravaggio's early years in Rome seem to confirm the fact that David's male beauty and Goliath's severed head also have an erotic meaning. In these early paintings some scholars claim to have detected Caravaggio's self-portrait among the semi-naked boys hiding in the shadows, or the figures of young men lustfully challenging the viewer.

The most important of these paintings, the New York *Concert* (page 493), highlights various problems in this fundamentally romantic search for real evidence about great artists.

It is certainly difficult to find in the New York painting the same face that Ottavio Leoni (page 497) later identified by the beard and the man's age. Both of the faces, which are turned towards the viewer, have powerful brows. Anyone who claims to see Caravaggio's self-portrait in the lute player must also accept that even as a young man in Rome the artist had already established himself as a commanding figure. In this case, the enchantingly androgynous picture the *Lute Player* in St. Petersburg (page 520) would also have to qualify as a self-portrait on physiognomic grounds.

All things considered, it seems more likely that this head is a portrait of the Sicilian painter, Mario Minitti (1576–1640), of whom Caravaggio was a very close friend for many years and who probably gave him shelter in Syracuse when he was fleeing from the Knights of Malta.

Caravaggio
David and Goliath, ca. 1605–1610
Oil on canvas, 125 x 101 cm
Museo Galleria Borghese, Rome

David is depicted against a deep black background as a kind of ideal portrait. He is holding the head of Goliath, whom he has felled with his sling. Accordingly, he will be presented to the virgins of Jerusalem, and then to King Saul. Yet Caravaggio shows us a melancholy hero, who looks at the chopped-off head with a pained expression, without taking any notice of the viewer. His pleated white shirt has slipped down his left shoulder. His coarse trousers, which are even open a little at the front, suggest that, as a shepherd boy, David fought the duel only by accident. The sling, his most important symbol, is of no interest to the artist.

Below:
Michelangelo
The Last Judgment (detail) St. Bartholomew,
1537–1541
Fresco
Capella Sistina, Vatican, Rome

As a sign of his martyrdom, the Apostle St. Bartholomew is holding his own flayed-off skin in his hand. Instead of repeating the saint's face on his skin, Michelangelo has painted his own self-portrait there. This unique step may have inspired Caravaggio to depict himself in the hacked-off head of Goliath.

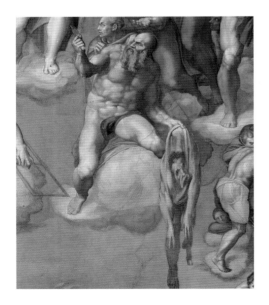

The hair, if not the complexion, argue in favor of this. In *La Pittura Trionfante*, Venice, 1615, Cesare Gigli wrote that with his strange sense of humor Caravaggio had pallid features and thick hair, that he was extremely tall and sturdy, and had bright, deep-set eyes.

Caravaggio completed the painting for Cardinal del Monte, a Prince of the Church of his generation and an important patron of the arts. In it love and wine, the lute and singing, combine into an urban Arcadia; but indoors rather than outside under the open sky.

The artist spirits his young men out of the land of Cupid and Bacchus and the temporal distance of myth, then locates them in a rather untidy looking cultural situation. Caravaggio was the first artist to make effective paintings of violins, and one lies in the foreground. These instruments represent the new music of Caravaggio's generation. Songbooks tell the young man in the front of the picture what songs and melodies he has to sing. They owe their appearance to the new art of printing.

The clothing Caravaggio paints shows what a sophisticated game he was playing. All the youths are semi-naked. Yet they have not clothed themselves in timeless robes that would have made sure they looked classical. That said, the main figure, the lute player, is wearing a modern-looking tailored shirt, with thick pleats. The shirt is worn loose, however, and thus does not match the naked knee. This means that instead of innocent nakedness we see a state of undress or a dressed state that is no longer respectable.

From the young man in the shadows near the New York *Lute Player*, we turn next to two paintings from Caravaggio's early days in Rome. Judging by the facial features, these two paintings, the *Sick Bacchus* (page 494) and the *Boy with a Basket of Fruit* (page 512), both in the Galleria Borghese, Rome, must also be self-portraits of the artist.

These two paintings both play with the idea of classicism in different ways. One of them alludes to an anecdote about the Greek painter, Zeuxis, and it depicts an anonymous boy along with its real subject, a still-life (page 512). However, anyone who shows Bacchus, the god of wine, as sick is ridiculing all the old gods (page 404). Most art experts see this paradoxical figure as a self-portrait. As seen in the mirror, the artist's painting hand would present a problem, of course: in this picture, the *Sick Bacchus*, that hand does not appear.

This painting is often compared to self-portraits in which Dürer (1471–1528) depicted himself in pain. Others see it as a manifesto of poetic painting in the Giorgione (1476/78–1510) sense against the historical painting of Rome.

Artists paint self-portraits in a mirror since although they depict everything around them the one thing they cannot look at is themselves. One's own features are linked to a secret which classical myth knows in a quite different, terrifying dimension. Only in a mirror can mortals endure to look upon the face of Medusa, because it turns to stone anyone who sees it; as Perseus found when he managed to overcome the monster.

Art history becomes pure speculation when it claims to see the self-portrait of a young man in the *Head of Medusa*. Yet it is still a fascinating idea. Scholars, at least, are agreed that Caravaggio used a boy, not a woman, as the model for the painting which Cardinal del Monte is supposed to have given to the Grand Duke of Tuscany, Ferdinando de' Medici (page 495).

If this face were a self-portrait, the artist would not only have combined shield and mirror into one entity but would have also seen his own features in the mirror, instead of the head of Medusa. A stroke of genius—the genius that is *stupor mundi* (that which astonishes the world)—might have inspired Caravaggio to take this step. Seeing one's own nature as something horrifying is certainly not beyond an artist who, like Caravaggio, has led a life marked by outbursts of violence and arrogance.

A totally different kind of horror distorts the features of a head in the *Martyrdom of St. Matthew* (page 498). This face is generally accepted as a self-portrait by Caravaggio because the features accord best with Ottavio Leoni's drawing (page 479). The face's serious, agonized features express the helplessness of someone who cannot prevent the murder, or even the perplexed face of the murderer himself.

It is more problematic to follow the widely held belief that Caravaggio also executed a self-portrait in the *Kiss of Judas* (page 545), which turned up in Dublin only a few years ago. In this picture the head in question appears in profile, in other words from a viewpoint the artist could hardly have seen even in a mirror. Caravaggio is also supposed to have mingled with Christ's persecutors, which has led many commentators to see the artist confessing to sin and seeking redemption. If this were indeed a self-portrait the figure holding a lantern would bring the light into the picture and thus play the part most appropriate to the artist, who sees history happening before his very eyes.

A LIFE OF VIOLENCE AND GENIUS

Especially in his period in Rome, when his fame was beginning to spread, our main impression of Caravaggio from old documents is that he is a veteran of many battles, constantly making himself conspicuous through insults, quarrels leading to bloody brawls, the illegal carrying of weapons, etc. Modern graphologists have detected the following characteristics in a handwritten note Caravaggio made on 8 April 1606: "violence and generosity, sensuality, pride and desperation when deprived of the place he considers his due, brilliant originality and bravery, stamina and swiftness of response."

According to the two epitaphs which Caravaggio's friend Marzio Milesi wrote after Caravaggio's death on 18 July 1610, the artist was "36 years, 9 months and 20 days old." This would mean he was born on 28 September 1573. He may, however, have come into the world in mid to late October 1571, since he was the first child of Fermo Merisi and his wife, Lucia Aratori, both from Caravaggio. As there is no documentary record of

Caravaggio
The Concert, ca. 1595
Oil on canvas, 92 x 118.5 cm
The Metropolitan Museum of Art, New York

A lute player, shown in the light and dominating the whole composition, along with a second youth, in his shadow, look out from a group of young men. The boy on the right in shadow is holding a crumhorn in his raised right hand. Both boys have been suggested as possible self-portraits of the artist. They are making music together with a singer on the right. A fourth youth on the left symbolizing the god Cupid is leaning towards a bunch of grapes. The wings on his shoulders had been painted over for some time, in order to make the painting look like a pure genre-picture. Baglione mentions the picture, under the title of *Musica*, painted for Cardinal del Monte.

Opposite page:
Caravaggio
Sick Bacchus, or *Satyr with Grapes*, 1592/93
Oil on canvas, 67 x 53 cm
Museo Galleria Borghese, Rome

Behind a dull greenish slab, on which two peaches and a
bunch of brilliantly black grapes lie, a half-naked youth is
crouching. A crown of ivy leaves—not vine leaves—is
woven into his hair. His face, which he has turned
towards the viewer, looks greenish, as does his whole
body. This explains why, in recent times at least, the
picture has been given the nickname of the *Sick Bacchus*.
Early sources called the painting simply a portrait of a
boy, though later it was said to depict a satyr. It belonged
to the Cavaliere d'Arpino (1568–1640), at whose house
Caravaggio spent a few months in 1592/93.

Caravaggio
The Head of Medusa, 1595–1600
Oil on a specially prepared shield covered with leather,
60 x 55 cm
Galleria degli Uffizi, Florence

This time Caravaggio did not paint a standard picture
surface, but a convex ceremonial shield. This shield from
the Medici armory was a decorative accompaniment to a
suit of armor that Shah Abbas of Persia had presented to
the Grand Duke of Tuscany. The myth of Perseus, who
cuts off the head of the monster Medusa, leads to a
curious paradox. On Caravaggio's shield, the head has
already been severed from the body, and blood pours out
of the neck. But life has not yet departed. Eyes widened
in horror, the monster looks at the world one last time,
whilst a scream of death is wrenched from its gaping mouth.

his birth either in the baptismal registers of Caravaggio
for the years 1569 to 1579 or in the appropriate Milan
register, we cannot even be sure of his place of birth.
After getting married, his parents lived in Milan, and so
it is more likely that Michelangelo was born there than
in Caravaggio. The family was petit bourgeois and
owned several smallish estates.

From 1576 onwards the artist lived for a while with
his family in the village of Caravaggio, presumably to
escape the plague that was raging in Milan. In 1584,
however, he returned to the big city. Here he was
apprenticed to Simone Peterzano (active between 1573
and 1592) for (so the contract said) four years. Peterzano
was not unknown as a painter in Milan, and called
himself a "pupil of Titian" (1479–1576). How long
Caravaggio stayed in Milan is not certain. Yet from 1589
onwards he was obviously back in Caravaggio. Here, he
sold his entire inheritance—his father had died in
1577—over the next three years. The documents of sale
confirm that he lived in Caravaggio until 1592. He may
have moved to Rome that year where, in 1593, he spent
a short time in the studio of the painter, Giuseppe Cesari
d'Arpino, later the Cavaliere d'Arpino (1568–1640).
Pictures which dated from his early years in Rome
include the *Boy with a Basket of Fruit* (page 512) and the
Sick Bacchus (page 494), which, after the Cavaliere
d'Arpino's goods were confiscated, became the property
of Cardinal Scipione Borghese, the Cardinal's "nephew."

In the following years, Caravaggio earned a living
from private pieces of work through which he built up a
small circle of wealthy admirers. About 1595, Cardinal
Francesco del Monte, a versatile, cosmopolitan man
with a strong humanist interest in art and science, gave
the painter accommodation in his house. For him,
Caravaggio painted pictures like the *Card Sharps* (page
538), the *Fortune Teller* (page 538), and *Lute Player*
(page 521). Caravaggio probably had del Monte to
thank for the commission originally intended for the
Cavaliere d'Arpino: the two history paintings (pages
552, 553) for the side walls of the Chapel of Cardinal
Matteo Contarelli in the church of San Luigi dei
Francesi, Rome.

Shortly after this, in September 1600, the artist
received his second public commission: Tiberio Cerasi,
bursar to Pope Clement VIII (1592–1605), had
acquired a family chapel in Santa Maria del Popolo, and
wanted paintings from Caravaggio for both of the side
walls. Caravaggio was due to deliver the *Crucifixion of
St. Peter* and the *Conversion of St. Paul* (page 554) in
late May 1601. However, after Cerasi died that same
month, the new owners (presumably the Ospedale della
Consolazione) rejected the pictures, so that Caravaggio
reconceived and repainted them (pages 555, 559).

Caravaggio received his third important commission
in February 1602, with the altarpiece for the Contarelli
Chapel. The first version of this painting, *St. Matthew
and the Angel*, was also rejected, and Caravaggio had to
redesign and re-execute it by September of the same year.
Whilst the first version, which was destroyed in the War
in Berlin in 1945 (page 564), found an admirer and
purchaser in Marchese Vincenzo Giustiniani, the second

version, also financed by this collector, is still hanging
above the altar in the Contarelli Chapel (page 563).

In 1603, Giovanni Baglione (1571–1644), who
wrote a biography of Caravaggio and is therefore of
great interest to scholars, brought an action for libel
against him and two other painters, as well as the
architect, Onorio Longhi. Caravaggio was imprisoned
for a few days, but soon released when the French
Ambassador intervened.

Yet such incidents did not lessen his fame as a painter
in the least. His services were much sought after both
by private collectors—such as, for example, Cardinal
Federico Borromeo, Vincenzo Giustiniani, whom we
have already mentioned, Marchese Ciriaco Mattei, and
the banker Ottavio Costa—and by Church authorities.
About 1603/04, for the Oratorian Church of Santa
Maria, Vallicella, known as the Chiesa Nuova,
Caravaggio painted his *Entombment of Christ* (page
569). In July 1605, however, he had a dispute with
Mariano Pasqualino, a notary, over a woman called
Lena, "donna del Caravaggio," in which he badly
injured Pasqualino. Caravaggio fled to Genoa, but later
apologized, whereupon the charges were dropped. He
returned to Rome, where, shortly afterwards, the
Confraternity of Sant'Anna dei Palafrenieri
commissioned him to paint a Madonna for the altar of
St. Peter's. This painting (page 570) stayed in its
appointed place only a short time, however, before
being given to Cardinal Scipione Borghese.

On 28 May 1606, Caravaggio and his friend,
Onorio Longhi, became involved in a brawl during a
ball game. Caravaggio killed one of their opponents.
The two friends fled from Rome: the injured
Caravaggio probably went into hiding on nearby land
owned by Prince Marzio Colonna, whilst Onorio fled
to Lombardy.

A document dated 16 October 1606 shows that
Caravaggio was now in Naples, where he was already
carrying out further commissions. Here, in 1607, he
was paid 400 ducats for the *Seven Acts of Mercy* (page
575), and in May of the same year, 290 ducats for the
Flagellation of Christ, formerly in San Lorenzo (page
577).

A court record of July 1607, calling the artist as a
witness, shows that Caravaggio was in Malta, where,
among other work, he painted the *Portrait of Alof de
Wignacourt* (pages 502, 503), and the *Beheading of
St. John the Baptist* (pages 578–579) for the cathedral.
On 14 July 1608, he was made a Knight of Malta *de
gratia* (Knight of Obedience of the Order of St. John),
and was clearly leading a respectable life. It is all the
more astonishing that by December of the same year
he had been expelled from the Order. He was
imprisoned, but managed to escape, and set sail for
Sicily. Here, a close friend from his time in Rome, the
Sicilian painter Mario Minnitti, gave him shelter in
Syracuse. Through Minnitti's good offices Caravaggio
was commissioned to paint the *Burial of St. Lucy* for
the altar of Santa Lucia (page 580). He traveled on to
Messina, where he painted the *Raising of Lazarus* (page
581) and the *Adoration of the Shepherds* (page 582). In

Michel.º da Caravaggio

IV

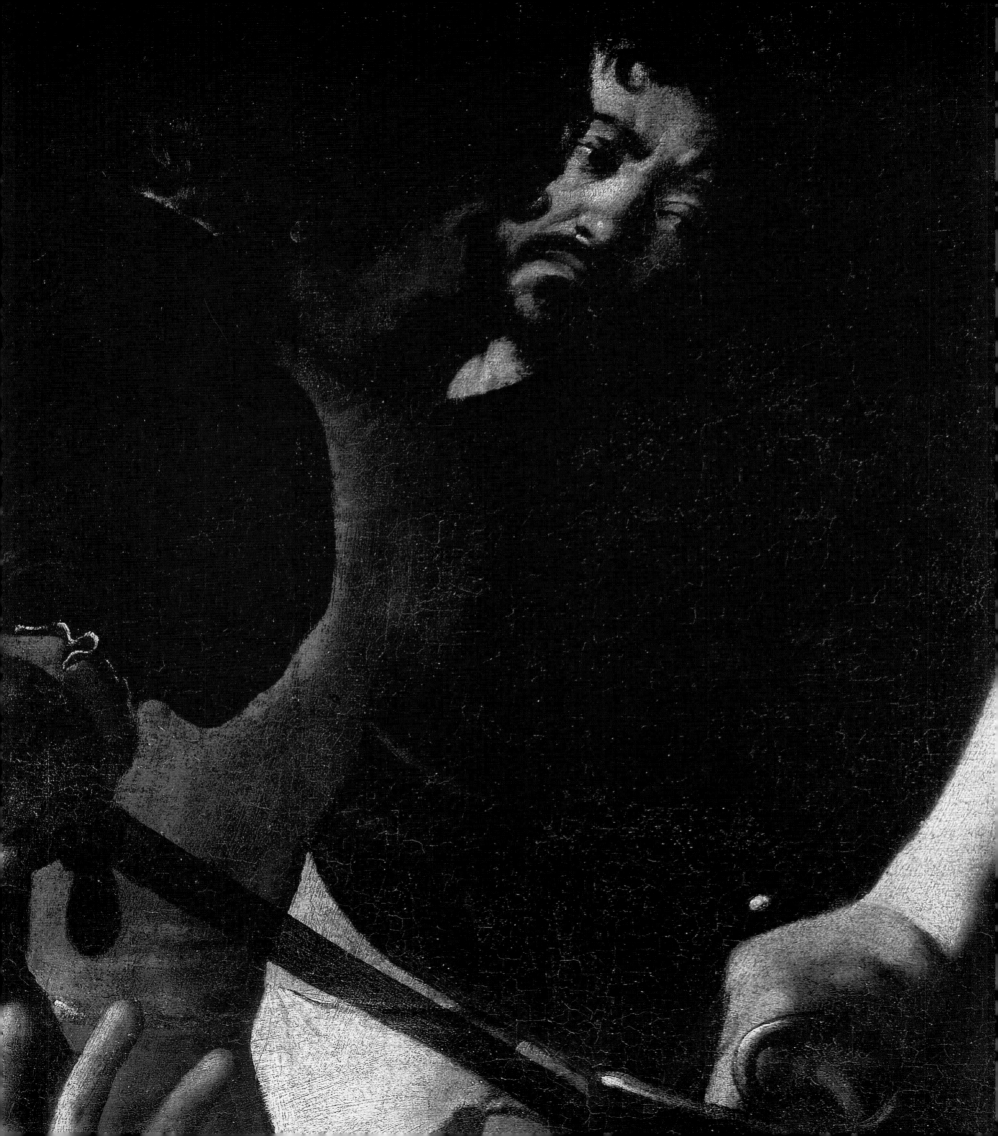

1609, in Palermo, Caravaggio was commissioned to paint the *Nativity with St. Francis and St. Lawrence* (page 583). By October of the same year, the artist was back in Naples. Here he was attacked and badly injured in the face, or, as an old document put it, "marked by the knife."

Caravaggio left the city in which he no longer felt safe. Cardinal Gonzaga had prevailed upon Pope Paul V (1605–1621) to grant him a pardon, but this had not yet been officially confirmed. He nevertheless embarked on a ship bound for Rome. After he landed he was arrested (probably due to mistaken identity) by Spanish soldiers, though he was soon released. He continued his journey on foot, and in Porto Ercole was afflicted with a fever, from which he died on 18 July 1610.

For a long time scholars thought that they knew the whole situation. Yet in recent times sensational attempts have been made to clarify the mystery of Caravaggio's death. It has been suggested that a mortally insulted Knight of Malta joined forces with the artist's papal pursuers and killed Caravaggio.

EARLY COMMENTATORS ON CARAVAGGIO'S LIFE AND WORK

There is one underlying tone to all the comments written about Caravaggio up to our own day. Anyone who regards the artist highly feels obliged to make a sharp distinction between the personality and the work. This already applies to the first detailed *vita* (life of the artist) contained in the *Considerazioni sulla pittura* by Giulio Mancini, personal physician to Urban VIII (1623–1644), dating from about 1620.

Searches made over the last few years in various archives have unearthed an extraordinary number of direct statements. Among these are commissions for several still extant major works, as well as documents recording payment for and storage of a large number of pictures. Old inventories list the paintings in the possession of the artist's major patrons. In letters and other writings contemporaries give reports about him or individual works by him. A letter from one of his patrons, the Marchese Vincenzo Giustiniani, written about 1620, even goes so far as to advance arguments for an evaluation of Caravaggio, in the context of a systematic theoretical study. Another highly placed owner of a Caravaggio, Cardinal Federico Borromeo of Milan, praised Caravaggio's Milan *Basket of Fruit* in his *Musaeum*, a text published in 1625, as a "unique work of art." This judgment was in fact predated by the fragmentary comments made by Giovan Battista Agucchi between 1607 and 1615, which explored Caravaggio's attitude to nature.

Court records give us information about incidents in which Caravaggio was involved. Evidence given by Caravaggio, Orazio Gentileschi (1563–1639) and others, in the libel action brought by Giovanni Baglione, give us an idea of how the artist used to speak and the competition that existed between them. We are even given a verbatim account of Caravaggio's attitude towards the characters and abilities of his most important contemporaries when he says: "I think I know almost all the painters in Rome ... They are almost all my friends, but not all of them are good painters ... those who are not my friends are Cesari [the Cavaliere d'Arpino], Baglione, Gentileschi, and Giorgio Tedeschi [Hoefnagel], for they do not talk to me ... the following are good painters: Cesari, Zuccari, Roncalli, Annibale Carracci." It is surprising here to see that he considers certain artists whom today we would regard as Caravaggesque, in other words, like him in style, neither his friends nor good painters.

The impression of Caravaggio which later generations developed was derived from a handful of printed texts. They began during the artist's lifetime with Karel van Mander's *Schilderboeck* of 1604. Writings like this seek to establish art theory. Models and so-called *topoi* (conventions) were quoted from classical antiquity: pithy situations and anecdotes that several different artists retail in much the same way. These need not be true as such but must offer the reader concrete criteria.

A writer as early as Karel van Mander described Caravaggio as an eccentric person with a highly exceptional view of art. Most other early commentators also saw him in a critical light. The most important of these is Giovanni Baglione, painter, competitor, and litigant. The book he wrote in 1625 or thereabouts was published in Rome in 1642 under the title: *Le vite de' pittori, scultori ed architetti. Dal pontificato di Gregorio XIII del 1572 in fino a tempi di papa Urbano Ottavo nel 1642*. In his *Microcosmo della Pittura*, published in Cesena in 1657, Francesco Scannelli took a detached attitude. Despite his sharp criticisms, however, Scannelli acknowledged the fascination that Caravaggio's work exercised. Another key work was the *vita* most influenced by *topoi*: in Gian Pietro Bellori's *Le vite de' pittori, scultori ed architetti moderni*, published in Rome in 1672. At the other end of the spectrum, Joachim von Sandrart's *Teutsche Academie* of 1675 took a thoroughly positive view of Caravaggio's work.

The Martyrdom of St. Matthew (detail page 553)

In the panic that breaks out in what first looks like total confusion at the altar, where the Apostle and Evangelist, St. Matthew, is thrown to the ground and slain, the victim's followers flee in horror. Only one head among several has the features that correspond to a portrait. Almost every authority agrees that this is Caravaggio's self-portrait. Whereas previously seen as a fleeing Christian, by now he is considered to be the actual murderer, the man who inflicted the first, fatal wound on the saint.

ESSENTIAL FEATURES OF CARAVAGGIO'S ART

St. Catherine of Alexandria (detail page 505)

The young woman who was in the destroyed Berlin portrait (opposite) posed for St. Catherine. Since Caravaggio probably only worked for a short period with the same models, scholars are able to get clues from them to help date the artist's works.

Opposite page:
Caravaggio
Phyllis, or Portrait of a Courtesan, ca. 1600 (1598?)
Oil on canvas, 66 x 53 cm
Formerly Kaiser-Friedrich-Museum, Berlin
(destroyed during World War II)

A young woman, holding a bunch of flowers in front of her breast, appears against a dark neutral background. Her intense eyes are looking almost straight at the viewer, in dramatic lighting. Although the woman depicted is more likely to have been one of the artist's models than a lady from an upper-class house, and was, for a while, known as Phyllis the Courtesan, the painting soon found a place alongside the Berlin *Cupid* (page 522), and the first version of St. Matthew in the magnificent Giustiniani Collection in Rome (page 563).

THE PRINCIPLES OF PORTRAITURE

The portrait, which developed into a major art form in both Italy and in northern Europe in the 15th and 16th centuries, was not a genre for leading artists in the two decades around 1600.

Several portraits attributed to Caravaggio are all disputed by scholars except one. This exception is a woman's portrait from the collection of Caravaggio's patron, Giustiniani, whose provenance has always kept it beyond suspicion. Furthermore, at the end of the World War II it was destroyed in Berlin, and that may be why it is virtually never mentioned nowadays (page 501). The painting did not depict the figure who had commissioned the picture, but rather a woman who modeled for other paintings by Caravaggio in historical costume (page 500). She is remembered as the Roman courtesan Phyllis. Yet this name has no historical value because it merely recalls the woman who made a fool even of the wise Aristotle.

The idea of simply painting an impressive face as an end in itself and considering the result a work of art, is relatively new. Only later generations came to regard full-length portraits of such people close to artists as common—to such an extent that the Dutch even has a word for it: *tronye*, slang for "face."

Official portraits do not constitute any high points in Caravaggio's work. According to Bellori, he painted a portrait of Pope Paul V (1605–1621) that has been linked with a painting in the Borghese Gallery, Rome. Two different versions of a portrait of Cardinal Maffeo Barberini have been attributed to him with greater confidence. The version in the Galleria Corsini, Florence, shows the future Pope Urban VIII (1623–1644) sitting beside a small table with a vase of flowers, similar to those Caravaggio painted near his anonymous young men (pages 519, 520). No such accessory belongs in an official portrait, which may explain why this motif is absent from the more impressive version in a private collection, Florence (page 502). Chiaroscuro alone, as well as a limpid palette of earth colors, combined with smoothly executed highlights, are hardly enough to reveal Caravaggio's fiery personality in these paintings.

Two paintings, considered authentic, which depict the Grand Master of the Order of the Knights of St. John on Malta, Alof de Wignacourt (pages 502, 503), are a quite different matter. Whilst the half-figure picture in Florence achieved the high standards of early Baroque portrait painting, the monumental portrait in the Louvre, on whose earth-colored background the Knight of Malta's powerful shadow falls, strikes me as being Caravaggio's most characteristic contribution to the genre. In one respect the painting demands comparison with other full-length official portraits like Titian's Philip II. Yet it does not fit comfortably into that tradition. In other words, wearing that armor, the man looks like a jointed doll. Caravaggio depicted Alof de Wignacourt as an arrangement of figure and accessories.

Below:
Caravaggio
Portrait of Maffeo Barberini, later Pope Urban VIII, 1598/99
Oil on canvas, 124 x 90 cm
Private collection, Florence

The still undeveloped features of this young cleric, who later became Pope Urban VIII (1623–1644) were portrayed as a much more distinguished figure by the skills of Gianlorenzo Bernini (1598–1680). Here, the face appears in chiaroscuro against a neutral background in such a way that a wall appears to be screening off the figure from the left. In order to give the figure more *rilievo*, or more three-dimensionality, the lit sections are painted against a dark, and the sections in shadow against a light, background.

Opposite page:
Caravaggio
Portrait of Alof de Wignacourt with a Pageboy, 1608
Oil on canvas, 195 x 134 cm
Musée du Louvre, Paris

The Grand Master of the Knights of Malta, wearing armor and wielding a heavy staff of office, has come in from the left, gently illuminated, and is standing against a neutral background which marks no division between wall and floor, but which suggests a wall on the right. His standing leg forms the midline of this unusual composition. The right-hand side of the picture is dominated by a pallid boy who is bringing in the helmet with a ceremonial plume. Many present-day experts doubt that this is an authentic Caravaggio. This is partly because it is historically inaccurate: Alof de Wignacourt's armor, which is preserved in Malta, looks very different. And it is partly because the spatial layout is inconsistent. However, since the Knight of Malta looks younger here than in the Florence portrait (left), a Caravaggesque painter must have strayed on to the island before his master.

Caravaggio
Portrait of Alof de Wignacourt, 1608
Oil on canvas, 118.5 x 95.5 cm
Galleria Palatina, Palazzo Pitti, Florence

Caravaggio's flight from Rome drove him first to Malta, where he quickly got to know the Grand Master of the Knights of Malta. The Grand Master playfully rests his left hand on his sword in its sheath, whilst in his right hand he is holding a rosary. The artist subtly dramatizes the contradiction between piety and brutality by the lighting and the fact that his subject is averting his eyes from the viewer. Only very recently was this painting identified in the gallery's storeroom, and related to a reference in Bellori's book of 1672.

Preceding pages, left:
Caravaggio
The Penitent Mary Magdalene, ca. 1595
Oil on canvas, 122.5 x 98.5 cm
Galleria Doria Pamphilj, Rome

The Mary Magdalene who is briefly mentioned in the Bible only became a person in her own right in later legends. According to these, she anointed Christ's feet with ointment in Bethany, asked him to raise her brother, Lazarus, from the dead (page 581), and was the first person to meet him after his resurrection. Even so, because of her dissolute former life (page 539), she was redeemed only after a hard process of atonement. In this picture, portrait in the usual sense and in the sense of a saint's image come to the same thing. From the young woman's dejected self-absorption, Caravaggio is able to achieve an expression of human tragedy.

Preceding pages, right:
Caravaggio
St. Catherine of Alexandria, ca. 1600 (1598?)
Oil on canvas, 173 x 133 cm
Museo Thyssen-Bornemisza, Madrid

St. Catherine of Alexandria cannot be depicted as casually as Mary Magdalene. This princess from Alexandria was a proud woman of great learning. She defied martyrdom on the wheel several times by breaking it, and finally had to be put to death by a sword. A young woman does not normally go around with a broken wheel and executioner's sword—nor martyr's palm frond, which lies in the foreground between the viewer and the saint. Caravaggio's vision is more artificial here. He has no qualms about adding a halo to emphasize the rapturous expression of this majestic head.

Right:
Caravaggio
St. Francis, 1606 (?)
Oil on canvas, 130 x 90 cm
Pinacoteca, Cremona

This seems to be an unconventional composition, and depicts the saint front-on, near a tree trunk, bending over a book. Even so, the artist decides not to depict the joyous devotion to nature expressed in St. Francis' canticle to the sun. Once again, the artist has reduced the founder of the Franciscan Order to a simple, ritual model, latterly in the tradition of *St. Jerome* (see page 529). The sole surviving example is in bad condition, but it is probably an authentic work by Caravaggio.

Opposite page:
Caravaggio
St. Francis, ca. 1605
Oil on canvas, 128 x 94 cm
Chiesa dei Cappuccini, deposited in the Galleria Nazionale d' Arte Antica, Palazzo Barberini, Rome

The founder of the Franciscan Order was the first person to experience the miracle of stigmatization on his own body. In other words, he was marked out by Christ's wounds. Here, he is reduced to the ideal state of penance in the wilderness: a state equally valid for saints and pious people. Caravaggio shows no sign of reinterpreting the story unconventionally. His rather traditional approach may derive from the fact that the composition is probably a commission from the papal family. They owned the township known as Carpineto, from where an almost identical second copy, at present in the Palazzo Venezia, Rome, originated. Stylistically, the painting is very closely related to the Brera *Supper at Emmaus* (page 541), which was probably painted in Latium.

According to Bellori, Caravaggio is supposed to have set out a painting, which is now in the Galleria Doria Pamphilj, Rome, as if it were a portrait (page 504): "He painted a girl, sitting on a chair, with her hands in her lap, drying her hair. He portrayed her [ritrasse] in a room, and by adding a jar of ointment on the floor, as well as jewelry and gemstones, he made a Mary Magdalene of her."

The author provided this explanation at the start of his *vita* in order to characterize Caravaggio's natural *modi* (manner of working) and his art of imitation.

As with Mary Magdalene, Caravaggio arranged a figure and still-life accessories into a picture of St. Catherine of Alexandria (page 505). His model for the face of this full-length painting was the woman Phyllis from the lost Berlin portrait of that name

(page 501). In the history of sacred paintings, both these canvases have played an exceptional role. In terms of subject, both the pictures are in fact devotional images. Whilst they were not meant to be worshipped as such, they were supposed to give an impression of those figures to whom the pious wished to turn. That said, Mary Magdalene avoids eye contact with anyone at prayer. Equally, it is difficult to imagine anyone praying fervently before St. Catherine, for she regards the viewer in too direct, too earthly a way.

Paintings like these two works by Caravaggio stood at a crossroads in time when both the Church and the art world became aware of the difference between sacred and gallery pictures. The fact that the Church also distinguished between secular and devotional art can be seen from a statement by the Jesuit, Pedro de Ribadeneira. As early as 1595, he considered that the highest praise for the pious series of pictures in which Juan de Mesa depicted the Life of St. Ignatius lay in the fact that this cycle would not be out of place in a collection of other paintings.

But even sacred pictures for pious worshippers were painted within Caravaggio's circle. Among these were several versions of St. Francis meditating, though the authorship is still disputed (pages 506, 507). His meditation on the death's head, with a crucifix on the floor, is executed with a simplicity and anonymity that explain why such pictures were never mentioned in older art literature.

Both versions probably date from the time when Caravaggio first fled Rome. Three related sacred paintings, two of St. John the Baptist and one Penitent Mary Magdalene, were found in the artist's luggage after his death.

THE STUDIO POSE

Around 1600 it was by no means self evident that an artist would simply paint reality in the form of an arranged scene with appropriate objects, then pass off the result as a figure from mythology or religion. Whilst it might cultivate noble religious thoughts to show an ordinary working-class girl as Mary Magdalene, Caravaggio had opened his art to new tendencies in the Roman Catholic Church, which, like the Oratorians

around Filippo Neri (1515–1595), did not wish to see saints remotely tucked away in heaven. Instead, they believed that their precursors among ordinary people had their feet firmly on the ground. In mentioning the episode of drying hair, Caravaggio's biographer, Bellori, emphasizes the artist's irreverence. But while doing so, he may be missing a deeper level of meaning which might make this into a very worthy Magdalenic gesture: for, after all, the saint did dry Christ's feet with her own hair.

How consciously Caravaggio sometimes arranged the reality of the studio as opposed to the world of the gods emerges very strongly from the earliest picture about whose authenticity scholars all agree, the Uffizi *Bacchus* (page 509).

To paint this picture, Caravaggio approached his task in an almost brazenly literal way. The boy who modeled Bacchus for him shows he is a child of the city, normally wears clothes, and only exposes his hands and his head to the light. He belongs to the same circle of young men who are playing the New York *Concert* (page 493). Since upper-class people of Caravaggio's day were conspicuous for the whiteness of their skin, under which veins full of blue blood stood out, the coarse sunburn on hands and face marks the boy out as lower class.

The Uffizi *Bacchus* shows even contemporary viewers why older theories of art rejected Caravaggio's work. The canvas reveals the whole process of artistic method. Caravaggio has the classical god represented so crudely by his model that he breaks entirely with his colleagues' game of disguises as he apparently follows it through with a naïve disregard for verisimilitude.

The real subject of the painting is neither the world of a Bacchus nor the hardships suffered by a genius who has just arrived in Rome from the provinces and is forced to use local boys as second-rate models. Caravaggio was more concerned to cast off the camouflage and pretense of historical painting. He thus turns ridicule about working in an untruthful way into a manifesto of his own style of painting.

Concentrating on accurate reproduction, this art makes precise imitation of nature decisively important. Even critics like Scannelli, writing in 1657, who think nothing of painting as reproduction, *copia*, are forced to acknowledge that Caravaggio and his school depict the elements of historical painting with such truth, power, and vitality that although they are not unequalled, they make the viewers' heads spin with astonishment.

Caravaggio
Bacchus, ca. 1595
Oil on canvas, 95 x 85 cm
Galleria degli Uffizi, Florence

We hardly imagine the gods of classical antiquity looking like this young man. He is sitting on a bed, at the edge of a table, which offers him a half-empty glass carafe of wine and an earthenware dish full of fruit. The white fabric he has wrapped around himself is draped so awkwardly that we can see the contemporary material of the mattress beneath it. Suntanned on his face and his hands, but otherwise pale, this would-be god reveals himself as a model from the city, affectedly holding an expensive wine glass. An especially eye-catching detail is the coarse canvas of the cushion that appears under the white linen. Pictures were sometimes painted on such fabric around the year 1600, here giving the impression that Caravaggio has literally brought the actual fabric on which the image is painted into view.

Caravaggio
Jupiter, Neptune, and Pluto, post-1596
Ceiling painting in oil, ca. 300 x 180 cm
Archivio Boncompagni Ludovisi, Rome

This technically unusual picture, which was mentioned by as early an authority as Bellori, is nowadays considered a work by Caravaggio painted for del Monte, who purchased the building in 1596. It decorates the ceiling of a small room where the cardinal apparently carried out experiments in alchemy. On his eagle, Jupiter swoops down towards Neptune and Pluto, who are standing at the opposite edge of the ceiling, as if he were making the sky light up with a crystal ball. Any interpretation of the gathering of the gods, seen (unusually) from below, must shift between mythology, astrology, alchemy, and even the Christian doctrine of salvation. An oddity in the artist's work, this ceiling painting does not fit into any stylistic category.

According to André Félibien, Nicolas Poussin (1593/94–1665) held the view that Caravaggio had come into the world solely to ruin painting. As early as 1642 Baglione had expressed the same opinion in his *vita*. Art theorists in particular complained about Caravaggio's influence on younger painters, whom he allegedly taught to be satisfied with unadulterated nature as a subject for painting.

As an artist who restricts his painting to confined spaces, Caravaggio certainly strikes contemporary viewers as being very far removed from painting nature in the raw. But for his own day, the concept of being true to nature was still too revolutionary. From the 15th century onwards artists had tended to study models in order to paint bodies and motion as well as accessories—but only on paper, not in oil.

In general, artists oriented themselves on the classical painter, Zeuxis (first half of the 4th century BC), of whom Cicero, Pliny, and others reported that five of the noblest virgins in Athens were put at his disposal so that he could study their naked bodies and put together an ideal image out of the best features of each: a Venus or a Helen. Such an undertaking demands from the artist not so much humility in the face of accidents of nature as an organizational sense that he must put at the service of visible phenomena.

The example of Caravaggio, on the other hand, was considered a warning against studying nature without preparatory training. A characteristic voice here was that of Charles-Alphonse Dufresnoy's didactic poem of 1668, which, from line 427, runs: "That anyone who begins should not be in too great haste to study everything he wants to do from nature, before he knows the proportions, the arrangement of the parts and their contours, before he has studied excellent originals thoroughly and before he is well versed in the sweet deceptions."

The notion of nature as the real mistress of art also has classical roots. The fact that this was well known is obvious from the comparison between Caravaggio and the Greek sculptor, Demetrios, who thought only nature was valid. This was how Bellori opened his *vita* as early as 1672. Yet Bellori was horrified that, far from selecting only what is worthwhile for art, both artists also borrow nature's vulgar aspects.

Caravaggio derived his energy from portraiture. By a unique form of paradox, an artist who could scarcely have achieved greater fame as a portrait painter, proved himself by relentlessly reproducing what he saw in front of him. Caravaggio subjugated his entire art to this talent, which Scannelli calls his "instinct for nature," so that he built up

something, which art theorists would dismiss as a wrong direction, into a whole system. The very first published book on Caravaggio, Karel van Manders's *Schilderboeck* of 1604, spread the story that the artist never put brush to canvas without having a model in front of him. The most outrageous point here is that he ventured to paint direct from nature in the studio. It was in what he saw in front of him there that he found truth: not in anything ideal or classically correct.

The whole issue of working from a model is more a *topos* than a verifiable fact, because it is clearly impossible to arrange and study everything that could be painted. All the same, Caravaggio's guiding principle—to paint direct from nature—explains a special characteristic of his art. Unlike almost all his contemporaries he declined to paint frescoes, thus turning his back on the noblest artistic activity of his age. In a small-scale picture in Berlin, Adolph von Menzel (1815–1905) once painted the crowd that gathered when Antoine Pesne (1683–1757) took a model on to the scaffolding with him for an illusionistic ceiling painting in Rheinsberg. We can see the absurdity of painting direct from nature while engaged on fresco work when we look at the only ceiling painting that can be attributed to Caravaggio with any certainty (page 511). He would have had to dangle between two sets of scaffolding: one to allow him to observe the model from below, and one to allow him to paint the ceiling. If the picture really is by him, this experience would have taught Caravaggio that this kind of painting was not his métier.

Inventio (invention) was regarded as the supreme quality. *Imitatio* (imitation) was subordinate to it and all that was required of it was to depict the product of some thought in a more plausible way. *Imitatio* was accorded no value in itself. But since objects themselves determined the hierarchy within art, a scale of values developed which judged painting according to its methods and subject matter.

All forms of imitation were seen as the lowest level of artistic creation. A human being in the image of God was seen as the very highest. Images of humans and the godhead supplied from the sphere of *inventio* crowned the hierarchy, whilst painting the likenesses of inanimate objects was frowned upon as the lowest form of art. In terms of hierarchy, everything else rose higher up the scale according to how animated it was or how far it was removed from pure imitation. The spectrum ranged from still-life to historical painting. Even before such hierarchies were established, so wrote Caravaggio's patron, Vincenzo Giustiniani, the artist denied that art was another ascending ladder of difficulty: "Human beings," he said, "were not one jot harder to paint than flowers and fruit."

CARAVAGGIO AND THE GRAPES OF ZEUXIS

Caravaggio
Boy with a Basket of Fruit
Oil on canvas, 70 x 67 cm
Museo Galleria Borghese, Rome

Grapes and vine leaves also dominate this even more generously filled basket of fruit, which includes not only apples, peaches, and pears, but cherries too. The basket is the main motif in an arrangement made up of a still-life and a figure. The basket is held by a boy whose white shirt is falling off his shoulders, thus showing Caravaggio's sure instinct for skin, even if the musculature is not nearly as effective as in later paintings. The expression on the boy's face, which many scholars see as a self-portrait, is curious. His lips enticingly parted, and his head thrown slightly back, the boy's eyes are half-mocking, half-longing. Two shadows, not cast by any object in the picture, intensify the bright light around his neck and head.

Pliny the Elder (before AD 79) gives the following account: "Parrhasios is said to have got into an argument with Zeuxis; the latter exhibited some grapes he had painted so convincingly that birds flew down to the exhibition site. Parrhasios, however, had exhibited a linen curtain he had painted so realistically that Zeuxis, who was most anxious to win the prize, demanded that the curtain finally be removed and the picture revealed; once he saw his error, he awarded the prize to his rival, deeply ashamed, because, although he had been able to deceive the birds, Parrhasios had deceived him as an artist. Later, Zeuxis was said to have painted a boy who was carrying some grapes. When some birds flew down, he angrily said of his work, with the same honesty: 'I painted the grapes better than the boy, for if I had achieved perfection with him as well, the birds would have been too frightened.'"

Even though this classical anecdote makes no mention whatever of still-life in the modern sense, from the very beginning ideas about this genre of painting have kept returning to this episode. That said, Caravaggio was the only first-rate artist to paint the grapes of Zeuxis as well as the boy of Zeuxis.

Whilst the Ambrosiana *Basket of Fruit* (below) can be regarded as the first unchallenged masterpiece of the still-life genre, the *Boy with a Basket of Fruit* (page 512) falls between genres. In competition with Zeuxis one could see how the birds responded to the painted grapes in the unprotected basket. If they had flown down to the pure still-life, but been scared off by the painted boy in the other picture, then Caravaggio would have triumphed over Zeuxis.

In the case of the *Boy with a Basket of Fruit* on its own, however, it would not have been possible to see whether the human figure indeed scared the birds off or whether the painter failed to achieve the necessary realism.

If Caravaggio really has immortalized himself in the features of the *Boy with a Basket of Fruit*, then he has gone far beyond his Athenian precursor in his competition with Zeuxis. If, instead of just any boy, he has used his own self-portrait to protect the grapes from the birds, then his own ego must have had a frightening effect.

Both works might be included among those reconstructions of lost classical pictures that have repeatedly been demanded of painters since the days of the humanists—even if Pliny was talking about convincingly painted fruit. Caravaggio's Milan still-life was meant to promote its creator as a new Zeuxis, whose imitation of nature surpasses the achievements of an artist very long ago, whom scholars only remember because of Pliny. In his own competition against painters from classical antiquity, Caravaggio is asserting that he could paint human beings with enough truth, energy, and vitality to scare off at least birds.

Caravaggio
Basket of Fruit
Oil on canvas, 31 x 47 cm
Pinacoteca Ambrosiana, Milan

A woven fruit basket, placed on a simple brown line rather than a badly painted table top, rises towards the viewer. As well as grapes and figs, we can see a lemon, a pear, an apple, and a peach. Against the yellow background, which is reminiscent of a distempered wall, the arrangement stands out principally because the leaves have been artfully spread out into the empty space. This makes me doubt the view that the yellow paint is covering a deeper background, modeled out of light and shadow. What looks at first sight like an accidental ensemble, arranged merely to create a trompe-l'œil effect, actually follows a careful geometric pattern. In accordance with the golden section, the basket has been moved to the left. The leaf projecting on the left follows the same geometric pattern. Even if the worm-eaten apple reminds us of Eve in Paradise, and a shriveled-up leaf on the right evokes the transience of all earthly things, the work's almost abstract character is still most impressive.

Arrangements of
Objects and Figures

This splendid work simply does not fit in with the idea
of Caravaggio's gradual development from still-life to
history painting. It depicts Narcissus in contemporary
dress but without any accessories. According to Ovid,
Narcissus saw his own reflection in a stream and fell so in
love with it that he never moved from the spot, and thus
died, metamorphosed into the narcissus flower. After
restoration in 1995, a fierce dispute about this Roman
painting's authenticity arose, as a result of which more
people favored its being attributed to Caravaggio. Despite
convincing similarities with one of the artist's major
works, the *Conversion of St. Paul* (page 555), I am not
certain that Caravaggio painted this very smooth picture
without accessories.

The way that Bellori describes the process (naturally
not observed by him) whereby Caravaggio made an
ordinary girl into a penitent Mary Magdalene relates to
still-lifes, not figure pictures. Here, we need to
remember that such pictures of inanimate objects were
not automatically a fit subject for art anywhere in
Europe at the turn of the 16th century. According to
Charles Sterling, an authentic still-life is born on the
day a painter makes the fundamental decision to take a
group of objects as a theme and to organize them into
a pictorial entity.

Like the French form, *nature morte*, the phrase "still-
life" principally reflects an artistic process. This
combination of words originating from the milieu of art
does not mean life that stands still or dead nature, but
the reproduction in paint of immobile or objects direct
from life or direct from nature. Accordingly, like the
portrait, the still-life aims at *imitatio*. In other words,
Caravaggio's principle of portraiture could just as well
be understood as his principle of still-life.

Part of Caravaggio's radical break with the artistic
practice of *inventio* lies in the fact that he does not base
his work on prototypes. According to his biographers,
he thought very little of classical artists and even of
Raphael (1483–1520). With only a few exceptions,
modern art historians also regard his work as being
independent of older tradition.

And yet early in his career Caravaggio was in conflict
with classical artists. The painter from the small town
in Lombardy known as Caravaggio, who so liked to
present himself as inexperienced, provincial, and
uncouth, clearly intervened personally in the dispute
between Parrhasios and Zeuxis.

In conflict with this episode from classical antiquity,
Caravaggio achieved a great deal for the genre of still-
life—with just one picture and accessories in figure
painting (pages 494, 509, 519). Considering the
impressive power the painting exercises, all the other
still-lifes attributed to the artist have until now had no
chance of being accepted as genuine Caravaggios.

The Milan *Basket of Fruit* (page 513) was a success
from the start. Cardinal Federico Borromeo purchased
the painting before 1607. Ever since then, it has been a
showpiece of the gallery he founded, the Ambrosiana in
Milan. As if he wanted to join battle over the relative
merits of different genres, Caravaggio—and we know
this from X-ray photographs—brazenly painted his still-
life over a figure that an inferior contemporary artist had
already completed. The brown brush stroke creating the
consummate optical illusion of the Milan *Basket of Fruit*
makes it abundantly clear that an artist painted this
picture, not a mathematician. It gives the basket the
rhetorical quality that Jan Bialostocki tried to define as
the main distinguishing feature of the Baroque.

Along with Scannelli and other early authors, more
recent art historians have seen Caravaggio's
development in the following terms: "Caravaggio's
formal development takes a remarkably unified,
consistent line. Unlike so many of his contemporaries,
he did not concern himself with conventional types of
picture, but began by concentrating on one type: close-
up half-length figures, which particularly suited his
talent for tactile sensuality and intimacy. He learnt not
from imitating acknowledged masterpieces but by
setting his ends as far away as his means would reach.
Step by step, he developed from single-figure to multi-
figure half-length pictures, and from half-length to
full-length pictures. He also moved from appropriate
calm through theatrical mobility to dynamic drama.
His painting style developed from the soft tones of
muted light to spectacular chiaroscuro contrasts, and
from strongly modeled surface relief to three-
dimensional fullness by way of broader modeling. His
formal technique moved on from layered parallel
surfaces to geometric spatial structures, and from a
dismembered, almost disconnected form of anatomy
through an abstract, not always successful, physicality
to sensual bodies of flesh and blood, and from simple
drapery and still-lifes to magnificent costumes, fragrant
flowers and fruits, as well as sparkling vessels and
jewelry. This development was all the more
extraordinary in that it can be only partially explained
by the general development taking place in art."
(Christoph Luitpold Frommel, *Storia dell'arte*, 1971)

For his early pictures, Caravaggio chose subjects
that diverge so sharply from convention that the
handful of paintings with traditional subjects hardly
fit into his work, despite being related stylistically

(page 515). It is certainly true that portraits of an artist's contemporaries, as well as imaginary portraits, had been part of European culture for a very long time. But in his half-length figures with accessories, Caravaggio does not depict any authors, or prophets and sibyls, or even any embodiments of the five senses, the four seasons, or other scholarly subjects. Instead, they are groupings of anonymous figures painted like portraits but arranged like still-lifes with accessories that have no especially expressive character. Most of them share one essential feature with the still-life: they depict not only flowers and fruit but also the half-length figures shown life-size.

Looking first at the *Sick Bacchus* in the Galleria Borghese in Rome (page 494), we start with an artist's own reflection on art, since gods—unlike models—cannot get sick. We can also find pure genre painting among the pictures attributed to Caravaggio. He considered his *Boy Peeling a Peach* worthy of painting. In a not very good example whose whereabouts are unknown, a model from the same circle of boys who posed for paintings like the New York *Concert* (page 493) plays an inattentive market lad. He is bitten by a small crab in a wooden tub, in which he has put the crabs ready for sale. Before Caravaggio, Dutch painters handled such subjects; and, virtually at the same time, so did Spanish artists. Nor should we forget that Bartolomeo Passarotti (1529–1592), as well as the Carracci brothers, indulged in this Dutch fashion in their own way in Rome.

We can see how sensitively Caravaggio differentiated between social levels if we compare the market lad's coarse expression of horror with the reaction of an upper-class boy who is bitten by a lizard. He exists in two good quality examples of the same size (pages 516, 517). Unlike the *Market Lad with the Crab* but like the *Boy with a Vase of Flowers*, owned by the Atlanta Art Association, Georgia—a version that is probably not an original Caravaggio—these two paintings are not representative of any genuine social genre. Rather, they are artistic products or studies of a particular expression. Yet they were clearly so successful that, as with the *Boy Bitten by a Lizard*, the artist reproduced them himself. The numerous non-authentic versions prove even more unequivocally that the more personal the subject matter of these pictures appeared to be, the more successful they were with the art-buying public of the day.

At the same time, both pictures show that the artist studied how to convey instantaneous effects, in order to astonish a viewer by arrestingly reproducing painful astonishment. That said, Caravaggio's art achieved its supreme expression when challenged by music, as the various versions of a lute player prove. These copies, executed by the artist, were meant for two important patrons of Caravaggio. After the Marchese Giustiniani had received the St. Petersburg version, Cardinal del Monte must have ordered a second version, which later found its way to the Barberini. Caravaggio used the same figure study for both versions, so that the artist can have made only one version from the live model, the second having been traced from the first.

Caravaggio's meticulous reproduction of musical notes suggests that he was painting for well-informed viewers, who would decipher the pictures by way of the melodies. Certainly, pictures showing half-length musicians had been traditional since Giorgione. Yet in Caravaggio's work there is a spectacular degree of concrete communication.

Thanks to art's astonishing affinity with music, for Caravaggio we can adapt Horace's formula that poetry is like painting. But instead of *ut pictura poesis*, we should say *ut musica pictura*. Together with the human figure, flowers, notes, and instruments are the raw material out of which he created paintings like pieces of music—as well as varying them in copies. If two versions of a picture were original to him, he would vary a once-observed arrangement in the same way that composers of his day used variations in sonatas.

THE NUDE

There are other paintings by Caravaggio that relate to classical antiquity. The most beautiful example is the breathtaking Berlin *Cupid Victorious* (page 522), which caused such a sensation in its day that Giovanni Baglione not only brought a libel action against Caravaggio but also attempted to rebuke his competitor in a picture of his own (page 523).

The most sensible title for Caravaggio's Cupid is Vergil's phrase *Omnia vincit Amor*. In order to show that "love conquers all," the artist proceeded in this picture, painted in 1602/03, to heighten a less than perfect figure into a sublime one. One crucial difference between this and earlier dated paintings with secular subject matter lies in the picture's size. Caravaggio now depicts full-size figures full-length. No longer draped in any form of clothing, the figure's nakedness strikes many viewers as obscene, since our eyes are directed not only at the young man's genitals, but lower still. It is also odd that Cupid's left hand is concealed behind his body.

The effect of a model posing as a god is again emphasized. The Berlin *Cupid* would be as unwelcome in polite society as he would be in the pantheon of the gods. *Ganymede* by Michelangelo (1475–1564) shows how little guidance on posing this model had at the outset.

The starry globe over which the naked boy is climbing might be a still-life object that indicates Cupid's descent from the sky. In the same way, the crown and staff denote worldly power. On top of the armor and the handwritten book, which lie scattered on the ground, we can make out a laurel wreath, which is awarded to poets and generals without distinction, and—in the light of Cupid's triumph—equally useless to both. A straightedge and pair of compasses can be seen near the divine model's foot. They stand for proportion in architecture as well as in God's Creation in general. However, they also represent something Caravaggio seems to have totally neglected in his

Caravaggio
The Lute Player, 1595
The Vincenzo Giustiniani version
Oil on canvas, 94 x 119 cm
Hermitage, St. Petersburg

Opposite page:
The Lute Player, ca. 1600
The Cardinal del Monte version
Oil on canvas, 100 x 126.5 cm
Private Collection. Photograph courtesy of the
Metropolitan Museum of Art, New York

Two oblong pictures of almost the same dimensions depict a boy with soft facial features and unusually thick dark brown hair, pouting lips, a half-open mouth, and a pensive expression beneath sharply drawn broad eyebrows. His white shirt is wide open at the front, again revealing the artist's intention to paint a nude. This figure has the same dimensions in both pictures, which suggests that Caravaggio traced one on to oilpaper. In this case, only one picture was completed from a fresh study of a model.

A sort of ribbon woven into the figure's hair emphasizes its almost androgynous features. The same applies (in the version in a private collection, right) to a broad yoke that divides his shirt under his chest like a woman's dress. This is undoubtedly why Bellori saw this as a female lute player, though recently it has been suggested that the model was a castrato. Light falls from a high window above left, creating a narrow triangle of brightness in the upper right-hand corner. That said, the brightly illuminated figure stands out boldly against the shadowy background.

The strongly foreshortened lute with its bent keyboard demonstrates Caravaggio's virtuoso handling of perspective. Tactile elements

project towards the viewer more successfully than in the New York *Concert* (page 493). As in the Uffizi *Bacchus* (page 509), the artist places a broad table top in front of the figure—in the St. Petersburg version it is made of marble, and in the other version, covered with an oriental carpet.

The objects in the picture include an open book of music lying on another that bears the inscription "Bassus" in Gothic script, whilst the body of a violin serves to hold the book open at the right page. In both versions Caravaggio has painted the scores of older compositions clearly enough for us to read them. The music in question is the base voice part of a popular collection, the *Libro primo* of Jacques Arcadelt, which contains other compositions as well as works by this composer. Although the artist has cut off one row of notes, he has reproduced the initial notes so exactly that in the St. Petersburg example we can recognize the Roman printer, Valerio Dorico, whereas in the second version (right) we can see that the book was published in Venice by Antonio Gardane.

In the St. Petersburg version, the message of this music is underlined by our being able to read the opening words of a madrigal. "Voi

sapete ch'" continues "io v'amo," so that cognoscenti could extend "you know that" with "I love you." The second madrigal is less easy to decipher, because Caravaggio has not shown the book open at connecting pages. The question "Chi potrà dir quanta dolcezza prova?" ("Who can express what sweetness I feel?"); also treats the topic of love.

In his version for Cardinal del Monte, Caravaggio combined two other pages. Francesco de Layolle, from Florence, set to music Petrach's sonnet 11: *Lassare il velo*, in which the lady is asked "to remove her veil." In the second madrigal, the Fleming, Jacques de Berchem, has adapted an anonymous poem: *Perchè non date voi?*, in other words, "Why do you not give yourself?" All these verses are addressed to a woman. Anyone looking for a homoerotic context should also remember that Shakespeare wrote his 150 sonnets for a young man, of whom he said: "Shall I compare thee to a summer's day?"

In the St. Petersburg picture, the violin bow lies across the strings and the open book of music—a prominent object for the observation of light and shade. In the second version, it is handled in a much less interesting way. Placed underneath the violin scroll, the bow can scarcely be distinguished from the brownish pattern of the carpet. In this version, a stout recorder and a triangular keyboard instrument are the other objects we see. The X-ray picture shows that they were painted over a still-life. The birdcage motif in the left-hand corner shows what unusual motifs Caravaggio liked to select, motifs similar to those preferred by Caravaggesque painters in the Netherlands.

The St. Petersburg version, on the other hand, plays with the motifs of Caravaggio's other early arrangements of still-life and individual figures. Pieces of fruit lie on the marble slab, extremely brightly colored and brilliantly painted. A crystal vase contains a bunch of flowers, which would have made even Jan Brueghel the Elder (1568–1625) jealous. The colors are applied uninhibitedly with a loaded brush, and with a richness and precision we do not see elsewhere in Caravaggio's work. It is hardly noticeable that so many flowers could not in fact fit into the narrow neck of the vase.

painting: the geometric fundamentals of *disegno*. Caravaggio gives a more prominent place to the art of music by depicting not only a lute and violin but also a book of music. This provides a mathematical note and leads the eye on to the straightedge and compasses. Paradoxes fascinate the artist. Thus, he depicts intact all the instruments with which people strive after success. Cupid's weapon, on the other hand, is no longer ready for action. The god of love is holding arrows for a bow whose string has broken. In other words, Cupid has either already triumphed or will triumph without any instrument. His body gives him power. The white drapery has fallen, a symbol of Cupid's victory.

In the Berlin *Cupid*, Caravaggio is not seeking to imagine a myth but to present a model playing a god, whilst elements of still-life, placed in front of the characterless studio wall, represent the world at large. Despite its playful lightheartedness, the Berlin painting nevertheless picks up two major themes of theological debate around 1600: the argument in the struggle over Copernicus's view of the universe, in which heavenly bodies revolve around the sun and around each other. Caravaggio's Cupid is about to spin around his own axis on his right foot. He thereby asserts that love revolves around itself, and is therefore a fixed star and not an ever-moving satellite! The second theme is the doctrine of Justification by Faith, which under Urban VIII led to the almost unique papal declaration that the matter cannot be resolved. With regard to the question of whether Man is justified by Grace alone or can achieve justification through good works, Caravaggio places his cupid in a striking position. Incapable of acting, with his weapons inoperative and his hands and wings entwined, the youth's meaning lies only in his own existence. He is neither good nor bad, but has no need of such categories, because in his nakedness he proclaims truth and is therefore justified merely through being, independent of his deeds.

This makes it all the more surprising that Caravaggio had so much success with nudes even in religious paintings. It is not only executioners at martyrdoms that he liked to depict almost unclothed, and with a pronounced sense of musculature and physical movement. The artist often depicted even saints naked, and sometimes without any kind of veil whatever. These figures are meant to be venerated, though not publicly in church. Here, Caravaggio was following an older tradition. In the Galleria Borghese in Rome, for example, next to his picture of St. John the Baptist there is an anonymous replica of Raphael's composition (page 260), as well as an impressive version by Agnolo Bronzino (1503–1572).

Painting figures in full-length, a principle which Raphael and Bronzino both respected, was also an essential prerequisite for Caravaggio's paintings on this subject: and three designs are, in fact, full-length (pages 524, 525, 527, 528). One of the exceptions uses the large format lengthways and finishes just underneath the figure's knees (page 526). The effect of four paintings that Caravaggio painted of St. John the Baptist in the desert depends on a color combination that was to become almost a trademark for the artist and his followers all over the world. Namely: light skin color, strongly brought out of the dark brown background, accompanied by brilliant white and contrasted with a rich red, whose shadows are often almost black in color.

Vegetation remains extremely sparse. All the same, in the earliest St. John the Baptist he has painted some marvelous foliage plants (page 524, 525). The later the version of this picture—at least in terms of scholarly classification—the more the green disappears. In the latest version, in the Galleria Borghese (page 528), vegetation appears only sparsely along the bottom edge.

The finest versions of this subject are astonishing iconographically, because instead of the Easter Lamb, which represents Christ suffering the Passion, as an attribute of the Baptist, Caravaggio has painted a powerful ram with strong horns, which John is embracing (pages 524, 525, 528). The boy's genitals are unmistakably evident. Even the very earliest picture of the Baptist (pages 524, 525), in which Caravaggio concerns himself deeply with Michelangelo's youth on the left above the Erythrean Sibyl (page 524), is divided more clearly by light and shade than by the musculature.

The nude in the Kansas City *St. John the Baptist* (page 527) also takes issue with Michelangelo. The black shadows which the vigorous chiaroscuro projects on to the model's pale skin introduce structures into the composition which do not originate from the *disegno*, but create a color phenomenon out of the light. In Florence, artists had spent a long time in front of Michelangelo's works, viewing them with their critical graphic insight and making an extensive study of the anatomical construction of the male body. After all this, Caravaggio's chiaroscuro offers a Venetian element that is often virtually intersected by the structure of the less fully developed body.

The version in the Galleria Nazionale d'Arte Antica (page 526) reveals itself to be a study of motion in the nude. This time the model's nakedness strikes the viewer as almost vulgar. After Caravaggio painted a boy in the earliest version, for the next two versions the models who pose for him are young men. Caravaggio clothes them both in a coarse robe and red cloak, leaving only the upper body above the navel and one leg uncovered. There is no sign of a lamb or a ram in either picture.

With its depiction of a situation in the forest that is left to the viewer's imagination, the oblong picture in Rome represents a kind of pastoral genre. In a composition which Caravaggio made on Malta in 1608 or possibly during his second stay in Naples in 1610 (*St. John at the Spring*, Collezione Bonello, Malta), he puts himself even more intensively into the situation of a hermit.

I would date the painting owned by the Kunstsammlung, Basel, much later than the two studies in motion after Michelangelo and the small-scale genre picture on Malta. I make a point of this because older art literature is entirely ignorant of it. This picture does not have the powerful red color of the other paintings of St. John the Baptist. The kind of boy who modeled for the

Opposite page:
Caravaggo
Cupid Victorious, 1602/03
Oil on canvas, 156 x 113 cm
Gemäldegalerie, Staatliche Museen, Berlin

Cupid makes his appearance above a still-life and some white drapery on a table. He has not descended from above—the picture is too dark in its upper section, and the weight of the body too earth-bound. It looks as if he has just climbed out of bed and is languidly searching for the wings on his back with his unseen left hand. The wing tip just resting on the boy's upper left thigh is especially impressive. As a silent art, painting produces neither sound nor movement. In depicting this Cupid, as he gingerly stretches one foot out of the disorder of worldly renown and gets his wing in a bit of a tangle in the process, Caravaggio has captured an extraordinary moment of movement. He has also added a tactile note: a gentle rustling of wing against skin.

Giovanni Baglione
Heavenly and Earthly Love, 1602/03
Oil on canvas, 179 x 118 cm
Gemäldegalerie, Staatliche Museen, Berlin

How detached contemporary art patrons in Rome were from pictures' ideological content is indicated by the juxtaposition of this painting with Caravaggio's Berlin *Cupid* (opposite page). Giovanni Baglione (1571–1644) depicted an angel figure in full armor, which Orazio Gentileschi (1563–1639) had already criticized. This angel was shown chastising a boy Cupid, painted in Caravaggio's style, with a sword of light. After Baglione made a gift of the painting to Cardinal Giustiniani, in 1621 it was acquired by his brother, the Marchese Vincenzo, and it has remained with the better-known Cupid until the present day.

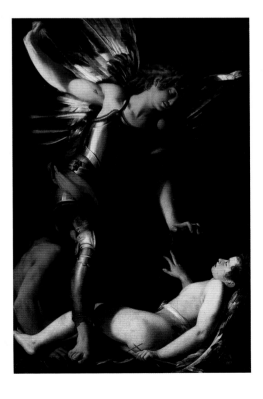

Caravaggio
St. John the Baptist, ca. 1600
Oil on canvas, 129 x 94 cm
Musei Capitolini, Rome

Lately, this depiction has wrongly been interpreted as
Isaac, happily hugging the animal to be sacrificed by
Abraham instead of him (page 534/535).

Michelangelo
Youth on the left above the *Erythrean Sibyl*,
1508–1512
Fresco
Ceiling, Capella Sistina, Vatican, Rome

Later generations remembered the anonymous boys of the
Sistine Chapel ceiling as *ignudi*. That said, they were
better known through graphic reproductions than in the
original fresco, to which it was not easy to gain access,
since the Sistine was the Pope's private chapel.
Michelangelo used the light solely to reinforce the
sculptural qualities of his strongly drawn bodily forms.

Opposite page:
Caravaggio
St. John the Baptist
Oil on canvas, 132 x 95 cm
Galleria Doria Pamphilj, Rome

In this almost identical picture, the totally naked
boy sits leaning far back, like the *ignudi* who adorn
Michelangelo's Sistine Chapel ceiling (above). Here, he
is propping his left elbow on some white drapery, has
straightened out his left leg behind him, and is supporting
his bent right leg by gripping the toes. A magnificent
piece of red fabric provides pictorial ornament at the
bottom on the left. The Baptist's body is so firmly
embedded in the yielding hide of his coarse garment that
the energetically black contours from his upper thigh to
his back stand out in a clear flow of lines. With his right
arm, the boy is reaching for a ram that has suddenly
materialized from the depths of the picture. Its nose and
mouth are nearly touching the smiling boy's cheek.

Caravaggio clearly based the figure on Michelangelo's
example, though he painted it according to his own
principles of working direct from a living model. The
figure does not reveal the great Florentine's feeling for
musculature, but the vigorous contouring of his back
shows his influence. Caravaggio is likely to have used a
study here. With great skill, and his instinct for dynamic
action, Caravaggio has placed the carefully built-up body
in such a way that the figure's left elbow almost bumps
against the edge of the picture. Otherwise, however, the
figure is completely free. This enables the apparition in
the light to develop dynamically from top left towards
the right.

Caravaggio
St. John the Baptist, ca. 1600
Oil on canvas, 94 x 131 cm
Galleria Nazionale d'Arte Antica, Palazzo Barberini,
Rome

In this horizontal version in Rome, the Baptist is sitting
in front of some somber tree stumps, without any sign of
dignity or saintliness. He is reaching towards the left for
his Jacob's staff. In the process, he abruptly turns to the
right, as if he has suddenly noticed a danger in the
wilderness. His not very attractive body, with its slack
stomach muscles, defies normal conventions of taste—not
only because of his crude suntan. Caravaggio's work on
the model is the only thing that makes this unappealing
painting an artistic sketch of first-rate quality.

Opposite page:
Caravaggio
St. John the Baptist, ca. 1600
Oil on canvas, 173 x 133 cm
The Nelson Atkins Museum of Art, Kansas City

In a remarkable variant of the arrogant boy on the left
above Isaiah in Michelangelo's Sistine Chapel ceiling
(page 524), this Baptist is almost an adult man. The eye
sockets of this figure, who is meditating with his head
lowered, are darkened by a black just as deep as the
background, in which a few leaves of vegetation are
suggested. This black background, which the figure has
not quite filled, and which was later to take up more
space in paintings by Caravaggio, has been tested and
found to be effective. Swinging his arm a long way back,
St. John is supporting himself, as if exhausted, on one of
the rocks that is covered with his red cloak. He is holding
a large bamboo cane. The small crossbar at the top, which
turns it into a Jacob's staff, is so much in shadow that only
cognoscenti will be aware of its existence.

Caravaggio
St. Jerome, ca. 1606
Oil on canvas, 112 x 157 cm
Museo Galleria Borghese, Rome

Caravaggio has placed the sitting figure in a rectangle, half of which is devoted to a tersely depicted still-life. Without averting his eyes from his text, his left hand clamped firmly to his book, where it is keeping track of parallel passages, St. Jerome stretches out his right hand a long way, in order to dip his quill into his inkpot. Yet, despite his sure instinct for a potential genre picture, the artist has not given any thought to what the Father of the Church is reading and writing.

Opposite page:
St. John the Baptist, ca. 1610
Oil on canvas, 159 x 124 cm
Museo Galleria Borghese, Rome

Here, too, the forerunner of Christ is accompanied not by a lamb but a full-grown ram, complete with strong horns. The powerful animal is turning away from the saint, now a boy again. Caravaggio has transformed the Baptist into a shepherd, resting in the wilderness. Although only a delicate fabric over his lap conceals his nakedness, his dejected expression drives out all sense of physical delight.

picture is not typical—and even less typical is a staff with a strip of writing on it. A device of this kind does not accord with Caravaggio's years in Rome. However, it does link the painting, which can also be compared to the Madrid *David and Goliath,* with the *Nativity* picture for Palermo (page 583). To me there seems to be an obvious connection, not only in the coloration but also in the execution of the leathery, earth-colored drapery, as well as the lamb's skin and pelt.

The pastoral game with the lamb, to which the youthful Baptist is holding out a bunch of flowers as if the animal was meant to snap at them, also expresses a theological thought. The forerunner of Christ holds out white and red roses to the lamb. As symbols of blood and water, they indicate passion and death. As the strip of writing in the foreground explains, the Basel canvas has less to do with the Baptist than the message about the Lamb of God.

The *St. John the Baptist* in the Galleria Borghese in Rome (page 528) is generally considered late Caravaggio. With its elegiac tone, its melancholy mood, and its lack of physicality, this painting seems to fit as well as the David with Goliath's head (page 491) at the end of Caravaggio's career.

On the other hand, the artist did not see painting the nude purely in terms of young men's bodies. Even the sufferings of Jesus in the *Flagellation of Christ* inspired him to create an impressive rendition of nude painting (page 577). But even more astonishing is a group of pictures devoted to naked old men, depicting the penitent Father of the Church, St. Jerome, in an interior.

For two of these pictures (pages 529, 530–531 both Monserrat Monastery) Caravaggio obviously used the same old man as a model. In the third example, however, he combined findings from portrait work with studies direct from a model. In his portrait in the role of St. Jerome, the artist seems to be paying his compliments to the man who commissioned the painting, Alof de Wignacourt, a powerful figure on the island of Malta (page 531). Caravaggio places him in a corner of the room to the left, whilst on the right a narrow strip of brown wood holds the eye in. It is as if a wooden door, bearing the coat-of-arms of Ippolito Malaspina, the Maltese Prior of Naples, who was a friend of Alof de Wignacourt, were about to open.

Two traditions appear to intersect in Caravaggio's pictures of St. Jerome. Northern Europe took the subject up for the sake of its magnificent interiors,

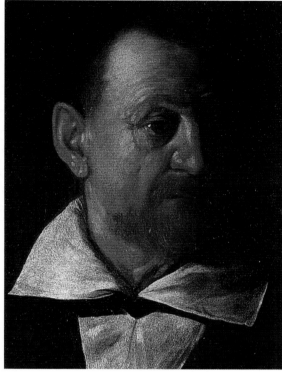

Portrait of Alof de Wignacourt (detail page 502)

For the face of St. Jerome (left) the artist aged the strained features of Alof de Wignacourt, Grand Master of the Knights of Malta, familiar from the portrait in the Palazzo Pitti, Florence, by adding wrinkles and strands of white hair in his beard and hair.

Caravaggio
St. Jerome, 1607/08
Oil on canvas, 117 x 157 cm
Museum of St. John's, Valletta, Malta

The half-naked old man turns away from the cardinal's hat on the left. With his left hand around the inkpot, he is making notes in a smallish book, in which there is already some writing. In the process, he turns his head, though not his eyes, towards a skull. Caravaggio skillfully shows the top of this skull leaning against the pebble that the saint uses to break open his breast when he is undergoing penance. An unlit candle stands on the right-hand edge of the table. A small crucifix, an indispensable symbol, reaches from near the skull to a considerable way beyond the table edge.

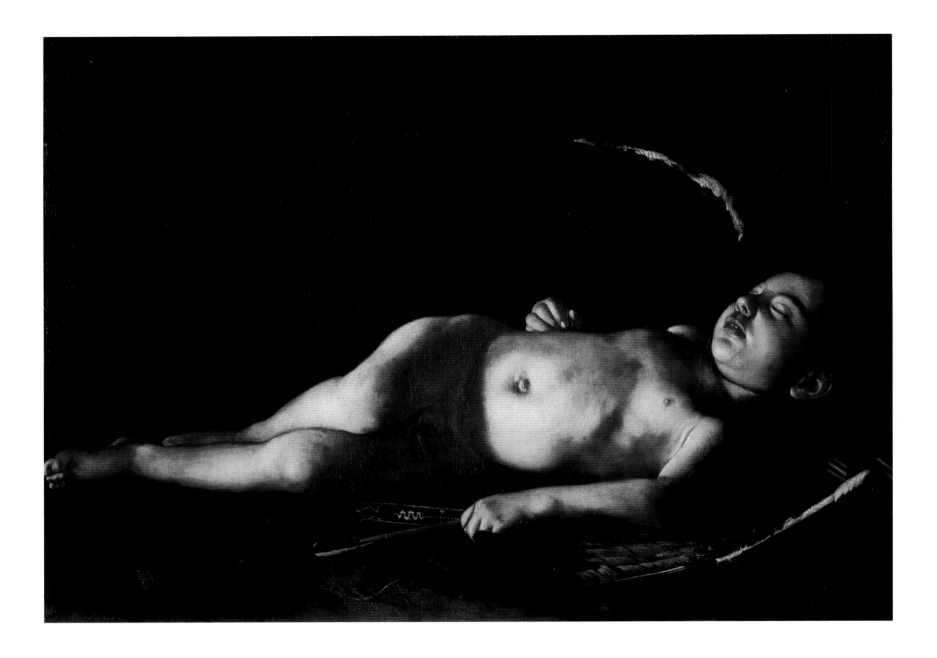

Caravaggio
Sleeping Cupid, ca. 1605–1610
Oil on canvas, 72 x 105 cm
Galleria Palatina, Palazzo Pitti, Florence

The child has spread his wings out on the ground in order to rest on them, holding his arrow and bow with its broken string in his left hand. A surprisingly broad strip of impenetrable black appears above the figure, enlivened only by the bold touch of the rim of a white wing. The artist may be suggesting night-time, which would fit in with the picture's subject, sleep, but in that case what is the source of the harsh highlight which floods on to the sleeping child? The figure's plump left arm appears to be separated from the rather stout body. Even more curiously, his right hand appears just above his belly.

which had prototypes in Italy. The subject achieved its supreme expression in Dürer's famous copperplate engraving, *St. Jerome in his Study*. In the North during the Renaissance, the saint continued to be depicted, but half-length rather than full length.

In Venice, on the other hand, the subject of a penitent St. Jerome in the wilderness was more popular until well into the 16th century. By removing the small-scale half-nude of the penitent from the Venetian landscape and placing it as a full-size three-quarter-length portrait in a chamber North of the Alps, he transforms this subject into a kind of genre picture that could be painted indoors direct from a model. Henceforth, it became possible to paint, on both sides of the Alps, not only the Father of the Church, St. Jerome, but also other saints not in a Flemish or Titianesque style, but in the style of Caravaggio. With scarcely any other subject did Caravaggio achieve such a triumph as he did in these paintings, with his chiaroscuro and his breathtaking combination of red next to skin color and black.

Yet it is not merely in the case of boys, youths, and old men that nude painting interested Caravaggio. The naked small child also inspired the artist to make a study (above). It may also have led to competition with Michelangelo, who painted a similar subject in a work now lost. In a painting long owned by the Medici, Caravaggio depicts Cupid as a full-length sleeping putto. Love and death meet in this subject. It was to return over and over again for centuries on tombs.

LANDSCAPE IN CARAVAGGIO'S PAINTINGS

Even for a commentator as early as Gian Pietro Bellori, Caravaggio's art was rooted in the Venetian painting of Giorgione. In his Dresden *Venus* (page 294), Caravaggio's great predecessor, who was painting shortly after 1500, was tackling a paradox that is similar to that in the Uffizi *Bacchus* (page 509).

The Venetian painter does not see the naked woman, who for him depicts Venus, on a meadow fit for gods in a godlike idyll, but near a farm. There she is lying on a cushion and some drapery: articles unfamiliar to gods of nature. She, too, is more a model than a goddess. Even earlier, in his pictures of St. Jerome, however, Caravaggio did not take advantage of Venice's supreme contribution to European art: he avoided landscape. A few plants dotted about like set pieces in front of an impenetrably dark background are not enough. Landscapes need distant views. These Caravaggio offers only in a handful of paintings, including *St. Francis in Ecstasy* (above) and the *Sacrifice of Isaac* (page 534–535).

In the nocturnal *St. Francis in Ecstasy*, the large figures are lit from the front. In the landscape behind, we see a narrow strip of light, but it does not illuminate the impenetrable darkness. We cannot make out the countryside any more clearly than we can the sky and the companion in the distance. For Caravaggio, highlights on angels and saints were more important than the firmament. It is debatable here whether this form of light

comes from God's heaven or only from the painter's vision. At all events, landscape does not give the figures something to look at, nor does it provide perspective for their movement. It merely indicates the depth of the night and the unreality of the location.

In the Uffizi *Sacrifice of Isaac* (page 534–535), too, the landscape is swallowed up by darkness. This is not night, however, but muted twilight in which the most distant mountains look just as bluish-gray as the clouds. Venetian artists adored views like this. Precisely for their lagoon city built on the sea, they used to paint the gently climbing slopes of the mainland, complete with trees, villages, and castles. Following this tradition, Caravaggio used the twilight ambience of a heightened view into the distance for narrative purposes: behind Abraham and Isaac lies the day during which they climbed the mountain. In this dramatic version of the theme, the angel appears on the left, and Isaac on the right, together with the ram. The angel has taken hold of Abraham's arm and, at the very last moment, the Patriarch appears ready to respond to the word of God.

Caravaggio
St. Francis in Ecstasy, 1595–1600
Oil on canvas, 92.5 x 128 cm
Wadsworth Atheneum, Hartford, Connecticut

With his eyes closed and his body rigid, St. Francis is pointing to the place where he will receive a wound in the side. Yet he does not see the angel who will ensure that he is stigmatized. Instead, he closes his eyes in an expression of ecstasy that has never been depicted before. An angel shelters him lovingly. They are both harshly lit.

Caravaggio
The Sacrifice of Isaac, ca. 1600
Oil on canvas, 104 x 135 cm
Galleria degli Uffizi, Florence

Movement from the left powers this painting. Standing
in front of dense, dark tree trunks that obstruct our view,
the Angel of the Lord intervenes to hold Abraham's arm,
just at the moment he is about to cut his son's throat.
According to the Bible story, he was ready to obey God's
command and sacrifice Isaac to him—at which point an
angel offered him a ram instead. The group of figures rises
powerfully in the harsh light from the left as far as the
patriarch's bald head, only to sink down towards Isaac.

Caravaggio's Contribution to Genre Painting

Caravaggio's revolutionary achievement consists, if not in his chiaroscuro, then in his genre painting, which draws its inspiration from the same sources as his paintings of St. Jerome. He mingled Venetian and Netherlandish sources in order to alter the status of this genre. His genre paintings gave rise to sensation, scorn, and recognition all at once. Only when the school of Caravaggio had established itself did this make its triumphant progress through the Netherlands, France, and Spain.

That said, Caravaggio himself completed surprisingly few genre pictures. Without making any attempt at portraiture, a genre painting depicts anonymous people in clothes appropriate to their social level who are carrying out typical, everyday activities.

If we can leave aside the individual figures with accessories reminiscent of a still-life, because, with only a few exceptions, their poses do not carry any social meaning, then Caravaggio's contribution to genre painting boils down mainly to two works. The more important of these, the *Fortune Teller*, exists in two versions with different claims to authenticity. The clothes, which distinguish the exotic fortune teller from the harmlessly dandified and dolled-up young man, are enough to characterize the two figures.

Bellori begins his Caravaggio *vita* with a fictitious account of how this subject came about. Through this anecdote, Bellori wishes to show how the artist distances himself from prototypes in classical antiquity, and approaches genre painting spontaneously, direct from a living model. He writes: "After Caravaggio had been shown the most famous pictorial works by Phidias and Glykon, so that he might learn from them, the painter responded merely by pointing to a crowd of people and remarking that nature had provided plenty of masters. In order to emphasize this, he called a passing gypsy woman in from the street and, after taking her back to her lodgings, painted her portrait, whilst she was predicting the future, as women of the Egyptian race are wont to do. Then he also painted a young man, who has one gloved hand on his sword and has opened his other palm to the woman, who is holding and reading it."

This episode, which has no basis in historical fact, helps explain the picture in two ways. For those who appreciate the picture's merits, it confirms the freshness of the artist's eye. For others, it makes the artist's unbridled arbitrariness crystal clear. Bellori follows the line he had already taken in the passage quoted earlier about Mary Magdalene in the Doria Pamphilj Gallery (page 504), a section that runs on from this episode in the *vita*, emphasizing the artist's deliberate decision to diverge from classical prototypes and make his own individual choices, irrespective of any hierarchies in art theory.

Bellori did not detect a deeper meaning in the picture. Levity of this kind does not appeal to modern art history, which will not allow artists to follow their impulses and paint works as the fancy takes them. When seduction is in the air, a young dandy is a Prodigal Son on his way to rack and ruin. In linking a picture like this to Christ's parables, we might imagine having a better reason for painting louche pictorial subjects.

Even if we choose not to follow Bellori, pictures could still limit themselves to the kind of human drama that develops anonymously and incidentally into art. Moving further out poetically, we reach Prosper Mérimée's and Bizet's "Carmen," who, although they do not read their Don José's palm in order to steal his ring, do tell his fortune from the cards.

A similar young man who falls victim to a fraudulent game of cards features in a second genre picture, which has only recently been acknowledged as original. In 1672, Bellori described the card trick exactly. He stated that the *Card Sharps* belonged to Cardinal Antonio Barberini, who must have purchased it from the estate of Cardinal del Monte. With card playing and card sharping, Caravaggio opens up a range of possibilities for genre pictures, which was to result in an endless series of paintings.

For Bellori, the *Card Sharps* and the *Fortune Teller* do not necessarily belong together, since he does not have an overriding idea of what genre painting is. In the battle of the genres, one of the genre paintings attributed to Caravaggio takes up a prominent position. The Musei Capitolini *Fortune Teller* was, like the Milan *Basket of Fruit* (page 531) and the New York *Lute Player,* painted over an older canvas. In the process of repainting, Caravaggio has in each case failed to respect the hierarchy of different genres, insofar as his still-life obliterated a putto and his genre subjects a praying saint, possibly even the Virgin Mary.

Caravaggio
The Card Sharps, 1595–1600
Oil on canvas, 94 x 131 cm
Kimbell Art Museum, Fort Worth

Whilst a stylishly turned-out youth hesitantly looks at his
cards, a man with tattered gloves peers over his shoulder,
putting up three fingers to show the youth's opponent
which of the cards hidden in his waistband he should
play. With dice and backgammon on display, gambling is
clearly in the ascendant here, and if the going gets rough,
violence, the dagger that the young cardsharp has placed
hilt uppermost and facing into the picture, shows where a
dispute will probably lead. Although the young card sharp
is standing in front of it, the edge of the table, which is in
shadow, and which the backgammon set overhangs, forms
the real boundary to the viewer. The light also extends the
pictorial space dynamically towards the right. It spills over
the card sharps in their blackish-crimson velvet, and
appears to promise them success.

By making the figures in his groundbreaking genre
scenes full-length Caravaggio is, in effect, saying that
he also painted these direct from life. Genre painting
after him kept to the same maxims. Painters in the style
of Caravaggio in Utrecht, Holland, liked to place their
figures in front of well-lit walls, just as Caravaggio
himself did. Painters like Manfredi (1587–1620/21)
and Valentin de Boulogne (ca. 1591–1632), on the
other hand, used black backgrounds for such pictures,
whereas Velázquez (1599–1660) preferred brown
backgrounds.

Caravaggio may also have influenced genre painting
through an unusually coarse and ugly picture, which was
painted hurriedly, and which deliberately flouts all
conventions of beauty. This tavern scene in the style of
the Hellenist painter, Peiraïkos, has come to light only

recently. As early as 1637, when owned by the Medici, it
was recorded as a Caravaggio (Palazzo del Montecitorio,
Rome).

Caravaggio's genre paintings reach beyond narrow
genre distinctions, and not merely because he was
convinced that one could only paint well direct from
nature. Just as he had moved on from half-length to
full-length genre pictures painted from models,
Caravaggio also revolutionized history painting.

The way Caravaggio set out his *Martha and Mary
Magdalene* makes the two figures look like a Venetian
portrait of courtesans. Scholars are almost unanimous
in thinking that, in inaugurating this series of paintings
(page 539), the artist continued to develop the
chiaroscuro he first put into effect in those pictures.
Caravaggio displayed a lot of feeling for the dissimilar

sisters. With great surety of touch he pinpoints the rigidity and humility that characterize the sisters, as well as the precise moment when proud Mary Magdalene begins to realize her destiny. To achieve this, he has no recourse to divine intervention, but only depicts what can be externally observed.

The very choice of subject is based on the principle of genre painting, because the kind of incidents Caravaggio depicts do not exist in the Bible. But even in the four Gospels some scenes originated from a pure genre situation. These revealed the presence of a divine agency only after the people involved thought they were going through an ordinary experience.

Yet there are some biblical subjects, like *Judith and Holofernes* (page 542–543), which even a Caravaggio could not reconstruct from models. The artist made a groundbreaking painting of Judith's heroic act in making Holofernes, the general of a besieging army, drunk in his tent, then beheading him in his sleep, so as to save her people. Whilst many artists before him had merely shown Judith and her maid hiding the hacked-off head in a cloth, Caravaggio shows Holofernes's death agony at the moment the sword cuts through his neck.

Caravaggio's gripping depiction owes little to studies of anatomy, the lack of which early art theorists always noticed in his work, or even to professional curiosity about public executions, which generations of Italian artists were said to have entertained. It is thanks rather to the artist's visual imagination, linked with Caravaggio's meticulous model studies. Whilst he has obviously painted the young woman from an observed

Caravaggio
Martha and Mary Magdalene, ca. 1595
Oil on canvas, 100 x 134.5 cm
The Detroit Institute of Arts, Detroit

Martha humbly points out to her sister, Mary Magdalene, how transient all worldly things are. Light strikes her only on her shoulder, so that her clothes—in disarray as a result either of work or of emotional upset—stand out clearly. Her face, however, disappears into the darkness, averted from the viewer almost in profile. A piece of soft fabric and a magnificent border form the boundary of Mary Magdalene's hands and generous décolleté. She is propping her left arm, over which she has thrown a piece of expensive green fabric, on a black convex mirror. She was in the process of testing the effect of a small white blossom (orange, or perhaps even edelweiss) on her breast. At this point, Martha came in, to reclaim her and make the mirror a symbol of *vanitas*.

Caravaggio
Supper at Emmaus, 1595–1600
Oil on canvas, 141 x 196.2 cm
The National Gallery, London

Already set out as a genre scene in the Bible, this story concerns two disciples who, on their way from Jerusalem to Emmaus on Easter morning, come across a stranger, also making the journey, with whom they go into an inn. The moment the stranger breaks the bread the disciples recognize him as the Risen Christ. Caravaggio depicted this scene twice in life-size half-length figures (above, opposite). These two pictures, which are virtually the same size, show how differently Caravaggio saw biblical subjects in the space of a few years.

A basket of fruit impudently intrudes near the front table edge. As in the Uffizi *Bacchus* (page 509), the still-life spreads out under the main figure, who, supported by the lines of the tablecloth, occupies the pictorial center in a pyramid shape. If the disciples had walked quite a long way with the Risen Lord, and only later recognized him by a gesture, then the figure who appeared at

Emmaus cannot have looked like Christ.

For this reason, the artist does not present the *vera icon*, that is, the usual image of the Redeemer, but a youthfully plump face without a beard. Whilst Caravaggio takes this aspect of the Gospel extremely literally, he does not depict the action accurately. The stranger blesses the whole meal, and does not need to break the bread, because everyone at table already has some. The landlord watches the stranger's gesture of blessing, his shadow on the wall offering the resurrected Christ an impressive framing.

Although the landlord has no idea what is happening, the two disciples offer the artist the opportunity to express surprise. The older one, on the right, spreads his arms out wide in an exaggerated example of foreshortening, with one much too large hand near Christ's shoulder. At the same time, the younger disciple is so astounded he almost jumps up from his chair. He grips the armrests with both hands, and sticks his head a long way forward. As he does so, light reflected naturally from the tablecloth makes his face look as if it has been illuminated by divine light.

pose, the man is an imaginary figure, and is therefore the weaker part of the painting. In cases where imagination was more straightforward, the gap between *imitatio* and *inventio* (between imitation and invention) is less striking. In his *Doubting Thomas* (page 544) Caravaggio often even succeeds in suggesting that he had an incredible Bible story happening before his very eyes.

The Potsdam picture of St. Thomas went to Prussia with the Giustiniani Collection. Baglione, however, mentioned a painting on this subject in the possession of Ciriaco Mattei. Perhaps it is another case of Caravaggio making several examples for competing patrons.

The Mattei Collection contained the *Kiss of Judas*, for which the artist received the not inconsiderable

sum of 125 scudi (page 545). Even if the dimensions of the painting do not match those of the Potsdam picture, the models make the two pictures form a pair. Caravaggio had the same men pose for the two main figures in both paintings as well as for Christ. It is true, however, that he painted Judas, the betrayer, as a coarser figure, with a knobly nose and with thinner hair, which consists only of a wreath, as if he had been tonsured.

Given that Caravaggio depicts half-length figures in the *Kiss of Judas*, it is probably not surprising that Peter, who cuts off one of Malchus' ears and is usually thrown to the ground, does not appear. Though this does not mean that the Prince of the Apostles should also be missing. In this picture Christ is shown gesturing helplessly. Deserted by his favorite disciple, he has to do

Caravaggio
Supper at Emmaus, 1606
Oil on canvas, 141 x 175 cm
Pinacoteca di Brera, Milan

Instead of the sumptuous still-life, we see only bread, a bowl, a tin plate, and a jug. The gestures of surprise are much the same, though differently distributed.

Caravaggio
Judith and Holofernes, ca. 1600
Oil on canvas, 145 x 195 cm
Galleria Nazionale d'Arte Antica, Palazzo Barberini,
Rome

A whole book in the Bible is devoted to Judith, because
as a woman she embodies the power of the people of
Israel to defeat the enemy, though superior in numbers,
by means of cunning and courage. She seeks out
Holofernes in his tent, makes him drunk, then beheads
him. The sight of their commander's bloodstained head
on the battlements of Bethulia puts the enemy to flight.
In the painting, Judith comes in with her maid,
surprisingly and menacingly, from the right, against the
direction of a usual reading of a picture. The general is
lying naked on a white sheet. Paradoxically, his bed is
distinguished by a magnificent red curtain, whose color
crowns the act of murder as well as the heroine's triumph.

Caravaggio
Doubting Thomas, ca. 1600
Oil on canvas, 107 x 146 cm
Schloss Sanssouci, Potsdam

Three disciples crowd in on Christ from the right, so that the head of Doubting Thomas and the head of a second Apostle form the painting's central axis. A strict color scheme divides the painting into a left-hand section, dominated entirely by flesh tint and muted white, whilst two red tones in the right-hand section shine out of the dark brown background. St. Thomas does not trust his eyes, but only what he can feel. One of the great qualities of good painting lies in conveying the tactile as a sensation that can be seen. The tactile aspect of painting, in the sense of *rilievo*, has to prove its worth against competition from sculpture. Before the highly observant eyes of the three Apostles, the action in this picture is enacted only by the two main figures' hands. Christ's brightly lit left hand grips his disciple tightly by the wrist, in order to push his outstretched index finger deep into the wound in his side. To make this easier, he draws back, with his right hand, the fold of the fabric that turns out to be his death shroud.

without the—admittedly unwelcome—support of the Prince of Apostles. Christ is kissed by a tonsured Judas, who looks like a monk in his yellowish cowl (in the copy owned by Odessa Museum, it is even the color of the Minorite Order). Everyone who sees Caravaggio as a tool of the official Roman Catholic Church ought to bear this picture in mind. With the agreement of his patrons, who were also closely associated with the papal Curia, the artist obviously allowed himself to take liberties with certain aspects of biblical history.

Chiaroscuro has different functions in Caravaggio's pictures of Christ. In the *Kiss of Judas*, deep black conveys night. As in most of the other equivalent scenes, the light source is above left, whilst the lamp in the hand of the man who is sometimes regarded as a Caravaggio self-portrait remains ineffectual. If we follow the increasingly common tendency to regard the *Crowning with Thorns*, in Vienna, as an authentic Caravaggio, we must add another picture, which

shows dawn breaking with the quality of light characteristic of the artist (page 546).

Any artist who changed his style so radically in so few years and painted even Christ's face direct from models, is bound to confuse art connoisseurs. They like to orient themselves on familiar faces as the personal stamp of the artist in question. Alongside the debatable picture from Vienna, we should add *Christ at the Column*, in Rouen (Musée des Beaux-Arts et de la Céramique), an episode from the Passion story. This is a painting in which the face of Christ again seems inappropriate. Yet the common model for one of the executioners' assistants lets us specify more exactly what place the underlying composition has in Caravaggio's work as a whole. The same assistant who is binding Christ to the column at which he will be flagellated, also appears in an artistically superior painting with half-length figures, in the National Gallery, London (page 549), holding the head of

St. John the Baptist. Furthermore, the Salome in this canvas is modeled on the same woman who posed as Caritas Romana for Caravaggio's most important Neapolitan work, the *Seven Acts of Mercy* (page 575).

Exactly how Caravaggio integrated once discovered pictorial formulas with painting direct from the model is evident in an original free variant, whose deep black background presumably dates it later in his career (page 548). Caravaggio reproduced the configuration of Salome and the maid with other models. The artist's imagination, his *inventio*, adapts to the layout that Caravaggio repeats exactly at different points, so that in each case he can paint it direct from life. In the later version, the artist has toned down indications of the executioner's bloody office. This fact should not be overlooked by those modern interpreters who look at all the bloodthirsty images in Caravaggio's successors, and conclude that Caravaggio himself, as the founder of this school,

had an unhealthy fascination with cruelty and contemporary methods of execution.

As well as oblong pictures of scenes from biblical history, early accounts suggest that Caravaggio also completed vertical pictures of scenes from Christ's Passion. Two vastly different paintings are the subject of fierce debate. In one of them, now in Prato, Christ is sitting in the *Crowning with Thorns* (Cassa di Risparmio), like the *Belvedere Torso*—in other words, like one of the most famous works of classical antiquity, which Michelangelo made the touchstone of sculptural art. However, in Genoa, where the artist fled in 1605, the painting he may have completed there —the *Ecce Homo* (Galleria di Palazzo Bianco)—makes use of totally different conventions which Caravaggio ignores elsewhere.

Towards the end of his life Caravaggio, recreated more biblical paintings with half-length figures. In 1672, Bellori described a *Denial of St. Peter* in Naples as

Caravaggio
The Kiss of Judas, before 2 January 1603
Oil on canvas, 133.5 x 169.5 cm
National Gallery of Ireland, Dublin

As in the *Doubting Thomas* (page 544), the main figures are pushed to the left, so that the right-hand half of the picture is occupied by soldiers, whose suits of armor absorb what little light there is, and whose faces are for the most part hidden. At the top right of the picture, an unhelmeted head emerges from the surrounding darkness. This is often regarded as the artist's self-portrait. Caravaggio has also concerned himself here with the act of seeing as one of a painter's tasks. Once again, the three men on the right are there mainly to intensify the visual core of the painting, underscored by the lantern. On the left, the tactile aspect is not forgotten. Judas vigorously embraces his master, whilst a heavily mailed arm reaches above him towards Christ's throat. Christ, however, crosses his hands, which he holds out well in front of him, whilst St. John flees shrieking into the deep night. His red cloak is torn from his shoulder. As it flaps open it binds the faces of Christ and Judas together—a deliberate touch on the artist's part.

Caravaggio
The Crowning with Thorns
Oil on canvas, 127 x 165.5 cm
Kunsthistorisches Museum, Vienna

The front boundary of the picture is articulated by a
wooden barrier, on which the captain is leaning in order
to observe the action but take no part in it. He watches
the executioner's half-naked assistants abuse Christ at his
behest. The powerful figure of the suffering victim, sitting
almost naked on a bench, seems larger than life. Christ's
shoulder line continues the shallow diagonal that begins
with the white feather of the captain's hat, on the left.
Christ's despair contradicts the ecclesiastical concept of
intentionally shouldered suffering. The Savior appears as
if he is vacantly gazing into nothing, an unsettling
thought for all pious believers.

Caravaggio
The Denial of St. Peter, 1606–1610
Oil on canvas, 94 x 125.5 cm
Shickman Gallery, New York

After the artist's many attempts to intensify the
dynamics of a scene from the right, this composition
offers a dramatic sequence of figures from the left. On
a very dark night with deep shadows and without any
indication of artificial light, a soldier wearing a helmet
and armor appears from the left. He is turning his face
so far round to the maid that it gets swallowed up by
the darkness. The maid herself, her face obscured by the
soldier's shadow, is peering at the soldier from close
quarters. She is pointing at St. Peter, who is holding both
hands against his chest in a gesture of questioning. For
the Apostle, Caravaggio has chosen a model who would
be equally ideal for an old satyr or for Socrates. The artist
usually introduced heads like this for executioners.

Caravaggio
Salome with the Head of St. John the Baptist,
after 1606 (?)
Oil on canvas, 116 x 140 cm
El Escorial, Madrid

Against a deep black background, the figure group,
consisting of Salome and her maid, has been moved
to the center of the picture, so that Salome's averted
gaze achieves greater pathos in the empty space. The
Baptist's head is already lying on the metal dish. The
executioner has to cram himself into the picture on
the right. Caravaggio has used a more prepossessing
model, painting him as the figure study of a half-naked
young man.

one of his best works. The authentication of paintings like this still occupies scholars, especially as good versions keep turning up with art dealers or in private collections (page 547).

The latest of these paintings which most recent research can consider to be original, the *Martyrdom of St. Ursula* (Banca Commerciale Italiana Naples), once again throws open the questions of pictorial arrangement and the use of the model. Sharply divided into two halves, the picture seems to be most like the group in *Doubting Thomas* (page 544) and the *Kiss of Judas* (page 545). Yet its sketchy execution distinguishes it decisively from these richly painted pictures from Caravaggio's Roman years shortly after 1600. The head

in profile, which again thrusts itself strikingly into the right-hand edge of the picture, has sometimes been regarded as a self-portrait of the artist (page 545).

Paintings like the picture of St. Ursula show the artist at less than his best. They support the view that towards the end of his life Caravaggio was more or less burnt out. Hurriedly dashed off, and furnished with set pieces from older sketches, expressively restrained and almost inept in its spatial layout, a work like this could well give ammunition to those critics of Caravaggio who argue that he was not always able to complete his projects convincingly. In this case, the Borghese *David* (page 491) would certainly not be one of Caravaggio's last paintings.

Caravaggio
Salome with the Head of St. John the Baptist, ca. 1606
Oil on canvas, 91.5 x 107 cm
The National Gallery, London

The artist has used a respectable looking Neapolitan
woman as the model for the lascivious female dancer
Salome, who has just seductively persuaded King Herod
to grant her wish. At the contrivance of her mother, she
demanded the head of John the Baptist, who had revealed
her mother's incestuous relationship with Herod. The
young woman much resembles *Judith* (pages 542–543).
She does not look at the chopped-off head, which the
rough executioner is handing her.

CARAVAGGIO'S HISTORY PAINTINGS IN ROME

The Calling of St. Matthew (detail page 552)

On the right, two youths are sitting opposite each other. The younger one, more strongly lit, is leaning back, putting his arm on St. Matthew's shoulder for protection. The youth opposite, with his sword dangling against his left upper thigh, spreads out his legs as he turns right.

Caravaggio's painting combines a remarkable feature with the Christian religion. The Word is made Flesh and the Supreme Being appears incarnate in an ordinary human being, who spontaneously calls other people away from their everyday activities in order to redeem them. In such a case, this God on earth has something to do with the painter who, in Bellori's tendentious description, suddenly recognizes the latent power contained in an everyday subject, a power that can be raised to higher spheres.

Caravaggio's earliest historical painting on a large scale (pages 551, 552) can be interpreted in this way. In the corner on the viewer's right it shows Christ seeing a room where money is changed calling out to one of the men present. The composition functions as a picture within a picture. The genre scene, which is built into the larger painting according to the principles of the golden section, could be cut out of the whole composition if one marked it out from the outline of the figure on the extreme right up to the lower edge of the window that lets in no light. Given the title, *At the Money Changer's*, this painting would have been a legitimate subject for a picture from about 1520 onwards, when the Antwerp artist Quentin Massys (1465/66–1530) was active.

When the Son of God intervenes in everyday affairs, he picks out a man who cannot be recognized at first, and whose calling scholars see differently. Some argue that St. Matthew is the young man sitting at the end of the table, engrossed in counting money and not looking up towards Christ. But, like Bellori and others, I believe that the dominating figure behind the table is the disciple. In pointing to his own breast with his left hand, he is repeating Christ's gesture, which Peter, also searching, imitates.

The light in this picture creates a strange effect. There is a window in the rear wall, but it is as dark as if it gave on to a narrow backyard or as if it were night outside. Through the slanting shutters, the left-hand section of the genre scene is immersed in deep black. However, the black shadow falling from an imaginary side wall on the right, which forms a background sloping at the top behind Christ and St. Peter, is even more vigorously black.

Normally, we would imagine that just as people come through a door, so light would, too. However, in an irritating but most convincing reversal, hard shadow falls from this direction. This breaks off right underneath the outside contour of the window shutter, as if the open door had created the shadow. Since, however, both Christ and St. Peter are standing quite close to the wall, they must both be within this shadow area. Without showing any concern for this, Caravaggio lights them from above right. Although himself in shadow, St. Peter even casts a shadow on to the floor into the center of the picture.

Effects which might at first seem too artificial, happening as it were on a theater stage, can be easily explained by the layout of the chapel. The painting hangs to the left of the entrance in a gloomy church, lit only by one window high up in the altar wall to the right. Caravaggio lets the windowless chapel wall project into the picture, without worrying about narrative logic.

Any artist who puts pictures together in such a way that a genre picture can only be elevated into a biblical historical painting by the device of two figures bursting in with rhetorically demonstrative gestures, is not really a narrative painter. Caravaggio's real subject is the everyday character of the powerfully depicted genre. The event, which picks out a man sitting at the table—first giving him a name among the nameless men

Caravaggio
The Calling of St. Matthew, 1599/1600
Oil on canvas, 322 x 340 cm
San Luigi dei Francesi, Rome

In his first public work, Caravaggio was concerned with
depicting powerfully three-dimensional figures by means
of chiaroscuro. This is Caravaggio's only painting to be
conclusively lit from the right. After *Mary Magdalene*
(page 504), it is the first to depict figures beneath a sharply
defined shadow boundary against a dark background and
illuminated by highlights.

Caravaggio
The Martyrdom of St. Matthew
Oil on canvas, 323 x 343 cm
San Luigi dei Francesi, Rome

The location is the steps up to a Christian altar, with a Greek cross marked on its front, and a candle burning. In the background on the left, we can just make out the shaft of a column in the almost impenetrable darkness. Steps ascend parallel to the picture towards the altar at the back. They also appear on the left, where churches do not normally have steps. For this reason, some experts have claimed to detect a baptismal font in the foreground, especially as men are lying nearby, half-

naked. One of them is propping himself up off the ground. He and the cowering youth in the foreground to the right frame the composition like the river gods on ancient reliefs. The most eye-catching figure of the picture is also half naked; this is not the martyr, but an athletic young man who, with sword in hand, looks like a murderer or executioner. He might have already mortally wounded the Apostle; the others have backed away from him. But since the men storming to the left appear more like *bravi*, foppish villains, it is now thought that the characters at the back, fleeing while looking

back at the scene, are the ones who have dealt the Apostle the deadly blow; of them, the bearded man at the rear of the group is held to be the main culprit, a figure considered to be a self-portrait of the painter. The gesture of the Herculean youth grasping the dying man by the wrist would then tell of the care of a candidate for baptism who has armed himself to chase away the villains. Only a painting by Caravaggio can inspire such an interpretation; in a mix of self-doubt and awareness of his own sinfulness, the painter would have cast himself in the role of a murderer!

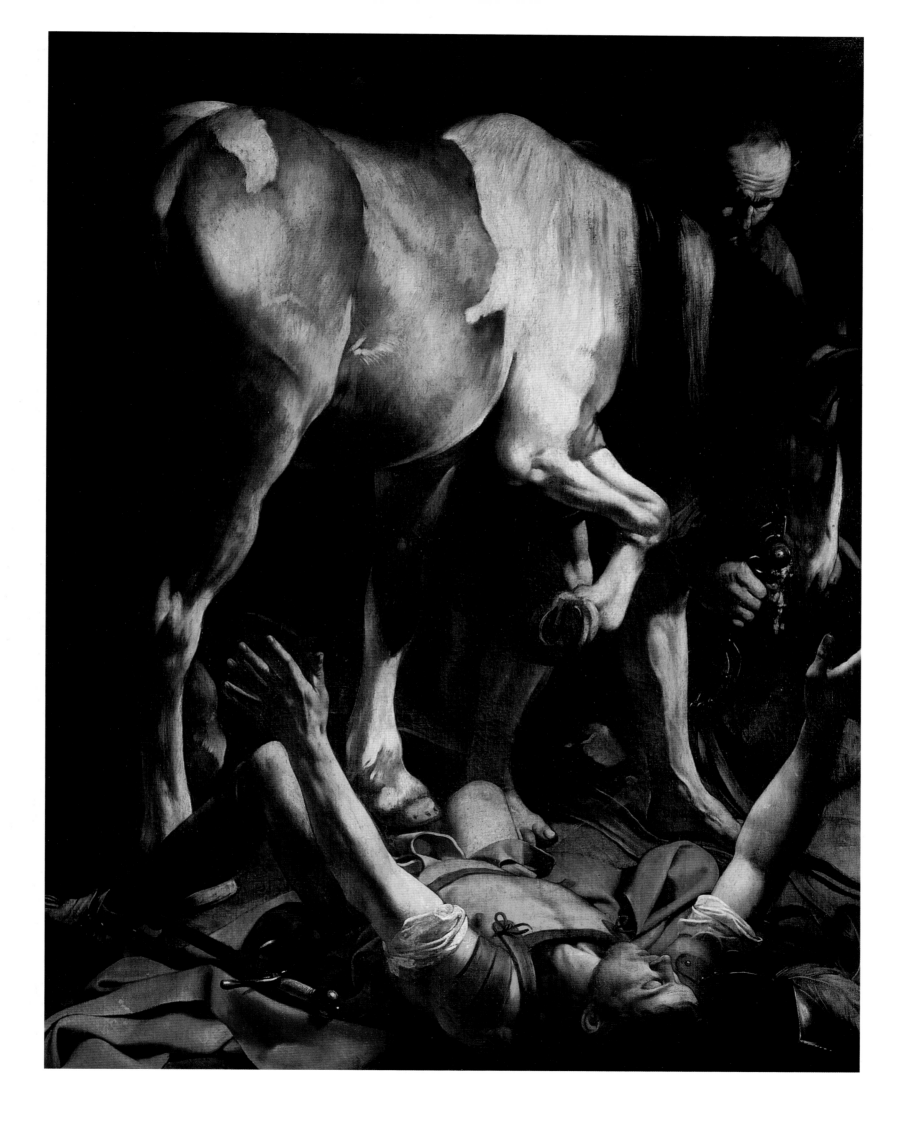

surrounding him—breaks into this everyday scene from outside, from the right, as a kind of afterthought. Thus, the unexpected entry of Christ and St. Peter suddenly transforms description into pictorial narrative.

At the same time two principles of Caravaggio's art become evident. Instead of building up his composition out of individual figures in the tradition of the *disegno*, he makes a sophisticated grouping around the money changers' table, with St. Matthew as the main figure. Free from older pictorial prototypes, he creates continuity in his work out of memories of possible poses and arrangements, which he has tried out in other subjects. In both the *St. Matthew* and the *Supper at Emmaus* (pages 540, 541), the right angle of the table, in foreshortened perspective, serves the artist as the foot of a pyramid above which he constructs a half-length portrait. As the full-size, full-length figures show, legs under the table present a problem, which the artist has avoided in Emmaus and other pictures showing half-length figures.

The smaller group of St. Peter and Christ also reveals an important peculiarity that has nothing to do with the development of its composition, as shown by X-ray photographs. Any artist who, like Caravaggio, creates movement not by physical structure but by light and shade, sections of color, and areas of profound darkness, will run into problems when painting several figures one behind the other. Caravaggio bunches the figures together, as it were, and depicts only St. Peter. Thus, Christ's head and arm tower behind St. Peter like a set piece. Anyone familiar with the old art of a stroboscopic figure, which can depict several different aspects of a related movement by means of figures standing one behind the other, will understand this brilliant device.

Caravaggio's figure is made up of two bodies developed during the course of a fairly lengthy design process. Interpreters who keep trying to explain Caravaggio's behavior in terms of Church politics, see his later addition of St. Peter as a concession to the Papal See. Only gullible popes would have read this work with the thrusting figures from the right, the bustling mockery of the Redeemer by the hectic antics of his deputy, as a profession of commitment.

Caravaggio completed this picture, together with its companion piece on the opposite wall, between 23 July 1599 and 4 July 1600. It was intended for the place

The Conversion of St. Paul (detail page 555)

As compared with the first version, the valid version, painted on canvas in contravention of the letter of the contract, reduces the incident to what is visible. Instead of looking like a figure modeled on a classical river god, as he does in the first version, Saul now appears boldly foreshortened. The model Caravaggio has chosen is markedly younger, though he is again wearing Roman leather armor, which follows the contours of his body. That said, powerful red coloring and clearly defined borders, as well as the shadow areas on Saul's neck, now emphasize the difference between skin and armor.

Preceding pages, left:
Caravaggio
The Conversion of St. Paul, 1600/01
Oil on cypress, 237 x 189 cm
Collezione Odescalchi Balbi, Rome

In the foreground, dressed in Roman leather armor, which exposes his body as if he were a nude, lies a general whose crimson cloak is crumpled about him in undignified confusion. At the bottom edge of the picture his helmet has come to rest on its side, so that we can see the skullcap inside. The fallen man is covering his eyes with both hands, to protect himself from the blinding light coming down from the top right-hand corner. It also illuminates an angel, who is holding Christ. Both have emerged from on high so clumsily that a poplar branch has broken under their weight. On earth, Caravaggio confronts them with a white-bearded giant, who is attempting to ward them off with his spear. His un-classical armor, with a golden crescent moon on an Oriental round shield, is a reminder that the Middle Ages—though not the Baroque period—equated heathens of ancient times with the Saracens.

Preceding pages, right:
Caravaggio
The Conversion of St. Paul, 1601
Oil on canvas, 230 x 175 cm
Santa Maria del Popolo, Rome

This version pays more attention to the development of the action. The helmet lies turned over near Saul's head in such a way that we can imagine it having revolved more than 180 degrees. The sword at his side lies flat on the ground. The rider has, as it were, fallen at a right angle from his horse. His sole companion is an old man, who, moved by the awkwardness of his general having fallen from his horse, tries to lead the animal away, without doing any harm to the rider. The horse also reacts to the miracle. It establishes eye contact with the viewer, and strides calmly away over Saul, whom, as a result of this event, Christ summons to be the Apostle Paul.

The Crucifixion of St. Peter (detail page 559)

Caravaggio has painted St. Peter's body with his astonishing feeling for anatomy and the skin structure of an elderly male physique. At the same time, he has chosen the very instant when the Prince of the Apostles is raised into the undignified position in which he will be crucified, upside down.

where it is still hanging now, the Sepulchral Chapel of Cardinal Matteo Contarelli, who stipulated in his will that the side-walls should be frescoed. After the project had become badly delayed with the Cardinal's death in 1585, Cavaliere d'Arpino (1568–1640) made a start on the ceiling frescoes, but did not concern himself with the walls. Probably with Cardinal del Monte's intercession, Caravaggio received contracts in July and August 1599. These pictures made Caravaggio an overnight celebrity.

The scene opposite called for a totally different kind of drama (page 553). In this picture, Caravaggio depicted the *Martyrdom of St. Matthew*. The kind of trouble this picture in a dark chapel caused for artists, too, can be gauged from an account by Joachim von Sandrart. He thought that this was a picture of the Expulsion of the Money Changers from the Temple, as if he took the central figure of the executioner for Christ.

The figuration is hard to follow here partly because of the tendency Caravaggio also shows in this painting to pack body movements tightly together. The two *ignudi* front right are so close together that it looks as if they have one body with two heads. The half-naked figure lying front left looks a little like a stroboscopic image of the murderer toppling forward. However, he also connects with the man above him, who is opening his hands in horror towards the man who is being murdered. His movement is echoed by another figure, whilst the two pairs of figures contrast youth and adulthood in men. Even the saint stretched out preparing to die, as well as his ministrant, act as if the figure of the boy draped in white fabric were trying to wriggle free from St. Matthew's movement. Finally, the angel with the small arm of a child, holding out a palm branch, is skillfully related to the terrifying, fully

grown arm of the murderer as he seizes the martyr. This is certainly not a traditional sort of composition. For it, as the X-ray photo shows, Caravaggio suppressed a triumphal arch in the center of the picture. He also made the figures look bigger by doing without a large number of figures customary in classical prototypes. By this means he made the expressive character of the painting subtler. He has succeeded very well with the Apostle's outstretched hand, whose palm only is illuminated. The artist apparently wished to develop the kind of tension inherent in all Baroque pictures of martyrdom. To achieve this here, he uses the highly unusual motif of a figure being thrown to the ground, then follows the saint's line of vision to open up the main lines of the composition. This also applies to a powerful light-line, which moves across several bodies, is transmitted by the Apostle's left leg, and ends in the head of the half-naked man front left. It is equally true of the vertical line leading at a right angle up to the angel. Finally, it also applies to the subsidiary lines, which radiate out from St. Matthew's head and describe parabolic arcs in the direction of both the murderer and the fleeing boy. In other words, the martyr's horror builds into a pictorial dynamic, in which even the magnificently drawn body of the murderer fails to retain its structure. The lighting deprives him of a firm base. At the same time the vision of his dying victim floods over his body from his knees up as far as his arms and head. Critics often overlook the fact that this picture has nothing to do with the execution practices of established authorities in Caravaggio's day—but instead depicts murder, assassination. The half-naked man with the sword embodies a coarseness that the artist does not usually give his nude figures. In other words, Caravaggio makes a distinction between the nakedness of Bacchus

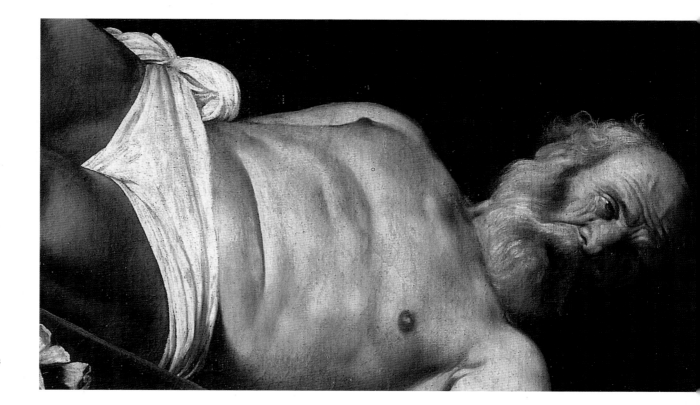

or St. John the Baptist and that of a heathen murderer. Shortly after his commission to paint the side walls of the Contarelli Chapel, Caravaggio received a similar commission for the Cerasi Chapel in Santa Maria del Popolo. The smaller vertical format of the pictorial areas allowed the artist to paint the figures life-size only by limiting their number. It is certainly true that both the *Crucifixion of St. Peter* (page 559) and the *Conversion of St. Paul* (page 555) take place in the open air. That said, Caravaggio suppressed landscape by obstructing distant views through backgrounds as dark as night, even though night is not mentioned in any of the historical accounts.

However, the viewer hardly notices this breach of narrative fidelity. Literature might well carefully ponder much less significant details, but it passes over this distortion of the facts in silence, for the artist's interpretation triumphs over any expectation that a picture will give a sensible account of an historical event.

At least two versions of virtually the same dimensions exist of the *Conversion of St. Paul*, one in wood and the other on canvas. We do not know whether the first version (page 554) was rejected by the artist or by the patron. It is one of Caravaggio's few landscapes. The evening sky, in which the domes of Damascus can be glimpsed in the far distance on the right, is in great turmoil. Here, Christ reveals himself to Saul to ask him why he is persecuting him, and he transforms him into the Prince of the Apostles, Paul. A large-leaved plant on the ground and a poplar tree at the picture's left-hand edge, which may allude to the name of Santa Maria del Popolo, are also evident.

After a lot of speculation about whether this painting was by Caravaggio at all and not, for instance, by Orazio Gentileschi, it is now certain that it was intended for the Cerasi Chapel in the church of Santa Maria del Popolo. According to the contract of 24 September 1600, Caravaggio was supposed to paint both pictures on cypress wood. This applies to this example, whereas in the church itself paintings on canvas are hanging.

The incident is narrated in a very round-about way. In the middle ground, the white horse has swerved round after throwing its rider off; it prances restlessly, and turns its head towards the light which comes from heaven. It looks much too small in relation to the figures, and its anatomy is so badly conceived that only the color of its pelt indicates that head and hindquarters belong to the same animal. Saul rears up, but at the same time leans back against his soldier's spear and knee. The foreshortening of Saul's body is just as unsuccessful as his legs, which are curved like sabers and disappear into the darkness. A mailed hand, a crumhorn, and a lance, which all peep out of the dark, suggest non-participants to the left. Normally, Caravaggio refrained from suggesting figures-off in this way.

In his use of lighting effects, Caravaggio overdoes his greatest artistic technique. The landscape and the figures are lit differently. This makes the landscape degenerate into something incidental, whilst the lighting on the figures is debased into a clumsy theatrical effect. Shadows virtually dismember the figures. The overall result is that, despite its magnificent concept, the picture cannot be taken quite seriously. Caravaggio repeatedly tried to capture momentary events. His tendency to take this task a little too literally shows itself here in the breaking branch with which he dramatically emphasizes how suddenly God intervenes. Yet the gravitational weight of Christ transported off to heaven—together with his angel—contradict our notions of how material heavenly bodies really are.

Although Caravaggio remains true to himself in this respect even when painting the miraculous scene of the Conversion of St. Paul, he is unable to set out the overall composition according to his own principles. Instead, like all painters of historical pictures, he has to combine different studies—direct from a model, as the skin color of Saul's hands and lower arms shows. One drawback—though a modern interpretation might see it as a revealing plus—of this early *Conversion of St. Paul* is that Caravaggio does not try to cover up the fissures and contradictions within his picture, all of which are fundamental to his methods. Taking a term from the early 20th century, we could speak of a collage of sections studied in advance.

The second version of the same subject, which Caravaggio obviously completed before November 1601, looks like a radical criticism of his first attempt (pages 555, 556). In this version the artist, who is a master only of what is visible on earth, restricts himself to Saul's reactions. Physical ecstasy, which, as in *St. Theresa* by Bernini (1598–1680), is not unlike erotic ecstasy, overcomes the general, who is still young. In foreshortening the lying body Caravaggio shows his familiarity with similar experiments in perspective, as practiced by Italian painters for many years.

That said, he adds the decisive device of chiaroscuro. He casts luridly bright light on to Saul, who lies stretched out with his legs open, his arms spread out wide, and shutting his eyes to block out the heavenly light. Diffuse streaks in the upper right-hand corner are enough for him to suggest the direction from which the light is falling into the picture. It illuminates only the ground, rock, boulder, clothes, and living creatures.

Caravaggio's blatant contravention of traditional Christian painting, which expressed heavenly light in terms of beams and, in pictures set at night, contrasted objects or figures against a painterly black background, may have something to do with revolutionary discoveries in optics. Even today, one of the most astonishing discoveries about light is the fact that even the strongest light will be visible in a black space only if a colored object is placed in its path. Beams are caused by dust and moisture. However, as soon as these atmospheric disturbances are removed, light will be visible only on the colored surfaces on which it shines. In this picture, the helmet proves that Caravaggio had wrestled with discoveries of this kind, for its blackness allows only reflections, not full illumination.

With impressive artifice, Caravaggio reduces the horse to a proportion in keeping with the human figures. Caravaggio fills out the verticals on the left with the animal's hindquarters and back, filling the

Caravaggio
The Crucifixion of St. Peter, 1601
Oil on canvas, 230 x 175 cm
Santa Maria del Popolo, Rome

With horrifying cold-bloodedness and a great instinct for the problems of the pull of gravity, Caravaggio shows three executioner's assistants erecting St. Peter's cross. The Prince of the Apostles has had four nails driven through his hands and feet. Now, at his own request, he is to be crucified upside down. Of Heaven, which, in the case of St. Matthew, sent down the angel with a martyr's palm branch, there is no sign here. The harsh light, which makes the figures stand out against the dark cliffs, seems to have no redeeming power. As in the *Conversion of St. Paul* (page 555), which forms the companion piece to this painting, the artist has distanced himself from historical fact. He has sound artistic reasons to envelop the event in darkness—as if his painting were competing with sculpture.

horizontals above in such a way that there is not much space left for the background, which falls away in blackish-brown tones. The horse lowers its head to its master, so that the pictorial surface can be used to maximum effect for majestic height.

Instead of a white horse, Caravaggio painted a piebald. White shines on its pelt, painted in muted earth colors, on its feet, over its back, and on a small patch of its hindquarters. Even in the horse's mane, colors vary.

In this version, Caravaggio tried to consolidate the spatial composition, which also failed miserably in the first version. He aligns the foreshortened figure of Saul at a right angle with the horse. Its body acts as the background for the event happening to the main character. At the same time, the horse is not standing in a visually parallel position, but at a slanting angle with its head turning toward Saul, who is lying at a corresponding angle. This enables the painter to stabilize the pictorial space.

Both the lighting effects and what remains of the narrative blend very well together. Although Caravaggio refrains from beams of light, the human figure and horse, both in the light, reproduce their effect. The apparition has not only thrown the general on to his back; it also fills him with a glow that is expressed by means of light. He tries to grasp it, as if it were a material quality, though the painter can depict it only in Saul's illuminated hands.

The horse responds to its rider's physical shock with supreme caution. The artist utilizes the fact that in a turmoil, horses are careful to avoid trampling on people. With an almost uncanny look, which shows no understanding for the fallen rider but at the same time identifies with the viewer, the animal strides off, led by an impassive stable lad, away from the miracle on the ground. The very gentleness of the horse's movement proves that Caravaggio, far from being the master of the terrifying instant, is at his most effective when surprise switches into careful observation.

As regards a first version of this picture's companion piece, the *Crucifixion of St. Peter* (page 559), opinion is more divided. In many respects the painting on canvas which has found its way into the church seems very well suited to the *Conversion of St. Paul* (page 555). The artist is concerned solely with the Apostle and the three executioners' assistants. After the not very successful foreshortenings in the *Martyrdom of St. Matthew* (page 553), Caravaggio tries out this well-established technique for depicting bodies with a new strength here—and to very much better effect.

An imposing, large figure seen from the back—one who also flouts the conventions of decency, or respectability—opens the picture. This man, with his flowing blond hair, is being assisted by a man with a rough, wrinkled face as well as short hair and a beard, who has put his arms around the cross to lift it. In the process, he looks up towards the right, where a third man, whose face is also hidden, is pulling a rope. Only a spontaneous artist's vision could depict two faceless individuals in such a way: an artist who does not wait until the men engaged in erecting the cross can be seen properly.

Peter, the Prince of the Apostles, is depicted skillfully foreshortened. With only his left lower arm concealed by one of the assistants, St. Peter's body is shown complete from his nailed feet to his head. Critics who accuse Caravaggio of being hostile to bodies should be reduced to silence by this sensitively observed nude. The artist has registered the nails in feet and hands with horrifying precision. St. Peter is forced to look for himself at this terrible method of fastening flesh to wood. His deeply furrowed head turns towards the fingers of his left hand, clenched around the nail. Anyone who remembers that St. Peter, who knew he was about to die on the cross, expressed the wish to be crucified upside down, and not, like his master, with his head uppermost, will see the old man's anxiety that the nail might not hold, rather than his contortions of agony.

This invests Caravaggio's perfectly valid depiction of the Crucifixion of St. Peter with a profound meaning.

To understand it would need a recapitulation of the whole story of St. Peter in Rome. He wanted to flee from the now imminent persecution of Christians. However, in the famous legend of *Quo vadis* he was stopped by Christ himself, as he was carrying his Cross, because he wanted to be crucified again in Rome.

The blue fabric draped at the bottom right is not without deeper meaning. It is one of St. Peter's traditional colors, but at the same time interrelates heaven with the dignity of the robe he wears. Turning to Christ, we should not forget that at his Crucifixion the victim's coat at the foot of the Cross also played a significant role.

The Cerasi Chapel receives hardly any light through its own lunette window with the family coat of arms, though more from the church's transept, especially in the afternoon. This means that there is no unambiguous light source. In other words, in the picture of St. Peter it is no surprise that the light comes from the left. Illuminated centrally, the picture of St. Paul, however, which adorns the right-hand side wall, fits the ambience perfectly.

Caravaggio's paintings do not stand alone. The artist's great competitor, Annibale Carracci (1560–1609), of all painters, received the commission for the main picture, an Assumption of the Virgin above the altar (page 560). This reminds us of the difference between narrative painting and the altarpiece. Caravaggio's paintings do not allow us to address the Apostle while praying. St. Peter is too preoccupied with the dignity of his crucifixion, and St. Paul much too enraptured.

Our only eye contact is with the horse of the young general, who will only very much later take on the majesty of a Prince of the Apostles. These pictures are narrative only in the sense that they refer the historical event back to the visible. Yet instead of using narrative to intensify what has happened, they concentrate on observing unforgettable genre painting images. By eliminating the divine element, the artist forces his viewers to focus initially on what happens on earth.

The appreciation thus gained can then develop into the kind of astonishment that makes Caravaggio's paintings acceptable even to those people who otherwise reject his art.

Annibale Carracci
The Assumption of the Virgin, 1600/01
Oil on canvas, 245 x 155 cm
Santa Maria del Popolo, Rome

Caravaggio's paintings of St. Peter and St. Paul flank the chapel's altarpiece by his rival Caracci. There is a radical difference between the Bolognese artist's beautifully bright colors, the powerful blue and red he applies, and Caravaggio's earth tones, which he varies only by blue on St. Peter and red on St. Paul. It is true that he also uses green as a complementary color to red. Furthermore, St. Peter's yellowish flesh tint seems like an indication of the complementary color to blue.

All in all, then, we can recognize a conscious use of color on Caravaggio's part over and above his use of chiaroscuro. Yet to view his pictures needs a different form of attention from the jubilation that Annibale Carracci proclaims.

Caravaggio
St. Matthew and the Angel
Oil on canvas, 295 x 195 cm
San Luigi dei Francesi, Rome

The angel flying above, there to communicate God's word, dominates the picture. Skillfully, Caravaggio shows his explanatory hands occupying the central axis, again demonstrating the artist's precise instinct for geometry. The sudden haste with which St. Matthew follows his inspiration and starts writing, determines the pictorial center. Caravaggio presents the full-length figure as a trompe-l'œil effect, as if he were appearing above the altar from a perspective that corresponds to eye-level in the chapel. The viewer gets a good view not only of the stool which is poised shakily over the top of a step, but also of the large table placed in the room at an angle. This continues a long way towards the right behind Matthew. So does the Gospel, as if Caravaggio wanted to make sure it was obvious.

In 1599, Caravaggio's commission for the Contarelli Chapel was limited to historical paintings for the side walls, as marble sculptures were initially meant to adorn the altar. However, the Evangelist intended for the Contarelli Chapel that was delivered by the Flemish sculptor, Jacob Cobaert, did not meet the requirements. The authorities thus approached Caravaggio again, and made a contract with him on 7 February 1602 for an altarpiece to be completed as early as the Pentecost festival, on 23 May of the same year. But his picture also caused displeasure.

Marchese Vincenzo Giustiniani offered to pay the same sum already paid for the painting installed at Pentecost. For this sum he received the rejected picture, whilst by 22 September 1602 payment could be made for Caravaggio's version, which still adorns the chapel (page 564).

Even in photographs, the rejected painting can puzzle modern viewers. Caravaggio sees the Evangelist as such a ponderous figure that there is almost a wrestling match when the inspirational angel tries to persuade the reluctant instrument of redemption to write down God's word. The version that dates from the spring of 1602, is, as it were, corrected by the picture that followed that summer and was paid for that autumn (page 563). Now the Evangelist can write, he only has to listen to the words of the angel.

One more thing changes. The Berlin canvas (page 564) depicted a dark-haired evangelist in the prime of life. His faun-like features, which are reminiscent of those of Socrates, hardly match the longish face of the well-dressed moneychanger whom Christ is calling (page 532). In the available version the artist depicts the same bald-headed man he had pose for the Uffizi *Sacrifice of Isaac* (page 535). By the way he paints his face, Caravaggio makes it seem probable that the Evangelist looked like this after losing the locks which he had when seated at the table in the Calling.

Whilst Caravaggio composed the Berlin version from in front, he tried now to make the Evangelist above the altar as convincing as in a trompe l'œil painting. Caravaggio draws our view to the upper edge of a stone step, observing the full-length figure and the table's surface from below.

Even if the picture that was finally accepted seems more conventional than the destroyed Berlin example, the organization of space and the spontaneity of movement compare very favorably even with the *Calling of St. Matthew* (page 552), which hangs next to it.

According to the recently discovered contract with Laerzio Cherubini, Caravaggio's largest painting for Rome was completed between the Cerasi Chapel and the two versions of the altarpiece for the Contarelli Chapel. This is the *Death of the Virgin Mary*, now in the Louvre, Paris (pages 556, 557). On 14 July 1601, the artist committed himself to delivering the painting in June 1602.

The *Death of the Virgin Mary* did not stay in its intended home for long. Today, the chapel is adorned by a painting on the same subject, which Carlo Saraceni (1585–1620) completed for the same patron (page 565). Precisely because this painter did not close his eyes to Caravaggio's influence, we can see his picture as a critical corrective to the *Death of the Virgin Mary* in the Louvre. Baglione reported that the Barefooted Carmelites had rejected Caravaggio's work. In 1607, the great Flemish painter, Sir Peter Paul Rubens (1577–1640), saw to it that the Gonzagas of Mantua purchased the painting, now removed from the altar. Before it was transported away, the painting was exhibited in Rome for another week, at the request of the artists in the city. During this exhibition the picture impressed even the Mantuan ambassador, who had, on his own admission, at first failed to appreciate its worth.

In this painting, Caravaggio's principle of genre painting reaches its apex. For him, the history of salvation expresses itself purely in terms of what is visible: which is why the Virgin Mary is really dying. Only the curtain in this picture has no straightforward genre painting meaning, because it does not serve the purpose of screening the dying woman. Thanks to its rich scarlet color, which wins out over the earth colors and even Mary's red dress, the magnificent drapery assumes the value of a luminous signal, which surpasses the profound despair of the Apostle, who remains in the dark.

The fact that the Barefooted Carmelites rejected one of Caravaggio's pictures should warn us not to assume

that Catholic ideals about reforming conditions of poverty are the artist's own convictions. Although Santa Maria della Scala is in one of the poorest areas of Trastevere and used to belong to a charitable institution, the Casa Pia, an honest look at earthly desperation was most unwelcome there. It was precisely the poor people and their carers who rejected the picture, whilst artists and art lovers in Rome recognized its extraordinary qualities. A glance at churches in poor areas nowadays will confirm the fact that those people who are really poor are no more able to endure seeing their destitution the subject of a genre painting than their benevolent carers are. Only a certain distance from the suffering allows one to objectify it into art. In his version, completed for the same patron, Laerzio Cherubini, shortly after the removal of Caravaggio's painting, Carlo Saraceni showed what the Barefooted Carmelites and the poor people in Trastevere really wanted (page 565).

After the Jesuits, the Oratorians were the most important mouthpiece of the Catholic reform in Rome. Their Chiesa Nuova, Santa Maria in Vallicella, once housed the *Entombment of Christ*, successfully and without any dispute (page 568).

In this case we are quite well informed about the circumstances surrounding the commission. Francesco Vittrice ordered the picture for a side chapel, which his uncle, Pietro (died 26 March 1600), had purchased for the family. The painting was completed between 19 January 1602 and 6 September 1604. Transported to Paris in 1797, it remained in the Vatican after its return to the Pope in 1815. Both the patron and the artist had to adhere to the proscribed decoration of the church with this picture. The chapel was dedicated to Our Lady of Sorrows. This makes the subject of the painting all the more astonishing. It depicts the darkness of the grave, the heavy tombstone, which juts out frighteningly into the viewer's vision, the dead Christ and the men who lay him to rest, as well as the lamentation of the women present—but only then does it show the Virgin Mary herself, albeit in the impressive position of the picture's geometric center.

Instead of the lament associated with the Marian Vespers, Caravaggio chose to depict the one connected with the compline of the Passion Office, in other words the station heralding the onset of night, when Christ was laid to rest in his tomb. Narrative mingles with genre-like observation. This picture, with its profound affinity with the missal sacrifice, in which this dead man is transformed into bread and wine, will offend any sensitive believer. Projecting out of the painting we see the stone slab that forms the basis for the full-length figures. This will seal up the tomb of Christ, who died on the Cross, after he has been lowered into the deep darkness of the tomb, where the priest's altar stands.

Amongst so much dense physicality, which varies from the warm orange of the men's garments to a bright flesh tint, the only figure conceived in a colorful way almost falls by the wayside. This is St. John, who puts his right hand under Christ's shoulders, and lets his left hand rest on the body, as if meditating. He is wearing a blue tunic and a red cloak, which makes a striking impact in the center of the painting, set against the white of the death shroud. The unity of the body dissolves in the contrast of colors and fabrics, which are separated by deep shadow. Furthermore, Christ's favorite disciple is bending his head so far forward that light falls only on his forehead and nose. Thus, his face does not offer a whole entity to be contemplated piously.

Caravaggio's altarpiece *Our Lady of Sorrows* in Santa Maria in Vallicella reflects, with frightening clarity, the presence in the Eucharist of the sacrificed Christ suffering his Passion. It also proves that the artist was able to visualize, in the truest sense of the word, a fundamental theological idea by means of bodies and lines of vision. At the same time, for the altarpiece of roughly the same size to St. Anne in St. Peter's, he had to combine a theological speculation with the presence of the saint who plays no part in the proceedings.

The *Madonna dei Palafrenieri* (page 570) is based on the first biblical promise of a Savior. After Eve's temptation by the serpent, the Lord of Creation curses the animal with the words: "And I will put enmity between thee and the woman, and between thy seed and her seed; it shall bruise thy head, and thou shalt bruise his heel" (Genesis 3: 15). During the Reformation, it was disputed whether Mary or Christ crushed the serpent's head. A papal decree decided that it was the Savior together with his mother, Mary.

Certainly, the boy's eagerness to reinforce the impact of his mother's foot by stamping his own little foot without losing his balance, adds a wonderful note of sympathy. Yet the artist is surely exaggerating when he makes the heavy breasts of the Holy Mother of God push out of her wide décolleté over the child's little head.

The Palafrenieri, or grooms in charge of the papal stables, were displeased, so that this major work by Caravaggio hung in St. Peter's Cathedral in Rome for only a few days. This had nothing to do with papal directives. From there the picture went directly to the gallery of the nepotistic Cardinal Scipione Borghese, who, under Pope Paul V (1605–1621), also arbitrated on matters of art from 1605 onwards.

In a quite different way Caravaggio also took a literal approach to the *Madonna di Loreto* (page 571), which he was supposed to paint for the Church of Sant' Agostino in Rome, and which to this day occupies its old place adorning the altar in the side chapel to the left. In this picture, only the pilgrims of Loreto, a place of pilgrimage in the Marches, remain. We see nothing at all of the legend that centers on this shrine and its Madonna. Angels had to transport the holy house in which the Annunciation had taken place from Nazareth to the Adriatic coast, in order to shelter it in Loreto. The painting would also need to show something of the Madonna di Loreto as the patroness of the battle against faithless Protestants. But all this, all the things that small-scale votive pictures depict, was not part of Caravaggio's art.

The artist reduces the cult of the Madonna di Loreto to her outcome, the pilgrimage to Loreto, and the warm affection felt by the Virgin Mary and her son, who gives his blessing to the pilgrims. A vague indication that the

Carlo Saraceni
The Death of the Virgin
Oil on canvas, 459 x 273 cm
Santa Maria della Scala, Rome

The Virgin Mary is sat on what looks like a throne. Her death happens in a state of rapture that allows her to hear the music of the angels. Above her in her dark room, clouds gather, from which putti with harps and roses flutter down, in order to receive unscathed the body of the Holy Mother of God in Heaven.

Opposite page:
Caravaggio
St. Matthew and the Angel, before Whitsun 1602
Oil on canvas, 232 x 183 cm
Kaiser-Friedrich-Museum, Berlin
(destroyed during World War II)

The slow-witted figure of St. Matthew, who is naked below his knees and elbows, and dressed in an ordinary cowl, acquires no real dignity even through the mantle laid over his folding chair. With his eyes wide open, and with heavy hands, he peers into the thick volumes on his knee. It is not easy to believe he can write. His angel has the greatest difficulty in leading his untrained hand to put the word of God into letters, which are far too big. In doing so, the angel inclines his charming figure, whose shape can clearly be seen beneath his light garment. And so can his androgynous face and long locks of hair, in contrast to the rough bald skull of St. Matthew. Against the almost black background, which has been trimmed on the left and at the top, we see the exquisite white of his enormous wings.

Opposite page:
Caravaggio
The Death of the Virgin, 1601/02
Oil on canvas, 369 x 245 cm
Musée du Louvre, Paris

The fact that the Virgin Mary could die, like any other woman, was something the Church was reluctant to imagine. In Caravaggio's case, however, no light from heaven can make up for the death of the Madonna. All eyes are on a dead woman, whose body shows the signs of a death struggle. As if death had come suddenly, the dying woman was laid on a bed too short for her. Her naked feet stick out over the end. A piece of cloth, which is earth colored and therefore not quite suitable for the Queen of Heaven, is lying forgotten over her lap and upper thigh.

The Virgin's bodice has been opened to help her breathe more easily. Her skin has discolored into a greenish tinge. Her face is swollen, and has sunk to the side, where her left arm is grasping at thin air, whilst her right hand is resting on her body. Her face, with eyes closed, is certainly turning towards the viewer, but anyone expecting help and intercession from the dead Madonna will be praying in vain. The universal horror this depiction aroused can be judged from derogatory reports that Caravaggio's model for this painting was a dead prostitute dragged from the Tiber.

On the left, one of the Apostles—open-mouthed—inclines his head, which follows the model of the first St. Matthew picture, towards the dead Madonna. Only a small part of his bald skull is illuminated, with some light reflected around the top of his head. Beside him, however, light floods over the next Apostle, who has sunk to his knees, in strong orange tones. He has buried his mouth and eyes in both hands, so that only his neck, right hand, and two fingers of his left hand are in the light. Another Apostle is standing close behind him: Caravaggio used him as the model for his second St. Matthew (page 563). He is expressing horror through his open hands, which form a strong shadow against his cloak. Once again, the light illuminates the figure's bald pate more than his face.

The same applies to the figure who is sinking down directly over the Madonna's body, and for whom the first St. Matthew was again the inspiration. Caravaggio brilliantly combines two motifs that he has prepared farther left. These are the gesture of this figure's right hand, now reaching for his eyes, and the tension created by the switch from illuminated sections of skin to the black hair. In the same way as Christ's favorite disciple stands beneath the Cross, a young man with thick locks, propping his head on one hand, stands behind the Madonna. He is probably meant to be St. John, whom Christ on the Cross entrusted to his mother for all time.

The Death of the Virgin (detail page 566)

In the foreground a woman, probably Mary Magdalene, who was sometimes described as an Apostle, is lamenting: drained of emotion and without any hope of redemption. However temporary the Madonna's makeshift bed may seem, a large brass bowl and towel are lying ready for the washing of her corpse. That said, the woman who has been summoned to do this is sitting on a low stool in the foreground, incapable of completing her task. Overwhelmed by her pain, she has let her head fall on to her hands. She has already rolled up her sleeves a little way. Yet the deep emotion she is feeling at the death of the Madonna has left her in helpless grief.

holy house in the Loreto legend is Mary's house in Nazareth, is evoked by the unusual location. The Madonna is leaning against a monumental reveal at her front door.

The picture has an unusual composition. Reading it from left to right, we first see the Holy Virgin and her child lingering in the doorway, illuminated as if by accident, then the two pilgrims nearby. Caravaggio suggests that his Madonna di Loreto is a simple woman, waiting for her worshippers. The weight of the large Christ child in Mary's arms makes it clear how humanly this Virgin Mary is experiencing the Incarnation of the Savior. By raising her one step higher, the artist creates just enough distance, whilst leaving Mary still in the sphere of ordinary people, so that the fingertips of the man praying almost touch Christ's left foot.

Caravaggio makes the middle of the composition an architectural set piece. However, by showing it very dilapidated, he robs the holy house of Loreto, which the building is meant to suggest, of the magnificence with which pious fantasy has endowed it. Together with the step, the edge of the stone separates the two worlds. On it falls the powerful shadow of the Holy Virgin, before her the face of the pilgrim, glowing with passionate joy.

The artist further characterizes the difference between the pure virgin and the pilgrims by his subtle use of different materials. The pilgrims are wearing coarse cloth, whose color looks dull and dirty after their journey. Only the cape that the man has round his shoulders bears any relation to the fine fabrics Mary is wearing. Does this suggest that pilgrimage is an ennobling activity? The Madonna, on the other hand, is robed in a dark gray silk dress, with red velvet sleeves.

Although the cut of this dress does not reveal the luxuriousness of upper-class society, the very softness of her flesh-tint indicates a social distance that reinforces Mary's beauty, youth, and purity.

Only if we take this possible aspect into account will we understand the deeper human meaning that Caravaggio has given his *Madonna di Loreto*. Along with the miracle-bringing house from Nazareth, which was not a palace, the heavenly Virgin Mary, in all her beauty and with the Savior in her arms, has descended, in order to look upon the pilgrims a step below. She has also come down to show them her son, so that he can give them his blessing. Although at first sight this might look like a genre scene in the doorway of a house in a dark side street, the contrast between the sublime nobility of Mary and her child and the coarse earthiness of the pilgrims invests the painting with a high degree of solemnity. This relates to the surprise element of a sudden vision of God, which Caravaggio expressed less subtly in his early work, the *Supper at Emmaus* (page 540).

Caravaggio's highly developed artist's instinct for what is only apparently a genre picture, through which the incarnation of God reveals itself in human form, is shown to perfection by the apparently casual manner in which he moves his Madonna figure (page 571) out of the picture's center to the left, as if this were a painting with half-length figures, with only the centrally placed architecture supporting her. By hinting, in the expectantly averted faces of the pilgrims, that they are about to have a vision of God, and by making an important pictorial theme of the way both the Madonna and her child look at them, the artist is showing his concern with the act of seeing.

Opposite page:
Caravaggio
The Entombment of Christ, 1602–1604
Oil on canvas, 300 x 203 cm
Pinacoteca Vatican, Rome

In this altarpiece, Caravaggio shows—with alarmingly sharp observation—the dead Christ being laid naked into his tomb. He depicts not only the muscular corpse but also the powerful gestures of the man who is lowering the dead Christ into the grave. This figure might well be one of the two biblical characters, Joseph of Arimathea or Nicodemus. He looks at the viewer on behalf of all the other figures in the pictures, his eyes heavy and dim with tears of pain. As a result, the picture appears to be looking at the viewer through him, rather than the other way about. An expression of such utter bewilderment will repulse any pious worshipper. It will also remind him or her to comprehend the full extent of the agony that is being expressed in three different ways by the three women behind the active figure in the foreground.

In church, however, a painting like this would offer quite a spectacle. We need to imagine it during Mass. The priests and their altar boys in their liturgical robes would play a prominent role. From above their heads there sinks down the dead Redeemer, full-size and showing all the horrifying signs of suffering and death: his flesh and blood returning to the altar in the form of sacramental bread and wine. Christ's favorite disciple, St. John, totally enveloped in darkness, is holding him.

The Entombment of Christ, (detail page 569)

The stone slab makes its appearance in the picture with terrifying power. According to one's attitude, one will detect in this painting either irreverence or profound religious bewilderment in the face of the death of Christ, because it presents the meaning of the sacred event—the unique occasion—which lies at the heart of Church ritual, in a tangible visual form.

Caravaggio
Madonna di Loreto (*Madonna dei Pellegrini*)
Oil on canvas, 260 x 150 cm
Sant'Agostino, Rome

At the bottom left corner a shadow falls into the picture
from the pillar of the altar frame. This area is illuminated
by a light-source that lies even lower. Leaning against a
door is the most beautiful Madonna Caravaggio
ever painted. She stands there with her legs crossed,
revealing—most unusually for a Madonna—her dainty,
immaculate feet. The feet of a man who is kneeling
alongside an older-looking woman in front of the high
front step that leads into the house are covered with dust
from their travels as pilgrims. Both of them lean a long
way forward, as they pray fervently.

Opposite page:
Caavaggio
Madonna dei Palafrenieri
Oil on canvas, 292 x 211 cm
Museo Galleria Borghese, Rome

The figures seem to be standing in a gloomy side street,
with lurid searchlights trained on them. Under her left
foot, the Madonna is crushing the head of a writhing
snake, with the naked Christ Child stamping his little
foot in support. Mary's mother, Anne, stands nearby, her
hands crossed over her lap, helplessly anxious, but still
upright, and a head taller than her daughter. She is
following what is happening with her mouth and eyes
wide open, though the latter remain dim in the shadow
of her old face's deep eye sockets. Caravaggio avoids any
overlap between the group consisting of Mary and the
Child and the majestic standing figure of the old woman,
Anne. The only point of contact is the index finger of the
boy's little left hand, which he is raising as if looking for
something. Originally intended for St. Peter's, the
painting was immediately acquired by the papal nephew
and cardinal, Scipione Borghese, for his own gallery,
allegedly because it was too shocking as an altarpiece.

ALTARPIECES BETWEEN ROME AND NAPLES

A fluted column stands on the left, disconnected from any other architectural features and suggesting an asymmetric niche cut off by the right-hand edge of the painting. The red drapery wound around it is more conventional than that in the *Death of the Virgin* (page 566), and therefore considered by some not to be by the artist. Mary sits enthroned above four Dominicans, St. Dominic, St. Thomas Aquinas, St. Peter Martyr, and St. Vincent Ferrer. Three barefoot men in robes reminiscent of the Apostles, as well as a woman and a small child wearing a thick diaper, crowd toward them from the foreground. A respectable gentleman, wearing a black robe with a crimped, white ruff-collar, kneels between the two groups to hold St. Dominic's habit.

According to recent findings, although the painting first surfaced in 1607 in Naples, it was originally from Rome. Acquired by Rubens and other Antwerp artists for the Painters' Chapel in St. Paul's in the same city, it had a greater influence on painting north of the Alps than any other work by Caravaggio.

Early biographies regarded the rejection of Caravaggio's commissioned altar paintings by ecclesiastical authorities as ground for characterizing the painter as a failed artist. However, these paintings were by no means thrown away, but integrated into galleries, where they attracted anything but contempt and were generally more appreciated than they were in an ecclesiastical setting. Detached from their original purpose, most of them have lost their utilitarian value and have thereby been raised to the sphere of art that serves no other rationale than aesthetics.

Only one painting is here an exception; it is the *Madonna of the Rosary* (page 573), currently to be found in Vienna. Following a period of wandering for more than a century, it again found its place on an altar, that of the Painters' Chapel in St. Paul's in Antwerp. Until recently, the story was thought to run as follows: in 1607, Caravaggio was in Naples, Ottavio Gentili and the Bruges painter Frans Pourbus II (1569–1622) sent the Gonzaga in Mantua a report from the city that a rosary painting by Caravaggio could be had for 400 ducats. Ten years later, in 1617, we learn from the testament of the Antwerp painter Louis Finson (before 1580–1617) that he had bought the work in Naples. Finson later offered the picture for sale from Amsterdam; it was acquired from his estate by Rubens, Jan Brueghel, Van Balen, and other painters of the Flemish commercial metropolis, with the intent of presenting it to the Dominicans of St. Paul in Antwerp. Displayed there from 1619 onward, the work was then acquired by Joseph II in 1781 and transported to Vienna in 1786.

This seems to confirm its Naples origin; however, examination of the painting's style in Vienna have provided certainty that this picture was by no means painted during the artist's first stay in Naples, but rather while he was still in Rome, at roughly the same time as the *Death of the Virgin* (pages 566, 567). Whereby the dissimilarity with the *Madonna di Loreto* (page 571) in Sant'Agostino in Rome is conceivably great and abrupt. It is made even greater by one thing they have in common—both paintings feature simply dressed people with dusty feet kneeling in devotion. The smooth style of the three kneeling men differs

clearly from the rough, earthy manner in which the pilgrims of the *Madonna di Loreto* are featured. The difference in Madonna style is even harsher; the wonderful model of his *Madonna in Sant'Agostino* could not be used by the artist in this case. Whereas the social distinction between the Mother of God and the simple pilgrims practically shrinks to no more than the single step separating them, the *Madonna of the Rosary* emphasizes the function of the Church and its wealthy benefactors in the hierarchy of god and man. Mary is enthroned above the powerful Dominican Order. Its saints force even the respectable gentleman who has made the painting possible to his knees; and it is not the Madonna's protective cloak that he is allowed to open, but that of the order's founder.

Now, in the light of such a multi-level hierarchy, it could be thought that the purpose of the picture lies in depicting ordinary people as subordinate to the Dominicans, who surround the enthroned majesty like ministers and advisors. But that nameless poor people practically push the commissioner of the work to the margin was by no means customary.

Here the painter reveals himself to be the same artist who painted the *Madonna di Loreto*; and this may be the reason why this painting, undoubtedly painted on commission, was initially refused its place on the altar. Although the Dominicans and the commissioner failed to grasp even a little of what Caravaggio has created, artists and art agents have obviously sensed the incredible qualities to be found in the work: the picture is opened by the mother and child on the bottom left, with only the mother allowed to look up to the Madonna, her son observing the three men coming from the right in a classical staggered depiction of the three ages of man. The older two fully dressed and the youth naked under a sheet, all three raise their arms to receive rosaries from the hand of St. Dominic, the founder of the order. The sole depiction of a donor in a painting by Caravaggio is given a key function: the gentlemen on the viewer's far left reassures himself with a glance over his shoulder. He is opening the saint's protective cloak for the common people, and is pushed aside by their impetuous piety in the process.

On the left, the hands of the Dominican form an imaginary horizontal boundary between the standing figures of the saints and the kneeling common people, among whom the figure of the respectable donor can be found. St. Dominic can be identified only by his prominent position in the picture and the legend of the Mother of God's command to the order's founder to spread devotion to the rosary. His appearance in profile corresponds to the magnificent *en face* figure on the right; the only person in this area of the picture to gaze in the direction of the viewer, he is pointing to the figures of Christ and Mary. It is intended to be St. Thomas Aquinas, behind whom the heads of St. Peter Martyr and St. Vincent Ferrer appear.

The Christ Child is standing in Mary's lap in a way that emphasizes his origin from his mother's body. While Mary is busy urging the founder of the order to distribute the rosaries to the poor, Christ embraces her shoulder, touches his belly in a moving gesture, playfully crosses his legs, and looks toward the viewer with a candid gaze; so that the immediacy with which Caravaggio otherwise shaped whole monumental paintings appears least in this geometrically defined center of the picture.

Even without the recent findings of restorers, the firm round forms should have opened the eyes of experts to the fact that the Viennese canvas does not yet possess the roughness of the Neapolitan works. Apart from the doubtlessly incomplete traditional provenance that begins in Naples, the preconception that stricter attention would have been paid to the orthodoxy of such paintings in Rome possibly also contributed to the view that the city could not be the place where this perfectly fitting Madonna for a mendicant order was painted. How the work came to Naples remains obscure. That Caravaggio himself traveled with paintings is shown by the situation after his death, when three works were found in his baggage; but they were most definitely not of the same grand size as the *Madonna of the Rosary*, which measures more than 2.5 meters wide (over 8 feet) when rolled up.

Without the apparent evidence of written sources, Naples would probably never have been considered as the work's point of origin; the only other work of similar monumentality created there is very different in appearance: Caravaggio painted the *Seven Acts of Mercy* (page 575) for the church of Pio Monte della Misericordia. Pictorial tradition demanded a banal painting that grouped the Seven Acts of Mercy around the Mother of God, preferably in separate medallions. Caravaggio, however, attempted to unite eight incompatible subjects in one collective event, in this his most unusual painting. There is no room left for Mary on the ground; therefore she descends from heaven to check that the works of mercy are actually being performed. No one below notices her, for each is diligently occupied with a task intended to express a work of mercy. Even so, Mary and the Christ Child are well shielded from view should anyone have the time to glance heavenward; for they are hovering above a pair of angels, embraced in a swirling descent, with symmetrically beating wings and lengths of opulent cloth.

From the heterogeneous concept of a Madonna with the Seven Acts of Mercy, the artist has developed a pictorial unity beyond conventional imagination: Samson from the Old Testament is quenching his thirst with the jawbone of an ass; to the left, Christ's Apostle St. James the Elder and the early Christian saint Martin of Tours encounter three unnamed figures: an innkeeper is showing the pilgrim James the way to a hostelry; in front of him cowers a nameless man, understood to be a sick person, who is lying on the ground, as is the half-naked figure in front of him, with whom St. Martin is sharing his cloak.

The figure of the beggar's back opens the composition in late-Mannerist style. On the right, a young woman appears before a window to nurse an imprisoned old man with milk from her breast—a motif known as Caritas Romana. A priest with a torch in his hand is consecrating a corpse whose legs are sticking out from around the corner of this prison building. In this, the folds of the Caritas Romana's dress, the shroud, and the priest's robes fall so closely together that there is no room for a rationalization of the space.

Exactly which acts of mercy are portrayed here cannot be deduced at first sight: the innkeeper is giving the Apostle shelter; Samson is given something to drink through a miracle, and not human help; St. Martin clothes the poor; a deceased person is receiving a burial; Caritas is visiting the prisoner and feeding him. Should the cowering figure next to St. Martin's beggar represent the sick, then he is being left, trembling and unattended, on the ground.

Caravaggio
The Seven Acts of Mercy
Oil on canvas, 390 x 260 cm
Pio Monte della Misericordia, Naples

In this monumental painting of the Madonna and the Seven Acts of Mercy, Caravaggio does something unknown in the rest of his work: he brings an exceptionally large number of figures together in such a way that a dynamic quality replaces the usual dramatic element. The subject itself is timeless, as we see from the nine figures below who come from different periods. Night is conveyed by chiaroscuro, even though some of the action must have happened in the daytime. Here, however, we see a torch burning, whereas Caravaggio normally never depicted light sources.

The painting technique of this work, definitely painted in Naples, differs decisively from the style of the *Madonna of the Rosary* (page 573), previously thought to have been done at the same time.

Caravaggio returns to the spirit of the *Madonna di Loreto* (page 571) with his movingly beautiful *Flagellation of Christ* (page 577) from San Lorenzo in Naples. Although time and again experts would like to believe they have discovered mannerist reminiscences in, of all works, this large altarpiece, none of the cited works come close to it. The sentiment of the *Madonna di Loreto* (page 571) is echoed most of all in the tilt of the head. In front of the altar, one has to imagine the devoted believers of the picture in Sant'Agostino addressed their prayers to Christ's face, although it is turned away in pain.

The *Crucifixion of St. Andrew* in the Cleveland Museum of Arts (page 576) is associated with a commission from the Spanish viceroy Benavente, who is said to have taken the painting home from Naples. In glaring contrast to the complex structure and extraordinary three-dimensionality of the *Flagellation of Christ* in the Museo Nazionale di Capodimonte in Naples (page 577), the martyrdom of the Apostle offers only a meager relief, rashly painted and disturbed by colors; so much so that Caravaggio's tendency to reduce almost completely the rich coloring in better paintings to sandy tones on a black background becomes understandable. The identity of the martyr is revealed by the X-shaped cross of St. Andrew, although the authenticity of this form of cross was challenged in Caravaggio's time by Cardinal Baronio, among others.

Caravaggio
The Crucifixion of St. Andrew
Oil on canvas, 202.5 x 152.7 cm
The Cleveland Museum of Art, Cleveland

Caravaggio positions the cross at a slight angle to the pictorial surface. From the left an old woman peers upwards, whilst a half-naked executioner's assistant, on a ladder, is untying the Apostle's right hand. He was ordered to do so by a captain in full armor, who is watching the proceedings with rapt attention. Like him, two other figures are watching what is happening. Whilst one of them is obscured by the captain, the other expresses great astonishment.

The Apostle hangs from the T-shaped cross usually associated with Christ, his legs crossed. According to legend, the old man remained alive for days in order to preach to the spectators; the henchman who was supposed to remove him from the cross was prevented from doing so by a sudden paralysis. This episode provided Caravaggio with his theme.

Opposite page:
Caravaggio
The Flagellation of Christ, 1607
Oil on canvas, 286 x 213 cm
Museo Nazionale di Capodimonte, Naples, on loan from the Dominicans of San Lorenzo

As with the *Crucifixion of St. Peter* (page 559), a kneeling figure on the left, cut off by the edge of the frame, leads the eye into the picture. Only as he presses forward does he turn his face towards the main figure, still tying a bundle of brushwood on the ground. A rough-looking character is already beating Christ, punching his neck at the same time, whilst the man on the right tightens his bonds. Christ, who is shown unusually plump and soft, moves his body helplessly towards the left, whilst his head is knocked to the right.

ON THE RUN IN MALTA AND SICILY

SIGNED WITH THE BLOOD OF THE BAPTIST: THE GREAT WORK IN MALTA

Caravaggio distinguished himself from most other Baroque painters by not making a sharp distinction between the genres of altarpiece and narrative painting.

An altarpiece for Malta has not survived. But there is a narrative picture that can attract devout attention; it is the artist's largest work (left).

The picture's laconic layout places both victim and murderers so center stage that, although the story gets told, pious worshippers, when they see the slain Baptist humiliated and thrown to the ground, are left in no doubt about what they are worshipping. That said, they must lower their eyes just as the people in the picture do. Although the living figures are so preoccupied with the pictorial action that the viewer cannot make any contact with their eyes, the face of St. John, still and relaxed in death, offers itself to meditation, with eyes which, although now blind, are free from pain.

This great work by the artist on the island of Malta was such an attraction that Joachim von Sandrart sailed there simply to see it. It is totally characteristic of Caravaggio's style of painting, which achieved its effects less through individual pictures than through the method the artist employed.

Caravaggio's hasty flight from prison in Malta took the artist to Sicily, where he painted a few more important pictures at great speed. The first one he completed was a rough altarpiece, one of the most intriguing works of European painting, which is still in the place for which it was intended, the church of Santa Lucia, Syracuse. Two pictures that almost equal Caravaggio's great Roman works in their inventive power have survived in Messina. Until 1969 Palermo also owned an altarpiece by Caravaggio, which has disappeared after a theft.

Bad colors, over-hasty execution, and possibly also artist's depression characterize the altarpiece in which St. Lucy suffered martyrdom (page 580). The poetry which is so markedly absent from the austere *Burial of St. Lucy* re-established itself in the other works which Caravaggio painted for Sicily. In these, allusions to earlier paintings

Caravaggio
The Beheading of St. John the Baptist, 1608
Oil on canvas, 361 x 520 cm
Museum of St. John's, Valletta, Malta

A weakly lit, sturdy barred gate, with the top of its arch cut off, appears just behind a frieze of life-size figures on the left. On the right, a barred window interrupts the line of the wall. Through it, two prisoners are watching what is happening on the left. With her sleeves rolled up, more like Judith than a lascivious dancer, Salome bends down to receive the head of John the Baptist on a large golden dish. Beside her, her maid is holding her head in silent horror, whilst looking down at the gleaming executioner's sword. It is lying near a man who has ordered the beheading. Sturdy, and seeming much larger than the three other figures, the half-naked executioner is bending over the Baptist's corpse. Whilst gripping his hair in his left hand, with his right hand he reaches for a short dagger in his belt, as if he needed this to help cut the head from the body. The Baptist, already beheaded, lies in a pool of his own blood, which pours out in diagonal spurts towards the right. In this blood, Caravaggio has signed his name on the floor. This is his only noticeable signature anywhere, limited to the letters *f michela*, which stand for *fecit* (or *frater*) *Michelangelus*. One interpretation of this would be that Michelangelo had created the picture. The other, however, would denote the artist as a Knight of Malta.

Following pages, left:
Caravaggio
The Burial of St. Lucy, 1608
Oil on canvas, 408 x 300 cm
Santa Lucia, Syracuse, stored in the Museum

The saint, who in Sweden is celebrated with a crown of lights before Christmas because she sacrificed her eyes in her martyrdom, is lying in dismal darkness on the bare floor of a bleak vault. She is being confirmed by a bishop and mourned by pious worshippers. Her dark eye sockets are allusions to her martyrdom. Only after several false starts, revealed by X-ray photographs, did Caravaggio decide on the exact form of her death, on which his contemporaries failed to agree. The artist eventually agreed with Cardinal Baronio's opinion that St. Lucy's throat was cut. Her dress is disordered, torn away from her shoulder to her breast.

Following pages, right:
Caravaggio
The Raising of Lazarus, 1609
Oil on canvas, 380 x 275 cm
Museo Regionale, Messina

Night, with light penetrating it, becomes a metaphor for death and resurrection through Christ, even though he himself gives off no light. On the right, level with Christ, and graduated like the helpers, the dead man's sisters, Mary Magdalene and Martha, appear. Even if, in this scene, they are normally shown asking Christ to raise their brother from the dead, here they are bending down towards the dead man's head in a gesture of lamentation.

Caravaggio
The Adoration of the Shepherds, 1609
Oil on canvas, 314 x 211 cm
Museo Regionale, Messina

At an astonishing distance from the viewer, and with a foreground which is filled in by a still-life of heaped-up implements on the left and a stone lying on the ground on the right, Mary is stretched out on straw, leaning against the wall of a crib for oxen and asses, holding her child tightly in her arms, without looking up towards the shepherds. They are pressing forward on the right behind Joseph, who is sitting watching mother and child.

Opposite page:
Caravaggio
The Nativity with St. Francis and St. Lawrence, 1609
Oil on canvas, 268 x 197 cm
San Lorenzo, Palermo, until 1969

Under the roof of the stable in Bethlehem, whose side walls are disappearing into a brownish darkness, shepherds and saints have gathered to worship the newborn Christ Child in such a way that we can make out Archdeacon Lawrence on the left only after a second look, and viewers may well mistake St. Francis for a shepherd. One figure, the patron, represents the church for which the picture was intended, and the other, the Order to which the church belonged. We cannot be entirely sure who Joseph, the foster father, is. As in the *Adoration of the Shepherds* in Messina (left), art literature has claimed to recognize him as the foreground figure seen from the back. This is true insofar as this man has sat down, which is not appropriate for shepherds. But where would Joseph have acquired a coiffure like that, and, despite his gray hair, how could he look so young? The center of the picture is shared out between the figures who have come to worship. The naked Christ Child lies there on a bed of straw and some white drapery. In his laterally inverted foreshortening, this figure is not totally unlike St. Paul in the Cerasi Chapel picture (page 556). Exhausted, the Holy Virgin is crouching on the ground behind him—wearing an unusually cut dress, which is falling from her right shoulder—looking at the child. The ox, which appears behind St. Lawrence, is also looking in that direction. Above all this, an angel is flying down from heaven. In his left hand he is holding a banner on which the words of the *Gloria* are written. His right hand is pointing upwards, as if, by also looking at the baby, he wanted to reassure the Christ Child that he really is the Son of God.

Caravaggio
The Annunciation, 1610 (?)
Oil on canvas, 285 x 205 cm
Musée des Beaux-Arts, Nancy

Caravaggio's figures are so self-absorbed, so much a part of the scene in which they find themselves, that even pious worshippers must, as it were, stand before the pictures in silence and without being noticed. This is the last monumental painting that is now regarded as being the artist's original work. The Madonna is kneeling humbly on the floor. From the left, on a cloud that looks solid enough to bear his weight, the angel descends, his wings still out-spread. He has turned away from the viewer towards the future Mother of God. A lily stalk appears in the center of the picture, as if this symbol of the Holy Virgin's purity were its most important object.

in Rome merged with echoes of older paintings. The pathos of the *Calling of St. Matthew* (page 552) lives on in the *Resurrection of Lazarus* (page 581). In this picture, Christ comes in, with the light from the left, so that the illumination of the gloomy scene and the entry of the divine element are well coordinated. The artist's geometric instinct leaves the outstretched hand of Lazarus isolated in the center of the figure composition. Morning light bathes the hand, a symbol of life returning. In a similar fashion, Caravaggio had filled the hand of the Apostle in the *Martyrdom of St. Matthew* (page 553) with heavenly promise, and structured St. Paul's fingers in his Conversion (page 556).

In the breathtakingly beautiful scene of the *Adoration of the Shepherds* in Messina (page 582), Caravaggio once again moves his figures dramatically against the usual direction of reading. In contrast to his normal method, he depicts the interior of the stable at Bethlehem in the Venetian manner, as if he wanted to prove his biographers right when they claimed Giorgione as a major influence. That said, he comes closer to later Venetian painters like Jacopo Bassano (1510/18–1592) and Correggio (1489/94–1534), the Upper Italian painter no longer connected with the city on the lagoon, especially his *Holy Night* in Dresden (page 417).

In the *Adoration of the Shepherds* in Messina, the figures bunch so closely together that an atmosphere of poetic intensity and veneration results, which may spill over on to the viewers, and make them also want to pray. In the *Nativity with St. Francis and St. Lawrence*, which Caravaggio painted for Palermo (page 583), we see again the form of Christian altarpiece which combines Mary and the Christ Child with saints of various epochs in the form of a *sacra conversazione*. The way the saints are ranked in order concentrates reverence on the Holy Virgin. The light also helps to make her, rather than her child, the center of the picture.

The paintings from Malta and Sicily are extremely well suited to embellishing an artist's life with romantic allusions. The large prison panorama makes us think of Caravaggio languishing in a Maltese jail. The *Burial in Syracuse* strikes us as being the absolute nadir of a brilliant career. That said, the picture of Lazarus shows new hope burgeoning—hope which will lead on to the exquisite Nativity scenes with the Shepherds in Messina and Palermo.

A LAST GREAT ALTARPIECE

There is still very little information about how Caravaggio spent his years after he had fled from Malta and Sicily. His spectacular fame as an artist, which had reached well beyond Rome by about 1600, must have been a heavy burden to him, when we consider that he was being pursued by the papal authorities and the Knights of Malta. Despite his frequent moves, however, Caravaggio was still receiving commissions from all over Europe.

An enigmatic painting in Nancy, which scholars have never fully addressed, was supposedly painted in 1609 in Rome by someone called Michelangelo (page 585). Even if scholars thought mistakenly that it was painted by Michelangelo Buonarroti (1475–1564), the information can be taken as a valuable source. So much speaks for Michelangelo da Caravaggio that, after restoration work in the early 1970s, the painting seems more and more to be his work. A gift to the future Cathedral of Nancy by Henri, Duke of Lorraine (in office 1608–1624), the painting might have been commissioned through the Gonzaga. Judging by its style, it dates from Caravaggio's last stay in Naples.

What is surprising about the not very well preserved painting at the Museum in Nancy is that Caravaggio suddenly introduced interior set pieces into the picture. Admittedly, they are in the background, but they are painted with great care, and are fully visible. The still-life of a basket and the piece of fabric distances the figure-relief a little. The same effect is achieved in the similarly lit *Adoration of the Shepherds* in Messina (page 582).

Perspectives of this kind opening up in Caravaggio's last paintings make us ask a question. How much further would this artist have taken European painting if he had not met an undignified and premature death in Porto Ercole after more brawling? His art may have degenerated into Mannerism. By the time he worked in Syracuse, his brilliant originality had deteriorated into a coarsened form of expressive painting. On the other hand, two completely new directions are suggested by the *Adoration of the Shepherds* and the *Annunciation* in Nancy. In the *Nativity* for Palermo (page 583), Caravaggio had proved how intensely he could paint the slightly unreal presence of different saints during Holy Night. In the other two pictures, he again altered his conception of space and figure very radically, as if he wished to re-organize his figures and their accessories in a completely different way.

EPILOGUE

Caravaggio
David with the Head of Goliath, ca. 1605
Oil on poplar, 90.5 x 116.5 cm
Kunsthistorisches Museum, Vienna

This version of David with the head of Goliath stands out from Caravaggio's half-length biblical paintings. Instead of an historical event, this picture offers a simple presentation of the youthful victor with his enemy's chopped-off head. Unlike in other paintings, the lighting from the left matches the movement towards the right. With shouldered sword, the young man looks out into the darkness. He looks more determined than the Borghese *David* (page 491) and expresses more deeply felt emotion. His eyes, however, are suffused by the melancholy that, in Caravaggio's paintings, sometimes affects not only the victors but also the executioners. This picture of David is painted over a Flemish or Roman depiction of Mars and Venus from the Mannerist period.

A study of an artist either gives an account of its hero's life in its various stages or orients itself to older predecessors that understand individual works as testimony of an exploration of the tasks which art sets itself.

To the irritation of many readers, this account may have helped bury the chronology of Caravaggio's life and work beneath an overall concept that has seen the artist grow with his projects. The starting point was Caravaggio's conflicted personality. It expressed itself in a life that often reads more like a police report. Yet a highly unusual character also spoke from the pictures themselves, and this has provided the impetus to go in search of self-portraits of the artist. There is a striking contrast between Caravaggio's life and work. The quick-tempered character who was always getting involved in fights, and who stylized himself into *Sick Bacchus* (page 494) or the hacked-off head of the giant, Goliath (page 491), also created paintings of human profundity and tenderness which completely redefined painting. Basing his art on the fundamental principle of painting direct from nature, to which no special feeling for the genre of portrait corresponded, the artist rebelled against the values of the great art of Rome. If at all, Caravaggio only once attempted the most distinguished monumental work available to an artist then: fresco painting. He rejected the idea of painting historical pictures out of his own imagination.

This is why it seemed appropriate to understand his work in terms of different genres, even if contemporary art theory still has no categories for them.

Anyone who makes painting as an act of reproducing into the guiding principle of his art will regard a still-life as equal to the depiction of a human being. Caravaggio constructed his early pictures out of still-lifes and models. He quickly grasped that landscape is not a field in which he could prove himself. With his very highly developed tactile sense, he explored the human body and became one of the greatest painters of the nude in the history of art. He attempted genre painting direct from life and with full-length figures in only a few pictures. Yet, along with his sole authentic still-life, he turned these into groundbreaking pioneer works of revolutionary impact. An even more important step was his radical decision to subjugate biblical history painting to the principles of portrait and genre painting. Transformed into monumental paintings in a public church context, Caravaggio's redefinition of art met strong resistance. More than once, he was obliged to withdraw a first version, in order to fulfill the wishes of his patron, even though the circle of his patrons included the most progressive minds in Rome. With their support, Caravaggio also opened up new markets for painting. Half-length and full-length biblical history-paintings immediately found a place in royal galleries—as did an advanced altarpiece that the Church authorities rejected. After Caravaggio, whole generations of painters were to earn their living by means of similar projects.

All the works which present-day scholars regard as original Caravaggios would fit into such a concept. Though this does not apply strictly to the Borghese *David* (page 491), which was discussed at the start of this book. Nor does it apply to another picture of the Old Testament hero, which now hangs in the Kunsthistorisches Museum, Vienna (page 587).

It would surely be artificial to include both paintings, as a kind of ideal portrait, with the early Roman works, which, constructed out of still-life and painting direct from a model, stand somewhere between mythology and genre pictures.

An artist who flouts all the conventions of his age cannot be properly classified into any conceptual system. This makes any exploration of Michelangelo Merisi da Caravaggio as fascinating for scholars as it still is for countless art-lovers, who may keep recognizing traces of their own human nature in his coldly calculated paintings.

Eberhard König

Sebastiano del Piombo
The Raising of Lazarus, ca. 1517–1519
Oil on wood, transferred to canvas, 381 x 287 cm
National Gallery, London

BIOGRAPHIES

Altichiero da Zevio

ca. 1330 Altichiero is born in Zevio near Verona. He trains and first matures as an artist in Verona, and is considered the founder of the Veronese School.

1370 Fresco with the Cavalli family in adoration of the Virgin Mary (Sant'Anastasia, Verona).

1376–1379 Frescoes in the Chapel of St. James in the Santo, Padua, commissioned by Bonifacio Lupi.

1377 Construction of the Oratorio di San Giorgio near Santo, Padua, as a burial chapel for Raimondino Lupi, Marquis of Soranzo.

1378 Painting of the Oratorio di San Giorgio with the legends of St. George, St. Lucy (Lucia), scenes from the story of Christ's childhood, and the Crucifixion above the altar (pages 42–44).

ca. 1390 Altichiero dies in Padua.

The relationship to Jacopo d'Avanzo, for whom there is also documentary evidence of activity in Padua alongside Altichiero da Zevio, depends on the chronological assessment of Avanzo's life and work: it is possible that he is identical to a painter who died in 1376 in Bologna; but he could also be a younger master who was active into the early 15th century, in which case the progressive frescoes on the interior façade wall of the Oratorio di San Giorgio, as well as other works, could be assigned to him (page 45).

Antonello da Messina

ca. 1430 Antonello da Messina is born the son of a stonemason in the Sicilian port of Messina.

early 1450s, or a little earlier, Antonello receives his training as an artist, probably in Naples in the workshop of Niccolò Colantonio (active around 1440–1470). In Naples, Antonello also becomes acquainted with the Early Netherlandish masters (works by Jan van Eyck and Rogier van der Weyden), who are particularly esteemed at the royal court. It is possible that he even travels to the Netherlands himself to continue his training.

ca. 1450–1453 One of his earliest known paintings is created: a small crucifixion panel that can be found today in Bucharest.

1457 First record of Antonello in his home city of Messina, where he is already running his own workshop. In the same year, the Brotherhood of San Michele dei Gerbini in Reggio Calabria commissions him to paint a procession banner. However, no such work by Antonello has survived.

late 1450s Antonello appears to live with his family on the mainland in Calabria for some time and possibly travels to Rome.

1461 Antonello is living in Messina again. His brother Giordano di Giovanni begins an apprenticeship with him. Various paintings documented as belonging to the following years have either not survived or are only available as fragments, such as *Abraham and Three Angels* (Museo Nazionale, Reggio di Calabria).

1465 The oldest signed and dated painting by Antonello depicts Christ behind a parapet, giving a blessing and turned to fully face the viewer. Around the same period, the *Maria Annunziata* (Museo Civico, Como) and *Madonna and Child* (National Gallery, London) attributed to Antonello are also painted.

1474 Antonello paints the signed and dated *Portrait of a Young Man* with its dark background (Gemäldegalerie, Berlin).

ca. 1474 One of Antonello's most significant works is commissioned by an unknown client: *St. Jerome in His Study* (Volume I, page 28).

1475/76 Antonello travels to Venice. Apart from the large *sacra conversazione* for San Cassiano (Kunsthistorisches Museum, Vienna), of which only fragments remain, he also paints two small crucifixion panels (page 132).

ca. 1476/77 Most likely shortly after his return to his Sicilian homeland, Antonello paints a *Pietà* (page 133)—probably with the participation of his son, Jacobello.

1478 The signed and dated *Portrait of a Young Man* captured in front of a landscape background (page 9) and *St. Sebastian* (page 131) are painted in Messina.

1479 Antonello da Messina dies in his home city of Messina. Several of his small-format pictures will be copied as icons, particularly by Antonio di Saliba (ca. 1466/67–1535).

Fra Bartolomeo

1472 Fra Bartolomeo (real name: Bartolomeo or Baccio della Porta) is born in Florence the son of a muleteer and carter.

from 1478 The family lives near the Porta San Pier Gattolini, the present-day Porta Romana, at the southeastern end of the Boboli Gardens (hence the name "della Porta").

1485 Apprenticeship with Cosimo Rosselli (1439–1507) and Piero di Cosimo (1461/62–1521).

mid-1490s The penitential sermons of the Dominican monk Girolamo Savonarola cause a religious crisis among many Florentine painters. And so Bartolomeo della Porta also burns many of his earlier profane paintings and drawings on the "Bonfire of the Vanities."

1497 Created in cooperation with Mariotto Albertinelli (1474–1515), another painter also trained in the Rosselli workshop, his first dated painting: the *Annunciation* in the cathedral at Volterra.

ca. 1498 Bartolomeo paints for Piero del Pugliese two small panels depicting the Annunciation (page 274), the Birth of Christ, as well as the Presentation in the Temple, which originally served to flank or frame a (now lost) Madonna relief by Donatello (Galleria degli Uffizi, Florence). At roughly the same time, he creates the *Madonna and Child with the Infant St. John the Baptist* (The Metropolitan Museum of Art, New York), inspired by Leonardo da Vinci; and the equally Leonardesque tondo the *Adoration of the Child* (Galleria Borghese, Rome).

1499 Commission for a monumental fresco the *Last Judgment* for a burial chapel in Santa Maria Nuova (today in the Museo di San Marco, Florence).

1500 He receives his initial consecration as a Dominican friar in San Domenico in Prato and enters the Florentine cloister of San Marco shortly afterwards. According to Vasari, he is not thought to have painted during the years that immediately followed.

1503 Mariotto Albertinelli finishes the *Visitation* (page 275) probably begun by Fra Bartolomeo around 1500.

ca. 1504 and 1507, paints the *Vision of St. Bernard* (Volume I, page 550), probably the first work after overcoming his crisis of belief, for the family chapel of Bernardo del Bianco in Badia.

1507 Altarpiece with the *Assumption* (formerly Kaiser-Friedrich-Museum, Berlin, lost during wartime).

1508 Journey to Venice. Altarpiece for the Murano Dominicans, God the Father with St. Mary Magdalene and St. Catherine of Siena, that never reached its intended destination, the church of San Pietro Martire. Sante Pagnini acquired it in 1513 for the San Romano church in Lucca (today in the Villa Guinigi).

1509 *Madonna and Child with John the Baptist and St. Stephen* in the cathedral at Lucca.

1510 Together with Mariotto Albertinelli, Fra Bartolomeo paints the *Madonna and Child with St. Catherine, St. Mary Magdalene, John the Baptist, St. Nicholas, St. Peter Martyr, and St. Benedict* for Piero Cambi's chapel in San Marco. A commission from the Signoria for the altarpiece of the Sala del Consiglio Maggiore in the Palazzo Vecchio (unfinished): *Madonna and Child with St. Anne and the Patron Saints of Florence* (page 273).

1511 The *Mystic Marriage of St. Catherine of Siena*, painted for San Marco, is acquired by the Signoria shortly afterwards and sent to France (Musée du Louvre, Paris) as a gift for Bishop Jacques Hurault, the French ambassador; Fra Bartolomeo therefore produces a second version the following year (Gallerie dell'Accademia, Florence).

1513 Fra Bartolomeo travels to Rome, possibly on the occasion of the election of the Medici pope, Leo X. There he paints *St. Paul and St. Peter* (Rome, Vatican, Musei Vaticani) for the prior of San Silvestro, Mariano Fetti; the painting remained unfinished when the painter became ill and returned to Florence.

1514 Three Madonna frescoes are painted for the hospice of Santa Maria Maddalena near Florence with the help of two assistants.

1515 *Madonna of Mercy* for the church of San Romano in Lucca (Villa Guinigi, Lucca); for San Marco in Florence two monumental choir frescoes with St. Mark and St. Sebastian, the nakedness of whom is said by Vasari to have irritated some female visitors to the church.

1517 Fra Bartolomeo dies in his home city of Florence.

Jacopo Bassano

1510 Jacopo Bassano (real name: Jacopo del Ponte) is born in Bassano del Grappa in the Veneto. As the son of a family of painters he initially receives his training as an artist in his father Francesco's workshop.

Early 1530s after completing his basic training, the young painter begins an apprenticeship in Venice with Bonifacio de' Pitati (1487–1553) and will afterwards often return to the lagoon city.

1534 Paints *Rest on the Flight to Egypt* (Museo Civico, Bassano del Grappa)—a repeated theme of the painter. Is still clearly influenced by his Venetian tutor, but now also by Titian.

1539 Following the death of his father, Jacopo takes over the running of the family business. Primarily altarpieces for churches in the area around Bassano del Grappa are painted in the years that follow. Many of his paintings—especially the diverse variations of the *Adoration of the Shepherds*—are enlivened by depictions of animals that lend the works a pastoral and sometimes genre character.

1548 Bassano is commissioned by the Venetian Antonio Zentani to paint *due brachi, cioè cani solo* ("two hunting dogs, that is, only dogs"), an extremely unusual commission for the time (page 424) the painting is not given any symbolic or allegorical significance. It is in fact one of the earliest genre works painted in Italy.

mid-1550s Elegant works are painted containing over-length figures that bear witness to the painter's preoccupation with the works of the Mannerist Parmigianino; for example the *Adoration of the Magi* (Kunsthistorisches Museum, Vienna) and *Susanna and the Elders* (National Gallery, Ottawa). At the same time, the "pastoral" elements in Bassano's works become more and more prominent.

1562/63 A new creative phase in the artist's painting emerges with works such as the *Crucifixion* (Museo Civico, Treviso) and *Thamar Being Led to the Stake* (Kunsthistorisches Museum, Vienna), in which he increasingly departs from Mannerism and embarks on a more "classical" path.

late 1560s and 1570s Jacopo Bassano now cooperates more closely with his sons, especially Francesco.

late 1570s The extremely productive Bassano workshop increasingly produces medium-sized paintings in which biblical themes are placed in genre settings (kitchen or court scenes).

1580s Jacopo primarily paints small devotional or collectors' works (especially dramatically lighted Passion scenes).

1592 Jacopo Bassano dies in Bassano del Grappa.

Bellini, Giovanni

ca. 1430 Giovanni Bellini, the second son of the painter Jacopo Bellini, is born in Venice, where he is to reside his entire life. Together with his one-year-older brother, Gentile (1429–1507), he receives his training in the father's workshop. He is later artistically influenced primarily by Andrea Mantegna, his brother-in-law of the same age, as well as by Antonello da Messina.

ca. 1455–1460 *Transfiguration*, possibly one of the side panels of the silver shrine on the high altar of San Salvatore (page 134).

1459 Giovanni is living in a house of his own near San Lio (not far from the Rialto Bridge) and appears in records for the first time. During this period he is mainly painting small pictures, mostly intended for private religious devotion (Madonna and *Pietà* depictions).

1460s He is still often working together with his father and brother, for example on a no-longer-existing series of paintings for the Scuola Grande di San Giovanni Evangelista (scenes from the life of Christ and the Virgin Mary) completed in 1465.

ca. 1464–1468 His first commission of his own: the *Polyptych of St. Vincent Ferrer* for the Dominican church of Santi Giovanni e Paolo (Zanipolo), Venice.

ca. 1465–1470 *Christ on the Mount of Olives* (page 25) is painted closely following a painting on the same theme by Andrea Mantegna (page 24).

ca. 1470 *Pietà* (page 136). Giovanni Bellini advances in the years that follow to become the leading Venetian painter of altar and devotional paintings, creating such works as *St. Francis in Ecstasy* (page 143).

ca. 1473 The only longer journey undertaken by the painter takes him to the Adriatic port city of Pesaro (the Marches), where he paints the large *Coronation of the Virgin Mary* (page 138) for the main altar of San Francesco as well as the *Pietà* (page 137) that tops it.

1474 The oldest of his relatively few portraits is painted (*Jörg Fugger*, Norton Simon Museum, Pasadena, CA).

late 1470s Bellini paints his earliest *sacra conversazione* in upright format with crowning coffered vault for the church of San Giobbe: the *San Giobbe Altarpiece* (page 140).

1479 Commission for paintings of historical events for the Doge's Palace. The paintings are carried out over a period of many years and with the help of numerous assistants (also including Vittore Carpaccio for a brief period). Destroyed by the great fire of 1577.

ca. 1480–1485 *Transfiguration* for the family chapel of Archdeacon Alberto Fioccardo in the cathedral at Vicenza (page 135).

1488 *Madonna and Child Enthroned, with Angels Playing Instruments, and Four Saints* for the vestry of the Franciscan church of Santa Maria Gloriosa dei Frari, commissioned by the Pesaro family (page 139).

ca. 1498 Titian comes to Venice and probably enters Bellini's workshop as an apprentice shortly afterwards.

ca. 1500–1505 The *Madonna with Sleeping Child* (*Madonna del Prato,* page 145) is painted for an unknown client.

ca. 1501–1504 Bellini's portrait of Doge Leonardo Loredan (Volume I, page 14).

1505 For the church of San Zaccaria, not far from the Doge's Palace and San Marco, he paints the *Madonna and Child Enthroned with Saints* (page 23) that can still be found there.

1513 Possibly with the participation of his pupil Titian, the already aged Bellini paints the *St. Jerome with St. Christopher and St. Augustine* (page 282).

1514 Paints the *Feast of the Gods* (National Gallery of Art, Washington) for Alfonso I of Ferrara—one of the painter's few mythological paintings.

1516 Giovanni Bellini dies in Venice.

Bellini, Jacopo

ca. 1400 Jacopo Bellini, father of Gentile and Giovanni Bellini, is born in Venice as the son of a pewter worker. He probably trains with Gentile da Fabriano, who is known to have resided in Venice between 1408 und 1413. Only fragments of his paintings have survived; the sketchbooks in the British Museum, London, and in the Musée du Louvre, Paris (page 49), form the most significant portfolios of his work.

1423 A certain "Jacopo Veneto" is mentioned in Florence as an assistant to Gentile da Fabriano. According to one legend, Jacopo Bellini allows himself to be beaten up for the master during an attack of Florentine painters on Gentile's workshop.

1424 Jacopo is known to be back in Venice.

1430 He signs a no-longer-existing altarpiece (*Archangel Michael Fighting a Dragon*) painted for San Michele in Padua.

1436 Jacopo paints a fresco with the Crucifixion (destroyed in 1759) in the Cappella di San Niccolò in the cathedral at Verona. According to Vasari, one of the figures under the Cross is a self-portrait of the artist.

1437 Becomes a member of the Scuola Grande di San Giovanni Evangelista, Venice.

1441 At the court of Ferrara, and in competition with Pisanello, Jacopo paints the portrait of Marquis Leonello d'Este (lost). His *Madonna and Child with a Member of the Este family* (page 52) dates from around the same period.

early 1440s *Annunciation* altarpiece and five predella panels depicting scenes from the life of Mary accredited to Jacopo that have survived intact (Sant'Alessandro, Brescia).

1448 The only dated painting of the master: *Madonna and Child* (Pinacoteca di Brera, Milan).

1453 Jacopo's daughter Nicolosia marries the painter Andrea Mantegna.

ca. 1455 A further Madonna panel, signed but not dated, has been preserved in the Galleria dell'Accademia di Belle Arti Tadini in Lovere (Province of Bergamo).

1465 Most comprehensive documented commission: a series of paintings on salvation for the Scuola di San Giovanni Evangelista, Venice.

1466 Two documented Passion scenes for the Scuola di San Marco (now lost).

1471/72 Jacopo Bellini dies in Venice.

Bordone, Paris

1500 Paris Bordone is born in Treviso, to the north of Venice.

1508 Moves to Venice after the death of his father.

ca. 1516 Apprenticeship with Titian, which he ends, however, after only two years.

1523 First signed and dated painting: *Portrait of a Bearded Man* (Alte Pinakothek, Munich).

ca. 1528–1530 The large *sacra conversazione* (including the two prominent saints of the plague, Roch and Sebastian) is painted for Santa Maria dei Battuti in Belluno (Gemäldegalerie, Berlin), probably in connection with the plague ravaging Venice at the time.

1530s Bordone paints the large-format painting *Christ in Limbo* (private collection) for Alvise Foscari.

1534 Bordone receives the prestigious commission to paint the *Presentation of the Ring to the Doge* for the Scuola Grande di San Marco (Gallerie dell'Accademia, Venice), a work that impresses most of all through its suggestive portrayal of architecture.

ca. 1538/39 The painter leaves Venice. According to Vasari, he goes to the court of French King Francis I at Fontainebleau, where he is mainly commissioned to paint numerous portraits. The painting *Jupiter and Io* in the Göteborg art museum and mentioned by Vasari possibly dates from this period.

ca. 1540 Bordone's return journey to the Veneto possibly takes him through southern Germany. In any case, his portrait of Thomas Stachel of Augsburg (Musée du Louvre, Paris) is dated to this time. Once again in his north Italian homeland, he paints an extensive cycle of frescoes in the church of Santa Croce in Pialdier (Province of Belluno).

1543 He is again living in Venice.

ca. 1549–1551 In Milan, he paints for courtier Carlo da Rhò *Mars and Venus Surprised by Vulcan* and *Bathsheba Bathing* (pages 426, 427), paintings probably conceived as counterparts.

mid-1550s Bordone's period in Augsburg is alternatively dated to this period. He paints a whole series of mythological themes for his clients there, who include the Fugger family.

ca. 1559 Whether the painter returns to the French king's court at Fontainebleau this year is today still a matter of debate.

1561 Bordone is working in the Ognissanti cloister in Treviso. Although the painter resides in Venice during his last years, he nevertheless primarily works for provincial clients, particularly in Treviso.

1571 Paris Bordone dies in Venice.

Bronzino, Agnolo

1503 Agnolo Bronzino (real name: Agnolo di Cosimo di Mariano) is born in Monticelli near Florence. Following a short apprenticeship with Raffaellino del Garbo (ca. 1466/70–1524), he enters Jacopo Pontormo's workshop, a painter with whom he would in later years repeatedly cooperate.

1523–1526 As Pontormo's assistant he participates in painting the frescoes at a Carthusian monastery located a few kilometers south of Florence at Galuzzo.

1526–1527 Bronzino paints two tondi for the Cappella Capponi in Santa Felicità, also decorated together with Pontormo.

1530/31 Bronzino participates in the painting of the Villa Imperiale of the Duke of Urbino in Pesaro (the Marches).

1532 Return to Florence, and a series of commissions for small altarpieces over the following years.

1535–1543 He decorates the Medici villas in Careggi and Castello with allegorical frescoes, once again in cooperation with Pontormo.

1539 Participates in painting the festive decorations for the marriage of Medici Grand Duke Cosimo I (1519–1574) with Eleonora of Toledo (1522–1562).

early 1540s Bronzino's career as court painter of the Medici begins with the painting of Eleonora of Toledo's private chapel in the Palazzo Vecchio and the first child portraits, as well as portraits of Florentine citizens among the Medici followers, such as Bartolomeo Panciatichi and his wife Lucrezia (pages 408, 409).

ca. 1540–1545 Commissioned by Cosimo I, he paints the enigmatic *Allegory of Love (Venus and Cupid)* (page 411) as well as the *Lamentation over the Dead Christ* as the altarpiece for the Grand Duchess' chapel (Musée des Beaux-Arts, Besançon).

mid-1540s The *Panciatichi Holy Family* (page 407); numerous drafts for tapestries.

1557/58 Following Pontormo's death, Bronzino finishes the frescoes the artist had begun in the choir of San Lorenzo: the *Deluge,* the *Resurrection of the Dead,* and the *Martyrdom of St. Lawrence* (destroyed in the 18th century).

1561 Altarpiece *Noli me tangere* for the Cappella Cavalcanti in Santo Spirito (Musée du Louvre, Paris) and *Deposition,* commissioned by Cosimo I for the Convento dei Zoccolanti on the island of Elba.

1563 Founding member of the Florentine Accademia del Disegno.

1565 Bronzino receives his last major commission by Cosimo I: in San Lorenzo he paints the large fresco the *Martyrdom of St. Lawrence.* That year he also participates in painting the festive decorations for the marriage of Francesco de' Medici with Johanna of Austria.

1571/72 The painter's final works include the *Raising of Jairus' Daughter* in the Florentine Dominican church of Santa Maria Novella, presumably painted with the participation of his pupil Alessandro Allori (1535–1607).

1572 Agnolo Bronzino dies in Florence.

Caravaggio

1571 Birth of Michelangelo Merisi da Caravaggio, the first child of Fermo Merisi and Lucia Aratori, probably toward the end of the year and presumably in Milan.

1576 Flight from the plague to Caravaggio.

1577 Death of his father, presumably of plague.

1584 Start of a four-year apprenticeship with the painter Simone Peterzano (1540–1596) in Milan.

1589–1592 The artist is living in Caravaggio.

1590 Death of his mother.

ca. 1592 Caravaggio is living in Rome and working in various workshops.

ca. 1593 He enters the workshop of the painter Giuseppe Cesare d'Arpino (1550–1640).

ca. 1595/96 He is admitted into the Palazzo Madama of Cardinal Del Monte.

1599 A contract is concluded in July for the painting of two historical scenes for the sidewalls of the Contarelli Chapel in San Luigi dei Francesi: the *Calling of St. Matthew* and the *Martyrdom of St. Matthew* (pages 552, 553).

1600 In September, a contract for two paintings for the chapel of Tiberio Cerasi in Santa Maria del Popolo (page 554).

ca. 1602/03 A commission for the altarpiece of the Girolamo Vittrice Chapel in the Chiesa Nuova of the Oratorians, Santa Maria in Vallicella (page 569).

1603 In August, the painter Giovanni Baglione accuses the painters Caravaggio, Orazio Gentileschi, and Filippo Trisegni, as well as the architect Onorio Longhi, of spreading defamatory poems. Caravaggio is arrested on 11 September. On 25 September he is released on the intervention of the French ambassador.

1604 He is rearrested in October for an attack on police henchmen.

1605 In May, he is arrested for the unauthorized carrying of a weapon. In July, he is accused of injuring the notary Mariano Pasqualone with a sword blow to the face; he flees to Genoa. In August, he returns to Rome. He is commissioned with the *Madonna dei Palafrenieri* (page 570).

1606 On 28 May, Caravaggio kills a fellow player during a ball game and has to flee to the country estate of Prince Marzio Colonna. From October he is living in Naples.

1607 On Malta from July at the latest.

1608 Admission to the Maltese order of Hospitallers on 14 July. In December he is excluded from the order and flees to Sicily.

1609 Caravaggio is attacked in Naples during October, receiving facial injuries.

1610 Embarkation for Rome. He dies of a sickness in Porto Ercole on 18 July, as recently discovered documents prove.

Carpaccio, Vittore

ca. 1460 Vittore Carpaccio, the son of a furrier, is born in Venice. Opinion is divided on the matter of his artistic training. Many painters, ranging from Gentile and Giovanni Bellini and Antonello da Messina to Lazzaro Bastiano and Jacometto Veneziano, have been considered potential tutors. Carpaccio achieved fame primarily as the creator of explanatory cycles of paintings for various Venetian lay fraternities, the so-called *scuole.*

late 1480s The devotional painting, signed *VETOR SCARPAZO* but not dated, depicting Christ as the savior of the world, standing behind a balustrade and surrounded by four male saints (Stanley Moss Collection, New York), is considered the oldest surviving work by Carpaccio.

ca. 1489/90 Carpaccio receives the commission from the Scuola di Sant'Orsola to paint an extensive cycle of pictures (completed in 1495) containing scenes from the life of St. Ursula (pages 150, 151). The *Arrival of St. Ursula in Cologne* from 1490 is the oldest signed and dated work by the artist.

1502–1508 Carpaccio paints another cycle of nine paintings (primarily depicting the legends of St. George and St. Jerome; pages 148, 149) for the comparatively small meeting room of the Scuola di San Giorgio degli Schiavoni, which can still be found there.

ca. 1505 In parallel to his work for the Scuola di San Giorgio, a cycle of paintings for the Scuola di San Giobbe is also created, of which only the *Meditation on the Passion of Christ* (The Metropolitan Museum of Art, New York) and *Preparation of Christ for the Grave* Gemäldegalerie, Berlin) have survived.

1507 Carpaccio acts for a brief period as assistant to Giovanni Bellini during the decorating of the Sala del Maggior Consiglio in the Doge's Place. In the same year he paints the altarpiece *St. Thomas Aquinas in Glory with St. Mark and St. Louis of Toulouse* (Staatsgalerie, Stuttgart) for the Dominican church of San Pietro Martire on the island of Murano.

1508 Carpaccio is a member of the committee of artists chosen to appraise Giorgione's frescoes for the Fondaco dei Tedeschi.

from 1510 During the last one-and-a-half years of his life, Carpaccio mainly works for clients on Terraferma (including Istria which at that time belonged to the Venetian Republic).

1511–1520 Scenes from the life of St. Stephen for the Scuola di Santo Stefano: *St. Stephen is Consecrated Deacon* (Gemäldegalerie, Berlin), the *Sermon of St. Stephen* (Musée du Louvre, Paris), the *Disputation of St. Stephen* (Pinacoteca di Brera, Milan), and the *Stoning of St. Stephen* (Staatsgalerie, Stuttgart).

1516 He paints the picture of the winged lion of St. Mark in front of a view of Venice that can today be seen in the Doge's Palace, but was probably intended for the Palazzo dei Camerlenghi.

1525/26 Vittore Carpaccio dies in Venice.

Cima da Conegliano

ca. 1459/60 Cima da Conegliano (real name: Giovanni Battista Cima), the son of a cloth cutter (Italian *cimatore*), is born in Conegliano, north of Venice and near Treviso. Although nothing is known about his training, the influence of both Giovanni Bellini and the School of Murano (painters of the Vivarini family) can hardly be overlooked.

mid-1480s Earliest (not yet signed or dated) works, including the polyptych in the parish church of Olera (near Bergamo).

1489 His first dated work, the *Madonna and Child with St. James and St. Jerome,* for the church of San Bartolomeo in Vicenza, has given rise to speculation over whether the artist had received his training here—perhaps in the workshop of Bartolomeo Montagna (ca. 1450–1523).

1492 First evidence of his presence in Venice. However, Cima is to remain closely connected to his hometown of Conegliano throughout his life.

ca. 1493–1495 Paints his first altarpiece in Venice, no doubt under the influence of works by Giovanni Bellini: it shows St. John the Baptist in front of a wide landscape and surrounded by four saints and sacred architecture that serves to provide an impression of antiquity (Madonna dell'Orto, Venice).

mid-1490s Numerous small altarpieces and devotional paintings such as the half-figure *Madonna and Child* (Pinacoteca Nazionale, Bologna).

ca. 1495–1497 The *Madonna and Child Enthroned, with St. Peter, St. Romuald, St. Benedict, and St. Paul,* (page 141) for the sacristy of the Camaldolese church of San Michele on the island of the same name located between Venice and Murano.

ca. 1497 *Madonna of the Orange Tree* (Gallerie dell'Accademia, Venice). At around the same time or a little later, a group of three or four painters are commissioned to decorate the chapel of the Lucchese silk weavers in the Venetian church of Santa Maria dei Crocicchieri with scenes from the life of St. Mark. *St. Mark Healing the Cobbler Anianus* is by Cima (page 146).

ca. 1499 Cima paints one of his larges altarpieces for the Cappella di San Giorgio in Santa Maria: a *sacra conversazione* with saints Catherine, George, Nicholas, Anthony, Sebastian, and Lucy (Gallerie dell'Accademia, Venice).

ca. 1504/05 *Christ with Doubting Thomas and Bishop St. Magnus of Oderzo,* an altarpiece commissioned by the Scuola dei Mureri for the church of San Samuele (page 147).

1505/06 The altar panel of St. Peter Martyr flanked by St. Nicholas and St. Benedict (Pinacoteca di Brera, Milan)—very much in the tradition of the Quattrocento—is painted for the Corpus Domini church. Two mythological tondi—possibly commissioned by Marchese Scipione della Rosa, an art collector from Parma—are painted at approximately the same time: *Endymion* and the *Judgment of Midas* (Galleria Nazionale, Parma).

ca. 1508 Cima paints an altarpiece for Canon Bartolomeo Montini, another client from Parma, for his burial chapel in Parma Cathedral (Galleria Nazionale, Parma).

ca. 1511–1513 The *Madonna and Child with St. John the Baptist and Mary Magdalene* from the Dominican church in Parma (Musée du Louvre, Paris), displays little of the artistic innovation of the early 16th century.

1517/18 Neither the exact date of his death, nor whether Giovanni Battista Cima died in Venice or his birthplace of Conegliano, has been recorded.

Correggio

1489/94 The painter Correggio (real name: Antonio Allegri) is born in Correggio (Emilia Romagna). His first lessons in drawing and painting are probably with his uncle Lorenzo Allegri, or perhaps with Francesco de' Bianchi Ferrari from Modena. He receives significant motivation primarily from Andrea Mantegna, who by 1506 has already died. In addition, many of his early works provide evidence of an intensive preoccupation with the art of Leonardo da Vinci as well as that of Albrecht Dürer.

1514 First record of his presence in Mantua, at around this time: the high altar of San Francesco, *Madonna and Child with St. Anthony of Padua, St. Catherine of Alexandria, and St. John the Baptist* (Gemäldegalerie Alte Meister, Dresden).

ca. 1516/17 Paints an altarpiece for a private chapel in Santa Maria della Misericordia in Correggio (The Metropolitan Museum of Art, New York).

ca. 1518–1520 His small *Adoration of the Child* (page 416). Contrary to Vasari's account, today's opinion is that Correggio has also been in Rome at about this time, since his following works betray knowledge of the frescoes by Michelangelo and Raphael in the Vatican.

ca. 1519/20 In Parma, Correggio receives the commission to paint the ceiling frescoes of the Camera di San Paolo in the Benedictine convent of the same name.

1520/21 The *Rest on the Flight into Egypt with St. Francis* for the Munari Chapel of San Francesco in Correggio (Galleria degli Uffizi, Florence).

1520–1525 Paints the frescoes of the dome *Vision of St. John on Patmos* and the apse vault *Coronation of the Virgin* for the new Benedictine church of San Giovanni Evangelista in Parma, with the assistance of his pupil Parmigianino.

1522 *Holy Night* (page 417), which from 1530 at the latest decorates the family chapel of its commissioner, Alberto Pratoneri, in the recently built church of San Prospero in Reggio Emilia.

ca. 1524 Correggio paints the *Madonna di San Sebastiano* (Gemäldegalerie Alte Meister, Dresden) for the Brotherhood of St. Sebastian in Modena. Around this time, paints the *Education of Cupid* (National Gallery, London) and *Venus, Cupid, and the Satyr* (Musée du Louvre, Paris), probably commissioned by Count Nicola Maffei, in Mantua.

1526–1534 Paints the large illusionist dome fresco the *Assumption of the Virgin Mary* (page 423) in Parma Cathedral.

1530 Completes the *Madonna di San Giorgio* (Gemäldegalerie Alte Meister, Dresden) for the Brotherhood of St. George in Modena.

1530–1532 The amours of Jupiter, the father of the gods, for the Duke of Mantua, Federico II Gonzaga: the *Rape of Ganymede* and *Jupiter and Io* (pages 418, 419), *Leda and the Swan* (page 420) and *Danaë* (page 421).

1534 Correggio dies in Correggio.

Cossa, Francesco del

1436 Francesco del Cristoforo Cossa is born in Ferrara.

1456 He paints a Deposition (now lost) while still a member of his father's household.

1460 He is declared fully competent as an artist by his father.

1462 Sojourn in Bologna.

1470 Cossa participates with Ercole de' Roberti in the decoration of the Salone dei Mesi in the Palazzo Schifanoia in Ferrara with depictions of the months of the year (page 128). In letter from Bologna, Cossa complains about the poor payment received for the frescoes.

1474 A *sacra conversazione* for the Foro dei Mercanti in Bologna (Pinacoteca Nazionale, Bologna).

1478 Cossa dies in Bologna, presumably of plague.

Crivelli, Carlo

1430/1435 Carlo Crivelli, the son of the painter Jacopo Crivelli, is born in Venice.

1456 at the latest He encounters the painter Francesco Squarcione (ca. 1397–1468), who at this time is staying in Venice.

7 March 1457 Crivelli is sentenced to six months in jail and a fine of 200 lire for adultery, rape, and the false imprisonment of the wife of the sailor Francesco Cortese.

1465 In Zara, Dalmatia, as a citizen *civis,* together with his brother Vittore and possibly also Giorgio Schiavone (ca. 1520–1582).

1468, 1470, 1472, 1487 Crivelli works, and is mentioned, in Fermo.

1470–1472 Polyptych for Macerata, today scattered around the world.

1469, 1473, 1476, 1477, 1478, 1480, 1482, 1486 Documents and works show he is available for and in Ascoli Piceno; in 1486 he paints the *Annunciation* for the Franciscan church of Sant'Annunziata (page 127).

1486 He names a lawyer for current and future litigation.

1488 Testament in Ascoli Piceno. He is in Camerino during the same year.

1489/90 Crivelli paints the *Blessed Gabriele Ferretti in Ecstasy,* for San Francesco in Alto, Ancona (National Gallery, London).

1490 In Francavilla, Crivelli is given the titles of *familiaris* (assistant) and *miles* (knight) by Prince Ferdinand of Capua. Around this time he signs the *Vision of the Holy Trinity* for San Francesco in Atri with his new title, *miles* (National Gallery, London).

1491, 1492, 1493 Employed in Fabriano and Pergola by the Franciscans.

1493 Last recorded mention of Crivelli in Fabriano: payment for his *Coronation of the Virgin* for San Francesco (Pinacoteca di Brera, Milan).

1494, 1495 or 1500 Crivelli dies, according to contradictory information about his legacy.

Dosso Dossi

ca. 1489 Dosso Dossi (real name: Giovanni Luteri) is probably born in Ferrara. His work proves to be heavily influenced both by the great Venetian painters of his day—especially Giorgione—and by the local artist trends of the Emilia-Romagna, leading to the painter Francesco del Cossa sporadically being considered to have been his tutor.

1512 Works for the Gonzaga in Mantua, and for the Este in Ferrara the following year.

ca. 1514 He travels to Venice and possibly also to Rome: *Holy Family with St. John and two Benefactors* (Philadelphia Museum of Art, Philadelphia) and *Madonna and Child with Five Saints* (Archbishop's Palace, Ferrara).

1515–1518 Two journeys to Venice and one to Florence in 1517: *Bacchanal* (National Gallery, London).

ca. 1518 Clearly inspired by Ludovico Ariosto's epic poem *Orlando Furioso,* he paints the enigmatic painting *The Sorceress Melissa* (also known as *Circe*) (page 385), no doubt for Duke Alfonso I d'Este.

1518–1522 Cycle on the life of Aeneas for the Este (scattered through various collections).

1520s *Jupiter, Mercury, and Virtue* (pages 386–387), also probably for Duke Alfonso, as well as a series of altar paintings such as the *sacra conversazione* in Modena Cathedral, and in the Galleria e Museo Estense, Modena.

1524–1526 Payments for the decoration of the ducal apartments on the Via Coperta in Ferrara (fragments in the National Gallery, London, and in private Florentine ownership).

ca. 1530 Together with his brother, Battista Dossi, and the Florentine painter Bronzino, he is summoned by Francesco Maria della Rovere I, Duke of Urbino, to Pesaro to decorate the Villa Imperiale.

1531/32 Dosso Dossi paints mythological scenes in the palace in Trento for Prince-Bishop Bernado Clesio, once again together with his brother and other North Italian artists.

ca. 1535 *Apollo and Daphne* (Galleria Borghese, Rome).

1540 *St. George and the Dragon* and *St. Michael* (Gemäldegalerie, Dresden).

1542 Dosso Dossi dies in Ferrara.

Giorgione

ca. 1477/78 Giorgione (real name: Giorgio or Zorzi da Castelfranco) is born in the small town of Castelfranco, situated between Venice, Padua, and Treviso. Possibly trained by Vincenzo Catena (ca. 1470–1531), he has close contact with Giovanni Bellini. The dates of his major works—the altarpiece for the church of San Liberale in his hometown of Castelfranco (page 283), and the painting the *Three Philosophers* (pages 288–289), possibly completed by Giorgione's pupil Sebastiano del Piombo—is still a matter of contention.

1506 *Portrait of a Young Woman (Laura)* (Kunsthistorisches Museum, Vienna).

1507/08 Façade frescoes of the Fondaco dei Tedeschi, the German Merchants' Hall in Venice, almost completely destroyed in the 18th century (remnants in the Galleria dell'Accademia). A further painting, for the Audience Hall of the Doge's Palace, was probably also destroyed during the great fires of 1574 and 1577.

1508/09 *Sleeping Venus* (page 294): after Giorgione's death it is completed by Titian, who is credited with the landscape as well as a cupid at the foot of the goddess of love's feet that was painted over in the 19th century.

ca. 1510 *Concert Champêtre* (pages 294/295); although long considered a work by Giorgione, the tendency today is to credit the painting to Titian.

1510 Giorgione dies in Venice of the plague.

Leonardo da Vinci

15 April 1452 Leonardo di Ser Piero da Vinci is born in the Tuscan town of Vinci.

1469 Leonardo's father is notary of the San Martire convent in Florence. The family household is relocated this year from Vinci to Florence. The apprenticeship in the workshop of Andrea del Verrocchio (1435–1488) probably begins.

1472 Leonardo becomes a registered member of the Florentine painters' guild.

5 August 1473 Earliest dated work by Leonardo, *Landscape Drawing for Santa Maria delle Neve* (church consecration day of Santa Maria Maggiore in Rome; page 154).

1476 Leonardo and several others are charged with homosexuality, but acquitted.

1478 The first pages of the *Codex Atlanticus* are created, a collection of drawings and notes from all phases of Leonardo's creativity. The British Museum is the custodian of the *Codex Arundel,* which, similar to the *Codex Atlanticus,* contains a temporally and thematically mixed collection of Leonardo's works. Leonardo notes that he is working on two Madonnas. Commission for San Bernardo Chapel in the Palazzo Vecchio.

1481 Contract signed for the altar panel the *Adoration of the Magi* for the monks of San Donato in Scopeto (unfinished; page 172).

1483 Contract for an altar panel, no doubt the *Madonna of the Rocks* (page 178), for the chapel of San Francesco Grande in Milan.

1487 Work begins on the *B* and *Ashburnham* manuscripts. The codex of the Biblioteca Trivulziana in Milan and *Codex Forster II* of the Victoria and Albert Museum in London also date from the years following 1487. Both Leonardo and Bramante participate in the competition for the dome louver of Milan Cathedral.

1489 Ludovico "il Moro" asks Lorenzo de' Medici for bronze casters for the Sforza monument. Work on the book *On the Human Body* begins on 2 April.

1490 Leonardo is commissioned with the decoration of the "Paradise Feast" for the marriage of Gian Galeazzo Sforza and Isabella d'Aragon.

1492 Giuliano da Sangallo stays briefly in Milan. Leonardo begins *Manuscript A* (Institut de France). He makes short journeys to Como, Valtellino, Valsassino, Bellagio, and Ivrea.

1493 He begins *Codex Madrid I* and the third part of *Manuscript H* in the Institut de France, Paris. The clay Sforza horseman monument is supposed to be ready on 30 December; on 20 December the decision is taken to cast the horse on its side and without its tail. Bellincioni calls Leonardo the "Apelles of Florence." Writes notes on the clock of Chiaravalle.

1495 Begins the work in *Manuscript M* of the Institut de France and is probably commissioned to paint the *Last Supper* (pages 190–191) in the refectory of Santa Maria delle Grazie. Leonardo decorates rooms in Castello Sforzesco.

1496 Drawings for *De divina proportione* by Luca Pacioli. Disagreement with Ludovico "il Moro" over the decoration of the rooms in Castello Sforzesco. Leonardo applies for the commission for the bronze doors for Piacenza Cathedral.

1498 Leonardo is in Genoa in March and assesses the city's harbor installations. He completes his work in the Sala delle Asse. In October, Ludovico "il Moro" presents Leonardo with a vineyard.

1500 On their way to Venice, Leonardo, Luca Pacioli and pupils are guests of the Gonzaga in Mantua. He paints the portrait of Isabella d'Este (page 186). He reaches Venice on 13 March; here, in the Friaul, he plans a defensive installation against a threatened invasion by the Turks. On 24 April, Leonardo is back in Florence. A note stating that he wants to travel to Rome, Vinci, and Naples with the Frenchman Ligny can be found in the *Codex Atlanticus.* His note "casa d'Adriana" gives rise to the supposition that he at least reached Tivoli, near Rome.

1501 On 3 April he is definitely back in Florence. Isabella d'Este requests a replica of her portrait. Pietro da Novellara refers to a Madonna with St. Anne and the *Madonna with the Yarn Winder* for Robertet, the secretary of the French King, Louis XII.

1502 Leonardo appraises vases from the collection of the deceased Lorenzo de' Medici for Isabella d'Este. On 18 August, Leonardo receives a travel permit from Cesare Borgia that allows him as "family architect and engineer general" to inspect all the defensive fortifications of cities under the rule of the Borgia.

1503 Studies for a project to divert the Arno so that Pisa would have been isolated from the sea. Drawings are done of Monte Verruca and the Pisan Mountains. In October, Leonardo receives the keys to the Papal Hall of the Florentine convent Santa Maria Novella, which is to serve him as a studio during his work on the *Battle of Anghiari.*

1504 Isabella d'Este requests a depiction of the infant Jesus. Leonardo notes: "my map of the world that Giovanni Benci has got." On 9 July he is told of his father's death. On 20 November, Leonardo is in Piombino and presents his city-planning and military blueprints. On 30 November, he notes that he has succeeded in squaring the circle.

1505 The Duke of Ferrara wishes to acquire *Bacchus* by Leonardo that has already been promised to the Cardinal of Rouen. Painting begins on the murals in the Palazzo Vecchio: entries in both the Milan *Codex Atlanticus* and in the *Codex Arundel* of the British Museum about "the existence of nothing," and in *Codex Forster I* of the Victoria and Albert Museum in London.

1506 Leonardo is summoned to Milan by Charles d'Amboise, the representative of the French king, and leaves Florence on 30 May, but has to commit himself by contract to return within three months. Charles d'Amboise requests extensions of the deadline on behalf of Leonardo on 18 August and 16 December.

1508 Leonardo dissects an old man and a woman in Santa Maria Nuova in Florence. On 22 March, he is guest in the Florentine home of Piero di Braccio Martelli and helps the sculptor Rustici with his bronze group above the north door of the Baptistery in Florence, which is still in place today. On 12 September, he is back in Milan and begins *Manuscript F* of the Institut de France. Plans for a villa for Charles d'Amboise.

1509 Urban planning for Milan, projects for a canal and water studies.

1510 Dissections at the University of Pavia with the anatomist Antonio della Torre. Leonardo participates in discussions about stables for Milan Cathedral in October. In December, Leonardo believes he will shortly finish his book on anatomy.

1511 Leonardo records the fires set by Swiss troops outside Milan; he was probably staying in Vaprio in the family villa of his pupil Francesco Melzi (ca. 1491/92–1570) at the time. He subsequently draws up plans for extending the villa.

1513 Leonardo is in Vaprio on 9 January. He leaves for Rome together with Francesco Melzi, Salai, and a certain Lorenzo on 24 September.

1514 On 7 July, at 11 pm, Leonardo notes that he is in his studio in the Belvedere, Rome; on 25 September, he is in Parma. Studies on the harbor facilities of Civitavecchia and projects for draining the Pontine Marshes. He is selected as a novice in the Arciconfraternità di San Giovanni dei Fiorentini in Rome.

1515 On 9 January, Leonardo records the departure of Cardinal Giovanni de' Medici from Rome. Leonardo is thrown out of the Hospital of San Spirito, where he wanted to continue his studies of anatomy, for "practicing black magic." Draws up plans for Giovanni de' Medici's stables and for a new Medici palace in Florence. The French King, Francis I, takes Milan. Leonardo probably takes part in the meeting in Bologna between the Medici Pope Leo X and Francis I.

1516 His patron Giovanni de' Medici dies on 17 March. In August, Leonardo is in Rome; he is engaged in surveying the church of San Paolo fuori le Mura.

2 May 1517 Leonardo is in Amboise, a residence of King Francis I, and becomes his prime painter, engineer, and architect.

1518 On 24 June he is in Clos-Lucé near Amboise.

1519 On 23 April 1519 he writes his testament. Leonardo dies on 2 May 1519 in Clos-Lucé near Amboise.

Lotto, Lorenzo

ca. 1480 Lorenzo Lotto is born in Venice. He is possibly trained by Alvise Vivarini (1445/46–1503/05).

1503–1506 Lotto is first documented in Treviso. His first known works include several portraits such as the *Portrait of Bishop Bernardino de' Rossi* (Galleria Nazionale di Capodimonte, Naples), in addition to altar paintings for churches in Treviso and Asolo.

1506–1508 Lotto moves to the Marches. He paints his work for the high altar of San Domenico (Pinacoteca Comunale, Recanati) in Recanati near Ancona.

1508/09 He moves to Rome, probably through the mediation of architect Donato Bramante (1444–1514), who is staying in Loreto near Recanati, where he is commissioned to paint the frescoes in the *stanze* of the Vatican that have, however, not survived.

1511 In the Marches again. The *Deposition* (Pinacoteca Comunale, Jesi) is painted for Brotherhood of Buon Gesù in Jesi (also near Ancona). Further altarpieces are painted for churches in Recanati.

1513–1525 In Bergamo (part of the Republic of Venice at the time): an unusually large painting (*Enthroned Madonna and Child with Ten Saints*, today in San Bartolomeo, Bergamo) commissioned by Count Alessandro Marinengo-Colleoni for the high altar of the Dominican church of Santo Stefano.

1521 The *Adoration of the Infant* (lost) and *Christ Taking Leave of His Mother* (page 374) commissioned by Domenico Tassi and his wife Elisabetta.

1524/25 The frescoes with scenes from the life of St. Barbara and St. Bridget of Ireland are painted in the Oratorio of the Villa Suardi in Trescore Balneario near Bergamo. Designs for the inlay work in the choir of Santa Maria Maggiore in Bergamo (scenes from the Old Testament).

1525–1532 Goes to Venice, where he temporarily lives in the Dominican cloister of San Giovanni e Paolo (Zanipolo). Although he remains a resident of the lagoon city, he is also still employed by clients in the Marches. The only altarpiece painted for a Venetian church during these years (around 1529) is the *St. Nicholas of Bari in Glory* (Santa Maria dei Carmini).

1527 Portrait of the Venetian merchant and antiquarian *Andrea Odoni* (page 381) as well as *Portrait of a Gentleman in his Study* (Gallerie dell'Accademia, Venice), *Goldsmith (?) in Three Views* (page 380), and the *Annunciation* (page 375).

ca. 1530 The *Crucifixion,* an altarpiece for Santa Maria della Pietà in Monte San Giusto (the Marches).

1532 Once again in Treviso.

1533–1539 Mainly in the Marches (Jesi, Ancona, and Macerata).

1540s The artist is employed in Venice and Trevisio for most of the decade.

1546 *Madonna and Child with Four Saints* for San Giacomo dall'Orio, Venice

from 1549 Spends his life in the Marches.

1550 He paints the *Assumption* for San Francesco delle Scale in Ancona.

1552 or 1554 The painter enters the cloister of Casa Santa in Loreto as a lay brother.

1556 Lorenzo Lotto dies in Loreto.

Mantegna, Andrea

1430/31 Birth of Andrea Mantegna, the son of a carpenter, probably in Isola di Carturo, between Vicenza and Padua.

ca. 1442 Apprenticeship with Francesco Squarcione (ca. 1397–1468) in Padua.

1447/48 First commission for Mantegna as a painter in his own right for Santa Sofia in Padua (Pinacoteca di Brera, Milan).

1448–1457 Frescoes of the Ovetari Chapel in the Eremitani church in Padua (pages 60–65; most destroyed by war).

1453/54 Marriage to Nicolosia, the daughter of the painter Jacopo Bellini from Venice; Mantegna is thereby related by marriage to Gentile and Giovanni Bellini.

1457–1460 Polyptych for the altar of San Zeno in Verona: the three panels of this *sacra conversazione* (pages 74–78) are unified by their classical aedicule frames.

1459–1460 He enters the service of the Gonzaga in Mantua.

ca. 1465–1474 Frescoes of the Camera degli Sposi (pages 89–101) of the Palazzo Ducale in Mantua: the actual space is expanded by the illusionary space of the paintings with their life-size figures on the side walls and a view of the sky.

1484–1495 The *Triumphs of Caesar* for Francesco Gonzaga (pages 104–105).

1488–1490 In the service of Pope Innocence VIII in Rome; there are no clear ideas of the works created there.

1494 Dürer's copies according to engravings by Mantegna, who claims to have gained a leading position in the history of book printing more through these copies than through his own copperplate engravings; during this period both profane and sacral themes are spread throughout Europe in this way.

1496 Mantegna's *Madonna of Victory* for Francesco Gonzaga in Manta (page 112): triumphal work with historical associations painted in the wake of persecution of the Jews.

1506 Mantegna dies on 13 September; he had designed his tomb in Sant'Andrea in Mantua himself.

Parmigianino

1503 Parmigianino (real name: Francesco Mazzola), the son of a relatively insignificant painter, is born in Parma. Serves an apprenticeship with Correggio.

ca. 1519 *Baptism of Christ* for Santissima Annunziata in Parma (Gemäldegalerie, Berlin).

ca. 1521 Paints the *Mystical Marriage of St. Catherine of Siena* for the church of San Pietro in Viadana, in the Province of Mantua (today in the parish church of Bardi in the Province of Parma).

1522 Works on the frescoes of San Giovanni Evangelista in Parma together with his teacher, Correggio.

1523/24 Paints a well-preserved cycle of frescoes depicting scenes from the myth of Diane and Actaeon in the moat castle of the Sanvitale family in Fontanellato, northwest of Parma.

1524 Moves to Rome, where his *Self-Portrait in a Convex Mirror* (page 412) and other works recommend him as an artist to the new Medici Pope Clement VII.

1526/27 The *Vision of St. Jerome* (National Gallery, London) is one of his major works from his period in Rome.

1527 He returns to the Emilia Romagna, initially to Bologna, following the Sacco di Roma, the plundering of the Eternal City by German and Spanish troops.

1527/28 The altarpiece *St. Roch and Donor* for San Petronio Cathedral in Bologna; at the same time the dramatic *Conversion of St. Paul* (Kunsthistorisches Museum, Vienna); and only slightly later the *Madonna with the Rose* (Gemäldegalerie Alte Meister, Dresden).

ca. 1530 *Madonna di San Zaccaria* for Bonifacio Gozzadini (page 414). The artist returns in the same year to his home city of Parma, where he is given the commission for two altar paintings for Santa Maria della Steccata. He begins the painting of the vault and apse of the same church the following year.

1530s Paints the *Portrait of a Man* (page 413), once thought to be a self-portrait, and a little later the *Bow-Whittling Cupid* (Kunsthistorisches Museum, Vienna).

1534–1540 The Baiardi family commissions perhaps the artist's most famous painting, the *Madonna of the Long Neck* (page 30, detail page 415).

ca. 1535–1537 *Portrait of a Woman* (page 413) was long considered to be a portrait of the artist's lover painted in the 1520s in Rome.

1540 Parmigianino dies in Casalmaggiore, to the north of Parma.

Piombo, Sebastiano del

ca. 1485 Sebastiano del Piombo (real name: Sebastiano Luciani) is probably born in Venice. According to Vasari, he received his first training with the already aged Giovanni Bellini, before moving to Giorgione's workshop.

ca. 1505 *Portrait of a Young Woman* (Museum of Fine Arts, Budapest) is the earliest known work by the painter. His *Judgment of Solomon,* probably painted for the Palazzo Loredan (present-day Palazzo Vendramin-Calergi), also dates from this period, but was previously credited to Giorgione.

1507/08 For San Bartolomeo, the church of the German merchants near the Rialto Bridge, Sebastiano paints the wings of the organ with saints (including the saint who gives the church its name).

1510 Main altar painting with a depiction of the Greek patron saint surrounded by other saints for the church of San Giovanni Crisostomo, also near the Rialto Bridge.

1511 While staying in Venice, the banker Agostino Chigi invites Sebastiano to accompany him back to Rome. There, Sebastiano at first participates in the decoration of Villa Farnesina, recently built by Baldassare Peruzzi for Agostino Chigi.

ca. 1512 The *Death of Adonis* (page 372–373), with its view of the city of Venice in the background, is probably also commissioned by Chigi.

ca. 1512/13 *Portrait of a Young Roman Woman* (page 369); the large *Pietà* for San Francesco in Viterbo is painted around this time.

1516–1524 The *Flagellation of Christ* in San Pietro in Montorio—a church on the slopes of the Gianicolo Hill.

ca. 1517–1519 In Rome, Cardinal Giulio de' Medici, later Pope Clement VII, orders two monumental paintings for the cathedral in Narbonne, which never reached their intended destination: Sebastiano paints the *Raising of Lazarus* (page 371) as a pendant to Raphael's *Transfiguration* (page 271).

1520 After the death of Raphael, Sebastiano rapidly advanced to become Rome's most sought-after portrait painter.

1522/23 During the short pontificate of Hadrian VI, Sebastiano begins a commission from a Dutch cardinal, called Enckenvoirt, for painting his chapel in Santa Maria dell'Anima. The murals, which have not survived, are completed in 1531 by Michiel Coxcie.

ca. 1526/27 Just before the Sacco di Roma Sebastiano paints the portrait of the Medici Pope Clement VII (page 368) who also commissions him to paint the Genoese admiral Andrea Doria (Galleria Doria Pamphilj, Rome).

1528/29 Visits Venice, the city of his birth.

1531 He is appointed keeper of the papal seal ("piombo," hence his name), and again paints the portrait of Pope Clement VII (Kunsthistorisches Museum, Vienna). He accompanies the Pope on numerous journeys.

1533 Ferrante Gonzaga commissions the artist to paint a *Pietà* for the burial chapel of the Imperial Chancellor, Francisco de los Cobos, in the church of San Salvador in Ubeda (about 80 km (50 miles) north of Granada). Sebastiano completes the painting in 1539 (now in Pilate House, Sevilla).

1537 *Christ Carrying the Cross* for the Count of Cifuente, Ferdinando da Silva (Hermitage, St. Petersburg). Shortly afterwards he begins work on the *Birth of the Virgin* for Santa Maria del Popolo, which is completed after his death by Francesco Salviati.

1540s Numerous portraits; among the painter's final works is *Christ Carrying the Cross,* now housed in the Museum of Fine Arts in Budapest.

1547 Sebastiano del Piombo dies in Rome on 15 June and is interred in Santa Maria Maggiore. In 1561, his mortal remains are transferred to the Accademia di San Luca, Rome.

Pisanello

1395 His father, a resident of Pisa, appoints Pisanello (real name: Antonio di Ser Puccino di Giovanni di Cereto) his sole heir and mentions that the young boy is staying with his mother, Elisabetta di Nicolò Zuperio, in Verona; two years later she is already a widow and remarries.

1408–1415 Apprenticeship in Venice in the milieu of Gentile Fabriano and Michelino da Besozzo (active around 1388–1445).

ca. 1415–1420 Historical painting for the Doge's Palace, Venice (now lost).

1422 He purchases of a plot of land in Verona.

1426 The *Annunciation* fresco in San Fermo, Verona.

1431/32 Murals in San Giovanni in Laterano (now lost).

1433 Based in Verona, he works for Leonello d'Este, Duke of Ferrara.

1435–1438 Paints the Cappella Pellegrini in Sant'Anastasia; only the work over the entrance arch has survived (page 50).

1436–1442 Fresco in the Gonzaga palace in Mantua (only the sinopiae (under drawings) have survived).

1438/39 Pisanello fashions the famous commemorative medal with the portrait of Byzantine Emperor John III Palaeologus at the Council of Ferrara; drawings with motifs from the emperor's entourage.

1439 Attending on the Gonzaga, Pisanello returns to Verona. He leaves the city again when the army from Mantua is driven out.

1441 He is declared an enemy of the Republic of Venice.

1442 He is convicted of diatribes against Venice. However, he is not sentenced to have his tongue cut out and be banished for life from the city's dominion. In November, he is allowed to leave Venice for Ferrara for only two months.

1447 He is taxed in Verona; he essentially remains in the service of the Este.

1448 In Naples he designs a medal for King Alfonso of Aragon that has first been dated 1448, then 1449.

1449 Pisanello is appointed a *familiaris* (part of the entourage) of the king.

1455 Pisanello dies, according to evidence provided by a letter by Carlo de' Medici from Rome.

Pontormo

1494 Jacopo Carrucci, the first child of the artist Bartolommeo di Jacopo Martino di Carrucci and his wife Alessandra Pasquale di Zanobi, is born on 24 or 25 May in Pontormo (hence his name), near Empoli, in Tuscany.

1499 Death of the father.

1504 Death of the mother. Jacopo grows up with his grandmother.

1508 Up to the end of his life, Pontormo remains in Florence where, as an orphan, he is initially a ward of court; he no doubt becomes acquainted with Leonardo da Vinci.

ca. 1510 Apprenticeship with Mariotto Albertinelli (1474–1515) and Fra Bartolommeo.

1512/13 Apprenticeship with Andrea del Sarto, together with Rosso Fiorentino.

1512 He participates in painting the festive decorations celebrating the return of the Medici.

1513 According to Vasari, Michelangelo is full of praise for Jacopo's allegorical fresco on belief and charity in Santissima Annunziata.

1514/16 Payments by the Servite Friars of Santissima Annunziata for his fresco the *Visitation* in the church courtyard (page 397).

1515 Festive decoration of the papal chapel in Santa Maria Novella to commemorate the visit of Medici Pope Leo X. Commission to embellish the Stanza Borgherini, together with Andrea del Sarto, Francesco Granacci, and Francesco Bachiacca.

1518 A *sacra conversazione* for the Pucci family altar in San Michele Visdomini.

1519 *Pomona and Vertumnus* fresco in the Villa Medicea in Poggio a Caiano.

1521 Work on the frescoes at Poggio a Caiano is discontinued following the death of Pope Leo X. Pontormo's painting of the eastern lunette is completed.

1523 On 4 February payments by Carthusian monks for the lunette frescoes in the cloister of Certosa del Galluzzo begin. They will continue up to 1528.

1525 *Supper at Emmaus* for the Certosa guesthouse (page 401); work on the Passion frescoes is completed in the fall. Return to Florence. Becomes a member of the Accademia del Disegno. Lodovico Capponi buys the chapel built by Brunelleschi in Santa Felicità; the commission to paint the *Annunciation* frescoes and the *Deposition* altarpiece (pages 403, 405) is probably awarded the same year.

1528 Work in the Capponi Chapel is completed.

1529 On 15 March, Pontormo acquires two plots of land on the Via Laura in the parish of San Giovanni from the orphanage and begins to convert the house there into living quarters and a workshop.

1536 On 13 December, the frescoes (now lost) in the Loggia of the Medici Villa at Careggi are unveiled.

ca. 1540 He works on the loggia frescoes (now lost) in the Medici Villa at Castello.

ca. 1546 Duke Cosimo I de' Medici awards him the commission to paint the frescoes in the choir of San Lorenzo.

1548 In a letter on 18 February, Pontormo answers a survey from Benedetto Varchi on whether painting or sculpture should be more highly valued.

from 1549 Pontormo draws a life annuity from the orphanage.

1554–1556 Diary-like notes in the so-called *Il libro mio* tell of the work on the choir frescoes in San Lorenzo.

1557 Pontormo is interred in the church of Santissima Annunziata on 2 January. The unfinished choir frescoes are completed by Angelo Bronzino within a year.

Raphael

6 April 1483 Raphael (Raffaelo di Giovanni Santi) is born the son of the painter Giovanni Santi di Pietro and his wife Màgia di Battista di Nicola Ciarla.

1 August 1494 Death of his father.

10 December 1500 Raphael and the older Evangelista da Piani Meleto are awarded the commission for the *Baronci Altarpiece* (sketch, page 209). Raphael is called *magister* (master) in the document, and named before his colleague.

13 September 1501 *Magister Rafael Johannis Santis de Urbino et Vangelista Andree de Piano Meleti* have completed the altar panel and received their payment.

1501–1503 The *Crowning of the Virgin* is commissioned by the Clarrisse family of Monteluce in Perugia.

1503 Documents from 19 January and 8 March provide evidence of Raphael's stay in Perugia.

1504 A letter of recommendation dated 1 October from Giovanna Felicia Feltria della Rovere to Gonfaloniere Sonderini of Florence announces Raphael's relocation to that city.

1505 On 12 December Raphael and Roberto di Giovanni di Marco declare themselves willing to paint a Crowning of the Virgin for Monteluce in the style of Ghirlandaio's work in San Girolamo di Narni. Raphael thereby lists where he may be staying: Perugia, Assisi, Gubbio, Rome, Siena, Florence, Urbino, Venice, and other places. He receives his first payment of 30 ducats from Monteluce for the *Crowning of the Virgin* on 23 December.

1509 A document dated 13 January is evidence of Raphael's presence in Rome. On 4 October, Raphael is appointed to the honorable papal position of "Letter Writer."

1511 A letter documents that Julius II Federico Gonzaga wants to have his portrait included in a fresco by Raphael in the Vatican Palace.

1512 The date MDXII can be found on the fresco below the *Mass at Bolsena* (page 244). A letter of 24 May reveals that Isabella d'Este wishes Raphael to paint a half-length portrait of Federico Gonzaga in armor.

1513 Julius II dies on 21 February. Giovanni de' Medici is elected his successor on 11 March. Raphael receives an initial payment of 50 ducats from the treasurer of the new pope, Leo X, on 7 July.

1514 Raphael is appointed the leading architect of St. Peter's Basilica. The letter to Castiglione, in which Raphael considers ideal beauty put together from many beautiful parts to be superior to natural beauty, also dates from this year.

1515 The tapestry cartoons for the Sistine Chapel are first mentioned in a payment made on 15 June. Raphael is appointed conservator of Rome's antiquities on 27 August.

1516 The *Stufetta* is completed on 20 June. The contract for the *Crowning of the Virgin* for Monteluce is renewed on 21 June. The final installment of payment for the tapestry cartoons is recorded on 20 December.

1517 Castiglione composes two sonnets on his portrait by Raphael. On 19 January, Sellaio tells Michelangelo that Raphael has been awarded the commission for the *Transfiguration* (page 271) and Sebastiano del Piombo the commission for the *Raising of Lazarus* (page 371). A letter reveals that Raphael has almost finished the Stanza dell'Incendio (pages 258–259), which includes a commission for a Triumph of Bacchus from the Duke of Ferrara.

1518 On 1 January, Sellaio reports to Michelangelo on the completion of the Loggia of Psyche in the Villa Farnesina. Letters mention a portrait of Lorenzo de' Medici by Raphael. The *Holy Family and St. Michael* for Francis I was already finished on 27 May. On 2 July, Sebastiano del Piombo reports to Michelangelo that Raphael has not yet begun the *Transfiguration*.

1519 On 16 June, Castiglione refers to the Loggia as completed.

1520 Payments for scaffolding in the Sala di Costantino are made between March and October.
Raphael dies on 6 April.

Rosso Fiorentino

1494 Rosso Fiorentino (real name: Giovanni Battista di Jacopo di Guaspare) is born in Florence. He probably receives his training as a painter in the workshop of Andrea del Sarto, together with Jacopo Pontormo.

1513 According to Giorgio Vasari, during this year Rosso studies Michelangelo's (now lost) cartoon on the *Battle of Cascina* and produces drawings of it.

1514–1514 Rosso, the younger painter, contributes the *Assumption* to the frescoes of his teacher, Andrea del Sarto, in the Chiostro dei Voti, the atrium of Santissima Annunziata.

1518 Commissioned by the hospital principal of Santa Maria Nuova in Florence, Rosso paints the *Madonna and Child with Four Saints* (page 390) for a burial chapel in Ognissanti.

1520/21 Travels to Volterra, where he paints one of his major works for the Cappella della Croce di Giorno in San Francesco: the monumental *Deposition* (page 391). His *Madonna Enthroned Between Two Saints* (St. John and St. Bartholomew) for the Pieve in Villamagna (15 km north of Volterra) is also painted during his stay in Volterra.

1522 Returns to Florence, where he is occupied with work on the *Dei Altar* (Palazzo Pitti, Florence).

1523 The paintings the *Betrothal of the Virgin* (San Lorenzo, Cappella Ginori) and *Moses Defending the Daughters of Jethro* (page 389) are painted in Florence.

1524 In the hope of receiving commissions from Clement VII, the Medici pope elected the previous year, Rosso Fiorentino travels to Rome, where he is primarily occupied with drawing. The two frescoes in the Cappella Cesi in Santa Maria della Pace (the *Creation of Eve* and *The Fall*) are among his first larger works there.

1525/26 He paints the *Dead Christ with Angels* (Museum of Fine Arts, Boston) for Bishop Lorenzo Tornabuoni.

1527 Rosso is imprisoned during the Sack of Rome by German and Spanish troops. He manages to escape and initially flees to Perugia in Umbria, and then to Sansepolcro (Borgo San Sepolcro), where he paints a *Pietà* for the Compagnia dei Battuti in San Lorenzo.

1528 He is commissioned to paint the *Risen Christ* for the cathedral in Città di Castello. Soon afterwards, he is in Arezzo, where he meets Vasari and is supposed to decorate the church of Santa Maria delle Lagrime with frescoes—a commission he does not fulfill.

1529 The artist is again staying in Sansepolcro, and shortly afterwards probably travels to Venice, where he is received by the poet Pietro Aretino. Rosso reputedly owes his contact with the French royal court to Aretino.

1530 Travels to the court of Francis I in Fontainebleau.

1532 He draws up plans for decorating the palace with frescoes and stuccowork. Several paintings are also done during the years in France. For example, Rosso is commissioned by the King of France's Marshal, Anne de Montmorency, to paint the *Lamentation over the Dead Christ* (page 393) for his palace in Ecouen, to the north of Paris.

1536–1539 Rosso supervises the implementation of his plans for decorating the palace in Fontainebleau (allegorical, mythological, and several historical scenes intended to glorify the king).

1540 Rosso Fiorentino dies in Fontainebleau, possibly—as Vasari says—by suicide.

Sarto, Andrea del

1486 Andrea del Sarto (real name: Andrea d'Agnolo) is born in Florence as the son of a tailor (Italian *sarto*).

ca. 1493 He initially begins an apprenticeship with a goldsmith at the early age of seven, before being trained as a painter in the workshop of Piero di Cosimo (ca. 1461/62–1521), a pupil of Rosselli. He is later mainly influenced by Leonardo, Michelangelo, Raphael, and Fra Bartolomeo.

beginning of 16th century Inspired by Raphael, he paints various images of the Madonna, including the *Madonna with the Goldfinch* (Galleria Nazionale d'Arte Antica — Palazzo Barberini, Rome), which can be dated to around 1506.

1507/08 He paints a fresco portraying Mary Magdalene being carried into heaven by angels for the Orsanmichele in the center of Florence.

1508 On 12 December, Andrea becomes a member of the Arte dei Medici e Speziali, guild of physicians and apothecaries, which is also responsible for painters, and opens a workshop together with Franciabigio (ca. 1482–1525), another pupil of Piero di Cosimo.

1509/10 Five frescoes in the Chiostro dei Voti of Santissima Annunziata commissioned by the Servi di Maria.

ca. 1510/11 The painter is supposed by some to have traveled to Rome.

1511 He paints a fresco of the Trinity in the refectory of the Vallombrosan monks of San Salvi (a decade and a half later the *Last Supper* follows).

ca. 1512/13 He paints a series of altarpieces, including the *Mystical Marriage of St. Catherine of Siena* (Gemäldegalerie Alte Meister, Dresden).

ca. 1514/15 From the Compagnia di San Giovanni Battista (Compagnia dello Scalzo), he receives the extensive commission to paint the cloister of their monastery with scenes from the life of St. John the Baptist. With numerous breaks, the artist is busy there until the mid-1520s.

1517 He paints the *Madonna of the Harpies* (page 277) for the Florentine convent of San Francesco de' Macci, and shortly afterwards the *Disputation on the Trinity* (Palazzo Pitti, Florence).

1518 In spring, he marries a woman by the name of Lucrezia. He then spends just over a year at the court of King Francis I of France in Fontainebleau. Vasari reports that he returns to Florence despite his promising career abroad because of his almost "foolish" love for his wife.

1519/20 After his return from France, Andrea del Sarto, Franciabigio, Pontormo, and others are commissioned by the Medici pope, Leo X, to decorate the villa in Poggio a Caiano near Florence (scenes from the history of Rome).

1525 He paints the *Madonna del Sacco* (page 276) in fresco in the Chiostro Grande of Santissima Annunziata in Florence.

ca. 1527/28 Andrea paints the *Sacrifice of Isaac* (page 279), originally intended for King Francis I.

1530 On 29 September, Andrea del Sarto dies of plague in Florence and is interred in the church of Santissima Annunziata.

Savoldo, Giovanni Girolamo

ca. 1480 Giovanni Girolamo Savoldo is either born in Brescia, Lombardy, or born as the son of a family from Brescia. Just as little is known about his exact origins as is known about his training as a painter. Lombard, Venetian, and even Netherlandish influences can be found in his work.

1506 First evidence of his name appears in Parma (Emilia Romagna).

1508 Savoldo is listed as a member of the Florentine guild of physicians and apothecaries (Arte dei Medici e Speziali). No further information about the painter during these years is available.

1520 A signed and dated painting of *St. Anthony Abbot and St. Paul* (Gallerie dell'Accademia, Venice), as well as the depiction of the Prophet Elijah (National Gallery of Art, Washington), clearly intended as its pendant, are painted this year.

1521 The painter is permanently based in Venice from this year at the latest. He paints *Enthroned Madonna and Child with Six Saints* for the Dominican church of San Niccolò in Treviso.

1524/25 In the Adriatic port of Pesaro (the Marches), where five decades earlier Giovanni Bellini had painted his large *Coronation of the Virgin* (page 138) for the main altar of San Francesco, Savoldo receives the commission from the Dominican rivals of the Franciscans for a *sacra conversazione* that apart from the substitution of St Dominic for St. Francis depicts the same saints as in Bellini's work (Pinacoteca di Brera, Milan).

ca. 1525 His two altarpieces of the *Transfiguration* (Galleria degli Uffizi, Florence, and Pinacoteca Ambrosiana, Milan) clearly show knowledge of Giovanni Bellini's earlier version (page 134).

1527 He paints the panel *St. Jerome the Penitent* (National Gallery, London) in horizontal format for the Averoldo family from Brescia, and four paintings with the *Rest on the Flight to Egypt* for Pietro Contarini of Venice who, according to present-day conjecture, intended to sell them to finance the furnishing of a chapel in Santi Apostoli. Savoldo marries a woman from Flanders in the same year.

ca. 1529 Paints *Portrait of a Man in Armor (Gaston de Foix)*, also sometimes considered a self-portrait (page 383).

ca. 1530 Paints *Tobias and the Angel* (page 382).

early 1530s Several nocturnal works by the painter are recorded for this period, probably commissioned by the Duke of Milan, Francesco Maria Sforza. A presumed journey by the artist to Genoa probably took place during these years.

ca. 1536 Savoldo paints altar panels with the *Adoration* for various churches.

mid-1530s through mid-1540s Paints several variations of Mary Magdalene (Palazzo Pitti, Florence; National Gallery, London; Gemäldegalerie, Berlin).

After 1548 Giovanni Girolamo Savoldo dies either in Venice or in Brescia.

Tintoretto

1519 Jacopo Tintoretto (real name: Jacopo Robusti) is born the son of silk dyer Battista Robusti in Venice.

1539 Recorded evidence of the painter as "master" on the Campo San.

1542 Tintoretto paints ceiling murals in the style of Giulio Romano (1499–1546), an artist greatly influenced by Raphael and Michelangelo, for the patrician Vettor Pisani.

1545 Tintoretto paints two mythological ceiling murals for Pietro Aretino, who thanks him with an effusive letter of praise.

1548 beginning of April Tintoretto is suddenly made famous by his canvas the *Miracle of the Slave* (page 431) in the chapter house of the Scuola Grande di San Marco.

1555 Tintoretto is working in the convent church of Madonna dell'Orto (pages 440–445) while the ten-year-younger Paolo Veronese is beginning in San Sebastiano.

1560 Birth of Tintoretto's son Domenico, who will become his most important colleague.

1562 In the year of the 1,500th anniversary of the death of St. Mark, Tintoretto is awarded the commission to paint a cycle of works on the miracles of St. Mark for the chapter house of the Scuola Grande di San Marco (pages 446–449).

1564 Tintoretto gains entry into the Scuola Grande di San Rocco by donating his oval ceiling canvas *Apotheosis of St. Roch* (page 451).

1566 Vasari is collecting material in Venice for the second edition of his *Vite*. Tintoretto becomes a member of the Florentine Accademia del Disegno, together with Titian, Palladio, and three other Venetian artists.

1570 The Turks threaten Venetian grain supplies. To ensure his own supply, "Jacobus de Robustis," alias Jacopo Tintoretto, acquires an estate near Padua.

1571 Following the Venetian victory in the Battle of Lepanto, Tintoretto presents the Venetian state with a painting of this sea battle and requests in return an agent's patent *sansaria* at the Fondaco dei Tedeschi (German Merchants' Hall).

1574 A fire at the Doge's Palace destroys Tintoretto's works. Jacopo participates in the festive decorations to celebrate the state visit of King Henry III. He acquires a house on the Fondamenta dei Mori.

1575–1577 Venice is ravaged by the plague.

1576 Short of money due to the plague, Tintoretto exchanges the estate he acquired in 1570 for a smaller one and 300 ducats. The decoration of the Scuola Grande di San Rocco (page 456) begins.

1580 Tintoretto travels with his wife Faustina to Mantua to supervise the mounting of a cycle of paintings in the ducal palace, and visits his brother, court musician Domenico Robusti.

1582/83 Works on the ground floor of the Scuola Grande di San Rocco.

1590 The portrait specialist Maria Robusti, known as "La Tintoretta," his favorite daughter and assistant, dies before reaching the age of 40.

1592 Tintoretto's eldest son, Giovanni Battista, dies in Padua or the surrounding area. Tintoretto is working in San Giorgio Maggiore.

1594 On 31 May Jacopo Tintoretto dies aged 75 in his house on the Rio della Sensa. He is interred three days later in Madonna dell'Orto.

Titian

ca. 1488–1490 Titian (real name: Tiziano Vecellio) is born in Pieve di Cadore.

ca. 1498 Titian and his brother move to Venice.

1508/09 Frescoes on the newly built Fondaco dei Tedeschi, the German Merchants' Hall near the Rialto, facing the Grand Canal.

1510 Fresco for the Scuola del Santo in Padua (page 299). Venice is ravaged by plague, to which Giorgione also falls victim.

1513 Invited to Rome by Pietro Bembo at the papal court, Titian offers his services to the Venetian senate and requests the "granting of a commission for the work on the pictures for the Sala del Gran Consiglio." He opens his first workshop of his own near San Samuele the same year.

1516 Starts to work for Alfonso d'Este in Ferrara. Titian also receives the commission for the *Assunta,* the high altar of Santa Maria Gloriosa dei Frari, Venice, which is unveiled on 19 May 1518 (page 307).

1519 On 24 April he is commissioned to paint the *Pesaro Altarpiece* in Santa Maria Gloriosa dei Frari, Venice, which is unveiled in 1526 (page 313).

1522 The Venetian senate demands that Titian delivers the promised painting for the Sala del Gran Consiglio and threatens to withdraw all privileges.

1523 Works in the Doge's Palace and for Alfonso d'Este in Ferrara. First contact to Federico Gonzaga.

1528 *Martyrdom of St. Peter Martyr* for the church of Santi Giovanni e Paolo (Zanipolo) in Venice, which is completed in 1530 (destroyed by fire; only a copper-plate engraving of it exists today).

1529 In October, Federico Gonzaga mediates Titian's first meeting with Emperor Charles V in Parma.

1530 He is working mainly for Federico Gonzaga.

1531 He moves to the house in Biri Grande in the community of San Canciano, where he is to live for the rest of his life.

1532 He is in contact with Francesco Maria della Rovere, Duke of Urbino.

1533 In January, Titian again meets Charles V in Bologna. He paints his portrait and is appointed Count Palatine and Knight of the Golden Spur by the Emperor.

1536 Begins work on the portraits of Eleonora Gonzaga and Francesco Maria della Rovere.

1537 The nuns of Santa Maria degli Angeli on Murano reject Titian's *Annunciation* and give the commission to Pordenone.

1538 Although Titian completes the long-promised battle painting for the Doge's Palace in August, privileges are withdrawn because of the delayed delivery. These privileges are then granted to his rival, Pordenone.

1539 The *Presentation of the Virgin at the Temple* in the Sala dell'Albergo of the Scuola della Carità is unveiled on 6 March (pages 326–327). Titian's privileges are reinstated.

1541 Delivers his painting *Alfonso d'Avalos Addressing His Troops* (page 325).

1543 Titian paints the portrait of Pope Paul III to commemorate the Pope's meeting with Charles V in Busseto.

1545 Accompanied by his son, Orazio, Titian travels to Rome via Urbino. Together with Sebastiano del Piombo and Giorgio Vasari, Titian views the ancient ruins of the Eternal City. He also meets Michelangelo.

1546 Titian returns to Venice after being granted Roman civic rights on 19 March.

1548 Journey to the Diet of Augsburg on the invitation of Charles V. It is October before Titian is again in Venice.

1550 Titian undertakes a second journey to the Diet of Augsburg at the request of Charles V.

1551 In August, he is back in Venice. Titian becomes a member of the Scuola di San Rocco.

1566 Titian demands from Cornelis Cort the rights to prints the latter has made of the painter's works. The Council of Ten agrees, and transfers both these rights and those to Niccolò Boldrini's prints to Titian. The artist is accepted into the Accademia dell' Disegno in Florence, together with Andrea Palladio and Tintoretto.

1575 He sends the painting *Religion Succored by Spain* (page 363) to Philip II on 24 September.

1576 The great plague epidemic that has been ravaging Venice since June 1575 will continue to rage until the summer of the following year and claim approximately 50,000 victims. Titian dies on 27 August, whether from plague or from old age is unclear. Shortly afterwards, the plague carries off his son, Orazio.

Tura, Cosimo

ca. 1430 Probably the year of birth of the painter Cosimo Tura of Ferrara. The date has previously been set as between 1379 and 1406, in which case the first mention of him, as "Gosme di Domenico Tura," is in a document from 1431 referring to property matters.

1451 Tura is employed to review works by Jacopo Turola, and is paid in this and the following year for his first works of his own, mostly of a decorative nature.

1458 Appointed court painter by Borso d'Este.

1460–1463 Works in the *studiolo* of Borso d'Este in Belfiore; afterwards he is often occupied with heraldic paintings and festive decorations.

1465–1467 Paints ten panels for the library of the humanist Pico della Mirandola (now lost).

1467–1468 Decorates the Cappella dei Sacrati in San Domenico, Ferrara (now lost).

1469 He starts his work in Belriguardo (now lost). Payment for the shutters of the cathedral organ on 11 June (Museo del Duomo, Ferrara).

ca. 1470 Paintings of the months of the year in the Palazzo Schifanoia, Ferrara.

1471 His first will, in favor of his assistant Domenico di Jacopo Valeri.

1474 Polyptych for Luigi Roverella for the church of San Giorgio fuori le Mura: *Madonna with Angels* (page 124); *Pietà* (Musée du Louvre, Paris), other panels either destroyed or scattered over various galleries.

1477–1480, 1485 Various portraits of members of the Este family, none of which have been identified.

1483 Litigation over outstanding payment for the *studiolo* of Borso d'Este, on which he had worked 1459–1463.

1486 Leaves his service at the court in Ferrara and together with the painter Teofilo di Jacopo da Cesena retreats to a tower in the city's fortification.

1487 Writes his second will.

1489 Arranges maintenance for his illegitimate son and the child's mother.

1490 He requests payment from Duke Ercole d'Este for work carried out six years earlier.

1491 In his third will, he names an illegitimate son, Damiano Cosimo Maria, as his heir and bequeaths 250 lire to Damiano's mother.

1495 Tura dies in Ferrara, where he is interred in San Lorenzo.

Veronese

1528 Veronese (real name: Paolo Caliari) is born the second eldest of stonemason Gabriele di Piero and his wife Caterina in the San Paolo quarter of Verona.

1538 Birth of his brother and later colleague, Benedetto Caliari.

ca. 1539 Apprenticeship with the painter Antonio Badile of Verona; first mentioned as his pupil and assistant in 1541. Further training with Giovanni Caroto follows.

1551 Works in the Villa Soranza near Castelfranco as the protégé of master builder Michele Sanmicheli. He makes his public debut in Venice with the *Holy Family with St. Antony Abbot, St. Catherine, and the Infant John the Baptist (Giustian Altarpiece)* (page 471) for the chapel of the same name in the church of San Francesco della Vigna.

1552 The *Temptation of St. Anthony,* commissioned by Cardinal Ercole Gonzaga for San Pietro Cathedral in Mantua (page 470).

1554–1556 Significantly involved in decorating the Sale del Consiglio dei Dieci (Sala delle Udienze, Sala della Bussola, and Stanza dei Tre Capi) in the Doge's Palace.

1555 Moves to Venice. First use of the name "Paulo Veronese" in the contract for an apartment in the Santi Apostoli quarter. Bernardo Torlioni, the prior of San Sebastiano in Venice, assigns the painting of the ceiling murals in the sacristy to "Paulo Caliaro Veronese." Numerous further works of art and illusionary frescoes are painted on the ceiling and sidewalls of the nave, in the choir, and in the refectory between 1555 and 1570.

1556–1557 Seven painters compete for paintings to decorate Sansovino's Libreria Vecchia. Veronese again proves his skill as a painter of ceilings and wins the competition with his tondo *Allegory of Music.* Working alongside the sculptor Alessandro Vittoria (1525–1608), he paints frescoes in the Palazzo Trevisan in Murano.

1559 Presumed journey to Rome in the entourage of the Venetian ambassador, Girolamo Grimani.

1560–1561 He decorates the Villa Barbaro built by Andrea Palladio in Maser (pages 475–477).

1562 On 7 January, he receives the commission for the large-scale painting *Frederick Barbarossa Kissing the Hand of the Antipope Victor IV* (page 474), which is destroyed in the fire in the Sala del Maggior Consiglio of the Doge's Palace in 1577.

1562–1563 He paints Venice's first monumental sacral banquet scene for the refectory of the Benedictine convent of San Giorgio Maggiore in Venice: the *Wedding at Cana* (pages 480–481).

1566 On 17 April, he marries Elena Badile, the daughter of his former teacher, in Verona.

1567–1570 Birth of his sons Gabriele and Carletto Caliari.

1572 Veronese is paid on 29 April for his *Feast of Gregory the Great* (page 482) painted for the sanctuary of the Madonna di Monte Berico in Vicenza. He moves to the Calle di Ca' Mocenigo in the parish of San Samule in Venice.

1573 His *Last Supper* in the refectory of the Dominican order of Santi Giovanni e Paolo in Venice causes offence. Veronese is summoned to appear before the Inquisition to justify himself. He compromises and changes the title to *Feast in the House of Levi* (pages 484–485).

1575 He is staying in Padua, together with Benedetto Caliari. He completes *Martyrdom of St. Guistina* for the high altar of the convent church of the same name. Plague is raging in Venice.

1575–1582 Paintings (page 486) for the ceilings and walls of the Sala del Collegio and Sala del Maggior Consiglio that had been destroyed by fires in the Doge's Palace in 1574 and 1577.

1585 Veronese declines the offer to work in the Escorial for the Spanish King.

1587 Commissioned by Bartolomeo Borghi, *Wonder of St. Pantaleon,* for the Venetian church of the same name.

1588 Following an eight-day illness, Veronese dies on 19 April, aged 60, of pleurisy and fever, and is interred in the church most adorned with his works, San Sebastiano in Venice.

Zoppo, Marco

1433 Marco Zoppo (real name: Marco di Antonio Ruggieri) is born in Cento. Is named "Marco the Lame" because of his physical disability.

1452 Payment for the restoration and mounting of an earlier statue of the Madonna.

1454 He enters the workshop of Francesco Squarcione (ca. 1397–1468) in Padua, who adopts him in 1455; the relationship is dissolved the same year. In Padua, he is confronted with Mantegna and Donatello, who exert a formative influence on him. Zoppo moves from Padua to Venice.

1455 *Madonna* (Musée du Louvre, Paris).

1462 He moves to Bologna.

1471 In Venice, where he has possibly been based since 1466/67, he signs and dates the *sacra conversazione* today in the Gemäldegalerie in Berlin (page 125), which may belong to the *Angel Pietà* in the Museum at Pesaro.

18 February 1478 Zoppo dies in Venice.

Adapted by Henrik Engel

SELECT BIBLIOGRAPHY

Acidini Luchinat, Cristina: Benozzo Gozzoli, Antella (Florence) 1994

Ackerman, James S.: Architectural Practice in the Italian Renaissance, in: Journal of the Society of Architectural Historians XIII, 1954, pp. 3–11

Aikema, Bernard: Jacopo Bassano and his public: Moralizing pictures in an age of reform c. 1535–1600, Princeton, NJ, 1996

Alberti, Leon Battista: Della Pittura (1436), Milan and Naples 1955

Alberti, Leon Battista: On Painting and On Sculpture, edited with translations, introduction and notes by Cecil Grayson, London 1972

Antal, Frederick: Florentine painting and its social background, New York, 1975

Arasse, Daniel: Leonardo da Vinci, Cologne 2002

Argan, Giulio Carlo: Fra Angelico, Geneva 1955

Aronberg-Lavin, Marylin: Piero della Francesca, San Francesco, Arezzo and New York 1993

Aronberg-Lavin, Marylin: Piero della Francesca and his Legacy, Washington 1995

Avery, Charles: Donatello, New York 1994

Avery, Charles, Andrew Butterfield and Ulrich Middeldorf: Early Renaissance Reliefs, New York, 2001

Baccheschi, Edi: L'opera completa di Giotto, Presentazione André Chastel, Milan 1966

Baccheschi, Edi: L'opera completa del Bronzino, Milan 1973

Bacci, Mina: L'opera completa di Piero di Cosimo, Milan 1976

Baggio, Luca, Gianluigi Colalucci and Daniela Bartoletti: Altichiero da Zevio nell'Oratorio di San Giorgio: Il restauro degli affreschi, Padua 1999

Baglione, Giovanni B.: Le vite de'pittori scultori et architetti: Dal Pontificato di Gregorio XIII. del 1572 in fino ai tempi di Papa Urbano Ottavo nel 1642, ed. by V. Mariani, Rome 1935

Baldini, Umberto: L'opera completa di Michelangelo scultore, Milan 1973

Baldini, Umberto: Masaccio, Milan 2001

Baldini, Umberto: Michelangelo scultore, Florence 1981

Baldini, Umberto and Elsa Morante: Fra Angelico, in: Klassiker der Kunst, Luzern, Freudenstadt and Vienna 1970

Ballarin, Alessandro: Dosso Dossi: La pittura a Ferrara negli anni del Ducato di Alfonso I, 2 vols, Padua 1994 and 1995

Bandera Bistoletti, Sandrina: Il Polittico di S. Luca di Andrea Mantegna in occasione del suo restauro, Florence 1989

Bandera Bistoletti, Sandrina: Giotto: Catalogo completo dei dipinti, Florence 1989

Barbera, Giocchino: Antonello da Messina, Milan 1998

Barolsky, Paul: Why Mona Lisa Smiles and Other Tales by Vasari, University Park 1991

Barolsky, Paul: Giotto's Father and the Family of Vasari's Lives, University Park 1992

Bartz, Gabriele: Guido di Piero, bekannt als Fra Angelico, um 1395–1455, Cologne 1998

Bartz, Gabriele and Eberhard König: Michelangelo Bonarroti: 1475–1564, Cologne 1998

Battisti, Eugenio: Piero della Francesca, Istituto editoriale italiano, Milan 1971

Battisti, Eugenio: Piero della Francesca, Milan 1992

Battisti, Eugenio, Bianca Bellardoni and Luciano Berti: Angelico a San Marco, Florence 1965

Bätzner, Nike: Andrea Mantegna: 1430/31–1506, Cologne 1998

Baxandall, Michael: Painting and Experience in Fifteenth Century Italy: A Primer in the Social History of Pictorial Style, Oxford 1972

Becherer, Joseph Antenucci: Pietro Perugino: Master of the Italian Renaissance, Grand Rapids, MI, and New York 1997

Beck, James: Raphael before Rome: Studies in the History of Art, in: National Gallery of Art, vol. 17, 1986

Beckers, Petra: Die Passionsfresken Pontormos für die Certosa del Galluzzo, 2 vols, Salzburg 1985

Béguin, Sylvie: Un nouveau Raphaël: Un ange du retable de Saint Nicolas de Tolentino, in: Revue du Louvre, vol. 31, 1982, pp. 99–115

Bellori, Giovanni P: Le vite de'pittori, scultori e architetti moderni, Rome 1672

Bellori, Giovanni P: The lives of the modern painters, sculptors and architects, trans. Alice Sedgwick Wohl, notes by Hellmut Wohl, introduction by Tomaso Montanari, New York 2005

Bellosi, Luciano: Buffalmacco e il Trionfo della Morte, Turin 1974

Bellosi, Luciano: Giotto, Florence 1981

Belting, Hans: Likeness and presence: a history of the image before the era of art, trans. Edmund Jephcott, Chicago 1996

Belting, Hans: Giovanni Bellini: Pietà, Ikone und Bilderzählung in der venezianischen Malerei, Frankfurt on Main 1985

Belting, Hans and Dieter Blume: Malerei und Stadtkultur in der Dantezeit, Munich 1989

Beltrami, Luca: Documenti e memorie riguardanti la vita e le opere di Leonardo da Vinci, Milan 1919

Benazzi, Giordana: Pintoricchio a Spello: La Cappella Baglioni in Santa Maria Maggiore, Milan 2000

Bennett, Bonnie A., and David G. Wilkins: Donatello, Oxford 1984

Berdini, Paolo: The religious art of Jacopo Bassano: Painting as visual exegesis, Cambridge 1997

Berenson, Bernard: Italian Painters of the Renaissance: Venetian School, 2 vols, London 1957; Florentine School, 2 vols, London 1963; Central and North Italian Schools, 3 vols, London 1968

Berenson, Bernard: Piero della Francesca or the Ineloquent in Art, London 1950

Bertelli, Carlo: Piero della Francesca, Milan 1991

Berti, Luciano: L'opera completa del Pontormo, Milan 1973

Berti, Luciano: L'opera completa di Masaccio, Presentazione Paolo Volponi, Milan 1968

Berti, Luciano and Umberto Baldini: Filippino Lippi, Florence 1991

Berti, Luciano, et al.: Gli Uffizi: Catalogo generale, Florence 1979

Bevilacqua, Alberto and Arturo Carlo Quintavalle: L'opera completa del Correggio, Milan 1970

Bialostocki, Jan: Spätmittelalter und beginnende Neuzeit, in: Propyläen-Kunstgeschichte, vol. 7, Frankfurt on Main and Berlin 1990

Bischoff, Uwe: Die "Cassonebilder" des Piero di Cosimo: Fragen der Ikonographie, Frankfurt on Main 1995

Blass-Simmen, Brigit: Sankt Georg: Drachenkampf in der Renaissance: Carpaccio – Raffael – Leonardo, Berlin 1991

Blum, Ilse: Andrea Mantegna und die Antike, Strasbourg 1936

Blume, Dieter: Wandmalerei als Ordenspropaganda: Bildprogramme im Chorbereich franziskanischer Konvente Italiens bis zur Mitte des 14. Jahrhunderts, Worms 1983

Bode, Wilhelm von: Sandro Botticelli, Berlin 1921

Bologna, Ferdinando: The Crowning Disc of a Trecento Crucifixion and Other Points Relevant to Duccio's Relationship to Cimabue, in: The Burlington Magazine, CXXXV, 1983, pp. 330–340

Bomford, David et al.: Art in the Making: Italian Painting before 1400, London 1989

Bonnet, Jacques: Lorenzo Lotto, Paris 1996

Bonsanti, Giorgio: Il Museo di San Marco, Milan 1985

Borsi, Franco and Stefano: Paolo Uccello, Milan 1992

Borsook, Eve and Johannes Offerhaus: Francesco Sassetti and Ghirlandaio at Santa Trinità, Florence: History and Legend in a Renaissance Chapel, Doornspijk 1981

Boskovits, Miklós: Pittura fiorentina alla vigilia del Rinascimento, Florence 1975

Boskovits, Miklós: Un'adorazione dei magi e gli inizi dell'Angelico, Bern 1976

Bovero, Anna: L'opera completa del Crivelli, Milan 1974

Brandi, Cesare: Il restauro della "Maestà" di Duccio, Rome 1959

Bredekamp, Horst: La Primavera: Florenz als Garten der Venus, Frankfurt on Main 1989

Brock, Maurice: Bronzino, Paris 2002

Brown, David Alan: Leonardo and the Ladies with the Ermine and the Book, in: Artibus et Historiae, 21, 1990, pp. 47–61

Brown, David Alan: Raphael, Leonardo, and Perugino: Fame and Fortune in Florence, in: Leonardo, Michelangelo, and Raphael in Renaissance Florence from 1500 to 1508, ed. by Serafina Hager, Washington 1992, pp. 29–53

Brown, Veverly Louise: Jacopo Bassano c. 1510–1592, Bassano and Fort Worth 1992

Buck, Stephanie and Peter Hohenstatt: Raffaello Santi, known as Raphael, Cologne and New York 1998

Bull, David: Two Portraits by Leonardo: Ginevra de'Benci and the Lady with the Ermine, in: Artibus et Historiae, 25, 1992, pp. 67–84

Burke, Peter: Culture and Society in Renaissance Italy, London 1972

Butterfield, Andrew: The sculptures of Andrea del Verrocchio, New Haven and London 1997

Calvesi, Maurizio: La realtà del Caravaggio: Seconda parte (i dipinti), Storia dell'arte 55, 1985, pp. 227–287

Calvi, Gerolamo: I manoscritti di Leonardo da Vinci, ed. by Augusto Marinoni, Busto Arsizio 1982

Camesasca, Ettore: Andrea Mantegna, Milan 1964

Camesasca, Ettore: Mantegna, Milan 1992

Camiz, Franca T. and Agostino Ziino: Caravaggio: Aspetti musicali e committenza, Studi musicali 12, 1983, pp. 67–83

Cämmerer, Monika: Giottos Polyptychon in der Baroncelli-Kapelle von Santa Croce: Nachträge und neue Beobachtungen, in: Mitteilungen des Kunsthistorischen Institutes in Florenz, vol. 39, 1995, pp. 374–392

Canova, Giordana: Paris Bordon, Venice 1964

Carli, Enzo: La "Maestà" di Duccio, Florence 1982

Carli, Enzo: La pittura senese del Trecento, Venice 1981

Castelfranchi Vegas, Liana: Italien und Flandern: Die Geburt der Renaissance, Stuttgart and Zurich 1994

Castelfranchi Vegas, Liana: L'Angelico e l'Umanesimo, in: Arte Storia Archeologia 1, Milan 1989

Castris, Pierluigi Leone de: La crocifissione di Masaccio a Napoli: Strana storia di un'attribuzione contesa e di un acquisto "conveniente," in: Confronto, 2002, No. 0, pp. 17–28

Cecchi, Alessandro: Nuovi contribuiti sulla committenza fiorentina di Masolino e di Masaccio, in: Masaccio e Masolino, ed. by Andrea Baldinotti, 2002, pp. 23–71

Cennini, Cennino: Il libro dell'arte, ed. by Franco Brunello, Vicenza 1982

Chastel, André: A chronicle of Italian Renaissance painting, Ithaca, NY, 1984

Chastel, André: Florentine drawings, XIV–XVII centuries, New York 1950

Chastel, André: The studios and styles of the Renaissance, New York 1966

Chastel, André: The flowering of the Italian Renaissance, New York 1965

Chastel, André: The crisis of the Renaissance, 1520–1600, Geneva 1968

Chastel, André: The myth of the Renaissance, 1420–1520, Geneva 1969

Chiari Moretto Weil, Maria A.: Tiziano: Corpus dei disegni, Milan 1989

Christiansen, Keith: Caravaggio and l'esempio davanti dal naturale, Art Bulletin 68, 1986, pp. 421–445

Cianchi, Marco: Die Maschinen Leonardo da Vincis, Florence 1988

Ciardi, Roberto Paolo and Alberto Mugnaini: Rosso Fiorentino: Catalogo completo dei dipinti, Florence 1991

Ciardi, Roberto Paolo, et al.: Il Rosso e Volterra, Exhibition Catalogue Volterra 1994

Cinotti, Mia: Michelangelo Merisi detto il Caravaggio, I pittori bergamaschi: il seicento, vol. 1, Bergamo, 1983, pp. 205–641

Cipriani, Renata: Tutta la pittura di Andrea Mantegna, Milan 1956

Clapp, Frederick Mortimer: Jacopo Carrucci da Pontormo: His Life and Work, New Haven and London 1916, reprint New York 1981

Clark, Kenneth: Leonardo da Vinci: An Account of his Development as an Artist (original ed. Cambridge 1939), with an introduction by Martin Kemp, London 1988

Clark, Kenneth: Piero della Francesca, London 1951, new ed. London 1969

Clark, Kenneth and Carlo Pedretti: A catalogue of the Drawings of Leonardo da Vinci in the Collection of Her Majesty the Queen at Windsor Castle, London 1968

Clark, Nicholas: Melozzo da Forlì: Pictor papalis, London 1990

Clayton, Martin: Leonardo da Vinci: A Curious Vision, London 1996

Cocke, Richard: Veronese, London 1980

Cocke, Richard: Veronese's Drawings: A catalogue raisonné, London 1984

Cole, Bruce: Sienese Painting, New York 1980

Cole Ahl, Diane: Benozzo Gozzoli, New Haven and London 1996

Cole Ahl, Diane: Benozzo Gozzoli's Frescoes of the Life of Saint Augustine in San Gimignano: Their Meanings in Context, in: Artibus et Historiae, No. 13, 1986, pp. 35–53

Cole Ahl, Diane: Fra Angelico: A new Chronology for the 1420's, in: Zeitschrift für Kunstgeschichte 43, 1980, pp. 360–381

Cole Ahl, Diane: Fra Angelico: A new chronology for the 1430's, in: Zeitschrift für Kunstgeschichte 44, 1981, pp. 133–158

Coletti, Luigi and Ettore Camesasca: La Camera degli Sposi, Milan 1959

Condivi, Ascanio: Vita di Michelangelo Buonarroti, Rome 1553

Condivi, Ascanio: The Life of Michel-Angelo, trans. Alice Sedgwick Wohl, edited Hellmut Wohl, University Park 1999

Contini, Roberto et al.: Un San Bastiano che par no li manchi se non il solo respiro: Paris Bordons Berliner Altarbild im Kontext, Berlin 2007

Costamagna, Philippe: Pontormo, Milan 1994

Covi, Dario A.: Andrea del Verrocchio: Life and Work, Florence 2005

Cox Raerick, Janet: The Drawings of Pontormo, Cambridge, MA, 1964

Crum, Roger J.: Roberto Martelli, The Council of Florence and the Medici-Chapel, in: Zeitschrift für Kunstgeschichte, vol. 3, 1996, pp. 403–417

Dahlhoff, Meinolf: Giovanni Bellini: Die Verklärung Christi. Rhetorik. Erinnerung. Historie, Münster 1997

Davies, Gerald S.: Ghirlandaio, London 1908

Degenhart, Bernhard and Annegrit Schmitt: Corpus der italienischen Zeichnungen: 1300–1450, 14 vols, Berlin 1968–2004

Degenhart, Bernhard and Annegrit Schmitt: Jacopo Bellini: Der Zeichnungsband im Louvre, Munich 1984

Degenhart, Bernhard and Annegrit Schmitt: Pisanello und Bono da Ferrara, Munich 1995

Deuchler, Florens: Duccio, Milan 1984

Didi-Hubermann, Georges: Fra Angelico: Dissemblance and Figuration, Chicago 1995

Dini, Daniela and Magnolia Scuderieri: Gli affreschi di S. Marco nella storia del Restauro, Florence 1990

Dobson, Christopher: Paolo Uccello: San Romano: The art of war, Suffolk 2001

Dolce, Lodovico: Dialogo della pittura intitolato l'Aretino, ed. by Paola Barocchi, in: Trattati d'arte del Cinquecento, II, Bari 1960–1962

Dolce, Lodovico: Aretin: A Dialogue on Painting, Menston 1970 (originally published 1770)

Douglas-Scott, Michael: Jacopo Tintoretto's Altarpiece of St. Agnes at the Madonna dell'Orto in Venice and the Memorialisation of Cardinal Contarini, in: Journal of the Warburg and Courtauld Institutes 60, 1997, pp. 130–163

Dreyer, Peter: Dantes Divina Commedia mit den Illustrationen von Sandro Botticelli, Zurich, 1986 (facsimile and commentary)

Dunkerton, Jill and Dillian Gordon: The Pisa Altarpiece, in: The Panel Paintings of Masolino and Masaccio: The Role of Technique, ed. by C. B. Strehlke and C. Frosinini, Milan 2002

Dussler, Luitpold: Die Zeichnungen des Michelangelo, Kritischer Katalog, Berlin 1959

Dussler, Luitpold: Raphael: A Critical Catalogue, London and New York 1971

Ebert-Schifferer, Sybille: Giovanni Gerolamo Savoldo und die Renaissance zwischen Lombardei und Venetien: Von Foppa und Giorgione bis Caravaggio, Milan and Frankfurt on Main 1990

Echols, Robert: Giovanni Galizzi and the Problem of the Young Tintoretto, in: artibus et historiae 31, 1995, pp. 69–110

Egger, Herman: Codex Escurialensis: Ein Skizzenbuch aus der Werkstatt Domenico Ghirlandaios, Vienna 1905

Einem, Herbert von: Michelangelo, Stuttgart 1959

Einem, Herbert von: Michelangelo: Bildhauer, Maler, Baumeister, Berlin 1973

Eisler, Colin: The Genius of Jacopo Bellini, New York 1989

Emmenegger, Oskar, Albert Knoepfli, Manfred Koller and André Meyer: Reclams Handbuch der künstlerischen Techniken: Wandmalerei und Mosaik, Stuttgart 1990

Ercoli, Giuliano: Arte e Fortuna del Correggio, Modena 1982

Ettlinger, Leopold D.: The Sistine Chapel Before Michelangelo: Religious Imagery and Papal Primacy, Oxford 1965

Ettlinger, Leopold D. and Helen S.: Botticelli, New York, 1977

Evers, Bernd, Architekturmodelle der Renaissance, exhib. cat., Munich and New York 1995

Farago, Claire J.: Leonardo's Battle of Anghiari: A Study in Exchange between Theory and Practice, in: The Art Bulletin, June 1994, pp. 301–330

Fehl, Philipp: Veronese and the Inquisition: A Study of the Subject Matter of the so-called "Feast in the House of Levi," in: Gazette des Beaux-Arts 58, 1961, pp. 325–354

Ferino-Pagden, Sylvia and Schianchi, Lucia Fornari: Parmigianino und der europäische Manierismus, Vienna 2003

Fermor, Sharon: Piero di Cosimo: Fiction, Invention and Fantasìa, London 1993

Fiocco, Giuseppe: L'arte di Andrea Mantegna, Venice 1959

Fiorio, Maria Teresia and Pietro C. Marani: I Leonardeschi a Milano: Fortuna e Collezionismo, Milan 1991

Flores d'Arcais, Francesca: Giotto, Milan 1995

Forssman, Erik: Über Architekturen in der venezianischen Malerei des Cinquecento, in: Wallraf-Richartz-Jahrbuch 29, 1967, pp. 105–139

Forster, Kurt W.: Pontormo: Monographie mit kritischem Katalog, Munich 1966

Foschi, Marina and Luciana Prati: Melozzo da Forlì: La sua città e il suo tempo, Milan 1994

Frangi, Francesco: Savoldo: Catalogo completo dei dipinti, Florence 1992

Franklin, David: Rosso in Italy: The Italian Career of Rosso Fiorentino, New Haven and London 1994

Franklin, David: The Art of Parmigianino, New Haven and London 2003

Freedberg, Sydney J.: Andrea del Sarto: Catalogue raisonné, 2 vols, Cambridge, MA, 1963

Frey, Karl: Die Dichtungen des Michelangelo Buonarroti, Berlin 1897

Frey, Karl: Die Handzeichnungen des Michelangelo Buonarroti, Berlin 1897

Friedlaender, Walter: Caravaggio Studies, Princeton 1955

Frommel, Christoph Luitpold: Storia dell'arte 1971

Frommel, Christoph Luitpold: Caravaggio und seine Modelle, Castrum Peregrini 96, 1971, pp. 21–55

Frommel, Christoph Luitpold: Caravaggios Frühwerk und der Kardinal Francesco Maria del Monte, Storia dell'arte 9/10, 1971, pp. 5–52

Frommel, Christoph Luitpold: Michelangelo und Tommaso dei Cavalieri, Amsterdam 1979

Frommel, Christoph Luitpold, Stefano Ray and Manfredo Tafuri: Raffaello architetto, Milan 1984

Frommel, Christoph Luitpold and Matthias Winner (eds.): Raffaello a Roma, Il Convegno del 1983, Rome 1986

Gatea Bertelà, Giovanna: Donatello, Florence 1991

Galuzzi, Paolo (ed.): Gli ingenieri del rinascimento da Brunelleschi a Leonardo da Vinci, Florence 1995

Gardner von Teuffel, Christa: Masaccio and the Pisa altarpiece: a new approach, in: From Duccio's Maestà to Raphael's Transfiguration, London 2005, pp. 1–71

Garibaldi, Vittoria: Perugino: catalogo completo, Florence 1999

Garibaldi, Vittoria and Simonetta Innamorati: Perugino, Milan 2004

Gärtner, Peter J.: Filippo Brunelleschi: 1377–1446, Cologne 1998

Gebhardt, Volker: Paolo Uccello. Die Schlacht von San Romano. Ein Bilderzyklus zum Ruhme der Medici, Frankfurt on Main 1995

Gemin, Massimo (ed.): Nuovi studi su Paolo Veronese, Venice 1990

Gentili, Augusto: Da Tiziano a Tiziano, Mito e allegoria nella cultura veneziana del Cinquecento, Rome 1988

Giampaolo, Mario di and Andrea Muzzi: Correggio. Catalogo completo dei dipinti, Florence 1993

Gibbons, Felton: Dosso and Battista Dossi. Court painters at Ferrara, Princeton, NJ, 1968

Giese, Elisabeth: Benozzo Gozzolis Franziskuszyklus in Montefalco, Frankfurt on Main 1986

Gilbert, Creighton: Change in Piero della Francesca, New York 1968

Gilbert, Creighton: Fra Angelico's Fresco Cycles in Rome: Their Number and Dates, in: Zeitschrift für Kunstgeschichte 38, 1975, pp. 245–265

Ginzburg, Carlo: Indagini su Piero, Turin 1981 (Erkundungen über Piero, Piero della Francesca, ein Maler der frühen Renaissance, Frankfurt 1981)

Gioseffi, Ducio: Giotto architetto, Milan 1963

Gisolfi Pechukas, Diana: Two oil sketches and the youth of Veronese, in: The Art Bulletin 64, 1982, pp. 388–413

Gizzi, Corrado (ed.): Signorelli e Dante, Milan 1991

Goffen, Rona: Giovanni Bellini, New Haven and London 1989

Goffen, Rona and Giovanna Nepi Scirè (eds.): Il colore ritrovato. Bellini a Venezia. Milan 2000

Golzio, Vincenzo: Raffaello nei documenti nelle testimonianze dei contemporanei e nella letteratura del suo secolo, Vatican 1971

Gombrich, Ernst H.: Symbolic Images: Studies in the art of the Renaissance, New York and London 1972

Gombrich, Ernst H.: Norm and Form, London 1966

Gordon, Dillian: The Altarpieces of Masaccio, in: The Cambridge Companion to Masaccio, Diane Cole Ahl, 2002, pp. 123–137

Gosebruch, Martin: Giotto und die Entwicklung des neuzeitlichen Kunstbewusstseins, Cologne 1962

Gosebruch, Martin: Giottos Stefaneschi-Altarwerk aus St. Peter in Rom, in: Miscellanea Bibliotheca Hertzianae zu Ehren von Leo Bruhns, Munich 1961, pp. 109–330

Gould, Cecil: Parmigianino, New York, London and Paris 1994

Gould, Cecil: The Paintings of Correggio, London 1976

Gould, Cecil: The Raising of Lazarus by Sebastiano del Piombo, London 1967

Gozzoli, Maria Cristina: L'opera completa di Simone Martini, Presentazione Gianfranco Contini, Milan 1970

Grave, Johannes: Landschaften der Meditation: Giovanni Bellinis Assoziationsräume, Freiburg im Breisgau 2004

Greco, Antonella: La capella di Niccoleò V del Beato Angelico, Rome 1980

Greenhalgh, Michael: Donatello and his Sources, London 1982

Gregori, Mina: Come dipingeva il Caravaggio: Atti della giornata di studio (Florence, 28.01.1991), Milan 1996

Grömling, Alexandra and Tilman Lingesleben: Alessandro Botticelli: 1444/45–1510, Cologne 1998

Guerrini, Mauro: Bibliografia leonardiana 1986–1989, in: Raccolta Vinciana, Milan 1989

Hale, John R.: Florence and the Medici: The pattern of control, London 1977

Hamann, Richard: Geschichte der Kunst, Berlin 1933

Hartt, Frederick: Michelangelo: The Complete Sculpture, London 1969

Hartt, Frederick: The Drawings of Michelangelo, London 1971

Haskell, Francis: Patrons and Painters, New York 1963

Haussherr, Reiner: Michelangelos Kruzifixus für Vittoria Colonna (Wissenschaftliche Abhandlungen der Rheinisch-Westfälischen Akademie der Wissenschaften, vol. 44), Opladen 1971

Hauvette, Henri: Ghirlandaio, Paris 1907

Held, Jutta: Caravaggio: Politik und Martyrium der Körper, Berlin 1996

Henning, Andreas and Günther Ohlhoff (eds.): Antonello da Messina. Der Heilige Sebastian, Dresden 2005

Hetzer, Theodor: Giotto, seine Stellung in der europäischen Kunst, Frankfurt on Main 1941

Hetzer, Theodor: Tizian: Geschichte seiner Farbe, Frankfurt am Main 1935

Heydenreich, Ludwig H.: Die italienische Renaissance in ihrer Entfaltung in der Zeit von 1400 bis 1460, Munich 1972

Heydenreich, Ludwig H.: Leonardo-Studien, Munich 1988

Hibbard, Howard: Caravaggio, New York 1985

Hibbard, Howard: Michelangelo: Painter, Sculptor, Architect, London 1979

Hirst, Michael: Sebastiano del Piombo, Oxford 1981

Hohenstatt, Peter: Leonardo da Vinci. 1452–1519, Cologne and New York 1998

Holmes, Megan: Fra Filippo Lippi: The Carmelite Painter, New Haven and London 1999

Hood, William: Fra Angelico at San Marco, New Haven, London 1993

Horne, Herbert P.: Alessandro Filipepi Commonly Called Sandro Botticelli, Painter of Florence, London, 1908

Horster, Marita: Andrea del Castagno: Complete Edition with a Critical Catalogue, Oxford 1980

Humfrey, Peter: Carpaccio: Catalogo completo dei dipinti, Florence 1991

Humfrey, Peter: Cima da Conegliano, Cambridge 1983

Humfrey, Peter: Lorenzo Lotto, London 1997

Humfrey, Peter (ed.): The Cambridge Companion to Giovanni Bellini, Cambridge 2004

Humfrey, Peter et al.: Dosso Dossi. Court Painter in Renaissance Ferrara, New York 1998

Huse, Norbert and Wolfgang Wolters: Venedig: Die Kunst der Renaissance, Architektur, Skulptur, Malerei, 1460–1590, Mich 1986

Jahnsen, Angeli: Perspektivregeln und Bildgestaltung bei Piero della Francesca, Munich 1990

Jannella, Cecilia: Duccio di Buoninsegna, Milan 1994

Janson, Horst W.: The Sculpture of Donatello, 2 vols, Princeton 1957

Justi, Carl: Michelangelo, Leipzig 1900 and Berlin 1909

Kaminski, Marion: Tiziano Vecellio, bekannt als Tizian. 1488/90–1576, Cologne 1998

Kanther, Laurence B. and Tom Henry: Luca Signorelli, Munich 2002

Kanter, Laurence B. et al.: Painting and Illumination in Early Renaissance Florence 1300–1450, New York 1994

Kecks, Roland G.: Ghirlandaio, catalogo completo, Florence 1995

Kehl, Ines: Vittore Carpaccios Ursulalegendenzyklus der Scuola di Sant'Orsola in Venedig. Eine venezianische Illusion, Worms 1992

Kemp, Martin: Leonardo da Vinci: The Marvellous Works of Nature and Man, London 1981

Kemp, Wolfgang: Die Räume der Maler. Bilderzählung seit Giotto, Munich 1996

Kempers, Bram: Kunst, Macht und Mäzenatentum. Der Beruf des Malers in der italienischen Renaissance, Munich 1989

Kempers, Bram und Sible de Blaauw: Jacopo Stefaneschi, Patron and Liturgist. A New Hypothesis Regarding the Date, Iconography, Authorship and Function of his Altarpiece for Old Saint Peter's, in: Medelingen van het Nederlands Instituut te Rome, Deel XLVII, n.s. 12, 1987, pp. 83–286

Kiel, Hanna: Das Sinopienmuseum im Camposanto am Dom zu Pisa, in: Pantheon, XXXIX, Book II, 1981, pp. 127–128

Kliemann, Jürgen: Vertumnus und Pomona. Zum Programm von Pontormos Fresko in Poggio a Caiano, in: Mitteilungen des Kunsthistorischen Instituts Florenz, vol. 16, 1972, pp. 293–328

Knab, Eckhart, Erwin Mitsch and Konrad Oberhuber: Raphael. Die Zeichnungen, Stuttgart 1983

Knapp, Fritz: Andrea Mantegna. Des Meisters Gemälde und Kupferstiche, Stuttgart, Leipzig 1910

König, Eberhard: Michelangelo Merisi da Caravaggio: 1571–1610, Cologne 1998

Krautheimer, Richard: Lorenzo Ghiberti (Princeton Monographs in Art and Archaeology XXXI), Princeton 1956, 1970 and 1982

Krischel, Roland: Jacopo Tintoretto. 1519–1595, Cologne 2000

Krischel, Roland: Tintoretto, Reinbek bei Hamburg 1994

Kristeller, Paul: Andrea Mantegna, London, New York 1901–1902

Kruft, Hanno-Walther: Altichiero und Avanzo. Untersuchungen zu oberitalienischen Malerei des ausgehenden Trecento, 1966

Krüger, Klaus: Der frühe Bildkult des Franziskus in Italien. Gestalt und Funktionswandel des Tafelbildes im 13. und 14. Jahrhundert, Berlin 1992

Krüger, Klaus: Das Bild als Schleier des Unsichtbaren. Ästhetische Illusion in der Kunst der frühen Neuzeit in Italien, Munich 2001

Krystof, Doris: Jacopo Carrucci, genannt Pontormo. 1494–1557, Cologne 1998

Küppers, Paul Erich: Die Tafelbilder des Domenico Ghirlandajo, Strasbourg 1915

Laskowski, Birgit: Piero della Francesca. 1416/1417–1492, Cologne 1998

Lauts, Jan: Carpaccio. Gemälde und Zeichnungen. Complete Edition, Cologne 1962

Lauts, Jan: Domenico Ghirlandajo, Vienna 1943

Lebensztejn, Jean-Claude: Jacopo da Pontormo. Paris 1992

Lecaldano, Paolo (ed.): The Complete Works of Andrea Mantegna (L'Opera completa di Andrea Mantegna), Scientific Appendix: Niny Garavaglia, Lucerne, Zurich, Milan 1967

Lightbown, Ronald William: Donatello and Michelozzo. An Artistic Partnership and its Patrons. In the Early Renaissance, 2 vols, London 1980

Lightbown, Ronald William: Mantegna: with a Complete Catalogue of the Paintings, Drawings and Prints, Oxford 1986

Lightbown, Ronald William: Piero della Francesca, New York, London, Paris 1992

Lightbown, Ronald: Sandro Botticelli, Leben und Werk, Munich, 1989

Lisner, Margrit: Die Gewandfarben der Apostel in Giottos Arenafresken. Farbgebung und Farbikonographie, in: Zeitschrift für Kunstgeschichte 1990, pp. 309–375

Lobbenmeier, Annette: Raum und Unendlichkeit. Die Perspektive als Bedeutungsträger in Florentiner Bildprogrammen des Quattrocento, Essen 1995

Lomazzo, Giovanni Paolo: Trattato dell'Arte de la Pittura (reprint of Milan 1584 edition), Hildesheim 1968

Lomazzo, Giovanni Paolo: A tracte containing the artes of curious paintinge, New York 1969 (facsimile of a 1598 translation)

Longhi, Robert: Giudizio sul Duecento, in: Proporzioni, II, 1984, pp. 5–54

Longhi, Roberto: Fatti di Masolino e di Masaccio, Florence 1940

Longhi, Roberto: Il Caravaggio, Milan 1952

Longhi, Roberto: Piero della Francesca, New York 1930

Longhi, Roberto: Venezianische Malerei, mit einem Vorwort von Heinz-Georg Held, Berlin 1995

Lorenzi, Alberto and Pietro C. Marani: Bibliografia Vinciana 1964–1979, Florence 1982

Ludwig, Heinrich (ed.): Leonardo da Vinci. Das Malereibuch, Osnabrück 1970 (new print of 1882 edition)

Lunghi, Elvio: Benozzo Gozzoli in Montefalco, Assisi 1997

Macioce, Stefania: Michelangelo Merisi da Caravaggio. La Vita e le Opere attraverso i Documenti. Atti del Convegno 1995, Rome 1996

Mancini, Guilio: Considerazioni sulla pittura, 2 vols, ed. by A. Marucchi, Rome 1956

Mandel, Gabriele: L'opera completa di Antonello da Messina, Milan 1967

Mannini, Maria Pia and Marco Fagioli: Filippo Lippi. Catalogo completo, Florence 1997

Manno, Antonio: Tintoretto. Sacre rappresentazioni nelle chiese di Venezia, 2 text portfolios, Venice 1994

Manselli, Raoul: Franziskus, Cologne 1984

Marani, Pietro C.: Leonardo, Milan 1994

Marani, Pietro C.: Leonardo. Das Werk des Malers, Munich 2001

Marchese, Vincenzo: Memorie dei più insigni Pittori, Scultori ed Architetti Domenicani, Florence 1854

Marchini, Giuseppe: Filippo Lippi, Milan 1975

Marini, Maurizio: Caravaggio. Michelangelo Merisi da Caravaggio pictor praestantissimus, Rome 1987

Marle, Raymond van: The Development of Italian Schools of Painting, 19 vols, The Hague, 1923–1938

Martin, Andrew John: Savoldos sogenanntes "Bildnis des Gaston de Foix." Zum Problem des Paragone in der Kunst und Kunsttheorie der italienischen Renaissance, Sigmaringen 1995

Martindale, Andrew: The "Triumphs of Caesar" by Andrea Mantegna, London 1979

Matile, Michael: Quadri laterali im sakralen Kontext. Studien und Materialien zur Historienmalerei in venezianischen Kirchen und Kapellen des Cinquecento, Munich 1997

Mazzarolli, Antonio et al.: Paris Bordon, Milan 1984

McCorquodale, Charles: Bronzino, London 1981

Mewiss, Millard: The Painter's Choice. Problems of the Interpretation of Renaissance Art, New York 1976

Meiss, Millard: Painting in Florence and Siena after the Black Death, London 1965

Mendogni, Pier Paolo: Il Correggio a Parma, Parma 1989

Menegazzi, Luigi: Cima da Conegliano, Treviso 1981

Mesnil, Jacques: Botticelli, Paris 1938

Meyer zur Capellen, Jürg and Bernd Roeck (eds.): Paolo Veronese. Fortuna Critica und künstlerisches Nachleben (Studi/Schriftenreihe des Deutschen Studienzentrums in Venedig, 8), Sigmaringen 1990

Micheletti, Emma: Domenico Ghirlandaio, Florence and Milan 1990

Middeldorf, Ulrich: L'Angelico e la scultura, in: Rinascimento 6, 1955, pp. 179–194

Milanesi, Gaetano: Le lettere di Michelangelo Buonarroti pubblicate con ricordi e i contratti artistici, Florence 1875

Milanesi, Giovanni: Documenti per la storia dell'arte senese, Siena 1854

Mittelstädt, Kuno (ed.): Eugène Delacroix. Dem Auge ein Fest. Aus dem Journal 1847–1863, Frankfurt on Main 1988

Molajoli, Rosemarie: Cosmè Tura e i grandi pittori ferraresi del suo tempo: Francesco Cossa e Ercole de'Roberti, Milan 1974

Moretti, Lino, Antonio Niero and Paola Rossi: La Chiesa del Tintoretto. Madonna dell'Orto, Venice 1994

Mueller von der Haegen, Anne: Giotto di Bondone, um 1267–1337, Cologne 1998

Muraro, Michelangelo and David Rosand: Tiziano e la silografia veneziana del Cinquecento, Venice 1976

Murray, Linda: Michelangelo. His Life, Work and Times, London 1984

Natali, Antonio: Andrea del Sarto. Maestro della "maniera moderna," Milan 1998

Natali, Antonio and Alessandro Cecchi: Andrea del Sarto. Catalogo completo dei dipinti, Florence 1989

Nichols, Tom: Tintoretto's Poverty, in: Francis Ames Lewis (ed.), New Interpretations of Venetian Painting, London 1994, pp. 99–110

Nigro, Salvatore S.: Pontormo. Il libro mio. Zeichnungen, Fresken, Gemälde. Mit einem Kommentar von Giorgio Manganelli, Munich 1996

Nova, Alessandro (ed.): Parmigianino. Zitat, Porträt, Mythos, Perugia 2006

Nucciarelli, Franco Ivan: Studi sul Pinturicchio. Dalle prime prove alla Cappella Sistina, Ellera Umbra 1998

Opitz, Marion: Benozzo Bozzoli. 1420–1497, Cologne 1998

Orlandi, Stefano: Beato Angelico, Florence 1964

Pächt, Otto: Venezianische Malerei des 15. Jahrhunderts. Die Bellinis und Mantegna, ed. by Margareta Vyoral-Tschapka and Michael Pächt, Munich 2002

Padoa Rizzo, Anna: Benozzo Gozzoli. Catalogo completo dei dipinti, Florence 1992

Padovani, Serena (ed.): L'età di Savonarola. Fra Bartolomeo e la Scuola di San Marco, Venice 1996

Pagden-Ferino, Sylvia and Maria Antonietta Zancan: Raffaello. Catalogo completo dei dipinti, Florence 1989

Pallucchini, Rodolfo: Tiziano, 2 vols, Florence 1969

Pallucchini, Rodolfo and Paola Rossi: Tintoretto: Le opere sacre e profane, 2 vols, Milan 1982

Panofsky, Erwin: Renaissance and Renascences in Western art, New York 1960

Passavant, Günter: Reflexe nordischer Graphik bei Raffael, Leonardo, Giulio Romano und Michelangelo, in: Mitteilungen des Kunsthistorischen Institutes in Florenz, vol. 27, 1983, pp. 193–222

Passavant, Günter: Andrea del Verrocchio als Maler, Düsseldorf 1959

Pedretti, Carlo: Leonardo da Vinci on Painting: A Lost Book (Libro A), Berkley and Los Angeles 1964

Pedretti, Carlo: Leonardo: A Study in Chronology and Style, London 1973

Pedretti, Carlo: The Codex Atlanticus of Leonardo da Vinci: A Catalogue of Its Newly Restored Sheets, New York 1979

Pedretti, Carlo: The Literary Works of Leonardo da Vinci. Commentary, Berkley and Los Angeles 1977

Pedretti, Carlo (ed.): Academia Leonardi Vinci, Florence 1988–1997

Pedretti, Carlo and Carlo Vecce (eds.): Leonardo da Vinci. Libro di Pittura, Florence 1995

Penny, Nicholas and Roger Jones: Raphael, New Haven and London 1983

Perrig, Alexander: Formen der politischen Propaganda der Kommune von Siena in der ersten Trecento-Hälfte, in: Karl Clausberg (ed.), Bauwerke und Bildwerke im Hochmittelalter, Gießen 1981, pp. 213–234

Pignatti, Terisio and Filippo Pedrocco: Veronese, 2 vols, Milan 1995

Piper, Ernst: Savonarola, Umtriebe eines Politikers und Puritaners im Florenz der Medici, Berlin, 1979

Pisani, Linda: L'arte di Masaccio e l'arte di Masolino: un dialogo e il suo contrario, in: Masaccio e Masolino, ed. by Andrea Baldinotti, 2002, pp. 189–206

Pisani, Rosanna Caterina Proto: Luce e disegno negli affreschi di Andrea del Castagno, Livorno 2000

Poeschel, Sabine and Alexander Maximus: Das Bildprogramm des Appartamento Borgia im Vatikan, Weimar 1999

Poeschke, Joachim: Die Kirche San Francesco in Assisi und ihre Wandmalereien, Munich 1985

Poeschke, Joachim: Wandmalerei der Giottozeit in Italien. 1280–1400, Munich 2003

Poletti, Federico: Antonio e Piero del Pollaiuolo, Milan 2001

Pons, Nicoletta: Botticelli, Milan, 1989

Pons, Nicoletta: I Pollaiuolo. Florence 1998

Pope-Hennessy, John: Donatello, Frankfurt and Berlin 1986

Pope-Hennessy, John: Fra Angelico, London 1952

Popp, Dietmar: Duccio und die Antike. Studien zur Antikenvorstellung und zur Antikenrezeption in der Sieneser Malerei am Anfang des 14. Jahrhunderts, Munich 1996

Prater, Andreas: Mantegnas Cristo in scurto, in: Zeitschrift für Kunstgeschichte 48, 1985, pp. 279–299

Preimesberger, Rudolf: Tragische Motive in Raffaels "Transfiguration," in: Zeitschrift für Kunstgeschichte 50, 1987, pp. 88–115

Previtali, Giorgio: Giotto e la sua bottega, 3rd edit., ed. by A. Conti, Milan 1993

Priever, Andreas: Paolo Caliari, genannt Veronese: 1528–1588, Cologne 2000

Priever, Andreas: Vorbild und Mythos: Die Wirkungsgeschichte der "Hochzeit zu Kana" Paolo Veroneses (Studi/Schriftenreihe des Deutschen Studienzentrums in Venedig, 16), Sigmaringen 1997

Prinz, Wolfram, and Iris Marzik: Die Storia oder die Kunst des Erzählens. In der italienischen Malerei und Plastik des späten Mittelalters und der Frührenaissance. 1260–1460, 2 vols, Mainz 2000

Prinz, Wolfram and Max Seidel: Domenico Ghirlandaio, Atti del Convegno Internazionale, Firenze, 16–18 ottobre 1994, Florence 1996

Quasimodo, Salvatore and Ettore Camesasca: L'opera completa di Michelangelo pittore, Milan 1967

Quermann, Andreas: Domenico di Tommaso di Currado Bigordi. Ghirlandaio. 1449–1494, Cologne 1998

Raabe, Rainald: Der imaginierte Betrachter. Studien zu Caravaggios römischem Werk, Hildesheim et al. 1996

Ramsden, E. H.: The Letters of Michelangelo, trans. from the original Tuscan, edited & annotated, 2 vols, Stanford, CA, 1963

Reti, Ladislao (ed.): Leonardo. Forscher, Künstler, Magier, Munich 1990 (original edition Lucerne 1987)

Ridolfi, Carlo: Le Maraviglie dell'arte ovvero le vite degli illustri pittori veneti e dello stato, Venice 1648, ed. by Detlev von Hadeln, 2 vols, Berlin 1914/1924

Riess, Jonathan B.: The Renaissance Antichrist: Luca Signorelli's Orvieto frescoes, Princeton, NJ, 1995

Rizzo, Anna Padoa: Paolo Uccello. Catalogo completo dei dipinti, Florence 1991

Roettgen, Steffi: Wandmalerei der Frührenaissance in Italien, vol. I: Anfänge und Entfaltung 1400–1470, Munich 1996

Roettgen, Steffi: Wandmalerei der Frührenaissance in Italien, vol. II: Die Blütezeit 1470–1510, Munich 1996

Romanini, Angiola Maria: L'itinerario pittorico del Mantegna, Padua 1966

Rosand, David: Painting in Cinquecento Venice. Titian, Veronese, Tintoretto, New Haven and London 1982

Rosand, David (ed.): Titian: His world and legacy, New York 1982

Rosen, Valeska von, Klaus Krüger and Rudolf Preimesberger (ed.): Reflexionen des Ästhetischen in der italienischen Malerei der frühen Neuzeit, Berlin 2003

Rosenauer, Artur: Donatello. L'opera completa, Milan 1993

Roskill, Mark W.: Dolce's "Aretino" and Venetian Art Theory of the Cinquecento, New York 1968

Rossi, Paola: L'opera completa del Parmigianino, Milan 1980

Rossi, Paola and Lionello Puppi (ed.): Jacopo Tintoretto nel quarto Centenario della Morte. Atti del Convegno Internazionale di Studi (Venezia, 24–26 novembre 1994) [= Quaderni di Venezia Arti 3], Padua and Venice 1996

Rowlands, Eliot W.: St. Andrew and the Pisa Altarpiece, Los Angeles 2003

Rubinstein, Nicolai: Florentine Government under the Medici, 1434–1494, Oxford, 1966

Ruda, Jeffrey: Fra Filippo Lippi: Life and Work, London 1993

Ruf, P. Gerhard: Franziskus und Bonaventura, Assisi 1974

Salmi, Mario (ed.): Mostra delle opere del Beato Angelico, Florence 1955

Salvini, Roberto: Tutta la pittura del Botticelli, 2 vols, Milan, 1958

Sandrart, Joachim von: Academie der Bau-, Bild- und Mahlerey-Künste 1675, ed. by A. R. Peltzer, Munich 1925

Santoro, Fiorella Sricchia: Antonello e l'Europa, Milan 1986

Scailliérez, Cécile: Rosso. Le Christ mort, Paris 2004

Scannelli, Federico: Il microcosmo della pintura, Cesena 1657, reprint, ed. by G. Giubbini, Milan 1966

Scarpellini, Pietro: Perugino, Milan 1991

Scarpellini, Pietro and Maria Rita Silvestrelli: Pintoricchio, Milan 2003

Schottmüller, Frida: Fra Angelico. Des Meisters Gemälde, Stuttgart 1924

Scirè, Giovanna Nepi: Carpaccio. Storie di Sant'Orsola, Milan 2000

Scudieri, Magnolia: San Marco, Florence 1996

Seidel, Max: Italian Art of the Middle Ages and the Renaissance (Series of the Kunsthistorisches Institut in Florenz. Max-Planck-Insitut 7–8), 2 vols, Venice 2003

Shearman, John: Andrea del Sarto, 2 vols, Oxford 1965

Shearman, John: Leonardo's Colour and Chiaroscuro, in: Zeitschrift für Kunstgeschichte 25, Berlin 1962, pp. 13–47

Shearman, John: Pontormo's Altarpiece in Santa Felicita, Newcastle upon Tyne 1971

Shearman, John: Raphael's Cartoons in the Collection of Her Majesty the Queen and the Tapestries for the Sistine Chapel, London 1972

Shearman, John: The Vatican Stanze: Functions and Decorations, Proceedings of the British Academy, vol. 57, London 1972

Shell, Janice and Grazioso Sironi: Salai and Leonardo's Legacy, in: Burlington Magazine 133, 1991, pp. 95–108

Signorini, Rodolfo: Opus hoc tenue: La Camera dipinta di Andrea Mantegna, Mantua, Parma 1985

Smyth, Carolyn: Correggio's Frescoes in Parma Cathedral, Princeton, NJ, 1997

Sonnenburg, Hubertus von: Beobachtungen zur Arbeitsweise Tintorettos, in: Maltechnik – Restauro 80, 1974, pp. 133–143

Sonnenburg, Hubertus von: Raphael in der Alten Pinakothek, Munich 1983

Spezzaferro, Luigi: La cultura del Cardinal del Monte e il primo tempo di Caravaggio, in: Storia dell'arte 9/10, 1971, pp. 57–92

Steinmann, Ernst: Ghirlandaijo, Bielefeld and Leipzig 1897

Steinmann, Ernst: Michelangelo im Spiegel seiner Zeit, Leipzig 1930

Steinmann, Ernst and Rudolph Wittkower: Michelangelo-Bibliographie 1510–1926, Leipzig 1927

Stubblebine, James H.: Assisi and the Rise of Vernacular Art, New York 1985

Stubblebine, James H.: Duccio di Buoninsegna and His School, Princeton 1979

Suida, Wilhelm and Adolfo Venturi: L'altare di Masaccio già nel Carmine a Pisa, in: Confronto, 2002, No. 0, pp. 14–16

Tazartres, Maurizia: Bronzino, Geneva and Milan 2003

Tempestini, Anchise: Giovanni Bellini, Munich 1998

Teza, Laura (ed.): Pietro Vannucci detto il Perugino: Atti del Convegno Internazionale di studio, 25–28 ottobre 2000, Perugia 2004

Thode, Henry: Franz von Assisi und die Anfänge der Kunst der Renaissance in Italien, Berlin 1885

Thode, Henry: Michelangelo und das Ende der Renaissance, Berlin 1902–1913

Tietze-Conrad, Erika: Mantegna, London, Florence 1955–1956

Tiziano e Venezia, Convegno Internazionale di Studi, Venezia 1976, Vicenza 1980

Tolnay, Charles de: Michelangelo, Princeton 1943–1960

Ullmann, Bertold L. and Philip A. Stadter: The Public Library of Renaissance Florence, Padua 1972

Vasari, Giorgio: Le vite dei più eccellenti architetti, pittori, et scultori italiani, Florence 1550

Vasari, Giorgio, Le vite de'più eccellenti pittori, scultori, et architettori, italiani, Florence 1568. In addition, diverse new editions and translations, including:
Lives of seventy of the most eminent painters, sculptors and architects, ed. and annotated in the light of recent discoveries by E.H. and E.W. Blashfield and A.A. Hopkins, New York 1913; Vasari's Lives of the Artists, abridged and ed. with commentary by Betty Burroughs, New York 1946; Lives of the Artists, selected and trans. by E.L. Seeley, introduction by Alfred Werner, New York 1957; Lives of the Artists: A Selection, trans. by George Bull, Harmondsworth and New York 1965; Lives of the Most Eminent Painters, selected, ed. and introduced by Marilyn Aronberg Lavin, trans. by Mrs. Jonathan Foster, Verona 1966; The Lives of the Artists, trans. with an introduction and notes by Julia Conaway Bondanella and Peter Bondanella, Oxford and New York 1991

Vecchi, Pierluigi de and Gianluigi Colalucci: Die Sixtinische Kapelle, Fribourg, Basel and Vienna 1996

Veltmann, Kim H.: Studies on Leonardo da Vinci, I. Linear Perspective and the Visual Dimensions of Science and Art, Munich 1986

Venturi, Adolfo: Storia dell'arte italiana, 11 vols, Milan 1901–1940

Verdon, Giorgio and John Henderson (eds.): Christianity and the Renaissance, Syracus 1990

Verga, Ettore: Bibliografia Vinciana 1493–1930, Bologna 1931

Vezzosi, Alessandro: Léonard de Vinci: Art et Science de l'Univers, Paris 1996

Volpe, Carlo and Mauro Lucco: L'opera completa di Sebastiano del Piombo, Milan 1980

Wackernagel, Martin: Der Lebensraum des Künstlers in der florentinischen Frührenaissance, Leipzig 1938

Warburg, Aby: Bildniskunst und Florentinisches Bürgertum: Domenico Ghirlandajo in Santa Trinità: Die Bildnisse des Lorenzo de'Medici und seiner Angehörigen, Leipzig 1902

Warburg, Aby: The renewal of pagan antiquity, introduction by Kurt W. Forster, Los Angeles 1999

Warburg, Aby: Gesammelte Schriften, Leipzig, Berlin, 1932

Wassermann, Jack: Leonardo da Vinci, Cologne 1977

Weber, Andrea: Duccio di Buoninsegna, um 1255–1319, Cologne 1997

Weddigen, Erasmus: Des Vulkans paralleles Wesen: Dialog über einen Ehebruch mit einem Glossar zu Tintorettos Vulkan überrascht Venus und Mars, Munich 1994

Weigelt, Curt H.: Duccio di Buoninsegna, Leipzig 1911

Weinberger, Martin: Michelangelo the Sculptor, London and New York 1967

Weinstein, Donald: Savonarola and Florence: Prophecy and Patriotism in the Renaissance, Princeton, 1970

Wethey, Harold E.: The Paintings of Titian, 3 vols, London 1969–1975

White, John: Donatello's High Altar in the Santo at Padua. Part One: The documents and their implications. Part Two: The reconstruction, in: The Art Bulletin 51, 1969, pp. 1–14 and 119–141

White, John: Duccio: Tuscan art and medieval workshop, London 1979

Wiemers, Michael: Zur Funktion und Bedeutung eines Antikenzitates auf Benozzo Gozzolis Fresko "Der Zug der Könige," in: Zeitschrift für Kunstgeschichte 4, 1987, pp. 441–470

Wilde, Johannes: Italian Drawings in the Department of Prints and Drawings in the British Museum, Michelangelo and his studio, London 1953

Wilde, Johannes: Michelangelo: Six Lectures, Oxford 1978

Wilmes, Ulrich: Rosso Fiorentino und der Manierismus: Ein Beitrag zur Entwicklung der Tafelmalerei im 16. Jahrhundert, Essen 1985

Windt, Franziska: Andrea del Verrocchio und Leonardo da Vinci: Zusammenarbeit in Skulptur und Malerei, Münster 2003

Winner, Matthias: Pontormos Fresko in Poggio a Caiano, in: Zeitschrift für Kunstgeschichte 35, 1972, pp. 153–197

Winner, Matthias: Progetti ed esecuzione nella Stanza della Segnatura, in: Raffaello nell'appartamento di Giulio II e Leone X, Milan 1993, pp. 247–291

Wirtz, Rolf C.: Donatello. 1386–1466, Cologne 1998

Wohl, Hellmut: The paintings of Domenico Veneziano, ca. 1410–1461: A study in Florentine art of the early Renaissance, New York and London 1980

Wolters, Wolfgang: Der Bilderschmuck des Dogenpalastes: Untersuchungen zur Selbstdarstellung der Republik Venedig im 16. Jahrhundert, Wiesbaden 1983

Wright, Alison: The Pollaiuolo Brothers: The Arts of Florence and Rome, New Haven and London 2005

Zambrano, Patrizia and Jonathan Katz Nelson: Filippino Lippi, Milan 2004

Zampetti, Pietro: L'opera completa di Giorgione: Presentazione Virgilio Lilli, Milan 1968

Zampetti, Pietro: Pittura nelle Marche, vol. I: Dalle orinigi al primo Rinascimento, Florence 1988

Zanardi, Bruno: Il cantiere di Giotto: le storie di San Francesco ad Assisi: Note storico-iconografiche di Chiara Frugoni, Milan 1996

Zapperi, Roberto: Tizian, Paul II. und seine Enkel, Nepotismus und Staatsportrait, Frankfurt 1990

Zeri, Federico (ed.): La pittura in Italia: Il Quattrocento, Milan 1987

Zöllner, Frank: Leonardo da Vinci: Sämtliche Gemälde und Zeichnungen, Cologne 2003

Exhibition Catalogues

Exhib. Cat. Altenburg 2001: Claritas: Das Hauptaltarbild im Dom zu Siena nach 1260: Die Rekonstruktion, ed. by Barbara John, Jochen Manzke and Jutta Penndorf, Altenburg 2001

Exhib. Cat. Avignon 1983: L'art gothique siennois: Enluminure, peinture, orfèvrerie, sculpture, ed. by Giulietta Chelazzi Dini and Marie-Claude Léonelli, Florence 1983

Exhib. Cat. Dublin 1993/94: Caravaggio: The Master Revealed, ed. by Sergio Benedetti, Dublin 1993

Exhib. Cat. Fabriano 2006: Gentile da Fabriano e l'altro Rinascimento, ed. by Laura Laureati and Lorenza Mochi Onori, 2 vols, Milan 2006

Exhib. Cat. Florence 1985: Omaggio à Donatello 1386–1986, Museo Nazionale del Bargello, Florence 1985–1986, Florence 1985

Exhib. Cat. Florence 1986: Donatello e i Suoi. Scultura fiorentina del primo Rinascimento, Florence 1986

Exhib. Cat. Florence 1986: Donatello e il restauro della Giuditta, Palazzo Vecchio, Sala dei Gigli, Florence 1986

Exhib. Cat. London 1983: The Genius of Venice: 1500–1600, ed. by Charles Hope, London 1983

Exhib. Cat. London 1983–1984: The Genius of Venice, 1500–1600, The Royal Academy of Arts, London 1983–1984

Exhib. Cat. London 1992: Andrea Mantegna, ed. by Jane Martineau, London 1992

Exhib. Cat. Milan 1990: Pittura di luce, ed. by Luciano Bellosi, Casa Buonarroti, Florence 1990, Milan 1990

Exhib. Cat. Mantua 2006: Mantegna. 1460–1506, ed. by Mauro Lucco, Milan 2006

Exhib. Cat. Mantua 2006: Mantenga e le Arti a Verona: 1450–1500, ed. by Sergio Marinelli and Paola Marini, Milan 2006

Exhib. Cat. New York 1985: In The Age of Caravaggio, ed. by Mina Gregori, The Metropolitan Museum of Art, New York 1985

Exhib. Cat. New York 1990: A Caravaggio Rediscovered: The Lute Player, ed. by Keith Christiansen, New York 1990

Exhib. Cat. New York 1994: Painting and Illumination in Early Renaissance Florence: 1300–1450, ed. by Laurence B. Kanter et al., New York 2004

Exhib. Cat. New York and Naples 1985: The Age of Caravaggio, ed. by Keith Christiansen, New York 1985

Exhib. Cat. New York, London 1992: Mantegna, ed. by Jane Martineau, Royal Academy London, Metropolitan Museum New York, New York, London 1992

Exhib. Cat. Padua 2006: Mantegna: 1445–1460, ed. by Davide Banzato et al., Milan 2006

Exhib. Cat. Paris 1975: Le Studiolo d'Isabelle d'Este, by Sylvie Beguin, Musée du Louvre, Paris 1975

Exhib. Cat. Paris 1993: Le Christ à la colonne d'Antonello de Messine, ed. by Dominique Thiébaut (Les dossiers du Musée du Louvre 42), Paris 1993

Exhib. Cat. Paris 1993: Le Siècle de Titien, Grand Palais, Paris 1993

Exhib. Cat. Paris 1996: Pisanello: Le peintre aux sept vertus, ed. by Dominique Cordellier and Paola Marini, Paris 1996

Exhib. Cat. Paris 2003: Léonard de Vinci: Dessins et manuscrits, ed. by Françoise Viatte and Varena Forcione, Paris 2003

Exhib. Cat. Paris and Washington 1999: Lorenzo Lotto 1480–1557, ed. by David Alan Brown, Paris 1999

Exhib. Cat. Rome 1992: Michelangelo Merisi da Caravaggio: Come nascono i capolavori, Florence 1991, Rome 1992

Exhib. Cat. Rome 2003: Antonello da Messina: L'opera completa, ed. by Mauro Lucco, Milan 2003

Exhib. Cat. San Giovanni Valdarno 2002: Masaccio e le origini del Rinascimento, ed. by Lucidano Bollori, Casa Masaccio, San Giovanni Valdarno 2002, Milan 2002

Exhib. Cat. Siena 2003: Duccio: Alle origini della pittura senese, ed. by Allessandro Bagnoli et al., Milan 2003

Exhib. Cat. Venice 1961: Andrea Mantegna, by Giovanni Paccagnini and Amalia Mezzetti, Palazzo Ducale Mantua, Venice 1961

Exhib. Cat. Venice 1990: Prince of Painters, Palazzo Ducale, Venice, National Gallery of Art, Washington, Munich, and Venice 1990

Exhib. Cat. Venice 1992: Leonardo & Venezia, ed. by Augusto Marinoni, Milan 1992

Exhib. Cat. Venice 1999: Renaissance Venice and the North: Crosscurrents in the Time of Bellini, Dürer and Titian, ed. by Bernard Aikema and Bevery Louise Brown, Milan 1999

Exhib. Cat. Verona 1988: Veronese e Verona, ed. by Sergio Marinelli, Museo di Castelvecchio, Verona 1988

Exhib. Cat. Vicenza 1988: Paolo Veronese: Disegni e dipinti, ed. by Alessandro Bettagno, Fondazione Giorgio Cini, Vicenza 1988

Exhib. Cat. Washington 1988: The Art of Paolo Veronese 1528–1588, ed. by William R. Rearick, National Gallery of Art, Washington 1988

Exhib. Cat. Washington and Vienna 2006: Bellini. Giorgione. Tizian und die Renaissance der venezianischen Malerei, ed. by David Alan Brown and Sylvia Ferino-Pagden, Milan 2006

Exhib. Cat. Vienna 1994: La prima donna del mondo: Isabella d'Este, Fürstin und Mäzenin der Renaissance, by Sylvia Ferino-Pagden, Kunsthistorisches Museum Wien, Vienna 1994

Exhib. Cat. Vienna and Venice 2004: Giorgione: Mythos und Enigma, ed. by Sylvia Ferino-Pagden and Giovanna Nepi Scirè, Milan 2004

Index

The index denotes all artists represented in this volume with an illustration.

Photographic Acknowledgements

Right up to the date of publication, the publisher has attempted intensively to locate all the holders of reproduction rights. If some claims remain outstanding, then the individuals or institutions concerned are asked to address themselves to the publisher.

akg-images, Berlin: © 26, 132, 525, 533, 545, © akg-images/Cameraphoto 456, 482, © akg-images/Andrea Jemolo 511, © akg-images/Erich Lessing 94, 300, 309, 379, 380, 386/387, 489, 538, 546, 573, © akg-images/Nimatallah 33, 493; Albertina, Vienna: 455;
Archivi Alinari, Florence: 60, 61;
Artothek, Weilheim: © 288/289, 417, © Bayer & Mitko 157, © Kusak 359, © Artothek/Photobusiness 286/287, 296, 377, 412, 418, 419, 437, © Artothek/Städel Museum 46, 69, 402;
Bibliothèque de l'Institut de France, Paris: © Bulloz 168;
Bildarchiv Preußischer Kulturbesitz, Berlin: © Jörg P. Anders 9, 22, 59, 72, 85, 87, 107, 124, 141, 147, 205, 285, 292, 334, 369, 374, 420, 426, 454, 461, 501, 522, 523, 564, Christoph Irrgang 107, RMN/Musée du Louvre, Paris (Jean-Gilles Berizzi) 48, (Gérard Blot) 49, (René-Gabriel Ojéda) 393;
Bridgeman Art Library, Berlin: © 8, 10, 24, 25, 34, 36/37, 51, 61, 61, 81, 117, 121, 125, 127, 131, 166, 179, 197, 213, 214, 228, 240, 248, 253, 262, 279, 294, 297, 301, 358, 371, 378, 411, 424, 428, 434/435, 445, 473, 539, 540, 544, 548, 549, 566, 588, © Bridgeman Art Library/Piero Codato 470, © Bridgeman Art Library/Oronoz 487, © Giraudon/Bridgeman Art Library 11;
Cameraphoto-Arte, Venice: 443, 444;
The Cleveland Museum of Art, Cleveland, Lenna C. Hanna, Jr., Fund: © 576;
Fondation Custodia/Collection Frits Lugt, Paris: 48;
The Frick Collection, New York: 143, 488;
Galleria Doria Pamphilj, Rome: © 266, 305, 504;
Herzog Anton Ulrich-Museum-Kunstmuseum des Landes Niedersachsen, Braunschweig: © Photo Michael Lindner 284;
Robert Janke, Boslar: 20;
The Metropolitan Museum of Art, New York: © 1987 Rogers Fund and The Elisha Whittelsey Collection, The Elisha Whittelsey Fund, 1986: 106; Purchase, Lila Acheson Wallace Gift, New York: 547; Anonymous Gift, 1932: 70;
Musée Jacquemart-André, Paris: 63;
Musei Vaticani, the Vatican, Rome: © 490, 524; National Gallery, London: © 116, 118/119, 145, 213, 316/317, 360, 517;
National Gallery of Art, Washington: © 2007 Board of the Trustees 115, 156, 158, 217, 378, 429, Photo Richard Carafelli: 126, Samuel H. Kress Collection © 86, 333, Photo José A. Naranjo 341;
The Pierpont Morgan Library/Art Resource, New York: 474;
Rheinisches Bildarchiv, Cologne: 427;
RMN, Paris: © Gérard Blot 470, Thierry Le Mage 198, Jacques Quecq d'Henripret 209, 249;
The Royal Collection, Windsor, Berkshire: © 2007 Her Majesty Queen Elizabeth II: 104, 105, 194, 207, 381;
Photo Scala, Florence: © 2, 7, 8, 9, 10, 12-19, 21, 23, 27-32, 35, 39-45, 47, 50, 52-56, 62, 63, 64-68, 71, 73-79, 82-84, 85, 88-93, 95-103, 109-114, 122, 123, 128, 129, 132, 133-140, 144, 146, 148-155, 158-165, 167, 170-178, 180-193, 195, 196, 199-204, 208, 210-212, 215, 218-227, 228-239, 241-247, 249-252, 254-261, 263-265, 267-277, 280-283, 287, 290, 294/295, 299, 301-304, 305-308, 310-314/315, 319-332, 335-340, 342-357, 361-368, 372/373, 375, 376, 382-385, 389-392, 395-409, 413-416, 421-423, 428, 431, 432/433, 438/439; 440/441, 446-452/453, 454, 455, 457-460, 463-467, 469, 471, 475-480/481, 484/485, 486, 491, 494-500, 502-503, 505-509, 512-516, 519, 520, 524, 526-532, 534/535, 537, 541, 542/543, 551-563, 567-571, 575, 577-587;
Soprintendenza per i Beni Artistici e Storici di Roma, Rome: 565;
Staatliche Kunstsammlungen, Gemäldegalerie Alte Meister, Dresden: © Photo Estel/Klut 120, Kupferstichkabinett 106;
Staats- und Universitätsbibliothek Göttingen, Göttingen: 468;
Studio Fotografico Quattrone, Florence: 456;
Toledo Museum of Art, Toledo (OH), Purchased with funds from the Libbey Endowment, Gift of Edward Drummond Libbey, 1977.41: 425.

Cover Volume I: Sandro Botticelli *The Birth of Venus,*
© Photo 1991 Scala, Firenze – Courtesy of the Ministero Beni e Att. Culturali

Cover Volume II: Titian *Bacchus and Ariadne,*
© The National Gallery, London

© 2007 Tandem Verlag GmbH
h.f.ullmann is an imprint of Tandem Verlag GmbH

Original title: *Die großen Maler der italienischen Renaissance*
ISBN 978-3-8331-2564-5

Project coordination: Nicole Weilacher
Editing: Ines Dickmann
Layout: Dorothee Seber
Cover Design: Sabine Vonderstein

© 2008 for the English edition:
Tandem Verlag GmbH
h.f.ullmann is an imprint of Tandem Verlag GmbH

Translation from the German: Paul Aston and Fiona Hulse (468-489), Anthea Bell/CPM (428-467), Russell
Cennydd (272-278, 280-291, 292-297, 368-387, 490, 508, 523, 553, 572-576, 588, 589-602, 603-609),
Phyll Greenhead (58-123), Fiona Hulse (154-207), Iain Macmillan (captions 394-404), Christine
Shuttleworth (6-33, 40-57, 58, 72, 73, 79, 124-129, 130-152, 172, 173, 176, 193, 200, 388-410, 412-427,
429, 468-470, 478-489), Christine Varley and Anthony Vivis (208-271), Anthony Vivis (34-39, 490-588)
Editing: Chris Murray
Project coordination: Lucas Lüdemann

Printed in China

ISBN 978-3-8331- 4441-7

10 9 8 7 6 5 4 3 2 1
X IX VIII VII VI V IV III II

www.ullmann-publishing.com